## Chapter 11

| | |
|---|---|
| $t_{obt}$ | obtained value in $t$-test |
| $t_{crit}$ | critical value of $t$-test |
| $s_{\bar{X}}$ | estimated standard error of the mean |
| $r_{obt}$ | obtained value of $r$ |
| $r_{crit}$ | critical value of $r$ |

## Chapter 12

| | |
|---|---|
| $n$ | number of scores in each sample |
| $s^2_{pool}$ | variance pooled |
| $s_{\bar{X}_1 - \bar{X}_2}$ | standard error of the difference |
| $\bar{D}$ | mean of difference scores |
| $\mu_D$ | mean of population of difference scores |
| $s_{\bar{D}}$ | standard error of the mean difference |
| $r^2_{pb}$ | effect size in a two-sample experiment |

## Chapter 13

| | |
|---|---|
| ANOVA | analysis of variance |
| $k$ | number of levels in a factor |
| $F_{obt}$ | obtained value from $F$-ratio |
| $F_{crit}$ | critical value of $F$ |
| $\sigma^2_{error}$ | population error variance |
| $\sigma^2_{treat}$ | population treatment variance |
| $MS_{wn}$ | mean square within groups |
| $df_{wn}$ | degrees of freedom within groups |
| $SS_{wn}$ | sum of squares within groups |
| $MS_{bn}$ | mean square between groups |
| $df_{bn}$ | degrees of freedom between groups |
| $SS_{bn}$ | sum of squares between groups |
| $SS_{tot}$ | total sum of squares |
| $df_{tot}$ | total degrees of freedom |
| $q_k$ | value used in HSD test |
| $HSD$ | Tukey's honestly significant difference |
| $\eta^2$ | eta squared; effect size in the sample |
| $\omega^2$ | omega squared; estimated effect size in the population |
| $F_{max}$ | obtained value in $F_{max}$ test |

## Chapter 14

| | |
|---|---|
| $F_A$ | obtained $F$ for factor A |
| $F_B$ | obtained $F$ for factor B |
| $F_{A \times B}$ | obtained $F$ for interaction of A and B |

## Chapter 15

| | |
|---|---|
| $f_o$ | observed frequency |
| $f_e$ | expected frequency |
| $\chi^2_{obt}$ | obtained value in chi square procedure |
| $\chi^2_{crit}$ | critical value in chi square procedure |
| $\phi$ | phi coefficient |
| $C$ | contingency coefficient |
| $\Sigma R$ | sum of ranks |
| $\Sigma R_{exp}$ | expected sum of ranks |
| $U_{obt}$ | obtained value in Mann-Whitney $U$ test |
| $T_{obt}$ | obtained value in Wilcoxon $T$ test |
| $H_{obt}$ | obtained value in Kruskal-Wallis $H$ test |
| $z_{obt}$ | obtained value in rank sums test |
| $\chi^2_{obt}$ | obtained value in Friedman $\chi^2$ test |

# BASIC STATISTICS FOR THE BEHAVIORAL SCIENCES

# BASIC STATISTICS FOR THE BEHAVIORAL SCIENCES

## Gary W. Heiman

State University of New York, College at Buffalo

**HOUGHTON MIFFLIN COMPANY**     **Boston**     Toronto

Dallas     Geneva, Illinois     Palo Alto     Princeton, New Jersey

Sponsoring Editor: Michael DeRocco
Project Editor: Suzanne Morris
Production Coordinator: Frances Sharperson
Manufacturing Coordinator: Priscilla Bailey
Marketing Manager: Diane McOscar

Cover photograph by Michel Tcherevkoff/The Image Bank

Printed in the U.S.A.

Library of Congress Catalog Card Number: 91-71989

ISBN: 0-395-51546-7

ABCDEFGHIJ-D-987654321

This book is dedicated to Jan, my most significant other.

# Contents

# 2

## Statistics and the Research Process    17

PART 2
_____

# DESCRIPTIVE STATISTICS: DESCRIBING SAMPLES AND POPULATIONS

# 3

## Frequency Distributions and Percentiles  42

# 4

## Measures of Central Tendency: The Mean, Median, and Mode 76

# 5

## Measures of Variability: Range, Variance, and Standard Deviation 105

PART **3**

## DESCRIBING RELATIONSHIPS

# 7

## Describing Relationships Using Correlations   172

# 8

## Linear Regression and Predicting Variability   205

PART 4

# INFERENTIAL STATISTICS

# 9

## Probability: Making Decisions About Chance Events    238

# 10

## Overview of Statistical Hypothesis Testing: The *z*-Test   266

# 11

## Significance Testing of a Single Sample Mean or a Correlation Coefficient: The *t*-Test   301

# 12

## Significance Testing of Two Sample Means: The *t*-Test   337

# 13

## One-Way Analysis of Variance: Testing the Significance of Two or More Sample Means   375

# 14

## Two-Way Analysis of Variance: Testing the Means from Two Independent Variables 411

# 15

## Nonparametric Procedures for Frequency Data and Ranked Data   451

## *APPENDIXES*

## $\mathcal{A}$

## Interpolation 493

## $\mathcal{B}$

## Additional Formulas for Computing Probability 498

## $C$

## One-Way Repeated Measures Analysis of Variance 504

## Statistical Tables   512

## Answers to Practice Problems   538

## Using HMSTAT   546

# Preface

Many of the undergraduates who enroll in my statistics course have a weak background in mathematics and some degree of "math phobia." By the end of the course, these same undergraduates must understand and be able to perform the descriptive and inferential statistical procedures that are commonly used in psychological and other behavioral research. In my fifteen-year search for a textbook that would help my students make this transition, I have never been fully satisfied.

A number of books dwell on the remarkable things statisticians do with statistics and say too little about the things *researchers* commonly do. Such books often present a catalog of procedures but do not explain the conceptual purposes of these procedures. Although students taught in this way can compute an answer on demand, they do not know why they should perform the procedure or what their answer reveals about the data.

## My Objectives

I wanted my students to have a textbook that takes their needs more fully into account: a book that *explains*—clearly, patiently, and with an occasional touch of humor—the way a good teacher does. In striving to write such a book, I pursued five objectives.

**1. Take a conceptual-intuitive approach** To help students understand why as well as how procedures are performed, the text emphasizes the context in which statistics are used to make sense out of data. Each procedure is introduced in the context of a simple study with readily understandable goals. I first focus on the purpose of research that examines relationships between variables, then delineate the procedures that describe and infer such relationships, and finally return to the conceptual purpose. Avoiding an abstract theoretical presentation, I instead provide students with simplified ways to think about statistical concepts and to see how these concepts translate into practical procedures for answering practical questions.

**2. Present statistics within an understandable research context**   I assume that students have not taken a research methods course. For this reason I have created the research examples in this book rather than drawing them from the professional literature. Understanding examples from the literature typically requires a level of methodological sophistication that introductory statistics students do not possess, and the result is that the student is distracted from the illustrative purpose of the example. The text does contain the basic principles and terminology of research and is intended to help prepare students for a subsequent course in research methods.

**3. Deal directly and positively with student weaknesses in mathematics**
The text presents no formulas or statistical statements without explanation. Formulas are introduced in terms of what they accomplish, and an example of each is worked out completely, step by step. To further reduce the apparent complexity of statistics, I have stressed the similarities among different procedures, showing how, despite slight variations in computations, they have similar components and answer similar questions.

**4. Introduce new terms and concepts in an integrated way**   I have strived to tie each new concept and procedure to previous material, briefly reviewing that material in every possible instance. Difficult concepts are presented in small chunks, which are then built into a foundation and later elaborated on. My guiding rule was, to paraphrase, "We will serve no statistic before its time."

**5. Create a text that students will enjoy as well as learn from**   To make the text readable and engaging, I have drawn on the many lessons I have learned from my students over the years. I repeatedly point out the everyday usefulness of statistics. I have tried to convey my own excitement about statistics and to dispel the notion that statistics (and statisticians) are boring. One can take a discipline seriously yet still recognize its quirks and foibles and have fun with it.

## Pedagogical Format and Features

A number of features have been built into the book to enhance its usefulness as both a tool for study and a reference.

Conceptual and procedural questions, as well as computational problems, are provided at the end of each chapter. Both the final and the intermediate answers for all odd-numbered questions are given in Appendix E. Answers to the even-numbered questions appear in the Instructor's Resource Manual, which accompanies the text.

Other features include the following:

1. Graphs and diagrams are thoroughly explained in captions and fully integrated into the discussion.

2. New statistical notations are introduced at the beginning of the chapter in which they are used, not before.

3. Each definition is highlighted and is presented in clear and concise terms. Many mnemonics and analogies are included to promote retention and understanding.

4. Each important procedural point is emphasized by a "STAT ALERT." This is a summary reminder, set off from the text, about the calculation or interpretation of a statistic.

5. Every chapter summary provides a substantive review of the material, not merely a list of the topics covered.

6. For quick reference, formulas are listed at the end of each chapter.

7. A glossary of terms is included at the end of the book, and a glossary of symbols appears on the inside covers of the text.

## Organization

The text is divided into four parts. In Part 1, *Getting Started,* Chapter 1 serves as a brief preface for the student and reviews basic math and graphing techniques. Chapter 2 then introduces the terminology, logic, and goals of statistics within the context of behavioral research. Chapters 3 through 6 make up Part 2, *Descriptive Statistics* (along with a discussion of linear interpolation in Appendix A). Part 3, *Describing Relationships,* consists of Chapters 7 and 8, in which correlation and regression are introduced as descriptive procedures, with emphasis on interpreting the correlation coefficient and the variance accounted for. (The point-biserial correlation is included to provide a bridge to measures of effect size in later chapters.)

Much of the text is organized around the bane of introductory students: inferential statistics. Extensive groundwork is laid in the chapters on descriptive statistics, with strong emphasis on understanding the proportion of the area under the normal curve. Along with $z$-scores, Chapter 6 introduces the description of sample means using a sampling distribution.

Part 4, *Inferential Statistics,* begins with Chapter 9, which introduces probability. (Such topics as the additive and multiplicative rules and binomial expansion are presented in Appendix B.) The focus is on using the normal curve to compute probability, with the goal of making decisions about the representativeness of sample means. In Chapter 10, hypothesis testing is formalized using the $z$-test.

Chapter 11 presents the single-sample $t$-test, the confidence interval for a single mean, and significance testing of correlation coefficients. Chapter 12 covers two-sample $t$-tests, confidence intervals for the difference between the means and for the mean of differences, and effect size. Chapter 13 introduces the one-way, between-subjects ANOVA, including *post hoc* tests for equal and unequal $n$'s, eta squared, and omega squared. The $F_{max}$ test is presented briefly. (The one-way repeated measures ANOVA is described in Appendix C.) Chapter 14 deals with the two-way between-subjects ANOVA, *post hoc* tests for main effects and for unconfounded comparisons in an interaction, as well as graphing and interpreting interactions. Chapter 15 covers the one-way and two-way chi square, as well as the nonparametric versions of all previous parametric tests (with appropriate *post hoc* tests and measures of effect size).

The text strives to teach students how to interpret their data—not just to report that a result is significant. Thus, I have emphasized such topics as plotting and interpreting graphs and understanding the relationships demonstrated by research. I've also included practical discussions of power and measures of effect size. These discussions occur at the end of a section or chapter so that instructors wishing to skip these topics can easily do so.

## Software

A data-analysis computer program called HMSTAT has been custom-tailored to this text by Dr. David Abbott of the University of Central Florida in Orlando. The program is packaged free with the student text. This menu-driven program can accept and store data, perform all the procedures discussed in the text, and be operated by students with a minimal computer background. The program is integrated with the text only through the final section in each chapter, "Using the Computer." Otherwise, use of the software is entirely optional.

## Other Ancillaries

Additional practice problems are available in the Student Workbook and Study Guide, which I co-wrote with my colleague Dr. Deborah Kohl. Each chapter contains a review of objectives, terms, and formulas, a programmed review, and conceptual/computational problems (answers are included). Each chapter also has a set of test-like questions for which answers are provided in the Instructor's Resource Manual. An additional chapter review facilitates student integration of the entire course.

The Instructor's Resource Manual, by Dr. David Chattin of St. Joseph College, Indiana, contains approximately 750 test items and problems, as well as suggestions for classroom activities and discussion. The test items are available on computer disk in an ASCII-file format.

## Acknowledgments

I gratefully acknowledge the help and support of many professionals at Houghton Mifflin Company. In particular, I want to thank my outstanding sponsoring editor, Michael DeRocco, who provided invaluable guidance and support, and Karen Donovan, who as developmental editor served above and beyond any reasonable expectation. I am grateful to Suzanne Morris and Sally Lifland for seeing the book through production and to Catherine Johnson for her excellent interior design. Dr. Kathleen Donovan of the University of Central Oklahoma checked the entire manuscript for accuracy, and I thank her for her diligence. Any errors that might remain, however, are mine and mine alone. Finally, I am grateful to the following reviewers who, in evaluating all or parts of this manuscript at one stage or another, provided invaluable feedback.

William Addison, Eastern Illinois University

Andrew A. Beveridge, Queens College, City University of New York

Elliott Bonem, Eastern Michigan University

David Chattin, St. Joseph College, Indiana

Charles L. Dufour, Colby College

William A. Frederickson, University of Central Oklahoma

Philip S. Gallo, Jr., San Diego State University

Jane A. Halpert, DePaul University

Milton H. Hodge, University of Georgia

Eric S. Knowles, Ohio State University

Suzanne Mannes, University of Delaware

Richard Rogers, Georgia Southern College

Glenn S. Sanders, State University of New York, Albany

Billy L. Smith, University of Central Arkansas

James L. Walker, Jr., Lamar University

Christine B. Ziegler, Kennesaw College

Gary W. Heiman

# BASIC STATISTICS FOR THE BEHAVIORAL SCIENCES

# PART 1

# GETTING STARTED

Okay, so you're taking a course in statistics. You probably wonder what's in store for you. Most students know that statistics involve math, but they don't know that studying statistics is much more interesting and educational than merely cranking out a bunch of math problems. A tour through the world of statistics will open up new vistas in how to think, reason, and apply logic, especially when it comes to drawing conclusions from scientific research. You will also learn new ways of simplifying enormous complexities, which will allow you to make confident decisions in seemingly chaotic situations. And statistics will increase your confidence in your own abilities to understand and master an important mental discipline. Moreover, statistics can be fun! Statistics are challenging, there is an elegance to their logic, and you can do nifty things with them. So, keep an open mind, be prepared to do a little work, and you'll be amazed by what happens. You will find that although statistics are a little unusual, they are not incomprehensible, they do not require you to be a math wizard, and they are very relevant to psychology and the behavioral sciences.

# Introduction

In this chapter, we will discuss some common misconceptions about statistics and consider the best way to approach the study of statistics. We will also review the basic math and graphing techniques used in statistics.

## SOME ANSWERS TO YOUR QUESTIONS AND CONCERNS ABOUT STATISTICS

Students repeatedly ask the same questions about studying statistics. The answers to these questions may teach you something about psychologists and their use of statistics, as well as relieve any anxiety you may have.

### What Are Statistics?

The word *statistics* means different things to different people. To psychologists and behavioral scientists, it is typically a shortened version of the phrase *statistical procedures*. These are computations performed as part of conducting psychological research. The answers obtained by performing certain statistical procedures are also called statistics. Thus, the word *statistics* refers both to statistical procedures and to the answers obtained from those procedures.

### What Do Psychologists Do with Statistics?

Psychology and other behavioral sciences are based on empirical research. The word *empirical* means knowledge obtained through systematic observation of events (instead of through intuition or faith). Empirical research involves measurement, and in psychological research we measure behaviors. Such measurement results in numbers, or scores. The scores obtained in research are the *data*. (The word *data*, by the way, is plural, referring to more than one score, so we say "the data are . . . .")

Researchers conduct research because they have a research question in mind, and statistics help them to answer the question. In any study, the researcher ends up with a large batch of data, which must be made manageable and meaningful. Statistical procedures are used to *organize, summarize*, and *communicate* data and then to *conclude* what the data indicate. In essence, statistics help a researcher to make sense out of the data.

## But I'm Not Interested in Research; I Just Want to Help People!

Even if you are not interested in conducting research yourself, you still must be an informed user of statistics so that you can understand and learn from other people's research. Let's say that you become a therapist or counselor, and you do not consider yourself a "scientist." You hear of a new therapy which says that the way to "cure" people of some psychological problem is to scare the living daylights out of them. This sounds crazy, but what is important is the quality of the research that does or does not support this therapy. As a responsible professional, you would evaluate the research supporting this therapy before you would use it. You could not do so without understanding statistics. However, after you have studied statistics, reading and learning from such research is relatively easy.

## But I Don't Know Anything About Research!

This book is written for the student who has not yet studied the way psychological or behavioral research is conducted. Whenever we discuss a statistical procedure, we will also discuss simple examples of research that employ the procedure, and this should be enough to get you by. Then, later, when you study research methods, you will know the appropriate statistical procedures to use.

## What If I'm Not Very Good at Statistics?

In the grand scheme of things, the application of statistics is one small, although extremely important step in the research process. Statistics are simply a tool used in the behavioral sciences, as a wrench is a tool used in the repair of automobile engines. A mechanic need not be an expert wrencher, and a psychologist need not be an expert statistician. Rather, in the same way that a mechanic must understand the correct use of wrenches in order to fix an engine, you must understand the correct use of statistics in order to evaluate research.

### But Statistics Aren't Written in English!

There is no denying that statistics involve many strange symbols and unfamiliar terms. But the symbols and terms are simply the shorthand "code" for communicating statistical results and statistical concepts. A major part of learning statistics is merely learning the code. Think of it this way: in order to understand research you must speak the language, and you are about to learn the language called statistics. Then you will be able to read, understand, and communicate statistical information using the appropriate symbols and terminology. Once you speak the language, much of the mystery surrounding statistics evaporates.

### What If I'm Not Very Good at Math?

Although statistics do involve mathematical computations, the math is simple. You only need to know how to add, subtract, multiply, divide, square a number, find a square root, and draw a simple graph. You can perform all statistical calculations with pencil, paper, and a calculator.

What makes statistical procedures *appear* difficult is that most formulas involve a sequence of mathematical operations (first you square the numbers, then you add them together, then you subtract some other number, then you divide by another number, and so on). Working through the formulas is not difficult, but because they are written in code it takes a little practice.

### So All I Have to Do Is Learn How to Compute the Answers?

No, there is more to statistics than merely crunching numbers through formulas. We will discuss each step in the math calculations so that you can see what a formula does and where the answer comes from. But, given the predominance nowadays of computer programs that perform statistical procedures, the computations are not a big worry. Don't get so carried away with formulas and calculations that you lose sight of the big picture. In the big picture, a statistical answer tells you something about data. Ultimately you want to make sense out of data, and to do that you must compute the appropriate statistic and correctly interpret it. More than anything else, you need to learn *when* and *why* to use each procedure and how to *interpret* the answer from that procedure. Be sure to put as much effort into this as you do into learning how to perform the calculations.

## What Should Be My Approach?

Your approach should be to become a competent user of statistics, in the same way that you are a user of telephones every day. Recognize that you can't be an intelligent user if you do not understand the system. To operate a telephone, you must understand the rules governing long distance and why you must dial different phone numbers to call different people. The same is true in statistics: your task is to learn the rules of the system. Fortunately, statisticians have already developed the internal workings of statistical procedures, so you need only be concerned with applying these procedures in an informed manner.

## All Right, So How Do I Learn Statistics?

Study.
Think.
Practice.
Think.
Practice some more.

The way to learn statistics is to do statistics. Remember, in part you are learning a foreign language called statistics. The way to learn a foreign language is to speak it every day. Therefore, from the outset, try to use precise statistical terminology. In this book, important statistical terms are printed in bold type or are preceded by such phrases as "in statistical language we say. . . ." There is also a glossary of terms at the back of the book.

Each new statistical concept builds on previous concepts, so move on only after you understand a topic. When we discuss a concept covered earlier, there is a brief review of the concept or a reference to a previous chapter. Go back and review the topic if necessary. (Practice, practice, practice.) Also, statistical concepts are often easier to comprehend if you look at graphs and tables. Take the time to find each table and graph discussed in the text and examine it. It is there to help you. Likewise, every time you encounter a new formula, work through the example presented in the text. Master the formulas and codes at each step, because they reappear later as part of more complicated formulas.

## What Should I Know About This Book?

This book takes an intuitive approach to statistical concepts. Explanations preceded by such phrases as "You can think of it as if . . ." are designed to give your mind something to grasp other than formulas and definitions. Use the examples and analogies to help you remember and understand a concept. However, statistics is a precise discipline, so pay attention to the "official" statistical definition of a concept as well.

The research examples tend to be very simple, and they may give you the impression that every study has about five people in it and that all scores are nice round numbers like 2 or 5. In fact, real research typically involves many individuals and the scores may be downright ugly numbers like $-104.387$. But if you learn to perform a procedure in a simple setting with simple numbers, you can perform it in a more complex setting.

This book contains several features to direct your attention to important information. At the beginning of most chapters is a section entitled "More Statistical Notation." It will explain the statistical symbols used in the chapter and give you a chance to familiarize yourself with the new code before you become immersed in the concepts of the chapter. Also, every so often you will see statements labeled "STAT ALERT." These refer to basic concepts you should remember. The last section in each chapter is called "Finally." It contains advice, cautions, and ways to integrate the material from different chapters. For quick reference, a list of the formulas discussed in each chapter is provided at the end of the chapter.

At the end of each chapter is a summary. You should read each statement and determine whether you understand it. There are also practice problems at the end of each chapter, which will help you identify weak spots in your understanding of the material (think of this as a self-test before the real test). After solving each problem, step back and determine whether your answer makes sense. (The correct answer *always* makes sense.) The answers to odd-numbered problems are provided in Appendix E at the back of the book. However, do not cheat yourself by looking at the answer before you have made a serious attempt to solve the problem. Remember, the goal is for *you* to be able to perform these procedures.

There is a computer program provided with this book. To operate the program, you merely tell the computer which procedure you want performed and give it the data; it will then print out the answer. At the end of each chapter, the section called "Using the Computer" explains how to instruct the computer to perform the procedures discussed in that chapter. But remember, the computer is only there to perform computations. Even the fanciest computer cannot tell you when to use a procedure or what the answer means. That's your job.

## REVIEW OF MATHEMATICS USED IN STATISTICS

The remainder of this chapter reviews the basic math operations used in performing statistical procedures. As you will see, there is a system for statistical notation, for rounding and transforming scores, and for creating graphs.

## Basic Statistical Notation

In statistical notation, we have a code for the mathematical operations performed in the formulas, a code for the order in which operations are performed, and a code for the answers we obtain.

**Using symbols for mathematical operations**   We write formulas in statistical notation so that we can apply them to any data. In statistical notation, we usually use the symbol $X$ or $Y$ to stand for each individual score obtained in a study. When a formula says to do something to $X$, it means to do it to all of the scores we are calling $X$ scores. When a formula says to do something to $Y$, it means to do it to all of the scores we are calling $Y$.

The mathematical operations required by the formulas are basic ones: addition is indicated by the plus sign ($+$), and subtraction is indicated by the minus sign ($-$). We read from left to right, so, for example, $P - Q$ is read as "$P$ minus $Q$", and we subtract $Q$ from $P$. If $P$ equals 10 and $Q$ equals 4, then $P - Q$ means $10 - 4$ and the answer is 6. (This *is* pretty basic, isn't it?) Notice, however, that $10 - 4$ actually results in $+6$ and is very different from $4 - 10$, which results in $-6$. In statistics, the correct answer is often a negative number. Therefore, with any subtraction, pay attention to what is subtracted from what and whether the answer is positive or negative.

We indicate division by forming a fraction, such as $P/Q$. If $P$ equals 1 and $Q$ equals 2, then $P/Q$ is 1/2. The number above the dividing line (the 1) is called the numerator, and the number down below the line (the 2) is called the denominator. (Remember, the $d$ in denominator stands for "down below.") *Always reduce fractions to decimals,* dividing the denominator *into* the numerator. (Remember: 1/2 equals .50, not 2!)

We indicate multiplication in one of two ways. We may place two components next to each other: $PQ$ means "multiply $P$ times $Q$." Or we may indicate multiplication by placing the components next to each other inside of parentheses. Thus, (4)(2) or 4(2) means "multiply 4 times 2."

The symbol $X^2$ indicates that we should square the score (multiply the number times itself). Thus, if $X$ is 4, $X^2$ is $4^2$, which equals 16. Conversely, $\sqrt{X}$ means "find the square root of $X$"—the number that multiplied times itself gives $X$. Thus, $\sqrt{4}$ is 2. (The symbol $\sqrt{\phantom{x}}$ also means "use your calculator.")

**Determining the order of mathematical operations**   Statistical formulas often call for a series of mathematical steps. Sometimes the steps are set apart by parentheses. Parentheses mean "the quantity," so we always find the quantity inside the parentheses first and then perform the operations outside of the parentheses on that quantity. For example, $(4(6)) + 3$ indicates that we add 3 to the quantity 4 times 6, so we first perform the multiplication, which gives us $(24) + 3$, or 27.

Most formulas are giant fractions. In solving such a formula, pay attention to how far the dividing line is drawn, because the length of the dividing line indicates the quantity that is in the numerator or denominator. For example, in

$$\frac{4 + 6}{2} = 5$$

the dividing line is under the entire quantity 4 + 6, so we add first: 4 + 6 is 10, so we have 10/2, or 5. On the other hand, in

$$\frac{4}{2} + 6 = 8$$

the dividing line is only under the 4. Therefore, first we divide the 4 by 2: 4/2 is 2. Then we add 2 + 6 to get 8. The most complicated formulas will look like this:

$$\frac{\frac{4}{2} + 6}{8} = 1$$

Here the large dividing line indicates that we divide by 8 last. After finding that 4/2 + 6 is 8, we divide by 8, for a final answer of 1.

A square root sign also indicates "the quantity," so we compute the quantity inside the square root sign before taking the square root. For example, $\sqrt{2 + 7}$ means "take the square root of the quantity 2 + 7," so $\sqrt{2 + 7}$ becomes $\sqrt{9}$, which is 3.

If you become confused in reading a formula, remember that there is an order of precedence of mathematical operations. *Unless otherwise indicated,* perform squaring or the taking of a square root first, then multiplication or division, and then addition or subtraction. Thus, for (2)(4) + 5, we multiply 2 times 4 first and then add 5. For $2^2 + 3^2$, we square first, so we have 4 + 9, which is 13. On the other hand, $(2 + 3)^2$ indicates the quantity 2 + 3 squared, so we work inside the parentheses first; after adding, we have $5^2$, which is 25.

**Solving equations to find the answer**   We perform the operations in a formula to find an answer, and we have symbols that stand for that answer. For example, in the formula $B = AX + K$, $B$ stands for the numerical answer we will obtain. Get in the habit of thinking of the *symbols* as quantities. Because $B$ stands for a number, we can discuss whether $B$ is larger than, smaller than, or equal to some other number or symbol.

In each formula, we will find the value of the single term that is isolated on one side of the equals sign, and we will know the values of the terms on the other side of the equals sign. For the formula $B = AX + K$, say that $A = 4$, $X = 11$, and $K = 3$. Now compute $B$. In working any formula, the first step is to copy the formula and then rewrite it, replacing the symbols with their known values. Thus, we start with

$B = AX + K$

Filling in the numbers gives

$B = 4(11) + 3$

To keep track of your calculations, it is very important to rewrite the formula again after each step in which you perform *one* mathematical operation. Above, 4(11) is multiplication, which takes precedence over addition, so we multiply and then write the formula as

$B = 44 + 3$

After addition, we have

$B = 47$

For simple procedures, you may have an urge to skip rewriting the formula after each step. Don't! That's one way to introduce errors.


## Rounding

Closeness counts in statistics, so you must carry out your calculations to the appropriate number of decimal places: there is a big difference between 1.644 and 1.646. Usually you must round off your calculations at some point. Always carry out calculations so that the *final* answer after rounding has two more decimal places than the original scores. *Do not round off to two decimal places at each intermediate step in the calculations; round off only at the end!* For example, if you have whole-number scores, carry out the intermediate calculations to three decimal places or round to three, and then round off the final answer to two decimal places.

To round off a calculation, mathematicians use the following rules:

If the number in the final decimal place is 5 or greater than 5, round up: 2.366 becomes 2.37.

If the number in the final decimal place is less than 5, round down: 4.524 becomes 4.52.

Since there are five digits between 5 and 9 and five digits between 0 and 4, these rules will have us rounding up about 50% of the time and rounding down about 50% of the time.

Recognize that we add zeroes to the right of the decimal point as a way of indicating the level of precision we are using. If rounding to two decimal places gives the whole-number answer 5, we should write it as 5.00.

## Transformations

A **transformation** is a systematic mathematical procedure for converting a set of scores into a different set of scores. Adding 5 to each score is a transformation; converting "number correct" into "percent correct" is a transformation. Many statistical procedures are nothing more than involved transformations.

We transform data for one of two reasons. First, if the original scores are awkward, we may perform a transformation to make them easier to work with. For example, if all of the scores contained a decimal (1.4, 3.7, etc.), we might transform the scores by multiplying every score by 10 so that we would have no decimals. Second, we perform a transformation to make different kinds of scores comparable. For example, if you obtained 8 out of 10 on a statistics quiz and 75 out of 100 on an English quiz, it would be difficult to compare the two scores. However, if you transformed the grades to 80% on statistics and 75% on English, you would no longer be comparing apples to oranges.

As the above example illustrates, we rely heavily on transformations to *proportions* and *percents*.

**Proportions**  The decimal equivalent of any fraction between 0 and 1 is a proportion; the term *proportion* means the portion of the total. To transform any score to a proportion, simply divide the score by the highest score that is possible. If you have a score of 5 correct out of a possible 10 on a statistics quiz, the proportion you have correct is .5 (5/10 = .5). Conversely, to determine what number constitutes a certain proportion, multiply the proportion times the highest possible score. Thus, to find how many questions out of a total of 10 you must answer correctly to get .5 correct, you multiply .5 times 10, and voilà, 5 is .5 of 10.

**Percents**  We can also transform a proportion into a percent. To transform a proportion into a percent, multiply the proportion times 100. Above, the proportion correct was .5, so you had (.5)(100), or 50%, correct. To transform the original test score of 5 out of 10 to a percent, first divide the score by the number possible to find the proportion and then multiply by 100. Thus, (5/10)(100) equals 50%.

To work in the other direction and transform a percent into a proportion, divide the percent by 100 (50/100 equals .50). To find the original test score that corresponds to a certain percent, transform the percent to a proportion and then multiply the proportion times the total number possible. Thus, to find the number that corresponds to 50% of 10, transform 50% to the proportion .5 and then multiply .5 times 10. Doing all of these steps simultaneously, we find that 50% of 10 is equal to (50/100)(10), or 5.

Recognize that percents are whole numbers: think of 50% as 50 of those things called percents. A decimal in a percent is a proportion of *one* percent. Thus, .2% is .2, or two-tenths, of one percent.

## Creating Graphs

One type of statistical procedure is none other than plotting graphs of data. In case it has been a long time since you have drawn a graph, recall that the horizontal line across the bottom of a graph is called the $X$ axis, and the vertical line at the left-hand side is called the $Y$ axis. The axes should be drawn so that the height of the $Y$ axis is about 60 to 75% of the length of the $X$ axis. Such a graph is shown in Figure 1.1. The basic approach in plotting any data is to use pairs of $X$ and $Y$ scores. Where the two axes intersect is always labeled as a score of 0 on $X$ and a score of 0 on $Y$. On the $X$ axis, scores become larger positive scores as we move to the *right,* away from zero. On the $Y$ axis, scores become larger positive scores as we move *upward,* away from zero.

Say that we measured the height and weight of several people. To plot their scores, we decide to place weight on the $Y$ axis and height on the $X$ axis. (How we decide this will be discussed later.) We plot the scores as shown in Figure 1.2 on page 12.

Notice that the lowest height score is 63, and so on the $X$ axis the lowest score is 63. Whenever there is a large gap between 0 and the lowest score we are plotting, the axis is compressed using two diagonal lines (//). The diagonal

**FIGURE 1.1** Arrangement of the $X$ and $Y$ Axes in a Graph

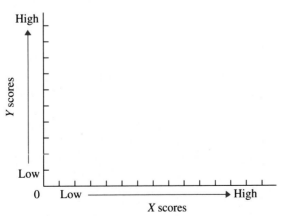

**FIGURE 1.2**  Plot of Height and Weight Scores

| Person | Height | Weight |
|--------|--------|--------|
| Jane   | 63     | 130    |
| Bob    | 64     | 140    |
| Mary   | 65     | 155    |
| Tony   | 66     | 160    |
| Sue    | 67     | 165    |
| Mike   | 68     | 170    |

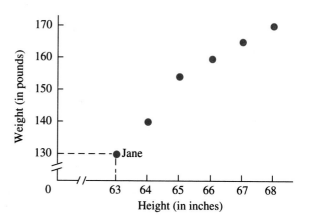

lines above indicate that we cut out, or compressed, the part of the $X$ axis between 0 and 63 and slid the graph over closer to 0. We did the same thing to the $Y$ axis, because the lowest weight is 130.

To fill in the body of the graph, we start with Jane. She is 63 inches tall and weighs 130 pounds, so we place a dot above the height of 63 and opposite the weight of 130. Bob is 64 inches tall and weighs 140 pounds, so there is a dot above 64 and opposite 140. And so on. Each dot on the graph is called a *data point*. Notice that we can read the graph using the scores on one axis and the data points. For example, to find the weight of the person who has a height of 67, travel vertically from 67 to the data point and then horizontally back to the $Y$ axis: 165 is the corresponding weight.

In later chapters you will learn when to connect the data points with lines and when to create other types of figures. A good habit to get into when reading any graph is to proceed from left to right along the $X$ axis and observe the pattern of change in the scores on the $Y$ axis. In essence we ask, "As the scores on the $X$ axis increase, what happens to the scores on the $Y$ axis?"

Regardless of the final form of a graph, always label the $X$ and $Y$ axes to indicate what the scores measure (not just $X$ and $Y$), and always give your graph a title, indicating what the figure describes.

In creating a graph, it is important to make the spacing between the labels identifying the scores on an axis reflect the spacing between the actual scores. In Figure 1.2, the labels 64, 65, and 66 are equally spaced on the graph, because the difference between 64 and 65 is the same as the difference between 65 and 66. However, in other situations, the labels may not be equally spaced. For

**FIGURE 1.3**  Plot of Height and Weight Scores Using a Different Scale on the *Y* Axis

| Height | Weight |
|--------|--------|
| 63 | 130 |
| 64 | 140 |
| 65 | 155 |
| 66 | 160 |
| 67 | 165 |
| 68 | 170 |

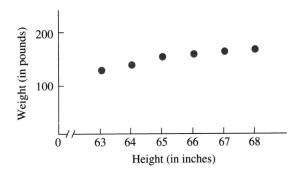

example, the labels for scores of 10, 20, and 40 would not be equally spaced, because the distance between 10 and 20 is not the same as the distance between 20 and 40.

Sometimes there are so many different scores that we cannot include a label for each score. The units we use in labeling each axis determine the impression the graph gives. Say that for the above weight scores, instead of labeling the *Y* axis in units of 10 pounds, we labeled it in units of 100 pounds (0, 100, 200). As shown in Figure 1.3, the graph now communicates a very different impression. This graph shows the same data as Figure 1.2, but changing the scale on the *Y* axis creates a much flatter pattern of data points. Here we have the misleading impression that regardless of their height, the people all have about the same weight. However, in looking at the actual scores, we see that this is not the case. Whenever you create a graph, label the axes in a way that honestly presents the data, without exaggerating or minimizing the pattern formed by the data points.

## FINALLY

That's all the basic math, algebra, and graphing you need to get started. You are now ready to begin learning to use statistics. In fact, you are already a user of statistics. If you compute your grade average or if you ask your instructor to "curve" your grades, you are using statistics. When you learn from the nightly news that Senator Fluster is projected to win the presidential election or when you learn from a television commercial that Brand X "significantly" reduces tooth decay, you are using statistics. You simply do not yet know the formal names for the procedures or the logic behind them. But you will.

## CHAPTER SUMMARY

*1.* Whether or not they are active researchers, psychologists and behavioral scientists rely on statistical procedures.

*2.* All empirical research involves some form of measurement. Research produces numbers, or scores. These scores are the *data.*

*3.* The term *statistics* has two meanings. First, it refers to a group of procedures and formulas used to analyze data. Second, it refers to the numerical answers researchers obtain by performing certain statistical procedures.

*4.* Statistical procedures are used to make sense out of data. We use statistics to organize, summarize, and communicate data and to draw conclusions about what the data indicate.

*5.* The goal in learning statistics is to know *when* to use a procedure and how to *interpret* the answer.

*6.* Unless otherwise indicated, the order of mathematical operations is to square or find the square root first, multiply or divide second, and then add or subtract.

*7.* Perform mathematical operations contained within a set of parentheses first, to find the quantity. Then perform additional operations outside of the parentheses on that quantity. Similarly, perform operations within the square root sign prior to finding the square root of the quantity, and perform operations above and below the dividing line of a fraction prior to dividing.

*8.* In rounding off decimals, if the final digit is equal to or greater than 5, round up; if the final digit is less than 5, round down.

*9.* A *transformation* is a systematic mathematical procedure for converting one set of scores into a different set of scores. We transform data to make scores easier to work with and/or to make different kinds of scores comparable.

*10.* The decimal equivalent of any fraction between 0 and 1 is a *proportion,* and it indicates the portion of the total. To transform any score to a proportion, divide the score by the highest possible score. To determine the score that constitutes a certain proportion, multiply the proportion times the highest possible score.

*11.* To transform a proportion to a *percent*, multiply the proportion times 100. To transform an original score to a percent, first find the proportion by dividing the score by the highest possible score and then multiply by 100. Conversely, to transform a percent to a proportion, divide the percent by 100. To find the original score that corresponds to a certain percent, transform the percent to a proportion and then multiply the proportion times the highest possible score.

*12.* In creating a graph, draw the $X$ and $Y$ axes so that the height of the $Y$ axis is 60 to 75% of the length of the $X$ axis. Scores on the $X$ axis start at zero and proceed to higher positive scores as we move to the *right*. Scores on the $Y$ axis start at zero and proceed to higher positive scores as we move *upward*.

*13.* Place the labels on each axis so that they accurately reflect the distance between scores and show how the scores change.

## PRACTICE PROBLEMS

(Answers are provided for odd-numbered problems.)

*1.* What four things do researchers use statistics for?
*2.* What are the rules for rounding a score up or down?
*3.* What is a transformation?
*4.* Why do we transform data?
*5.* How is a proportion computed?
*6.* What is a percent?
*7.* How does one transform a percent to a proportion?
*8.* When you create a graph, how long should the $Y$ axis be relative to the $X$ axis?
*9.* What is a data point?
*10.* Some calculations based on whole-number scores give us the intermediate answers $X = 4.3467892$ and $Y = 3.3333$. We now want to find $X^2 + Y^2$. What values of $X$ and $Y$ do we use?
*11.* Round off the following numbers to two decimals places.
  *a.* 13.7462
  *b.* 10.043
  *c.* 10.047
  *d.* .079
  *e.* 1.004
*12.* If $Q = (X + Y)(X^2 + Y^2)$, find $Q$ for $X = 3$ and $Y = 5$.
*13.* Using the formula in question 12, find $Q$ for $X = 8$ and $Y = -2$.
*14.* For $X = 14$ and $Y = 4.8$, find $D$:

$$D = \left(\frac{X - Y}{Y}\right)(\sqrt{X})$$

15. Using the formula in question 14, find $D$ for $X = 9$ and $Y = -4$.
16. Of the 40 students in a gym class, 13 played volleyball, 12 ran track (4 of whom did a pushup), and the remainder were absent.
    a. What proportion of the class ran track?
    b. What percent played volleyball?
    c. What percent of the runners did a pushup?
    d. What proportion of the class was absent?

# 2

# Statistics and the Research Process

To understand how psychologists use statistics, you need to first understand why and how they conduct research. As you begin to understand behavioral research, you will see how statistics fit in. In this chapter, we discuss the basics of behavioral research, present an overview of statistical procedures, and get you started in the language of statistics.

## THE LOGIC OF SCIENTIFIC RESEARCH

In any science, the goal is to understand the "laws of nature." A law of nature describes how some portion of the universe operates. Behavioral scientists study the laws of nature that govern behavior. Implicitly, they assume that for any behavior, there is one or more specific cause. A law of nature applies to a particular group of living organisms, so the same cause has, more or less, the same effect on the behavior of all members of that group. Thus, the goal of behavioral science is to understand those factors which cause a behavior in a particular group. When psychologists study the mating behavior of sea lions or the development of language in humans or the factors influencing learning in white rats, they are studying the laws of nature.

### Variables

In reality the laws of nature are extremely complex, with many factors all combining to cause or influence behavior. Psychologists try to simplify things by examining a law of nature in terms of one specific factor that causes or influences one specific behavior. Thus, we describe a law as something, *X*, that causes or influences some behavior, *Y*. In the language of research, the factors that cause or influence a behavior, as well as the behaviors they influence, are called variables. A **variable** is anything that, when measured, can produce two or more different scores. Some of the variables in psychological research are age, gender, intelligence, type of personality, attitudes, how loud a noise is to you, how noisy you are, how much you are paid to do something, how hard you will work, how much information you are supposed to remember in a particular situation, how much you forget in a situation, and how long it takes you to make a particular decision.

We can separate variables into two general categories. If a score indicates the amount of a variable that is present, the variable is called a *quantitative* variable. A person's height, for example, is a quantitative variable because a score indicates the quantity of height that is present. Some variables cannot be measured in amounts. Instead, they classify an individual on the basis of a characteristic. Such variables are called *qualitative*, or classification, variables. A person's gender, for example, is a qualitative variable, because the "score" of male or female indicates a *quality*, or category.

In conducting research, we study a law of nature by studying the relationship between variables.

## Relationships Between Variables

A **relationship** occurs when a change in one variable is accompanied by a consistent change in another variable. Since, in any research, we measure individuals' scores on variables, a relationship is a *pattern* in which certain scores on one variable are paired with certain scores on another variable. As the scores on one variable change, the scores on the other variable change in a consistent manner. For example, one common law of nature is that studying influences grades. We can translate this law into a relationship between two variables: one variable is the number of hours you spend studying for a test, and the other variable is your grade on the test. Theoretically anyway, the more time you study, the higher your grade will be on the test, and the less time you study, the lower your grade will be on the test.

What might this relationship look like? Say that we asked some students how long they studied for a test and their subsequent grades on the test. We might find the scores shown in Table 2.1. These scores form a relationship, because as the scores on the variable of study time change (increase), the scores on the variable of test grades also change in a consistent fashion (also increase). Further, when the scores on the study time variable do *not* change (for example, Jane and Bob both studied for 1 hour), the scores on the grade variable do not change either (for example, they both received F's). In statistics,

**TABLE 2.1**  Scores Showing a
Relationship Between Two Variables:
Study Time in Hours and Test Grades

| *Student* | *Study time in hours* | *Test grades* |
|-----------|------------------------|---------------|
| Jane      | 1                      | F             |
| Bob       | 1                      | F             |
| Sue       | 2                      | D             |
| Tony      | 3                      | C             |
| Sidney    | 3                      | C             |
| Ann       | 4                      | B             |
| Rose      | 4                      | B             |
| Lou       | 5                      | A             |

we often use the term *association* when talking about relationships. In the same way that your shadow's movements are associated with your movements, low study times are associated with low test grades and high study times are associated with high test grades.

The simplest relationships fit either the phrase "the more you $X$, the *more* you $Y$" or the phrase "the more you $X$, the *less* you $Y$." Thus, the saying "the bigger they are, the harder they fall" describes a relationship, as does that old saying "the more you practice statistics, the less difficult they are." Relationships may also form more complicated patterns where, for example, more $X$ at first leads to more $Y$, but beyond a certain point even more $X$ leads to *less* $Y$. For example, the more you exercise, the better you feel, but beyond a certain point more exercise leads to feeling less well, as pain, exhaustion, or death sets in.

Although the above examples reflect relationships involving quantitative variables, behavioral research also studies relationships involving qualitative variables. In a relationship involving a qualitative variable, as the category or quality changes, scores on the other variable change in a consistent fashion. Consider, for example, the fact that men typically are taller than women. If you think of male and female as "scores" on the variable of gender, then this is a relationship because as gender scores change (going from male to female), height scores change in a consistent fashion. We can study any combination of qualitative and/or quantitative variables in a relationship.

**Degree of association in a relationship**  In Table 2.1, there was perfect consistency between the amount of study time and test grades: all those who studied the same amount received the same grade. In the real world, however, all of the people who study the same amount of time will not receive the same test grade. (Life is not fair.) Still, a relationship can be present even if the association between scores is not perfectly consistent. There can be some *degree* of consistency so that as the scores on one variable change, the scores on the other variable *tend* to change in a consistent fashion. For example, Table 2.2 presents a relationship between the variables of number of hours spent studying and number of errors made on a test. To some degree, higher scores on the study time variable tend to be associated with lower scores on the error variable. However, every increase in study time is not matched perfectly with a decrease in errors, and sometimes the same studying score produces different error scores. The degree of association is also called the *strength* of the relationship.

Relationships are not perfectly consistent because of individual differences. The term **individual differences** refers to the fact that no two individuals are identical and that differences in genetic makeup, personal history, intelligence, aptitude, personality, and many other variables all influence their behavior in a given situation. Remember that each score reflects a behavior and that different scores reflect different behaviors. Because of individual differences, everyone who studies the same amount will not exhibit the same behavior and make the same number of errors on a test. Further, because of individual differences, an increase in the number of hours studied will not have the same effect on everyone and produce an identical change in the number of errors.

In psychological research, individual differences always produce relationships that contain only some degree of consistent association. Theoretically, perfectly consistent relationships are possible, but they do not occur in the real world.

> **STAT ALERT**  In statistics and research, we are concerned not only with the existence of a relationship but also with the degree of association, or strength, of the relationship.

**TABLE 2.2**  Scores Showing a Relationship Between Study Time in Hours and Number of Errors on Test

| Student | Study time in hours | Number of errors on test |
|---------|---------------------|--------------------------|
| Amy   | 1 | 13 |
| Joe   | 1 | 11 |
| Cleo  | 2 | 11 |
| Jack  | 3 | 10 |
| Terry | 3 | 9  |
| Chris | 4 | 9  |
| Sam   | 4 | 7  |
| Gary  | 5 | 4  |

**TABLE 2.3** Scores Showing No Relationship Between Number of Chocolate Bars Consumed per Day and Number of Eye-Blinks per Minute

| Student | Number of chocolate bars consumed per day | Number of eye-blinks per minute |
|---------|-------------------------------------------|---------------------------------|
| Mark    | 1                                         | 20                              |
| Ted     | 1                                         | 22                              |
| Ray     | 2                                         | 20                              |
| Denise  | 2                                         | 23                              |
| Maria   | 3                                         | 23                              |
| Irene   | 3                                         | 20                              |

**No relationship**  The scores on two variables can produce any degree of association from perfectly consistent association to no association. When there is no consistent association between two variables, there is no relationship. For example, there is (I think) no relationship between the number of chocolate bars people consume each day and the number of times they blink each minute. If we measured the scores of individuals on these two variables, we might have the data shown in Table 2.3. Here there is no consistent change in the scores on one variable as the scores on the other variable change. Instead, the same blinking scores tend to show up for each chocolate bar score. Notice that, because there is no relationship, *differences* in the amount of chocolate consumed are not associated with consistent differences in blinking. Ultimately, when we look for a relationship, we look for differences among the scores: for each different score on one variable, there should be a different group of scores on the other variable. Much of statistics boils down to trying to identify such differences. When researchers say they have found a difference, they mean they have found a relationship. When they find no difference, they have not found a relationship.

To summarize, then, when there is a relationship, certain scores on one variable tend to be associated with certain scores on the other variable, and when the scores on one variable change, there tends to be a consistently different group of scores on the other variable.

**Graphing relationships**  It is important that you be able to recognize a relationship and its strength when looking at a graph. Figure 2.1 on page 22 shows the data points from four sets of data. In Graph A, each $X$ is associated with one value of $Y$, and as the $X$ scores increase, the $Y$ scores consistently change (also increase). Because all the data points fall in a perfect line, the graph indicates that everyone who obtained a particular value of $X$ obtained the same value of $Y$, so there is perfectly consistent association. In Graph B, there is

**FIGURE 2.1**   Plots of Data Points from Four Sets of Data

*Each data point is the dot formed by a pair of X-Y scores.*

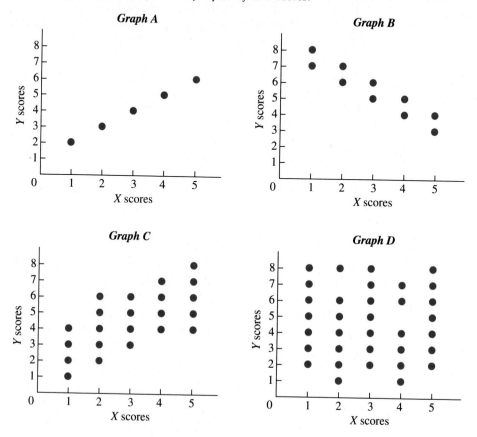

also a pattern of changing (decreasing) values of $Y$ as the $X$ scores increase. However, because there are different values of $Y$ at an $X$ score, this relationship is weaker and less than perfectly consistent. In Graph C, there is again a pattern reflecting a relationship, but here a relatively wide range of different values of $Y$ are paired with each $X$, reflecting an even less consistent and weaker relationship than in Graph B. Graph D shows no consistent pattern of change, with more or less the same values of $Y$ associated with each value of $X$. This graph reflects zero association and no relationship.

**Using relationships to discover laws**   Now you can see the basis for scientific research. The goal of science is to discover the laws of nature, and relationships are the telltale signs that a law of nature is at work. If we think we have identified something about a law of nature, we translate it into variables we can measure. Then we conduct research to see if there is a relationship between the variables. If we find a relationship, we determine the degree of association between the variables and we try to understand the relationship. Then we relate this back to the law of nature, and we have learned something about how the universe operates. For example, based on the previous examples, we have reason to believe that there is a law of nature that the amount of time spent studying somewhat consistently influences the number of errors on a test, but there is apparently no law that eating chocolate influences blinking. That, more or less, is the logic of science.

> *STAT ALERT*  The focus of all scientific research is the study of relationships.

## SAMPLES AND POPULATIONS

Any law of nature applies to a specific group of individuals (all mammals, all humans, all male white rats, all four-year-old English-speaking children). The entire group to which the law applies is called a **population.** The population contains all possible members of the group, so we usually consider a population to be infinitely large. Although ultimately scientists discuss the population of *individuals,* in statistics we talk of the population of *scores,* as if we had already measured the behavior of everyone in the population in a particular situation. Thus, you can think of a population as the infinitely large group of all possible scores we would obtain if we could measure the behavior of everyone of interest in a particular situation.

Of course, to measure an infinitely large population would take roughly forever! Instead, therefore, we study a sample of the population. A **sample** is a relatively small subset of a population that is intended to represent, or stand for, the population. It is the sample or samples that we measure, and the scores from the sample(s) constitute the data. The individuals measured in a sample are called the **subjects.** However, as with a population, in statistics we discuss a sample of scores, as if we had already measured the subjects in a particular situation. The logic behind samples is this: because we cannot measure a population, we use the scores in a sample to estimate the scores we would expect to find if we could measure the entire population.

Notice that the definitions of a sample and a population depend on your perspective. Say that we measure the students in your statistics class on some variable. If these are the only individuals we are interested in discussing, then we have measured the population of scores. On the other hand, if we are interested in the population of all college students studying statistics, then we have collected a sample of scores that represents that population. If we are interested in both the population of college males studying statistics and the population of college females studying statistics, then the males in the class are one sample and the females in the class are another sample, and each sample represents its respective population.

There is one other way to view a sample and a population. One or more scores from *one* subject can be considered a sample representing the population of all possible scores that subject might produce.

Thus, a population is any complete group of scores that would be found in a particular situation, and a sample is a subset of those scores that we actually measure in that situation. Remember, though, that scores reflect behavior, so the behavior of the sample represents the behavior of the population. Thus, when the nightly news predicts who will win the presidential election based on the results of a survey, researchers are using a sample to represent or estimate a population. The scores from the sample survey (usually containing about 1200 voters) are used to represent the voting behavior of the population of over 50 million voters.

Ultimately, the goal of any research is to describe the relationship found in the population. Ideally, based on our sample, we can conclude that as *everyone's* score on one variable changes, his or her score on the other variable tends to change in a consistent fashion. By describing how a relationship applies to everyone in the population, we are describing one aspect of how the universe or nature operates. We have reached our goal of understanding a law of nature.

Because the conclusions we draw about the population all depend on our samples, we need to create samples we can rely on.

## Representativeness of a Sample

For us to draw accurate conclusions about a population, our sample must be representative of that population. In a **representative sample,** the characteristics of the sample accurately reflect the characteristics of the population. The characteristics of the population include such things as how often each score occurs, what the highest and lowest scores are, and what the average score is. Thus, if the average score in the population is 12, then the average score in a representative sample will be around 12. If 30% of the scores in the population are 13, then around 30% of the scores in a representative sample will be 13, and so on. To put it simply, a representative sample accurately represents the population.

Whether a sample is representative depends on how we select the sample. From a statistical standpoint, the most important aspect of creating representative samples is random sampling.

## Random Sampling

**Random sampling** is a method of selecting a sample whereby (1) all possible scores in the population have the same chances of being selected for a sample and (2) all possible samples have the same chances of being selected. Since we obtain scores from subjects, random sampling means that we are unbiased, or unselective, in choosing our subjects, so that all members of the population have an equal chance of being selected. To create a random sample from a population, we select subjects based on the luck of the draw. We might place the names of all potential subjects on slips of paper in a very large hat, stir them up, and then draw the names of the subjects to be in our sample. Or we might use a computer to generate random numbers and select subjects with corresponding social security numbers. Any way we do it, we are as unbiased as possible in selecting subjects, and we try to select from all segments of the population of interest. We may be selective in choosing the population, but then we use random sampling to select the sample from that population. For example, if I want to study only 12-day-old babies, I will randomly select from the population of 12-day-old babies to create my sample.

> *STAT ALERT*  It is an implicit assumption of all statistical analysis that samples are selected through random sampling.

A random sample *should* turn out to be representative of the population, because random sampling allows the characteristics of the population to occur in the same way in the sample. For example, if 30% of the individuals in the population have a score of 13, then 30% of the subjects we select through random sampling should also have a score of 13. It is as if we randomly wandered through the population of subjects. Out of every 100 subjects we encountered, 30 of them should have a score of 13. In the same way, random sampling should produce a sample having all of the characteristics of the population.

At least we *hope* it works that way! I keep saying that random samples "should" be representative, but this is a very big should. There is nothing that forces a random sample to be representative of a particular population. The trouble is that with random sampling we are dealing with the luck of the draw. Whether a sample is representative is determined by which scores and thus which subjects we select to be in the sample. Which subjects we select is determined by random chance. Therefore, whether a sample is representative depends on who happens to be selected for the sample. We can, just by the luck of the draw, obtain a very unusual sample of subjects who are not at all representative of most subjects in the population. Thus, for example, 30% of the individuals in the population may have a score of 13, but through random sampling we may not select *any* subjects who have this score. Likewise, the sample average may not accurately represent the population average, and so on.

Thus, random sampling is a double-edged sword. We use random sampling to produce a representative sample, and usually it works pretty well. But random sampling may backfire on us, producing a very unrepresentative sample. This is one of the most important concerns we have when interpreting research. As we shall see, one of the reasons behavioral scientists use statistics is to enable them to determine whether a sample is representative of a particular population. For now, the lesson is that we can never take a sample at face value, automatically assuming that it represents a particular population.

## RESEARCH DESIGNS

Although virtually all research uses random samples to represent populations, there are many ways to set up, or design, a study. A **research design** is the way in which a study is laid out: how many samples there are, how the subjects are tested, and the other specifics of how a researcher goes about demonstrating a relationship. As we shall see, different research designs require different statistical procedures. However, research designs can be broken down into two major types: experiments and correlational studies.

### Experiments

Not all research is an experiment. Technically, an **experiment** involves a procedure in which the researcher actively changes or manipulates one variable, measures the scores on another variable, and keeps all other variables constant. The logic of an experiment is extremely simple, and you use it every day. For example, if you believe a certain light switch controls a certain light, you flip that switch, keep all other switches constant, and see whether the light comes on. In an experiment, if we believe there is a relationship in which variable $X$ influences behavior $Y$, we produce different amounts of $X$, keep all other variables constant, and see whether the scores on variable $Y$ change in a consistent fashion.

Say that we are conducting an experiment to examine the relationship between the variables of amount of time spent studying statistics and number of errors made on a statistics test. We decide to compare 0, 1, 2, and 3 hours of study time, so we randomly select four samples of students. We give one sample of subjects 0 study time, administer the test, and then count the number of errors each subject makes. We give another sample 1 hour of study time, administer the test, and then count the errors, and so on for our remaining samples. If we understand the laws of nature governing learning and test taking, then as the length of study time increases, the number of errors should decrease.

There are names for the components of any experiment, and you will use them daily in research and statistics.

**The independent variable**  In any experiment, there is at least one variable called the independent variable. An **independent variable** is a variable that is changed or manipulated by the experimenter. Implicitly, it is the variable that we think causes a change in the other variable. In our studying experiment, we manipulate how long subjects study, because we think that longer studying causes fewer errors. Thus, amount of study time is the independent variable. In an experiment to determine whether eating more chocolate causes people to blink more, amount of chocolate consumed would be the independent variable, because the experimenter controls the amount of chocolate a subject eats. You can remember the independent variable as the variable that the experimenter manipulates independently of what the subject wishes. (Above, some subjects studied for 3 hours whether they wanted to or not.)

Technically, a true independent variable is manipulated by doing something *to* subjects. However, there are many behavior-influencing variables that an experimenter cannot change by doing something to subjects. For example, we might hypothesize that growing older causes a change in some behavior. However, we cannot randomly select subjects and then *make* some of them 20 years old and some of them 40 years old. In such situations, the experimenter must manipulate the variable in a different way. Here we would randomly select one sample of 20-year-olds and one sample of 40-year-olds. Similarly, if we wanted to examine whether a qualitative variable such as gender was related to some behavior, we would select a sample of females and a sample of males. In our discussions, we will *call* such a variable an independent variable, because the experimenter controls the variable by controlling a characteristic of the samples. Technically, though, such variables are called *quasi-independent variables.*

Thus, the experimenter is always in control of the independent variable, either by determining what is done to a sample or by determining a characteristic of the subjects in each sample. In essence, a subject's "score" on the independent variable is determined by the experimenter. Above, subjects in the sample that studied 0 hours have a score of 0 on the study time variable, and subjects in the 20-year-old sample have a score of 20 on the age variable.

In any experiment, we test subjects under certain conditions of the independent variable. A **condition** is a specific amount or category of the independent variable that creates the specific situation under which the subjects' scores on some other variable are measured. Above, our independent variable was amount of study time, and the conditions of that variable were 0, 1, 2, or 3 hours of study. Or, if we compare the errors of males and females, then "male" and "female" are each a condition of the independent variable of gender. A condition is also known as a **treatment:** having subjects study 1 hour is one way to treat subjects.

**The dependent variable**   If a relationship exists, then as we change the conditions of the independent variable, we will observe a consistent change in the scores on the dependent variable. The **dependent variable** is the variable that is measured under each condition of the independent variable. Scores on the dependent variable are presumably caused or influenced by the independent variable, so scores on the dependent variable *depend* (in part, at least) on the conditions of the independent variable. In our studying experiment above, the number of errors on the test is the dependent variable, because we believe that the number of errors depends on how long subjects study. Since we measure subjects' scores on the dependent variable, it is also called the dependent measure.

>   *STAT ALERT*   The independent variable is always manipulated by the experimenter, and the dependent variable is always what the subjects' scores measure.

After we have conducted our experiment examining the relationship between amount of study time and number of test errors, we need to examine our data. Table 2.4 shows a useful way to diagram the design of an experiment, label the components, and organize the data.[1] Each number is a subject's score on

**TABLE 2.4**   Diagram of an Experiment Involving the Independent Variable of Number of Hours Spent Studying and the Dependent Variable of Number of Errors Made on a Statistics Test

*Each column contains subjects' scores measured under one condition of the independent variable.*

|  | *Independent variable: number of hours spent studying* | | | |
|---|---|---|---|---|
|  | *Condition 1: 0 hours* | *Condition 2: 1 hour* | *Condition 3: 2 hours* | *Condition 4: 3 hours* |
| Dependent variable: number of errors made on a statistics test | 13 12 11 | 9 8 7 | 7 6 5 | 5 3 2 |

[1]The data presented in this book are a work of fiction. Any resemblance to real data is purely coincidence.

the dependent variable of number of test errors. Is there a relationship here? Yes. Why? Because as subjects' scores on the variable of amount of study time change (increase), their scores on the variable of number of test errors also tend to change (decrease) in a consistent fashion.

**Drawing conclusions about the population**    Ultimately, we want to describe the population of all students with respect to amount of time spent studying and number of errors made on a test. If our samples are representative, then we can assume that each sample of scores under a particular condition represents a different population of scores that occurs under that condition. For example, our sample that studied 0 hours produced scores of 11, 12, and 13 errors. Therefore, we expect that if all college students studied for 0 hours, they would produce a population consisting of error scores generally around 11 to 13. Our sample that studied for 1 hour produced scores of between 7 and 9 errors. Therefore, we expect that if we had all students study for 1 hour, the population would consist of scores around 7 to 9 errors. Similarly, we expect that studying for 2 hours would produce a population of scores around 5 to 7 errors, and studying for 3 hours would produce a population of scores around 2 to 5 errors.

The above example illustrates the type of conclusions we hope to draw from any experiment. If we can conclude that different populations of error scores would be associated with different amounts of study time, we can conclude that there is a *relationship in the population:* as scores on the variable of amount of study time change, *all* scores on the variable of number of errors tend to change in a consistent fashion. This means that there is one group (population) of error scores having certain values associated with one score on the variable of amount of study time and there is a different group (population) of error scores associated with a different score on amount of study time. If we can say that the relationship applies to the population, we are saying that the relationship applies to *all* students. Therefore, we have demonstrated how the laws of nature operate when it comes to studying and test errors.

On the other hand, if we cannot conclude that there are different populations of error scores associated with different amounts of study time, then we have *not* demonstrated a relationship in the population. Then, we have not learned about how a law of nature operates.

Thus, from a statistical perspective, the goal of any experiment is to show that there is a different population of scores on the dependent variable associated with each condition of the independent variable.

**The problem of causality**    When we conclude that an experiment shows a relationship in the population, we then discuss the relationship as if changing the independent variable "caused" the scores on the dependent variable to change. However, it is important to realize that we cannot definitively prove that $X$ causes $Y$. Implicitly we recognize that some other variable may actually be the cause. In our studying experiment, for example, perhaps the subjects who studied for 0 hours had headaches and the actual cause of high error scores was not lack of study time, but headaches. Or perhaps the subjects who studied for 3 hours were more motivated, and this motivation produced lower error scores. Or perhaps some subjects cheated, or perhaps the moon was full, or who knows what! Although we try to eliminate and control such extraneous variables through well-designed research, we are never completely certain that we have done so. Therefore, in any relationship we demonstrate, there is always the possibility that some unknown variable is actually causing the scores to change.

This is especially true when we examine a quasi-independent variable. For example, if we find that a sample of males has different scores than a sample of females, we *cannot* claim that the sex of the subjects causes differences in scores. This is because not only would the samples differ in terms of the gender variable, but coincidentally the females would tend to differ from the males along a host of other variables, including height, hair length, amount of makeup, interests, and attitudes. Any one of these variables might actually be causing the differences in scores.

Recognize that statistics are not a solution to this problem. There is no statistical procedure that will prove that one variable causes another variable to change. Think about it: how could some formula written on a piece of paper "know" what causes certain scores to occur? How could a statistical result prove any statement you make about the real world?

**Statistics do not prove anything!**

An experiment merely provides evidence, like the evidence in a court of law. How the experiment was conducted and how well the experimenter controlled extraneous variables are part of the evidence supporting a certain conclusion. Statistical results are additional evidence to support the conclusion. Such evidence helps us to *argue* for a certain point of view, but it is not proof. As scientists, we always know there is the possibility that we are wrong.

## Correlational Studies

Sometimes we choose not to manipulate certain variables and conduct an experiment. Instead, we may design the research as a correlational study. In a **correlational study,** we simply measure subjects' scores on two variables and then determine whether there is a relationship. We could, for example, use a correlational approach to study the relationship between amount of study time and number of test errors. We would simply ask a random sample of students how long they studied for a particular test and how many errors they made on the test. Then we would again determine whether a relationship exists, asking "Did subjects who studied longer make fewer errors?" As in an experiment, the goal of a correlational study is to describe the relationship we expect would be found in the population. We seek to show that for all students who study for a certain amount of time there is one population of error scores, and for those students who study for a different amount of time there is a different population of error scores.

Notice that in correlational research the researcher does not actively manipulate or control any variables. Therefore, even more so than in an experiment, there are potentially a host of extraneous variables that actually may be causing scores to change. Thus, we can *never* say, based on a correlational study, that changes in one variable cause the other variable to change. All we can say is that there is a relationship, or association, between the scores on the two variables. (We will explore this issue further when we discuss correlation in Chapter 7.)

## USING STATISTICAL PROCEDURES TO ANALYZE DATA

Regardless of the design of our experiment, we use statistical procedures to make sense out of it. What does "make sense" mean? First of all, since we conduct research to demonstrate a relationship, we use statistical analysis to determine whether a relationship is present. In our studying experiment, we want to determine whether there is a relationship between subjects' error scores and the amount of time they studied. Second, making sense of the data means describing the scores and the relationship we find in a study. We want to know how many errors are associated with a particular amount of study time, how much errors decrease with increased study time, how consistently errors decrease, and so on. Third, if we understand a relationship, then we should be able to use a subject's score on one variable to accurately predict his or her behavior and corresponding score on some other variable. If we know how many hours subjects study, we should be able to accurately predict the number of errors they make on the test. Thus, we use statistical procedures to analyze data so that we may (1) determine whether a relationship is present, (2) describe the relationship and the scores in it, and (3) predict the scores on one variable using the scores on another variable.

In statistics, however, we are always talking about two things: the sample data we have collected and the population of scores being represented. Therefore, statistical procedures can be broken down into two categories: descriptive statistical procedures, which deal with samples, and inferential statistical procedures, which deal with populations.

## Descriptive Statistics

Recall that individual differences ensure that there is no such thing as a perfectly consistent relationship. Therefore, in real data, there will be many different scores in each sample. Researchers are invariably confronted with a mind-boggling array of different numbers which may have a relationship hidden in it. The purpose of descriptive statistics is to bring order to this chaos. **Descriptive statistics** are procedures for organizing and summarizing data so that we can communicate and describe the important characteristics of the data. (Descriptive statistics are used to describe data, so when you see *descriptive,* think *describe.*)

How do descriptive statistics work? In our studying experiment, of the three subjects who studied for 0 hours, one made 11 errors, one made 12 errors, and one made 13 errors. To simplify the data, we can say that this sample produced around 11 to 13 errors. In fact, split the difference: close to 12 errors are associated with zero study time. By saying that zero study time produced close to 12 errors, we have used descriptive statistics. We summarized the data by reducing the results to one number (12). We communicated an important characteristic of the data by saying that the scores are around 12 (and not around 33). We described another important characteristic of the data by stating that the scores are *close* to 12 (as opposed to being spread out around 12).

Statisticians have developed descriptive procedures that enable us to answer five basic questions about the characteristics of a sample.

1. *What scores did we obtain?* To answer this question, we organize and present the scores in tables and graphs.

2. *Are the scores generally high scores or generally low scores?* We can describe the scores with one number that is the "typical" score.

3. *Are the scores very different from each other, or are they close together?* As we shall see, there are mathematical ways of computing "close."

4. *How does any one particular score compare to all other scores?* Certain statistical transformations allow us to easily compare any score to the rest of the scores.

5. *What is the nature of the relationship we have found?* We can describe the important characteristics of a relationship and use this information to predict scores on one variable if we know a score on another variable.

Parts 2 and 3 of this book discuss the specific descriptive procedures used to answer these five questions. When we have answered these questions, we have described the important characteristics of a sample. Realize, however, that even though we compute a precise mathematical answer, it will not precisely describe every score in the sample. (Above, every score in the zero study time condition was not 12.) In any summary, less accuracy is the price we pay for less complexity and less quantity, so descriptive statistics always imply "around" or "more or less."

## Inferential Statistics

After we have answered the five questions above for our sample, we want to answer the same questions for the population represented by the sample. Thus, although technically, descriptive statistical procedures are used to describe samples, the logic of descriptive statistics is also applied to describing populations. Of course, since we usually cannot measure the scores in the population, we must *estimate* the description of the population. However, we cannot automatically infer that a sample accurately estimates the population. Remember, the inferences we draw about a population will be accurate only if the sample is representative of the population. Although previously we saw that random sampling should produce representative samples, we also saw that it may not. Therefore, for example, even though the subjects in our sample who studied for 0 hours made around 12 errors, this does not mean that everyone in the population who studies for 0 hours will make around 12 errors. Only when the sample is representative of the population can we assume that the average error score in the population is around 12.

The problem is that we never know whether a sample is representative of a particular population. We would have to measure the entire population and see how well the sample and population matched. But if we could measure the entire population, then we would not need the sample to begin with! Thus, there is always the possibility that a sample is *not* representative of the corresponding population.

For this reason, before we can draw any conclusions about the population being represented by our sample, we must first perform inferential statistics. **Inferential statistics** are procedures that allow us to decide whether a sample we have obtained is or is not representative of a particular population. As the name implies, inferential procedures help us to make accurate *inferences* about the population being represented by our sample.

How do we do this? Previously we said that whether a sample is representative depends on chance, the luck of the draw by which subjects are selected to be in the sample. Although we never know whether random chance produced an unrepresentative sample, we do have models of how random chance operates. Through such models, inferential statistics allow us to decide whether a sample is representative of a particular population. If the sample is deemed representative of a particular population, then we assume that the sample gives us a reasonably accurate estimate of the population.

Part 4 of this book discusses inferential statistics in great detail. Until then, simply think of inferential procedures as ways of determining whether a sample is representative of a particular population. For now, we will assume that a sample is representative of the corresponding population.

### Statistics and Parameters

In all research, then, whether experimental or correlational, we set up a situation in which we measure the scores of a randomly selected sample. We use descriptive procedures to describe the sample, and then we use inferential procedures to make estimates about the corresponding population of scores we expect we would find if we could measure the entire population. From our description of the population of scores, we may be able to infer that a relationship exists in the population and thereby learn something about a law of nature.

So that we know when we are describing a sample and when we are describing a population, statisticians use the following system. A number that describes a characteristic of a *sample* of scores is called a **sample statistic** or simply a **statistic.** Different statistics describe different characteristics, and the symbols for different statistics are different letters from the English alphabet. On the other hand, a number that describes a characteristic of a *population* of scores is called a **population parameter** or simply a **parameter.** The symbols for different parameters are different letters from the Greek alphabet. For example, if we compute your bowling average from a sample of your scores, we are computing a descriptive statistic. The symbol for a sample average is a letter from the English alphabet. If we then estimate the average of the population of all your bowling scores based on the sample average, we are estimating a population parameter. The symbol for a population average is a letter from the Greek alphabet.

## TYPES OF VARIABLES

Whether we conduct an experiment or a correlational study, we measure subjects on variables, so we end up with a batch of scores. Depending on the variables, the numbers that comprise the scores can have different underlying mathematical characteristics. The particular mathematical characteristics of a variable determine which particular descriptive or inferential procedure we should use. Recall that one of your goals is to learn when to use a particular statistical procedure. Therefore, you must always pay attention to two important characteristics of your variables: the type of measurement scale involved and whether the scale is continuous or discrete.

## The Four Types of Measurement Scales

Numbers mean different things in different contexts. The meaning of the number 1 on a license plate is different from the meaning of the number 1 in a race, which is different still from the meaning of the number 1 in a hockey score. The kind of information that scores convey depends on the *scale of measurement* that is used in measuring the variable. There are four types of measurement scales—nominal, ordinal, interval, and ratio scales—and each has unique mathematical characteristics.

With a **nominal scale,** each score does not actually indicate an amount; rather, it is used simply for identification, as a name. (When you see *nominal,* think *name.*) License plate numbers and the numbers on the uniforms of football players reflect a nominal scale of measurement. In research, a nominal scale is used to identify the categories of a qualitative, or classification, variable. For example, we cannot perform any statistical operations on the words *male* and *female.* Therefore, we might assign each male subject a 1 and each female subject a 2. However, because this scale is nominal, we could just as easily assign males a 2 and females a 1, or we could use any other two numbers. Because we assign numbers in a nominal scale arbitrarily, they do not have the mathematical properties normally associated with numbers. For example, as used here, the number 1 does not indicate more than 0 but less than 2 as it usually does.

When a variable is measured using an **ordinal scale,** the scores indicate rank order: the score of 1 means the most or least of the variable, 2 means the second most or least, and so on. (For *ordinal,* think *ordered.*) In psychological research, ordinal scales are used, for example, to rank subjects in terms of their aggressiveness or to have subjects rank the importance of certain attributes in their friends. Each score indicates an amount of sorts, but it is a relative amount. For example, relative to everyone else being ranked, you may be the number 1 student, but we do not know how good a student you actually are. Further, with an ordinal scale there is not an equal unit of measurement separating each score. In a race, for example, first may be only slightly ahead of second, whereas second may be miles ahead of third. Also, there is no number 0 in ranks (no one can be "zero-ith").

When a variable is measured using an **interval scale,** each score indicates an actual amount, and there *is* an equal unit of measurement separating each score: the difference between 2 and 3 is the same as the difference between 3 and 4. (For *interval,* think *equal* interval.) Interval scales include the number 0 but it is not a "true" zero. It does not mean zero amount; it is just another point on the scale. Because of this feature, an interval scale allows negative numbers. Temperature (measured in centigrade or Fahrenheit) is an interval scale. A measurement of zero degrees does not mean that zero amount of heat is present; it only means that there is less than 1 degree and more than $-1$ degree. Interval scales are often used with quantitative variables measured by psychological tests, such as intelligence or personality tests. Although a score of zero may be possible, it does not mean zero intelligence or zero personality.

Finally, when a variable is measured using a **ratio scale,** the scores measure an actual amount, there is an equal unit of measurement, *and* 0 truly means that zero amount of the variable is present. Therefore, ratio scales cannot include negative numbers. Only with ratio scales can we make ratio statements, such as "4 is twice as much as 2." (So for *ratio,* think *ratio!*) In psychological research, ratio scales are used to measure quantitative variables, such as the number of errors made on a test, the number of friends someone has, or the number of calories consumed in a day.

To help you remember the four scales of measurement, Table 2.5 summarizes their characteristics.

## Discrete and Continuous Scales

In addition to being nominal, ordinal, interval, or ratio, a measurement scale is either continuous or discrete. A **continuous scale** allows for fractional amounts; it "continues" between the whole-number amounts. With a continuous scale, decimals make sense. Age is a continuous variable because it is perfectly intelligent to say that someone is 19.6879 years old. (In fact, age is a continuous

**TABLE 2.5**   Summary of Types of Measurement Scales

*Each column describes the characteristics of the scale.*

| | Type of scale | | | |
|---|---|---|---|---|
| | *Nominal* | *Ordinal* | *Interval* | *Ratio* |
| What does the scale indicate? | Quality | Relative quantity | Quantity | Quantity |
| Is there an equal unit of measurement? | No | No | Yes | Yes |
| Is there a true zero? | No | No | No | Yes |
| How might the scale be used in research? | To identify males and females as 1 and 2 | To judge who is 1st, 2nd, etc., in aggressiveness | To convey the results of intelligence and personality tests | To state the number correct on a test |

ratio variable.) To be continuous, a variable must be at least theoretically continuous. For example, intelligence tests are designed to produce whole-number scores. You cannot obtain an IQ score of 95.6. But theoretically an IQ of 95.6 makes sense, so intelligence is a theoretically continuous interval variable.

On the other hand, some variables involve a **discrete scale,** and then the variables can only be measured in whole-number amounts. Here, decimals do not make sense. Usually, nominal and ordinal variables are discrete. In addition, some interval and ratio variables are discrete. For example, the number of cars someone owns and the number of children someone has are discrete variables. It sounds strange when the government reports that the average family has 2.4 children and owns 1.78 cars, because these are discrete variables being treated as if they were continuous. (Imagine a .4 child driving a .78 car!)

There is a special type of a discrete variable. When there can be only two amounts or categories of the variable, it is a **dichotomous** variable. Pass/fail, male/female, and living/dead are examples of dichotomous variables.

> *STAT ALERT*   Whether a variable is continuous or discrete and whether it is measured using a nominal, ordinal, interval, or ratio scale are factors used to determine which statistical procedure to apply.

### *FINALLY*

The terms and logic introduced in this chapter are used throughout the scientific world. Psychologists and behavioral scientists thoroughly understand such terms as relationship, independent and dependent variable, condition, and descriptive statistic. These terms are a part of their everyday vocabulary, and they think using these terms. For you to understand research and apply statistical procedures (let alone understand this book), you too must learn to think in these terms. The first step is to always be careful to use the appropriate terminology.

## CHAPTER SUMMARY

*1.* The goal of psychological research is to discover the laws of nature governing behavior. To do this, we study the relationships between variables.

*2.* A *variable* is anything that, when measured, can produce two or more different scores. Variables may be *quantitative,* measuring a quantity or amount, or *qualitative,* measuring a quality or category.

3. A *relationship* occurs when a change in scores on one variable is associated with a consistent change in scores on another variable.

4. The term *individual differences* refers to the fact that no two individuals are identical. Because of individual differences, relationships can have varying *strengths*, showing only some *degree* of consistent association between the scores on two variables.

5. The large group of all individuals for which a relationship applies is known as the *population*. In statistics, the population is the entire group of scores that we wish to describe. The subset of the population that is actually measured is the *sample*.

6. In conducting research, we select subjects using *random sampling*. For a sample to be random, all possible scores in the population must have the same chances of being selected and all possible samples must have the same chances of being selected.

7. Random sampling is used to produce *representative samples*. Representative means that the characteristics of the sample accurately reflect the characteristics of the population.

8. In an *experiment*, a relationship is demonstrated by the experimenter's manipulating or changing the *independent variable* and then measuring scores on the *dependent variable*. Each specific amount or category of the independent variable used in an experiment is known as a *condition* or *treatment*.

9. In *correlational research*, neither variable is actively manipulated or controlled. Scores on both variables are simply measured as they occur, and then a relationship is determined.

10. In any type of research, if a relationship is observed, it may or may not mean that changes in one variable *cause* the other variable to change.

11. *Descriptive statistics* are procedures used to organize, summarize, and describe the characteristics of a sample. *Inferential statistics* are procedures used to decide whether a sample is representative of a particular population.

12. A *statistic* is a number that describes a characteristic of a sample of scores. The symbols for statistics are letters from the English alphabet. A sample statistic is used to infer or estimate the corresponding *population parameter*. A parameter is a number that describes a characteristic of a population of scores. The symbols for parameters are letters from the Greek alphabet.

13. Which particular descriptive or inferential procedure we use is in part determined by the *scale of measurement* used to measure the variables.

We may use (1) a *nominal scale*, in which numbers name or identify a quality or characteristic; (2) an *ordinal scale*, in which numbers indicate a rank order; (3) an *interval scale*, in which numbers measure a specific amount, but with no true zero; or (4) a *ratio scale*, in which numbers measure a specific amount and 0 indicates truly zero amount.

*14.* Which procedures we use also depends on whether a variable is *continuous*, in which case decimals make sense, or *discrete*, in which case decimals do not make sense. A *dichotomous variable* is a special type of discrete variable that has only two amounts or categories.

## USING THE COMPUTER

Accompanying this book is a computer disk containing a program that performs the descriptive and inferential statistical procedures we will discuss. To carry out a procedure, you answer some questions and enter your data, and the program does the rest. (In the instructions given in this text, any answers that you are to give the program are displayed in **bold** print. Remember that, when you give an answer, usually the computer won't proceed until you press the key that is labeled either "Return" or "Enter.")

The program can be used on most IBM-compatible computers. To use the program, first load the DOS program that comes with your computer. Then insert the statistics program disk into the computer. To start the program, type **RUN** (and press the Return key). The title page of the program will then appear, and at the bottom of the screen you will see "To continue to Main Menu, strike a key when ready." Do so, and you will see the Main Menu. This is a list of the major procedures that the program performs. Each procedure is numbered. Number **1**, entitled "Instructions," tells you about the program, including your options of saving your data on a disk and of printing out the data and the results you compute. Under the Main Menu is a request for you to type the number of the procedure you want. Then, to perform the procedure, simply answer as instructed the questions displayed on the screen. On completion of a procedure, the program will return to the Main Menu. Then you can select another procedure or select number **14** to exit the program.

Refer to Appendix F for further information about hardware and software requirements.

## PRACTICE PROBLEMS

(Answers are provided for odd-numbered problems.)
1. How can you recognize that a relationship exists between two variables?
2. What is the difference between an experiment and a correlational study?

3. What is meant by the condition of an independent variable?
4. What is the dependent variable?
5. What is random sampling?
6. Why do random samples occur that are representative of the population? Why do unrepresentative samples occur?
7. What is the purpose of descriptive statistics?
8. What are inferential statistics used for?
9. What is the difference between a statistic and a parameter?
10. What types of symbols are used for statistics and parameters?
11. In which of the following samples is a relationship present?

| Sample A | | Sample B | | Sample C | | Sample D | |
|---|---|---|---|---|---|---|---|
| X | Y | X | Y | X | Y | X | Y |
| 1 | 1 | 20 | 40 | 13 | 20 | 92 | 71 |
| 1 | 1 | 20 | 42 | 13 | 19 | 93 | 77 |
| 1 | 1 | 22 | 40 | 13 | 18 | 93 | 77 |
| 2 | 2 | 22 | 41 | 13 | 17 | 95 | 79 |
| 2 | 2 | 23 | 40 | 13 | 15 | 96 | 74 |
| 3 | 3 | 24 | 40 | 13 | 14 | 97 | 71 |
| 3 | 3 | 24 | 42 | 13 | 13 | 98 | 69 |

12. In question 11, which sample shows the strongest degree of association?
13. Using the words "statistic" and "parameter," describe a relationship in the population.
14. In the chart below, identify the characteristics of each variable.

| Variable | Qualitative or quantitative | Continuous, discrete, or dichotomous | Type of measurement scale |
|---|---|---|---|
| gender | ———— | ———— | ———— |
| academic major | ———— | ———— | ———— |
| time | ———— | ———— | ———— |
| restaurant ratings | ———— | ———— | ———— |
| speed | ———— | ———— | ———— |
| money | ———— | ———— | ———— |
| position in line | ———— | ———— | ———— |
| change in weight | ———— | ———— | ———— |

# PART 2

# DESCRIPTIVE STATISTICS: DESCRIBING SAMPLES AND POPULATIONS

So, we're off! In research we attempt to discover the laws of nature by looking for a relationship between variables. We use statistical analysis of the scores we obtain in a study as a tool to look with. In Chapter 2 we saw that descriptive statistical procedures can answer five questions about a set of data:

*1.* What scores did we obtain?

*2.* Are the scores generally high scores or generally low scores?

*3.* Are there large differences between the scores, or are there small differences between the scores?

*4.* How does any one particular score compare to all other scores?

*5.* What is the nature of the relationship we have found?

Using the answers from these questions, we then estimate the answers to the same questions about the population that is represented by the sample. In each of the four chapters of Part 2, we will discuss the procedures used to answer one of the first four questions above. In Part 3 we will answer the final question.

# 3

# Frequency Distributions and Percentiles

We call the scores we measure in a study the *raw data* or the *raw scores:* the scores are "uncooked" and not yet "digestible." Descriptive statistical procedures help us to cook down the raw scores into an organized and interpretable form. One way to organize raw scores is to display them in graphs and tables. In creating a graph or table, we present the scores so as to answer our first question about the data: what scores did we obtain? A basic rule for you is always to organize the raw data into a table or to plot a graph. As the saying goes, "a picture is worth a thousand words," and nowhere is this more appropriate than in organizing a large group of scores. Such organization is imperative if you are to make sense out of the data. Also, descriptive statistical procedures allow you to communicate your results to others, and creating a table or graph is often the most efficient way to do so. Finally, we want to look for relationships in our data, and an organized table or graph allows us to see a relationship.

In this chapter we will discuss four ways to organize and display data: using each score's simple frequency, relative frequency, cumulative frequency, or percentile.

But first . . .

## MORE STATISTICAL NOTATION

By constructing a table or graph, we create what statisticians call a distribution. A **distribution** is the general name for any organized set of data. We organize scores in different ways so that we can see the pattern formed by the scores.

In statistical language, the pattern, or arrangement, of the scores is the way in which the scores are *distributed* in the sample or population.

Throughout statistics we use the important symbol $N$. In most procedures we must count how *many* scores we have. $N$ stands for the number of scores in a set of data. (When you see $N$, think *Number*.) An $N$ of 10 means that we have 10 scores, or $N = 43$ means that we have 43 scores. Note that $N$ stands for the total number of scores, *not* the number of different scores. For example, if the 100 scores in a sample are all the same number, $N$ still equals 100. When we have one score for each subject, $N$ corresponds to the number of subjects in the sample. In the terminology of statistics, $N$ is the *sample size:* $N$ indicates how big a sample is in terms of the number of scores it contains. Get in the habit of treating the symbol $N$ as a quantity itself so that you will understand such statements as "the $N$ subjects in the sample" or "increasing $N$" or "this sample's $N$ is larger than that sample's $N$."

We are concerned with how often each score occurs within a set of data. How often a score occurs is the score's **frequency,** symbolized by $f$. Also learn to treat $f$ as a quantity: one score's $f$ may be larger than another score's $f$, we can add the $f$'s of different scores, and so on. Since there are several different ways to describe a score's frequency, we use frequency and $f$ with other terms and symbols.

## CREATING SIMPLE FREQUENCY DISTRIBUTIONS

The most common way to organize a distribution of scores is to create a simple frequency distribution. A **simple frequency distribution** shows the number of times each score occurs in a set of data. The symbol for a score's simple frequency is simply $f$. To find $f$ for a score, count how many times that score occurs in the data. If three subjects scored 13, there are three scores of 13 in the data, so the frequency of 13 (its $f$) is 3. Creating a simple frequency distribution involves counting the frequency of every score in the data.

### Presenting Simple Frequency in a Table

To see how we present a simple frequency distribution in a table, let's begin with the following sample of raw scores. (Perhaps these scores measure some deep psychological process, or perhaps they are something silly like the number of chocolate Bing-Bongs each subject eats in a day; it makes no difference.)

| | | | | | | | | |
|---|---|---|---|---|---|---|---|---|
| 14 | 14 | 13 | 15 | 11 | 15 | 13 | 10 | 12 |
| 13 | 14 | 13 | 14 | 15 | 17 | 14 | 14 | 15 |

There are only 18 scores here, but in this disorganized arrangement, it is difficult to make sense out of them. Watch what happens, though, when we arrange them into a simple frequency table. We create the table by counting the number of times each score occurred. Then we create a score column and an $f$ column, as shown in Table 3.1. Notice that the score column begins with the highest score in the data at the *top* of the column. Below that in the column are all *possible* whole-number scores in decreasing order, down to the lowest score that occurred. Thus, although no subject obtained a score of 16, we still include it.

Now we can easily see the frequency of each score and discern how the scores are distributed. We can also determine the combined frequency of several scores by adding together their individual $f$'s. For example, in Table 3.1, the score of 13 has an $f$ of 4 and the score of 14 has an $f$ of 6. The combined frequency of 13 and 14 is $4 + 6$, or 10. Notice too that there are 18 scores, so $N$ equals 18. If we add together all the values in the $f$ column, the sum will equal 18.

**The sum of all individual frequencies always equals $N$.**

The 1 subject who obtained 17, plus the 0 subjects scoring 16, plus the 4 subjects who scored 15, and so on will equal the $N$ of 18. As a check on any frequency distribution you create, add up the frequencies. If the sum of the individual frequencies does not equal $N$, you made a mistake.

**TABLE 3.1**  Simple Frequency Distribution Table

*The left-hand column identifies each score, and the right-hand column contains the frequency with which the score occurred.*

| Score | $f$ |
|-------|-----|
| 17 | 1 |
| 16 | 0 |
| 15 | 4 |
| 14 | 6 |
| 13 | 4 |
| 12 | 1 |
| 11 | 1 |
| 10 | 1 |
| Total: | 18 $= N$ |

That is how we create a simple frequency distribution. Such a distribution is also called a plain old *frequency distribution* or a *regular frequency distribution*.

## Graphing a Simple Frequency Distribution

We create graphs because they provide an easy way to communicate the overall distribution of a set of scores. The graph of a simple frequency distribution shows the relationship between each score and the frequency with which it occurs. We place the scores on the $X$ axis and the frequency of the scores on the $Y$ axis. Then we look to see how the frequency changes as the scores change.

> *STAT ALERT* A graph of a frequency distribution always shows the scores on the $X$ axis.

Recall from Chapter 2 that a variable may involve one of four types of measurement scales—nominal, ordinal, interval, or ratio. As you will see in the following sections, we graph a frequency distribution as either a bar graph, a histogram, or a polygon, depending on the type of scale involved.

**Bar graphs**   Recall that in nominal data, each score is merely a name for some category, and in ordinal data, each score indicates rank order. We produce a frequency distribution of nominal or ordinal scores using a bar graph. A **bar graph** is a graph in which we draw a vertical bar centered over each score on the $X$ axis. *In a bar graph, adjacent bars do not touch.*

Figure 3.1 on page 46 shows two bar graphs of simple frequency distributions. Here the frequency table is included so that you can see how each score was plotted, but usually we do not include the table. The upper graph shows the nominal variable of political affiliation of subjects, where a score of 1 indicates Republican, a 2 indicates Democrat, a 3 indicates Socialist, and a 4 indicates Communist. The lower graph shows ordinal data reflecting the frequencies with which a certain baseball team has ranked in the top four positions nationally in the last 20 years. In both graphs, the height of each bar corresponds to the score's frequency.

The reason we crate bar graphs here is that, in both nominal and ordinal scales, no equal unit of measurement separates the scores. The space between the bars indicates this fact.

**Histograms**   When plotting the frequency distribution of a small range of interval or ratio scores, we create a histogram. A **histogram** is similar to a bar graph except that *in a histogram adjacent bars touch.* Recall that interval and ratio scales have an equal unit of measurement between scores. The absence of a space between the bars in a histogram communicates this fact. Histograms

**FIGURE 3.1**   Simple Frequency Bar Graph for Nominal and Ordinal Data

*The height of each bar indicates the frequency of the corresponding category on the X axis.*

| *Nominal variable of political affiliation* | |
| --- | --- |
| *Score* | *f* |
| 4 | 1 |
| 3 | 3 |
| 2 | 8 |
| 1 | 6 |

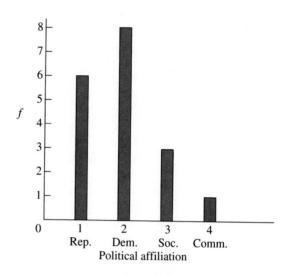

| *Ordinal variable of baseball team rankings* | |
| --- | --- |
| *Score* | *f* |
| 4 | 3 |
| 3 | 8 |
| 2 | 4 |
| 1 | 5 |

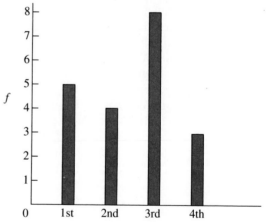

are especially appropriate when the variable is discrete (that is, there can be no fractions).

For example, say that we measured a sample of subjects on the variable of number of parking tickets received, and we obtained the data in Figure 3.2. The scale is a ratio scale because there is a true zero, and we measure parking

**FIGURE 3.2** Simple Frequency Histogram

| Score | f |
|-------|---|
| 7 | 1 |
| 6 | 4 |
| 5 | 5 |
| 4 | 4 |
| 3 | 6 |
| 2 | 7 |
| 1 | 9 |

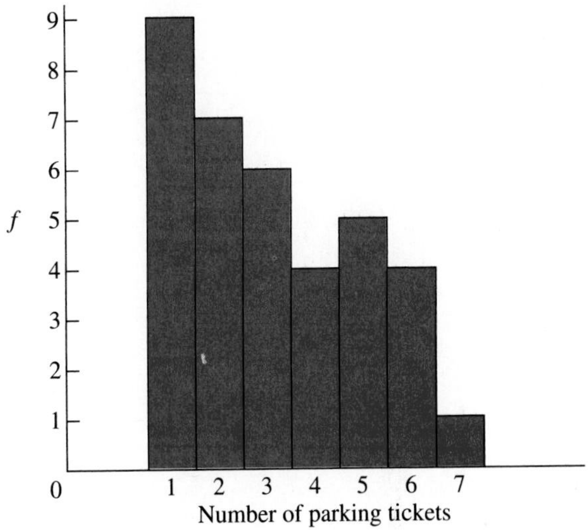

tickets in discrete units. The histogram for these data appears to the right of the scores.

Generally we do not create a histogram to show the frequencies of a large range of different scores, because such a histogram would be difficult to read. Also, sometimes we plot more than one sample of scores on the same graph, and if histograms overlap, they are extremely difficult to read. Instead, in such situations we create a frequency polygon.

**Frequency polygons** To construct a **frequency polygon** we place a data point over each score on the $X$ axis at the height on the $Y$ axis corresponding to the appropriate frequency. Then we connect the data points using straight lines. Figure 3.3 on page 47 shows our parking ticket data plotted as a frequency polygon.

Notice that unlike a bar graph or histogram, a simple frequency polygon includes on the $X$ axis the next score above the highest score in the data and the next score below the lowest score (in Figure 3.3 scores of 0 and 8 are included). These added scores have a frequency of 0, so the polygon touches the $X$ axis. In this way the polygon forms a complete geometric figure, with the $X$ axis as its base.

Often in statistics you must read the frequency of a score directly from the polygon. To do this, locate the score on the $X$ axis and then move upward until you reach the line forming the polygon. Then, moving horizontally, locate the frequency of the score. For example, as shown by the dashed line in Figure

**FIGURE 3.3**  Simple Frequency Polygon Showing the Frequencies of Parking Tickets in a Sample

| Score | f |
|:-----:|:-:|
| 7 | 1 |
| 6 | 4 |
| 5 | 5 |
| 4 | 4 |
| 3 | 6 |
| 2 | 7 |
| 1 | 9 |

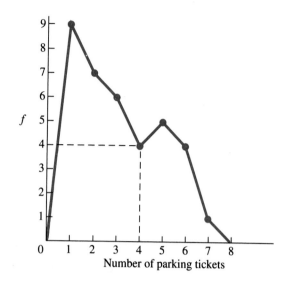

3.3, the score of 4 has an *f* equal to 4. It is very important to remember that the *height* of the polygon above any score corresponds to the *frequency* with which that score occurred.

## TYPES OF SIMPLE FREQUENCY DISTRIBUTIONS

In statistics we have special names for polygons having certain characteristic shapes. Each shape comes from an idealized frequency distribution of an infinite population of scores. By far the most important frequency distribution is the normal distribution. (This is the big one, folks.)

### The Normal Distribution

Figure 3.4 shows the polygon of the ideal theoretical normal distribution. For reference, we might assume that these are test scores from the population of college students. Although specific mathematical properties define this polygon, in general it is a bell-shaped curve. However, we don't call it a bell curve. Because this shape occurs so often, the polygon itself is called the *normal distribution* or the *normal curve,* or we say that the scores are *normally distributed.*

To get a sense of the normal curve (or any polygon for that matter), imagine

**FIGURE 3.4**   The Ideal Normal Curve

*Scores farther above and below the middle scores occur with progressively lower frequencies.*

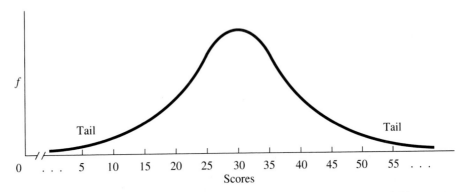

that you are flying in a helicopter over a parking lot. The *X* and *Y* axes are laid out on the ground, and the entire population of subjects, representing all possible scores, is present (it's a very big parking lot). Those subjects who received a particular score stand in line in front of the marker for their score on the *X* axis. The lines of subjects are packed so tightly together that, from the air, all you see is a dark mass formed by the tops of many heads. This view is shown in Figure 3.5.

   If you painted a line that went behind the last subject in line at each score, you would have the outline of the normal curve shown previously in Figure 3.4. The height of the curve above any score indicates how many subjects are

**FIGURE 3.5**   Parking Lot View of the Ideal Normal Curve

*The height of the curve above any score reflects the number of subjects receiving that score.*

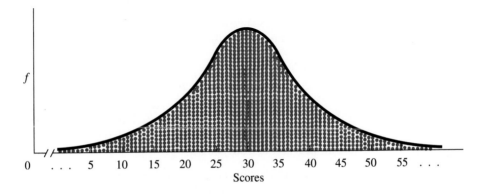

standing in line at that score, which tells how many subjects obtained that score. If we count the number of people in line at a score, we have that score's simple frequency. If we add together the numbers of subjects in all the lines (the frequencies of all the scores), we have the total number of subjects in the parking lot, which is $N$.

As you can see in Figures 3.4 and 3.5, the normal distribution has the following characteristics. The score with the highest frequency is the middle score between the highest and lowest scores (the longest single line of subjects in the parking lot is at the score of 30). The normal curve is *symmetrical*, meaning that the left half (containing the scores below the middle score) is a mirror image of the right half (containing the scores above the middle score). As we proceed away from the middle score toward the higher or lower scores, the frequencies at first decrease only slightly. As we proceed farther from the middle score, each score's frequency decreases more drastically, with the highest and lowest scores having relatively very low frequency.

In statistics, the scores that are relatively far above and below the middle score of any distribution are called the **extreme scores.** In a normal distribution, the extreme scores have a relatively low frequency. In the language of statistics, the left and right portions of a normal curve containing the relatively low frequency, extreme scores are called the **tails** of the distribution. In Figures 3.4 and 3.5, the tails are roughly below the score of 15 and above the score of 45.

Because the ideal normal curve represents a theoretical infinite population of scores, it has several characteristics that are not found with polygons created from actual sample data. First, with an infinite number of scores, we cannot label the $Y$ axis with specific values of $f$. (Simply remember that the higher the curve, the higher the frequency.) Second, the theoretical normal curve is a smooth curved line. There are so many different scores that we do not need to connect the data points with straight lines. The individual data points form a solid curved line. Finally, there is no limit to the extreme scores in the ideal normal curve: regardless of how extreme a score might be, theoretically such a score will sometimes occur. Thus, as we proceed to ever more extreme scores in the tails of the distribution, the frequency of each score decreases, but there is never a frequency of zero so the theoretical normal curve approaches but never actually touches the $X$ axis.

Before you proceed, be sure that you are comfortable reading the normal curve. Can you see in Figure 3.4 that the most frequent scores are between 25 and 35? Do you see that a score of 15 has a relatively low frequency and a score of 45 has the same low frequency? Do you see that there are relatively few scores in the tail above 50 or in the tail below 10? Above all, you must be able to see this in your sleep:

> **On a normal distribution, the farther a score is from the central score of the distribution, the less frequently the score occurs.**

**FIGURE 3.6**  Overlapping Distributions of Male and Female Height

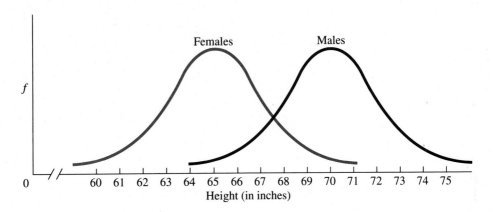

**Overlapping normal distributions**   Sometimes we have two or more overlapping normal distributions plotted on the same set of $X$ and $Y$ axes. For example, say that we wish to compare the populations of males and females on the variable of height. Figure 3.6 shows two idealized normal distributions of the data. Generally males tend to be taller than females, but the overlapping parts of the polygons show that some males and females are the same height. (If this were a parking lot full of males and females, then in the overlapping portions of the curve, members of one sex would be standing on the shoulders of those of the other sex.) In examining overlapping distributions, simply ignore one distribution when looking at the other: we count only males when looking at the male distribution and only females when looking at the female distribution. The height of each polygon at a score indicates the frequency with which the score occurred in that distribution. Thus, for example, the score of 69 inches occurs more frequently in the male distribution than in the female distribution.

**Approximations to the normal distribution**   Not all bell-shaped curves fit the mathematical requirements of the true normal curve. In statistics and research, we often talk of distributions that are approximately normal distributions. Consider the three curves in Figure 3.7 on page 52. In statistical terminology, the word *kurtosis* refers to how skinny or fat a distribution is. Curve A is generally what we think of when we discuss the ideal normal distribution; such a curve is called mesokurtic (*meso* means middle). Curve B is skinny relative to the normal curve, and it is called leptokurtic (*lepto* means thin). Leptokurtic distributions occur when only a few scores around the middle score have a relatively high frequency. On the other hand, Curve C is fat relative to the normal curve, because many different scores around the middle

**FIGURE 3.7**  Variations of Bell-Shaped Curves

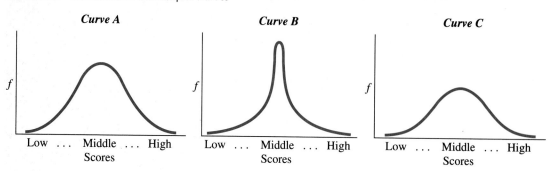

score have a relatively high frequency. Such a curve is called platykurtic (*platy* means flat).

These terms help us to more precisely describe approximations to the normal distribution. For statistical purposes, however, as long as we have close approximations to the normal curve, differences in shape are not all that critical.

**The normal curve model**   It turns out that in nature, middle scores or ordinary events tend to occur most frequently and more extreme scores or unusual events occur less frequently. We noted in Chapter 2 that inferential statistics are based on models of how nature operates. The most common model is based on the normal curve, and hence we call it the **normal curve model.** Whenever we say that we *assume* that scores are normally distributed, we are using the normal curve model. Scores from the real world never conform exactly to the precise mathematical normal curve, but usually they are close enough to forming a normal distribution that we can use the ideal normal curve as a model.

Notice what this model enables us to do. Recall that the goal of research is to describe the laws of nature so that we understand how everyone will behave in a particular situation. In statistical terms, this means describing the entire population of scores we would find in a particular situation. Saying that the population forms a normal distribution is a major part of describing the population, so we are well on the way to our goal.

## Other Common Frequency Polygons

The distributions from all variables do not conform to a normal distribution. When a distribution does not fit the normal curve, it is called a *nonnormal* distribution. The three most common types of nonnormal distributions are *skewed,* *bimodal,* and *rectangular* distributions.

**FIGURE 3.8**  Idealized Skewed Distributions

*The direction in which the distinctive tail is located indicates whether the skew is positive or negative.*

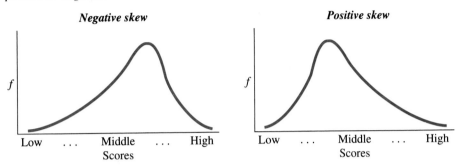

Skewed distributions   A **skewed distribution** is similar in shape to a normal distribution except that it is not symmetrical: the left half of the polygon is not a mirror image of the right half. A skewed distribution has only one pronounced tail. A distribution may be either negatively skewed or positively skewed, and the skew is where the tail is.

A **negatively skewed distribution** contains low frequency, extreme low scores, but does not contain corresponding low frequency, extreme high scores. The left-hand polygon in Figure 3.8 shows an idealized negatively skewed distribution. Remember that in a negative skew the pronounced tail is in the direction of lower scores, toward zero, toward where the negative scores would be.

On the other hand, a **positively skewed distribution** contains low frequency, extreme high scores, but does not contain corresponding low frequency, extreme low scores. The right-hand polygon in Figure 3.8 shows a positively skewed distribution. Remember that in a positive skew the tail is over in the direction of positive higher scores, above zero.

Bimodal and rectangular distributions   An idealized bimodal distribution is shown in the left-hand side of Figure 3.9 on page 54. A **bimodal distribution** is a symmetrical distribution containing two distinct humps where there are relatively high frequency scores. At the center of each hump is a score that occurs more frequently than the surrounding scores, and technically the center scores in each hump have the same frequency.

The right-hand side of Figure 3.9 presents a rectangular distribution. A **rectangular distribution** is a symmetrical distribution shaped like a rectangle. There are no discernible tails, because the extreme scores do not have relatively low frequencies.

**FIGURE 3.9**   Idealized Bimodal and Rectangular Distributions

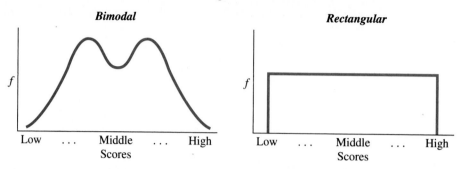

**Distributions of real data versus ideal distributions**   Recall that we use descriptive statistics to describe the important characteristics of a set of data. One important characteristic of data is the shape of the frequency distribution it forms, so we apply the names of the previous ideal distributions to sample data as well. However, real research data are never pretty, and the distribution of a sample of scores will tend to be a bumpy, rough approximation to the smooth idealized curves we have discussed. Figure 3.10 shows several frequency

**FIGURE 3.10**   Simple Frequency Distributions of Sample Data with Appropriate Labels

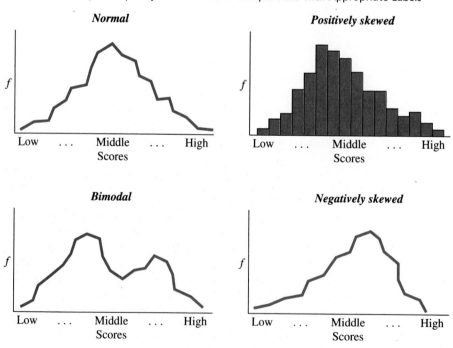

distributions of sample data, as well as the corresponding labels we might use. (Notice that we can apply these names even to choppy histograms or bar graphs.) We generally assume that the sample represents a population that more closely fits the corresponding ideal polygon.

We shall return to simple frequency distributions throughout the remainder of this book. However, counting each score's simple frequency is not the only thing we do in statistics.

## CREATING RELATIVE FREQUENCY DISTRIBUTIONS

Another way to organize scores is to transform each score's simple frequency into a relative frequency. **Relative frequency** is the proportion of the total $N$ comprised by a score's simple frequency. While simple frequency is the number of times a score occurs in a sample, relative frequency is the proportion of time the score occurs in the sample. The symbol for relative frequency is rel. $f$. We use relative frequency to interpret a score's simple frequency. For example, the finding that a score has a simple frequency of 60 is difficult to interpret, because we have no frame of reference. However, we can easily interpret the finding that a score has a relative frequency of .30, because this means that the score's $f$ comprises .30 of the total $N$; the score occurred .30 of the time in the sample.

Here is your first statistical formula.

---

*THE FORMULA FOR COMPUTING A SCORE'S RELATIVE FREQUENCY IS*

$$\text{rel. } f = \frac{f}{N}$$

---

This formula says that to compute the relative frequency of a score, divide that score's frequency by the total $N$.

For example, say that out of an $N$ of 10 scores, the score of 7 has a simple frequency of 4. What is the relative frequency of the score of 7? Using the formula, we have

$$\text{rel. } f = \frac{f}{N} = \frac{4}{10} = .40$$

The score of 7 has a relative frequency of .40; 7 occurred .40 of the time in the sample.

## Presenting Relative Frequency in a Table

A distribution based on the relative frequency of the scores is called a **relative frequency distribution.** To create a relative frequency table, first create a simple frequency table, as we did previously. Then add a third column labeled "rel. $f$" for the relative frequency of each score.

As an example, say that we asked several mothers how many children they had, and then we compiled the results as shown in Table 3.2. To compute rel. $f$, we need $N$, which is the total number of scores in the sample. Although there are 6 scores in the score column, $N$ is not 6. As shown by the sum of the $f$'s, there are a total of 20 scores in this sample. The relative frequency for each score is the $f$ for that score divided by $N$. The score of 1, for example, has $f = 4$, so the relative frequency of 1 is 4/20, or .20. Thus, in our sample, .20 of the subjects have 1 child.

We can determine the combined relative frequency of several scores by adding the individual relative frequencies together. For example, in Table 3.2, a score of 1 has a relative frequency of .20, and a score of 2 has a relative frequency of .50. Therefore, the relative frequency of 1 and 2 is .20 + .50, or .70; these scores occurred .70 of the time, so mothers having 1 or 2 children comprise .70 of our sample.

You may find that working with relative frequency is easier if you transform the decimals to percents. (Remember that officially relative frequency is a proportion.) If we convert relative frequency to percent, we have the percent of time that a score or scores occurred. To transform a proportion to a percent, multiply the proportion times 100. Above we saw that .20 of the scores were

**TABLE 3.2**  Relative Frequency Distribution

*The left-hand column identifies the scores, the middle column shows each score's frequency, and the right-hand column shows each score's relative frequency.*

| Score | $f$ | rel. $f$ |
|:-----:|:---:|:--------:|
| 6 | 1 | .05 |
| 5 | 0 | .00 |
| 4 | 2 | .10 |
| 3 | 3 | .15 |
| 2 | 10 | .50 |
| 1 | 4 | .20 |
| Totals: | 20 | 1.00 = 100% |

the score of 1. Since $(.20)(100) = 20\%$, 20% of all scores were 1. To transform a percent back to a relative frequency, divide the percent by 100.

To check your work, remember that the sum of all the relative frequencies in a distribution should equal 1.0: all scores together should constitute 1.0, or 100%, of the sample.

## Graphing a Relative Frequency Distribution

As with simple frequency, we graph relative frequency with a bar graph if the scores are from a nominal or ordinal scale and with a histogram or polygon if the scores are from an interval or ratio scale. Figure 3.11 presents examples using the relative frequency distribution we created in Table 3.2. These graphs are drawn in the same way as corresponding graphs of simple frequency except that here the $Y$ axis reflects relative frequency and is labeled in increments between 0 and 1.0.

## Finding Relative Frequency Using the Normal Curve

We can determine relative frequency directly from the normal curve. One reason for visualizing the normal curve as the outline of a parking lot full of people is so that you think of the normal curve as forming a solid geometric figure having an area underneath the curve. What we consider to be the total space occupied by subjects in the parking lot is, in statistical terminology, the **total area under the curve.** We visualize the total area under the curve as the space occupied by all subjects, which represents the total frequency of all scores.

**FIGURE 3.11**  Examples of Relative Frequency Distributions

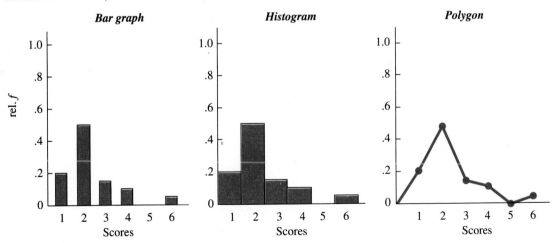

As with any geometric figure, we can divide up the area under the normal curve. We can take a vertical "slice" of the polygon that constitutes some proportion of the total. Any vertical slice is over certain scores, so we have *the proportion of the total area under the curve* above those scores.

Here's an example. In Figure 3.12 a vertical line has been drawn through the middle score so that .50 of the total area under the curve is over the scores to the left of the line and .50 of the area is over the scores to the right of the line. Visualize the figure as a parking lot, and assume that the line is razor thin so that no subjects are on the line and one-half of all subjects are standing to each side of it. Now here is the important part:

**The proportion of the total area under the normal curve above any scores corresponds to the relative frequency of those scores.**

The subjects standing to the left of the line are there because they received scores below the middle score. If .50 of all subjects in the parking lot had scores below the middle score, then the scores below the middle score occurred .50 of the time. Thus, the combined relative frequency of the scores below the middle score is .50.

In the same way, we can identify any proportion of the total area under the curve. Think of any proportion of the area under the curve as the proportion of all subjects who are standing in that part of the parking lot. The proportion of all subjects standing in a part of the parking lot is the proportion of all scores that are in that part of the distribution. The proportion of all scores that are in a part of a distribution is the relative frequency of the scores in that part of the distribution.

Of course, statisticians do not fly around in helicopters, eye-balling parking

**FIGURE 3.12**   Normal Curve Showing .50 of the Area Under the Curve

*The vertical line is through the middle score, so 50% of the distribution is to the left of the line and 50% is to the right of the line.*

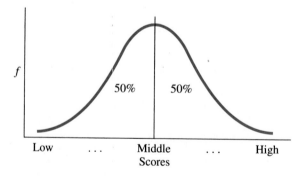

lots. If, using the formula for rel. $f$, we added the simple frequencies of the scores below the middle score and divided by $N$, we would again find that the scores below the middle score had a total relative frequency of .50. Thus, whether we look at the proportion of the area under the curve or directly compute the relative frequency, we will obtain the same answer. This is because the area under the curve depends on the curve's height, which is created by each simple frequency. Therefore, a proportion of the total area equals that proportion of the total frequency. A proportion of the total frequency is what we call relative frequency.

In Chapter 6 you will learn how to determine the relative frequency of any score by determining the corresponding proportion of the area under the curve.

## CREATING CUMULATIVE FREQUENCY DISTRIBUTIONS

Another way we can organize data is to compute cumulative frequency. **Cumulative frequency** is the frequency of all scores at or below a particular score. The symbol for cumulative frequency is $cf$. We use cumulative frequency when we want to know how many subjects scored at or below a particular score. The word *cumulative* implies accumulating. To compute a particular score's cumulative frequency, we accumulate, or add, the simple frequencies below the score and then add the score's frequency, to get the frequency of scores at or below the score.

### Presenting Cumulative Frequencies in a Table

To create a cumulative frequency distribution, first create a simple frequency distribution. Then add a third column labeled *"cf."*

As an example, say that we have collected some data, shown in Table 3.3, in which we measured the ages of subjects. To compute cumulative frequency, we begin with the *lowest* score. In Table 3.3, we see that no one scored below 10 and 1 subject scored 10, so we put 1 in the $cf$ column opposite 10: there is one subject who is 10 years of age or younger. Next there were two scores of 11. We add this $f$ to the $cf$ for 10, so the $cf$ for 11 is 3: there are 3 subjects at or below the age of 11. Next, no one scored 12 and three subjects scored below 12, so the $cf$ for 12 is also 3. In the same way, the $cf$ of each score is the frequency for that score plus the cumulative frequency for the score immediately below it.

As a check on any cumulative frequency distribution you create, verify that the $cf$ for the highest score equals $N$: all of the $N$ subjects obtained either the highest score or a score below it.

**TABLE 3.3** Cumulative Frequency Distribution

*The left-hand column identifies the scores, the center column contains the simple frequency of each score, and the right-hand column contains the cumulative frequency of each score.*

| Score | f | cf |
|-------|-----|-----|
| 17 | 1 | 19 |
| 16 | 2 | 18 |
| 15 | 4 | 16 |
| 14 | 5 | 12 |
| 13 | 4 | 7 |
| 12 | 0 | 3 |
| 11 | 2 | 3 |
| 10 | 1 | 1 |
| Total: | 19 | |

**FIGURE 3.13** Cumulative Frequency Polygon Showing the Cumulative Frequencies of the Scores in Table 3.3

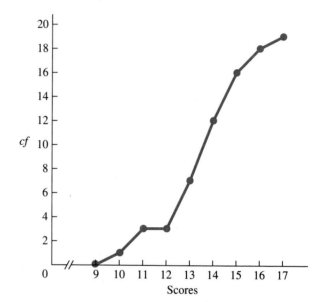

### Graphing a Cumulative Frequency Distribution

Usually it makes sense to compute cumulative frequency only for interval or ratio data, and the convention is to create a polygon. Figure 3.13 shows the cumulative frequency polygon of the distribution we created in Table 3.3.

In a cumulative frequency distribution, the $Y$ axis is labeled "$cf$." As in plotting simple frequency, we include on the $X$ axis the next score below the lowest score in the data: 10 is the lowest score in the data, but 9 is included on the graph. Unlike the polygon of a simple frequency distribution, however, a cumulative frequency distribution does not include the next score above the highest score in the data.

Cumulative frequencies never decrease. There cannot be fewer subjects having a score of 13 or below than received a score of 12 or below. Therefore, when you plot cumulative frequency, as the scores on the $X$ axis increase, the height of the polygon must either remain constant or increase.

## CREATING GROUPED FREQUENCY DISTRIBUTIONS

A rule of thumb for creating any type of frequency table is that there should be between about 8 and 18 rows in the table. Fewer than 8 scores tend to produce a very small, often unnecessary table, while more than 18 scores tends to produce a very large, inefficient table. In the previous examples we presented each individual score, so we created *ungrouped distributions.* When there are too many individual scores to produce a manageable ungrouped distribution, we create a grouped distribution. In a **grouped distribution** we combine different scores together into small groups and then report the total $f$, rel. $f$, or $cf$ of each group.

To see how this is done, we will create a grouped distribution out of the following scores:

$$3 \quad 4 \quad 4 \quad 18 \quad 4 \quad 28 \quad 26 \quad 41 \quad 5 \quad 40 \quad 4 \quad 6 \quad 5$$
$$18 \quad 22 \quad 3 \quad 17 \quad 12 \quad 26 \quad 4 \quad 20 \quad 8 \quad 15 \quad 38 \quad 36$$

The scores are between a low of 3 and a high of 41, spanning 39 possible different scores. In creating a grouped distribution, the first step is to decide how to group the scores so that each group spans the same range of scores. To facilitate this, we can operate as if the sample continued a wider range of scores than was actually in the data. For example, we will operate as if the above scores were from 0 to 44, spanning 45 possible different scores. This conveniently allows us to create nine groups, each spanning 5 scores. Thus, we turn the above raw scores into the grouped distribution shown in Table 3.4.

The group labeled "0–4" contains the scores 0, 1, 2, 3, and 4, while "5–9" contains scores 5 through 9. Each group is called a *class interval,* and the number of possible scores spanned by each class interval is the *interval size.* Here we have used an interval size of 5. It may not appear that each group includes five scores, but if you count them, each contains five possible scores.

**TABLE 3.4**  Grouped Cumulative Frequency Distribution

*The left-hand column identifies the lowest and highest score in each class interval.*

| Scores | $f$ | rel. $f$ | $cf$ |
|--------|-----|----------|------|
| 40–44 | 2 | .08 | 25 |
| 35–39 | 2 | .08 | 23 |
| 30–34 | 0 | .00 | 21 |
| 25–29 | 3 | .12 | 21 |
| 20–24 | 2 | .08 | 18 |
| 15–19 | 4 | .16 | 16 |
| 10–14 | 1 | .04 | 12 |
| 5– 9 | 4 | .16 | 11 |
| 0– 4 | 7 | .28 | 7 |
| Total: | 25 | 1.00 | |

Mathematically, the interval size is the difference between the low score in an interval and the high score in the interval plus 1, or

High − low + 1

Thus, 4 − 0 + 1 gives an interval size of 5. We typically choose an interval size that is easy to work with (such as 2, 5, 10, or 20), rather than something unfriendly (like 17). Also, we choose an interval size that will result in between 8 and 18 class intervals.

Notice several things about the layout of the score column in Table 3.4 above. First, each class interval is labeled with the low score on the left. Second, the low score in each interval is a whole-number multiple of our interval size of 5. Third, every class interval has the same interval size, including the highest and lowest intervals. (Even though the highest score in the data is only 41, we have the complete interval of 40–44.) Finally, the intervals are arranged so that we proceed to higher scores as we proceed toward the top of the column.

To complete the table, we find the $f$ for each class interval by summing the individual frequencies of all scores in the group. In the original raw data above, there were no scores of 0, 1, or 2, but there were two 3's and five 4's. Thus, the 0–4 interval has a total $f$ of 7. For the 5–9 interval, there were two 5's, one 6, no 7's, one 8, and no 9's, so the 5–9 interval has a total $f$ of 4. And so on.

In the relative frequency column, the rel. $f$ for each interval is computed by dividing the $f$ for the interval by $N$. Remember, $N$ is the total number of raw scores (here 25), not the number of class intervals.

In the cumulative frequency column, the $cf$ for each interval gives the number of scores in the data that are at or below the *highest* score in the interval. Begin with the lowest scores in the data. There are 7 scores of 4 or below, so the $cf$ for interval 0–4 is 7. Next, $f$ is 4 for the scores between 5 and 9; adding the 7 scores below the interval, we find that the $cf$ for interval 5–9 is 11. The $cf$ for each interval is the $f$ for that interval plus the $cf$ for the interval immediately below it.

We can summarize the steps in creating a grouped distribution as follows:

*1.* Select a low score and a high score that include all the scores in the sample and that allow the scores to be divided into intervals having the same interval size.

*2.* Arrange the intervals, starting with the highest interval, and label each interval with the lowest and highest scores in the interval, putting the lowest score on the left.

*3.* Compute the frequency and relative frequency for each interval based on the scores that fall in the interval. List as the cumulative frequency for each interval the cumulative frequency of the highest score in that interval.

In deciding how to create a distribution, you must weigh the advantages and disadvantages of grouping the data. The disadvantage is that grouped distributions present the individual scores less precisely than do ungrouped distributions. For example, the above 0–4 interval has an $f$ of 7, so all we know from the table is that 7 subjects scored somewhere between 0 and 4. If we had chosen a larger interval size, say 10, then we would have even less precision. The advantage is that grouped distributions shrink a large number of different scores into a manageable form, so that we can comprehend the overall distribution better than if we examined a mass of individual scores.

## Real Versus Apparent Limits

What if one of the scores in the above example were 4.6? This score is too large to be in the 0–4 interval, but too small to be in the 5–9 interval. To allow for scores with decimals, we must define each interval more clearly. The upper and lower numbers that we show for each group in the score column of a frequency table are called the *apparent upper limit* and the *apparent lower limit*, respectively. However, apparent limits always imply another type of limit, called the *real limit*. The left-hand portion of Table 3.5 shows the apparent limits for the previous grouped data, and the right-hand portion gives the implied real limits for each interval.

As you can see, the *lower real limit* of an interval is always halfway between the lower apparent limit of the interval and the upper apparent limit of the interval below it. Thus, the lower real limit of the 5–9 interval is 4.5. The *upper real limit* of an interval is always halfway between the upper apparent limit and the lower apparent limit of the interval above it. Thus, the upper real limit of the 5–9 interval is 9.5. Notice that the lower real limit of one

**TABLE 3.5** Real and Apparent Limits

*The apparent limits in the left-hand column imply the real limits in the right-hand column.*

| Apparent limits (lower–upper) | imply | Real limits (lower–upper) |
|---|---|---|
| 40–44 | → | 39.5–44.5 |
| 35–39 | → | 34.5–39.5 |
| 30–34 | → | 29.5–34.5 |
| 25–29 | → | 24.5–29.5 |
| 20–24 | → | 19.5–24.5 |
| 15–19 | → | 14.5–19.5 |
| 10–14 | → | 9.5–14.5 |
| 5– 9 | → | 4.5– 9.5 |
| 0– 4 | → | – 0.5– 4.5 |

interval is the upper real limit of the interval below it. Also, notice that the difference between the lower real limit and the upper real limit always equals the interval size.

Real limits allow no gaps between the intervals, so now we can place all scores. We know that a score such as 4.6 falls in the interval 5–9, because it falls between 4.5 and 9.5. If we have scores equal to a real limit (such as two scores of 4.5), we place half of them in the lower interval ($-0.5$–4.5) and half in the upper interval (4.5–9.5). If there is one such score left over, we flip a coin to pick the interval.

The principle of real limits also applies to ungrouped data. Implicitly, each individual score is actually a class interval with an interval size of 1. Thus, when we label the score column in an ungrouped distribution with the score of 6, we are writing both the upper and the lower apparent limit. However, the lower real limit for this interval is 5.5, and the upper real limit is 6.5.

As we shall see, real limits are important in graphing grouped distributions and in computing percentiles.

## Graphing Grouped Distributions

Grouped distributions are graphed in the same way as ungrouped distributions *except* that we label the $X$ axis differently.

**Graphing grouped simple and relative frequency distributions**   To graph a grouped simple frequency distribution, label the $X$ axis using the *midpoint* of each class interval. To find the midpoint, multiply .5 times the interval size, and add the result to the lower real limit. In Table 3.4, the interval size was 5, and .5 times 5 is 2.5. For the interval 0–4, the lower real limit was $-.5$. Adding 2.5 to $-.5$ yields 2. Thus, we use the score of 2 on the $X$ axis to represent the class interval 0–4. Similarly, for the interval 5–9, 2.5 plus 4.5 is 7, so we represent this interval using the score of 7.

As usual, for nominal or ordinal scores we create a bar graph of the simple frequencies, and for interval or ratio scores we create a histogram or polygon. Figure 3.14 presents a histogram and polygon for the grouped simple frequency distribution created back in Table 3.4. The height of each bar or data point corresponds to the simple frequency of all scores in the class interval. We plot a relative frequency distribution in the same way except that the $Y$ axis is labeled in increments between 0 and 1.0.

**Graphing grouped cumulative frequency distributions**   To graph a grouped cumulative frequency distribution, we label the $X$ axis using the *upper real limit* of each interval. Thus, for example, the interval 0–4 is represented at 4.5 on the $X$ axis, and the interval 5–9 is at 9.5. Then we create a polygon in

**FIGURE 3.14**  Grouped Frequency Polygon and Histogram

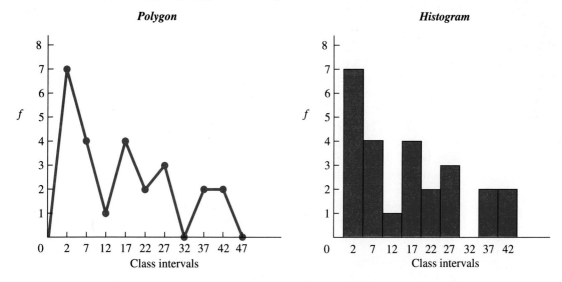

which each data point is the *cf* for a group. Figure 3.15 presents the grouped cumulative frequency polygon for the preceding data.

Now that you understand cumulative frequency and real limits, we can discuss our final topic: percentile.

**FIGURE 3.15**  Grouped Cumulative Frequency Polygon

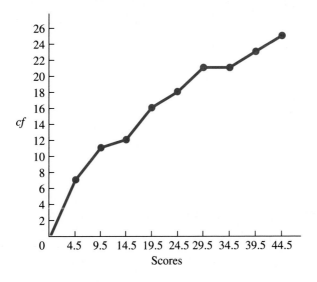

## COMPUTING PERCENTILE

One reason for computing a score's cumulative frequency is so that we can then compute the score's percentile. A **percentile** is a cumulative percentage—the percent of all scores in the data that are at or below a certain score. While a cumulative frequency indicates the number of subjects who obtained a particular score or below, a percentile indicates the percentage of subjects who obtained a particular score or below. Percentile gives us a frame of reference for evaluating the relative standing of any score. Thus, for example, if a score is at the 25th percentile, we know that 25% of all the scores in the sample are at or below that score.

Computing percentiles can be cumbersome, so the easiest way to compute a percentile is with a computer. In case there is no computer handy, the following sections explain how to determine the score that corresponds to a given percentile and how to determine the percentile of a given score.

### Determining the Score at a Given Percentile

We compute percentiles from cumulative frequency distributions. As an example, say that we have collected scores from laboratory rats, where each score reflects the number of minutes required for the rat to find the end of a maze. The cumulative frequency distribution for these data is presented in Table 3.6.

Say that we wish to determine the score at the 50th percentile; 50% of the scores are at or below this score. To find the score at a particular percentile, we find the score that has a $cf$ that corresponds to that particular percentage of $N$. Here we are looking for the score with a $cf$ that is 50% of $N$. Since $N$ is 10, the score at the 50th percentile is the score having a $cf$ of 5.

The trouble is that no score in the table has a $cf$ of exactly 5. The score of

**TABLE 3.6** Cumulative Frequency Distribution of Maze-Running Times for Laboratory Rats

| Score | $f$ | $cf$ |
|-------|-----|------|
| 5 | 1 | 10 |
| 4 | 1 | 9 |
| 3 | 2 | 8 |
| 2 | 3 | 6 |
| 1 | 3 | 3 |
| | $N = 10$ | |

1 has a *cf* of only 3, and the score of 2 has a *cf* of 6. Obviously, the score having a *cf* of 5 is somewhere between the scores of 1 and 2. As this example illustrates, the percentile we seek may not correspond to one of the scores that actually occurred in the sample.

To compute a percentile, we first treat the scores as if they were from a continuous variable that allowed for decimals. Then we look at the real limits. Looking at the real limits for the scores of 1 and 2, we see

| *Scores* | *f* | *cf* |
|----------|-----|------|
| 1.5–2.5  | 3   | 6    |
| .5–1.5   | 3   | 3    |

Because the score we seek has a *cf* of 5, we are looking for a score that is larger than 1.5 (with *cf* = 3) but smaller than 2.5 (with *cf* = 6). Thus, the score we seek is in the interval 1.5–2.5.

We assume that the interval's total frequency is evenly distributed throughout the interval so that any proportion of the interval includes an equal proportion of the interval's frequency. Thus, for example, if we go to a score that is one-half of the way between the upper and lower limits of an interval, we accumulate one-half of the frequency in the interval. Conversely, if we accumulate one-half of the frequency in the interval, we assume that we are at the score that is halfway between the upper and lower limits.

Since the score we seek has a *cf* of 5, we want the score above 1.5 that increases the *cf* by 2. If we went to a score of 2.5, we would accumulate an additional *f* of 3 and increase the *cf* by 3. We want 2 rather than 3, so we want two-thirds of the total frequency in the interval. To accumulate two-thirds of the total frequency in the interval, we go to the score that is two-thirds of the way between the lower and upper limits. To find the score that is two-thirds of the way between 1.5 and 2.5, we multiply two-thirds, or .667, times the interval size of 1, which is .667. Then adding .667 to 1.5 takes us to the score of 2.17. Thus, we assume that the score of 2.17 has a *cf* of 5, so the score at the 50th percentile is 2.17. We conclude that 50% of our rats completed the maze in 2.17 minutes or less.

Luckily, we have a formula that accomplishes everything above all at once.

*THE FORMULA FOR DETERMINING THE SCORE AT A GIVEN PERCENTILE IS*

$$\text{Score} = \text{LRL} + \left( \frac{\text{target } cf - cf \text{ below interval}}{f \text{ within interval}} \right)(\text{interval size})$$

In English, the formula says that we need these components.

1. target *cf:* the cumulative frequency of the score we seek. To find it, we transform the percentile we seek into a proportion and then multiply the proportion by *N*. The interval containing this *cf* contains the score we seek. (In our example above, the target *cf* is 5.) You must find the target *cf* before you can find any other component.

2. LRL: the lower real limit of the interval containing the score we seek. (In the example above, it is 1.5.)

3. *cf* below interval: the cumulative frequency of the interval below the interval containing the score we seek. (In the example, it is 3.)

4. *f* within interval: the frequency of the interval containing the score we seek. (In the example, it is 3.)

5. interval size: the interval size used to create the frequency distribution. (Above, it is 1.)

Table 3.7 shows where in the original cumulative frequency distribution you would find the components needed to determine the score at the 50th percentile.

We put these numbers into the formula for computing the score at a given percentile:

$$\text{Score} = \text{LRL} + \left(\frac{\text{target } cf - cf \text{ below interval}}{f \text{ within interval}}\right)(\text{interval size})$$

which becomes

$$\text{Score} = 1.5 + \left(\frac{5 - 3}{3}\right)(1)$$

We must first deal with the fraction. After subtracting $5 - 3$, we have 2/3, which is .667. So

$$\text{Score} = 1.5 + (.667)(1)$$

After multiplying, we have

$$\text{Score} = 1.5 + .667$$

So finally,

$$\text{Score} = 2.17$$

Again, the score at the 50th percentile in these data is 2.17.

Although this example has an interval size of 1, we can use the above formula for any grouped distribution having any interval size.

### Finding a Percentile for a Given Score

We can also work from the opposite direction, if we have a score in mind and wish to determine its percentile. To find the percentile for a given score, we find the *cf* of the score within the interval, plus the *cf* below the interval, and then determine the percent of scores that are at or below the score.

Mathematically we accomplish this using the following formula.

> **THE FORMULA FOR COMPUTING THE PERCENTILE OF A GIVEN SCORE IS**
>
> $$\text{Percentile} = \left( \frac{cf \text{ below interval} + \left( \dfrac{\text{score} - \text{LRL}}{\text{interval size}} \right) \left( \begin{matrix} f \text{ within} \\ \text{interval} \end{matrix} \right)}{N} \right)(100)$$

This formula requires the following components:

*1.* score: the given score for which we are computing the percentile.

*2.* *cf* below interval: the cumulative frequency of the interval below the interval containing the given score.

*3.* LRL: the lower real limit of the interval containing the given score.

*4.* *f* within interval: the frequency of the interval containing the given score.

*5.* interval size: the interval size used to create the grouped cumulative frequency distribution.

*6.* *N*: the total number of scores in the sample.

**TABLE 3.7** Cumulative Frequency Distribution Showing Components for Computing the Score at the 50th Percentile

| Score | *f* | *cf* | |
|-------|-----|------|---|
| 4.5–5.5 | 1 | 10 | target *cf* of 5 is in this interval |
| 3.5–4.5 | 1 | 9 | |
| 2.5–3.5 | 2 | 8 | |
| LRL→ 1.5–2.5 | 3 | 6 | *cf* below interval |
| .5–1.5 | 3 | 3 | |

interval size = 1    *f* within interval

**TABLE 3.8** Cumulative Frequency Distribution Showing Components for Computing the Percentile of a Given Score of 4

| | Score | *f* | *cf* | |
|---|-------|-----|------|---|
| score of 4 is in this interval | 4.5–5.5 | 1 | 10 ←N |
| LRL→ | 3.5–4.5 | 1 | 9 |
| | 2.5–3.5 | 2 | 8 ← *cf* below interval |
| | 1.5–2.5 | 3 | 6 |
| | .5–1.5 | 3 | 3 |

interval size = 1    *f* within interval

To use this formula to find the percentile of the score of 4 in our rat data, we find the components for the formula as shown in Table 3.8.

We then put these numbers into the formula for finding the percentile of a given score:

$$\text{Percentile} = \left( \frac{cf \text{ below interval} + \left( \dfrac{\text{score} - \text{LRL}}{\text{interval size}} \right) \left( \begin{array}{c} f \text{ within} \\ \text{interval} \end{array} \right)}{N} \right) (100)$$

which becomes

$$\text{Percentile} = \left( \frac{8 + \left( \dfrac{4.0 - 3.5}{1} \right)(1)}{10} \right) (100)$$

Working on the fraction in the numerator first, we find that 4.0 minus 3.5 is .5, which divided by 1 is still .5, so we have

$$\text{Percentile} = \left( \frac{8 + (.5) \ (1)}{10} \right) (100)$$

Multiplying .5 by 1 gives .5, so we have

$$\text{Percentile} = \left( \frac{8 + .5}{10} \right) (100)$$

After adding, we have

$$\text{Percentile} = \left( \frac{8.5}{10} \right) (100)$$

and after dividing, we have

$$\text{Percentile} = (.85)(100)$$

Finally, the answer is

$$\text{Percentile} = 85$$

Thus, the score of 4.0 in the above distribution is at the 85th percentile, so 85% of the rats completed the maze in 4 minutes or less.

## Finding Percentile Using the Area Under the Normal Curve

Earlier in this chapter we discussed using the proportion of the total area under the normal curve to compute relative frequency. We can also use the proportion of the area under the curve to compute percentile. A percentile corresponds

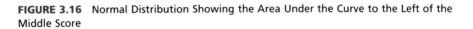

**FIGURE 3.16**  Normal Distribution Showing the Area Under the Curve to the Left of the Middle Score

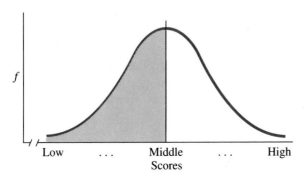

to the percent of the total area under the normal curve that is to the *left* of that score. For example, on the distribution in Figure 3.16, 50% of the area under the curve is to each side of the solid vertical line marking the middle score. Because scores to the left of the middle score are below that score, 50% of the distribution is below that score (50% of the subjects are standing to the left of the line in the parking lot). Thus, the score at the vertical line is at the 50th percentile.

Notice that we make a slight change in our definition of a percentile when using the normal curve. Previously we defined a percentile as the percent of all scores that are at or below a certain score. Technically, with small samples, we should not say that 50% of the scores are above the 50th percentile and 50% of the scores are below it. If 10% of the scores are the score at the 50th percentile, we will end up with a total of 110% of the sample! However, when we are describing a very large sample or population using the normal curve, we treat the scores *at* the percentile as a negligible proportion of the total, and we consider the percentile to be the percent of all scores that are *below* a certain score. Thus, for example, on the normal distribution above, the score at the 50th percentile is the one that has 50% of the scores below it and 50% above it. The 70th percentile has 70% of the scores below it and 30% above it, and so on.

## *FINALLY*

In this chapter we saw that we can describe scores using simple frequency, relative frequency, cumulative frequency, or percentile. Each technique provides a slightly different perspective on the data, allowing us to interpret the information in a slightly different way. As a researcher, you must decide which technique to use. However, you will not know automatically which is the best technique for a given situation, so use the trial-and-error method: try everything, and then choose the technique that most accurately and efficiently communicates and summarizes the data.

As an aid to learning statistics, start drawing graphs. In particular, draw the normal curve. When you are working problems or taking tests, draw the normal curve and indicate where the low, middle, and high scores are located. Being able to see the frequencies of the different scores will greatly simplify the task.

## CHAPTER SUMMARY

*1.* The number of scores in a sample is symbolized by *N*.

*2.* A *simple frequency distribution* organizes data by showing the frequency with which each score occurred. The symbol for *simple frequency* is *f*. In a simple frequency distribution, *N* is equal to the sum of the individual *f*'s of all the scores in the sample.

*3.* When graphing a simple frequency distribution, plot the scores along the *X* axis and the frequency of the scores along the *Y* axis. If the variable involves a nominal or ordinal scale, create a *bar graph,* in which the adjacent bars do not touch. If the variable involves an interval or ratio scale and there are relatively few different scores, create a *histogram.* It is similar to a bar graph except that adjacent bars do touch. If there are many different scores from an interval or ratio variable or there is more than one sample of scores, create a *polygon:* place a data point above each score at the corresponding frequency and then connect adjacent data points with a straight line. Also include the score above the highest score and below the lowest score.

*4.* A *normal distribution* forms a symmetrical, bell-shaped curve known as the *normal curve,* where extreme high and low scores occur relatively infrequently, scores closer to the middle score occur more frequently, and the middle score occurs most frequently. The low frequency, extreme low and extreme high scores are in the *tails* of the distribution.

*5.* The *normal curve model* assumes that the frequency distribution for a population of scores or events generally fits the normal curve.

*6.* A *negatively skewed distribution* is a nonsymmetrical distribution containing low frequency, extreme low scores, but not containing corresponding low frequency, extreme high scores. A *positively skewed distribution* is a nonsymmetrical distribution containing low frequency, extreme high scores, but not containing corresponding low frequency, extreme low scores.

7. A *bimodal distribution* is a symmetrical distribution containing two areas where there are relatively high frequency scores.

8. A *rectangular distribution* is a symmetrical distribution in which the extreme scores do not have relatively low frequencies.

9. The *relative frequency* of a score, symbolized by rel. *f*, is the proportion of time that the score occurred in a distribution. A relative frequency distribution is graphed in the same way as a simple frequency distribution except that the *Y* axis is labeled in increments between 0 and 1.0.

10. Relative frequency also corresponds to the *proportion of the total area under the curve*. If the area under the curve above a score or scores constitutes a certain proportion of the total area, then the frequency of the score or scores will constitute that same proportion of the total *N*.

11. The *cumulative frequency* of a score, symbolized by *cf*, is the frequency of all scores at or below the score. A cumulative frequency polygon is graphed in the same way as a simple frequency polygon except that the *Y* axis is labeled cumulative frequency and we do not include the score above the highest score.

12. In a *grouped distribution*, we combine different scores into small groups and then report the total *f*, rel. *f*, or *cf* for each group. Each group of scores is called a *class interval*, and the range of scores in the interval is called the *interval size*. The lowest score shown in each class interval is the lower apparent limit, and the highest score shown in a class interval is the upper apparent limit.

13. The lower real limit of an interval is the score that is halfway between the lower apparent limit and the upper apparent limit of the interval below. The upper real limit of an interval is the score that is halfway between the upper apparent limit and the lower apparent limit of the interval above.

14. When graphing a grouped simple frequency distribution or a grouped relative frequency distribution, label the *X* axis using the *midpoint* of each class interval. When graphing a grouped cumulative frequency distribution, label the *X* axis using the *upper real limit* of each interval.

15. *Percentile* indicates the percent of all scores at or below a given score. On the normal curve, the percentile of a score is the percent of the area under the curve to the left of the score.

## USING THE COMPUTER

Once you are at the Main Menu of the computer program, type in **2** to select the procedure entitled "Frequency Tables and Percentile." It will create an ungrouped frequency table that shows simple, relative, and cumulative frequency for the scores in your data. It will also compute the percentile of any score in the data.

## PRACTICE PROBLEMS

(Answers are provided for odd-numbered problems.)

1. What does $N$ stand for?
2. What does $f$ stand for?
3. With what type of data is a bar graph used?
4. With what type of data is a histogram used?
5. With what type of data is a polygon used?
6. What are the characteristics of the normal curve?
7. Describe a positively skewed distribution.
8. Describe a negatively skewed distribution.
9. Describe a bimodal distribution.
10. What is relative frequency?
11. What does a proportion of the area under the normal curve reflect?
12. What is cumulative frequency?
13. What does a percentile indicate in a small sample?
14. How is a score's percentile related to the area under a normal curve?
15. Organize the scores below in a table showing simple frequency, relative frequency, and cumulative frequency.

| 49 | 52 | 47 | 52 | 52 | 47 | 49 | 47 | 50 |
|----|----|----|----|----|----|----|----|----|
| 51 | 50 | 49 | 50 | 50 | 50 | 53 | 51 | 49 |

16. Organize the scores below in a table showing simple frequency, cumulative frequency, and relative frequency.

| 16 | 11 | 13 | 12 | 11 | 16 | 12 | 16 | 15 |
|----|----|----|----|----|----|----|----|----|
| 16 | 11 | 13 | 16 | 12 | 11 |    |    |    |

17. In question 15, what score is at the 50th percentile?
18. In question 15, what is the percentile for the score of 51?

## *SUMMARY OF FORMULAS*

*1. The formula for computing a score's relative frequency is*

$$\text{rel. } f = \frac{f}{N}$$

where $f$ is the score's simple frequency and $N$ is the number of scores in the sample.

*2. The formula for determining the score at a given percentile is*

$$\text{Score} = \text{LRL} + \left( \frac{(\text{target } cf - cf \text{ below interval})}{f \text{ within interval}} \right)(\text{interval size})$$

where target $cf$ is the cumulative frequency of the score we seek, LRL is the lower real limit of the interval containing the score we seek, $cf$ below interval is the cumulative frequency of the interval below the interval containing the score we seek, $f$ within interval is the frequency of the interval containing the score we seek, and interval size is the interval size used to create the frequency distribution.

*3. The formula for computing the percentile of a given score is*

$$\text{Percentile} = \left( \frac{cf \text{ below interval} + \left( \frac{\text{score} - \text{LRL}}{\text{interval size}} \right)\left( \frac{f \text{ within}}{\text{interval}} \right)}{N} \right)(100)$$

where score is the score for which we are computing a percentile, $cf$ below interval is the cumulative frequency of the interval below the interval containing the score, LRL is the lower real limit of the interval containing the score, $f$ within interval is the frequency for the interval containing the score, interval size is the interval size used in creating the distribution, and $N$ is the total number of scores in the sample.

# 4

# Measures of Central Tendency: The Mean, Median, and Mode

The graphs and tables discussed in the previous chapter are important ways of presenting data. The purpose of descriptive statistics is to describe the important characteristics of a set of data, and the shape of the polygon formed by graphing a distribution is one important characteristic. However, graphs and tables are not the most efficient way to summarize all the characteristics of a distribution. We can compute a single number that summarizes and describes each important characteristic of a sample or population of scores.

Recall from Chapter 2 that numbers describing samples are called statistics, and from them we estimate the numbers that describe populations, called parameters. In this chapter we discuss the important statistics and parameters called measures of central tendency. A measure of central tendency allows us to answer the question "Are the scores generally high scores or generally low scores?"

## MORE STATISTICAL NOTATION

Recall that the symbol $X$ stands for a subject's raw score. If a formula requires us to perform a particular mathematical operation on $X$, then we perform that operation on each score in a sample. Also, recall that parentheses mean "the quantity." We first perform the operations inside the parentheses and then perform any operations outside of the parentheses on the quantity.

A new important symbol is $\Sigma$, the Greek capital letter $S$, called sigma. Sigma is used in conjunction with a symbol for scores, so you will see such notations as $\Sigma X$. In words, $\Sigma X$ is pronounced **"sum of $X$"** and literally means to find the sum of the $X$ scores. Thus, $\Sigma X$ for the scores 5, 6, 9, and 7 is 27, and in code we would say $\Sigma X = 27$. Notice that we do not care whether each $X$ is a different score. If the scores are 4, 4, and 4, then $\Sigma X = 12$.

This chapter also introduces a symbol used in performing certain transformations on scores. The symbol $K$ stands for a constant number. This symbol is used when we add the same number to each score or when we multiply, divide by, or subtract a constant.

Now, on to central tendency.

## WHAT IS CENTRAL TENDENCY?

To understand central tendency, you need to alter your perspective of what a score indicates. You should think of a score as indicating a *location* on a variable. For example, if I am 6 feet tall, do not think of my score as indicating that I have 6 feet of height. Instead, think of me as being located on the variable of height at the point marked 6 feet. Think of any variable as an infinite continuum, a straight line, and think of a score as indicating a subject's location on that line. Thus, as shown in Figure 4.1, my score locates me at the address labeled 6 feet. If my brother is 4 feet tall, then he is located at the point marked 4 on the height variable. The idea is not so much that he is two feet shorter than I am, but rather that we are separated by a *distance* of 2 units—in this case, 2 "feet" units. In statistics, scores are locations, and the difference between any two scores is the distance between them.

From this perspective, a frequency polygon for an entire sample or population shows the location of each score. Again visualize the parking lot view of the normal curve: subjects' scores determine where they stand. A high score puts them on the right side of the lot, a low score puts them on the left side, and a middle score puts them in a crowd in the middle. Further, if two distributions contain different scores, then the *distributions* have different locations on the variable. Figure 4.2 on page 78 shows the polygons for two samples of height scores, one consisting of low scores and the other consisting of high scores.

We began this chapter by asking, "Are the scores generally high scores or generally low scores?" From the above perspective you can see that we are

**FIGURE 4.1**   Locations of Individual Scores on the Variable of Height

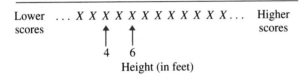

**FIGURE 4.2**   Two Sample Polygons on the Variable of Height

*Each polygon indicates the locations of the scores and their frequencies.*

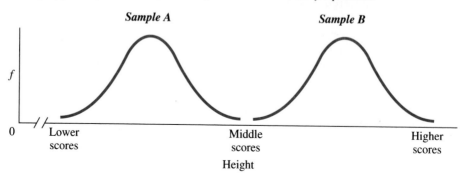

actually asking, "*Where* on the variable is the distribution located?" Because there are usually many different scores in a distribution, we must summarize the general location of the distribution. A **measure of central tendency** is a score that summarizes the location of a distribution on a variable. In essence, the score is used to describe *around* where most of the distribution is located. This means that ideally the distribution is centered around the measure of central tendency, with the majority of the scores close to this score. Thus, the purpose of a measure of central tendency is to indicate where the *center* of the distribution *tends* to be located. It provides us with one score that serves as a reasonably accurate address for the entire distribution.

> *STAT ALERT*   The first step in summarizing any set of data is to compute the appropriate measure of central tendency.

There are three common measures of central tendency. In the following sections we will discuss first the mode and then the median. With this background, we will finally discuss the most common measure of central tendency, the mean. As we shall see, we decide which measure to use by deciding which measure most accurately summarizes the location of the entire distribution we are describing. This decision is based on (1) the scale of measurement we used and (2) the shape of the distribution.

## THE MODE

If we are trying to describe where most of the scores tend to be located, then one way to summarize the distribution is to use the one score that occurs most frequently. The most frequently occurring score is called the **modal score** or simply the **mode.** Consider the scores 2, 3, 3, 4, 4, 4, 4, 5, 5, and 6. The score of 4 is the mode, because its frequency is higher than that of any other score in the sample. You can see how the mode summarizes this distribution in Figure 4.3, which presents the polygon for these scores. Most of the scores are at or around 4. Notice that Figure 4.3 is roughly a normal curve, with the highest point on the curve over the mode. When a polygon has one hump, such as on the normal curve, the distribution is called **unimodal,** indicating that one score qualifies as the mode.

There may not always be a single mode in a set of data. For example, Figure 4.4 on page 80 shows the polygon for the scores 2, 3, 4, 5, 5, 5, 6, 6, 7, 8, 9, 10, 10, 10, 11, and 12. Here two scores, 5 and 10, are tied for the most frequently occurring score. In Chapter 3 we saw that such a distribution is called **bimodal,** meaning that it has two modes. Describing this distribution as bimodal and identifying the two modes does summarize where most of the scores tend to be located, because most scores are either around 5 or around 10.

## Uses of the Mode

The mode is typically used to describe central tendency when the scores reflect a nominal scale of measurement. Recall that a nominal scale is used when we categorize subjects on the basis of a qualitative, or classification, variable. For example, say that we asked subjects their favorite flavor of ice cream and counted the number of responses in each category. A useful way to summarize

**FIGURE 4.3**   A Unimodal Distribution

*The vertical line marks the highest point on the distribution, thus indicating the most frequent score, which is the mode.*

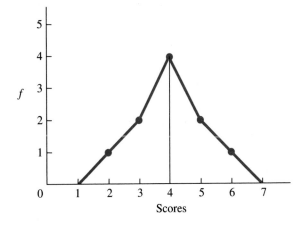

**FIGURE 4.4**  A Bimodal Distribution

*Each vertical line marks one of the two equally high points on the distribution, so each indicates the location of one of the two modes.*

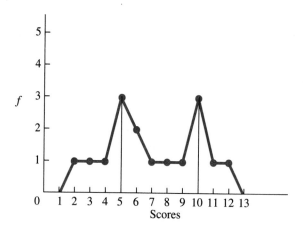

such data would be to indicate the most frequently occurring category. Reporting that the modal response was a preference for "goopy chocolate" would be very informative. When our data are ordinal, interval, or ratio, it is useful to know the mode, but we focus on other measures of central tendency.

## Problems with the Mode

Two potential problems arise in using the mode to describe central tendency. One problem is that, depending on the distribution we obtain, many scores may have the same highest frequency. In distributions with more than two modes, we begin to fail to summarize the data. In the most extreme case, we might obtain a rectangular distribution with scores such as 4, 4, 5, 5, 6, 6, 7, and 7. Here the mode should not be determined. Depending on your perspective, either there is no mode or all scores are the mode. Either way, the mode will not summarize the data.

A second problem is that we ignore much of the information in the data when we compute the mode. Because it does not take into account any scores other than the most frequent score(s), the mode may not accurately describe where the majority of the scores are located. For example, say we have the sample 7, 7, 7, 18, 18, 19, 19, 20, 20, 21, 22, 22, 23, and 23. The mode is 7 because it is the most frequently occurring score. The problem is that the majority of the sample is not located at 7 or even around 7: most of the scores are between 18 and 23. Thus, depending on the actual distribution of the data, the mode may produce a very misleading summary of the distribution.

## THE MEDIAN

A better measure of central tendency is the median score, or simply the median. The **median** is the score located at the 50th percentile. Recall that 50% of all scores fall at or below the 50% percentile, so 50% of the scores in the distribution are at or below the median. If the median score is 10, then 50% of all scores are either the score of 10 or a score less than 10. (Note that the median will not always be one of the actual scores that occurred.) The median is typically a better measure of central tendency than the mode, because (1) only one score can be the median and (2) the median will usually be around where most of the scores in the distribution tend to be located.

In Chapter 3 we discussed the procedure for determining the score that lies at a given percentile. To compute the median, we follow this procedure to determine the score at the 50th percentile. The symbol for the median is usually its abbreviation, Mdn.

---

*THE FORMULA FOR COMPUTING THE MEDIAN IS*

$$\text{Mdn} = \text{LRL} + \left( \frac{.5(N) - cf \text{ below interval}}{f \text{ within interval}} \right)(\text{interval size})$$

---

This formula is similar to the previous formula for percentile except that this formula contains $.5(N)$ instead of target $cf$. By multiplying $.5$ times $N$, we find the target cumulative frequency that corresponds to the 50th percentile. Then LRL is the lower real limit of the interval containing the median, $cf$ below interval is the cumulative frequency of the interval below the interval containing the median, $f$ within interval is the frequency of the interval containing the median, and interval size is the interval size used to create the frequency distribution. Table 4.1 shows a cumulative frequency distribution for a sample of data, indicating the above components. In the formula, multiplying $.5$ times $N$ we have $.5(10)$, or 5, so the $cf$ of the median score is 5. Then, from the table we know that the interval 25–34 contains the median. Putting the remaining numbers into the formula for finding the median, we have

$$\text{Mdn} = 24.5 + \left( \frac{5 - 4}{2} \right)(10)$$

After subtracting $5 - 4$, we have

$$\text{Mdn} = 24.5 + \left( \frac{1}{2} \right)(10)$$

**TABLE 4.1**
Components of a
Cumulative Frequency
Distribution Used in
Computing the
Median

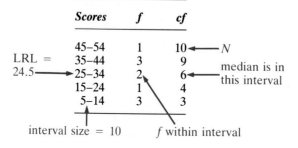

| Scores | f | cf | |
|--------|---|----|---|
| 45–54 | 1 | 10 ◄——— N | |
| LRL = 35–44 | 3 | 9 | |
| 24.5 ——► 25–34 | 2 | 6 ◄— median is in this interval | |
| 15–24 | 1 | 4 | |
| 5–14 | 3 | 3 | |

interval size = 10          f within interval

So finally,

$$\text{Mdn} = 24.5 + 5 = 29.5$$

Thus, 29.5 is the score at the 50th percentile, so it is the median in these data.

In a large sample or population, the median is the score in the middle of the distribution, separating the lower 50% of the distribution from the upper 50% of the distribution. We can see this by looking at the frequency polygon in Figure 4.5.

In Chapter 3 we saw that the proportion of the area under the normal curve to the left of a score corresponds to the score's percentile. In Figure 4.5 we

**FIGURE 4.5**  Location of the Median in a Normal Distribution

*The vertical line indicates the location of the median. One-half of the distribution is on each side of it.*

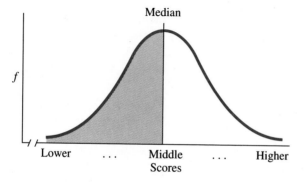

see that 50% of the area under the curve is to the left of the center vertical line. Recall our parking lot view: 50% of the subjects are standing to the left of the line because they obtained scores below the score at the vertical line. Therefore, the score at the line is the median. Notice that in a normal distribution, the median is the most frequently occurring score, so it is the same score as the mode.

### Uses of the Median

The median is not used to describe nominal data: to say that 50% of the subjects fall in the categories below some category is usually meaningless. On the other hand, the median is often the preferred measure of central tendency when the data are ordinal (rank-ordered) scores. For example, say that a group of students ranked how well a college professor teaches. If we report that the professor's median ranking was 2, we communicate that 50% of the students rated the professor as number 1 or number 2.

As we shall see in a later section, the median is also the most appropriate measure of central tendency when interval or ratio scores form a very skewed distribution. In addition, for any distribution, the median may be one of the measures of central tendency we compute, because it's nice to know where the 50th percentile is located.

### Problems with the Median

In computing the median we still ignore some information in the data. The median reflects only the frequencies of the scores, ignoring the specific value of each score. Therefore, it is not our first preference for describing the central tendency of most distributions.

## THE MEAN

By far the all-time measure of central tendency in psychological research is the mean score, or simply the mean. The **mean** is the score located at the exact mathematical center of a distribution. Although technically we call this statistic the arithmetic mean, it is what most people call the average. We compute a mean exactly the same way we compute an average: we add up all the scores and then divide by the number of scores we added. Unlike the mode or the median, the mean does not ignore any information in the data. In computing the mean, we include the exact value of each score, and the number of times a score is included is the same as its frequency.

The symbol for a *sample* mean is $\overline{X}$. It is pronounced "the sample mean" (not "bar $X$": bar $X$ sounds like the name of a ranch!). As with other symbols, get in the habit of thinking of $\overline{X}$ as a quantity itself, so that you understand statements such as "the size of $\overline{X}$" or "this $\overline{X}$ is larger than that $\overline{X}$." To compute $\overline{X}$, recall that the symbol meaning "add up all the scores" is $\Sigma X$ and the symbol for the number of scores is $N$. Then,

---

**THE FORMULA FOR COMPUTING A SAMPLE MEAN IS**

$$\overline{X} = \frac{\Sigma X}{N}$$

---

As an example of how the formula works, take the scores 1, 1, 3, and 4. The sum of $X$ ($\Sigma X$) is all the scores added together, or $1 + 1 + 3 + 4$, which equals 9. There are four scores, so $N$ is 4. The mean is equal to $\Sigma X$ divided by $N$, so $\overline{X} = 9/4 = 2.25$. Thus, the mean of these scores is 2.25. This tells us that the exact mathematical center of this distribution is located at the score of 2.25. As you can see, the mean can be a score that does not actually occur in the sample, but it is still the location of the center of the distribution.

What is the exact mathematical center of a distribution? We can think of the mathematical center of a distribution as its balance point. Visualize a polygon as a teeter-totter on a playground. A score's location on the teeter-totter corresponds to its location on the $X$ axis. The left-hand side of Figure 4.6 shows the scores of 3, 4, 6, and 7 sitting on the teeter-totter. The mean on the left is 5 (because $\Sigma X/N = 20/4 = 5$), and it balances the distribution. The right-hand side of Figure 4.6 shows the mean as the balance point even when all of the scores do not have the same frequency (the score of 1 has an $f$ of 2). Here the mean is 4 (because $\Sigma X/N = 20/5 = 4$), and it balances the distribution.

**FIGURE 4.6**   The Mean as the Balance Point of a Distribution

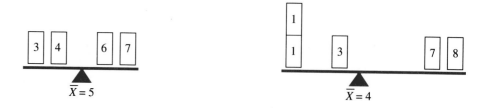

## Uses of the Mean

We do not use the mean when describing nominal data. For example, say we are studying political affiliation and we arbitrarily assign a 1 if a subject is a Democrat, a 2 if a Republican, a 3 if a Socialist, and so on. It is meaningless to say that the mean political affiliation is 2.3; the mode or percentages would be much more informative. Likewise, we usually prefer the median when describing ordinal data. This leaves us with using the mean to describe interval or ratio data (where there is a consistent unit of measurement and zero). The mean is especially useful when the variable is at least theoretically continuous (decimals are permitted).

We must also consider the shape of the distribution, however. The mean is most appropriate when the scores form a symmetrical distribution (where the left half of the distribution mirrors the right half). The mean is used with a symmetrical distribution because the balance point is located halfway between the highest and lowest scores. This fact is especially important for our ultimate symmetrical distribution: the normal distribution. Consider the scores 1, 2, 3, 3, 4, 4, 4, 5, 5, 6, and 7, which form the approximately normal distribution shown in Figure 4.7. The mean is truly that point around which most of the scores are located.

Notice that, as Figure 4.7 illustrates, on a normal distribution all three measures of central tendency are located at the same score. The mean score of 4 divides the distribution into two equal halves, so the mean score is also the median score. At the same time, the mean score is the most frequently occurring score, so the mean is also the mode.

**FIGURE 4.7** Location of the Mean on a Normal Distribution Formed by the Scores 1, 2, 3, 3, 4, 4, 4, 5, 5, 6, and 7

*The vertical line indicates the location of the mean score, which is the balance point of the distribution.*

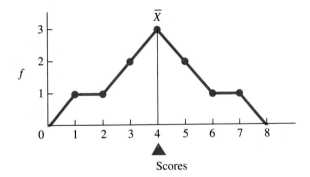

If a distribution is only roughly normal, then the mean, median, and mode will be close to but not exactly the same score. In such a situation, you might think that any one of the measures of central tendency would be close enough. Not true. Because the mean uses all of the information in the data, the mean is the preferred measure of central tendency. Further, most inferential statistical procedures are based on the mathematical properties of the mean. Therefore, the rule for you as a researcher should be that the mean is the preferred statistic to use with interval or ratio data unless it clearly provides an inaccurate description of the central tendency of the distribution.

## Problems with the Mean

The mean does not accurately describe a highly skewed distribution. The scores 1, 2, 2, 2, 3, and 14 form the skewed distribution shown in Figure 4.8. Picture this graph as a teeter-totter with some little guys (1's, 2's and 3's) at one end trying to balance the big guy (the 14) at the other end. The mean of 4 balances the distribution, but the extreme score of 14 can be balanced with the many low scores only if the mean is pulled toward the extreme high score. Likewise, your college grade average (a mean) drops like a rock when you receive one very low grade. That one low score produces a negatively skewed distribution, pulling your mean down, away from most of your scores. The problem is that a measure of central tendency is supposed to describe where most of the scores tend to be located, but in a skewed distribution the mean is not where most of the scores are located. In Figure 4.8, there are no scores located at 4, and most scores are not around 4. The mean is where the mathematical center is, *but in a skewed distribution the mathematical center is not the point around which most of the scores tend to be located.*

The solution is to use the median to summarize a very skewed distribution.

**FIGURE 4.8**   Location of the Mean on a Skewed Distribution Formed by the Scores 1, 2, 2, 2, 3, 14

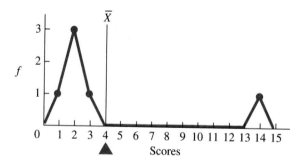

**FIGURE 4.9** Measures of Central Tendency for Skewed Distributions

*The vertical lines show the relative positions of the mean, median, and mode.*

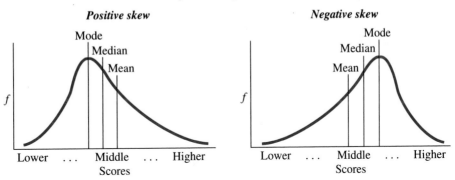

Figure 4.9 shows the relative positions of the mean, median, and mode in skewed distributions. When the distribution is positively skewed, the mean is larger than the median. When the distribution is negatively skewed, the mean is less than the median. In both cases, the mean is pulled toward the extreme tail of the distribution and does not accurately describe the central tendency of the entire distribution. Likewise, the mode tends to be toward the side away from the extreme tail, so most of the distribution is not centered around the mode either. However, the median is not thrown off by extreme scores occurring in only one tail of the distribution, because it does not take into account the actual values of the scores. Yet it is usually centered around where the majority of the scores are located.

It is for the above reasons that the government typically uses the median to summarize such skewed distributions as that of yearly income or the price of houses. For example, the median income in the United States is around $33,000 a year. But there are a relatively small number of corporate executives, movie stars, professional athletes, rock stars, and the like who make millions! When we average these extreme high incomes with everyone else's, the mean income works out to be close to $50,000. However, because most incomes are not located at or around $50,000, the median is a much better summary of the distribution, reflecting the many lower incomes instead of being drawn off by the few extremely high incomes.

Although skewed distributions do occur in psychological research, most variables produce more or less symmetrical, unimodal distributions that are best described by the mean.

**STAT ALERT** Whenever we have a normal or symmetrical unimodal distribution of interval or ratio scores, we describe the central tendency of the distribution by computing the mean.

Because the mean is used so extensively in statistics, in the following sections we will delve further into the characteristics and uses of the mean.

## TRANSFORMATIONS AND THE MEAN

We perform transformations on raw scores so that the scores are easier to work with or so that we can compare scores from different variables. The simplest transformation is to add, subtract, multiply, or divide each score by a constant. This brings up the burning question of how transformations affect the mean.

If we add a constant value, $K$, to each raw score in a sample, the new mean of the transformed scores will equal the old mean of the raw scores plus $K$. For example, the scores 7, 8, and 9 have a mean of 8. If we add the constant 5 to each score, we have 12, 13, and 14. The new mean is 13. The old mean of 8 plus the constant 5 also equals 13. Thus, the rule is that new $\overline{X}$ = old $\overline{X}$ + $K$. The same logic applies for other mathematical operations. If we subtract $K$ from each score, new $\overline{X}$ = old $\overline{X}$ − $K$. If we multiply each score by $K$, new $\overline{X}$ = (old $\overline{X}$)$K$. If we divide each score by $K$, new $\overline{X}$ = (old $\overline{X}$)/$K$.

The above rules also apply to the median and to the mode. Whenever we use a constant, we merely change the location of each score on the variable by $K$ points. We move the entire distribution to higher scores or to lower scores, so we also move the address of the distribution by a corresponding amount.

## DEVIATIONS AROUND THE MEAN

To understand why the mean is the center of any distribution, you must understand that, *in total*, the mean is just as far from the scores above it as it is from the scores below it. The distance separating a score from the mean is called the score's **deviation**, because it indicates the amount the score *deviates* from the mean.[1] A score's deviation is equal to the score minus the mean. In symbols, a deviation is the quantity $(X - \overline{X})$.

> *STAT ALERT* Always subtract the mean score *from* the raw score when computing the score's deviation.

Thus, if the sample mean is 47, a score of 50 deviates by +3, because 50 − 47 is +3. A score of 40 deviates from the mean of 47 by −7, because 40 − 47

---

[1] In some textbooks, the lowercase letter $x$ is the symbol for the amount a score deviates from the mean, and thus $x = (X - \overline{X})$.

$= -7$. Notice that a score's deviation consists of a number and a sign. A positive deviation indicates that the score is greater than the mean. A negative deviation indicates that the score is less than the mean. The size of the deviation (regardless of its sign) indicates the distance the score lies from the mean. The larger the deviation, the farther the score is from the mean. Conversely, the smaller the deviation, the closer the score is to the mean. A deviation of 0 indicates that the score is equal to the mean.

When we determine the deviations of all the scores above the mean in a sample and the deviations of all the scores below the mean, we find the *deviations around the mean*. The *sum of the deviations around the mean* is the sum of all differences between the scores and the mean. The reason the mean is the mathematical center of any distribution is this:

**The sum of the deviations around the mean always equals zero.**

For example, for the scores 3, 4, 6, and 7, the mean is 5. Table 4.2 shows how we compute the sum of the deviations around the mean for these scores. As you can see, the sum of the deviations is zero. For any sample of scores you can imagine, having a distribution of any shape, the sum of the deviations around the mean will always equal zero. This is because the sum of the positive deviations equals the sum of the negative deviations, so the sum of all deviations is zero. In the same way that the center of a rectangle is an equal distance from both sides, the mean is the center of a distribution, because, in total, it is an equal distance from scores above and below it.

Many of the formulas we will eventually use involve something similar to finding the deviations around the mean. In the formulas, the statistical code for finding the sum of the deviations around the mean is $\Sigma(X - \overline{X})$. We always start inside the parentheses, so we first find the deviation for each score, $(X - \overline{X})$. The $\Sigma$ indicates that we then find the sum of the deviations. Thus, as in Table 4.2, $\Sigma(X - \overline{X}) = -2 + -1 + 1 + 2$, which equals zero.

**TABLE 4.2**  Computing Deviations Around the Mean

*The mean is subtracted from each score, resulting in the score's deviation.*

| Score | minus | Mean score | equals | Deviation |
|-------|-------|------------|--------|-----------|
| 3 | − | 5 | = | −2 |
| 4 | − | 5 | = | −1 |
| 6 | − | 5 | = | +1 |
| 7 | − | 5 | = | +2 |
| | | | Sum: | 0 |

## Using the Mean to Predict Individual Scores

As part of understanding the laws of nature, we want to predict what will happen in a given situation. This translates into predicting the scores we will find in that situation. The mean of a sample forms the basis for predicting any unknown scores. Because the mean is located in the exact mathematical center of any distribution, it is the most representative single score from a sample of scores. It is, more or less, the typical score in the distribution. In saying that the mean is the typical score, we imply that if all the scores in the sample were the same score, they would all be the mean score. Therefore, when we do not know anything else about the scores, the mean score is our best prediction or estimate of any individual score.

Think about the grades you predict for your friends who have a B average in college. They may not always get Bs, but you operate as if they did. Your best estimate of what they will receive in statistics is a B. For every other course, you also predict a grade of B. In fact, if you had to guess what grade they had received in some prior course, you would guess a B. Based on the sample mean, you predict a grade of B for every grade. In the same way, if we predict any individual score, we will predict the sample mean score and we will predict it for every subject.

Of course, our predictions will be wrong sometimes, because every raw score will not equal the mean score. To determine the amount of error in our predictions, we must compare our predicted scores to the actual scores the subjects obtain. The only scores we know are the scores in our sample. Thus, we determine the error in predicting the scores in a known sample, and then we use this error as an estimate of the error we would have in predicting any unknown scores. (In statistics, the amount of error in our predictions of unknown scores is always based on how well we can predict the known scores in a sample.)

Since we predict the mean score for any score, the amount of error in a particular prediction is the difference between the mean score and the actual score the subject obtains. In symbols, the error in our prediction of any single score is equal to $(X - \overline{X})$. We have already seen that $(X - \overline{X})$ is the amount by which a score deviates from the mean. The *total* error in predicting all the scores in the sample is the sum of these deviations, or $\Sigma(X - \overline{X})$. The reason we use the mean score as a predicted score is that then the total error in our predictions equals the sum of the deviations around the mean, *which always equals zero*. Consider the scores 5, 6, 8, and 9, which have a $\overline{X}$ of 7. One of the subjects, Quasimodo, scored the 5. We would predict a score of 7 for Quasimodo, so we would be wrong by $-2$. But another subject, Attila, scored the 9; in predicting a 7 for him, we would be off by $+2$. In the same way, the errors in our predictions for the rest of the sample will cancel out so that our total error is zero. Likewise, we assume that if we use the mean to predict unknown scores, our errors will cancel out so that the total error is zero.

If, instead of the mean, we used any other single score as the predicted score for every subject, the total error would be greater than zero. Say we predict a score of 6 for the scores of 5, 6, 8, and 9: the sum of the deviations around 6 is +4. Or, if we predict 8, the sum of the deviations is −4. Having a total error of +4 or −4 is not as good as having a total error of zero. A total error of zero means that, over the long run, we overestimate and underestimate by the same amount. In statistics, this is considered to be the next best thing to having no error. (There is an old joke about two statisticians who are shooting targets. One shoots one foot to the left of the target, and the other shoots one foot to the right of the target. "Congratulations," one says. "We got it!") If we cannot perfectly predict every score, we want our over- and underestimates to cancel out.

Of course, this is not the whole story. Although the *total* error in our predictions will equal zero, a prediction of an *individual* score may be off by a country mile. In later chapters we will see how to reduce our error in predicting each individual score. For now, however, simply remember that *unless you have additional information about the scores,* the mean is the best score to use when predicting scores, because the total error in your predictions, considering both over- and underestimates, will balance out to zero.

The concept of deviations around the mean has one other important aspect. We can use deviations from the mean as the basis for describing each score in a distribution.

## Using Deviations to Indicate a Score's Location in a Distribution

In computing the deviations around the mean, we have simply performed a transformation on the raw scores (we subtracted $K$ from each score, where $K = \overline{X}$). Recall that we perform transformations so that scores are easier to interpret. Calculating a score's deviation from the mean is a transformation that provides an easy way of describing the score's relative location within the distribution.

Look at the approximately normal distribution in Figure 4.10, which shows the scores 1, 2, 3, 3, 4, 4, 4, 5, 5, 6, and 7. Below each raw score is the score's deviation. Since a positive deviation occurs when the score is larger than the mean, a positive deviation indicates that the score is located to the right of the mean on the distribution. Conversely, a negative deviation indicates that the score falls to the left of the mean. The larger the deviation, whether positive or negative, the farther from the mean the score lies. Thus, by examining a

**FIGURE 4.10**   Frequency Polygon Showing Deviations from the Mean

*The first row under the X axis indicates the raw scores, and the second row indicates the amounts the raw scores deviate from the mean.*

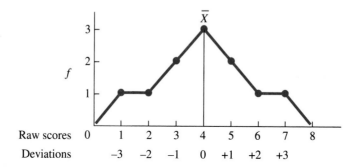

score's deviation, we can determine the score's location relative to the mean and, indirectly, the score's location relative to the rest of the distribution.

The deviations of scores in a normal distribution also tell us about the scores' frequencies. The larger the deviation, whether positive or negative, the farther in the tail of the distribution the score lies. As you know, scores lying farther in the tail of a normal distribution occur less frequently. Thus, the larger a score's deviation, the less frequently the score occurs. Also, notice that the larger a score's deviation, the less frequently the *deviation* occurs. In the data above, there is one score of 7, so there is one deviation of +3. In fact, the frequency of any score's deviation will equal the frequency of that score. As shown in Figure 4.10, whether we label the *X* axis using scores or deviations, we have the same frequency polygon.

We will elaborate on deviations around the mean in subsequent chapters. For now, remember that on the normal curve, the larger the deviation (whether positive or negative), the farther the score is from the mean and thus the less frequently the score and its deviation occur.

## USING THE SAMPLE MEAN TO DESCRIBE THE POPULATION MEAN

Recall that research ultimately is designed to describe the entire population of scores we would find in a given situation if we could measure all the scores. Populations are unwieldy, so we summarize a population using a measure of central tendency. Here is what we want to know: If we examined the population, around which point would most of the scores be located?

Since we usually assume that the population forms an approximately normal distribution, we usually describe the population using the mean. Recall that parameters are numbers that describe the important characteristics of a population and that they are symbolized using letters from the Greek alphabet. The mean score of a population is one such parameter, and it is symbolized by the Greek letter $\mu$, pronounced "mew." Thus, saying that $\mu$ equals 143 is the same as saying that the population mean is 143. A population mean has all the characteristics of a sample mean:

1. $\mu$ is the arithmetic average of all the scores in the population.
2. $\mu$ is the score at the mathematical center of the distribution, so $\mu$ is the balance point.
3. The sum of the deviations around $\mu$ is zero.
4. The value of $\mu$ is our best estimate or prediction of each and every score in the population.

We use the symbol $\mu$ to show that we are talking about a population mean, just as we use $\overline{X}$ to show that we are talking about a sample mean.

How do we determine the value of $\mu$? If we know all the scores in the population, then we compute $\mu$ using the same formula we used to compute $\overline{X}$:

$$\mu = \frac{\Sigma X}{N}$$

Of course, usually we think of a population as being infinitely large and unmeasurable, so we cannot directly compute $\mu$. Instead we estimate the value of $\mu$ based on the mean of a random sample. If, for example, a random sample's mean in a particular situation is 99, then our best guess is that if we could actually compute it, the population $\mu$ in that situation would also be 99. This is because a population having a mean of 99 is most likely to produce a sample having a mean of 99. If the population $\mu$ is 99, many subjects score at or close to 99. When we randomly select a sample, we are very likely to run into many of those subjects, so we are very likely to have a sample mean of 99. On the other hand, if the population mean is 4000, relatively few subjects will score around 99, so we are very unlikely to obtain a sample having a mean of 99. Therefore, a random sample mean is usually a good estimate of the corresponding population mean (assuming, of course, that the sample is representative of the population).

Now that we have discussed the characteristics of sample and population means, we can discuss how they come together in an experiment.

## SUMMARIZING THE RESULTS OF EXPERIMENTS

As we discussed in Chapter 2, in an experiment we obtain a sample of scores on the dependent variable for each condition of the independent variable. If a relationship exists, then as the conditions of the independent variable change, there will be a consistent change in the scores on the dependent variable: the scores will have certain values under one condition and different values under the other conditions.

Say that we are interested in the relationship between the amount of information that subjects must remember and the number of errors they make when recalling the information. Specifically, we predict that subjects will make more errors in recalling a long list of words than in recalling a short list. We conduct an overly simplistic experiment to demonstrate the relationship between the length of the list to be remembered and the number of errors produced during recall. We randomly select three samples of subjects. Subjects in one sample read a list containing 5 words and then recall it. Subjects in another sample read a 10-item list and then recall it, and those in the third sample read a 15-item list and then recall it. What is our independent variable? It is the length of list to be remembered, with the three conditions being 5-, 10-, and 15-item lists. Our dependent variable is the number of errors subjects make in recalling their list. If a relationship exists, then as we change the length of the list, there will be a consistent change in subjects' error scores.

Say we study this relationship using the unrealistically small $N$ of 3 subjects per sample. The error scores for the three conditions appear in Table 4.3. Most experiments involve much larger $N$s, and with many different scores it is difficult to detect a relationship by looking at the raw scores. That's why we have measures of central tendency: so that we can summarize the scores and at the same time summarize and simplify the relationship.

**TABLE 4.3**  Numbers of Errors Made by Subjects Recalling a 5-, 10-, or 15-Item List

*Note the different mean for each condition.*

| *Condition 1: 5-item list* | *Condition 2: 10-item list* | *Condition 3: 15-item list* |
|:---:|:---:|:---:|
| 3 | 6 | 9 |
| 4 | 5 | 11 |
| 2 | 7 | 7 |
| $\overline{X} = 3$ | $\overline{X} = 6$ | $\overline{X} = 9$ |
| $N = 3$ | $N = 3$ | $N = 3$ |

## Summarizing a Relationship Using Measures of Central Tendency

Which measure of central tendency we should compute for each condition in an experiment is determined by the characteristics of the *dependent variable*. We choose the mean, median, or mode, depending on (1) the scale of measurement we used to measure the dependent variable and (2) how the population is assumed to be distributed. How do we know how a population is distributed? Fortunately, we do not perform an experiment in a vacuum, so from previous research, books, and other sources we can determine the assumed shape of the population.

In our experiment above, number of recall errors is a ratio variable that is assumed to form an approximately normal distribution, so we compute the mean score for each condition. Because most dependent variables in psychological research are interval or ratio variables that are assumed to be normally distributed, computing the mean score for each condition is the predominant method of summarizing experiments.

Examining the means in Table 4.3, we quickly recognize evidence of a relationship:

| *Condition 1:* 5-item list | *Condition 2:* 10-item list | *Condition 3:* 15-item list |
|---|---|---|
| $\overline{X} = 3$ | $\overline{X} = 6$ | $\overline{X} = 9$ |

Remember that the mean is the location of the center of the distribution of scores on the variable—the point around which most of the scores in the sample fall. Thus, recalling a 5-item list results in one distribution of scores located around the mean of 3 errors, recalling a 10-item list results in a different distribution located around the mean of 6 errors, and recalling a 15-item list results in a different distribution located around the mean of 9 errors. Thus, the means indicate that a relationship exists, because as the conditions of the independent variable change (from 5 to 10 to 15 items), the scores on the dependent variable also tend to change in a consistent fashion.

Our experiment "worked" in that it demonstrated a relationship between the length of the list and the number of recall errors. Length of list is a variable that literally makes a difference in recall scores. Whenever an experiment works, it demonstrates that different conditions of the independent variable result in different locations for the distributions of dependent scores. Because we summarize locations by computing sample means, we have evidence of a relationship whenever the means for two or more conditions of an experiment have different values.

In the language of statistics, we describe any relationship using the phrase *as a function of.* In an experiment, if there is a relationship, then the scores on the dependent variable change as a function of changes in the independent variable. If no relationship exists, then scores on the dependent variable do not change as a function of changes in the independent variable.

> **STAT ALERT**  In an experiment, we describe the relationship by stating whether changes occur in the dependent variable as a function of changes in the independent variable.

So that we can easily see a relationship when it is present, we summarize experiments by creating graphs.

## Graphing the Results of an Experiment

The convention for graphing the results of an experiment is to place the independent variable on the $X$ axis and the dependent variable on the $Y$ axis. We place the independent variable on the $X$ axis because we usually treat the variable on the $X$ axis as a given. Then we read the graph to determine the $Y$ scores for each given value of $X$. In an experiment, we want to see the scores on the dependent variable for each given condition of the independent variable. In essence, we ask, "As the condition of the independent variable changes, what happens to the scores on the dependent variable?"

> **STAT ALERT**  Although in our formulas we use the symbol $X$ to stand for each subject's score on the dependent variable, on a graph of the results of an experiment, subjects' scores on the dependent variable are plotted on the $Y$ axis.

Thus, to show how the dependent variable changes as a function of changes in the independent variable, we show the changes in $Y$ scores as a function of changes in $X$. (Any time we use the phrase *as a function of,* it is $Y$ as a function of $X$.)

In graphing the results of an experiment, we create either a line graph or a bar graph. The type of graph we create is determined by the characteristics of the *independent variable.*

**Line graphs**  Whenever an independent variable is an interval or ratio variable, we connect the data points with straight lines. This type of graph is called a **line graph.**

In our recall study, the independent variable of length of list involves a ratio scale, because it has an equal unit of measurement and a true zero. Therefore, we create the line graph shown in Figure 4.11. First we label the $X$ and $Y$ axes with the specific variables (not "independent variable" and "dependent variable"). Note that the label on the $Y$ axis is *mean* recall errors. The numbers on the $X$ axis correspond to the values of the independent variable in the various conditions. Then we place a data point above the 5-item condition opposite 3 errors, because the mean error score for the 5-item list was 3. Similarly, we place a data point above the 10-item condition at 6 errors, and a data point above the 15-item condition at 9 errors. Then we connect adjacent data points with straight lines. We use straight lines with interval or ratio data because we assume that the relationship continues in a straight line between the points shown on the $X$ axis. For example, we assume that if there had been a 6-item list, the mean error score would have fallen on the line connecting the means for the 5- and 10-item lists.

The graph in Figure 4.11 conveys the same information as the sample means in Table 4.3. The different sample means indicate that for each condition there is a different distribution of scores, located at a different position on the dependent variable. In the graph, the different position of each distribution on the dependent variable is reflected by a different position on the $Y$ axis, producing a line that is not horizontal. Because the position of the mean of the $Y$ scores changes as the conditions of the independent variable change, the raw scores also change, so there is a relationship. Thus, *on any graph, if the data points form a line that is not horizontal, the Y scores change as the X scores change and there is a relationship present.*

**FIGURE 4.11**  Line Graph Showing Mean Errors in Recall as a Function of List Length

*Each data point is the mean score for a condition.*

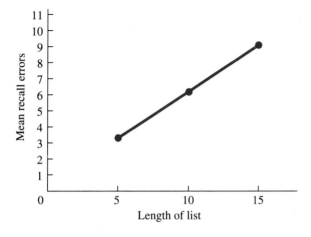

**FIGURE 4.12**   Line Graph Showing Mean Recall Errors as a Function of List Length

*The flat line indicates that the mean is the same in each condition, so there is no relationship present.*

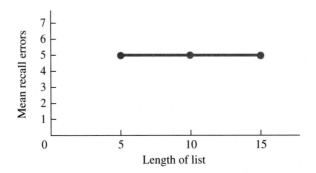

On the other hand, say that each condition had produced a mean of 5 errors. As shown in Figure 4.12, plotting the same mean score of 5 for each condition results in a horizontal line. A horizontal (flat) line indicates that as the $X$ scores change, the mean error score stays the same. This implies that the distribution of individual scores stays the same, regardless of the condition. If the scores on the dependent variable stay the same as the conditions of the independent variable change, there is no relationship present. Thus, *on any graph, if the data points form a horizontal line, the Y scores do not change as the X scores change and there is not a relationship present.*

**Bar graphs**   When the independent variable is a nominal or ordinal variable, we plot the results of the experiment by creating a bar graph. Each bar is centered over a condition on the $X$ axis, and the height of the bar corresponds to the mean score for the condition.

For example, say that we conducted another recall experiment in which we compared the errors made by samples of psychology majors, English majors, and physics majors. Here, the independent variable of college major is a nominal, or categorical, variable, so we have the bar graph shown in Figure 4.13. The bars implicitly indicate that on the variable of college major, we arbitrarily assigned psychology a nominal score to the left of that of English, closer to zero. The bars also indicate that there is an unknown or undefined gap between categories. If, for example, we inserted an additional category of sociology between psychology and English, we could not assume that the mean scores of sociology majors would fall on a line running between the means for psychology and English majors.

The bar graph in Figure 4.13 shows that a relationship is present, because the tops of the bars do not form a flat, or horizontal, line. This tells us that

**FIGURE 4.13**   Bar Graph Showing Mean Errors in Recall as a Function of College Major

*The height of each bar corresponds to the mean score for the condition.*

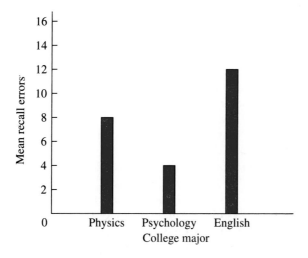

we have different means for different conditions, so the recall scores change as a function of changes in college major.

## Describing the Relationship in the Population

So far we have summarized the results of our recall experiment in terms of the sample data. But this is only part of the story. The big question remains: Do these data reflect a law of nature? Do longer lists produce more errors in recall for everyone in the population?

   To make inferences about the population, we must compute the appropriate inferential statistics in order to determine if the sample is representative. For the moment we'll assume that our data passed the inferential test. Then we can conclude that each sample mean represents the population mean that would be found for that condition. The mean error score for the 5-item condition was 3, so we infer that if we had the population recall a 5-item list, the mean of the population of error scores would be located at 3. In essence, we expect that everyone would have around 3 errors. Similarly, we infer that if the population recalled a 10-item list, $\mu$ would equal our sample mean of 6, and if the population recalled a 15-item list, $\mu$ would be 9.

   We conceptualize the populations of error scores in the following way. Assuming that each sample mean provides a good estimate of the corresponding population mean, we know approximately where on the dependent variable each population of scores would be located. Further, assuming that recall errors are normally distributed in the population, we also have a good idea of the shape of each population distribution. Thus, based on our data and our assumptions, we can use the simple frequency distributions shown in Figure 4.14 to describe the population of recall errors we would expect to find for each list length.

The population means in Figure 4.14 are located at the same points on the dependent variable as are the sample means in the line graph in Figure 4.11. Because Figure 4.14 depicts frequency distributions, however, the scores on the dependent variable are back on the $X$ axis. The overlap among the distributions simply shows that some subjects in one condition make the same number of errors as other subjects in adjacent conditions.

Because these population distributions have different values of $\mu$, we have described the relationship that we think exists in the population: as the conditions of the independent variable change, the scores on the dependent variable tend to change in a consistent fashion so that there is a different population of scores for each condition. In essence, it appears that for every 5 items in a list, everyone's score tends to increase by about 3 errors, and thus the distribution slides 3 units to the right for each condition.

Since a population of scores reflects the behavior of everyone of interest, a change in a population of scores indicates a change in everyone's behavior. If, as some independent variable changes, *everyone's* behavior changes, then we have learned about a law of nature involving that behavior. Above, we changed everyone's behavior in terms of recall errors by changing the list length, so we have evidence of how a law of nature works: for every 5 items in a list, recall

**FIGURE 4.14**  Locations of Populations of Error Scores as a Function of List Length

*Each distribution contains the recall scores we would expect to find if the population were tested under each condition.*

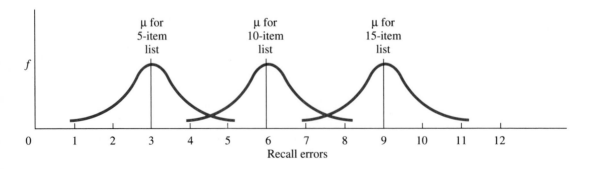

errors go up by about 3. That is about all there is to it: we have reached the goal of our research.

   If the process by which we arrived at the above conclusion sounds easy, it's because it is easy. In essence, statistical analysis of most experiments merely involves three steps: (1) computing each sample mean (and other descriptive statistics) so that we can summarize the scores and the relationship found in the experiment, (2) performing the appropriate inferential procedure to determine whether each sample is representative of a particular population, and (3) describing the location of the population of scores that we expect would be found for each condition by describing the value of each $\mu$. Once we have described the expected population for each condition, we are basically finished with statistical analysis.

### FINALLY

As you may have noticed, psychological research and the statistical procedures therein rely on the mean as *the* measure of central tendency. To be literate in statistics, you should understand the mode and the median, but the truly important topics in this chapter involve the mean and its characteristics, especially when applied to the normal distribution. These topics form the basis for virtually everything else that we will discuss.

## CHAPTER SUMMARY

*1.* *Measures of central tendency* summarize the location of a distribution of scores on a variable. Each measure is a way of indicating around where the center of the distribution tends to be located. So that we accurately summarize the location of the distribution, we base our choice of measure on (1) the scale used to measure the variable we are describing and (2) the shape of the distribution.

*2.* The *mode* is the most frequently occurring score or scores in a distribution. The mode is used primarily to summarize nominal data.

*3.* The *median,* symbolized by Mdn, is the score in a distribution located at the 50th percentile. The median is used primarily for describing ordinal data and for describing interval or ratio data that form a very skewed or nonsymmetrical distribution.

*4.* The *mean* is the score located at the exact mathematical center of a distribution, and it is computed in the same way as an average. The mean is used to describe interval or ratio data that form a symmetrical unimodal distribution such as the normal distribution. The symbol for a sample mean is $\overline{X}$, and the symbol for a population mean is $\mu$.

5. Transforming raw scores by using a *constant*, $K$, results in a new value of the mean, median, or mode. The new value is equal to the one that would be obtained if the transformation were performed directly on the old value.

6. The amount a score *deviates* from the mean is computed as the score minus the mean, or $X - \overline{X}$. A *deviation* consists of a number and a sign ($+$ or $-$) and it indicates the location of the raw score relative to the mean and relative to the distribution. A positive deviation indicates that the score is above the mean and, when graphed, to the right of the mean. A negative deviation indicates that the score is below the mean and, when graphed, to the left of the mean. The size of the deviation, whether positive or negative, indicates the *distance* the score lies from the mean. In a normal distribution, scores having larger deviations lie farther in the tail of the distribution. Thus, the larger the deviation, the less frequently the score and the deviation occur.

7. The *sum of the deviations around the mean*, or $\Sigma(X - \overline{X})$, always equals zero. When we do not know anything else about the scores, the mean is the best score to use as any individual's *predicted score*. This is because the *total error* across all predictions will be the sum of the deviations around the mean, which will always equal zero.

8. In graphing the results of an experiment, we plot the independent variable along the $X$ axis and the dependent variable along the $Y$ axis. When the independent variable is measured using a ratio or interval scale, we create a *line graph*. When the independent variable is measured using a nominal or ordinal scale, we create a *bar graph*.

9. On any graph, if the data points form a line that is not horizontal, then the $Y$ scores change *as a function of* changes in the $X$ scores and there is a relationship present. If the data points form a flat, or horizontal, line, then the $Y$ scores do not change as a function of changes in the $X$ scores and there is no relationship present.

10. If the samples in an experiment are representative of the population, then we can infer that each condition of the experiment would produce a population of scores having a $\mu$ equal to the sample mean for that condition. If a relationship is present, there will be different values of $\mu$ for two or more conditions of the independent variable. Then we can conclude that the variables are related in nature, because we can infer

that each condition of the independent variable would result in a different population of scores on the dependent variable.

---

## USING THE COMPUTER

In your computer program, routine number **3** in the Main Menu is entitled "One Group Descriptive Statistics." This program will compute the mode, median, and mean of a sample (as well as several statistics you will learn about in the next chapter). With experience analyzing data, you'll find that routine **3** usually provides you with everything you need to fully describe and summarize a sample. Because of this, routine **3** will often be your first stop in the program, even if you then perform additional routines. To prevent a great deal of busy work, you will want to learn how to save data (permanently record it) on a computer disk. Data can be saved right on your program disk. If you save your data, you can run different routines from the Main Menu or you can come back another day and run routines, all without retyping the data each time.

---

## PRACTICE PROBLEMS

(Answers are provided for odd-numbered problems.)

1. What does a measure of central tendency indicate?
2. What is the mode, and with what type of data is it most appropriate?
3. What is the median, and with what type of data is it most appropriate?
4. What is the mean, and with what type of data is it most appropriate?
5. For the data below, compute the mean.

| 18 | 16 | 19 | 20 | 18 | 19 | 23 | 54 | 20 | 16 |
|----|----|----|----|----|----|----|----|----|----|
| 18 | 19 | 18 | 19 | 18 | 40 | 30 | 19 | 18 | 38 |

6. *a.* For the data in question 5, what is the mode?
   *b.* By comparing the mean and the mode, determine what shape the distribution has. How do you know?
7. What two pieces of information about the location of a score does a deviation score convey?
8. On a normal distribution of scores, four subjects obtained the following deviation scores: $-5$, $0$, $+3$, and $+1$.
   *a.* Which subject obtained the lowest raw score? How do you know?
   *b.* Which subject's raw score had the lowest frequency? How do you know?

    *c.* Which subject's raw score had the highest frequency? How do you know?

    *d.* Which subject obtained the highest raw score? How do you know?

9. Why do we use the mean score in a sample to predict any score that might be found in that sample?

10. What is $\mu$, and how do we usually determine its value?

11. *a.* When graphing the results of an experiment, when do you create a line graph and when do you create a bar graph?

    *b.* Which variable do you plot on the $Y$ axis, and which do you plot on the $X$ axis?

12. The line graph of the results of an experiment slants upwards as a function of increases in the amount of the independent variable.

    *a.* What does this tell you about the mean scores for the conditions?

    *b.* What does this tell you about the raw scores for each condition?

    *c.* Assuming that the samples are representative, what does this tell you about the population $\mu$'s?

    *d.* What do you conclude about whether there is a relationship between these variables in nature?

## *SUMMARY OF FORMULAS*

**1.** *The formula for computing the median is*

$$\text{Mdn} = \text{LRL} + \left(\frac{.5(N) - cf \text{ below interval}}{f \text{ within interval}}\right)(\text{interval size})$$

where $N$ is the total frequency of scores in the sample, LRL is the lower real limit of the interval containing the median, *cf* below interval is the cumulative frequency of the interval below the interval containing the median, *f* within interval is the frequency of the interval containing the median, and interval size is the interval size used to create the frequency distribution.

**2.** *The formula for computing the sample mean is*

$$\overline{X} = \frac{\Sigma X}{N}$$

where $\Sigma X$ stands for the sum of the scores and $N$ is the number of scores.

# 5

# Measures of
# Variability:
# Range, Variance, and
# Standard Deviation

As we saw in the previous chapter, measures of central tendency provide a shorthand summary of a distribution of scores. If the scores form a normal or symmetrical distribution, the mean best describes central tendency. The mean is the mathematical center of the distribution, and the sum of the deviations of all scores around the mean equals zero. We use the symbol $\overline{X}$ to describe the mean of a sample of scores, and we use the symbol $\mu$ to describe the mean of a population. We think of $\overline{X}$ or $\mu$ as the typical score, and we use it to represent or predict all the scores in a distribution.

Of course, usually all the scores will not equal the mean score; there will be many different scores. In this chapter we discuss procedures for describing and summarizing the differences between scores. Then we can answer the third question posed by descriptive statistics: Are there large differences between the scores, or are there small differences between the scores? First, though, we need to look at a couple of new symbols that will appear in our discussions.

## MORE STATISTICAL NOTATION

As part of our statistical calculations, we will square each score in a sample. This operation is symbolized by $X^2$. Usually, we then add up the squared scores. This operation is symbolized by $\Sigma X^2$. The notation $\Sigma X^2$ indicates the **sum of the squared Xs:** it tells us to first square each $X$ score and then find the sum of the squared $X$s. Thus, to find $\Sigma X^2$ for the scores 2, 2, and 3, we take $2^2 + 2^2 + 3^2$, or $4 + 4 + 9$, which adds up to 17.

Learn right here to avoid confusing $\Sigma X^2$ with a similar looking, yet very different operation symbolized by $(\Sigma X)^2$. The symbol $(\Sigma X)^2$ stands for the **squared sum of X.** In Chapter 1 we saw that parentheses indicate to first find the quantity inside of the parentheses and then perform any other operations on that quantity. Because $\Sigma X$ is inside the parentheses, we must first find the sum of the $X$ scores and then square that sum. To find $(\Sigma X)^2$ for the scores 2, 2, and 3, we have $(2 + 2 + 3)^2$, which is $(7)^2$, or 49. Notice that for scores of 2, 2, and 3, $\Sigma X^2$ gives 17, while $(\Sigma X)^2$ gives the different answer of 49.

With this chapter we will begin using subscripts. A *subscript* is a symbol placed below and to the right of a statistical symbol which identifies the scores used in computing the statistic. Pay attention to subscripts, because they are part of the complete symbols for certain statistics.

Finally, prepare yourself for the fact that many statistics have two different formulas, a definitional formula and a computational formula. A definitional formula defines a statistic. The reason you need to pay attention to this formula is so you understand where the answer comes from when you compute the statistic. However, definitional formulas tend to be very time-consuming to use, especially when $N$ is large. Therefore, statisticians have reworked the formulas to produce computational formulas. As the name implies, we use the computational formula when actually computing a statistic. Trust me, computational formulas give exactly the same answers as definitional formulas, and they are much easier to use.

## THE CONCEPT OF VARIABILITY

The mean may sound like a great invention, but by itself it provides an incomplete description of any distribution. The mean tells us the central score and often where the most frequently occurring scores are, but it tells us little about scores that are not at the center of the distribution and/or that occur infrequently.

Consider the three samples of data shown in Table 5.1. As you can see, each sample has a mean of 6. If we did not look at the raw scores, we might believe that the three samples formed identical distributions. Obviously, they do not. Sample A contains relatively large differences between many of the scores, Sample B contains smaller differences between the scores, and Sample C contains no differences between the scores.

Thus, to accurately describe a set of data, we need to know not only the central tendency but also how much the individual scores differ from each other. The type of statistic we need is called a measure of variability. **Measures of variability** summarize and describe the extent to which scores in a distribution

**TABLE 5.1** Three Different Distributions
Having the Same Mean Score

| Sample A | Sample B | Sample C |
|----------|----------|----------|
| 0 | 8 | 6 |
| 2 | 7 | 6 |
| 6 | 6 | 6 |
| 10 | 5 | 6 |
| 12 | 4 | 6 |
| $\overline{X} = 6$ | $\overline{X} = 6$ | $\overline{X} = 6$ |

differ from each other. When there are many relatively large differences between the scores, the data are said to be relatively *variable* or to contain a large amount of *variability*. Thus, when we ask whether there are large differences between the scores or small differences between the scores, we are asking the statistical question "How much variability is there in the data?"

In Chapter 4 we saw that a score indicates a subject's location on the variable and that the difference between two scores is the distance that separates them. From this perspective, by telling us the extent to which scores in a distribution differ from each other, measures of variability tell us how *spread out* the scores are.

In Figure 5.1 we see a graphic representation of the distances separating the scores in Samples A, B, and C of Table 5.1. There are relatively large differences between the scores in Sample A, so the distribution in Sample A is spread out. There are smaller differences between the scores in Sample B, so the distribution is not as spread out. There are no differences between the scores in Sample C, so there is no spread in this distribution. Thus, of the three samples, we can describe Sample A as having the largest differences

**FIGURE 5.1** Distance Between the Locations of Scores in Three Distributions

*An X over a score indicates a subject who obtained that score. Each arrow indicates how spread out the scores in the sample are.*

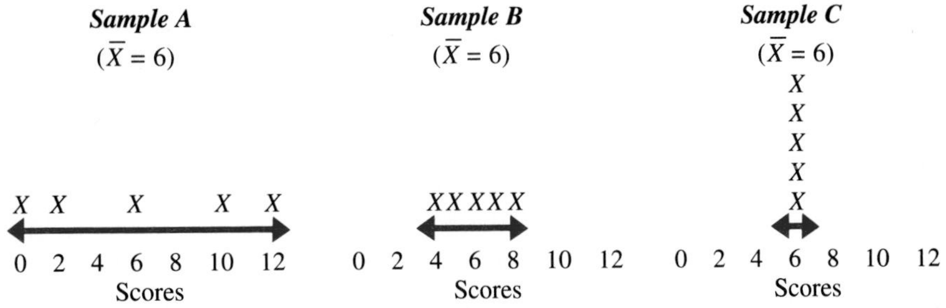

between scores, or we can say that the scores in Sample A are spread out the most. In the language of statistics, we say that the scores in Sample A show the greatest variability.

We always measure the variability of a distribution, because the amount of variability in the data determines how accurately the measure of central tendency describes the distribution. The greater the variability, the more the scores are spread out and the less accurately they are represented by one central score. Because of different amounts of variability in the above samples, 6 is a very accurate representative score for Sample C, but it is not so accurate for Sample B, and not even close for Sample A.

> *STAT ALERT* Measures of variability provide a number that indicates how spread out the scores are. While measures of central tendency indicate the *location* of most scores in a distribution, measures of variability indicate the *distance* between the scores in the distribution.

In the following sections we will discuss three common measures of variability: the range, the variance, and the standard deviation.

## THE RANGE

One way to describe the variability in scores is to determine how far the lowest score is from the highest score. In Figure 5.1, Sample A is spread out the most because the lowest and highest scores are farther apart than in the other two groups. The descriptive statistic that indicates the distance between the two most extreme scores in a set of data is called the **range.**

> *THE FORMULA FOR COMPUTING THE RANGE IS*
>
> Range = highest score − lowest score

In Sample A, the highest score is 12 and the lowest score is 0, so the range is 12 − 0, which equals 12. The range in Sample B is 8 − 4, or 4, and the range in Sample C is 6 − 6, or 0.

Although each of these ranges does give an indication of the amount of spread in the sample, the range is a rather crude measure. Since it involves only the two most extreme scores, the range is based on the least typical and often least frequent scores. Therefore, the range is our sole measure of variability only with rank-ordered data or when interval or ratio scores form distributions that cannot be accurately described using other, better measures.

## The Semi-interquartile Range

A special version of the range is the semi-interquartile range, which is used in conjunction with the median to describe highly skewed distributions. *Quartiles* are the scores at the 25th and 75th percentiles. The *semi-interquartile range* is one-half of the distance between the scores at the 25th and 75th percentiles.

*THE FORMULA FOR COMPUTING THE SEMI-INTERQUARTILE RANGE IS*

$$\frac{\text{Score at 75th percentile} - \text{score at 25th percentile}}{2}$$

We determine the scores at the 25th and 75th percentiles using the formula in Chapter 3 for finding the score at a given percentile. Then we subtract the score at the 25th percentile from the score at the 75th percentile and divide by 2.

To see what the semi-interquartile range tells us, consider the distribution shown in Figure 5.2. We have determined that the score of 12 is at the 25th percentile and the score of 17 is at the 75th percentile. Using the above formula, we find that the semi-interquartile range is (17 − 12)/2, which is 5/2, or 2.5.

**FIGURE 5.2** Semi-interquartile Range on a Positively Skewed Distribution

*A total of 25% of all subjects scored between 12 and 14, and 25% scored between 14 and 17.*

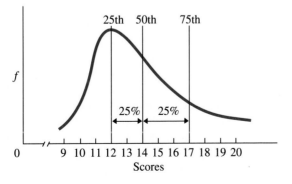

The semi-interquartile range is the average range between the median and the scores at the two quartiles. Thus, we can recalculate the semi-interquartile range by first finding that the range between the 25th percentile and the median (the 50th percentile) is 14 − 12, or 2. The range between the 50th and 75th percentile is 17 − 14, or 3. The average of 2 and 3 is 5/2, or again 2.5. We have determined that the 25% of the distribution immediately below or above the median is, on average, within 2.5 points of the median. The semi-interquartile range describes the majority of the scores in the distribution more accurately than the overall range does, because the semi-interquartile range describes the range of scores more toward the center of the distribution and does not include the most infrequent extreme scores.

## UNDERSTANDING VARIANCE AND STANDARD DEVIATION

Most of the time in psychological research we have interval or ratio data that more or less fit a normal or at least a symmetrical distribution, so the mean is the best measure of central tendency. When the mean is the appropriate measure of central tendency, we use two measures of variability, called the variance and the standard deviation. Recognize from the outset that the variance and the standard deviation are two very similar ways to describe the variability in a distribution of scores. They are the best measures of variability because in computing them we consider every score in the distribution.

The variance and the standard deviation describe how different the scores are from each other, but we compute them using the mean score as our reference point. We do this because the mean is always the center of a distribution. When the scores are spread out from each other, they are also spread out from the center. If a high score is far from a low score, both scores are relatively distant from the mean. If all scores are close to each other, they are also close to the mean. Thus, it is important to understand that although we use these measures of variability to communicate how much the scores differ from each other, we actually measure how much the scores differ from the mean.

The variance and standard deviation are most appropriate with normal or other symmetrical distributions, because these distributions are balanced above and below the mean. The mean is the point *around* which a distribution is located. The variance and standard deviation allow us to quantify "around." For example, if the grades in your statistics class form a normal distribution with a mean of 80, then you know that most people have a score around 80. But does this mean that most scores are between 79 and 81, or between 60 and 100, or what? By computing the variance and standard deviation, you can define "around."

The distance between a score and the mean is the numerical difference between the score and the mean. This difference is symbolized by the quantity $(X - \overline{X})$. Recall from Chapter 4 that $(X - \overline{X})$ defines the amount by which a score deviates from the mean. Thus, a deviation indicates how much a score is spread out from the mean. Of course, some scores will deviate from the mean more than other scores. Because we want to summarize the variability of many scores that deviate by different amounts, it makes sense to determine the average amount that the scores deviate from the mean. We could call this amount the "average of the deviations." The larger the average of the deviations, the greater the spread, or variability, between all of the scores and the mean.

To compute an average, we sum the scores and divide by $N$. We *might* find the average of the deviations by first computing $(X - \overline{X})$ for each subject, then summing these deviations to find $\Sigma(X - \overline{X})$, and finally dividing by $N$, the number of deviations we summed. Altogether, the formula for the average of the deviations[1] would be

$$\text{Average of the deviations} = \frac{\Sigma(X - \overline{X})}{N}$$

We *might* compute the average of the deviations using this formula, except for a *big* problem. Recall from Chapter 4 that the sum of the deviations around the mean, $\Sigma(X - \overline{X})$, always equals zero, because the positive deviations cancel out the negative deviations. This means that, for any set of scores, the numerator of the average of the deviations will always be zero, so the average of the deviations will always be zero. So much for the average of the deviations!

But remember our purpose here: we want a statistic that tells us something *like* the average of the deviations, so that we know the average amount the scores are spread out around the mean. The trouble is, mathematically, the average of the deviations is always zero, so we will have to calculate this statistic in a more complicated way. Nonetheless, you should think of the variance and standard deviation as producing a number that, like an average, indicates the typical amount by which the scores differ from the mean.

## DESCRIBING THE SAMPLE VARIANCE

So how do we compute the average of the deviations? The problem is that the positive and negative deviations always cancel out to produce a sum of zero. The solution to this problem is to *square* the deviations. That is, we will find

---

[1] In advanced statistics there is a very real statistic called the average deviation. This isn't it.

the difference between each score and the mean and then square that difference. This removes all the negative deviations, so that the sum of the squared deviations is not necessarily zero and neither is the average of the squared deviations. (As we shall see, we also choose this solution because squaring the deviations results in statistics that have unique and very useful characteristics.)

In finding the average of the squared deviations, we are computing the variance. The **variance** is the average of the squared deviations of the scores around the mean. When we calculate this statistic for a sample of scores around the sample mean, we are computing the *sample variance*. The symbol for a sample variance is $S_X^2$. You must always include the squared sign ($^2$), because it is part of the symbol for variance. The capital $S$ indicates that the quantity describes a sample, and the subscript $X$ indicates that it is computed for a sample of $X$ scores.

---

*THE DEFINITIONAL FORMULA FOR THE SAMPLE VARIANCE IS*

$$S_X^2 = \frac{\Sigma(X - \overline{X})^2}{N}$$

---

Finding the average of the squared deviations around the mean is simply a way of describing variability. In essence, $S_X^2$ stands for the answer we obtain when we use this formula to describe our sample, and this answer is called the sample variance. Recognize that we use the above formula *only* when we are describing a sample of data (as opposed to the population), simply to determine the variance of those scores in the sample.

> *STAT ALERT*  The symbol $S_X^2$ stands for the variance of the scores in a sample.

Say that a sample consists of the scores 2, 3, 4, 5, 6, 7, and 8, so the mean is 5. To compute $S_X^2$ using the above formula, we arrange the data as shown in Table 5.2. First we compute each deviation, $(X - \overline{X})$, by subtracting the mean from each score. Next, as shown in the far right column, we square each of these deviations to get $(X - \overline{X})^2$. Then we add the squared deviations to find $\Sigma(X - \overline{X})^2$, which here is 28. The number of scores in the sample, $N$, is 7. Filling in our formula for $S_X^2$, we have

$$S_X^2 = \frac{\Sigma(X - \overline{X})^2}{N} = \frac{28}{7} = 4.0$$

**TABLE 5.2**  Calculation of Variance Using the Definitional Formula

| Subject | Score | − | $\overline{X}$ | = | $(X - \overline{X})$ | $(X - \overline{X})^2$ |
|---------|-------|---|----|---|------------|-------------|
| 1 | 2 | − | 5 | = | −3 | 9 |
| 2 | 3 | − | 5 | = | −2 | 4 |
| 3 | 4 | − | 5 | = | −1 | 1 |
| 4 | 5 | − | 5 | = | 0 | 0 |
| 5 | 6 | − | 5 | = | 1 | 1 |
| 6 | 7 | − | 5 | = | 2 | 4 |
| 7 | 8 | − | 5 | = | 3 | 9 |
| | $N = 7$ | | | | $\Sigma (X - \overline{X})^2 = 28$ | |

Thus, in this sample, the variance, $S_X^2$, equals 4.0. In other words, the average squared deviation of the scores around the mean is 4.0.

## Computational Formula for the Sample Variance

To simplify the preceding definitional formula for variance, we replace the symbol for the mean with the formula for the mean. After reducing the formula, we have the computational formula. Like the definitional formula, this computational formula is used only when we wish to know the variance of the scores in a sample.

*THE COMPUTATIONAL FORMULA FOR THE SAMPLE VARIANCE IS*

$$S_X^2 = \frac{\Sigma X^2 - \dfrac{(\Sigma X)^2}{N}}{N}$$

The long dividing line tells us to calculate everything above the line first. Likewise, the short dividing line tells us to calculate the quantity $(\Sigma X)^2$ before dividing. Thus, we first find the sum of the $X$s, $\Sigma X$, square that sum, and divide the squared sum by $N$. The next step is to subtract that amount from the sum of the squared $X$s, $\Sigma X^2$. Finally, we divide that quantity by $N$. The answer is the sample variance, $S_X^2$.

Using the same scores we used with the definitional formula, we arrange the scores as shown in Table 5.3. The sum of the $X$s, $\Sigma X$, is 35, the sum of the

**TABLE 5.3**  Calculation of
Variance Using the
Computational Formula

| $X$ score | $X^2$ |
|---|---|
| 2 | 4 |
| 3 | 9 |
| 4 | 16 |
| 5 | 25 |
| 6 | 36 |
| 7 | 49 |
| 8 | 64 |
| $\Sigma X = 35$ | $\Sigma X^2 = 203$ |

squared $X$s, $\Sigma X^2$, is 203, and $N$ is 7. Putting these quantities into the computational formula, we have

$$S_X^2 = \frac{\Sigma X^2 - \frac{(\Sigma X)^2}{N}}{N} = \frac{203 - \frac{(35)^2}{7}}{7}$$

The squared sum of $X$, $(\Sigma X)^2$, is $35^2$, which is 1225, so we have

$$S_X^2 = \frac{203 - \frac{1225}{7}}{7}$$

Now, 1225 divided by 7 equals 175, so

$$S_X^2 = \frac{203 - 175}{7}$$

Since 203 minus 175 equals 28, we have

$$S_X^2 = \frac{28}{7}$$

Finally, after dividing, we have

$$S_X^2 = 4.0$$

Thus, as we found using the definitional formula, the sample variance for these scores is 4.0.

Do not read any further until you are sure that you understand how to work this formula!

### Interpreting Variance

The good news is that the variance provides a direct way of measuring variability using all the scores in the data. Ideally, though, we want the average of the deviations, and the bad news is that the variance does not make much sense as an average deviation. Because the variance is the average of the *squared* deviations—the squared distances between the scores and the mean—it is always an unrealistically large number. As we saw, for the scores of 2, 3, 4, 5, 6, 7, and 8, $\overline{X}$ is 5 and $S_X^2$ is 4. To say that these scores differ from the mean of 5 by an average of 4 would be plain silly! Not one score actually deviates from the mean by as much as 4 points, so how can we interpret the variance as telling us that the "average" deviation is 4? Well, the answer is that we can't. As a measure of variability, the variance is difficult to relate directly to the original data. (Because it measures in squared units, variance is also rather bizarre: if the scores reflect the ages of the subjects, the variance measures squared ages!)

Does this mean that computing the variance is a waste of time? No, because variance is used extensively in the statistics we will discuss later. Also, variance does communicate the variability of scores. If someone reports that one sample has $S_X^2 = 1$ and another sample has $S_X^2 = 3$, you know that the second sample is more variable, or spread out, because it has a larger average squared deviation. Thus, think of variance as a number that simply tells us how variable the scores are: the larger the variance, the more the scores are spread out.

The measure of variability that more directly communicates the average deviation of the raw scores is the standard deviation.

## DESCRIBING THE SAMPLE STANDARD DEVIATION

The variance turns out to be an unrealistically large number because we square each deviation. We solve this problem by taking the square root of the variance. The answer is called the standard deviation. The **standard deviation** is the square root of the variance, or the square root of the average squared deviation of scores around the mean. To create the formula for the standard deviation, we simply add the square root to the formula for variance.

*THE DEFINITIONAL FORMULA FOR THE SAMPLE STANDARD DEVIATION IS*

$$S_X = \sqrt{\frac{\Sigma(X - \overline{X})^2}{N}}$$

Notice that the symbol for the sample standard deviation is the square root of the symbol for the sample variance, because $\sqrt{S_X^2}$ is $S_X$. Conversely, if we square the standard deviation, we have the variance. (To remember all of this, think of the capital $S$ in $S_X$ as indicating the sample standard deviation and $S_X^2$ as the squared sample standard deviation, which we call the sample variance.)

> **STAT ALERT**  The symbol $S_X$ stands for the standard deviation of the scores in a sample.

To compute $S_X$ using this formula, we first compute everything inside the square root sign, which gives us the variance: we square each score's deviation, sum the squared deviations, and then divide that sum by $N$. In the previous example, the variance ($S_X^2$) was 4. We then take the square root of this number to find the standard deviation. In this case,

$$S_X = \sqrt{4.0}$$

which gives us

$$S_X = 2.0$$

The standard deviation of these scores is 2.0.

## Computational Formula for the Sample Standard Deviation

We create the computational formula for the standard deviation merely by adding the square root symbol to the computational formula for the variance.

> THE COMPUTATIONAL FORMULA FOR THE SAMPLE STANDARD DEVIATION IS
> $$S_X = \sqrt{\dfrac{\Sigma X^2 - \dfrac{(\Sigma X)^2}{N}}{N}}$$

This formula is used only when we are describing the standard deviation of a *sample* of scores.

To see how the formula works, we will again use the scores 2, 3, 4, 5, 6, 7, and 8. From Table 5.2 we know that $\Sigma X$ is 35, $\Sigma X^2$ is 203, and $N$ is 7. Putting these values in the formula gives

$$S_X = \sqrt{\dfrac{203 - \dfrac{(35)^2}{7}}{7}}$$

Completing the computations inside the square root symbol, we have the variance, which is 4.0. Thus, we have

$$S_X = \sqrt{4.0}$$

Taking the square root of 4.0, we once again find that the standard deviation is

$$S_X = 2.0$$

## Interpreting the Standard Deviation

The standard deviation is as good as our measures of variability get: computing the standard deviation is as close as we come to computing the "average of the deviations." For the previous scores, $S_X$ equals 2.0. We interpret this statistic as indicating that the scores differ, or deviate, from the mean by an "average" of about 2. Some scores will deviate by more and some by less, but overall the scores will deviate from the mean by something like an average of 2. Further, the standard deviation measures in the same units as the raw scores. So if, for example, the above scores indicated the ages of our subjects in years, we would know that the scores differed from the mean age by an "average" of 2 years.

   Since the standard deviation provides us with a number that indicates the average amount the scores are spread out above or below the mean, we can further summarize a distribution by describing the scores that lie at "plus one standard deviation from the mean" ($+1S_X$) and "minus one standard deviation from the mean" ($-1S_X$). For example, our previous scores of 2, 3, 4, 5, 6, 7, and 8 produced $\overline{X} = 5.0$ and $S_X = 2.0$. The score that is $+1S_X$ from the mean is the score of $5 + 2$, or 7. The score that is $-1S_X$ from the mean is the score of $5 - 2$, or 3. Thus, a good way to summarize these scores is to say that the mean score is 5 and the majority of the scores are between the scores of 3 and 7.

## Applying the Standard Deviation to the Normal Curve

By describing a distribution in terms of the scores that are between $+1S_X$ and $-1S_X$, we specify *around* where most of the scores lie. This is especially useful if the scores form a normal distribution. For example, earlier in this chapter we imagined a statistics class with a mean score of 80. Say that $S_X$ for the class is 5. The score at $80 - 5$ is the score of 75, and the score at $80 + 5$ is the score of 85. Figure 5.3 shows where these scores are located on a normal distribution. First, by saying that the mean is 80, we imply that most scores are around 80. Then, by finding the scores at $-1S_X$ and $+1S_X$, we define "around": most of the scores are between 75 and 85 (from our parking lot perspective, this is where most of the subjects are standing).

**FIGURE 5.3**    Normal Distribution Showing Scores at Plus or Minus One Standard Deviation

*With $S_X = 5.0$, the score of 75 is at $-1S_X$ and the score of 85 is at $+1S_X$. The percentages are the approximate percentages of the scores falling in each portion of the distribution.*

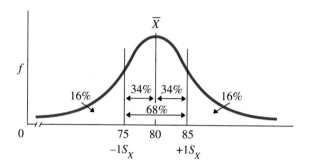

In fact, as illustrated in Figure 5.3, we see that about 34% of all students have scores between 75 and 80, and 34% have scores between 80 and 85. Thus, approximately 68% of all scores in the distribution fall between the scores of 75 and 85. One reason we compute the standard deviation is that there is a precise mathematical relationship between the standard deviation and the normal distribution: approximately 34% of the scores in *any* normal distribution fall between the mean and the score that is one standard deviation from the mean, so approximately 68% of the scores are always between the scores at $+1S_X$ and $-1S_X$ from the mean. Conversely, about 32% of the scores are outside of this range.

Of course it is very unlikely that the scores of a small statistics class would produce an ideal normal distribution. However, this example shows how we apply the normal curve model to real data. If we can assume that statistics grades are generally normally distributed, we can operate as if the class formed the ideal normal distribution. Then we *expect* about 68% of the scores in the class to fall between 75 and 85. The more closely the distribution conforms to the ideal normal curve, the closer to about 68% of the scores will be between 75 and 85.

Different data produce different normal distributions. By finding the scores at $-1S_X$ and $+1S_X$ from the mean, we can see how the standard deviation communicates these differences. Figure 5.4 shows three variations of the normal curve. The larger the standard deviation (and variance), the wider the distribution. This is because the differences in shape are determined by the differences in the frequency of the scores that are close to the mean. In Distribution A, $S_X$ is 4.0. This tells us that, as shown in the figure, the most frequent scores are between about 46 and 54. Because the majority of the deviations are

**FIGURE 5.4**   Three Variations of the Normal Curve

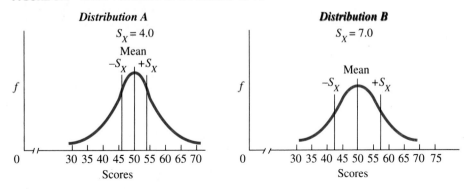

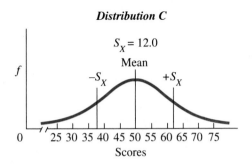

smaller than or equal to $+4$ and $-4$ and there are relatively few larger deviations, the "average" of these deviations is 4. But look at Distribution B. Here $S_X$ is 7.0, and this tells us that the relatively frequent scores are spread over a wider range, between about 43 and 57. Now the majority of the deviations are larger, up to $+7$ and $-7$, producing an "average" deviation of about 7. Finally, in Distribution C, $S_X$ is 12. This tells us that the relatively frequent scores are between about 38 and 62, producing many deviations between $+12$ and $-12$. With so many large deviations, we have a large "average" deviation of about 12. Thus, a larger standard deviation (or variance) indicates that a distribution is wider, because in a wider distribution the relatively extreme scores occur more frequently, producing a larger "average" deviation.

   Despite these differences, a normal distribution will always have approximately 68% of the scores between the scores at $+1S_X$ and $-1S_X$ from the mean. This is because, mathematically, 68% of the *area* under the normal curve falls between $+1S_X$ and $-1S_X$. To understand this, visualize the above distributions as parking lots full of people. Say that each parking lot contains 1000 subjects: 68% of 1000 is 680. In Distribution A, the greater height of the curve indicates that more subjects are standing in line at those scores close to the mean. With so many small deviations, we will compute a small standard deviation. Correspondingly, because each line contains so many subjects, we will not travel very far above and below the mean before we accumulate 680 subjects. On the other hand, in Distribution C, there are fewer subjects standing in line at each score near the mean. Here relatively large deviations are more frequent, producing a larger standard deviation. Correspondingly, because each line contains fewer subjects, we will travel farther above and below the mean before we accumulate 680 subjects. Thus, regardless of the size of $S_X$, approximately 68% of the area under the normal curve, and thus 68% of the scores, falls between the scores at $+1S_X$ and $-1S_X$ from the mean.

In summary, then, here is how our descriptive statistics are used to describe the important characteristics of a normal distribution. The mean describes the location of the distribution. The standard deviation describes the "average" amount the scores are spread out around that location, and we expect to find about 68% of the scores between the scores at $+1S_X$ and $-1S_X$ from the mean.

## Avoiding Some Common Errors in Computing $S_X$

Because the computations for $S_X$ (and $S_X^2$) are somewhat involved, you should always examine your answers to be sure that they are correct. There are some answers you should never obtain.

First, remember that variability can never be a negative number. If you state that $S_X$ is $-5$, for example, you are claiming that the amount of spread between scores is less than zero. All our formulas involve squared numbers, and squared numbers can never be negative numbers.

Second, watch for answers that simply do not make sense. If the raw scores range between 35 and 65, what should you conclude if you find that $S_X$ is 20? My first guess is that you made a mistake! If these scores form anything like a normal distribution, the mean score will be around 50. If so, then the largest deviation for the extreme scores of 35 and 65 will be only about 15 points, so the "average deviation" for all scores cannot be 20. Similarly, it is unlikely that the $S_X$ for these scores is extremely small, such as .25. If there are only two extreme deviations of 15, imagine how many small deviations from the mean it would take to create an average of only .25. (Similarly, you can evaluate any variance you compute by first finding its square root, the standard deviation.)

Strange numbers for $S_X$ and $S_X^2$ may be correct for strange distributions, but you should always be alert to whether statistical answers make sense. (They *do* make sense, you know.) Checking your calculations is the best way to ensure that you have the correct answer. However, a general rule of thumb for any roughly normally distributed data is that the standard deviation is about one-sixth of the overall range of scores in the data.

## Mathematical Constants and the Standard Deviation

As we discussed in Chapter 4, we sometimes transform scores by adding, subtracting, multiplying, or dividing by a constant. What effect do such transformations have on the standard deviation and variance? The answer depends on whether we add (subtracting is adding a negative number) or multiply (dividing is multiplying by a fraction).

When we add a constant to the scores in a distribution, we merely shift the entire distribution to higher or lower scores. We do not alter the relative position of any score, so we do not alter the spread in the data. For example, take the scores 4, 5, 6, 7, and 8. The mean is 6. Now add the constant 10. The resulting scores of 14, 15, 16, 17, and 18 have a mean of 16. Before the transformation, the score of 4 was 2 points away from the mean of 6. In the transformed data, that score is now 14, but it is still 2 points away from the new mean of 16. In the same way, each score's distance from the mean is unchanged, so the standard deviation is unchanged. If the standard deviation is unchanged, then the variance is unchanged.

> **Adding or subtracting a constant does not change the value of the standard deviation or variance.**

When we multiply by a constant, we alter the relative positions of scores, and therefore we change the variability. If we multiply the scores 4, 5, 6, 7, and 8 by the constant 10, they become 40, 50, 60, 70, and 80. The original raw scores that were 1 and 2 points from the mean of 6 are now 10 and 20 points from the new mean of 60. Each transformed score produces a deviation that is 10 times the original deviation, so the new standard deviation is also 10 times greater.

> **Multiplying or dividing the scores by a constant produces the same standard deviation as multiplying or dividing the old standard deviation by that constant.**

Note that this rule does not apply to the variance. The new variance will equal the square of the new standard deviation.

---

# THE POPULATION VARIANCE AND THE POPULATION STANDARD DEVIATION

In every chapter so far, we have seen how researchers and statisticians always discuss two things: samples and the populations they represent. The same is true when it comes to variance and standard deviations. We have described the variability of a sample, and now we will describe the variability of the population.

In Chapter 2 you learned that Greek letters symbolize numbers that describe a population (population parameters). To represent the true population standard deviation, we use the symbol $\sigma_X$. The $\sigma$ is the lowercase Greek letter s, or sigma. Since the squared standard deviation is the variance, the symbol for the true population variance is $\sigma_X^2$. (In each case, the subscript $X$ indicates that we have a population of $X$ scores.)

The definitional formulas for $\sigma_X$ and $\sigma_X^2$ are similar to those we saw previously for describing a sample:

***Population Standard Deviation***

***Population Variance***

$$\sigma_X = \sqrt{\frac{\Sigma(X - \mu)^2}{N}} \qquad\qquad \sigma_X^2 = \frac{\Sigma(X - \mu)^2}{N}$$

The only difference is that, in describing the population, we determine how far each score deviates from the population mean, $\mu$. Otherwise the standard deviation and variance of the population tell us exactly the same things about the population that the sample standard deviation and variance tell us about the sample. Both are ways of measuring how much, "on average," the scores differ from $\mu$, indicating how much the scores are spread out in the population.

> **STAT ALERT** Anytime we are discussing the true population variability, we use the symbols $\sigma_X^2$ and $\sigma_X$.

Of course, we usually think of a population as being infinitely large. Since we usually cannot obtain all the scores in the population, we usually cannot use the above formulas to compute the true values of $\sigma_X$ and $\sigma_X^2$. Instead, we make estimates, or inferences, about the population based on a random sample of scores. In Chapter 4 we saw that we can estimate the population mean, $\mu$, by computing the sample mean, $\overline{X}$. We estimate that if we could measure the entire population, the population mean would equal our sample mean. Now we ask the question "What is our estimate of the variability of the scores around $\mu$?"

## Estimating the Population Variance and Population Standard Deviation

You might think that we would compute the sample variance as described previously and then use it to estimate the population variance (and, likewise, that we would use the sample standard deviation to estimate the population standard deviation). If, for example, the sample variance, $S_X^2$, is 4, then should we guess that the population variance, $\sigma_X^2$, is also 4? Nope! The sample variance and standard deviation are used *only* to describe the variability of the scores in the sample. The values we compute using the previous formulas are not the best estimates of the corresponding population parameters.

To understand why this is true, say that we measure an entire population of scores and compute its true variance, $\sigma_X^2$. We then draw a series of random samples of scores from the population and compute the variance of each sample, $S_X^2$. Sometimes the sample variance will equal the actual population variance, but other times the sample will not be perfectly representative of the population. Either the sample variance will be smaller than, or underestimate, the population variance, or the sample variance will be larger than, or overestimate, the population variance. Over many random samples, it turns out that, more often than not, the sample variance will *underestimate* the population variance. The same thing happens if we perform the above operations using the standard deviation.

In statistical terminology, the formulas for $S_X^2$ and $S_X$ are called the *biased estimators* of the population variance and standard deviation: they are biased toward underestimating the true population parameters. Using the biased estimators is a problem because, as we saw in Chapter 4, if we cannot be perfectly accurate in our estimates or predictions, we at least want our under- and overestimates to cancel out over the long run. (Remember the statisticians shooting targets?) With the biased estimators, the under- and overestimates will not cancel out. Thus, although the sample variance ($S_X^2$) and sample standard deviation ($S_X$) accurately describe the variability of the scores in a sample, they are too often too small to serve as estimates of the true population variance ($\sigma_X^2$) and standard deviation ($\sigma_X$).

Why do $S_X^2$ and $S_X$ produce biased estimates of the population variance and standard deviation? Because their formulas are intended to describe the variability in the sample and are not intended to estimate the population. Remember that to accurately estimate a population, we should have a random sample. We want the variability, or deviation, of each score to be random so that we can accurately estimate the variability of the scores in the population. Yet, when we measure the variability of a sample, we use the mean as our reference point. In doing so, we encounter the mathematical restriction imposed by the mean that the sum of the deviations, $\Sigma(X - \overline{X})$, must equal zero. Because of this restriction, not all of the variability in the sample reflects random variability.

Say that the mean of five scores is 6.0, and from the sample we select the four scores 1, 5, 7, and 9. Their deviations are $-5$, $-1$, $+1$, and $+3$, so the sum of the deviations is $-2$. Without even looking at the final score, we know that it must be 8, because it must have a deviation of $+2$ so that the sum of the deviations is zero. Thus, given the sample mean and the deviations of the other scores, the deviation of the score of 8 is not random; rather, it is determined by those of the other scores. Therefore, only the deviations of the four scores 1, 5, 7, and 9 reflect the variability found in the population. The same would be true for any four of the five scores. Thus, when $N$ is 5, only four of the scores actually reflect the variability of the scores in the population. In general, out of the $N$ scores in a sample, only $N - 1$ of them are free to actually reflect the variability in the population.

The result is that when we compute the variability using our previous formulas for the biased estimators, we use five scores to compute $\Sigma(X - \overline{X})^2$, but this statistic reflects the random variability of only four scores. The formulas for $S_X$ and $S_X^2$ are inappropriate, because we want the "average deviation" reflected by the four scores, but these formulas require us to divide by an $N$ of 5. Because we are dividing by too large a number, our answer tends to be too small, underestimating the actual variability in the population.

Obviously, in the above example, to accurately estimate the average variability based on the four scores that are free to vary, we should divide by 4, or $N - 1$. By so doing, we compute the unbiased estimators of the population variance and standard deviation.

---

**THE DEFINITIONAL FORMULAS FOR THE UNBIASED ESTIMATORS OF THE POPULATION VARIANCE AND STANDARD DEVIATION ARE**

$$\textit{Estimated Population} \atop \textit{Variance}$$

$$s_X^2 = \frac{\Sigma(X - \overline{X})^2}{N - 1}$$

$$\textit{Estimated Population} \atop \textit{Standard Deviation}$$

$$s_X = \sqrt{\frac{\Sigma(X - \overline{X})^2}{N - 1}}$$

---

As you can see from these formulas, we are still computing a number that is analogous to the average of the deviations in the sample, *but* (and this is the big but) here we divide by the number of scores in the sample minus one. We include all of the scores when we are computing the sum of the squared deviations in the numerator, but then we divide by $N - 1$.

Notice that the symbol for the unbiased estimator of the population standard deviation is $s_X$ and the symbol for the unbiased estimator of the population variance is $s_X^2$. To keep all of your symbols straight, remember that the symbols for the sample variance and standard deviation involve the capital, or big, $S$, and in those formulas we divide by the entire, or big, value of $N$. The symbols for estimates of the population variance and standard deviation involve the lowercase, or small, $s$, and we divide by a number slightly smaller than $N$, the quantity $N - 1$. Further, the small $s$ is used to estimate the true population value, symbolized by the small Greek s, $\sigma$. Finally, think of $s_X^2$ and $s_X$ as the inferential variance and the inferential standard deviation, because the *only* time we use them is to estimate, or infer, the variance or standard deviation of the population based on a sample. You can think of $S_X^2$ and $S_X$ as the descriptive variance and standard deviation, because they are used to describe the sample.

> **STAT ALERT** We use the symbols $S_X^2$ and $S_X$ and the corresponding formulas to describe the variability of scores in a sample of scores. We use the symbols $s_X^2$ and $s_X$ and the corresponding formulas to estimate the variability of scores in the population.

For future reference, the quantity $N - 1$ has a special name; it is referred to as the degrees of freedom. The **degrees of freedom** is the number of scores in a sample that are free to vary. The symbol for degrees of freedom is *df*. We shall use degrees of freedom frequently in later chapters, and they are not always equal to $N - 1$. Here, however, $df = N - 1$. In the final analysis, you can think of degrees of freedom, or $N - 1$, as simply a correction factor. Since $N - 1$ is a smaller number than $N$, dividing by $N - 1$ produces a slightly larger answer than does dividing by $N$. Over the long run, this larger answer will prove to be a more accurate estimate of the population variability.

### Computational formula for the estimated population variance

*THE COMPUTATIONAL FORMULA FOR ESTIMATING THE POPULATION VARIANCE IS*

$$s_X^2 = \frac{\Sigma X^2 - \dfrac{(\Sigma X)^2}{N}}{N - 1}$$

The only difference between this computational formula for the estimated population variance and the previous computational formula for the sample variance is that here the final division is by $N - 1$. Notice that in the numerator we still divide by $N$.

In our previous computational examples, the scores were 2, 3, 4, 5, 6, 7, and 8, with $N = 7$, $\Sigma X^2 = 203$, and $\Sigma X = 35$. Putting these quantities into the above formula gives

$$s_X^2 = \frac{\Sigma X^2 - \dfrac{(\Sigma X)^2}{N}}{N - 1} = \frac{203 - \dfrac{(35)^2}{7}}{6}$$

We work through this formula in exactly the same way we worked through the formula for the sample variance, except that here the final division involves $N - 1$, or 6. Since $35^2$ is 1225, and 1225 divided by 7 equals 175, we have

$$s_X^2 = \frac{203 - 175}{6}$$

Now 203 minus 175 equals 28, so we have

$$s_X^2 = \frac{28}{6}$$

and the final answer is

$$s_X^2 = 4.67$$

Notice that this answer is slightly larger than the one we obtained when we computed the sample variance for this same set of scores. There $S_X^2$ was 4.0. Although 4.0 accurately describes the sample variance, it is likely to underestimate the actual variance of the population; 4.67 is more likely to be the population variance. In other words, if we measured all the scores in the population from which this sample was drawn and then computed the population variance, $\sigma_X^2$, we would expect it to equal 4.67.

**Computational formula for the estimated population standard deviation**
Creating the formula for the unbiased estimator of the population standard deviation involves merely adding the square root sign to the previous formula for the estimated population variance.

*THE COMPUTATIONAL FORMULA FOR ESTIMATING THE POPULATION STANDARD DEVIATION IS*

$$s_X^2 = \sqrt{\frac{\sum X^2 - \frac{(\sum X)^2}{N}}{N - 1}}$$

In the previous section, we computed the estimated population variance from our sample of scores to be $s_X^2 = 4.67$. Using the above formula, we find that the estimated population standard deviation, $s_X$, is $\sqrt{4.67}$, or 2.16. Thus, if we could compute the standard deviation using the entire population of scores, we would expect $\sigma_X$ to be 2.16.

### Interpreting the Estimated Population Variance and Standard Deviation

We interpret the estimated variance and standard deviation in the same way as we did $S_X^2$ and $S_X$, except that now we are describing the population. Assuming that our sample is representative of the population, we have largely reached the ultimate goal of research: to describe an unknown population of scores. If we can assume that the distribution is normal, we have described its overall shape. Based on our sample mean, $\overline{X}$, we have calculated a good estimate of the population mean, $\mu$. The size of $s_X^2$ or $s_X$ is our estimate of how spread out the population is—an estimate of the "average amount" that the scores in the population deviate from $\mu$. Further, we expect that approximately 68% of the scores in the population lie between the scores at $+1s_X$ and $-1s_X$ from $\mu$.

Recall that there is one other important goal of research: to be able to predict individual scores. As we shall see in the next section, the concept of variability plays an important role in meeting this goal as well.

## VARIANCE IS THE ERROR IN PREDICTIONS

In Chapter 4 we saw that the mean of a sample is the best single score to use to predict unknown scores. We employ measures of variability to determine how well we can predict these scores. As usual, we first determine how well we can predict the scores in a known sample: pretending that we don't know the scores, we predict them, and then we see how close we came to the actual scores.

For example, if a statistics class has a mean score of 80, then our best guess is that any student in the class has a grade of 80. Of course not every student will actually obtain a grade of 80. When we use the mean score to predict the actual scores in a sample, the amount by which we are wrong in a single prediction is the quantity $(X - \overline{X})$, the amount that the actual score differs, or deviates, from the predicted mean score. Since some predictions in a sample will contain more error than others, we want to summarize our error by finding the average amount that the actual scores deviate from the mean. As we have seen, our way of finding the average amount that scores deviate from the mean is by computing the variance and standard deviation. Because these statistics measure the difference between each score and the mean, they also measure the error in our predictions when we predict the mean score. Thus, we have a slightly novel way of thinking about measures of variability. In this context, the larger the variability, the larger the differences between the mean and the scores, so the larger our error when we use the mean to predict the scores.

For example, if the mean score in the statistics class is 80 and the standard deviation is 5, then the actual scores differ from the mean by an "average" of 5 points. This indicates that if we predict a score of 80 for every member of the class, the actual scores will differ from our predicted score by an "average" of 5 points. Sometimes we will be wrong by more, sometimes by less, but overall we will be wrong by an amount equal to the sample standard deviation, $S_X$.

Similarly, the variance, $S_X^2$, indicates the average of the squared deviations from the mean, so the variance is the average of the "squared errors" we will have when we predict the mean score for each subject in a sample. Unfortunately, the concept of squared errors is rather abstract. This is too bad, because in statistics the proper way to describe the amount of error in our predictions is to compute the variance. In fact, the variance is sometimes called *error:* it is our way of measuring the average error between the predicted mean score and the actual raw scores. Thus, for our purposes, we will simply remember that when we use the mean to predict scores, the larger the variance, the larger the error and the smaller the variance, the smaller the error. To keep this concept in focus, think of the extreme case in which all the scores in a statistics class are the same score of 80. Then the mean is 80, and the variance, $S_X^2$, is zero. In this case, when we use the mean of 80 as the predicted score for each subject, we are never wrong: there is zero error, and that is exactly what $S_X^2 = 0$ indicates.

We can always compute the mean and use it as the predicted score. Thus, the value of $S_X^2$ is the largest error we are forced to accept when predicting the scores in a sample.

> **STAT ALERT**  The sample variance, $S_X^2$, is the largest "average" error we have in predicting the scores in a sample. It occurs when we use the sample's mean score as the predicted score for every subject in the sample.

## Estimating the Error in Predictions in the Population

Of course, we can also estimate the amount of error we expect to have if we predict unknown scores not in our sample. The unknown scores we are predicting are the other scores in the population. Our best estimate of any score in the population is the population mean, $\mu$, which we assume is equal to our sample mean (assuming that our data are representative of the population). Thus, for example, based on our statistics class mean of 80, we estimate that the population mean is 80. Then our best prediction is that any student in the population who takes this statistics class will receive a grade of 80.

To determine the error in our predictions for the population, we use the same logic that we used above for the sample. We measure the amount of error in our predictions using the population variance, because it describes the differences between the population mean, which we predict for each subject, and the actual scores in the population. Since we usually cannot compute the true population variance, we instead compute the estimated population variance, $s_X^2$. Say that the $s_X^2$ for our statistics class is 4.75. This tells us that the scores differ from the $\mu$ of the population by an "average" of about 4.75. Therefore, when we predict that students taking this statistics class will receive a grade equal to the $\mu$ of 80, the average amount by which we expect to be wrong is 4.75.

> ***STAT ALERT*** The estimated population variance, $s_X^2$, is the amount of error we expect when we predict the scores in the population. It occurs because we assume that our sample mean equals the population mean and then use this score as the predicted score for every subject in the population.

Because we can always use a mean to predict scores, the variance forms our reference point, indicating the worst that we can do. Anything we can do to improve the accuracy of our predictions and reduce our error is measured relative to this variance.

## Accounting for Variance

We use the mean to predict scores unless we have other information about the scores. As scientists, we look for ways to improve the accuracy of our predictions, and the additional information we look for is in relationships. When a relationship exists between two variables, a particular score on one variable tends to be consistently associated with a particular score on the other variable. Therefore, we can more accurately predict the score on one variable if we know the corresponding score on the other variable. For example, for children, the variable of height forms a consistent relationship with the variable of weight: the taller the child, the more he or she tends to weigh. If we know a child's height, we can use this relationship to more accurately predict his or her weight.

But our predictions will be "more accurate" than what? They will be more accurate than if we used the mean of all the subjects' weights as the predicted score for each subject. In other words, our error will be less than that reflected by the variance. Table 5.4 shows a sample of weight scores grouped by height. Using the height-weight relationship, we predict a weight of around 81 pounds for children who are 46 inches tall, around 91 pounds for children who are 47 inches tall, and around 98 pounds for children who are 48 inches tall. These

**TABLE 5.4** Data Showing the Relationship Between Height and Weight

*The scores in each column show the weights of children of one height.*

| Height | | |
| --- | --- | --- |
| *46 inches* | *47 inches* | *48 inches* |
| 80 | 90 | 97 |
| 81 | 91 | 98 |
| 82 | 92 | 99 |
| Overall mean weight = 90 | | |

predictions are, on average, closer to each subject's actual weight score than if we predicted the overall sample mean of 90 pounds for each child. Therefore, our average error when we predict weight scores based on subjects' heights is less than the value of $S_X^2$ when we predict the mean score for all subjects.

To describe how well we predict scores using a relationship, we compare our error when we use the relationship to our error when we do not use the relationship. In the language of statistics, we say that by using a subject's height to predict his or her weight, we can *account for* the variance in weight scores. We account for the variance in weight scores in the sense that we explain the differences in weight scores described by $S_X^2$. When we predict the overall mean score for each subject, we predict the same score for each subject, so even though the subjects' weight scores change (contain variance), our predictions do not. However, when we use the relationship between height and weight, we predict a particular weight score for children of one height and a different weight score for children of a different height. Our predictions tend to change, or vary, in the same way as the weight scores change. Thus, there is variability in our predictions that tends to match the variability in the actual weight scores. We account for, or explain, this variance in weight scores in terms of the changing height scores. In essence, we know when subjects tend to have a certain weight score (when they are a certain height) and when subjects tend to have a different weight score (when they are a different height). Thus, when we say we account for the variance in weight scores, what we mean in simple English is that by using the height-weight relationship, we come closer to predicting the actual weight scores. The errors in our prediction of weight scores are smaller than when we predict weight scores using only the overall mean score of the sample.

Of course, a relationship usually does not eliminate all of our errors in prediction. Instead, it reduces our errors by some proportion. We describe the error in our predictions that we have eliminated as the proportion of variance accounted for. The **proportion of variance accounted for** is the proportion of the error in our predictions when we use the mean that is eliminated when we use the relationship with another variable to predict scores. Thus, the proportion of variance accounted for is the proportional improvement in our predictions that is achieved by using a relationship to predict scores.

For example, using procedures we'll discuss later, we might find that when we use subjects' height to predict their weight, the relationship accounts for 85% of the variance in weight scores. This means that if we know a subject's height, our average error in predicting his or her weight is 85% smaller than if we do not know his or her height and base our predictions solely on the overall mean weight score. In essence, we are, on average, 85% more accurate, or 85% closer to predicting each individual weight score, when we utilize the relationship than when we do not.

> **STAT ALERT** When we say that Variable A accounts for a certain percent or proportion of the variance in Variable B, we mean that knowing subjects' scores on Variable A allows us to more accurately predict their scores on Variable B. The size of that proportion indicates how much our errors are reduced, relative to what they would be if we used only the overall mean of scores on Variable B to predict all scores on Variable B.

In later chapters we will discuss methods for computing the proportion of variance accounted for when using a relationship to predict scores in our sample, as well as methods for estimating the proportion of variance accounted for when using a relationship to predict scores in the population. Determining the amount of variance accounted for is a very important procedure, because it is variance and variability that lead to scientific inquiry in the first place. When researchers ask, "Why does a person do this instead of that?" they are trying to predict and explain differences in scores. In other words, they are trying to account for variance. Ultimately, as behavioral scientists, we want to understand the laws of nature so that we know with 100% accuracy when a subject will get one score, reflecting one behavior, and when a subject will get a different score, reflecting a different behavior. In statistics, this translates into accounting for 100% of the variance in scores.

## FINALLY

You can organize your thinking about measures of variability using the diagram in Figure 5.5. Remember that variability refers to the differences between

**FIGURE 5.5**   Organizational Chart of Descriptive and Inferential Measures of Variability

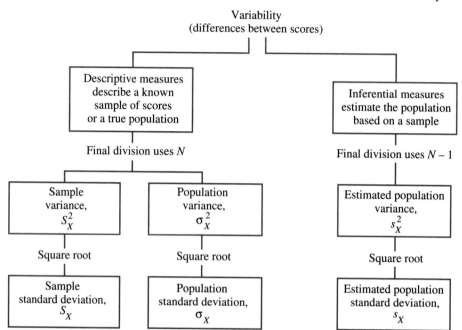

scores. The variance and standard deviation are simply two related methods for describing variability, or differences. Constructing any formula for the standard deviation merely requires adding the square root to the corresponding formula for variance. For either the variance or the standard deviation, we can compute the descriptive sample version, which is a biased estimator of the population, or we can compute the inferential, or estimated, version, which is an unbiased estimator of the population. The difference is that inferential formulas require a final division by $N - 1$ instead of by $N$.

---

## CHAPTER SUMMARY

*1.* In order to accurately describe any set of scores, we must know how different the scores are from each other. *Measures of variability* describe how much the scores differ from each other, or how much the distribution is spread out.

*2.* One measure of variability is the range. The *range* is computed as the difference between the highest score and the lowest score, so it describes the distance between the two most extreme scores in a distribution.

3. The *semi-interquartile range* is used in conjunction with the median to describe skewed distributions. It is the average range between the median score and the scores at the 75th and 25th percentiles.

4. The *variance* is used in conjunction with the mean to describe symmetrical and normally distributed data. It is the average of the squared deviations of the scores around the mean.

5. The *standard deviation* is also used in conjunction with the mean to describe symmetrical and normally distributed data. It is computed as the square root of the variance. It can be thought of as indicating the "average" amount by which the scores deviate from the mean.

6. If we transform scores by adding or subtracting a constant, we do not alter the standard deviation. If we transform scores by multiplying or dividing by a constant, we alter the standard deviation by the same amount as if we had multiplied or divided the original standard deviation by the constant.

7. There are three versions of the formula for variance. The version identified by $S_X^2$ is used to describe how far sample scores are spread out around a sample mean. The version identified by $\sigma_X^2$ describes how far the true population of scores is spread out around the population mean. The version identified by $s_X^2$ is computed using sample data, but it is used as the inferential, unbiased estimate of how far the scores in a population are spread out around a population mean.

8. There are three versions of the formula for the standard deviation. The version identified by $S_X$ is used to describe how far the sample scores are spread out around a sample mean. The version identified by $\sigma_X$ describes how far the true population of scores is spread out around the population mean. The version identified by $s_X$ is computed using sample data, but it is used as the inferential, unbiased estimate of how far the scores in a population are spread out around a population mean.

9. The difference between the formulas for descriptive and inferential measures of variability is that the descriptive formulas (for $S_X^2$ and $S_X$) use $N$ as the final denominator whereas the inferential formulas (for $s_X^2$ and $s_X$) use $N - 1$. The quantity $N - 1$ is known as the *degrees of freedom* of the sample.

10. When we predict the scores in a sample by predicting the mean score for each subject, the amount of error in our predictions is measured by the sample variance, $S_X^2$. Since the variance indicates differences between

the actual scores and the mean score, it also indicates our error when we predict the actual scores using the mean score. When we predict the scores in the population by predicting the population mean score for each subject, we estimate the amount of error in our predictions using the estimated population variance, $s_X^2$.

11. When there is a relationship between two variables, knowing the scores on one variable allows us to more accurately predict the scores on the other variable. The improvement in prediction is described as the *proportion of variance accounted for*. It indicates the proportion of the error using the mean as the predicted score that is eliminated by using the relationship to predict scores.

## USING THE COMPUTER

As part of the descriptive statistics computed by routine **3**, the computer program calculates the highest and lowest score in your data, the range, the sample standard deviation, and the sample variance, as well as the estimated population standard deviation and the estimated population variance. Note that you must supply the appropriate symbols for these statistics, because the computer cannot print them.

## PRACTICE PROBLEMS

(Answers are provided for odd-numbered problems.)

1. What do measures of variability communicate about the scores in a distribution?
2. What is the range?
3. Define the variance and relate it to the standard deviation.
4. For the following data, compute the range, the variance, and the standard deviation.

| 3 | 2 | 1 | 0 | 7 | 4 | 8 | 6 | 9 | 1 |
|---|---|---|---|---|---|---|---|---|---|
| 6 | 8 | 6 | 9 | 4 | 5 | 0 | 8 | 7 | 6 |

5. *a.* For the data in question 4, estimate the central tendency, the variance, and the standard deviation in the population.
   *b.* Between which two scores do you expect to find about 68% of the scores in the population?
6. Sample 1 has $\overline{X} = 60$ and $S_X = 20$, and Sample 2 has $\overline{X} = 60$ and $S_X = 5$. For which sample does the mean provide a more accurate description of the central tendency and why?
7. In question 6, which sample will result in the more accurate predictions of scores and why?

8. Distinguish between $S_X^2$ and $s_X^2$ in terms of their calculation.
9. Distinguish between $S_X^2$ and $s_X^2$ in terms of their use.
10. Distinguish between $\sigma_X$ and $s_X$.
11. A researcher has found that a sample has $\overline{X} = 100$ and $S_X^2 = 36$. If the researcher predicts the mean for each subject in the sample, what will be her "average error" in prediction?
12. The researcher in question 11 has found a relationship between the scores in the sample and the scores on another variable. If she uses these other scores to predict the scores in the sample, what can you say about her average error now, relative to her error in question 11?
13. If she compares the error when using the relationship to predict scores to the error when using the mean of the sample to predict scores, what statistical information is she computing?
14. In the phrase *proportion of variance accounted for*, what does the variance reflect, and how do we account for it?

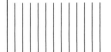

## SUMMARY OF FORMULAS

**1.** *The formula for the range is*

$$\text{Range} = \text{highest score} - \text{lowest score}$$

**2.** *The formula for the semi-interquartile range is*

$$\frac{\text{Score at 75th percentile} - \text{score at 25th percentile}}{2}$$

**3.** *The computational formula for the sample variance is*

$$S_X^2 = \frac{\Sigma X^2 - \dfrac{(\Sigma X)^2}{N}}{N}$$

**4.** *The computational formula for the sample standard deviation is*

$$S_X = \sqrt{\frac{\Sigma X^2 - \dfrac{(\Sigma X)^2}{N}}{N}}$$

5. *The computational formula for estimating the population variance is*

$$s_X^2 = \frac{\Sigma X^2 - \dfrac{(\Sigma X)^2}{N}}{N - 1}$$

6. *The computational formula for estimating the population standard deviation is*

$$s_X = \sqrt{\frac{\Sigma X^2 - \dfrac{(\Sigma X)^2}{N}}{N - 1}}$$

# 6

# z-Score Transformations and the Normal Curve Model

The techniques discussed in the preceding chapters for graphing, measuring central tendency, and measuring variability comprise the descriptive procedures used in the vast majority of research in the behavioral sciences. Most notably, keep in mind that the mean indicates where most of the scores tend to be located on the variable, and the standard deviation can be thought of as the "average" amount that the scores deviate from the mean.

Also remember that the farther a score deviates from the mean, the lower the score's simple frequency and the lower its relative frequency. The relative frequency of a score is the proportion of time the score occurred, which corresponds to the proportion of the total area under the normal curve at that score. The percentile—the percent of scores at or below a particular score—is equal to the percent of the total area under the normal curve to the left of the score.

If you understand the above concepts, then congratulations, you are learning the language of statistics. In this chapter we will use these concepts to answer another question about our data: How does any one particular score compare to the other scores in a sample or population? We answer this question by performing what is known as the z-score transformation. Recall that we transform scores for two reasons: to compare scores on different variables and to make scores within the same distribution easier to work with and interpret. The z-score transformation is the Rolls-Royce of statistical transformations because it allows us to interpret and compare scores from virtually any distribution.

In the following sections we will first examine the logic of z-scores and discuss their computation. Then we will look at the various uses of z-scores, especially when applied to a normal distribution.

### MORE STATISTICAL NOTATION

Statistics often involves negative and positive numbers. Sometimes, however, we want to consider only the size of a number, ignoring, for the moment, its sign. When we are interested in the size of a number, regardless of its sign, we are concerned with the *absolute value* of the number.

In this chapter we will encounter the symbol $\pm$, which means "plus or minus." It provides a shorthand method for describing two numbers or the range of numbers between them. If we talk about $\pm1$, we mean $+1$ and $-1$. If we describe the scores "between $\pm1$," we mean all possible scores from $-1.0$, through $0.0$, up to and including $+1.0$.

## UNDERSTANDING z-SCORES

Let's say that we conduct a study at Prunepit University in which we determine the attractiveness of a sample of male subjects. We train several judges to evaluate subjects on the variable of attractiveness, and each subject's score is the total number of points assigned by the judges. We want to analyze these attractiveness scores, especially those of three men: Slug, who scored 35; Binky, who scored 65; and Biff, who scored 90.

How do we interpret these scores? We might develop an absolute definition of attractiveness: if a subject scores above $X$, he is attractive. However, attractiveness is not easily defined in this way. Like many other variables in psychology, attractiveness is a relative term: whether a score is good, bad, or indifferent depends on how everyone else scored. To evaluate an individual score, we must compare it to the entire distribution of scores. Let's say that our sample of attractiveness scores forms the normal curve shown in Figure 6.1. By looking at the distribution and using the statistics we have learned, we can make several statements about each man's score.

What would we say to Slug? "Bad news, Slug. Your score is to the left of the mean, so you are below average in attractiveness in our sample. What's worse, you are below the mean by a large distance. Down in the tail of the distribution, the height of the curve above your score is not large, indicating a low $f$: not many men received this low score. The proportion of the total area under the curve at your score is also small, so the relative frequency—the proportion of all men who received your score—is small. (In terms of our parking lot approach to the normal curve, the proportion of all subjects standing

**FIGURE 6.1** Frequency Distribution of Attractiveness Scores at Prunepit U.

*Scores for three individual subjects are shown on the X axis.*

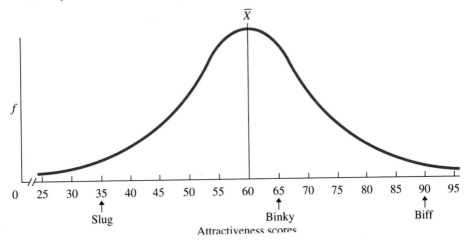

at Slug's score is small.) Finally, Slug, your percentile rank is low: a small percentage of men scored below your score, while a large percentage scored above it. So, Slug, scores such as yours are relatively infrequent, and few scores are lower than yours. Relative to the others, you're fairly ugly!"

What would we tell Binky? "Binky, we have some good news and some bad news. The good news is that your score of 65 is above the mean of 60, which is also the median, or 50th percentile: you are better looking than more than 50% of the men in our study. The bad news is that your score is not *that* far above the mean. The area under the curve at your score is relatively large, and thus the relative frequency of your score is large: this means that the proportion of equally attractive men is large. What's worse, there is a relatively large part of the distribution with higher scores."

And then there is Biff. "Yes, Biff, as you expected, you are above average in attractiveness. In fact, as you have repeatedly told everyone, you are one of the most attractive men in our study. The area under the curve at your score, and thus the relative frequency of your score, is quite small, meaning that only a small proportion of the men are equally attractive. Also, the area under the curve to the left of your score is relatively large. This means that if we cared to figure it out, we'd find that you scored at a very high percentile rank: a large percentage of scores are below your score, while a small percentage are above your score."

Recognize that, although Biff is better looking than most men in our study, he may in fact have a face so ugly that it could stop a clock! Or Slug might be considered highly attractive at some other school. However, since we have defined attractive and ugly relative to the distribution, we have described each score's relative standing. The **relative standing** of a score reflects a systematic evaluation of the score relative to the characteristics of the sample or population in which the score occurs.

Above, we first determined each score's location relative to the mean. Based on this information, we then determined other measures of relative standing, such as the score's relative frequency and percentile. Thus, the essence of determining a score's relative standing is to determine how far it is above or below the mean.

## Describing a Score's Relative Location as a z-Score

In previous chapters we saw that the distance between a raw score and the mean is the amount that the score deviates from the mean, which equals ($X - \overline{X}$). To quantify a score's relative standing, we begin by computing the score's deviation. For example, Biff's raw score of 90 deviates from the mean of 60 by $+30$ ($90 - 60 = +30$). (The $+$ sign indicates that he is above the mean.) A deviation of $+30$ *sounds* as if it might be a large deviation, but is it? When we examined the distribution, we saw that only a few scores deviated to such an extent, and that is what makes Biff's score an impressively high score. Similarly, Slug's score of 35 deviates from the mean of 60 by $-25$ ($35 - 60 = -25$). This too is impressive, because only a few scores deviate from the mean by such an amount. Thus, a score is impressive if it is far from the mean, and "far" is determined by how frequently other scores are that distance from the mean.

To interpret a score's location, we need a way to compare an individual deviation to all deviations. For Biff, we need to quantify whether his deviation of $+30$ is impressive relative to all the deviations in the sample. To do this, we need a standard to compare to Biff's deviation: we need a standard deviation. As we saw in Chapter 5, calculating the standard deviation is our way of computing the average deviation between each score and the mean. By comparing a score's deviation to the standard deviation, we can describe the location of an individual score in terms of the "average" deviation of all scores.

Say that for the data from Prunepit U., the sample standard deviation is 10 (10 attractiveness points). Biff's deviation of $+30$ attractiveness points is equivalent to 3 standard deviations: $3(10) = 30$. Thus, another way to describe Biff's raw score is to say that it is located 3 standard deviations above the mean. We have simply described Biff's score in terms of its distance from the mean, measured in units of standard deviation. We do the same type of thing when we convert inches to feet. In that case, the unit of measurement called a foot is defined as 12 inches, so a distance of 36 inches is equal to 3 of those units, or 3 feet. In our study, the unit of measurement called a standard deviation is defined as 10 attractiveness points. Since Biff's deviation from the mean is 30 attractiveness points, Biff's score is a distance of 3 of those units, or 3 standard deviations, from the mean.

By transforming Biff's deviation into standard deviation units, we have performed a z-score transformation and computed Biff's z-score. A **z-score** describes the location of a raw score in terms of the distance, measured in standard deviations, that the score deviates from the mean. Biff's z-score of $+3.00$ provides us with a number that summarizes his relative standing: Biff's raw score deviates from the mean by an amount that is three times the "average" amount that all scores in the sample deviate from the mean. Since his z-score is positive, he is 3 standard deviations above the mean.

## Computing z-Scores

The symbol for a z-score is $z$. Above, we performed two mathematical steps in computing Biff's $z$. First we found the score's deviation by subtracting the mean from the raw score. Then we divided the score's deviation by the standard deviation.

*THE FORMULA FOR TRANSFORMING A RAW SCORE IN A SAMPLE INTO A z-SCORE IS*

$$z = \frac{X - \overline{X}}{S_X}$$

Technically, this is the definitional formula of $z$, but it is also the easiest computational formula. If we are starting from scratch with a sample of raw scores, we first compute $\overline{X}$ and $S_X$ and then substitute their values into the formula. Notice that we are computing a z-score from a known sample of scores, so we use the descriptive sample standard deviation, $S_X$ (the formula in Chapter 5 that involves dividing by $N$, not $N - 1$).

To find Biff's z-score, we substitute into the above formula his raw score of 90, the $\overline{X}$ of 60, and the $S_X$ of 10:

$$z = \frac{X - \overline{X}}{S_X} = \frac{90 - 60}{10}$$

We find the deviation in the numerator first, so we subtract 60 from 90 (always subtract $\overline{X}$ from $X$). Rewriting the formula gives

$$z = \frac{+30}{10}$$

We then divide, to find that

$$z = +3.00$$

Binky's raw score of 65 produces a z-score of

$$z = \frac{X - \overline{X}}{S_X} = \frac{65 - 60}{10} = \frac{+5}{10} = +0.50$$

Binky's raw score is literally one half of 1 standard deviation above the mean. Slug's raw score is 35, so his z is

$$z = \frac{X - \overline{X}}{S_X} = \frac{35 - 60}{10} = \frac{-25}{10} = -2.50$$

Here 35 minus 60 results in a deviation of minus 25, which, when divided by 10, results in a z-score of $-2.50$. Slug's raw score is 2.5 standard deviations *below* the mean. In working with z-scores, always pay close attention to the positive or negative sign: it is part of the answer.

Usually our purpose is to describe the relative standing of a subject in a sample, so we use the previous formula. However, we can also compute a z-score for a score in a population, if we know the population mean, $\mu$, and the true standard deviation of the population, $\sigma_X$.

---

**THE FORMULA FOR TRANSFORMING A RAW SCORE IN A POPULATION INTO A z-SCORE IS**

$$z = \frac{X - \mu}{\sigma_X}$$

---

This formula is identical to the previous formula except that now the answer we obtain indicates how far the raw score lies from the population mean, measured in units of the true population standard deviation. (Note that we do not compute z-scores using the estimated population standard deviation, $s_X$.)

### Computing a Raw Score When z Is Known

Sometimes we know a z-score and want to find the corresponding raw score. For example, in our study at Prunepit U. (with $\overline{X} = 60$ and $S_X = 10$), Bucky scored $z = +1.0$. What is his raw score? He is 1 standard deviation above the mean, or 10 points above 60, so he has a raw score of 70. What did we just do? We multiplied his z-score times the value of $S_X$ and then added the mean.

**THE FORMULA FOR TRANSFORMING A z-SCORE IN A SAMPLE INTO A RAW SCORE IS**

$$X = (z)(S_X) + \overline{X}$$

Substituting values into the formula to transform Bucky's z-score of $+1.00$, we have

$$X = (+1.0)(10) + 60$$

so

$$X = +10 + 60$$

so

$$X = 70$$

To check this answer, compute the z-score for the raw score of 70. You should end up with the z-score you started with: $+1.0$.

Say that Fuzzy has a negative z-score of $z = -1.3$ (with $\overline{X} = 60$ and $S_X = 10$). Then

$$X = (-1.3)(10) + 60$$

so

$$X = -13 + 60$$

Adding a negative number is the same as subtracting its positive value, so

$$X = 47$$

Fuzzy has a raw score of 47.

After transforming raw scores or z-scores, always determine whether your answer makes sense. At the very least, negative z-scores must correspond to raw scores smaller than the mean, and positive z-scores must correspond to raw scores larger than the mean. Further, as we shall see, with a normal distribution we seldom obtain z-scores greater than $\pm 3.00$ (plus or minus 3.00). You should be suspicious if you obtain z-scores greater than $\pm 3.00$ and should double-check your work.

## How Variability Influences z-Scores

It is important to recognize that a z-score describes the location of a raw score in terms of both the raw score's deviation from the mean *and* the variability (standard deviation) of all scores in the distribution. Thus, the z-score that a particular deviation produces will depend on the amount of variability. For example, Biff's deviation of +30 produced a z-score of +3.00 when the standard deviation was 10. If, however, the data had produced a standard deviation of 30, then Biff's z-score would be $z = (90 - 60)/30 = +1.0$. Then Biff's deviation would equal the "average" deviation, indicating that his raw score was relatively close to the mean, located among very frequent scores. In that case Biff's score would not be as impressive.

Thus, bear in mind that there are two factors that produce a z-score having a large absolute value: (1) a large absolute deviation from the mean and (2) a small standard deviation.

**STAT ALERT**  The magnitude of a z-score depends on the size of the raw score's deviation and the size of the standard deviation.

## INTERPRETING z-SCORES: THE z-DISTRIBUTION

A **z-distribution** is the distribution of z-scores produced by transforming all raw scores in a distribution into z-scores. The easiest way to interpret z-scores is to plot the z-distribution. Transforming all the attractiveness scores in our study into z-scores, we have the z-distribution shown in Figure 6.2.

Notice that the z-score for the mean raw score of 60 is 0.0: the mean score is zero distance from the mean. For any other score, think of the z-score as having two parts: the number and the sign in front of it. The number indicates the absolute distance the score is from the mean, measured in standard deviations. The sign indicates the *direction* the score lies in relation to the mean. A + indicates that the score is above and graphed to the right of the mean. A − indicates that the score is below and graphed to the left of the mean. From this perspective, z-scores become increasingly larger numbers with a positive sign as we proceed to raw scores farther above and to the right of the mean. Conversely, z-scores become increasingly larger numbers with a negative sign as we proceed to raw scores farther below and to the left of the mean. However, remember that the farther below the mean the raw score is, the lower it is. Thus, for example, a z-score of −2.0 corresponds to a *lower* raw score than does a z-score of −1.0.

By creating a z-distribution, we have only transformed the way in which we describe each score's location. Saying that Biff has a deviation of +30 or a z of +3 is merely another way to describe his raw score of 90. Recognize that Biff's z-score of +3.00 and his deviation of +30 have the same frequency, relative frequency, and percentile rank as his raw score of 90.

**FIGURE 6.2**   z-Distribution of Attractiveness Scores at Prunepit U.

*The labels on the X axis show first the raw scores, then the deviations, and then the z-scores.*

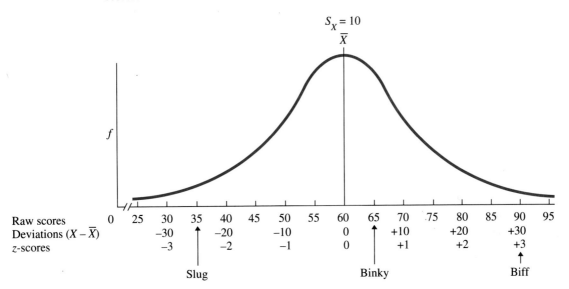

| Raw scores | 0 | 25 | 30 | 35 | 40 | 45 | 50 | 55 | 60 | 65 | 70 | 75 | 80 | 85 | 90 | 95 |
|---|---|---|---|---|---|---|---|---|---|---|---|---|---|---|---|---|
| Deviations $(X - \overline{X})$ | | | $-30$ | | $-20$ | | $-10$ | | 0 | | $+10$ | | $+20$ | | $+30$ | |
| z-scores | | | $-3$ | | $-2$ | | $-1$ | | 0 | | $+1$ | | $+2$ | | $+3$ | |

Slug                                    Binky                                    Biff

**STAT ALERT**   The farther a raw score is from the mean, the larger its corresponding z-score. On a normal distribution, the larger the z-score, whether positive or negative, the less frequently that z-score and the corresponding raw score occur.

It is important to recognize that a negative z-score is not automatically a bad score. How we interpret z-scores depends on the nature of the raw score. For some variables, the goal is to have as low a raw score as possible (for example, errors on a test, number of parking tickets, amount owed on a credit card bill). With these variables, negative z-scores are best. For example, say that we count the number of errors made by students on a statistics test, and we find that the $\overline{X}$ for the class is 5 and the $S_X$ is 1.0. Figure 6.3 shows the z-distribution for the class. Since students want to give 0 incorrect answers, their goal is to produce the score that is the greatest distance below the mean. Here, a z-score of $-3.0$ would be very good because it corresponds to only 2 incorrect answers. Conversely, a z-score of $+3.0$ would be very bad because it corresponds to 8 incorrect answers.

**FIGURE 6.3**   z-Distribution of Number of Errors on a Statistics Test and Corresponding z-Scores

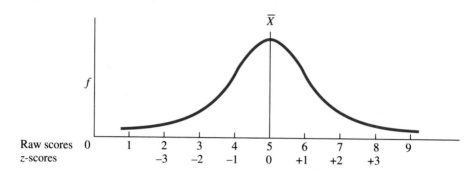

## Characteristics of the *z*-Distribution

The previous examples illustrate three important characteristics of any z-distribution.

1. *A z-distribution always has the same shape as the raw score distribution.* The preceding distributions form normal distributions only because the raw scores form normal distributions. Transforming a nonnormal distribution into z-scores will *not* "normalize" the distribution, making it form a normal curve.

2. *The mean of any z-distribution always equals 0.* The mean of the raw scores has a z-score of 0. If we computed the mean of all z-scores, the result would also be 0: the sum of the positive and negative z-scores is the sum of the deviations around the mean, and this sum always equals 0, so the mean z-score is 0.

3. *The standard deviation of any z-distribution always equals 1.0.* This is because 1 standard deviation unit for raw scores transforms into 1 z-score unit. Whether the standard deviation is equal to 10 or to 35 in the raw score distribution, it is still 1 standard deviation, and 1 standard deviation is 1 z-score unit.

## Transforming *z*-Scores

When we must communicate z-scores to people who are statistically unsophisticated, we can transform the z-scores into numbers that are easier to understand. The principal advantage of such transformations is that they eliminate negative scores and reduce the number of decimal places.

College entrance exams such as the Scholastic Aptitude Test (SAT) involve a transformation of $z$-scores. A grade on the SAT is actually a $z$-score, which is then transformed using the formula

SAT score $= z(100) + 500$

For $z$-scores, the mean is $z = 0.0$, so for SAT scores, the mean is 500. Similarly, the standard deviation of $z$ is 1.0, which becomes 100. You may have heard that the highest possible SAT score is 800. This is because a score of 800 corresponds to $z = +3.00$. Since $z$-scores beyond $+3.00$ are so infrequent, for simplicity these scores are rounded to $+3.00$, or 800. Likewise, the lowest score is 200.

One general way of transforming $z$-scores is to produce $T$-scores.

---

*THE FORMULA FOR A T-SCORE IS*

$$T = z(10) + 50$$

---

For example, $z = -1.30$ becomes $T = -13.0 + 50$, which is 37. Multiplying $z$ times 10 eliminates one decimal place, and adding 50 eliminates the negative sign of any $z$ up to $-5.00$. The mean, which is 0 for $z$, becomes a $T$ of 50, and the standard deviation, which is 1.0 for $z$-scores, becomes 10. Thus, $T$-scores range between 0 and 100, with a mean of 50 and a standard deviation of 10. We interpret such transformed scores in the same way that we interpret their corresponding $z$-scores.

The $z$-distribution provides us with a very useful statistical tool. As we shall see, we can use a $z$-distribution to (1) make comparisons between scores from different distributions, (2) determine the relative frequency for raw scores within any distribution, and (3) define psychological attributes and categories.

---

## USING THE z-DISTRIBUTION TO COMPARE DIFFERENT DISTRIBUTIONS

In research, comparing a score on one variable to a score on another variable may be a problem, because the two variables may not be directly comparable. For example, say that Althea received a grade of 38 on a statistics quiz and a grade of 45 on an English paper. If we say that she did better in English, we are comparing apples to oranges. These grades reflect scores on different kinds of variables, assigned by different instructors using different criteria. We can avoid this problem by transforming the raw scores from each class into $z$-scores. This gives us two $z$-distributions, each with a mean of 0, a standard deviation of 1, and a range of between about $-3$ and $+3$. Each z-score indicates an individual's relative standing in his or her respective class. Therefore, we can compare Althea's relative standing in English to her relative standing in statistics, and we are no longer comparing apples and oranges. Note: With the z-transformation, we equate, or standardize, the distributions. For this reason, z-scores are often referred to as **standard scores.**

Say that for the statistics quiz, the $\overline{X}$ was 30 and the $S_X$ was 5. We transform all of the statistics grades to z-scores, including Althea's grade of 38, which becomes $z = +1.60$. For the English paper, the $\overline{X}$ was 40 and the $S_X$ was 10, so Althea's grade of 45 becomes $z = +.50$. (Did you get the same answers?) Figure 6.4 shows the locations of Althea's z-scores on their respective z-distributions. A z-score of $+1.60$ is farther above the mean than a z-score of $+.50$. Thus, in terms of her relative standing in each class, Althea did better in statistics, because she is farther above the statistics mean than she is above the English mean. Another student, Millie, obtained raw scores that produced $z = -2.00$ in statistics and $z = -1.00$ in English. In which class did Millie do better? Millie's z-score of $-1$ in English is better, because it is less distance below the mean.

Notice that we labeled the $X$ axis for each distribution with equally spaced raw scores and then marked the location of each corresponding z-score. Because the English raw score distribution is spread out over a wider range than the statistics raw score distribution, the English distribution produced a larger standard deviation. The values of $S_X$ in the two distributions are not the same, so the spacing of the z-scores in the two distributions is not the same.

**FIGURE 6.4**  Comparison of Two Distributions for Statistics and English Grades, Plotted Using Raw Scores

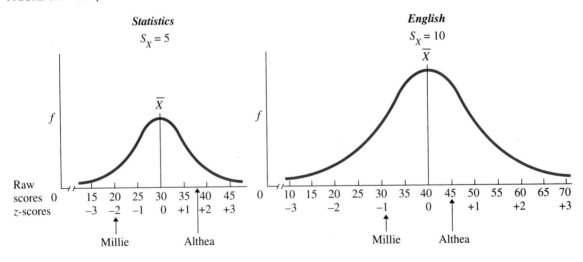

Of course, it would be easier to compare these two distributions if we plotted them on the same set of axes. Fortunately, z-scores enable us to do just that.

## Plotting Different z-Distributions on the Same Graph

For two distributions to be graphed on the same set of axes, the scores must reflect the same variable. By transforming both the statistics and English scores into z-scores, we establish a common variable. If we label the $X$ axis with equally spaced z-score units, we can graph both of the above distributions on one set of axes, as shown in Figure 6.5. Clearly, Althea scored better in statistics and Millie scored better in English.

Compare these distributions to the original distributions in Figure 6.4. There, because we created the distributions using raw scores, the z-scores were not spaced the same in both distributions. Here, because we created the distributions using z-scores, the raw scores are not spaced the same. However, since both z-distributions have the same standard deviation of 1, the result is virtually identical z-distributions.

Do not be concerned about the difference in the heights of the two z-distributions. The greater height of the English distribution merely reflects a larger $f$ for each score. Overall, the English class simply had a larger $N$. If the two raw score distributions had contained the same $N$, the z-distributions would be identical.

**FIGURE 6.5**  Comparison of z-Distributions for Statistics and English Grades, Plotted Using z-Scores

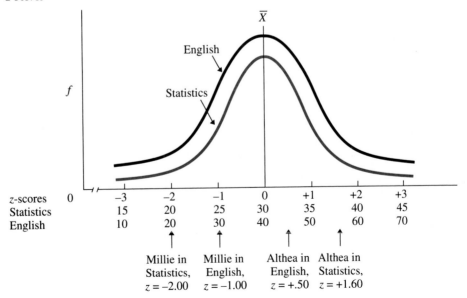

## Comparing the Relative Frequency on Different z-Distributions

The two z-distributions in Figure 6.5 illustrate a critical point:

> **Even though normal distributions may not contain an equal N, the relative frequency of a particular z-score will be the same on all normal z-distributions.**

Recall that relative frequency is the proportion of time that a score occurs, and it can be computed as the proportion of the total area under the curve. For example, you know from previous chapters that 50% of all scores on a normal curve are to the left of the mean score. Thus, regardless of their raw score, students with negative z-scores in Figure 6.5 constitute 50% of their respective distributions. On *any* normal z-distribution, the relative frequency of the negative z-scores is .50.

Having determined the relative frequency of the z-scores, we can work backwards to find the relative frequency of the corresponding raw scores. In the statistics distribution in Figure 6.5, those students having negative z-scores have raw scores ranging between 15 and 30, so the total relative frequency of 15 to 30 is .50. Similarly, in the English distribution, those students having negative z-scores have raw scores ranging between 10 and 40, so the relative frequency of 10 to 40 is .50.

Likewise, recall from Chapter 5 that approximately 68% of all scores on a normal distribution fall between the score that is 1 standard deviation below the mean and the score that is 1 standard deviation above the mean. As you can see from Figure 6.5, regardless of their raw scores, students with z-scores between $\pm 1.0$ are between $\pm 1 S_X$ on their respective distributions. Therefore, they constitute approximately 68% of their distributions. On *any* normal z-distribution, the relative frequency of z-scores between $\pm 1.0$ is approximately .68. Having determined this, we can again work backwards to the raw scores. We see that statistics grades between 25 and 35 constitute approximately 68% of the statistics distribution, and English grades between 30 and 50 constitute approximately 68% of the English distribution.

These examples illustrate our second use of the z-distribution: determining the relative frequency of raw scores in any normal distribution.

---

## USING THE z-DISTRIBUTION TO DETERMINE THE RELATIVE FREQUENCY OF RAW SCORES

Since the relative frequency of a z-score is always the same on any normal z-distribution, we conceptualize any normal z-distribution as conforming to one standard curve. In fact, this curve is called the standard normal curve. The **standard normal curve** is a theoretical perfect normal curve, which serves as a model of the perfect normal z-distribution. (Since it is a z-distribution, the mean of the standard normal curve is 0, and the standard deviation is 1.0.)

We use the standard normal curve to determine the relative frequency of z-scores in a perfect normal curve. As we saw above, once we know the relative frequency of certain z-scores, we can work backwards to determine the relative frequency of the corresponding raw scores. Thus, the first step is to find the relative frequency of the z-scores. To do this, we look at the area under the standard normal curve.

## The Area Under the Standard Normal Curve

As shown in Figure 6.6, statisticians have determined the proportion of the area under the standard normal curve between the mean and any z-score. Above the $X$ axis, the numbers between the vertical lines indicate the proportions of the total area between z-scores. Below the $X$ axis, the number on each arrow indicates the proportion of the total area between the mean and the indicated z-score.

The proportion of the total area under the curve is the same as relative frequency, so each proportion is the relative frequency of the z-scores located in

**FIGURE 6.6**   Proportions of Total Area Under the Standard Normal Curve

*The curve is symmetrical: 50% of the scores fall below the mean, and 50% fall above the mean.*

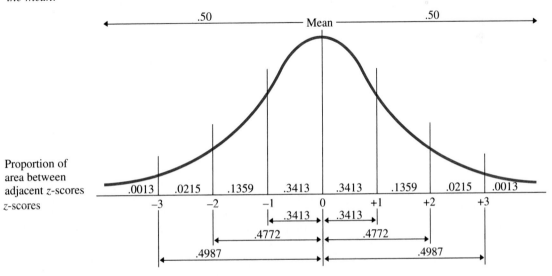

that section of the ideal normal curve. Thus, on a perfect normal distribution, .3413 of the z-scores are located between $z = 0.00$ and $z = +1.00$. Since we can express a proportion as a percent by multiplying the proportion times 100, we can say that 34.13% of all z-scores fall between $z = 0.00$ and $z = +1.00$. Similarly, z-scores between $+1.00$ and $+2.00$ occur 13.59% of the time, and z-scores between $+2.00$ and $+3.00$ occur 2.15% of the time. Because the distribution is symmetrical, the same proportions occur between the mean and the corresponding negative z-scores.

To determine the relative frequency for larger areas, we add the above proportions. For example, .3413 of the distribution is located between $z = -1.00$ and the mean, and .3413 of the distribution is between the mean and $z = +1.00$. Thus, a total of .6826, or 68.26%, of the distribution is located between $z = -1.00$ and $z = +1.00$ (see, approximately 68% of the distribution really is between $\pm 1S_X$ from the mean). Likewise, we can add together non-adjacent portions of the curve. For example, .0228, or 2.28%, of the distribution is in the tail of the distribution beyond $z = -2.00$, and 2.28% is beyond $z = +2.00$. Thus, a total of 4.56% of all scores fall in the tails beyond $z = \pm 2.00$. (Don't worry: you won't need to memorize these proportions.)

Figure 6.6 shows why we seldom obtain z-scores greater than $\pm 3$. This is a theoretical distribution representing an infinitely large distribution (the tails of the polygon never touch the X axis). Even so, only .0013 of the scores are above $z = +3$ and only .0013 are below $z = -3.00$. In total, only .0026, or .26 of 1 percent, of the scores are beyond $\pm 3.00$. This leaves 99.74% of all scores (100% $-$ .26% $=$ 99.74%) located between $z = \pm 3$. Thus, for all practical purposes, the range of z is between $\pm 3$. Also, now you can see why, in Chapter 5, we said that for normally distributed scores, the value of $S_X$ should be about one-sixth of the range of the raw scores. The range of the raw scores is approximately between $z = -3$ and $z = +3$, a distance of six times the standard deviation. If the range is six times the standard deviation, then the standard deviation is one-sixth of the range.

## Applying the Standard Normal Curve Model

By using the standard normal curve, we can quickly determine the relative frequency of any score or scores in any normal sample or normal population. This is true even though real data will not form a perfect normal curve. As we have seen in previous chapters, the normal curve model assumes that most populations of raw scores "more or less" form a normal distribution and that most samples represent such a distribution. When we conceptualize this model, however, we do not draw a "more or less" normal curve: we draw the ideal perfect normal curve. We then use this curve as a model of our distribution of raw scores, operating as if the scores formed a perfect normal curve. If we operate as if the raw scores formed a perfect normal curve, then when we transform the raw scores to z-scores, the z-distribution also forms a perfect normal curve. As we have seen, the perfect normal z-distribution is the standard normal curve.

> **STAT ALERT**  The standard normal curve is our model for any roughly normal distribution when transformed to z-scores.

To use the model, we first transform a raw score into a z-score. From the standard normal curve, we then determine the proportion of the total area between the mean and this z. This proportion is the same as the relative frequency of the z-scores between the mean and this z on a perfect normal curve. The relative frequency of these z-scores is the same as the relative frequency of the corresponding raw scores in a perfect normal distribution. Thus, the relative frequency we obtain from the standard normal curve is the *expected* relative frequency of the raw scores in our data, if the data were to form a perfect normal distribution.

How accurately the expected relative frequency from the model describes our actual data depends on three aspects of the data:

1. The closer the raw scores are to forming a normal distribution, the more accurately the model describes the data. Therefore, the standard normal curve model is appropriate *only* if we can assume that our data are at least approximately normally distributed.

2. The larger the sample $N$, the more closely the sample tends to fit the normal curve and the more accurate the model tends to be. The model is most accurate when applied to very large samples or to populations.

3. The model is most appropriate if the raw scores are theoretically continuous scores (which can include decimals) on ratio or interval variables (which have equal intervals between scores and measure actual amounts).

Our original sample of attractiveness scores from Prunepit U. meets the above requirements, so we can apply the standard normal curve model to these data. Say that Cubby has a raw score of 80, which, with $\overline{X} = 60$ and $S_X = 10$, is a z of $+2.0$. What proportion of scores are expected to fall between the mean and Cubby's score? From the standard normal curve we see that .4772 of the total area falls between the mean and $z = +2.00$. Thus, we can show Cubby's location on the distribution as in Figure 6.7. Since .4772 of all z-scores fall between the mean and a z of $+2$, we expect .4772, or 47.72%, of all attractiveness scores at Prunepit U. to fall between the mean score of 60 and Cubby's score of 80.

We can also convert the above relative frequency to simple frequency by multiplying the $N$ of the sample times the relative frequency. Say that the sample $N$ at Prunepit was 1000. If we expect .4772 of all scores to fall between the mean and $z = +2$, then $(.4772)(1000) = 477.2$, so we expect about 477 scores to fall between the mean and Cubby's raw score of 80.

**Finding percentile rank for a raw score**   Looking again at Figure 6.7, you'll see that we can also use the standard normal curve model to determine Cubby's expected percentile. Recall that a percentile is the percent of all scores *below* (graphed to the left of) a score. On a normal distribution, the mean is the median (the 50th percentile). Any positive $z$-score is above the mean, so Cubby's $z$-score of $+2$ is above the 50th percentile. In addition, as Figure 6.7 shows, Cubby's score is above the 47.72% of the scores that fall between the mean and his $z$-score. To the 50% of the scores below the mean we add the 47.72% of the scores between the mean and his score, and we find that a total of 97.72% of all $z$-scores are below Cubby's $z$-score. We usually round off the percentile to a whole number, so we conclude that Cubby's $z$-score is at the 98th percentile. Likewise, Cubby's raw score of 80 is expected to be at the 98th percentile. Conversely, if 97.72% of the curve is below $z = +2.00$, then, as shown in Figure 6.7, only 2.28% of the curve is above $z = +2.00$ (100% − 97.72% = 2.28%). Thus, anyone scoring above $z = +2.00$, or the raw score of 80 would be in about the top 2% of all scores.

On the other hand, say that Elvis obtained an attractiveness score of 40, for a $z$-score of $-2.00$. We can find Elvis's percentile using Figure 6.8. Because

**FIGURE 6.7**   Location of Cubby's Score on the z-Distribution of Attractiveness Scores

*Cubby is at approximately the 98th percentile.*

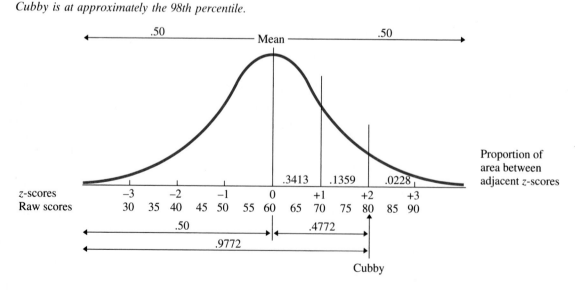

**FIGURE 6.8**   Location of Elvis's Score on the z-Distribution of Attractiveness Scores

*Elvis is at approximately the 2nd percentile.*

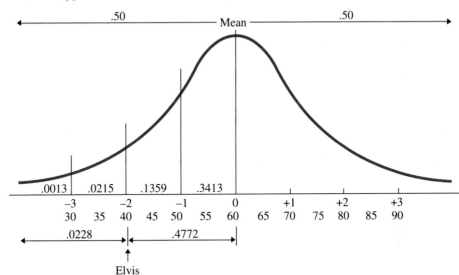

.0215 of the distribution is between $z = -2$ and $z = -3$, and .0013 of the distribution is below $z = -3$, there is a total of .0228, or 2.28%, of the distribution below (to the left of) Elvis's score. With rounding, Elvis ranks at the 2nd percentile.

**Finding a raw score at a given percentile rank**   We can also use the standard normal curve model to find a raw score at a particular percentile. Say that we want to find the raw score at the 16th percentile. Because the 16th percentile is below the 50th percentile, we are looking for a negative z-score. Consider Figure 6.9 on the next page. If 16% of all scores are below the unknown score, then 34% of all scores are between it and the mean (50% − 16% = 34%). We saw that 34.13% of a normal z-distribution is between $z = -1$ and the mean, so that leaves 15.87% of the distribution to the left of a z of −1.0 (50% − 34.13% = 15.87%). Thus, with rounding, $z = -1.0$ is at approximately the 16th percentile.

We then use the formula $X = (z)(S_X) + \overline{X}$ to find the raw score at $z = -1.0$. With $\overline{X} = 60$ and $S_X = 10$ for this sample, we have $X = (-1.0)(10) + 60 = 50$. Thus, the raw score of 50 is expected to be at approximately the 16th percentile.

**Using the z-table**   In the above examples, we rounded off the z-scores to keep things simple. With real data, however, we do not round z-scores containing

**FIGURE 6.9**  Proportions of the Standard Normal Curve at Approximately the 16th Percentile

*The 16th percentile corresponds to a z-score of about −1.0.*

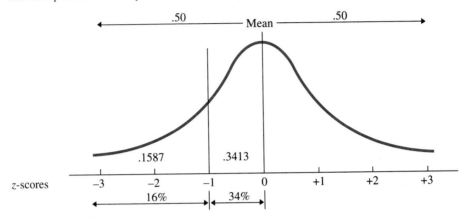

decimals to whole numbers. Further, fractions of z-scores do *not* result in proportional divisions of the corresponding area. For example, even though $z = +.50$ is one-half of $z = +1.0$, the area between the mean and $z = +.50$ is *not* one-half of the area between the mean and $z = +1.0$. Instead, the proportion of the total area under the standard normal curve for any two-decimal z-score is found in Table I of Appendix D. This table is called the **z-table.** A portion of the z-table is reproduced in Table 6.1.

Say that we seek the proportions corresponding to $z = +1.63$. First we

**TABLE 6.1**  Sample Portion of the z-Table

| (A)<br>z | (B)<br>*Area between the mean<br>and z* | (C)<br>*Area beyond z* |
|---|---|---|
| 1.60 | .4452 | .0548 |
| 1.61 | .4463 | .0537 |
| 1.62 | .4474 | .0526 |
| 1.63 | .4484 | .0516 |
| 1.64 | .4495 | .0505 |
| 1.65 | .4505 | .0495 |

locate $z = 1.63$ in column (A), labeled "$z$," and then move to the right. Column (B), labeled "Area between the mean and $z$," contains the proportion of the total area under the curve between the mean and the $z$ identified in column (A). Thus, .4484 of the curve, or 44.84% of all $z$-scores, is between the mean ($z = 0$) and $z = +1.63$. Column (C), labeled "Area beyond $z$," contains the proportion of the total area under the curve for all $z$-scores larger than (beyond) the $z$-score in column (A). Thus, .0516 of the curve, or 5.16% of all $z$-scores, is in the tail of the distribution beyond $z = +1.63$. We can translate the information in the table as shown in Figure 6.10. If you get confused, look at the normal distribution at the top of each column of the table. The shaded portion indicates the part of the curve described in that column.

We can also read the columns in the opposite order to find the $z$-score that corresponds to a particular proportion. First find the proportion in column (B) or (C), depending on the area you seek, and then identify the corresponding $z$-score in column (A). For example, say that we seek the $z$-score corresponding to 44.84% of the curve between the mean and $z$. In column (B) of the table, we find .4484, which corresponds to the $z$-score of 1.63.

Notice that the $z$-table contains no positive or negative signs. Because the normal distribution is symmetrical, only the proportions for one-half of the standard normal curve are given. *You* must decide whether $z$ is positive or negative, based on the problem you are working. Sometimes you will not want to round off to a proportion given in the $z$-table, or you will need the proportion for a $z$-score containing three decimal places. In such cases, you use a mathematical procedure called interpolation. Instructions for interpolating $z$-scores or their corresponding proportions are given in Appendix A.

In most of the remainder of this book, we will be working with $z$-scores or

**FIGURE 6.10**  Distribution Showing the Area Under the Curve Above $z = +1.63$ and Between $z = +1.63$ and the Mean

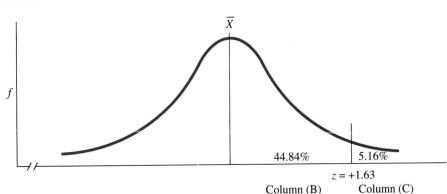

their equivalent, so it is *very* important that you become comfortable with interpreting their location on a normal distribution. To do so, always sketch a normal curve. Then, as we did in the previous examples, label the location of the mean score, identify the relevant portions under the curve, and indicate the corresponding *z*-scores and raw scores. By giving yourself a curve to look at, you'll greatly simplify the problem.

## USING THE STANDARD NORMAL CURVE MODEL TO DEFINE PSYCHOLOGICAL ATTRIBUTES

Many psychological attributes are difficult to define in an absolute sense: What must someone do to be considered a genius? How do we define an "abnormal" personality? To answer such questions, psychologists often use a statistical definition. That is, if the variable being measured is normally distributed, then we apply the standard normal curve and define an attribute in terms of a *z*-score. For example, we might statistically define the old-fashioned term "genius" as a person with a *z*-score of more than $+2.00$ on an intelligence test. Since a *z* greater than $+2.00$ falls in about the highest 2% of the distribution, we have defined a genius as anyone with a score in the top 2% of all scores on the intelligence test. Similarly, we might define as "abnormal" any person with a *z*-score beyond $-1.5$ on a personality test. Such scores are "abnormal" in a statistical sense, because they are very infrequent in the population and are among the most extreme low raw scores.

Instructors who "curve" grades generally use the normal curve and *z*-scores. They assume that grades are normally distributed, so they assign letter grades based on proportions of the area under the normal curve. If the instructor defines an A student as one who is in the top 2%, then students with *z*-scores greater than $+2$ receive A's. If the instructor defines B students as those in the next 13%, then students having *z*-scores between $+1$ and $+2$ receive B's, and so on.

## USING THE STANDARD NORMAL CURVE MODEL TO DESCRIBE SAMPLES

So far we have discussed using *z*-scores and the standard normal curve model to describe the relative standing of any single raw score. Now, using the same logic, we will use *z*-scores and the standard normal curve to determine the relative standing of an entire sample. Recall that a sample statistic is a number that describes the sample. We can think of a sample statistic as the "score" for an entire sample, so we can evaluate it in the same way we have evaluated an individual's score. We evaluated an individual raw score by determining its relative standing within the distribution of raw scores. Now we will evaluate a sample statistic by determining its relative standing within a distribution of sample statistics.

To understand how we determine the relative standing of a sample statistic, you must first understand what we mean by a distribution of sample statistics. Therefore, in the following section we will discuss one such distribution, called the sampling distribution of means.

## The Sampling Distribution of Means

Say that we wish to describe the mean of a randomly selected sample of SAT scores. To determine its standing relative to other sample means, we will first create a distribution of all possible random SAT sample means.

One way to do this would be to record each raw score from the entire population of SAT scores on a slip of paper and deposit all the slips in a hat (a very large hat). We could then hire a statistician to sample this population an infinite number of times (she would be very bored, so the pay would have to be good). The statistician would randomly select from the hat a sample with a particular size $N$ (say, 25), compute the sample mean, replace the scores in the hat, draw another 25 scores, compute the mean, and so on. Because the scores selected in each sample would not be identical, all samples would not be identical, and thus all sample means would not be identical. By constructing a frequency distribution of the different sample means, the statistician would create a sampling distribution of means. The **sampling distribution of means** is the distribution of all possible random sample means when an infinite number of samples of the same size $N$ are randomly selected from one raw score population. Thus, the sampling distribution of means is the population of all possible sample means that can occur when a raw score population is exhaustively sampled using a particular size $N$.

In subsequent chapters we will discuss the sampling distributions of many statistics. In general, a sampling distribution for any statistic has four important characteristics:

*1.* All the samples contain raw scores from the same population.
*2.* All the samples are randomly selected.
*3.* All the samples have the same size $N$.
*4.* The sampling distribution reflects the infinite population of all possible values of the sample statistic.

Of course, our bored statistician could not actually sit down and sample the population an infinite number of times. However, she could create a *theoretical* sampling distribution by applying the central limit theorem. The **central limit theorem** is a statistical principle that defines the mean, the standard deviation, and the shape of a theoretical sampling distribution. From the central limit theorem, we know that the sampling distribution of means for SAT scores, for example, would look like the curve shown in Figure 6.11.

You can conceptualize a sampling distribution of means in the same way that you conceptualize a distribution of raw scores. The only difference is that here each "score" along the $X$ axis is a sample mean. (We can still think of the distribution as a parking lot full of people, except that now each person is the captain of a sample, having the sample's mean score and thus representing the sample.)

The central limit theorem states that, regardless of the shape of the raw score distribution, *a sampling distribution of means is always an approximately normal distribution.* The larger the $N$ in the samples used to create the sampling distribution, the more closely the sampling distribution conforms to the perfect normal curve. The sampling distribution is always normal because, over an infinite number of random samples, most often the sample mean will equal the population mean, $\mu$. Sometimes, however, a sample will contain a few more high scores or low scores than the population, so the sample mean will be close to $\mu$ but slightly greater than or less than $\mu$. Less frequently, random sampling will produce rather strange samples, with sample means farther above or below $\mu$. Once in a great while, some very infrequent and unusual scores will be drawn, resulting in a sample mean that deviates greatly from $\mu$. Notice that

**FIGURE 6.11**   Sampling Distribution of Random Sample Means of SAT Scores

*The X axis is labeled to show the different values of $\overline{X}$ we obtain when we sample a population where the mean for SAT scores is 500.*

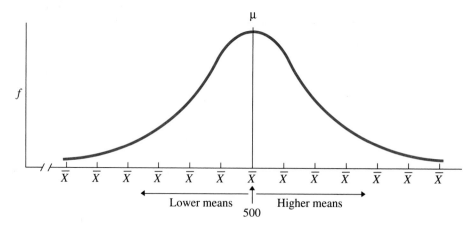

the different values of the sample means in a sampling distribution occur simply because of the luck of the draw by which subjects were selected. For example, the bored statistician would sometimes obtain a high SAT sample mean because, *by chance,* she would randomly select a sample of subjects with predominantly high SAT scores.

The central limit theorem also states that *the mean of the sampling distribution always equals the mean of the raw score population,* $\mu$. Above, the $\mu$ of the population of SAT raw scores is 500, so the mean of all sample means of SAT scores will also equal $\mu$, or 500. This is because the raw scores in a population are balanced around $\mu$, so the sample means created from those scores will also be balanced around $\mu$. Therefore, those means above and below $\mu$ will average out, and overall the mean of the sampling distribution will equal the mean of the raw score population.

Finally, the central limit theorem states that *there is a mathematical relationship between the variability of raw scores and the variability of sample means.* If the population of raw scores is spread out so that there are many large differences between raw scores, then there will be many large differences between sample means. Conversely, if the raw scores are very close together, then the sample means will also be very close together. Thus, if we know the standard deviation of the raw score population, we can determine the standard deviation of the sampling distribution.

As you will eventually see, the sampling distribution of means forms the basis for many inferential statistics. Therefore, you must know how to compute the standard deviation of the sampling distribution of means.

## The Standard Error of the Mean

The standard deviation of the sampling distribution of means is called the **standard error of the mean.** We call it the standard error so that we know we are describing the deviations of sample means and not the deviations of raw scores. The standard error of the mean can be thought of as the "average" amount that the sample means deviate from the mean of the sampling distribution, $\mu$.

For the moment, we will discuss the *true* standard error of the mean, as if we had actually computed it using the entire sampling distribution. The symbol for the true standard error of the mean is $\sigma_{\bar{X}}$. Be careful, because the symbol for the true standard error of the sampling distribution is very similar to the symbol for the true standard deviation of the population of raw scores, $\sigma_X$. In $\sigma_{\bar{X}}$, the $\sigma$ indicates that we are describing the population, but the subscript $\bar{X}$ indicates that we are describing the population of sample means—what we call the sampling distribution of means. Also, be careful because we compute the true standard error using the true standard deviation.

*THE FORMULA FOR THE TRUE STANDARD ERROR OF THE MEAN IS*

$$\sigma_{\overline{X}} = \frac{\sigma_X}{\sqrt{N}}$$

In the formula, $\sigma_X$ is the true standard deviation of the population of raw scores and $N$ is the number of scores used to compute each sample mean in the sampling distribution.

> **STAT ALERT**  The true standard deviation of the population of random sample means, $\sigma_{\overline{X}}$, is computed using the true standard deviation of the population of raw scores, $\sigma_X$.

We can compute $\sigma_{\overline{X}}$ for the sampling distribution of SAT scores because, through recordkeeping, we *know* that the true standard deviation of the population of SAT scores is 100. Since our bored statistician used $N = 25$ to create the sampling distribution, the above formula says that the standard error of the mean for this distribution is

$$\sigma_{\overline{X}} = \frac{100}{\sqrt{25}}$$

The square root of 25 is 5, so

$$\sigma_{\overline{X}} = \frac{100}{5}$$

and thus

$$\sigma_{\overline{X}} = 20$$

A value of $\sigma_{\overline{X}} = 20$ indicates that in the sampling distribution of all SAT sample means, the means will, "on average," deviate from the $\mu$ of 500 by 20 SAT points when the $N$ of each sample is 25.

## Using the Sampling Distribution to Determine Relative Frequency of Sample Means

The sampling distribution of means is important because we can use it to describe the relative standing of any single sample mean that we might obtain in our research. For example, say that a random sample of 25 students at Prunepit U. produced SAT scores with $\overline{X} = 520$. We can evaluate this sample mean by determining its relative location within the sampling distribution of all SAT sample means. We determine a mean's relative location on a sampling distribution by using—you guessed it—z-scores.

Previously we saw that when we know the population mean, $\mu$, and we know the true population standard deviation, $\sigma_X$, the formula for transforming a raw score into a z-score is

$$z = \frac{X - \mu}{\sigma_X}$$

Since the sampling distribution of means is the population of sample means and we know the true standard deviation, $\sigma_{\overline{X}}$, we can transform a sample mean into a z-score using a similar formula.

---

*THE FORMULA FOR TRANSFORMING A SAMPLE MEAN INTO A z-SCORE IS*

$$z = \frac{\overline{X} - \mu}{\sigma_{\overline{X}}}$$

---

Do not be confused by the minor difference in symbols between the two above formulas. Conceptually we are doing the same thing in both: we are simply finding how far a score on a distribution falls from the mean of the distribution, measured in standard deviations of that distribution. With a sample mean, we treat the mean as the sample's score and find how far the sample mean is from the mean of the distribution, $\mu$, measured in standard error units, or $\sigma_{\overline{X}}$.

> **STAT ALERT**  We use the above formula only when we know the true population standard deviation, $\sigma_X$, because only then can we compute $\sigma_{\overline{X}}$.

Using the above formula, we can describe our sample of 25 students from Prunepit U. for which $\overline{X} = 520$. From our previous discussion, we know that $\mu = 500$ and $\sigma_{\overline{X}} = 20$ when $N = 25$. Filling in the above formula for z, we have

$$z = \frac{\overline{X} - \mu}{\sigma_{\overline{X}}} = \frac{520 - 500}{20} = \frac{+20}{20} = +1.0$$

Thus, a sample mean of 520 has a z-score of $+1.0$ on the sampling distribution of means when $N$ is 25 and the sampling distribution is created from the SAT raw score population where $\mu = 500$, and $\sigma_X = 100$.

Everything we said previously about a z-score for an individual raw score applies to a z-score for a sample mean. It makes no difference that the z-score now refers to the location of a sample mean: a z-score is a z-score! Thus, since our sample mean has a z-score of +1.0, we know that it is above the mean of the sampling distribution by an amount equal to the "average" amount that sample means deviate from the mean of the sampling distribution.

And here is the nifty part: because the sampling distribution of means always forms at least an approximately normal distribution, if we transformed *all* of the sample means in a sampling distribution into z-scores, we would have a roughly normal z-distribution. The standard normal curve is our model of *any* normal z-distribution, even if it is a z-distribution of random sample means! Thus, using the standard normal curve model, we can determine the relative frequency of random sample means in any portion of a sampling distribution. For example, Figure 6.12 shows the standard normal curve applied to z-scores for sample means on our SAT sampling distribution.

The curve in Figure 6.12 is the same curve, with the same proportions, that we saw when describing individual raw scores. Once again we see that the farther a score (here $\overline{X}$) is from the mean of the distribution (here $\mu$), the larger the absolute value of the z-score. The larger the z-score, the smaller the relative frequency and simple frequency of the z-score and of the corresponding sample mean. As we did with raw scores, we can now use the standard normal curve (and the z-table) to determine the proportion of the area under the curve between the mean and a z. This proportion is also the expected relative frequency of the corresponding sample means in our sampling distribution of means.

For example, our random sample from Prunepit U. had an SAT mean of

**FIGURE 6.12**   Proportions of the Standard Normal Curve Applied to the Sampling Distribution of SAT Means

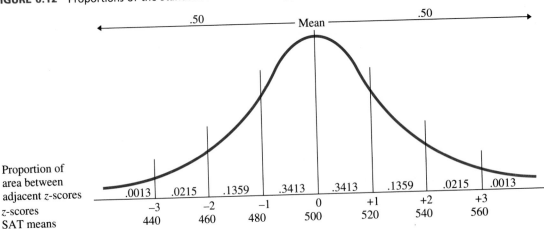

520, so it has a z of +1.0. As we have seen, .3413, or 34.13%, of all scores fall between the mean and $z = +1.00$ on a normal distribution. Therefore, 34.13% of all random SAT sample means are expected to fall between the $\mu$ of 500 and a sample mean of 520 on this sampling distribution of SAT means. Similarly, a sample mean of 540, for example, has a z of +2.00 on this sampling distribution. Since we know that about 2% of all z-scores are above a z of +2.00, we expect that about 2% of all random sample means will be larger than 540 when the sample contains 25 SAT scores. In the same way, we can determine the relative frequency of any random sample means falling in any part of the sampling distribution of means.

In fact, as we shall see in later chapters, we can use a similar procedure to determine the relative frequency of any sample statistic on the appropriate sampling distribution. Why would we want to do this? Because eventually we will perform inferential statistical procedures. In the final analysis, inferential statistical procedures are nothing more than methods for computing something like a z-score for a particular value of a sample statistic so that we can determine its relative frequency on a sampling distribution. We will elaborate on these procedures in later chapters. For now it is enough to understand that the basic approach is to compute z-scores and apply the standard normal curve model.

### FINALLY

In this chapter we saw that we should apply the standard normal curve model to a distribution of raw scores only when we can make certain *assumptions* about the data. In subsequent chapters we will apply other statistical models and discuss their assumptions. Always bear in mind that a statistical model indicates what we can expect, assuming the rules and regulations of the model are being met.

The most important concept for you to understand is that any normal distribution of scores can be described using the standard normal curve model and z-scores. To paraphrase a famous saying, a normal distribution is a normal distribution is a normal distribution. Any normal distribution contains the same proportions of the total area under the curve between z-scores. Therefore, picture a normal distribution and repeat after me: the larger the z-score, whether positive or negative, the farther the z-score and the corresponding raw score are from the mean of the distribution. The farther they are from the mean, the lower the relative frequency of the z-score and the corresponding raw score. This is true whether the raw score is an individual score or a sample statistic.

By the way, what was Biff's percentile?

## CHAPTER SUMMARY

*1.* The *relative standing* of a score reflects a systematic evaluation of the score relative to the characteristics of a sample or population of scores. We determine a score's relative standing by first computing its *z-score,* which indicates the distance the score is above or below the mean, measured in standard deviations.

*2.* The larger the value of a positive *z*-score, the farther the raw score is above the mean. The larger the absolute value of a negative *z*-score, the farther the raw score is below the mean. On a normal distribution, the larger the *z*-score, whether positive or negative, the less frequently it occurs, and thus the less frequently the corresponding raw score occurs.

*3.* By transforming an entire raw score distribution into *z*-scores, we create a *z-distribution.* The *z*-distribution will have the same shape as the raw score distribution, but the mean of a *z*-distribution is always 0 and the standard deviation is always 1.0. The *z*-distribution enables us to compare scores from different variables by transforming these scores to one common scale.

*4.* The *standard normal curve* is a mathematically perfect normal curve that can be used as a model of any *z*-distribution when (a) the distribution is at least roughly normally distributed and (b) the corresponding raw scores reflect an interval or ratio scale of measurement.

*5.* The *z-table* gives the proportion of the total area under the standard normal curve between the mean and any value of *z*. The proportion of the area under the curve is equal to the relative frequency of *z*-scores falling between the mean and *z*.

6. Using the relative frequency of *z*-scores in any portion of the standard normal curve, we can determine the *expected* relative frequency, simple frequency, and percentile rank of corresponding raw scores. These are the expected values, assuming the raw score distribution conforms to the perfect normal curve.

*7.* A *sampling distribution* is a theoretical distribution of the different values of a sample statistic obtained when samples of a particular size *N* are randomly selected from a particular raw score population an infinite number of times. The *sampling distribution of means* is the distribution of sample means when samples of a particular size *N* are randomly selected from one raw score population. The different sample means in a sampling distribution of means occur solely because of chance—the luck of the draw when each sample is randomly selected.

**8.** The *central limit theorem* shows that (a) the sampling distribution of means will be an approximately normal distribution, (b) the mean of the sampling distribution of means will equal the mean of the raw score population, and (c) the variability of the sample means is related to the variability of the raw scores.

**9.** The true *standard error of the mean* is the standard deviation of the sampling distribution of means, and its symbol is $\sigma_{\overline{X}}$. The value of $\sigma_{\overline{X}}$ can be thought of as the average amount that each sample mean deviates from the $\mu$ of the sampling distribution. We compute $\sigma_{\overline{X}}$ *only* when we know the true standard deviation of the raw score population, $\sigma_X$.

**10.** The location of a random sample mean on the sampling distribution of means can be described as a $z$-score: the distance the sample mean score ($\overline{X}$) is from the mean of the distribution ($\mu$), measured in standard error units ($\sigma_{\overline{X}}$).

**11.** We can apply the standard normal curve model to the sampling distribution of means. From the $z$-table, we determine the proportion of the area under the curve between the $\mu$ and a $z$. This tells us the expected relative frequency of the sample means between the $\mu$ and the corresponding $\overline{X}$ on the sampling distribution of means.

**12.** Biff's percentile was 99.87.

## USING THE COMPUTER

The computer program will not compute $z$-scores for a raw score in a sample of data. However, by running the routine entitled "One Group Descriptive Statistics" (number **3** on the Main Menu), you can obtain the mean and sample standard deviation for your data. Then you can easily compute any $z$-score using the formula you learned in this chapter.

The computer program will compute a $z$-score for a sample mean in routine number **5**, if you know the $\mu$ and the true standard deviation of the population. However, recognize that this is part of the inferential statistical procedure known as the $z$-test, so there will be additional information presented that you don't yet understand.

## PRACTICE PROBLEMS

(Answers are provided for odd-numbered problems.)

1. What does a z-score indicate?
2. On what factors does the absolute value of a z-score depend?
3. What is a z-distribution?
4. What are the three uses of z-distributions in describing individual scores?
5. For the data

    9    5    10    7    9    10    11    8    12    7    6    9

    a. compute the z-score for the raw score of 10.
    b. compute the z-score for the raw score of 6.
6. In the data in question 5, find the raw scores that correspond to
    a. $z = +1.22$
    b. $z = -0.48$
7. Which z-score in each of the following pairs corresponds to the smaller raw score?
    a. $z = +1.0, z = +2.3$
    b. $z = -2.8, z = -1.7$
    c. $z = -.70, z = +.20$
    d. $z = 0.0, z = -2.0$
8. In each pair in question 7, which z-score has the higher frequency?
9. In a normal distribution of scores, what proportion of all scores are expected to fall in each of the following areas?
    a. between the mean and $z = +1.89$
    b. below $z = -2.30$
    c. between $z = -1.25$ and $z = +2.75$
    d. above $z = +1.96$ and below $-1.96$
10. For a distribution where $\overline{X} = 100$, $S_x = 16$, and $N = 500$,
    a. what is the relative frequency of scores between 76 and the mean?
    b. how many subjects are expected to score between 76 and the mean?
    c. what is the percentile of someone scoring 76?
    d. how many subjects are expected to score above 76?
11. Two consumers' groups publish studies on how reliable various brands of automobiles are. The car you are interested in buying is rated a 92 by Group A ($\overline{X} = 80$, $S_x = 4$), but only a 40 by Group B ($\overline{X} = 35$, $S_x = 2$). Why should you buy or not buy the car?
12. a. What is a sampling distribution of means?
    b. What are the four characteristics of a sampling distribution?
13. What is $\sigma_{\overline{x}}$ and what does it tell us?
14. A researcher obtained a sample mean of 68.4 when he gave a test to a random sample of 49 subjects. For everyone who has ever taken the test, the mean is 65 (and $\sigma_x = 10$). The researcher believes that his sample mean is rather unusual.
    a. How often can he expect to obtain a sample mean that is higher than 68.4?
    b. Why might the researcher obtain such an unusual mean?
15. If you took 1000 random samples of 50 subjects each from a population where $\mu$

$= 19.4$ and $\sigma_X = 6.0$, how many samples would you expect to produce a mean below 18?

## SUMMARY OF FORMULAS

1. *The formula for transforming a raw score in a sample into a z-score is*

$$z = \frac{X - \overline{X}}{S_X}$$

where $X$ is the raw score, $\overline{X}$ is the sample mean, and $S_X$ is the sample standard deviation.

2. *The formula for transforming a z-score in a sample into a raw score is*

$$X = (z)(S_X) + \overline{X}$$

3. *The formula for a T-score is*

$$T = z(10) + 50$$

4. *The formula for the true standard error of the mean is*

$$\sigma_{\overline{X}} = \frac{\sigma_X}{\sqrt{N}}$$

where $\sigma_X$ is the true standard deviation of the raw score population.

5. *The formula for transforming a sample mean into a z-score on the sampling distribution of means is*

$$z = \frac{\overline{X} - \mu}{\sigma_{\overline{X}}}$$

where $\overline{X}$ is the sample mean, $\mu$ is the mean of the sampling distribution (which is also equal to the $\mu$ of the raw score distribution), and $\sigma_{\overline{X}}$ is the standard error of the mean of the sampling distribution of means.

# PART 3

# DESCRIBING RELATIONSHIPS

As you know by now, the purpose of research is to understand the laws of nature, and psychologists do this by describing relationships between variables. The final question that we answer with descriptive statistics is "What is the nature of the relationship we have found?" In the next two chapters we will discuss the descriptive statistics that directly summarize and describe a relationship. In Chapter 7 we will discuss the procedure known as correlation, and in Chapter 8 we will discuss the procedure known as linear regression.

If it seems that the topics in the upcoming chapters are different from previous topics, it is because they *are* different. Although correlation and regression are major statistical procedures, their perspective is somewhat different from that of our previous techniques, which focused on an individual sample mean and standard deviation. Therefore, think of the upcoming chapters as somewhat of a detour. After we complete the detour, we will return to describing a sample using the mean and standard deviation. In particular, we will return to describing the location of a sample mean on a sampling distribution of sample means. Don't forget those procedures, because they form the basis for inferential statistics.

# 7

# Describing Relationships Using Correlations

Recall that in a relationship, as the scores on one variable change, there is a consistent pattern of change in the scores on the other variable (for example, the bigger they are, the harder they fall). In research, in addition to demonstrating a relationship, we also want to describe its characteristics: What is the nature of the relationship? How consistently do the scores change together? In what direction do the scores change? In this chapter we discuss the descriptive statistical procedure used to answer such questions. This procedure is known as *correlation*.

In the following sections we will consider correlational research procedures, and then we will examine those characteristics of a relationship that are described by correlation. Finally, we will see how to calculate different types of correlation statistics. First, though, we will look at several new statistical symbols that are used with correlation.

## MORE STATISTICAL NOTATION

We perform correlational analysis when we have scores from two variables. We use $X$ to stand for the scores on one variable and $Y$ to stand for the scores on the other variable. Usually, we obtain an $X$ score and a $Y$ score from the same subject, and then each subject's $X$ is paired with the corresponding $Y$. If the $X$ and $Y$ scores are not from the same subject, there must be some other rational system for pairing the scores (for example, we might pair the scores of roommates).

In our computations, we use the same conventions for $Y$ that we have previously used for $X$. Thus, $\Sigma Y$ is the sum of the $Y$ scores, $\Sigma Y^2$ is the sum of the squared $Y$ scores, and $(\Sigma Y)^2$ is the squared sum of the $Y$ scores. The mean of the $Y$ scores is symbolized by $\overline{Y}$ and is equal to $\Sigma Y/N$. Similarly, the variance of a sample of $Y$ scores is $S_Y^2$, and the standard deviation of $Y$ is $S_Y$. To find $S_Y^2$ and $S_Y$, we use the same formulas that we used to find $S_X^2$ and $S_X$, except that now we plug in the $Y$ scores instead of the $X$ scores.

We will also encounter three new mathematical notations. We will see the notation $(\Sigma Y)(\Sigma X)$, which is the sum of $X$ multiplied times the sum of $Y$. This tells us to first find the sum of the $X$s and the sum of the $Y$s and then multiply the two sums together. We will also see the notation $\Sigma XY$, which is called the sum of the cross products. This tells us to first multiply each $X$ score in a pair times its corresponding $Y$ score and then sum all of the resulting products. Finally, we will see the symbol $D$. This stands for the numerical *difference* between the $X$ and $Y$ scores in a pair, which we find by subtracting one from the other.

Table 7.1 shows how we compute each of the above quantities. Notice that we are comparing pairs of scores, so there must be the same number of $X$ and $Y$ scores. Then, as the first two columns show, $\Sigma X$ is 6 and $\Sigma Y$ is 8. Therefore, $(\Sigma X)(\Sigma Y)$ is (6)(8), which is 48. On the other hand, we obtain $\Sigma XY$ by first multiplying each $X$ times the corresponding $Y$ and then summing, so $\Sigma XY = 18$. As shown in the far right-hand column, we compute each $D$ by subtracting each $Y$ from its corresponding $X$.

Now, on to correlation.

## UNDERSTANDING CORRELATIONAL RESEARCH

A statistical statement that captures the flavor of a relationship is "The scores on variables $X$ and $Y$ *covary*." By this we mean that the scores on the two

**TABLE 7.1**  Computing $\Sigma XY$, $(\Sigma X)$ $(\Sigma Y)$, and $D$ for Three Subjects' $X$ and $Y$ Scores

| Subject | X | Y | XY | D |
|---------|---|---|----|---|
| 1 | 1 | 2 | 2 | −1 |
| 2 | 2 | 2 | 4 | 0 |
| 3 | 3 | 4 | 12 | −1 |
| | $\Sigma X = 6$ | $\Sigma Y = 8$ | $\Sigma XY = 18$ | |
| | $(\Sigma X)$ $(\Sigma Y) = (6)$ $(8) = 48$ | | | |

variables vary, or change, together. For example, it is commonly believed that as people drink more coffee, they become more nervous. Thus, if there is a relationship, amount of coffee consumed and nervousness will covary.

Recall that one way to demonstrate such a relationship is through the correlational approach. In correlational research, the researcher does not manipulate or select particular conditions of an independent variable, as in an experiment. Instead, the researcher merely measures subjects' scores on two variables and then describes the relationship that is present. Thus, in a correlational study, we might simply ask each subject to report the amount of coffee he or she had consumed that day, and we might use physiological measures to determine how nervous each subject was.

As the name implies, in correlational research we use a correlational statistic to summarize the relationship. The word *correlation* is synonymous with *relationship*. (Think of a correlation as the shared, or "co," relation between two variables.) A correlation is found by examining the individual pairs of *X-Y* scores in the data. If a relationship exists, then as the *X* scores change, the corresponding *Y* scores will change in a consistent fashion. Thus, we might find a relationship between coffee consumption and nervousness by determining that as individual subjects reported consuming more coffee, they also had higher nervousness scores.

Because of the manner in which the data are collected in correlational research, we must be very careful when we interpret the results.

## Correlation and Causality

Whenever we hear of a relationship between *X* and *Y,* we have a natural tendency to conclude that it is a *causal* relationship—that *X* causes *Y*. In Chapter 2 we discussed the problems of inferring causality from an experiment. The problems are even greater with correlational research. Say that in our correlational study we discovered that subjects who reported drinking more coffee also tended to be more nervous. You might want to conclude that drinking more coffee causes people to be more nervous. In a correlational study, however, we only describe how the *X* and *Y* scores are paired, or match up, to form a relationship. *The fact that there is a relationship between two variables does not mean that changes in one variable cause the changes in the other variable.* A statistical relationship can exist even though one variable does not cause or influence the other. Therefore, correlational research *cannot* be used to infer a causal relationship between two variables.

There are two obvious requirements for concluding that *X* causes *Y*. First, *X* must occur before *Y*. In correlational research, we have no way of knowing which factor occurred first. For example, in our study above, we simply measured the scores for amount of coffee and nervousness. Perhaps subjects who were more nervous subsequently drank more coffee. If so, then it is greater nervousness that actually causes greater coffee consumption. In any correlation it is possible that $Y$ causes $X$. Second, $X$ must be the only variable that can influence $Y$. In correlational research, we do not control or eliminate any variables that may potentially cause scores to change. For example, in the above coffee study, some of the subjects may have had less sleep than other subjects the night before we tested them. Perhaps the lack of sleep caused those subjects to be more nervous *and* to drink more coffee. In any correlation some other variable may cause both $X$ and $Y$ to change.

Thus correlation by itself does not allow us to conclude causality. Quite simply, the relationship between the variables that we describe in a correlation may be a *coincidence*. Sometimes the coincidental nature of the relationship is obvious. For example, there is a relationship between the number of toilets in a neighborhood and the number of crime victims in the neighborhood: the more toilets, the more crime. Based on this correlation, should we conclude that indoor plumbing causes crime? Of course not! We recognize that crime tends to occur more frequently in large cities, especially in crowded neighborhoods. Coincidentally, there are more indoor toilets in crowded neighborhoods in large cities.

The problem is that it is easy to be trapped by more mysterious relationships involving variables that we do not understand. For example, there is a correlation between the amount of "adult literature" (pornography) sold in a state and the incidence of rape in the state: the more pornography sold, the more rape. Based solely on this correlation, can we conclude that pornography causes rape? Not unless we can conclude that indoor plumbing causes crime! For all of the reasons stated above, since we cannot use correlation to infer causality in one situation, we cannot use it in another.

> *STAT ALERT* We never infer causality based solely on the existence of a correlation.

## Distinguishing Characteristics of Correlation

There are three major differences between how we handle data in correlational analysis and how we handle data in an experiment. First, since we examine pairs of $X$-$Y$ scores, correlational procedures involve *one* sample containing all *pairs* of $X$ and $Y$ scores.

**In correlational analysis, $N$ stands for the number of pairs of scores in the data.**

Second, in a correlational study, neither variable is called the independent or dependent variable, and either variable may be called the $X$ or $Y$ variable. How do we decide which variable is $X$ and which is $Y$? As we have seen, we discuss any relationship in terms of changes in $Y$ scores as a function of changes in $X$ scores. This means that we take each $X$ score as a given and then look at what happens to the $Y$ scores. Thus, for example, if we ask, "For a given amount of coffee, what are the nervousness scores?" then amount of coffee is the $X$ variable (plotted on the $X$ axis) and nervousness is the $Y$ variable (plotted on the $Y$ axis). Conversely, if we ask, "For a given nervousness score, what is the amount of coffee consumed?" then nervousness is the $X$ variable and amount of coffee is the $Y$ variable.

Third, as we shall see in the next section, we graph the data differently in correlational research than we do in an experiment. We use the individual pairs of scores to create a scatterplot.

## Plotting Correlational Data: The Scatterplot

A **scatterplot** is a plot of the individual data points from a set of $X$-$Y$ pairs. The scatterplot in Figure 7.1 shows the data we might obtain if we actually conducted a study of coffee drinking and nervousness (for reference, the raw scores are also listed). We are interested in how nervousness scores change as a function of coffee consumption, so nervousness is the $Y$ variable and coffee consumption is the $X$ variable. Real research typically involves a larger $N$ than

**FIGURE 7.1**   Scatterplot Showing Nervousness as a Function of Coffee Consumption

*Each data point is created using a subject's coffee consumption as the $X$ score and the subject's nervousness as the $Y$ score.*

| Cups of coffee: X | Nervousness scores: Y |
|:---:|:---:|
| 1 | 1 |
| 1 | 1 |
| 1 | 2 |
| 2 | 2 |
| 2 | 3 |
| 3 | 4 |
| 3 | 5 |
| 4 | 5 |
| 4 | 6 |
| 5 | 8 |
| 5 | 9 |
| 6 | 9 |
| 6 | 10 |

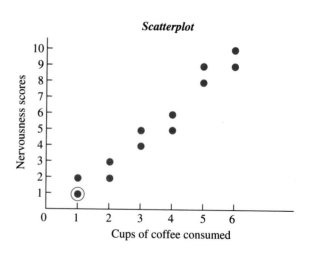

we have here, and the data points may not form such a pretty pattern. Nonetheless, a scatterplot does summarize the data somewhat. In the table of raw scores on the left, we see that two subjects had raw scores of 1 on both coffee consumption and nervousness. On the scatterplot there is one circled data point for these subjects. Sometimes we circle a data point to indicate that two data points are plotted on top of each other. In real data, many subjects with a particular $X$ score may score the same value of $Y$, so the number of data points may be considerably smaller than the number of pairs of raw scores.

Remember that the lower left-hand corner of the graph always has the low scores on the $X$ and $Y$ variables. The scores get larger as the $Y$ variable goes up and as the $X$ variable goes to the right. We ask, "As the $X$ scores increase, what happens to the $Y$ scores?" In Figure 7.1, as the $X$ scores increase, the $Y$ scores tend to increase. The scatterplot illustrates how we conceptualize a relationship: one value or a few values of $Y$ tend to be paired with one value of $X$. As the $X$ scores change, the $Y$ scores tend to change consistently so that a different value or values of $Y$ tend to be paired with a different value of $X$. Thus, we can see that the more coffee subjects drink, the more nervous they tend to be: subjects drinking 1 cup of coffee tend to have nervousness scores around 1, subjects drinking 2 cups of coffee tend to have nervousness scores around 2, and so on.

STAT ALERT  When a relationship exists, a particular value of $Y$ tends to be paired with one value of $X$ and a different value of $Y$ tends to be paired with a different value of $X$.

*Always draw the scatterplot* of a set of correlational data. A scatterplot allows you to see the nature of the relationship that is present and map out the best way to accurately summarize and describe it.

The shape of the scatterplot is an important indication of both the presence of a relationship and the nature of the relationship. We can visually summarize a scatterplot by drawing a line around its outer edges. As we shall see, a scatterplot may have any one of a number of shapes when a relationship is present. When no relationship is present, however, the scatterplot will be either circular or elliptical, oriented so that the ellipse is parallel to the $X$ axis. The scatterplots in Figure 7.2 show no relationship. There is no relationship in either scatterplot, because as the $X$ scores change, the $Y$ scores do not consistently change. No particular value of $Y$ tends to be associated with a particular value of $X$. Instead, virtually every value of $Y$ is associated with every value of $X$.

The scatterplots in Figure 7.2 are further summarized by the line drawn through the long dimension of each scatterplot that seems to best fit the center of the scatterplot. This best-fitting summary line is called the **regression line.** We will discuss the procedures for drawing a regression line in the next chapter.

**FIGURE 7.2**  Scatterplots Showing No Relationship Present

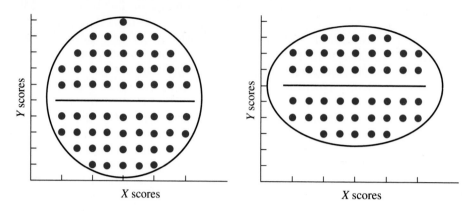

However, as you can see in Figure 7.2, the orientation of the regression line matches the orientation of the scatterplot. Thus, when no relationship is present, the regression line forms a horizontal straight line.

## THE CORRELATION COEFFICIENT

When a relationship is present, the scatterplot will form some shape other than a circle or a horizontal ellipse, and the regression line will not be a horizontal straight line. The particular shape and orientation of a scatterplot reflect the characteristics of the relationship formed by the data. To summarize these characteristics, we compute the statistic known as the correlation coefficient. A **correlation coefficient** is a number that summarizes and describes the important characteristics of a relationship. There are two important characteristics of a relationship: the type of relationship and the strength of the relationship. In the following sections, we discuss these characteristics.

## TYPES OF RELATIONSHIPS

The **type of relationship** that is present in a set of data is determined by the overall direction in which the $Y$ scores change as the $X$ scores change. There are two general types of relationships: linear and nonlinear relationships.

## Linear Relationships

The term *linear* means "straight line," and a linear relationship has a summary regression line that is a straight line. The scatterplots in Figure 7.3 illustrate two linear relationships. The scatterplot on the left illustrates the relationship between the amount of time students study and their test performance. The scatterplot on the right illustrates the relationship between the number of hours students spend watching television and the amount of time they spend sleeping.

Both scatterplots show a relationship because, although they are elliptical in shape, they are not horizontal. Both indicate linear relationships because they are best summarized by a straight line. Any scatterplot that forms a *slanted ellipse* and has a *slanted straight* regression line indicates that a linear relationship is present. In a **linear relationship,** as the $X$ scores increase, the $Y$ scores tend to change in only one direction. On the left, as students study longer, their grades tend only to increase. On the right, as students watch more television, their sleep tends only to decrease.

The above scatterplots reflect two different types of linear relationships. The type of linear relationship depends on the *direction* in which the $Y$ scores change. The study-test relationship is an example of a positive relationship. In a **positive linear relationship,** as the scores on the $X$ variable increase, the scores on the $Y$ variable also tend to increase. Thus, low $X$ scores are paired with low $Y$ scores, and high $X$ scores are paired with high $Y$ scores. Any relationship that fits the general pattern "the more $X$, the more $Y$" is a positive linear relationship. Examples of positive linear relationships include the more you eat, the more you weigh, and the more long-distance phone calls you make,

**FIGURE 7.3**  Scatterplots Showing Positive and Negative Linear Relationships

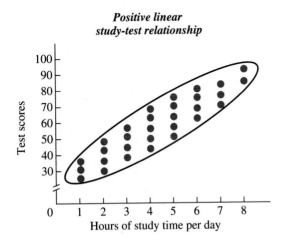

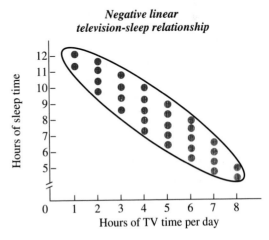

the more you must pay. You can remember that such relationships are positive by remembering that as the $X$ scores increase, the $Y$ scores change in the direction away from zero, toward *positive* scores.

On the other hand, the television-sleep relationship is an example of a negative relationship. In a **negative linear relationship,** as the scores on the $X$ variable increase, the scores on the $Y$ variable tend to decrease. Low $X$ scores are paired with high $Y$ scores, and high $X$ scores are paired with low $Y$ scores. Any relationship that fits the general pattern "the more $X$, the less $Y$" is a negative linear relationship. Examples of negative linear relationships include the more you study statistics, the less difficult it is, and the more you eat, the less hungry you are. You can remember that such relationships are negative by remembering that as the $X$ scores increase, the $Y$ scores change in the direction toward zero, heading for negative scores.

It is important to understand that the term *negative* does not mean that there is anything wrong with the relationship. Negative relationships are no different from positive relationships *except* in terms of the direction in which the $Y$ scores change as the $X$ scores increase.

## Nonlinear Relationships

If a relationship is not linear, then it is called nonlinear. *Nonlinear* does not mean that the data cannot be summarized by a line; it means that the data cannot be summarized by a *straight* line. Thus, another name for a nonlinear relationship is a curvilinear relationship. In a **nonlinear, or curvilinear, relationship,** as the $X$ scores change, the $Y$ scores do not tend to *only* increase or *only* decrease: the $Y$ scores change their direction of change.

Nonlinear relationships come in many different shapes. Figure 7.4 shows two common nonlinear realtionships. The scatterplot on the left illustrates the relationship between subjects' age and the amount of time they require to move from one place to another. Very young children locomote slowly, but as age increases, movement time decreases. Beyond a certain age, however, the time scores change direction so that as age continues to increase, movement time increases. Because of the shape of the scatterplot, such a relationship is called a *U-shaped function.* The scatterplot on the right illustrates the relationship between the number of alcoholic drinks subjects consume and their sense of feeling well. At first, people tend to report feeling better as they drink, but beyond a certain point, drinking even more makes them feel progressively worse. Such a relationship is called an *inverted U-shaped function.*

Curvilinear relationships may be even more complex than those shown in Figure 7.4, producing a wavy regression line that repeatedly changes direction. However, such relationships are rare in psychological research.

**FIGURE 7.4** Scatterplots Showing Nonlinear Relationships

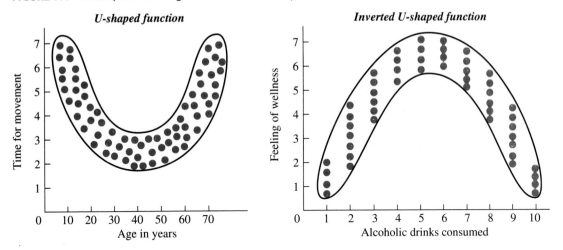

## How the Correlation Coefficient Describes the Type of Relationship

Although there are correlation coefficients that describe nonlinear relationships, in this chapter we discuss only linear correlation. How do we know whether our data form a linear relationship? We make a scatterplot of the data. If the scatterplot seems to be best fit by a straight line, then linear correlation is appropriate. Sometimes, however, we may want to describe the extent to which a nonlinear relationship has a linear component and partially fits a straight line. In this case linear correlation is also appropriate. However, to summarize a nonlinear relationship, we do not compute a linear correlation coefficient. Describing a nonlinear relationship with a straight line is like putting a round peg into a square hole: the relationship will not fit a straight line very well, and the correlation coefficient will not accurately describe the relationship.

With a correlation coefficient we communicate two things about the type of relationship we are describing. First, by virtue of the fact that we compute a linear correlation coefficient, we communicate that we are describing a linear relationship. Second, we communicate whether the linear relationship is positive or negative. If the coefficient we compute has a minus sign in front of it, we know that the linear relationship is negative. If the coefficient does not have a minus sign, then it is positive and we put a plus sign in front of it to indicate a positive linear relationship. Thus, a positive correlation coefficient indicates a positive linear relationship, and a negative correlation coefficient indicates a negative linear relationship.

The other characteristic of a relationship communicated by the correlation coefficient is the strength of the relationship.

## STRENGTH OF THE RELATIONSHIP

In a relationship, as the $X$ scores change, the $Y$ scores change consistently so that one value of $Y$ tends to be associated with one and only one value of $X$. However, different relationships will exhibit different degrees of consistency. The **strength of relationship** between two variables is the extent to which one value of $Y$ is consistently associated with one and only one value of $X$. As we saw in Chapter 2, the strength of a relationship is also referred to as the *degree of association* between the two variables. In stronger relationships, there is more consistently one value of $Y$ or close to one value of $Y$ associated with only one value of $X$. In weaker relationships, there is not one value of $Y$ or close to one value of $Y$ consistently associated with only one value of $X$.

The absolute value of the correlation coefficient (the size of the number) indicates the strength of the relationship. The largest absolute value we can obtain is 1.0, and the smallest value we can obtain is 0.0. Thus, when we include the positive or negative sign, the correlation coefficient may be any value from $-1.0$ to 0.0 or from 0.0 to $+1.0$. The *larger* the absolute value of the coefficient, the *stronger* the relationship. In other words, the closer the coefficient is to $\pm 1.0$, the more consistently one value of $Y$ is paired with one and only one value of $X$.

> *STAT ALERT*  A correlation coefficient contains two components: the sign and the absolute value. The sign indicates either a positive or a negative linear relationship. The larger the absolute value, the stronger the relationship.

As we will eventually see, computing the correlation coefficient is not difficult. The difficulty comes in interpreting the strength of the relationship, because correlation coefficients do not measure in equal units of "consistency." Thus, if one correlation coefficient is $+.40$ and another is $+.80$, we *cannot* conclude that $+.80$ describes a relationship that has twice as much consistency as the one with $+.40$. Instead, we evaluate any correlation coefficient by comparing it to the extreme values of 0.0 and $\pm 1.0$. First we will discuss a coefficient of $\pm 1.0$.

## Perfect Association

A correlation coefficient of $\pm 1.0$ describes a perfect linear relationship that is as strong as it can be. Figure 7.5 shows the data and resulting scatterplots for examples in which the correlation coefficient is $+1.0$ and $-1.0$.

There are four ways to think about what a correlation coefficient of $\pm 1.0$ tells us about a relationship. First, it tells us that *every* subject who obtains a particular $X$ score obtains one and only one value of $Y$. Every time $X$ changes, the $Y$ scores all change to one new value. Thus, $\pm 1.0$ indicates a one-to-one correspondence, or perfect consistency, between the $X$ and $Y$ scores.

**FIGURE 7.5**   Data and Scatterplots Reflecting Perfect Positive and Negative Correlations

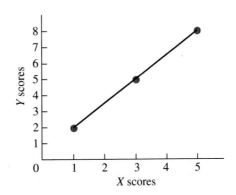

*Perfect positive*
*coefficient = +1.0*

| X | Y |
|---|---|
| 1 | 2 |
| 1 | 2 |
| 1 | 2 |
| 3 | 5 |
| 3 | 5 |
| 3 | 5 |
| 5 | 8 |
| 5 | 8 |
| 5 | 8 |

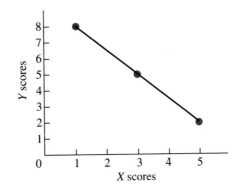

*Perfect negative*
*coefficient = −1.0*

| X | Y |
|---|---|
| 1 | 8 |
| 1 | 8 |
| 1 | 8 |
| 3 | 5 |
| 3 | 5 |
| 3 | 5 |
| 5 | 2 |
| 5 | 2 |
| 5 | 2 |

Second, a coefficient of $\pm 1.0$ indicates that there are no differences among the $Y$ scores associated with a particular $X$. In statistics, we describe differences between scores as variability, so $\pm 1.0$ indicates that there is no variability, or spread, in the $Y$ scores at each $X$.

Third, a coefficient of $\pm 1$ ensures perfect predictability. Pretend that we do not know a particular subject's $Y$ score. Since each $Y$ score is associated with only one $X$ score, if we know the subject's $X$ score, then we know the subject's $Y$ score. Thus, when the coefficient is $\pm 1.0$, knowing subjects' $X$ scores allows us to perfectly predict their corresponding $Y$ scores. (We'll discuss how we predict the $Y$ scores in the next chapter.)

Fourth, because it indicates that there is no spread in the $Y$s at each $X$, a coefficient of $\pm 1.0$ tells us that the data points for the subjects at an $X$ are all on top of one another. When we summarize this scatterplot with a regression line, all of the data points lie *on* the regression line.

## Intermediate Association

The essence of understanding any other value of the correlation coefficient is this: the strength of a linear relationship is the extent to which the data tend to form a perfect linear relationship. Thus, any correlation coefficient that is not equal to $\pm 1.0$ indicates that only to some degree do the data form a perfect linear relationship.

> *STAT ALERT* The absolute value of a correlation coefficient indicates the extent to which the data conform to a perfect linear relationship.

The way to interpret any value of the correlation coefficient is to compare it to $\pm 1.0$. For example, Figure 7.6 shows data and the resulting scatterplot that produce a correlation coefficient of $+.98$. Again we interpret the coefficient in four ways. First, a correlation coefficient with an absolute value less than 1.0 indicates that there is less than perfectly consistent association. Every subject obtaining a particular $X$ did not obtain the exact same $Y$. However, since a coefficient of $+.98$ is close to a value of $\pm 1.0$, it tells us that there is "close" to perfect consistency between the $X$ and $Y$ scores.

Second, when the correlation coefficient is not $\pm 1.0$, *different* $Y$ scores are associated with a single $X$ score, so there is variability between the $Y$ scores at each $X$. For example, subjects obtaining an $X$ of 1 obtained a $Y$ of 1 or 2, and subjects obtaining an $X$ of 3 scored a $Y$ of 4 or 5. However, since $+.98$ is close to $+1.0$, it tells us that the variability of the $Y$ scores at each $X$ is small *relative* to the overall variability of all $Y$ scores in the data. Think of it this way: over the entire sample, $Y$ scores range from 1 to 8, so the overall range is 8. At each $X$ score, however, the $Y$s span a range of only 1. It is this

**FIGURE 7.6**  Data and Scatterplot Reflecting a Correlation Coefficient of $+.98$

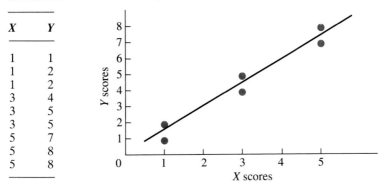

| X | Y |
|---|---|
| 1 | 1 |
| 1 | 2 |
| 1 | 2 |
| 3 | 4 |
| 3 | 5 |
| 3 | 5 |
| 5 | 7 |
| 5 | 8 |
| 5 | 8 |

small variability in $Y$ at each $X$ relative to the overall variability in all $Y$ scores that produces a correlation coefficient close to $+1.0$.

Third, pretending for a moment that we do not know a particular subject's $Y$ score, if we know his or her $X$ score, we can only predict *around* what the $Y$ score would be. However, since a coefficient of $+.98$ is close to $+1.0$, we know that the predicted $Y$ score will be close to the actual $Y$ score the subject obtained.

Fourth, because there is now spread in the $Y$s at each $X$, all data points do not all fall *on* the regression line: they fall above and below it. However, a coefficient of $+.98$ is close to $+1.0$, so we know that the $Y$ scores are close to, or hug, the regression line. The spread between the lowest and highest $Y$ scores at each $X$ is small, resulting in a scatterplot that is a narrow, or skinny, ellipse. (The absolute value of the correlation coefficient always tells us how skinny the scatterplot is. When the coefficient is $\pm 1.0$, the scatterplot forms a straight line, which is the skinniest ellipse possible. The closer the coefficient is to $\pm 1.0$, the skinnier the scatterplot, and vice versa.)

The greater the variability, or spread, in the $Y$ scores at each $X$, the weaker the strength of a relationship. Therefore, as the spread, or variability, in the $Y$s at each $X$ becomes larger relative to the overall variability in the sample, the value of the correlation coefficient approaches $0.0$. In Figure 7.7 we see an example of data and the resulting scatterplot that produce a much smaller correlation coefficient of $-.28$. The fact that this is a negative relationship has nothing to do with its strength. On a scale of $0.0$ to $\pm 1.0$, a coefficient of $-.28$ is not very close to $\pm 1.0$, so this relationship is not very close to forming a perfectly consistent linear relationship. In fact, only barely does one value of $Y$ or even close to one value of $Y$ tend to be associated with one value of $X$. Such a small coefficient indicates that the variability in the $Y$s at each $X$ is

FIGURE 7.7   Data and Scatterplot Reflecting a Correlation Coefficient of −.28

| X | Y |
|---|---|
| 1 | 9 |
| 1 | 6 |
| 1 | 3 |
| 3 | 8 |
| 3 | 6 |
| 3 | 3 |
| 5 | 7 |
| 5 | 5 |
| 5 | 1 |

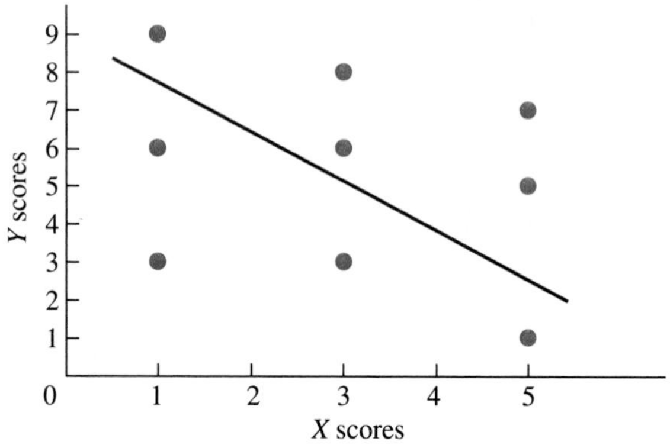

almost as large as the spread across all *Y* scores in the data. This means that knowing a subject's *X* score will not allow us to closely predict the *Y* score he or she would obtain. Finally, the coefficient tells us that there is a large vertical distance between the *Y*s at each *X,* so the scatterplot is fat and does not hug the regression line.

## Zero Association

The lowest possible value of the correlation coefficient is 0.0, indicating that no linear relationship is present. Figure 7.8 shows an example of data and the resulting scatterplot that produce a correlation coefficient of 0.0. A scatterplot having this shape is as far from forming a slanted straight line as possible, and a correlation coefficient of 0.0 is as far from a correlation coefficient of ±1.0 as possible. Therefore, we know that there is no value or values of *Y* consistently associated with one and only one value of *X.* Instead the *Y*s found at one *X* are the same as the *Y*s found at any other *X.* This means that knowing a subject's *X* score will not in any way help us to predict the corresponding *Y* score. Finally, the spread in *Y* at any *X* equals the overall spread of *Y* in the data, producing a scatterplot that is a circle or horizontal ellipse that in no way hugs the regression line.

> *STAT ALERT*   The larger the correlation coefficient, whether positive or negative, the stronger the relationship and the closer it is to forming a perfect linear relationship. The stronger the relationship, the less the *Y*s are spread out at each *X,* the more accurately we can predict

**FIGURE 7.8**  Data and Scatterplot Reflecting a Correlation Coefficient of 0.0

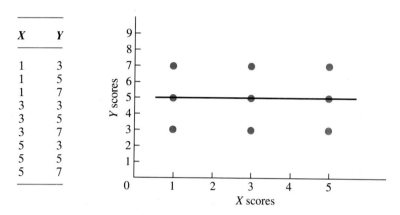

| X | Y |
|---|---|
| 1 | 3 |
| 1 | 5 |
| 1 | 7 |
| 3 | 3 |
| 3 | 5 |
| 3 | 7 |
| 5 | 3 |
| 5 | 5 |
| 5 | 7 |

a subject's $Y$ score by knowing the subject's $X$ score, and the closer the $Y$ scores come to all falling on a straight line.

Although theoretically a correlation coefficient may be as large as $\pm 1.0$, in real research such values do not occur. Remember that the $X$ and $Y$ scores reflect the behaviors of living organisms, and living organisms do not show a great deal of consistency. Therefore, in psychological research, a correlation coefficient in the neighborhood of $\pm .50$ is considered to be quite respectable, and coefficients above $\pm .50$ are downright impressive. A correlation of $\pm 1.0$ is so unlikely to occur with real data that, if you ever obtain one, you should assume you've made a computational error. (If you obtain a coefficient greater than $\pm 1.0$, you have definitely made an error, because $\pm 1.0$ indicates a perfect relationship and you cannot do better than that.)

## COMPUTING THE CORRELATION COEFFICIENT

In the following sections we will discuss the three most common linear correlation coefficients: the *Pearson correlation coefficient,* the *Spearman rank-order correlation coefficient,* and the *point-biserial correlation coefficient.* In each case a value of between 0 and $\pm 1.0$ describes the degree of linear relationship in a sample, and everything we have said previously about the interpretation of the correlation coefficient applies. The major difference among the three coefficients is that each is appropriate for describing a relationship between certain types of variables.

## The Pearson Correlation Coefficient

By far the most common correlation coefficient in psychological research is the Pearson correlation coefficient. The **Pearson correlation coefficient** is used to describe the linear relationship between two variables that are both interval or ratio variables. (Technically this statistic is the Pearson product moment correlation coefficient, but it is usually called the Pearson correlation coefficient. It was invented by Karl Pearson.) The symbol for the Pearson correlation coefficient is $r$. When you see $r$, think "relationship." (All of the examples in the previous section involved $r$.)

The underlying statistical basis of $r$ is that it compares how consistently each value of $Y$ is paired with each value of $X$ in a linear fashion. In the previous chapter we saw that to compare scores from different variables, we first transform the scores from each variable into $z$-scores. In computing $r$, we transform each $Y$ score into a $z$-score (call it $z_Y$), and we transform each $X$ score into a $z$-score (call it $z_X$). Then we determine the correspondence between each $z_Y$ and its paired $z_X$. Usually, every pair will not exhibit the same degree of correspondence. Therefore, $r$ indicates the "average" amount of correspondence between the $z_Y$'s and the $z_X$'s in the sample. The Pearson correlation coefficient is defined as

$$r = \frac{\Sigma(z_X z_Y)}{N}$$

Mathematically, when we multiply each $z_X$ times the corresponding $z_Y$ of the pair, sum the products, and then divide by $N$ (the number of pairs), we have computed the average correspondence within all $z_Y$-$z_X$ pairs.

Of course, there's an easier way to compute $r$.

**Computing the Pearson correlation coefficient**    We have derived a computational formula from the above definitional formula. First we replaced the symbols $z_X$ and $z_Y$ with their formulas. Then, in these formulas, we replaced the symbols for the mean and standard deviation with their own computational formulas. As you can imagine, this produced a monster of a formula. When we reduce the formula to its simplest form, we have the smaller monster below.

*THE COMPUTATIONAL FORMULA FOR THE PEARSON CORRELATION COEFFICIENT IS*

$$r = \frac{N(\Sigma XY) - (\Sigma X)(\Sigma Y)}{\sqrt{[N(\Sigma X^2) - (\Sigma X)^2][N(\Sigma Y^2) - (\Sigma Y)^2]}}$$

Say that we have collected scores from ten subjects on two variables: the number of times they visited a doctor in the last year and the number of glasses of orange juice they drink daily. We want to describe the linear relationship between juice-drinking and doctor visits. Table 7.2 shows a good way to set up the data to compute $r$.

From the computational formula for $r$, we see that we need the values of $\Sigma X$, $\Sigma X^2$, $(\Sigma X)^2$, $\Sigma Y$, $\Sigma Y^2$, $(\Sigma Y)^2$, $\Sigma XY$, and $N$. To find each $XY$, we multiply each $X$ times its corresponding $Y$, as shown in the far right-hand column in Table 7.2. Summing each column then gives us $\Sigma X$, $\Sigma X^2$, $\Sigma Y$, $\Sigma Y^2$, and $\Sigma XY$. Squaring $\Sigma X$ and $\Sigma Y$ gives us $(\Sigma X)^2$ and $(\Sigma Y)^2$.

Once we have obtained the above quantities, we put them in the formula for $r$. Thus,

$$r = \frac{N(\Sigma XY) - (\Sigma X)(\Sigma Y)}{\sqrt{[N(\Sigma X^2) - (\Sigma X)^2][N(\Sigma Y^2) - (\Sigma Y)^2]}}$$

becomes

$$r = \frac{10(52) - (17)(47)}{\sqrt{[10(45) - 289][10(275) - 2209]}}$$

TABLE 7.2  Sample Data for Computing the $r$ Between Doctor Visits (the $X$ variable) and Orange Juice Consumed (the $Y$ variable)

| Subject | Glasses of juice per day | | Doctor visits per year | | |
| | X | X² | Y | Y² | XY |
| --- | --- | --- | --- | --- | --- |
| 1 | 0 | 0 | 8 | 64 | 0 |
| 2 | 0 | 0 | 7 | 49 | 0 |
| 3 | 1 | 1 | 7 | 49 | 7 |
| 4 | 1 | 1 | 6 | 36 | 6 |
| 5 | 1 | 1 | 5 | 25 | 5 |
| 6 | 2 | 4 | 4 | 16 | 8 |
| 7 | 2 | 4 | 4 | 16 | 8 |
| 8 | 3 | 9 | 4 | 16 | 12 |
| 9 | 3 | 9 | 2 | 4 | 6 |
| 10 | 4 | 16 | 0 | 0 | 0 |
| $N = 10$ | $\Sigma X = 17$ | $\Sigma X^2 = 45$ | $\Sigma Y = 47$ | $\Sigma Y^2 = 275$ | $\Sigma XY = 52$ |
| | $(\Sigma X)^2 = 289$ | | $(\Sigma Y)^2 = 2209$ | | |

Let's compute the numerator first. Since multiplication takes precedence over subtraction, we multiply 10 times 52, which is 520, and we multiply 17 times 47, which is 799. Rewriting the formula, we have

$$r = \frac{520 - 799}{\sqrt{[10(45) - 289][10(275) - 2209]}}$$

We complete the numerator by subtracting 799 *from* 520, which is $-279$. (Note the negative sign.)

Now compute the denominator. First we perform the operations within each bracket. In the left bracket, we multiply 10 times 45, which is 450, and from that we subtract 289, obtaining 161. In the right bracket, we multiply 10 times 275, which is 2750, and from that we subtract 2209, obtaining 541. Rewriting one more time, we have

$$r = \frac{-279}{\sqrt{[161][541]}}$$

Now we multiply the quantities in the brackets together; 161 times 541 is 87,101. Then we take the square root of 87,101, which is 295.129. Now we have

$$r = \frac{-279}{295.129}$$

We divide, and there you have it: $r = -.95$.

The value of $r$ is not greater than $\pm 1.0$, so our calculations may be correct. Also, we have computed a negative $r$, and in the raw scores we see that there is a negative relationship: as the orange juice scores increase, the number of doctor visits decreases. (If you have any doubt, make a scatterplot.) Had this been a positive relationship, the numerator of the formula would not contain a negative number and $r$ would not be negative.

Thus, we conclude that there is a negative linear relationship between juice-drinking and doctor visits. On a scale of 0.0 to $\pm 1.0$, where 0.0 is no relationship and $\pm 1.0$ is a perfect linear relationship, this relationship is a $-.95$. Relatively speaking, this is a very strong linear relationship: each amount of orange juice is associated with one relatively small range of doctor visits, and as juice scores increase, doctor visits consistently decrease.

### The Spearman Rank-Order Correlation Coefficient

Sometimes our data involve ordinal or rank-order scores (first, second, third, etc.). The **Spearman rank-order correlation coefficient** describes the linear relationship between pairs of ranked scores. The symbol for the Spearman correlation coefficient is $r_s$. (The subscript s stands for Spearman; it is named for Charles Spearman.)

In psychological research, ranked scores often arise in cases where variables are difficult to measure quantitatively. Instead, we evaluate each subject by making qualitative judgments, and then we use these judgments to rank-order the subjects. We use $r_s$ to correlate the ranks on two such variables. Or, if we want to correlate one ranked variable with one interval or ratio variable, we transform the interval or ratio scores into ranked scores: we might rank the subject with the highest interval score as 1, the subject with the second highest score as 2, and so on. Either way, $r_s$ tells us the extent to which subjects' ranks on one variable consistently match their ranks on the other variable to form a linear relationship. If every subject has the same rank on both variables, $r_s$ will equal $+1.0$. If every subject's rank on one variable is the opposite of his or her rank on the other variable, $r_s$ will equal $-1.0$. If there is some degree of consistent pairing of the ranks, $r_s$ will be between $\pm 1.0$ and 0.0, and if there is no consistent pairing, $r_s$ will equal 0.0.

Since $r_s$ describes the consistency with which ranks match, or agree, one use of $r_s$ is to determine the extent to which two observers agree. For example, say that we ask two observers to judge how aggressively a sample of children behave while playing. Each observer assigns the rank of 1 to his or her choice for most aggressive child, 2 to the second-most-aggressive child, and so on. Figure 7.9 shows the sets of ranked scores and the resulting scatterplot the two observers might produce for 9 subjects.

In creating the scatterplot and computing $r_s$, we treat each observer as a variable: the scores on one variable are the rankings assigned by one observer

**FIGURE 7.9** Sample Data for Computing $r_s$ Between Rankings of Observer A and Rankings of Observer B

| Subject | Observer A: X | Observer B: Y |
|---------|---------------|---------------|
| 1 | 4 | 3 |
| 2 | 1 | 2 |
| 3 | 9 | 8 |
| 4 | 8 | 6 |
| 5 | 3 | 5 |
| 6 | 5 | 4 |
| 7 | 6 | 7 |
| 8 | 2 | 1 |
| 9 | 7 | 9 |

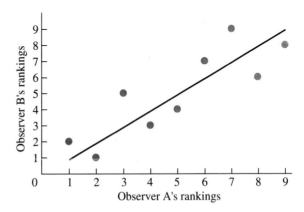

to the subjects, and the scores on the other variable are the rankings assigned by the other observer. Judging from the scatterplot, it appears that there is a positive relationship here. To describe this relationship, we compute $r_s$.

## Computing the Spearman correlation coefficient

*THE COMPUTATIONAL FORMULA FOR THE SPEARMAN RANK-ORDER CORRELATION COEFFICIENT IS*

$$r_s = 1 - \frac{6(\Sigma D^2)}{N(N^2 - 1)}$$

$N$ is the number of pairs of ranks, and $D$ is the difference between the two scores in each pair. (Notice that the formula always contains the 6 in the numerator.)

In using this formula, first arrange the data as shown in Table 7.3. The column labeled $D$ contains the difference between the rankings in each pair. Here we have subtracted each $Y$ from the corresponding $X$, but you can subtract $X$ from $Y$. In the right-hand column, after finding the $D$s, we compute $D^2$ by squaring the difference in each pair. Finally, we determine the sum of the squared differences, $\Sigma D^2$ (here $\Sigma D^2$ is 18). To compute $r_s$, we also need $N$, the number of $X$-$Y$ pairs (here $N = 9$), and $N^2$ ($9^2 = 81$). Placing these quantities in the formula, we have

$$r_s = 1 - \frac{6(\Sigma D^2)}{N(N^2 - 1)} = 1 - \frac{6(18)}{9(81 - 1)}$$

**TABLE 7.3**   Data Arrangement for Computing $r_s$

| Subject | Observer A: X | Observer B: Y | D | D² |
|---------|---------------|---------------|-----|-----|
| 1 | 4 | 3 | 1 | 1 |
| 2 | 1 | 2 | −1 | 1 |
| 3 | 9 | 8 | 1 | 1 |
| 4 | 8 | 6 | 2 | 4 |
| 5 | 3 | 5 | −2 | 4 |
| 6 | 5 | 4 | 1 | 1 |
| 7 | 6 | 7 | −1 | 1 |
| 8 | 2 | 1 | 1 | 1 |
| 9 | 7 | 9 | −2 | 4 |
|   |   |   | $\Sigma D^2 =$ | 18 |

In the numerator, 6 times 18 equals 108. In the denominator, $81 - 1$ is 80, and 9 times 80 is 720. Now we have

$$r_s = 1 - \frac{108}{720}$$

After dividing, we have

$$r_s = 1 - .15$$

Subtracting yields

$$r_s = +.85$$

Thus, on a scale of 0 to $\pm 1.0$, the rankings form a linear relationship to the extent of $r_s = +.85$. This tells us that a child receiving a particular ranking from one observer tended to receive close to the same ranking from the other observer.

Notice that a negative $r_s$ would indicate that the observers did not agree, because low ranks by one observer would tend to be paired with high ranks by the other observer, and vice versa.

**Tied ranks**   A problem arises with ranked data when we have tied ranks. A **tied rank** occurs when two subjects receive the same rank-order score on the same variable. For example, say that Observer B assigned two children the rank of 1. We must resolve such ties before computing $r_s$.

We resolve tied ranks using the following logic: if the two children had not tied for first, then one of them would be 1 and one would be 2, using up the ranks of 1 and 2. *To resolve any tie, we assign the mean of the ranks that would have been used had there not been a tie.* The mean of 1 and 2 is 1.5, so we assign each of the two children the score of 1.5. This approach is illustrated in Table 7.4. In a sense, we have now used up 1 and 2, so we assign the next-most-aggressive child the rank of 3, and so on. Any subsequent ties are resolved in the same way.

Once we have resolved all ties in the $X$ and $Y$ ranks, we compute $r_s$, using the new ranks and the above formula.

## The Point-Biserial Correlation Coefficient

Sometimes we want to correlate the scores from a continuous, interval or ratio variable with the scores from a dichotomous variable (which has only two categories). The **point-biserial correlation coefficient** describes the linear relationship between the scores from one continuous variable and one dichotomous

**TABLE 7.4**  Sample Data with Tied Ranks

| Subject | Observer A: X | Observer B: Y | To resolve ties | New Y |
|---------|--------------|---------------|-----------------|-------|
| 1 | 4 | 1⎫ | Tie uses up ranks | ⎧1.5 |
| 2 | 3 | 1⎭ | of 1 and 2 | ⎩1.5 |
| 3 | 2 | 2⎬ | Becomes 3rd | {3 |
| 4 | 1 | 3⎬ | Becomes 4th | {4 |
| . | . | . | | . |
| . | . | . | | . |
| . | . | . | | . |

variable. The symbol for the point-biserial correlation coefficient is $r_{pb}$ (the pb stands for point-biserial, and no, no one named Point and Biserial invented this one).

**Computing the point-biserial correlation coefficient**   Here is an example of a study that calls for $r_{pb}$. Say that we wish to correlate the dichotomous variable of gender (male/female) with the interval scores from a personality test. We cannot quantify "male" and "female," so we first arbitrarily assign numbers to represent these categories. We can assign any numbers, but an easy system is to use 1 to indicate male and 2 to indicate female. Think of each number as indicating whether a person scored "male" or "female." Then $r_{pb}$ describes how consistently certain personality test scores are paired with one and only one gender score.

---

THE COMPUTATIONAL FORMULA FOR THE POINT-BISERIAL CORRELATION COEFFICIENT IS

$$r_{pb} = \left( \frac{\overline{Y}_2 - \overline{Y}_1}{S_Y} \right) (\sqrt{pq})$$

---

We always call the dichotomous variable the $X$ variable and the interval or ratio variable the $Y$ variable. Then $\overline{Y}_1$ stands for the mean of the $Y$ scores for one of the two groups of the dichotomous variable. (In our example, $\overline{Y}_1$ will be the mean personality score for males.) The symbol $\overline{Y}_2$ stands for the mean of the $Y$ scores for the other group. In our example, $\overline{Y}_2$ will be the mean personality score for females. The $S_Y$ is the standard deviation of *all* the $Y$ scores. The $p$ stands for the proportion of all subjects in one of the groups of the dichotomous variable, and $q$ stands for the proportion of all subjects in the other group. Each proportion is equal to the number of subjects in that group divided by the total $N$ of the study.

Say that we tested 10 subjects and obtained the scores and scatterplot shown in Figure 7.10. The first thing we must do is compute the standard deviation of $Y$, $S_Y$. Below is the formula for the sample standard deviation, written using $Y$s. We substitute into the formula the data in Figure 7.10:

$$S_Y = \sqrt{\frac{\Sigma Y^2 - \frac{(\Sigma Y)^2}{N}}{N}} = \sqrt{\frac{31344 - \frac{(544)^2}{10}}{10}} = 13.23$$

To compute $r_{pb}$, we see that the first four subjects scored "male," and their mean test score, $\overline{Y}_1$, is 38.5. The remaining six subjects scored "female," and their mean test score, $\overline{Y}_2$, is 65.00. The $S_Y$ for all $Y$ scores is 13.23. We will call $p$ the proportion of subjects who scored "male," so $p$ is 4/10, or .40. We will call $q$ the proportion of subjects scoring "female," which is 6/10, or .60.

Now we put these values into the formula for $r_{pb}$.

$$r_{pb} = \left(\frac{\overline{Y}_2 - \overline{Y}_1}{S_Y}\right)(\sqrt{pq}) = \left(\frac{65.00 - 38.50}{13.23}\right)(\sqrt{(.40)(.60)})$$

When we subtract 38.50 from 65.00, we obtain 26.50, so we have

$$r_{pb} = \left(\frac{26.50}{13.23}\right)(\sqrt{(.40)(.60)})$$

**FIGURE 7.10**   Example Data for Computing $r_{pb}$

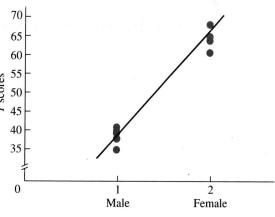

| Subject | Gender: X | Test: Y | |
|---------|-----------|---------|---|
| 1 | 1 | 35 | |
| 2 | 1 | 38 | $\overline{Y}_1 = 38.50$ |
| 3 | 1 | 41 | |
| 4 | 1 | 40 | |
| 5 | 2 | 60 | |
| 6 | 2 | 65 | |
| 7 | 2 | 65 | $\overline{Y}_2 = 65.00$ |
| 8 | 2 | 68 | |
| 9 | 2 | 68 | |
| 10 | 2 | 64 | |
| $N = 10$ | | $\Sigma Y = 544$ | |

We divide 26.50 by 13.23, which is 2.003. Also, .40 times .60 is .24, and the square root of .24 is .489. Thus, we have

$$r_{pb} = 2.003(.489)$$

Multiplying, we find that

$$r_{pb} = +.979$$

Thus, with rounding, our $r_{pb}$ is $+.98$. We interpret this statistic as indicating that, on a scale of 0.0 to $\pm1.0$, one or close to one test score is very consistently associated with each gender score.

It is important to recognize that in this example the dichotomous variable is a qualitative variable, so the arbitrary scores of 1 and 2 do not reflect an amount of the gender variable. Our $r_{pb}$ is positive only because we arbitrarily assigned a 1 to males and a 2 to females. Had we assigned females a 1 and males a 2, their locations on the $X$ axis of the scatterplot would be reversed, and we would have a negative relationship. Similarly, in the formula is $\overline{Y}_2 - \overline{Y}_1$, so above we had $65.00 - 38.50$. Had we chosen to call the female mean $\overline{Y}_1$ and the male mean $\overline{Y}_2$, we would have had $38.50 - 65.00$, which would have resulted in a negative $r_{pb}$ of $-.98$. Thus, for any qualitative variable, the value of $r_{pb}$ describes the strength of the relationship, but whether it is positive or negative depends on how we have arbitrarily arranged the data.

## The Restriction of Range Problem

In collecting scores for a correlation, it is important to avoid the restriction of range problem. **Restriction of range** arises when the range between the lowest and highest scores on one or both variables is too small, or too restricted.

Recall that the correlation coefficient reflects the spread in $Y$ at each $X$ *relative* to the overall spread in all $Y$s. Look at Figure 7.11. When we have the full range of $X$ scores, the spread in the $Y$ scores at each $X$ is small relative to the overall variability in $Y$. The data form a narrow ellipse that hugs the regression line. Therefore, $r$ will be relatively large, and we will conclude that there is a strong relationship.

If, however, we restrict the range of the $X$ scores by collecting scores only between score A and score B, we will have just the shaded part of the scatterplot in Figure 7.11. Now the spread in $Y$s at each $X$ will be large relative to the overall spread in all $Y$s in the shaded area. For this reason, if we calculate a correlation coefficient using only the data in the shaded portion, it will be relatively small and we will conclude that there is a weak relationship. However, this conclusion will be erroneous in the sense that if we did not restrict the range, we would find a much stronger relationship. Thus, restriction of range

**FIGURE 7.11**   Scatterplot Showing Restriction of Range in *X* Scores

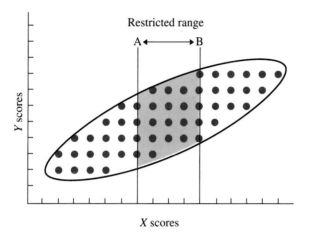

leads to an erroneous *underestimate* of the degree of association between two variables. (Since either variable can be called the *X* or *Y* variable, restricting the range of *Y* has the same effect.)

How might we avoid restricting the range when collecting data? Generally, restriction of range occurs when researchers are too selective in obtaining scores or subjects. Thus, if we are interested in the relationship between subjects' high school grade averages and their subsequent salaries, we should not restrict the range of grades by including only honor students: we should measure the entire range of grades. Or, if we are correlating personality types and degree of emotional problems, we should not restrict our study to only college students. People with severe emotional problems tend not to be admitted to or remain in college, so use of a college sample eliminates their scores and thus restricts the range. Instead, we should include the full range of subjects from the general population. In all cases, if we measure a wide range of scores on both variables, we have a more accurate description of the relationship.

## CORRELATIONS IN THE POPULATION

As we have seen in previous chapters, ultimately we want to use our sample to describe the population we would find if we could measure it. Here we want to use our sample correlation coefficient to estimate the corresponding population correlation coefficient we would obtain if we could correlate the $X$ and $Y$ scores of everyone in the population.

The symbol for a population correlation coefficient is $\rho$. This is the Greek letter rho (the Greek r). Technically $\rho$ is the symbol for the population correlation coefficient when the Pearson $r$ is used. Thus, we compute $r$ for a random sample, which gives us an estimate of the value of $\rho$. If our data involve ranked scores, then we compute $r_s$ and have an estimate of the population coefficient symbolized by $\rho_s$. If our data involve one continuous variable and one dichotomous variable, we compute $r_{pb}$ to estimate $\rho_{pb}$. Remember that before we can estimate any population parameter with confidence, we *must* determine whether the sample is representative. (In Chapter 11 we will discuss the inferential statistical procedures used with correlation coefficients.) Once we have decided that a sample is representative, we interpret the population correlation coefficient the same way we interpret the sample correlation coefficient. Thus, $\rho$ stands for a number between 0.0 and $\pm 1.0$, indicating either a positive or a negative linear relationship in the population. The larger the absolute value of $\rho$, the stronger the relationship: the greater the extent to which one and only one value of $Y$ is associated with each $X$ and the more closely the scatterplot for the population hugs the regression line. We interpret $\rho_s$ and $\rho_{pb}$ in the same manner.

### *FINALLY*

In our discussion of the Spearman rank-order correlation coefficient, we determined how well our observers agreed in their rankings of aggressiveness in children. In psychological research, using any type of correlation for this purpose is known as determining "inter-rater reliability." The term *reliability* means consistency. As we have seen, a positive correlation coefficient indicates the degree to which $X$ and $Y$ scores are consistently paired. Thus, we often determine reliability by demonstrating that there is a relatively large positive correlation. For example, a test is reliable if the subjects' scores we measured yesterday correlate positively with the same subjects' scores we obtain today: low scores today are consistently paired with low scores yesterday, and high scores today are consistently paired with high scores yesterday. (Note that this does not mean the test is "valid" and measures what it is supposed to measure. It just means that whatever the test measures, it measures consistently.) Although an in-depth discussion of reliability is beyond the scope of this text, remember that when researchers describe a measurement as reliable, they mean that the measurement is consistent and typically that they have examined scores in a way that produced a high positive correlation.

## CHAPTER SUMMARY

*1.* A *relationship* exists when the scores on one variable change consistently as the scores on another variable change, so that one value of $Y$ tends to be associated with one value of $X$. No relationship is present when, as the $X$ scores change, the $Y$ scores do not form a consistent pattern of change.

*2.* There are three types of relationships. In a *positive linear relationship,* as the $X$ scores increase, the $Y$ scores tend to increase. In a *negative linear relationship,* as the $X$ scores increase, the $Y$ scores tend to decrease. In a *nonlinear,* or *curvilinear, relationship,* as the $X$ scores increase, the $Y$ scores do not only increase or only decrease.

*3.* A *scatterplot* is a graph that shows the relative location of each pair of $X$-$Y$ scores in the data.

*4.* We summarize a relationship and its resulting scatterplot by drawing a best-fitting line called the *regression line.*

*5.* The shape and orientation of the scatterplot and regression line correspond to the type of relationship. Circular or elliptical scatterplots that produce horizontal regression lines indicate no relationship. Sloped elliptical scatterplots with regression lines oriented so that as $X$ increases, $Y$ increases indicate a positive linear relationship. Sloped elliptical scatterplots with regression lines oriented so that as $X$ increases, $Y$ decreases indicate a negative linear relationship. Scatterplots producing curved regression lines indicate curvilinear relationships.

*6.* The existence of a relationship does not necessarily mean that there is a causal relationship between the two variables. A relationship can occur when neither variable is the causal variable. Therefore, we never infer causality based solely on a correlation.

*7.* A *correlation coefficient* is a statistic that describes two important characteristics of a relationship: the *type* of relationship and the *strength* of the relationship.

*8.* A *positive correlation coefficient* indicates that a positive linear relationship is present. A *negative correlation coefficient* indicates that a negative relationship is present.

*9.* The absolute value of the coefficient may be as small as 0.0 (indicating no linear relationship) or as large as 1.0 (indicating a perfect linear relationship). The absolute value of the correlation coefficient is a measure of the *strength of the relationship,* which is the extent to which one value of $Y$ is consistently paired with one and only one value of $X$. When the coefficient equals $\pm 1.0$, one value of $Y$ is paired with one and only one value of $X$, and we can perfectly predict a subject's $Y$ score if we know the subject's $X$ score. The smaller the absolute value of the coefficient, the greater the variability, or spread, in the $Y$s associated with a particular value of $X$, and the less accurately we can predict $Y$ scores.

10. The absolute value of the coefficient also tells us the extent to which the scatterplot hugs the regression line. A large value indicates a relatively narrow scatterplot, with most data points relatively close to the regression line. A small value indicates a relatively wide scatterplot, with many data points more distant from the regression line.

11. The *Pearson correlation coefficient, r,* describes the linear relationship between two interval or ratio variables.

12. The *Spearman rank-order correlation coefficient, $r_s$,* describes the linear relationship between two variables that have been measured using ranked scores.

13. The *point-biserial correlation coefficient, $r_{pb}$,* describes the linear relationship between scores from one continuous interval or ratio variable and one dichotomous variable.

14. The *restriction of range problem* occurs when the range of scores collected on one or both variables is too restricted. The resulting correlation coefficient erroneously underestimates the strength of the relationship that would be found if the range were not restricted.

15. Ultimately, after performing the appropriate inferential statistical procedures, we use a sample correlation coefficient to estimate the corresponding population correlation coefficient, symbolized by the Greek letter rho. We use $r$ to estimate $\rho$, $r_s$ to estimate $\rho_s$, and $r_{pb}$ to estimate $\rho_{pb}$.

## USING THE COMPUTER

From the Main Menu of the computer program, routine **4,** entitled "Correlation and Regression," computes the various correlation coefficients discussed in this chapter. After you enter **4,** the program will ask you to select either the Pearson, the Spearman, or the point-biserial correlation. For each, the program will also create a scatterplot of your data. Be forewarned that the routine also performs and displays descriptive statistics discussed in the next chapter, as well as providing information used in the inferential procedures discussed in Chapter 11.

## PRACTICE PROBLEMS

(Answers are provided for odd-numbered problems.)

1. Why can't we conclude that we have demonstrated a causal relationship based on correlational research?
2. What is a scatterplot?
3. What two characteristics of a linear relationship are described by a correlation coefficient?
4. *a.* Define a positive linear relationship.
   *b.* Define a negative linear relationship.
   *c.* Define a curvilinear relationship.
5. As the value of *r* approaches ±1.0, what does it indicate about the following?
   *a.* the shape of the scatterplot
   *b.* the variability of the *Y* scores at each *X*
   *c.* the closeness of *Y* scores to the regression line
   *d.* the accuracy with which we can predict *Y* if *X* is known
6. What does a correlation coefficient equal to 0.0 indicate about the four characteristics in question 5?
7. For each of the following pairs of variables, give the symbol for the correlation coefficient you should compute.
   *a.* SAT scores and IQ scores
   *b.* tea taste rankings by experts and tea test rankings by novices
   *c.* presence or absence of head injury and scores on a vocabulary test
   *d.* finishing position in a race and amount of liquid consumed during the race
8. Why can't one obtain a correlation coefficient greater than ±1.0?
9. What is the restriction of range problem?
10. *a.* What does $\rho$ stand for?
    *b.* How is the value of $\rho$ determined?
    *c.* What does $\rho$ tell you?
11. *a.* Compute *r* for the data below.

| Subject | X | Y |
|---------|-----|---|
| 1       | 9   | 3 |
| 2       | 8   | 2 |
| 3       | 4   | 8 |
| 4       | 6   | 5 |
| 5       | 7   | 4 |
| 6       | 10  | 2 |
| 7       | 5   | 7 |

*b.* What do you conclude about this relationship?

12. The data below reflect whether or not a subject is a college graduate (Y or N) and the score he or she obtained on a life-satisfaction test. To what extent is there a positive or negative linear relationship here?

| Subject | X | Y |
|---------|---|----|
| 1 | Y | 8 |
| 2 | Y | 7 |
| 3 | Y | 12 |
| 4 | Y | 6 |
| 5 | Y | 10 |
| 6 | N | 2 |
| 7 | N | 8 |
| 8 | N | 6 |
| 9 | N | 1 |
| 10 | N | 9 |

13. *a.* Resolve the tied ranks in the ordinal data below.

| Subject | X | Y |
|---------|---|---|
| 1 | 2 | 3 |
| 2 | 9 | 7 |
| 3 | 1 | 2 |
| 4 | 5 | 7 |
| 5 | 3 | 1 |
| 6 | 7 | 8 |
| 7 | 4 | 4 |
| 8 | 6 | 5 |
| 9 | 8 | 6 |

*b.* Compute $r_s$ for these data.

*c.* What do you conclude about the extent to which the rankings form a linear relationship?

14. What do you conclude about the extent to which there is a linear relationship in the following ratio data?

| Subject | X | Y |
|---------|---|---|
| 1 | 2 | 4 |
| 2 | 1 | 7 |
| 3 | 2 | 6 |
| 4 | 3 | 9 |
| 5 | 4 | 6 |
| 6 | 4 | 8 |
| 7 | 7 | 7 |
| 8 | 7 | 10 |
| 9 | 8 | 11 |

15. *a.* Compute $r_{pb}$ for the data below.

| Subject | X | Y |
|---------|---|---|
| 1 | 0 | 4 |
| 2 | 0 | 6 |
| 3 | 0 | 11 |
| 4 | 0 | 5 |
| 5 | 1 | 8 |
| 6 | 1 | 5 |
| 7 | 1 | 8 |
| 8 | 1 | 11 |
| 9 | 1 | 7 |
| 10 | 1 | 4 |

*b.* What do you conclude about the linear relationship in these data?

16. What do you conclude about the linear relationship in the ordinal data below?

| Subject | X | Y |
|---------|---|---|
| 1 | 1 | 10 |
| 2 | 2 | 8 |
| 3 | 5 | 6 |
| 4 | 4 | 7 |
| 5 | 9 | 5 |
| 6 | 7 | 3 |
| 7 | 3 | 9 |
| 8 | 6 | 4 |
| 9 | 8 | 1 |
| 10 | 10 | 2 |

## SUMMARY OF FORMULAS

1. *The computational formula for the Pearson correlation coefficient is*

$$r = \frac{N(\Sigma XY) - (\Sigma X)(\Sigma Y)}{\sqrt{[N(\Sigma X^2) - (\Sigma X)^2][N(\Sigma Y^2) - (\Sigma Y)^2]}}$$

where $X$ and $Y$ stand for the scores on the $X$ and $Y$ variables and $N$ is the number of pairs in the sample.

2. *The computational formula for the Spearman rank-order correlation coefficient is*

$$r_s = 1 - \frac{6(\Sigma D^2)}{N(N^2 - 1)}$$

where $N$ is the number of pairs of ranks and $D$ is the difference between the two ranks in each pair.

3. *The computational formula for the point-biserial correlation coefficient is*

$$r_{pb} = \left(\frac{\overline{Y}_2 - \overline{Y}_1}{S_Y}\right)(\sqrt{pq})$$

where

$\overline{Y}_1$ is the mean of the scores on the continuous variable for one group of the dichotomous variable,

$\overline{Y}_2$ is the mean of the scores on the continuous variable for the other group of the dichotomous variable,

$S_Y$ is the standard deviation of all the continuous $Y$ scores,

$p$ is the proportion of all subjects in the sample in one dichotomous group and $q$ is the proportion of all subjects in the sample in the other dichotomous group. Each is found by dividing the number of subjects in the group by $N$, the total number of $X$-$Y$ pairs in the study.

# Linear Regression and Predicting Variability

As we saw in the previous chapter, the best-fitting summary line drawn through a scatterplot is called the regression line. The stronger the relationship, the more consistently certain $Y$ scores are associated with each $X$ score, so the more the $Y$ scores tend to hug the regression line. If we know an individual's $X$ score and the relationship between $X$ and $Y$, we can predict the individual's $Y$ score. As we shall see in this chapter, it is through the regression line that we predict $Y$ scores from the corresponding $X$ scores. In the following sections we will first examine the logic behind the regression line and then discuss how to predict scores using a regression line. Finally, we will look at ways of measuring the amount of error in our predictions.

## MORE STATISTICAL NOTATION

In this chapter we will discuss the variance and standard deviation of the $Y$ scores, or $S_Y^2$ and $S_Y$. Be sure that you understand that we compute the variance and standard deviation of the $Y$ scores in the same ways that we compute these values for the $X$ scores. This is also a good time to review three important concepts from Chapter 5:

1. In measuring variability, we think of the variance and standard deviation as ways of indicating the average difference between the individual scores and the mean.

2. When we predict that each subject's score is the mean score, the error in our predictions is the difference between the mean score and the

actual scores, so variance and standard deviation are measures of the "average" error in our predictions.

3. Using a relationship to predict subjects' Y scores allows us to reduce this error, or to account for the variance in the scores.

## UNDERSTANDING LINEAR REGRESSION

**Linear regression** is the procedure for describing the best-fitting straight line that summarizes a linear relationship. The procedures discussed here go hand in hand with the Pearson correlation: $r$ is the statistic that summarizes a relationship, and the regression line is the line that summarizes a scatterplot of the relationship. However, we do not always create the regression line. We first compute $r$ to determine whether a relationship exists. If $r = 0.0$, then there is no linear relationship present and regression techniques are unnecessary. All that the regression line would tell us is "Yup, there really is no relationship here." If the correlation coefficient is not 0.0, then we produce the linear regression line to further summarize the relationship.

### Summarizing the Scatterplot Using the Regression Line

An easy way to understand a regression line is to compare it to a line graph. In Chapter 4 we created a line graph by computing the mean of the $Y$ scores at each $X$. After graphing each $X$-$\overline{Y}$ data point, we connected the mean scores using straight lines. The left-hand scatterplot in Figure 8.1 shows the line graph of a study in which subjects produced $Y$ scores at one of four values of $X$. We summarize the data by drawing a straight line from the $\overline{Y}$ at $X_1$ to the $\overline{Y}$ at $X_2$, another line from the $\overline{Y}$ at $X_2$ to the $\overline{Y}$ at $X_3$, and a third line from the $\overline{Y}$ at $X_3$ to the $\overline{Y}$ at $X_4$. To read the graph, we travel vertically from any $X$ until we intercept the line, and then we travel horizontally until we intercept the $Y$ axis. For example, as the arrows indicate, the mean of $Y$ at $X_3$ is 3.0. Because this mean is the central score, it is the one score that best represents those scores. In essence, those subjects scoring at $X_3$ also scored around a $Y$ of 3.0, so a score of 3.0 is our best single description of their scores. Further, if we know that a subject scored at $X_3$, then the mean $Y$ score for that group (3.0) is our best prediction of that subject's $Y$ score.

Instead of creating a line graph, we can summarize the data with the regression line shown in the right-hand graph in Figure 8.1. Think of a regression line as a straightened-out version of the line graph. The regression line is drawn so that it comes as close as possible to connecting the mean of $Y$ at each $X$ and yet still produces one straight line. All of the means may not fall in a perfectly straight line, but across the entire relationship, the distance that

**FIGURE 8.1**  Comparison of a Line Graph and a Regression Line

*Each data point is formed by a subject's X-Y pair. Each asterisk (∗) indicates the mean Y score at an X.*

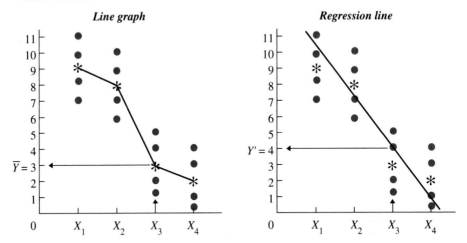

some means are above the line will average out with the distance that other means are below the line. Thus, the regression line is the best-fitting line, because "on average" it passes through the center of the various $Y$ means. Since each $Y$ mean is located in the center of those $Y$ scores, by passing through the center of the $Y$ means, the regression line passes through the center of the $Y$ scores. Thus, the **linear regression line** may be defined as the straight line that summarizes the scatterplot of a linear relationship by, on average, passing through the center of all $Y$ scores.

We read the regression line by traveling vertically from any $X$ until we intercept the regression line. Then we travel horizontally until we intercept the $Y$ axis. As the arrows on the right-hand graph of Figure 8.1 indicate, the value of $Y$ at $X_3$ is now 4. The symbol for this value is $Y'$, pronounced "$Y$ prime." Like the means of a line graph, each $Y'$ is a summary of the $Y$ scores for that $X$. However, the advantage of the regression line is that each $Y'$ summarizes the scores based on the linear relationship across *all X-Y pairs* in the data. Thus, considering the entire linear relationship in Figure 8.1, we find that subjects at $X_3$ scored around 4.0, so a score of 4.0 is our best single description of their scores. Further, if we know that a subject scored at $X_3$, then the $Y'$ of 4.0 is our best prediction of that subject's $Y$ score. Thus, the symbol $Y'$ stands for a **predicted Y score.** In statistics, $Y'$ is our best description and prediction of the $Y$ scores at a particular $X$, based on the linear relationship that is summarized by the regression line.

It is important to recognize that the $Y'$ for the subjects who score at any value of $X$ is the value of $Y$ falling *on* the regression line. In essence, the regression line is composed of the different values of $Y'$ that occur with the different values of $X$. The value of $Y'$ at each $X$ is the value of $Y$ that would occur if all the $Y$s at an $X$ were the same value *and* if, overall, the data formed a perfect linear relationship.

## Predicting Scores Using the Regression Line

Why are we interested in predicting $Y$ scores? After all, we have the $Y$ score of every subject in the sample right in front of us. The answer is that regression techniques are a primary statistical device for predicting *unknown* scores in a linear relationship. To do this, we first establish the relationship in a sample by computing the correlation. Then, by performing the inferential procedures for $r$ (described in Chapter 11), we determine whether the relationship in the sample represents a relationship in the population. If the correlation "passes" the inferential test, we use the regression line to determine the $Y'$ for each $X$. Then we can measure the $X$ scores of other subjects who are not in our sample. By using the relationship established in our sample, we can predict these other subjects' $Y$ scores; $Y'$ is our best prediction of their $Y$ scores. Thus, the importance of linear regression is that it allows us to predict subjects' unknown $Y$ scores if we know their $X$ scores on a correlated variable.

The reason students must take the Scholastic Aptitude Test (SAT) to be admitted to college is that researchers have established that SAT scores are positively correlated with college grades: to a certain extent, the higher the SAT score, the higher the college grades. Therefore, by using the SAT scores of students who are about to enter college, we can predict their future college performance. Applying regression techniques, we use a student's $X$ score on the SAT to obtain a predicted $Y'$ of the student's college grade average. If the predicted grades are too low, then the student is not admitted to the college.

The emphasis on prediction in correlation and regression brings two important terms into play. In the discussions of regression procedures in this text, we will use the $X$ variable to predict scores on the $Y$ variable. (There are procedures out there for predicting $X$ scores from $Y$.) In statistical lingo, when the $X$ variable is used to predict unknown scores, then $X$ is called the **predictor variable** (as in $X$ does the predicting). When the unknown scores being predicted are on the $Y$ variable, then $Y$ is called the **criterion variable.** In our SAT example, SAT scores are the predictor variable, and college grade average is the criterion variable. (To remember the word "criterion," remember that your predicted grades must pass a certain criterion for you to be admitted to the college.)

We base our predictions of $Y$ on the relationship between the pairs of $X$ and $Y$ scores found in our sample. Thus, after we determine that there is a correlation in the sample, the next step is to determine the regression line for the sample. To do this, we compute the linear regression equation.

## THE LINEAR REGRESSION EQUATION

To draw the regression line that summarizes a particular relationship, we don't simply eyeball the scatterplot and sketch in something that looks good. Instead, we use the linear regression equation. This is a mathematical equation for computing the value of $Y'$ at each $X$. When we plot the data points formed by the $X$-$Y'$ pairs, they all fall in a perfectly straight line. Then when we draw a line connecting the data points, we have the regression line that summarizes the scatterplot and the underlying relationship. Thus, the **linear regression equation** is an equation that, by describing the value of $Y'$ at each $X$, defines the straight line that summarizes a linear relationship. The regression equation describes two characteristics of the regression line: its slope and its $Y$-intercept.

The **slope of a line** is a number that indicates how slanted the line is and the direction in which it slants. In algebra, the slope is defined as the ratio of the average change in $Y$ scores to the average change in $X$ scores. Figure 8.2 shows examples of regression lines having different slopes. When there is no relationship, the regression line is horizontal, such as line A. Then the slope of the line is zero. A positive linear relationship yields a regression line such as line B or C; each of these has a slope that is a positive number. Because line

**FIGURE 8.2** Regression Lines Having Different Slopes and Y-Intercepts

*Line A indicates no relationship, lines B and C indicate positive relationships having different slopes and Y-intercepts, and line D indicates a negative relationship.*

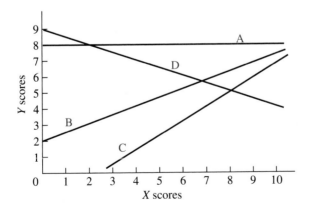

C is steeper, its slope is a larger positive number. A negative linear relationship yields a regression line such as line D, with a slope that is a negative number.

The **Y-intercept of a line** is the value of $Y$ at the point where the regression line intercepts, or crosses, the $Y$ axis. At the $Y$ axis, the value of $X$ is 0, so the $Y$-intercept is the value of $Y'$ when $X$ equals 0. In Figure 8.2 above, line B intercepts the $Y$ axis at $+2$, so its $Y$-intercept is $+2$. If we extended line C, it would intercept the $Y$ axis at a point below the $X$ axis, so its $Y$-intercept is a negative $Y$ score. Because line D reflects a negative relationship, its $Y$-intercept is the relatively high $Y$ score of 9. Finally, line A exhibits no relationship, and its $Y$-intercept equals $+8$. Notice that here the value of $Y'$ for any value of $X$ is always $+8$. *When there is no relationship, the slope of the regression line is zero, and every $Y'$ equals the Y-intercept.*

The regression equation works in the following manner. The slope and $Y$-intercept of a particular line determine the orientation and location of the line. In turn, the orientation and location of the line determine the value of $Y'$ at each $X$. For example, in Figure 8.2, at $X = 4$, each of the four regression lines gives a different value of $Y'$. Thus, when we know the slope and $Y$-intercept, we can compute the $Y'$ at each $X$.

The symbol for the slope of the regression line is $b$. The symbol for the $Y$-intercept is $a$.

*THE LINEAR REGRESSION EQUATION IS*

$$Y' = bX + a$$

This formula says that to find the value of $Y'$ for a given $X$, multiply the slope ($b$) times $X$ and then add the $Y$-intercept ($a$).

Suppose that a researcher has developed a paper-and-pencil test to identify people who will be productive widget-makers. To find out whether test scores help to predict "widgetability," the researcher first determines whether subjects' test scores are correlated with their widget-making ability. The researcher gives the test to an unrealistically small $N$ of 11 subjects and then measures the numbers of widgets they make in an hour. Figure 8.3 shows the resulting scatterplot, with test scores as the predictor ($X$) variable. The raw scores are also listed, arranged for computing $r$.

The first step is to find $r$:

$$r = \frac{N(\Sigma XY) - (\Sigma X)(\Sigma Y)}{\sqrt{[N(\Sigma X^2) - (\Sigma X)^2][N(\Sigma Y^2) - (\Sigma Y)^2]}}$$

$$r = \frac{11(171) - (29)(58)}{\sqrt{[11(89) - 841][11(354) - 3364]}}$$

**FIGURE 8.3**  Scatterplot and Data for Widgetability Study

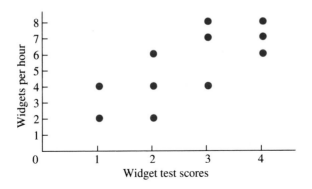

| Subject | Widget test score: X | Widgets per hour: Y | XY |
|---------|---------------------|---------------------|-----|
| 1 | 1 | 2 | 2 |
| 2 | 1 | 4 | 4 |
| 3 | 2 | 4 | 8 |
| 4 | 2 | 6 | 12 |
| 5 | 2 | 2 | 4 |
| 6 | 3 | 4 | 12 |
| 7 | 3 | 7 | 21 |
| 8 | 3 | 8 | 24 |
| 9 | 4 | 6 | 24 |
| 10 | 4 | 8 | 32 |
| 11 | 4 | 7 | 28 |
| $N = 11$ | $\Sigma X = 29$ | $\Sigma Y = 58$ | $\Sigma XY = 171$ |
| | $\Sigma X^2 = 89$ | $\Sigma Y^2 = 354$ | |
| | $(\Sigma X)^2 = 841$ | $(\Sigma Y)^2 = 3364$ | |
| | $\overline{X} = 29/11 = 2.64$ | $\overline{Y} = 58/11 = 5.27$ | |

The result is $r = +.736$, which rounds to $r = +.74$. (What did you get?) Thus, as confirmed by our scatterplot, we have a positive linear relationship, which, with $r = +.74$, is reasonably strong.

To summarize this relationship so that we can predict widget-making scores, we compute the linear regression equation. To do that, we compute the slope and the $Y$-intercept. (In statistical language, the following formulas produce a regression line using the *least-squares method,* a term we shall explain in a later section.)

Compute the slope first.

## Computing the Slope

*THE FORMULA FOR THE SLOPE OF THE LINEAR REGRESSION LINE IS*

$$b = \frac{N(\Sigma XY) - (\Sigma X)(\Sigma Y)}{N(\Sigma X^2) - (\Sigma X)^2}$$

$N$ is the number of pairs of scores in the sample, and $X$ and $Y$ are the scores in the sample. This is not a difficult formula, because we typically compute the Pearson $r$ first. The numerator of the formula for $b$ is the same as the numerator of the formula for $r$, and the denominator of the formula for $b$ is the left-hand quantity in the denominator of the formula for $r$.

For our widget study, we substitute the appropriate values from our computations of $r$ into the formula for $b$, and we have

$$b = \frac{N(\Sigma XY) - (\Sigma X)(\Sigma Y)}{N(\Sigma X^2) - (\Sigma X)^2} = \frac{11(171) - (29)(58)}{11(89) - 841}$$

In the numerator, 11 times 171 is 1881, and 29 times 58 is 1682. Subtracting 1682 from 1881 gives 199. Rewriting the formula, we have

$$b = \frac{199}{11(89) - 841}$$

In the denominator, 11 times 89 is 979. Subtracting 841 from 979 gives 138, so we have

$$b = \frac{199}{138} = +1.44$$

Thus, the slope of the regression line for our widgetability data is $b = +1.44$. This positive slope indicates a positive relationship. (As a double check, note that the data do form a positive relationship, with $r = +.74$.) Had the relationship been negative, the formula would have produced a negative number for the slope.

We are not finished yet! Now we compute $a$, the $Y$-intercept.

## Computing the Y-Intercept

> *THE FORMULA FOR THE Y-INTERCEPT OF THE LINEAR REGRESSION EQUATION IS*
>
> $$a = \overline{Y} - (b)(\overline{X})$$

First we multiply the mean of all $X$ scores, $\overline{X}$, times the slope of the regression line, $b$. (See why we compute $b$ first?) Then we subtract that quantity from the mean of all $Y$ scores, $\overline{Y}$.

For our widgetability data in Figure 8.3, $\overline{Y}$ is 5.27, $\overline{X}$ is 2.64, and $b$ is $+1.44$. Filling in the above formula for $a$, we have

$$a = 5.27 - (+1.44)(2.64)$$

Multiplying $+1.44$ times 2.64 gives $+3.80$. Rewriting again, we have

$$a = 5.27 - (+3.80) = +1.47$$

Thus, the $Y$-intercept of the regression line for our widgetability study is $a = +1.47$: when $X$ equals 0, $Y'$ equals $+1.47$.

We are still not finished!

## Describing the Linear Regression Equation

Once we have computed the $Y$-intercept and the slope, we rewrite the regression equation, substituting our computed values for $a$ and $b$. Thus,

$$Y' = +1.44X + 1.47$$

This is the finished regression equation that describes the linear regression line for the relationship between widget test scores and widgets-per-hour scores.

Putting all of this together, we summarize the preceding computations in Table 8.1.

Our final step is to plot the regression line.

## Plotting the Regression Line

To plot the regression line, we must have some pairs of $X$ and $Y'$ scores to use as data points. Therefore, we choose some values of $X$, insert each in the finished regression equation, and calculate the value of $Y'$ for that $X$. Actually,

**TABLE 8.1**   Summary of Computations for the Linear Regression Equation

1. Compute $r$.
2. Compute the slope, $b$, where $b = \dfrac{N(\Sigma XY) - (\Sigma X)(\Sigma Y)}{N(\Sigma X^2) - (\Sigma X)^2}$.
3. Compute the $Y$-intercept, $a$, where $a = \overline{Y} - (b)(\overline{X})$.
4. Substitute the values of $a$ and $b$ into the formula for the regression equation
$$Y' = (b)(X) + a$$

we need only two data points to draw a straight line: an $X$-$Y'$ pair where $X$ is low and an $X$-$Y'$ pair where $X$ is high. (An easy low $X$ to use is $X = 0$: when $X$ equals 0, $Y'$ equals the $Y$-intercept, $a$.)

To see how the calculations work, we will compute $Y'$ for all of the $X$ scores in our widget study given in Figure 8.3. We begin with the finished regression equation:

$$Y' = +1.44X + 1.47$$

First we find $Y'$ for $X = 1$. Substituting 1 for $X$, we have

$$Y' = +1.44(1) + 1.47$$

Multiplying 1 times $+1.44$, and adding 1.44 to 1.47 yields a final value of $Y' = 2.91$. Thus, we predict that anyone scoring 1 on the widget test will make 2.91 widgets per hour. Using the same procedure, we obtain the values of $Y'$ for the remaining $X$ scores of 2, 3, and 4. These are shown in Figure 8.4.

To graph the regression line, we simply plot the data points for the $X$-$Y'$ pairs and draw the line. (Note that, as shown, we typically do not include the scatterplot, nor do we draw the regression line through the $Y$-intercept.)

Now we are finished. (Really.)

## Using the Regression Equation to Predict Y Scores

When we compute $Y'$ for a particular $X$, we are computing the predicted $Y$ score for all subjects who have that $X$ score. Above, for example, we found that those subjects scoring an $X$ of 1 had a predicted $Y'$ of 2.91. Therefore, in essence, we predict that anyone scoring an $X$ of 1 will have a $Y'$ of around 2.91. Further, we can compute $Y'$ for any value of $X$, even one that was not obtained in the original sample data. On the regression line in Figure 8.4, we can travel vertically above any value of $X$ to the line and then travel horizontally to the $Y$ axis to find $Y'$. Likewise, we can use any value of $X$ in our regression equation. No subject in our original sample obtained a widget test score of 1.5. Yet, inserting an $X$ of 1.5 into the regression equation yields a $Y'$ of 3.63.

**FIGURE 8.4** Regression Line for Widgetability Study

| Widget test scores: X | Predicted widgets per hour: Y |
|---|---|
| 1 | 2.91 |
| 2 | 4.35 |
| 3 | 5.79 |
| 4 | 7.23 |

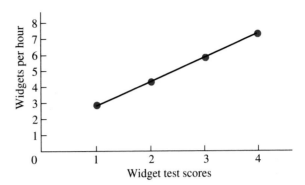

Thus, we predict that any individual who scores an $X$ of 1.5 on our test will have a $Y$ score of 3.63 widgets per hour.

Of course, as you know by now, any prediction we make may be wrong by some amount. Therefore, whenever we use the regression equation to predict $Y$ scores, we also want to describe the amount of error in our predictions. The remaining sections of this chapter are devoted to describing errors in prediction. This topic is important for two reasons. First, a complete description of our data includes the descriptive statistics that summarize the amount of error we have when we use our linear regression equation to predict $Y$ scores. Second, understanding how we describe the amount of error in predictions based on the regression equation sets the stage for understanding how we describe the amount of error in predictions based on other statistical procedures. (In other words, the following topics will not go away.)

## ERROR WHEN THE LINEAR REGRESSION EQUATION IS USED TO PREDICT SCORES

We describe the amount of error in our predictions by describing how well each $Y'$ predicts the actual $Y$ scores in our sample. In this imperfect world, our predictions for some subjects will be close to their actual $Y$ scores and contain little error, while our predictions for other subjects may contain considerably more error. To summarize the error across the entire relationship, we compute something like the average error between all of the actual $Y$ scores and the corresponding $Y'$ scores.

The amount of error in any single prediction is the amount that a subject's actual score differs, or deviates, from the corresponding $Y'$: in symbols this is

$(Y - Y')$. To find the average error, we will find something like the average of the deviations (yes, here we go again). The first step is to find the deviations for all subjects. We compute $Y'$ for each subject in our data and then subtract each $Y'$ from its corresponding $Y$ score. However, we cannot merely sum these deviations and find the average. Because the $Y'$ scores lie in the center of the $Y$ scores, the sum of the deviations of the $Y$ scores from their $Y'$ scores is always zero (as usual, the positive and negative deviations cancel out). If $\Sigma(Y - Y')$ is always zero, then the average deviation between the $Y$ and $Y'$ scores is always zero also.

To solve this problem, we *square* each deviation. The sum of the squared deviations of $Y - Y'$ is not necessarily zero, so neither is the average squared deviation. (Does this sound familiar?) When we find the average of the squared deviations between the $Y$ and corresponding $Y'$ scores, the answer we obtain is a type of variance. With this variance, we are describing the "average" spread of the actual $Y$ scores around their predicted $Y'$ scores.

## Computing the Variance of the Y Scores Around Y'

The symbol for the variance of a sample of $Y$ scores around $Y'$ is $S_{Y'}^2$. The $S^2$ indicates that we are computing the sample variance or error, and the subscript $Y'$ indicates that it is the error associated with using $Y'$ to predict the $Y$ scores.

THE DEFINITIONAL FORMULA FOR THE VARIANCE OF THE Y SCORES AROUND THEIR CORRESPONDING Y' SCORES IS

$$S_{Y'}^2 = \frac{\Sigma(Y - Y')^2}{N}$$

This formula tells us to subtract each $Y'$ we predict for a subject from his or her corresponding $Y$ score, square each deviation, sum the squared deviations, and finally divide by $N$. The answer we obtain gives us the average squared difference between each $Y$ and the corresponding $Y'$ in our sample. It is one way to measure the amount of error we have when we use $Y'$ to predict $Y$ scores.

Remember our widgetability study? Table 8.2 shows the $X$ and $Y$ scores we obtained, as well as the $Y'$ scores we computed for each $X$ using our regression equation. In the column labeled $Y - Y'$, we subtract each $Y'$ from the corresponding $Y$. In the column labeled $(Y - Y')^2$, we square each difference. Then we sum the squared differences to find $\Sigma(Y - Y')^2$. Here $\Sigma(Y - Y')^2$

**TABLE 8.2**  Widgetability Data with Computed Y' Scores

| Subject | Widget test score: X | Widgets per hour: Y | Predicted widgets: Y' | Y − Y' | (Y − Y')² |
|---------|---------|---------|---------|---------|---------|
| 1 | 1 | 2 | 2.91 | − .91 | .83 |
| 2 | 1 | 4 | 2.91 | 1.09 | 1.19 |
| 3 | 2 | 4 | 4.35 | − .35 | .12 |
| 4 | 2 | 6 | 4.35 | 1.65 | 2.72 |
| 5 | 2 | 2 | 4.35 | − 2.35 | 5.52 |
| 6 | 3 | 4 | 5.79 | − 1.79 | 3.20 |
| 7 | 3 | 7 | 5.79 | 1.21 | 1.46 |
| 8 | 3 | 8 | 5.79 | 2.21 | 4.88 |
| 9 | 4 | 6 | 7.23 | − 1.23 | 1.51 |
| 10 | 4 | 8 | 7.23 | .77 | .59 |
| 11 | 4 | 7 | 7.23 | − .23 | .05 |
| N = 11 | | $\Sigma Y = 58$ | | | $\Sigma(Y - Y')^2 = 22.07$ |
| | | $\Sigma Y^2 = 354$ | | | |
| | | $(\Sigma Y)^2 = 3364$ | | | |

$= 22.07$, and $N = 11$. Filling in the formula for $S_{Y'}^2$, we have

$$S_{Y'}^2 = \frac{\Sigma(Y - Y')}{N} = \frac{22.07}{11}$$

After dividing, we have

$$S_{Y'}^2 = 2.006$$

With rounding,

$$S_{Y'}^2 = 2.01$$

Using the definitional formula for $S_{Y'}^2$ is very time consuming. Luckily, we compute $r$ before we compute $S_{Y'}^2$, and there is a mathematical relationship between the value of $S_{Y'}^2$ in a set of data and the value of $r$. From this relationship we derive a quick computational formula.

*THE COMPUTATIONAL FORMULA FOR THE VARIANCE OF Y' SCORES AROUND Y IS*

$$S_{Y'}^2 = S_Y^2(1 - r^2)$$

This formula says that we first find the variance of the raw $Y$ scores in the data. Then we compute $r$ and square it. Finally, we subtract $r^2$ from 1 and then multiply the result times $S_Y^2$. The answer is $S_{Y'}^2$.

In our widget study, $r$ was $+.736$. Using the data from Table 8.2, we compute $S_Y^2$. to be 4.38. Placing these numbers in the above formula, we have

$$S_{Y'}^2 = 4.38(1 - .736^2)$$

Squaring $+.736$ gives .542, which when subtracted from 1 gives .458. Thus, we have

$$S_{Y'}^2 = 4.38(.458)$$

so

$$S_{Y'}^2 = 2.01$$

Again the average squared difference between the actual $Y$ scores and their corresponding values of $Y'$ is 2.01. This indicates the amount of error that occurs when we use $Y'$ to predict each widgets-per-hour score based on each subject's widget test scores.

> **STAT ALERT**  $S_{Y'}^2$ is a way to describe the average error we have when we predict the actual $Y$ scores using the corresponding $Y'$ scores.

Now we can explain the term *least-squares regression method*. We said that using $Y'$ to predict the $Y$ scores results in a sum of deviations, $\Sigma(Y - Y')$, of zero. Obviously, zero is the minimum that the sum can be. Because the sum of deviations is the minimum we can obtain, the sum of the squared deviations is also the minimum we can obtain. We shorten the term *squared deviations* to *squares*. Then, the least-squares method is the name for a way of computing the regression equation so that the sum of the squares between $Y$ and $Y'$ is the least that it can be. Any other method leads to greater error in our predictions, resulting in a larger sum of squared deviations between $Y$ and $Y'$ and a larger value of $S_{Y'}^2$.

There is a problem with $S_{Y'}^2$, however. The answer we obtain is difficult to interpret, because by squaring the difference between each $Y$ and $Y'$, we obtain an unrealistically large number. (This *must* sound familiar.) To solve this problem, we take the square root of the variance, and the result is a type of standard deviation. To distinguish the standard deviation found in regression from other standard deviations, we call this standard deviation the *standard error of the estimate*.

## Computing the Standard Error of the Estimate

The **standard error of the estimate** is the standard deviation indicating the amount that the actual $Y$ scores in a sample differ from, or are spread out around, their corresponding $Y'$ scores. It is a way of describing the average amount of error we have when we use $Y'$ to predict $Y$ scores. The symbol for the standard error of the estimate is $S_{Y'}$. (Remember, $S$ measures the error in the sample, and $Y'$ is our estimate of a subject's $Y$ score.)

*THE DEFINITIONAL FORMULA FOR THE STANDARD ERROR OF THE ESTIMATE IS*

$$S_{Y'} = \sqrt{\frac{\Sigma(Y - Y')^2}{N}}$$

This is the same formula we used previously for the variance of $Y$ scores around $Y'$, except that here we have added the square root sign. Thus, to compute $S_{Y'}$, we first compute the variance of the scores around $Y'$, or $S_{Y'}^2$, and then we find its square root.

In our widgetability study, we computed the variance of the $Y$ scores around their corresponding $Y'$ scores as $S_{Y'}^2 = 2.01$. Taking the square root of this variance produces

$\quad S_{Y'} = 1.42$

Previously we saw that the shortcut way to compute the variance of $Y$ around $Y'$ was to use the formula

$\quad S_{Y'}^2 = S_Y^2(1 - r^2)$

By taking the square root of each component, we construct the computational formula.

*THE COMPUTATIONAL FORMULA FOR THE STANDARD ERROR OF THE ESTIMATE IS*

$\quad S_{Y'} = S_Y \sqrt{1 - r^2}$

This formula says that after we find the variance of the actual $Y$ scores in the data, we take the square root and find the standard deviation, $S_Y$. Then, after we find the quantity $1 - r^2$, we take the square root and multiply it times $S_Y$. The answer is $S_{Y'}$.

For our widget study, $S_Y^2$ was 4.38, so $S_Y$ is 2.093, and $r$ was $+.736$. Placing these numbers in the above formula, we have

$\quad S_{Y'} = 2.093 \sqrt{1 - .736^2}$

Squaring $+.736$ yields $.542$, which when subtracted from 1 gives $.458$. Then the square root is $.677$. Thus, we have

$$S_{Y'} = 2.093(.677)$$

so again

$$S_{Y'} = 1.42$$

The standard error of the estimate is 1.42. Because the $Y$ scores measure the variable of widgets per hour, the standard error of the estimate is 1.42 widgets per hour. Therefore, we conclude that when we use the regression equation to predict widgets-per-hour scores based on widget test scores, we are wrong by an "average" of about 1.42 widgets per hour.

> **STAT ALERT**  The standard error of the estimate describes the amount of error in our predictions of the actual $Y$ scores when we use $Y'$ from the regression equation as the predicted score.

## Assumptions of Linear Regression

As we have seen, $S_{Y'}$ measures the differences between $Y$ and $Y'$ and thus indicates the amount the $Y$ scores are spread out around the $Y'$ scores. Since all values of $Y'$ fall *on* the regression line, $S_{Y'}$ also describes the amount the actual $Y$ scores are spread out around the regression line. In order for $S_{Y'}$ to accurately describe this spread, we must be able to make two assumptions about how the $Y$ scores are distributed.

First, we assume that the $Y$ scores are equally spread out around the regression line throughout the relationship. This assumption goes by the funny little name of homoscedasticity. **Homoscedasticity** occurs when the $Y$ scores at each $X$ are spread out to the same degree as they are spread out at every other $X$. The left-hand scatterplot in Figure 8.5 shows homoscedastic data. Since the vertical distance separating the $Y$ scores is the same at each $X$, the spread of the $Y$ scores around the regression line and around $Y'$ is the same at each $X$. Therefore, $S_{Y'}$ will be reasonably accurate in describing this spread and in describing the error in predicting the $Y$ scores throughout the relationship. Conversely, the right-hand scatterplot shows an example of heteroscedastic data. **Heteroscedasticity** occurs when the spread in $Y$ is not equal throughout the relationship. In such cases, $S_{Y'}$ will not accurately describe the "average" error throughout the entire relationship: it will be much greater than the actual average error in predictions for some $Y$ scores and much less than the average error for other scores.

Second, we assume that the sample of $Y$ scores at each $X$ represents an approximately normal distribution. That is, if we constructed a frequency polygon of the $Y$ scores at each $X$, we would expect to have a normal distri-

**FIGURE 8.5**   Illustrations of Homoscedastic and Heteroscedastic Data

*The vertical width of the scatterplot above an X indicates how spread out the corresponding Y scores are. On the left, the Ys have the same spread at each X.*

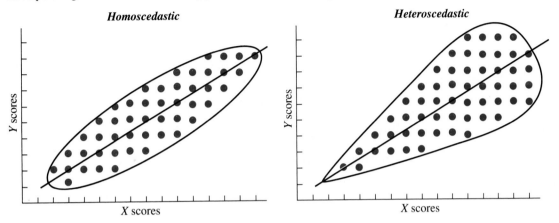

bution centered around $Y'$. Figure 8.6 illustrates this assumption for our widgetability study. If the distributions are normal, $S_{Y'}$ accurately indicates the average amount the distributions are spread out above and below $Y'$. Further, in the same way that we expect approximately 68% of all scores in a normal distribution to fall between $\pm 1$ standard deviations from the mean, we expect approximately 68% of all $Y$ scores to be between $\pm 1 S_{Y'}$ from the regression line. In our widget study, the standard error of the estimate is 1.42, so we

**FIGURE 8.6**   Scatterplot Showing Normal Distribution of $Y$ Scores at each $X$

*At each X, there is a normal distribution of different Y scores centered around $Y'$.*

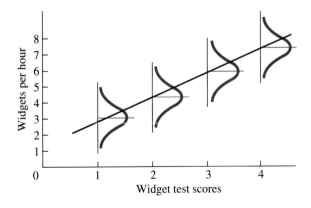

expect approximately 68% of the actual $Y$ scores to be between $\pm 1.42$ from each value of $Y'$.

In summary, $S_{Y'}$ and $S_{Y'}^2$ tell us how much the $Y$ scores are spread out around the $Y'$ scores and thus indicate the amount of error we have when we use $Y'$ to predict the $Y$ scores. However, $S_{Y'}$ and $S_{Y'}^2$ are not the only statistics that indicate how spread out the $Y$ scores are. Recall that the correlation coefficient, $r$, also reflects how much the scatterplot is spread out around the regression line. For this reason, $r$ indirectly tells us the amount of error in our predictions.

### Strength of the Relationship and Amount of Prediction Error

As you know, the larger the absolute size of $r$, the stronger the relationship: the more consistently one value of $Y$ is associated with one and only one value of $X$. In turn, the more consistent the association, the smaller the spread in $Y$ scores and the smaller the amount of error we have when we use $Y'$ scores to predict $Y$ scores.

Our minimum error occurs when $r$ is $\pm 1.0$. In the previous chapter we saw that when $r = \pm 1.0$, there is no spread in the $Y$ scores and the scatterplot *is* the regression line. The left-hand graph in Figure 8.7 shows such a perfect relationship. The $Y'$ for each $X$ equals the one $Y$ score every subject obtained for that $X$. Therefore, the difference between each $Y$ and corresponding $Y'$ is zero, so the error in our predictions, $S_{Y'}$, equals zero (as does $S_{Y'}^2$).

At the other extreme, $r$ equals 0.0 in the right-hand graph of Figure 8.7. Here the regression line is horizontal, and all values of $Y'$ equal the $Y$-intercept. In order to understand the error in prediction here, recognize that

**FIGURE 8.7**   Scatterplots and Regression Lines When $r = +1.0$ and when $r = 0.0$

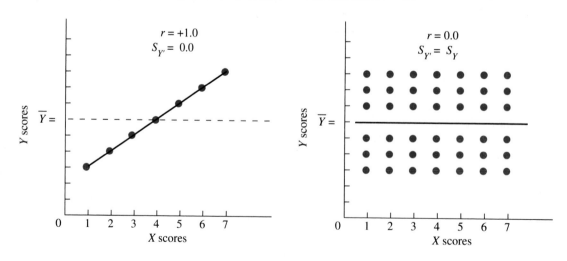

the $Y$-intercept is the overall mean of all $Y$ scores, or $\overline{Y}$. This is because when there is no relationship, the $Y$ scores at each $X$ are virtually the same as the $Y$ scores at any other $X$. Thus, the regression line passes through the center of all $Y$ scores in the sample, and the central score in a sample is the mean. *When $r = 0.0$, the Y-intercept is equal to the mean of all Y scores in the sample, and the predicted Y' for all subjects is the overall mean of Y.* As we saw in previous chapters, when we have no additional information about the scores, we should predict the overall mean for each score. When $r = 0.0$, there is no relationship to provide additional information about $Y$ scores, so, even through the regression equation, we end up predicting $\overline{Y}$ for each $Y$ score.

When $r = 0.0$, the standard error of the estimate is at its maximum value, and that value is equal to $S_Y$, the standard deviation of all the actual $Y$ scores in the sample. Why? Because when no relationship exists, the value of $Y'$ for every subject is always the overall mean of the $Y$ scores, $\overline{Y}$. We can call it $Y'$ or we can call it $\overline{Y}$, but it is the same score. Therefore, we can replace the symbol $Y'$ with the symbol $\overline{Y}$ in the formula for the standard error of the estimate, as shown here:

$$S_{Y'} = \sqrt{\frac{\Sigma(Y - Y')^2}{N}} = \sqrt{\frac{\Sigma(Y - \overline{Y})^2}{N}} = S_Y$$

The resulting formula on the right is the formula for the standard deviation of all $Y$ scores, $S_Y$. Thus, when $r = 0.0$, the standard error of the estimate, $S_{Y'}$, is equal to the total variability, or spread, in the $Y$ scores, $S_Y$. (Likewise, $S_{Y'}^2$ is equal to $S_Y^2$.)

Thus, the absolute size of $r$ is *inversely* related to the size of $S_{Y'}$. When $r$ is $\pm 1.0$, we have the minimum amount of error in our predictions, which is zero, yielding a value of zero for $S_{Y'}$. When $r$ is 0.0, we have the maximum amount of error in our predictions, with the value of $S_{Y'}$ equal to $S_Y$. When $r$ is any value between 0.0 and $\pm 1.0$, the value of $S_{Y'}$ is less than $S_Y$ but greater than zero. Figure 8.8 shows two such intermediate relationships.

The scatterplot on the left shows a relationship with an $r$ close to $-1.0$. The $Y$ scores at each $X$ are not spread out much around the corresponding $Y'$ on the regression line, so the actual $Y$ scores are relatively close to the predicted $Y'$. Therefore, $S_{Y'}$ (and $S_{Y'}^2$) will be relatively close to zero. Conversely, the scatterplot on the right shows a relationship with an $r$ much closer to 0.0. The $Y$ scores at each $X$ are spread out around the corresponding $Y'$ on the regression line, so many of the actual $Y$ scores are relatively far from the predicted $Y'$. Therefore, there will be considerable error when $Y'$ is used to predict subjects' $Y$ scores, and $S_{Y'}$ (and $S_{Y'}^2$) will be relatively large.

*Now we arrive at the essence of understanding how correlation and regression work together.* Returning to Figures 8.7 and 8.8, notice that when $r$ is close to $\pm 1.0$, the actual $Y$ scores are considerably closer to the corresponding values

**FIGURE 8.8**   Scatterplots of Strong and Weak Relationships

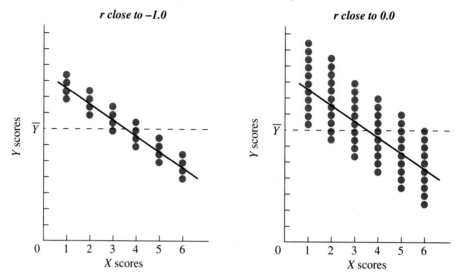

of $Y'$ than they are to the overall mean of $Y$, $\overline{Y}$. However, when $r$ is close to 0.0, the actual $Y$ scores are not that much closer to the corresponding values of $Y'$ than they are to the value of $\overline{Y}$. Thus, think of $r$ as indicating how much better our predictions are if we use subjects' $X$ scores and the regression equation to predict $Y$ scores, rather than merely predicting $\overline{Y}$ for every subject.

When $r$ is 0.0, the $X$ scores are no help whatsoever in predicting $Y$ scores. If we use the $X$ scores and the regression equation to compute $Y'$, each predicted $Y'$ score is the mean of $Y$. If we do not use the $X$ scores and the regression equation, we still predict that each $Y$ score is the mean of $Y$. Thus, when there is no relationship, our error when we use the $X$ scores, $S_{Y'}$, equals our error when we do not use the $X$ scores, $S_Y$ (and $S_{Y'}^2$ equals $S_Y^2$).

If $r$ is not 0.0, however, using the $X$ scores reduces our error in prediction. When there is a relationship, the actual $Y$ scores are closer to the corresponding values of $Y'$ than to the mean of $Y$. Therefore, our error when we use the regression equation to predict $Y$ scores, $S_{Y'}$, is less than our error when we use the overall mean of $Y$ to predict $Y$ scores, $S_Y$ (and $S_{Y'}^2$ is less than $S_Y^2$). As the strength of the relationship increases and $r$ approaches $\pm 1.0$, the actual $Y$ scores become even closer to the corresponding values of $Y'$, producing even less error (and $S_{Y'}$ is even smaller relative to $S_Y$).

> **STAT ALERT**   The larger the absolute value of $r$, the smaller our error in prediction if we use the relationship, $S_{Y'}$, compared to our error if we do not use the relationship, $S_Y$.

Obviously, if we decrease the error in our predictions as $r$ approaches $\pm 1.0$, we increase the accuracy of our predictions. Although the value of $r$ implicitly communicates the accuracy of our predictions, to directly compute the amount that we have improved the accuracy of our predictions, we compute the proportion of variance accounted for by the relationship.

## PREDICTING VARIABILITY: THE PROPORTION OF VARIANCE ACCOUNTED FOR

As we saw in Chapter 5, when we use a relationship with $X$ to more accurately predict $Y$ scores, we say that we *account for the variance* in $Y$ scores. The variance we account for is $S_Y^2$, the variance of the $Y$ scores around the overall $\overline{Y}$. This is our frame of reference; we can always use $\overline{Y}$ to predict scores, so $S_Y^2$ is the greatest error we can have in predictions. If a relationship allows us to reduce this error, we account for some of the variance in $Y$. We express the amount by which we reduce our error as the proportion of variance accounted for. This is the proportional improvement achieved in our predictions when we use a relationship with $X$ to predict $Y$ scores, rather than using the overall $\overline{Y}$ to predict $Y$ scores. In essence, this proportion tells us how much closer we are to accurately predicting each different $Y$ score when we use the relationship than when we do not use the relationship.

Calculation of the proportion of variance accounted for can be difficult to conceptualize. Therefore, we will first calculate it for only one subject, and then we will see how it is computed for an entire sample.

### Understanding the Variance Accounted For

Say that in a study where we have discovered a relationship, we want to predict the $Y$ score of one subject, Dorcas. The overall mean of the $Y$ scores in the sample is 9, but Dorcas obtained an actual $Y$ score of 4. Using the mean as her predicted score, we predict a score of 9 for her and we are wrong by 5 points ($9 - 4 = 5$). Since our error in prediction when we use the overall mean of $Y$ is the worst that we can do, think of this amount as the *total error*.

Say that, using the relationship and the regression equation, we predict a $Y'$ of 6 for Dorcas. We are now off by 2 points ($6 - 4 = 2$). Thus, of the 5 points of error we have without using the relationship, we are still off by 2 of those points when we use the relationship. Think of this amount as the *error remaining*.

By reducing our error from 5 points of total error to 2 points of error remaining, we are now 3 points closer to Dorcas's actual $Y$ score than we were when we predicted her score as the overall $\overline{Y}$. Think of this improvement as the *error eliminated*.

Figure 8.9 shows the total error, the error remaining, and the error eliminated in our prediction of Dorcas's score. The total error in our prediction without using the relationship breaks into two components: error remaining when using the relationship and error eliminated when using the relationship:

$$
\begin{array}{c}
\text{Total prediction error} \\
\text{without using the} \\
\text{relationship}
\end{array}
=
\begin{array}{c}
\text{error remaining} \\
\text{when using the} \\
\text{relationship}
\end{array}
+
\begin{array}{c}
\text{error eliminated} \\
\text{when using the} \\
\text{relationship}
\end{array}
$$

In statistics, we want to describe the improvement in predictions, so we want to describe the error eliminated. However, we do not directly measure the error eliminated. Instead, we measure the total error without using the relationship and the error remaining when using the relationship. Then, by subtracting the error remaining from the total error, we obtain the error eliminated: Thus,

$$
\begin{array}{c}
\text{Total error} \\
\text{without using the} \\
\text{relationship}
\end{array}
-
\begin{array}{c}
\text{error remaining} \\
\text{when using the} \\
\text{relationship}
\end{array}
=
\begin{array}{c}
\text{error eliminated} \\
\text{when using the} \\
\text{relationship}
\end{array}
$$

So that they can compare the error eliminated in different relationships (wherein one error might be measured in units of 1 or 2 and the other measured in units of 50 or 60), statisticians describe the above components in terms of

**FIGURE 8.9**   Error in Prediction of Dorcas's Scores

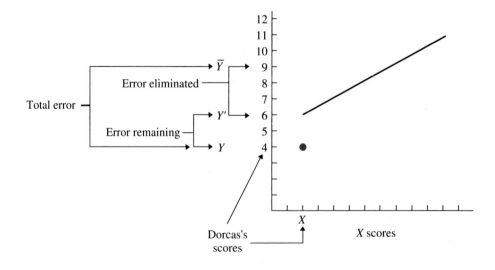

the proportion each represents of the total error in the sample. Thus, we end up with

$$\frac{\text{Total error}}{\text{Total error}} - \frac{\text{error remaining}}{\text{total error}} = \frac{\text{error eliminated}}{\text{total error}}$$

On the left, the total error divided by the total error equals 1.0, or 100%, of the total error. On the right, the error eliminated divided by the total error is the proportion of total error that is eliminated by using the relationship. Therefore, we can state the above formula as

$$1.0 - \left(\frac{\text{error remaining}}{\text{total error}}\right) = \text{proportion of total error eliminated}$$

This is the formula we use to find the proportion of total error eliminated.

For Dorcas, the error remaining when using the relationship (2 points) divided by the total error without using the relationship (5 points) is 2/5, or .40. Thus, when we use the relationship, we still have .40, or 40%, of the error we have when we do not use the relationship. Since .40 of the total error remains when we use the relationship, the error eliminated is $1.0 - .40$, or .60. (The 3 points of error eliminated is .60 of 5.) Thus, .60, or 60%, of the total error we have when we do not use the relationship is eliminated when we use the relationship to predict her score. We are .60, or 60%, closer to Dorcas's score if we use the regression equation to predict her $Y$ score than if we use the overall mean of the $Y$ scores as her predicted score.

Of course, we never examine only one subject. Instead, we compute the proportion of variance we have accounted for in the entire sample.

## Computing the Proportion of Variance Accounted For

To describe the entire sample, we use the above logic except that we compute the appropriate measures of variance.

The overall variance in $Y$, $S_Y^2$, measures the differences between the $Y$ scores and $\overline{Y}$, so it indicates the error we have when we use the mean score as the predicted $Y$ score. Thus, $S_Y^2$ is analogous to the total error we have without using the relationship.

The variance of the $Y$ scores around $Y'$, $S_{Y'}^2$, measures the differences between $Y$ and $Y'$, so it indicates the error we have when we use $Y'$ as the predicted $Y$ score. Thus, $S_{Y'}^2$ is analogous to the error remaining when we use the relationship.

From here, we follow the same procedure as we did with Dorcas. There we saw that

$$\text{Proportion of total error eliminated} = 1.0 - \left(\frac{\text{error remaining}}{\text{total error}}\right)$$

Since we measure the total error using the variance in $Y$ scores, the proportion of total error eliminated is the proportion of variance accounted for. Substituting the symbols $S_{Y'}^2$ and $S_Y^2$, we have the following definitional formula.

---

*THE DEFINITIONAL FORMULA FOR THE PROPORTION OF VARIANCE IN Y THAT IS ACCOUNTED FOR BY A LINEAR RELATIONSHIP WITH X IS*

$$\text{Proportion of variance accounted for} = 1 - \left(\frac{S_{Y'}^2}{S_Y^2}\right)$$

---

Using this formula, we can return to our widgetability study and, by finding the proportion of variance accounted for, determine how much help subjects' test scores are in predicting their widget-making scores. From the data back in Table 8.2, we computed that the variance in the $Y$ scores, $S_Y^2$, was 4.38, and $S_{Y'}^2$ was 2.01. The proportion of variance in widgets-per-hour scores that is accounted for by knowing test scores is

$$1 - \frac{2.01}{4.38} = 1.00 - .459 = .54$$

This relationship accounts for .54 of the variance in $Y$ scores: if we know subjects' scores on the widget test, we are "on average" .54, or 54%, more accurate at predicting their widgets-per-hour scores than we would be if we did not use this relationship. In other words, when we use the relationship to compute $Y'$, our predictions are, on average, 54% closer to the actual $Y$ scores than when we do not use the relationship and instead use $\overline{Y}$ as the predicted $Y$ score for each subject.

> *STAT ALERT* In a relationship, variable $X$ will account for a certain proportion of the variance in variable $Y$. This is the proportion by which we can improve our accuracy in predicting scores on variable $Y$ by using the relationship with $X$.

### Using *r* to Compute the Proportion of Variance Accounted For

Computing the proportion of variance accounted for with the above definitional formula is rather time consuming. However, we saw that the size of $r$ is related to the amount of error in our predictions, $S_{Y'}^2$, by the formula

$$S_{Y'}^2 = S_Y^2(1 - r^2)$$

If we solve this formula to isolate $r^2$, we have

$$r^2 = 1 - \frac{S_{Y'}^2}{S_Y^2}$$

The squared correlation coefficient equals 1 minus the ratio $S_{Y'}^2/S_Y^2$. Since 1 minus this ratio is the definitional formula for the proportion of variance accounted for, we have the following computational formula.

> *THE COMPUTATIONAL FORMULA FOR THE PROPORTION OF VARIANCE IN Y THAT IS ACCOUNTED FOR BY A LINEAR RELATIONSHIP WITH X IS*
>
> Proportion of variance accounted for $= r^2$

Not too tough! All we do is compute $r$ (which we would do anyway) and square it. Then we have computed the proportion of variance in $Y$ scores that is accounted for by using the relationship with $X$ to predict $Y$. (Yes, it has taken a long time to get to such a simple method, but to understand $r^2$ you must understand $1 - S_{Y'}^2/S_Y^2$.)

Above we computed that in our widgetability study, the relationship accounted for .54 of the variance in $Y$ scores. Since $r$ for this study was $+.736$, we can also compute the proportion of variance accounted for as $(.736)^2$, which again is .54.

In statistical language, $r^2$ is called the *coefficient of determination,* which is merely another name for the proportion of variance accounted for. The proportion of variance *not* accounted for is called the *coefficient of alienation.*

> *THE COMPUTATIONAL FORMULA FOR THE PROPORTION OF VARIANCE NOT ACCOUNTED FOR IS*
>
> Proportion of variance not accounted for $= 1 - r^2$

This value equals the ratio $S_{Y'}^2/S_Y^2$, so it is the proportion of total error remaining. In our widget study, the coefficient of determination is .54, so we still cannot account for $1 - .54$, or .46, of the variance in the $Y$ scores.

Note that $r^2$ describes the proportion of *sample* variance that is accounted for by the relationship. If the $r$ passes the inferential statistical test, we can conclude that this relationship holds for the population. Then the value of $r^2$ is a *rough* estimate of the proportion of variance in $Y$ scores in the population that is accounted for by the relationship. Thus, we expect to be roughly 54% more accurate if we use the relationship with our widget test scores to predict other, unknown widgetability scores in the population.

## Using the Variance Accounted For

The logic of $r^2$ can be applied to any relationship. For example, in the previous chapter we discussed the correlation coefficients $r_s$ and $r_{pb}$. Squaring these coefficients also indicates the proportion of variance accounted for. (It is as if we performed the appropriate regression analysis, computed $S_{Y'}^2$ and $S_Y^2$, and so on.) Likewise, as we shall see in later chapters, we can determine the proportion of variance accounted for in experiments. We describe the proportion of variance in the dependent variable (the $Y$ scores) that is accounted for by the relationship with the independent variable (the $X$ scores). This proportion tells us how much more accurately we can predict subjects' scores on the dependent variable if we take into account the condition of the independent variable under which the subjects were tested, rather than merely using the overall mean of the dependent scores as the predicted score.

Although theoretically a relationship may allow us to account for any proportion of the variance, in the behavioral sciences we get very excited if we find a relationship that accounts for around 25% of the variance. Remember, this is an $r$ of $\pm.50$, which is pretty good. Given the complexity of the behaviors of living organisms, we are unlikely to find an $r$ that is very close to $\pm 1.0$, so we are also unlikely to find that a relationship accounts for close to 100% of the variance. (If we ever found a relationship that accounted for 100% of the variance, we'd get ready for the Nobel prize!)

The reason we make such a big deal out of the proportion of variance accounted for is that it is the statistical measure of how "important" a particular relationship is. Remember, scores reflect behavior. When we use a relationship with $X$ to predict $Y$ scores, we are predicting differences in behavior $Y$. The greater the proportion of variance accounted for by the relationship, the more accurately we can predict behavior, and thus the more scientifically important and informative the relationship is.

When we wish to compare two correlation coefficients to see which relationship is more important, we square each $r$. Say that we find a relationship between the length of a person's hair and his or her creativity, but $r$ is only $+.02$. Yes, this $r$ indicates a relationship, but such a weak relationship is virtually useless. The fact that $r^2 = .0004$ indicates that knowing a subject's hair length improves predictions about creativity by only four-hundredths of *one* percent! However, say that we also find a relationship between a subject's age and his or her creativity, and here $r$ is $-.40$. This relationship is more important, at least in a statistical sense, because $r^2 = .16$. If we want to predict creativity, then age is a more important variable than hair length, because knowing subjects' ages gets us 16% closer to accurately predicting their creativity. Knowing their hair length gets us only .04% closer to accurately predicting their creativity.

## A WORD ABOUT MULTIPLE CORRELATION AND REGRESSION

Sometimes we discover several *X* variables that help us to more accurately predict a *Y* variable. For example, there is a positive correlation between a person's height and his or her ability to shoot baskets in basketball: the taller people are, the more baskets they tend to make. There is also a positive correlation between how much people practice basketball and their ability to shoot baskets: the more they practice, the more baskets they tend to make. Obviously, to be as accurate as possible in predicting how well people shoot baskets, we want to know both how tall they are and how much they practice. In this example there are two predictor variables (height and practice) that predict the criterion variable (basket shooting). In other words, there are multiple predictor variables. When we have multiple predictor variables for one criterion variable, we use the statistical procedures known as *multiple correlation* and *multiple regression.*

Although the computations involved in multiple correlation and multiple regression are beyond the introductory level of this text, the logic is the same as the logic of the procedures we have discussed here. The correlation coefficient, called the *multiple r*, indicates the strength of the relationship between the multiple predictors and the criterion variable. The multiple regression equation allows us to predict a subject's *Y* score using the subject's scores on all *X* variables. The squared multiple *r* is the proportion of variance in the *Y* variable accounted for (the proportion of error eliminated) by using the relationship with the *X* variables to predict *Y* scores.

### *FINALLY*

This chapter and the previous one have introduced many new symbols and concepts. However, they boil down to three major topics.

1.  *Correlation.* When there is a relationship between the *X* and *Y* variables, a particular value or range of *Y* tends to be paired with one value of *X*. The stronger the relationship, the more consistently one and only one value of *Y* is paired with one and only one value of *X*. The type and strength of a relationship are described by *r*.

2.  *Regression.* In a relationship, the *X* and *Y* scores are paired in a certain way. If we know the relationship, we can use a particular *X* score to

help us predict the corresponding $Y$ score. We predict $Y$ scores using the linear regression equation, and graph the predictions as the linear regression line.

3. *Error in prediction.* The proportion of variance in $Y$ that is accounted for by $X$ is the amount by which our errors in predicting $Y$ scores are reduced when we use the relationship, compared to what they would be if we did not use the relationship. This proportion is described by $r^2$.

## CHAPTER SUMMARY

1. *Linear regression* is the procedure for describing the best-fitting straight line that summarizes a linear relationship. The line is called the *linear regression line,* and it runs through the center of the $Y$ scores.

2. The *linear regression equation* describes the regression line. The equation includes the *slope,* which indicates how much and in what direction the line slants, and the *Y-intercept,* which indicates the value of $Y$ at the point where the line crosses the $Y$ axis.

3. Using the regression equation, we compute for each $X$ the summary $Y$ score that best represents the $Y$ scores at that $X$. This summary score is $Y'$, the predicted $Y$ score at each $X$. The regression line is formed by drawing a line that connects all $X$-$Y'$ pairs.

4. The *error in our predictions* is the difference between an actual $Y$ score at an $X$ and the predicted $Y'$ at that $X$. The error in predictions across the entire relationship may be summarized by the *standard error of the estimate,* symbolized by $S_{Y'}$. The $S_{Y'}$ is a type of standard deviation indicating the spread in the $Y$ scores around the $Y'$ scores, and thus the spread in the $Y$ scores above and below the regression line. The differences (and error) between $Y$ and $Y'$ also may be summarized by the *variance of the Y scores around $Y'$,* which is symbolized by $S_{Y'}^2$, the square of $S_{Y'}$.

5. We assume that the $Y$ scores are *homoscedastic*—that the spread in the $Y$ scores around any $Y'$ is the same as the spread in the $Y$ scores around any other $Y'$. We also assume that the $Y$ scores at each $X$ are normally distributed around the corresponding value of $Y'$.

6. The stronger the relationship and the larger the absolute value of $r$, the smaller the values of $S_{Y'}$ and $S_{Y'}^2$. This is because the stronger the relationship, the closer the $Y$ scores are to $Y'$ and thus the smaller the difference, or error, between $Y$ and $Y'$.

7. When $r$ equals $\pm 1.0$, every $Y$ score equals its corresponding $Y'$, and thus there is zero error in predictions and both $S_{Y'}$ and $S^2_{Y'}$ equal zero. When $r$ equals 0.0, $S_{Y'}$ equals $S_Y$ and $S^2_{Y'}$ equals $S^2_Y$. This is because when no relationship exists, the overall mean of $Y$ is the predicted score for all subjects, and thus the differences between the actual $Y$ scores and the predicted scores equal $S_Y$ (or $S^2_Y$). When $r$ is between 0.0 and $\pm 1.0$, the value of $S_{Y'}$ is between the value of $S_Y$ and 0.0.

8. The *proportion of variance in Y that is accounted for by X* describes the proportional improvement in our predictions that is achieved when we use the relationship to predict $Y$ scores, rather than predicting $Y$ scores without using the relationship. It indicates the proportion of the total prediction error that is eliminated when we use $Y'$ as the predicted score instead of $\overline{Y}$. The proportion of variance accounted for is computed by squaring the correlation coefficient, or finding $r^2$.

9. The proportion of variance not accounted for is computed as $1 - r^2$. This is the proportion of the total prediction error that is not eliminated when we use $Y'$ as the predicted score instead of $\overline{Y}$.

10. The proportion of variance accounted for indicates the statistical importance of a relationship.

11. *Multiple correlation* and *multiple regression* are procedures for describing the relationship when multiple predictor variables (several $X$ variables) are used to predict scores on one criterion variable ($Y$ variable).

---

## USING THE COMPUTER

By selecting routine **4** in your computer program and then selecting the Pearson correlation coefficient, you can perform linear regression. The program computes the linear regression equation, the standard error of the estimate, and $r^2$. Using the regression equation, it will also compute the predicted value of $Y'$ for any value of $X$ that you enter.

---

## PRACTICE PROBLEMS

(Answers are provided for odd-numbered problems.)
1. What is the linear regression line?
2. What is the linear regression procedure used for?
3. What is $Y'$?

4. What is the general form of the linear regression equation?
5. What does the $Y$-intercept of the regression line indicate?
6. What does the slope of the regression line indicate?
7. *a.* What does the standard error of the estimate tell you about the spread in the $Y$ scores?
   *b.* What does the standard error of the estimate tell you about your errors in prediction?
8. What two assumptions must we be able to make about the data for the standard error of the estimate to provide an accurate description of the data?
9. *a.* How is the value of $S_{Y'}$ related to $r$?
   *b.* When is $S_{Y'}$ at its maximum value and why?
   *c.* When is $S_{Y'}$ at its minimum value and why?
10. When are multiple regression procedures used?
11. *a.* In statistical terminology, what does $r^2$ indicate?
    *b.* How do you interpret $r^2$?
12. A researcher finds that variable A accounts for 25% of the variance in variable B. Another researcher finds that variable C accounts for 50% of the variance in variable B. Which relationship is scientifically more important and why?
13. *a.* Compute $r$ for the data below.

| Subject | X | Y |
|---------|---|----|
| 1 | 2 | 8 |
| 2 | 6 | 14 |
| 3 | 1 | 5 |
| 4 | 3 | 8 |
| 5 | 6 | 10 |
| 6 | 9 | 15 |
| 7 | 6 | 8 |
| 8 | 6 | 8 |
| 9 | 4 | 7 |
| 10 | 2 | 6 |

   *b.* Compute the linear regression equation for these data.
   *c.* What is the value of $Y'$ for a subject who obtains an $X$ score of 9?
14. *a.* Compute $S_{Y'}$ for the data in question 13.
    *b.* What does this value tell you about the errors in prediction in these data?
15. *a.* For the relationship in question 13, what is the proportion of variance in $Y$ that is accounted for by $X$?
    *b.* What is the proportion of variance not accounted for?
    *c.* Why is or is not this a valuable relationship?
16. *a.* Compute the statistic that describes the nature of the relationship described by the following interval data.

| Subject | X | Y |
|---------|----|----|
| 1 | 10 | 7 |
| 2 | 8 | 6 |
| 3 | 9 | 11 |
| 4 | 6 | 4 |
| 5 | 5 | 5 |
| 6 | 3 | 7 |
| 7 | 7 | 4 |
| 8 | 2 | 5 |
| 9 | 4 | 6 |
| 10 | 1 | 4 |

b. What is the predicted $Y$ score for a subject scoring at $X = 3$?

c. Assuming that your prediction is in error, what is the amount of error you expect to have?

d. How much smaller will your error be if you use the regression equation than if you merely predict the mean of the $Y$ scores?

## SUMMARY OF FORMULAS

1. *The formula for the linear regression equation is*

$$Y' = bX + a$$

where $b$ stands for the slope of the line, $X$ stands for an $X$ score, and $a$ stands for the $Y$-intercept.

2. *The formula for the slope of the linear regression line is*

$$b = \frac{N(\Sigma XY) - (\Sigma X)(\Sigma Y)}{N(\Sigma X^2) - (\Sigma X)^2}$$

where $N$ is the number of pairs of scores in the sample and $X$ and $Y$ are the scores in the sample.

3. *The formula for the Y-intercept of the linear regression equation is*

$$a = \overline{Y} - (b)(\overline{X})$$

where $\overline{Y}$ is the mean of all $Y$ scores, $b$ is the slope of the regression line, and $\overline{X}$ is the mean of all $X$ scores.

**4.** *The definitional formula for the standard error of the estimate is*

$$S_{Y'} = \sqrt{\frac{\Sigma(Y - Y')^2}{N}}$$

where $Y$ is each score in the sample, $Y'$ is the corresponding predicted $Y$ score, and $N$ is the number of pairs in the sample.

**5.** *The computational formula for the standard error of the estimate is*

$$S_{Y'} = S_Y \sqrt{1 - r^2}$$

where $S_Y$ is the standard deviation of the $Y$ scores in the sample.

**6.** *To find the variance of the Y scores around Y', $S^2_{Y'}$, square the value of $S_{Y'}$.*

**8.** *The definitional formula for the proportion of variance in Y that is accounted for by a linear relationship with X is*

$$\text{Proportion of variance accounted for} = 1 - \frac{S^2_{Y'}}{S^2_Y}$$

where $S^2_{Y'}$ is the squared standard error of the estimate and $S^2_Y$ is the variance of all $Y$ scores in the sample.

**9.** *The computational formula for the proportion of variance in Y that is accounted for by a linear relationship with X is*

$$\text{Proportion of variance accounted for} = r^2$$

**10.** *The computational formula for the proportion of variance not accounted for is*

$$\text{Proportion of variance not accounted for} = 1 - r^2$$

# PART 4

# INFERENTIAL STATISTICS

Now that we have covered the various methods for describing scores and relationships, we are finally ready to discuss inferential statistical procedures. Inferential statistics are procedures that allow us to answer this question: Based on our sample, what would we expect to find if we could perform this study on the entire population? Would we expect to find that the population has approximately the same mean as our sample? Or, if different samples produce different means, would we expect to find approximately the same difference between the population means? Or, would we expect to find that the population has about the same correlation coefficient as the sample? The problem is that since we cannot know what the population would contain, the best we can do is to place an intelligent bet. In essence, inferential statistical procedures are ways to make decisions about the population that have a high probability of being correct.

The first step in understanding these procedures is to understand probability. In the next chapter we will discuss the concept of probability and see how probability is used to make statistical decisions. Subsequent chapters will then deal with the various inferential procedures we use, depending on the design of a particular study and the types of variables we are measuring. As you read each chapter and become familiar with the names and symbols for the different procedures, remember to keep one eye on the big picture: all inferential procedures are basically a variation on the concept of making decisions about the scores and relationship we would find in the population.

# Probability: Making Decisions About Chance Events

In Chapter 6 we saw that we can use a $z$-score to describe any score, even if the "score" is a sample mean. From that chapter, be sure you remember the following. A $z$-score indicates how far the score is from the mean of the distribution, with the distance measured in standard deviation units. If the distribution forms a normal curve, then we apply the standard normal curve model. For raw scores, we apply the model to a raw score distribution, and for a sample mean, we apply the model to a sampling distribution of means. In either case, the proportion of the area under the normal curve between the mean and $z$ is the relative frequency of the $z$-scores falling between the mean and that $z$. This relative frequency is also the expected relative frequency of the corresponding raw scores or sample means.

This chapter introduces the wonderful world of probability. As we shall see, psychologists combine their knowledge of probability with the standard normal curve model to make decisions about their data. We will keep the discussion simple, because psychologists do not need to be experts in probability. However, they do need to understand the basic logic of chance.

## MORE STATISTICAL NOTATION

In daily conversation we use the words *chances, odds,* and *probability* interchangeably. In statistics, however, there are subtle differences among these terms. Odds are expressed as fractions or ratios ("The odds of winning are 1 in 2"). Chance is expressed as a percentage ("There is a 50% chance of winning"). Probability is expressed as a decimal ("The probability of winning is .50"). You should express the answers you compute as probabilities.

The symbol we use to represent probability is the lowercase letter $p$. When we describe the probability of a particular event such as event A, we write it as $p(A)$, which is pronounced "$p$ of A" or "the probability of A."

## THE LOGIC OF PROBABILITY

Probability is used to describe random chance events. Random chance events occur when nature is being fair—when there is no bias toward one event over another (no rigged roulette wheels or loaded dice). A chance event occurs or does not occur merely because of the luck of the draw. In statistical work, luck is a very important concept, and probability is our way of mathematically describing how luck operates to produce an event.

But hold on! How can we describe an event that happens only by luck? Well, we begin by paying attention to how often the event occurs when only luck is operating. The probability of any event is based on how often the event occurs *over the long run*. Intuitively, we use this logic all the time: if event A happens frequently over the long run, then we tend to think that A is likely to happen and we say that it has a high probability. If event B happens infrequently, then we tend to think that B is unlikely to happen and we say that it has a low probability.

When we decide that event A happens frequently, we are making a relative judgment. Compared to anything else that might happen in this situation, event A happens relatively frequently. Intuitively, we determine the *relative frequency* of event A: the proportion of time that event A occurs, out of all possible events that might occur in this situation. In statistical terminology, we call all possible events that can occur in a given situation the *population* of events. Thus, the probability of an event is equal to the event's relative frequency in the population of all possible events that can occur.

> *STAT ALERT* The relative frequency of an event in the population equals the probability of the event.

If a population is thought of as all possible events that can occur, then a sample contains the event or events that do occur. Previously we saw that a score's relative frequency in the population is also the score's expected relative frequency in the sample. We use probability as a way of expressing an event's expected relative frequency in any single random sample. For example, I am a rotten typist, and while typing the manuscript for this book, I randomly made typos 80% of the time. This means that in the population of my typing, typos occur with a relative frequency of .80. We expect the relative frequency of typos to continue at a rate of .80 in any random sample of my typing. We can express this expected relative frequency as a probability. Thus, the probability is .80 that I will make a typo when I type the next woid.

As the above example illustrates, a **probability** is a mathematical statement indicating the likelihood of an event when we randomly sample a particular population. It is our way of expressing what we expect to occur when we randomly sample a population, and it indicates our confidence in any particular event. For example, if event A has a relative frequency of zero in a particular situation, then the probability of event A is zero. This means that we do not expect A to occur in this situation, because it never does. But if event A has a relative frequency of .10 in this situation, then A has a probability of .10. This means that we have some, but not much, confidence that the event will occur in any particular sample. Because it occurs only 10% of the time in this situation, we expect it to occur in only 10% of our samples. On the other hand, if event A has a probability of .95, we are confident that A will occur. Because it occurs 95% of the time in this situation, we expect it to occur in 95% of our samples. At its most extreme, event A's relative frequency can be 1.0. If event A is 100% of the population, its probability is 1.0. Then we are positive it will occur in this situation because it always does.

Notice that an event cannot happen less than 0% of the time or more than 100% of the time, so a probability can *never* be less than 0 or greater than 1.0. Notice also that all events in a population constitute 100% of the time, or 1.0 of the population. This means that the relative frequencies of all events must add up to 1.0, so the probabilities of all events in the population must also add up to 1.0. Thus, if the probability of my making a typo at any moment is .80, then because $1.0 - .80 = .20$, there is a probability of only .20 that any word I type will be error free.

It is important to remember that except when $p$ equals either 0 or 1, we are never absolutely certain that an event will or will not occur in a particular situation. The probability of an event is its relative frequency over the long run, or in the infinite population. It is up to luck whether a particular sample contains the event. For example, even though I make typos at a rate of .80 over the long run, I may go for quite a while without making a typo. That 20% of the time I make no typos has to occur sometime. Thus, although the probability is .80 that I will make a typo in each word, it is only over the long run that we truly expect to see precisely 80% typos.

## COMPUTING PROBABILITY

Computing the probability of an event is rather simple: we need only determine its relative frequency in the population. When we know the relative frequency of every possible event in a population, we have a probability distribution. A **probability distribution** tells us the probability of every possible event in a population.

## Creating Probability Distributions

There are two ways to create a probability distribution. One way is to actually measure the relative frequency of every event in the population. If we empirically (through observation) determine the relative frequencies of all events in a population, we create an *empirical probability distribution*. Typically, however, we cannot measure all of the events in a population, so we create an empirical probability distribution from samples of those events. We assume that the relative frequency of an event in a random sample represents the relative frequency of the event in the population.

For example, say that Dr. Fraud is sometimes a very cranky individual, and as near as we can tell, his crankiness is random. To sample his behavior, we observe him on 18 days and determine that he is cranky on 6 of these days. Since relative frequency equals the frequency of an event divided by N, the relative frequency of Dr. Fraud's crankiness is 6/18, or .33. Assuming that this sample represents the population of how Dr. Fraud always behaves, we expect that he will continue to be cranky on 33% of all days. Thus, the probability that he will be cranky today is $p = .33$. Conversely, he is not cranky on 12 of the 18 days we observe him, so the relative frequency of his not being cranky is 12/18, or .67. Thus, the probability that he will not be cranky today is $p = .67$. Since his cranky days plus his noncranky days constitute all possible events, we have an empirical probability distribution for his crankiness.

Statistical procedures usually rely on the other way to create a probability distribution, which is to create a theoretical probability distribution. A **theoretical probability distribution** is a theoretical model of the relative frequencies of events in a population. As with previous models, we devise theoretical probability distributions based on a model of how we assume nature distributes events in the population. From such a model, we determine the relative frequency of each event in the population. This relative frequency is then the probability of the event in any random sample.

Let's first look at common random events such as tossing a coin and drawing playing cards. (As we shall see, determining probability in such situations is analogous to determining probability in research.) With coin tossing, we assume that we are discussing random flips of a fair coin. When we toss a coin in the air, there are a total of two possible outcomes that can occur: we may obtain a head, or we may obtain a tail. We assume that heads and tails are equally distributed in the population, with 50% heads and 50% tails. In other words, we expect the relative frequency of heads to be .50 and the relative frequency of tails to be .50. Since relative frequency in the population *is* probability, we have devised our theoretical probability distribution. The probability of a head on any toss of the coin is $p = .50$, and the probability of a tail is $p = .50$.

When we draw a playing card, we select 1 of the 52 cards in the deck. We assume that there is no bias favoring one card over another, so each has the same relative frequency in the population. Over the long run, we expect each card to occur at a rate of once out of every 52 draws, so each card has a relative frequency of 1/52, or .0192. Therefore, the probability of drawing any specific card on a single random draw is $p = .0192$.

And that is the logic of probability. We either theoretically or empirically devise a model of how events are assumed to be distributed in the population. This model gives us the expected relative frequency of each event in the population. From this, we derive the expected relative frequencies of events in any sample, expressed as $p$. By computing the probability for all possible events in a particular situation, we create the probability distribution for that situation.

## General Formula for Computing Probability

Hidden in the above examples is the method for directly computing the probability of a specific event. The way we do this is to first determine the number of outcomes that satisfy the requirements of the event we are describing. In the case of flipping a coin, there is one outcome that satisfies the condition of showing a head. Then we determine the total number of possible outcomes that can occur. There are two possible outcomes that can occur when we flip a coin: head or tail. Since all possible events are equally likely in this situation, over the long run we expect to satisfy the event "head" at a rate of 1 out of every 2 coin tosses. Therefore, the probability of a head is 1 out of 2, or .5. Likewise, earlier we saw that Dr. Fraud was cranky 6 out of 18 days. Since 6 out of the 18 total possible outcomes satisfied the event we call cranky, $p$(cranky) is 6/18, or .33.

Thus, to compute the probability of any event, we form a ratio. In the numerator we place the number of possible outcomes that can satisfy the event. In the denominator we place the total number of possible outcomes that can occur.

---

*THE FORMULA FOR COMPUTING THE PROBABILITY OF AN EVENT IS*

$$p(\text{event}) = \frac{\text{number of outcomes that satisfy event}}{\text{total number of possible outcomes}}$$

We might, for example, define the event as randomly drawing a king from a deck of cards. There are four kings in a deck, so any one of these 4 outcomes would satisfy the event. With a total of 52 possible outcomes that can occur, the probability of randomly drawing a king on any single draw is 4/52, or .0769.

We can even apply this formula to real life! For example, raffle tickets are sometimes sold one for a dollar and sometimes sold three for a dollar. Many people think they have a better chance of winning when everyone gets three tickets for a dollar. Boy, are they wrong! By applying the above formula, we can see why. Say that 100 people each spend a dollar and get one ticket. Then each person's probability of winning is equal to 1/100, or .01. However, if 100 people each buy 3 tickets for a dollar, then each person's probability of winning equals 3/300. The kicker is that 3/300 is equal to 1/100, so each person still has a probability of winning equal to .01.

The above formula can be used to find the probability of any event when all possible events are equally likely. However, using this formula is rather tedious when the event can be satisfied by complex sequences or alternatives, such as when we describe the event using the word "and" or "or." Therefore, shortcut formulas for three of the most common complex events are provided in Appendix B at the back of this book.

## Factors Affecting the Probability of an Event

All random events are not the same. In computing the probability of an event, we must consider two important factors. First, events may be either independent or dependent. Two events are **independent events** when the probability of one event is *not* influenced by the occurrence of the other event. For example, contrary to popular belief, washing your car does not make it rain. These are independent events, so the probability of rain does not increase when you wash your car. On the other hand, two events are **dependent events** when the probability of one event is influenced by the occurrence of the other event. For example, whether you pass an exam usually depends on whether you study: the probability of passing increases or decreases depending on whether studying occurs.

Second, the probability of an event is affected by the type of sampling we perform. **Sampling with replacement** is the procedure in which we replace, or return, any previously selected samples to the population before drawing any additional samples. Say we are to draw two cards from a deck of playing cards. Sampling with replacement occurs if, after drawing the first card, we return it to the deck before drawing the second card. The probabilities on the first and second draw are each based on 52 possible outcomes, and the probability of any particular card's being selected either time is constant. On the other hand, **sampling without replacement** is the procedure in which we do *not* replace, or return, any previously selected samples to the population before drawing additional samples. Sampling without replacement occurs if we discard the first playing card after drawing it. In that case, the probability of a card's being selected on the first draw is based on 52 possible outcomes, but the probability of a card's being selected on the second draw is based on only 51 possible outcomes. With fewer possible outcomes, the probability of drawing a particular card is slightly larger on the second draw than on the first draw. (Of course, the probability of drawing the first card again is zero, because the card is no longer in the deck.)

In statistics we usually assume that the events we are considering are independent and sampled with replacement.

The reason we discuss probability is not that we have an uncontrollable urge to flip coins and draw cards. Researchers use probability to make decisions about scores and samples of scores. To do that, they use the standard normal curve.

## OBTAINING PROBABILITY FROM THE STANDARD NORMAL CURVE

As we saw with flipping coins and drawing playing cards, once we know how events are distributed in the population, we can determine their relative frequencies and thus their probabilities. In statistics we usually assume that the events—the scores—in the population form a normal distribution. For this reason, our most common theoretical probability distributions are based on the standard normal curve. Here is how it works. In Chapter 6 we saw that by using z-scores, we can find the proportion of the total area under the normal curve in any part of a distribution. This proportion corresponds to the relative frequency of the scores in that part of the distribution. Remember that the relative frequency of scores in the population equals the probability of those scores. Thus,

> **The proportion of the area under the standard normal curve for scores in any part of the distribution equals the probability of those scores!**

For example, as shown in Figure 9.1, we know that 50% of the area and thus 50% of all scores fall below the mean on the standard normal curve. Since negative z-scores occur .50 of the time in the population, the probability of randomly selecting a negative z-score is .50. To understand this, think of the curve as again representing a parking lot full of people. Say that we put everyone's name in a large hat and stir thoroughly. As we randomly select names from the hat, we will be satisfied by any one of the 50% of them that

**FIGURE 9.1** *z*-Distribution Showing the Area Below the Mean

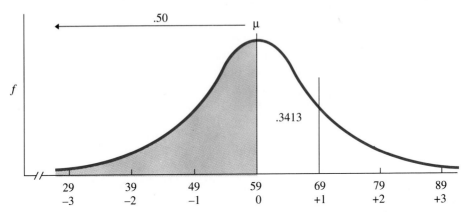

| Raw scores | 29 | 39 | 49 | 59 | 69 | 79 | 89 |
| z-scores | −3 | −2 | −1 | 0 | +1 | +2 | +3 |

have negative *z*-scores. Therefore, the probability that the next name we draw will satisfy the event "negative *z*-score" is .50.

We obtain the same answer by using the formula for probability. We know that out of a total of 100% of the possible scores in the population, 50% of them satisfy the event "negative *z*-score." So, 50%/100% equals *p* = .50.

Once we know the probability of selecting any range of *z*-scores, we know the probability of selecting the corresponding raw scores. In Figure 9.1 we have applied our model to a distribution of raw scores where the mean is 59. Raw scores below the mean of 59 produce negative *z*-scores. Thus, the probability is .50 that any individual we select will have a raw score below 59.

We can obtain the proportion under the curve, and thus the probability for any part of a normal distribution, by using the *z*-tables in Appendix D. For example, from the *z*-tables we know that scores between the mean and a *z* of +1.0 occur .3413 of the time in the population. What is the probability of randomly selecting a *z*-score between the mean and *z* = +1.0? Since these *z*-scores occur .3413 of the time in the population, the probability of randomly selecting any one of them is .3413. Looking again at the distribution in Figure 9.1, we see that if the mean raw score is 59 and a score of 69 produces a *z*-score of +1.0, then the probability of randomly selecting a raw score between 59 and 69 in this distribution is also .3413.

Likewise, we can determine the probability of randomly selecting any score greater than a certain *z*-score. For example, what is the probability of selecting a *z*-score larger than +2.0? From the *z*-tables we see that all of the *z*-scores above *z* = +2.0 comprise .0228 of the population and thus occur .0228 of the time. Therefore, the probability of randomly selecting a score above *z* = +2.0 is *p* = .0228.

What is the probability of selecting a score that is beyond a *z* of ±2.0? The phrase "beyond ±2.0" means that we will be satisfied by any score above +2.0 or below −2.0, so we must determine the probability of drawing a score from either of the shaded areas shown in Figure 9.2. All scores beyond z = +2.0 constitute .0228 of the curve, and all scores beyond z = −2.0 constitute .0228 of the curve. In total, .0228 + .0228, or .0456, of the curve contains scores that will satisfy us. Since scores beyond ±2.0 occur .0456 of the time, the probability of randomly selecting a z beyond ±2.0 is p = .0456. On the distribution below, a raw score of 39 corresponds to a z of −2.0, and a raw score of 79 corresponds to a z of +2.0. Therefore, the probability is .0456 that we will randomly select a raw score below 39 or above 79.

Using the above procedure, we can determine the probability of randomly selecting any range of scores from any portion of any normal distribution. In fact, we can even use this procedure to find the probability of randomly selecting "scores" that are sample means.

## Determining the Probability of Sample Means

In Chapter 6 we saw that by applying the central limit theorem, we can create the theoretical normal distribution of sample means called the sampling distribution of means. We conceptualized the sampling distribution of means as a frequency distribution of all possible sample means that would result if our bored statistician randomly sampled a raw score population an infinite number of times using a particular sample size N. The sampling distribution is graphed like any other normally distributed population except that sample means, instead of raw scores, are plotted along the X axis. Since a sampling distribution shows how sample means are distributed in the population, it forms the basis for a theoretical probability distribution. The most important theoretical probability distributions in statistics are sampling distributions.

**FIGURE 9.2**   Area Under the Curve Beyond z = ±2.0

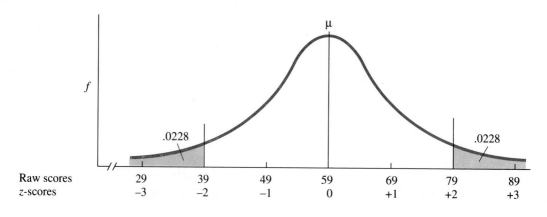

In Chapter 6 we also found a sample mean's location on a sampling distribution by computing the standard error of the mean (the standard deviation of the sampling distribution) using the formula $\sigma_{\bar{X}} = \sigma_X/\sqrt{N}$. Then we computed a $z$-score using the formula $z = [\bar{X} - \mu]/\sigma_{\bar{X}}$. Then, by applying the standard normal curve model, we determined the relative frequency of sample means falling above or below that $z$-score. In the same way that we just determined the probability of randomly selecting certain raw scores, we can now determine the probability of randomly selecting certain sample means.

Let's look again at the sampling distribution of SAT means discussed in Chapter 6, which is shown in Figure 9.3. The population mean, $\mu$, of this distribution is 500, and when $N$ is 25, the standard error of the mean is 20. First we examine the portion of the sampling distribution containing means with $z$-scores between 0 and $+1.0$. Since the relative frequency of such $z$-scores is .3413, the relative frequency of sample means that produce these $z$-scores is also .3413. Because an event's relative frequency in the population equals its probability, the probability of randomly selecting a sample mean with a $z$-score between 0 and $+1.0$ from this population is $p = .3413$. On this SAT sampling distribution sample means between 500 and 520 produce $z$-scores between 0 and $+1.0$. Thus, when $N$ is 25, the probability is .3413 that we will randomly select a sample mean between 500 and 520 from this SAT raw score population.

Think about this: randomly selecting a sample mean is the same as randomly selecting a sample of raw scores and then computing their mean. Likewise, randomly selecting a sample of raw scores is the same as randomly selecting a sample of subjects and then measuring their raw scores. Therefore, because the area under a portion of the curve provides the probability of selecting certain sample means, it also provides the probability of selecting the corre-

**FIGURE 9.3** Sampling Distribution of SAT Means When $N = 25$

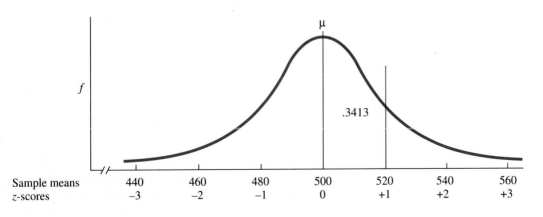

| Sample means | 440 | 460 | 480 | 500 | 520 | 540 | 560 |
| --- | --- | --- | --- | --- | --- | --- | --- |
| $z$-scores | $-3$ | $-2$ | $-1$ | 0 | $+1$ | $+2$ | $+3$ |

sponding samples. Thus, we can rephrase our above finding: when we randomly select 25 subjects from this SAT population, the probability of selecting a sample that produces a mean between 500 and 520 is .3413.

We can determine the probability of selecting any range of sample means from a particular raw score population. We saw in the previous section that $z$-scores beyond $\pm 2.0$ have a probability of .0456. Thus, the probability that we will select a random sample that produces a sample mean having a $z$-score beyond $\pm 2.0$ is also .0456. On the above SAT sampling distribution, $z$-scores of $\pm 2.0$ correspond to means of 540 and 460, respectively. Therefore, when we sample this SAT population, the probability is .0456 that we will randomly select a sample of 25 scores producing a mean below 460 or above 540.

In the same way, we can determine the probability of selecting any range of sample means from any normally distributed raw score population. From a different distribution of, for example, personality test scores, say that we compute that sample means of 88 and 78 have $z$-scores of $\pm 2.0$, respectively. Then the probability of selecting a random sample of subjects who produce a mean personality test score above 88 or below 78 is also .0456.

Computing a $z$-score for sample data and then determining its probability on a sampling distribution is the basis for all inferential statistical procedures. Therefore, think of a sampling distribution as a "picture of chance." It shows us how often, over the long run, we can expect random chance to produce samples having certain sample means when we randomly sample a particular raw score population using a particular $N$.

> *STAT ALERT* A sampling distribution of means provides us with a theoretical probability distribution that describes the probability of obtaining any range of sample means when we randomly select a sample of a particular $N$ from a particular raw score population.

Recall that the reason we are discussing probability is so that ultimately we can make decisions about our data. Now that you understand how to compute probability, the next step is to understand how to make decisions using probability.

## MAKING DECISIONS BASED ON PROBABILITY

The probability that I will make a typo at any moment is .80. Should you decide that I will make a typo on the next word? Yes, it's a good bet. Over the long run, I make typos 80% of the time, so on any word you are likely to win the bet. What is the probability that you made the correct decision? The probability of a correct decision equals the probability that chance will produce the event you are predicting. To figure this probability, assume that you make the same decision every time, over the long run. If 100% of the time you bet that I will make a typo and 80% of the time I make a typo, then you will be correct 80% of the time. Thus, the relative frequency of your winning the bet is .80, so the probability of winning any single bet is $p = .80$. Remember, though, that I do not make typos 20% of the time, so out of 100%, you will lose the bet 20% of the time. Since the relative frequency of your losing is .20, the probability of losing any single bet is $p = .20$. Conversely, if you bet that I will not make a typo, $p = .20$ of winning the bet, and $p = .80$ of losing the bet.

As this example illustrates, we decide in favor of high probability events, because by doing so, we maximize the probability of having made a correct decision. Conversely, we do not decide in favor of low probability events, because if we did, the probability of having made a correct decision would be low.

In statistics, we also make bets. As we shall see, the bet we make involves deciding whether random chance produced a particular event from a particular population.

## Deciding Whether Chance Produced a Particular Event

It is essential to remember that probability is based on the population of events over the long run. For example, even though we expect 50% heads and 50% tails, we do not expect that in a series of flips we will have precisely head, tail, head, tail, etc. Say we flip a coin 7 times and obtain 7 heads in a row. This will not concern us, *assuming that we have a fair coin!* If we see 7 heads (or 70 heads) in a row, we still assume that over the long run, the relative frequencies of heads and tails will each be .50. We understand that any single random sample of coin tosses may not be *representative* of the population of coin tosses because a head's relative frequency in the sample may not equal its relative frequency in the population. We have merely shown up at a time when luck produced an unrepresentative sample.

People who fail to understand this principle fall victim to the "gambler's fallacy." If we have obtained 7 heads in a row, the fallacy is that a head is now less likely to occur, because it has already occurred too frequently (as if the coin said, "Hold it. That's enough; no more heads for a while!"). If it is a fair coin, the probability of a head on the next toss is still .50. The mistake of the gambler's fallacy is failing to recognize that each coin toss is an independent event and we have merely observed an unrepresentative sample of coin tosses.

But what if we are not certain whether the coin is a fair coin? What if we are not certain whether random chance is operating? If you are betting money on the flips of a coin and another player obtains 7 heads in a row, you should stop playing: it's a good bet that the coin is rigged. How do we reach this decision? We compute the probability of obtaining such an outcome if the coin is fair (if the coin is crooked, we don't know how it is rigged, so we cannot determine any probabilities).

To compute a probability, we must determine the total number of possible outcomes. Therefore, we determine all possible series of heads and tails we could obtain by flipping a coin 7 times. In addition to the one way of obtaining all 7 heads,

head, head, head, head, head, head, head

there are many ways we can obtain 1 tail, such as

tail, head, head, head, head, head, head

or

head, tail, head, head, head, head, head

or

head, head, tail, head, head, head, head

and so on. Next we determine all the ways we can obtain 2 tails in 7 tosses, 3 tails in 7 tosses, and so on. We will find a total 128 different arrangements of heads and tails that can be obtained when a coin is tossed 7 times in a row. Only one of these outcomes will satisfy us, and that is obtaining all 7 heads. Thus, the probability of obtaining 7 heads in 7 coin tosses is 1/128, or about .008. (A shortcut formula for computing such probabilities, called the binomial expansion, is presented in Appendix B.)

Now we can decide about the fairness of the coin. If this coin is fair, then 7 heads in a row will hardly ever happen by chance. We expect its relative frequency to be 8 out of every 1000 times, or .8% of the time that the coin is flipped 7 times in a row. Since it is difficult to believe a player would be that lucky, we reject the idea that random chance has produced such an unlikely outcome, and we leave the game.

Notice that we have made a definitive, all or nothing decision: we reject the idea that chance produced the 7 heads, period. The probability suggests that the coin is crooked, so we decide that it is definitely crooked. In statistics, whenever we use probability to make a decision, our decision is a definite yes or no.

However, our decision could be wrong!

## The Probability of Incorrectly Rejecting Chance

Even though 7 heads in a row occurs relatively infrequently, we cannot be certain that the coin is rigged. Unlikely events are just that: they are unlikely, not impossible. Random chance does produce unusual samples every once in a while. In fact, we computed that we would expect chance to produce 7 heads in a row .8% of the time. Perhaps this was one of those times. Thus, regardless of the probability, we can never *know* whether random chance was operating or not. The best we can do is determine the probability that we mistakenly rejected the explanation that chance produced the event.

We determine the probability that we incorrectly rejected the chance explanation in the same way that we determine the probability of losing any bet. When chance is operating (and the coin is fair), it produces 7 heads in a row .8% of the time. Because this is such an infrequent event, 100% of the time that we see seven heads in a row, we will bet that chance did not produce the result. If we make the bet 100% of the time and chance does produce 7 heads .8% of those times, then .8% of the time that we reject chance, chance *will be* operating. Thus, over the long run, we will be incorrect .8% of the time. Since the relative frequency of our losing the bet is .008, the probability of losing any single bet is $p = .008$.

> **STAT ALERT** Anytime we reject the idea that chance produced an event, the probability that we are incorrect is equal to the relative frequency with which chance does produce the event.

Be sure that you feel comfortable with the above logic of deciding we had a crooked coin and then determining the probability that we were wrong. You need to understand this logic, because we apply it when making statistical decisions.

---

## USING PROBABILITY TO MAKE DECISIONS ABOUT THE REPRESENTATIVENESS OF A SAMPLE

Recall that in research, we use a random sample of data to draw conclusions about the behavior of the population of our subjects. In essence, we want to say that the way in which the sample behaves indicates the way in which the population would behave. However, there is an insurmountable problem: we can never be certain how that population would behave, because there is no guarantee that our sample accurately reflects that population. In other words, we are never certain that a sample of scores is *representative* of a particular population of scores.

Back in Chapter 2 we said that a representative sample is a mini-version of the population, having the same characteristics as the population. However, representativeness is not all or nothing. A sample can be more or less representative, having more or less the same characteristics as the population. This is because how representative a sample is depends on random chance. The sample may be somewhat different from the population from which it is selected by *chance*—the luck of the draw by which scores were selected—and thereby poorly represent that population. The problem is that when a sample is different from the population it actually represents, it has the characteristics of some other population and thus appears to represent that other population. The end result is that although a sample always represents some population, we are never sure *which* population it represents: the sample may poorly represent one population, or it may represent another population.

This was the problem we faced with the crooked coin: we were uncertain whether the sample of coin tosses was representative of the population of tosses for a fair coin or the population of tosses for a crooked coin. We decided whether our sample represented the population of fair coin tosses by determining the probability of obtaining our sample from that population. Implicitly, we used this logic: if we flip a coin several times and obtain 55% heads and 45% tails, this sample appears reasonably representative of the population of fair coin tosses containing 50% heads and 50% tails. Even 60% heads and 40% tails is reasonably representative of fair coin tosses. In these situations, the fact that we do not have a 50-50 split between heads and tails is written off as being due to chance, because chance is likely to produce a less than perfectly representative sample.

Beyond a certain point, however, we begin to doubt that random chance is operating. For example, with 70% heads and 30% tails, we grow suspicious about whether our sample of coin tosses represents the population of fair coin tosses. When we saw 7 heads in a row, we seriously doubted the honesty of the other player: it was *too unlikely* that we would obtain such a sample by chance if the sample actually represented the population of fair coin tosses. Therefore, we rejected the idea that luck merely produced a less than perfectly representative sample from that population. We decided that the sample was not merely a poor representation of the population of fair coin tosses, but rather that it represented the population of tosses from a crooked coin.

To summarize our decision making above, we used a theoretical probability distribution based on the population of fair coin tosses. We determined that if the sample represents this population, the probability of obtaining a sample of 7 heads by chance is only $p = .008$. Because the probability of obtaining this sample from this population is so small, we concluded that the sample does not represent this population. Instead, we concluded that our sample represents the population of coin flips when the coin is crooked.

Here is another example. You obtain a sample paragraph of someone's typing, but you do not know whose. Is it mine? Does this sample represent the population of my typing? Say that you find zero typos in the paragraph. You cannot know for certain whether I typed this paragraph, but there is a good chance that I did not. Since I type errorless words only 20% of the time, the probability that I would type an entire errorless paragraph is very small.

Thus, the probability of obtaining such a sample paragraph is very small if the sample represents the population of my typing. It could occur simply by chance, but this is unlikely. Because chance is unlikely to produce such a sample when you randomly sample the population of my typing, you decide against this low probability event. You reject the idea that chance produced this unrepresentative sample from the population of my typing and.instead conclude that the sample represents some other population, such as that of a competent typist who makes few errors.

On the other hand, say that there are typos in 79% of the words in the paragraph. Since I make typos 80% of the time, this paragraph is reasonably consistent with what you would expect if the sample represents my typing. Although you expect 80% typos from me over the long run, you do not expect precisely 80% typos in every sample. Rather, a sample with 79% errors seems likely to occur simply by chance when the population of my typing is sampled. Thus, you can accept that this paragraph is more or less representative of my typing, but because of random chance, there are slightly fewer typos in the sample than in the population.

As we shall see, we use this same logic in research to decide whether a sample of scores is representative of a particular population of scores. This is the essence of all inferential statistical procedures: based on the probability of obtaining a particular sample from a particular population, we decide whether the sample represents that population. If the sample is likely to occur when the population is sampled, then we decide that it may represent that population. If the sample is unlikely to occur when the population is sampled, then we decide that it does not represent that population and instead represents some other population.

> **STAT ALERT**  The essence of all inferential statistical procedures is to decide whether a sample of scores is likely or unlikely to represent a particular population of scores.

The next chapter puts all of this in a research context. Meanwhile, in the following sections of this chapter, we will consider the basics of deciding whether a sample of scores represents a particular population of scores.

## Making Decisions About Samples of Scores

Say that we have returned to Prunepit U. and obtained a random sample of SAT scores having the surprising mean of 550! This is surprising because we think that the students at Prunepit U. are terminally average. Since the everyday, national population of SAT scores has a $\mu$ of 500, we should have obtained a sample mean of 500 if our sample was perfectly representative of this population. How do we explain having a sample mean of 550? On the one hand, the simplest explanation is that we obtained a sample of relatively high SAT scores merely because of random chance—the luck of the draw that determined who was selected to be in the sample. It is possible that chance produced a less than perfectly representative sample of the population where $\mu$ is 500. On the other hand, perhaps our sample represents some other population of SAT scores having some other $\mu$.

To decide whether this sample represents the population of SAT scores where $\mu$ is 500, we will determine the probability of randomly selecting a sample mean of 550 from the population having a $\mu$ of 500. As we saw previously, to determine the probability of obtaining a particular sample mean from a particular raw score population, we create the sampling distribution of means for that raw score population. Then, using $z$-scores, we determine the location of our sample mean on the sampling distribution and thereby determine the probability of obtaining that mean. If it is likely that random chance would produce a sample mean of 550 from the SAT population where $\mu$ is 500, we will accept that our Prunepit sample may represent this population. Conversely, if it is unlikely that chance would produce a sample mean of 550 from this population, we will reject the idea that chance is operating and conclude that our sample represents some other population of scores, having some other $\mu$.

Notice that we have two tasks to perform: we must determine the probability of obtaining our sample from this population, and we must decide whether our sample is too unlikely to be representing this population. In statistics, we perform both of these tasks simultaneously. To do so, we first set up the sampling distribution of means.

## Setting Up the Sampling Distribution of Means

Before we can do anything else, we must decide what it will take to convince us that a sample mean is too unlikely to be representing a particular population. Earlier we decided that we did not have a fair coin because the occurrence of 7 heads in a row was too unlikely for us to believe that chance produced it. Implicitly, we had defined "too unlikely": we had some probability in mind, and any probability less than that convinced us that the event was too unlikely to have resulted from sampling the population of fair coin tosses. In this way we had defined the *criterion* that formed the basis of our decision. (In Chapter 8 we saw that the $Y$ variable is called the criterion variable. Here we use the term "criterion" differently, to refer to a probability.) The **criterion** is the probability that we use to decide whether a sample is too unlikely to occur by chance to be representing a particular population. When the probability that a sample occurred by chance from a particular population is *less* than our criterion probability, then we decide not to accept the idea that the sample occurred by chance from that population. Instead, we decide that the sample is "too unlikely" to be representing that population, so it must be representing some other population.

Psychologists usually use the probability of .05 as their criterion. Because we must make a yes or no decision (yes, the sample represents the particular population, or no, the sample does not represent the population), we will reject the idea that chance produced *any* of the sample means that, together, have only a .05 probability of occurring in a particular population.

> **STAT ALERT**  The criterion probability that defines samples as too un-
> likely is usually $p = .05$.

As you know, on a normal distribution, the scores having a low frequency and thus a low probability lie in the tails of the distribution. Because probability is the same as the proportion of the total area under the curve, those sample means having a total probability of .05 comprise the extreme 5% of the curve. Thus, all samples falling in the extreme 5% of the sampling distribution are treated the same and considered too unlikely to accept as representing the particular population. Because there are two tails, we divide this 5% in half and demarcate the extreme 2.5% in each tail of the sampling distribution, as shown in Figure 9.4.

Quite literally, we have drawn a line in each tail of the distribution that defines "too unlikely." In statistical terms, the shaded areas beyond the lines comprise the region of rejection. The **region of rejection** is that portion of a sampling distribution containing values that are considered to be too unlikely to occur by chance. The size of the area under the curve that comprises the region of rejection is always equal to our criterion. Usually our criterion is .05, so the total region of rejection usually comprises .05 of the curve.

**FIGURE 9.4**  Setup of Sampling Distribution of Means Showing the Region of Rejection

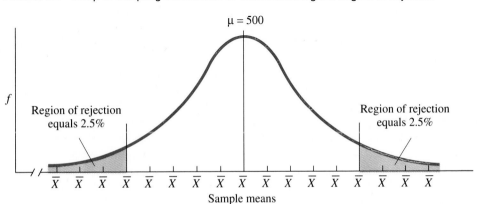

We use the sampling distribution as our model of how often various sample means occur when random samples are drawn from a raw score population having certain characteristics. For our Prunepit problem, it is as if the sampling distribution showed the frequencies of different means that our bored statistician would obtain if she randomly sampled this SAT population using our $N$. Thus, we see how often each sample mean is expected to occur when samples *are* drawn from the SAT raw score population where $\mu$ is 500 and when the samples *do* represent that population.

Remember, we are asking whether our sample from Prunepit U. is merely a poor representation of this SAT raw score population. Since the $\mu$ of the population is 500, sample means of 500 are perfectly representative. The more unrepresentative a sample, the more the sample mean differs from 500. Looking at the sampling distribution, we see that very infrequently are samples *so* poor at representing the population that they have means lying in the region of rejection. In essence, the region of rejection contains the worst, most unrepresentative sample means that we can obtain when representing this population. With our criterion, we have simply defined the most unrepresentative means as the most unlikely, extreme 5%. If our Prunepit sample mean lies in the region of rejection, then either our sample is an extremely unrepresentative sample produced by chance from this population or it represents some other population. Given how unlikely it is that the mean of a sample representing this SAT population will be in the region of rejection, if our sample mean is in this region, then it is not a good bet that chance produced it. Therefore, in statistical terms, we *reject* the idea that the sample is merely an unrepresentative sample produced by chance from this population. In essence, because we are too unlikely to obtain such means representing this population, if we obtain such a mean we reject the idea that the sample represents this population.

Conversely, if our Prunepit sample mean is not in the region of rejection, then it is not so unrepresentative as to be too unlikely to occur by chance if we are sampling this SAT population. In fact, by our criterion, sample means not in the region of rejection are likely to occur by chance when this population is sampled. In statistical terms, in this case we *retain* the idea that chance may have produced our particular sample mean and that the sample may represent, although possibly poorly, this population of SAT scores.

We locate our sample mean on the sampling distribution by computing a $z$-score for it. Since the absolute values of $z$-scores get larger as we go farther into the tail of the distribution, if the absolute value of our $z$-score is large enough, then our sample mean falls in the region of rejection. How large must the $z$-score be? With a criterion of .05, the total region of rejection equals 5% of the total area under the curve. However, we set up the region of rejection so that each tail constitutes half that amount, or .025 of the total area under the curve. From the $z$-table we see that the extreme .025 of the curve lies beyond the $z$-score of $\pm 1.96$. Therefore, the region of rejection lies beyond the z-score of either +1.96 or −1.96. Thus, as shown in Figure 9.5, for a sample mean to lie in the region of rejection, its z-score must lie *beyond* ±1.96. In this example, ±1.96 is the critical value of z. A **critical value** marks the edge of the region of rejection and thus defines the value required for a sample to be in the region of rejection.

Now, deciding whether our sample represents the SAT population where μ is 500 boils down to comparing the sample's z-score to ±1.96. Any sample mean producing an absolute value of z that is larger than the critical value of 1.96 lies in the region of rejection: it is among those means that we consider too unlikely to occur by chance when this SAT population is sampled. Therefore, we will reject the idea that chance produced our sample mean from this population and thus reject the idea that the sample represents this raw score population.

Conversely, any sample mean producing an absolute value of z that is smaller than or equal to the critical value is *not* in the region of rejection: it is among those means that we consider to be likely to occur by chance when this raw score population is sampled. Therefore, we will retain the idea that chance may have produced the sample mean from this raw score population and retain the idea that our sample may represent this SAT population.

> **STAT ALERT** When the z-score for our sample lies beyond the critical value, we *reject* the idea that the sample represents the particular raw score population reflected by the sampling distribution. When the z-score does not lie beyond the critical value, we *retain* the idea that our sample may represent that raw score population.

**FIGURE 9.5** Setup of Sampling Distribution of SAT Means Showing Region of Rejection and Critical Values

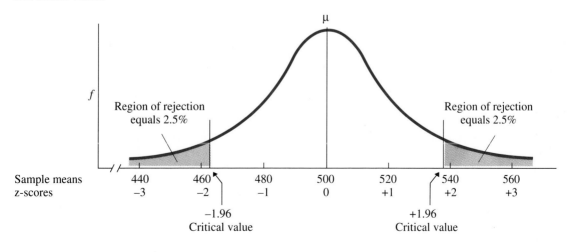

## Deciding If a Sample Is Representative

Now, at long last, we can evaluate our sample mean of 550 from Prunepit U. On the sampling distribution created from the population of SAT scores for which $\mu$ is 500, $\sigma_X$ is 100, and $N$ is 25, the standard error of the mean is $100/\sqrt{25}$, which is 20. Then our sample mean of 550 has a $z$-score of $(550 - 500)/20$, which is $+2.5$. Think about this $z$-score. If the sample represents this SAT raw score population, it seems to be doing a very poor job of it. Since the population mean is 500, a perfectly representative sample would also have a mean of 500 and thus have a $z$-score of 0. Good old Prunepit produced a $z$-score of $+2.5$! To confirm our suspicions, we examine the sampling distribution.

We can envision our sample mean as being located on the sampling distribution as shown in Figure 9.6. The sample's $z$-score of $+2.5$ is beyond the critical value of $\pm1.96$, so it is in the region of rejection. Because the $z$-score is in the region of rejection, the corresponding sample mean of 550 is also in the region of rejection. This tells us that our sample mean of 550 is among those means that we consider to be too unlikely to occur by chance when sampling the population of SAT scores having a $\mu$ of 500. It is not a good bet that, through random chance, we merely obtained an unrepresentative sample from that population: samples that are this unrepresentative hardly ever happen. Therefore, we reject the idea that chance produced this sample from this population and that our sample represents the population of SAT raw scores having a $\mu$ of 500. Notice that, as with the crooked coin, we make a yes or no

**FIGURE 9.6** Sampling Distribution of SAT Means Showing Location of the Prunepit U. Sample Relative to the Critical Value

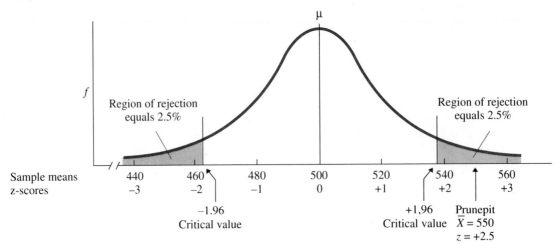

decision. Because our sample would be unlikely to occur if it represented the SAT raw score population where $\mu$ is 500, we decide that no, it definitely does not represent that population.

Once we reject the idea that our sample represents the raw score population reflected by the sampling distribution, we conclude that the sample represents some other population of scores, where such a sample mean is more likely. For example, a sample mean of 550 is more likely if students lie about their SAT scores. Perhaps our Prunepit subjects obtained a mean of 550 because they lied about their SAT scores, so they may represent the population of students who lie about the SAT. Or, since Prunepit U. is located on a toxic waste dump, perhaps toxic wastes produce higher SAT scores. This sample may represent the population of SAT scores of students who live on toxic waste dumps. Thus, in sum, as we did when betting on my typos, we decide against the low probability event that the sample represents the SAT population where $\mu$ is 500, and we decide in favor of the high probability event that the sample represents some other population.

On the other hand, say that our sample mean had been 474, resulting in a $z$-score of $(474 - 500)/20$, which is $-1.30$. Since $-1.30$ does not lie beyond our critical value of $\pm 1.96$, our sample would not be in the region of rejection. Looking at the sampling distribution, we see that when our bored statistician sampled this population, such a $z$-score and corresponding sample mean were relatively frequent and thus likely. Because of this, we can accept that random chance produced a less than perfectly representative sample for us, and thus that our sample may represent this SAT population.

In essence, we have described a system for evaluating the *difference* between our sample mean and what we would expect to obtain if the sample represented a particular population. We expect a representative sample mean to be "close" to the population mean. We cannot clearly recognize whether our sample is representative of the population, because we don't know which sample means should be considered to be close to the population mean of 500. Because a $z$-score describes a sample mean's relative standing, it allows us to determine whether or not the sample mean is relatively close to the population mean. From this perspective, the critical value of $\pm 1.96$ defines "close." If our sample has a $z$-score lying beyond the critical value, the sample mean is not close to the population mean. Then, the difference between our sample mean and the population mean is so large that we do not consider the sample to be representing that population.

## Other Ways to Set Up the Sampling Distribution

In the above example, we placed the region of rejection in both tails of the distribution because we wanted to make a decision about any sample mean having an extreme positive or negative $z$-score. However, we can also set up the distribution to examine only negative z-scores or only positive z-scores. (In the next chapter we shall discuss why we might want to do this.)

Say that we are interested only in sample means less than 500, having negative z-scores. Then we place the entire region of rejection in the lower left-hand tail of the sampling distribution, as shown in Figure 9.7. Notice that this produces a different critical value of −1.645. From the z-table (and using the interpolation procedures described in Appendix A), we see that the extreme lower 5% of the means in the sampling distribution lie beyond a z-score of −1.645. If the z-score for our sample is beyond this critical value, our z-score and our sample mean lie in the region of rejection. Therefore, we conclude that such a sample is too unlikely to occur in sampling the SAT raw score population where $\mu = 500$, so we reject the idea that our sample represents this population.

On the other hand, say that we are interested only in sample means greater than 500, having positive z-scores. Here we place the entire region of rejection in the upper, right-hand tail of the sampling distribution, as shown in Figure 9.8. We again use a criterion of .05, so the region of rejection constitutes 5% of the curve. Here, however, the critical value that defines the beginning of our region of rejection is a z-score of *plus* 1.645. If the z-score for our sample is beyond +1.645, our z-score and our sample mean lie in the region of rejection. Therefore, we conclude that such a sample is too unlikely to occur when the underlying raw score population is randomly sampled, so we reject the idea that our sample represents it.

**FIGURE 9.7**   Setup of SAT Sampling Distribution to Test Negative z-Scores

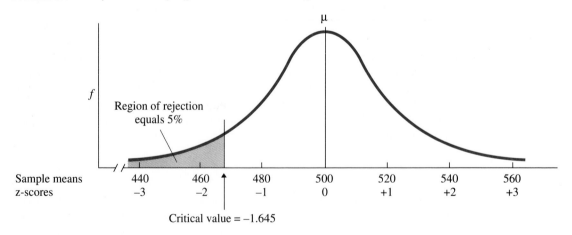

**FIGURE 9.8**  Setup of SAT Sampling Distribution to Test Positive *z*-Scores

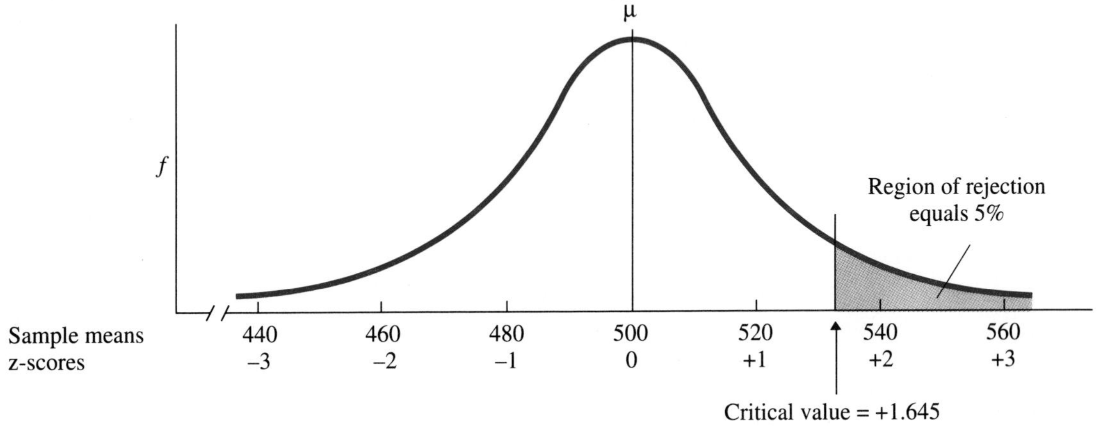

On Being Wrong When We Decide About a Sample

When we rejected the idea that we were playing with a fair coin, we might have been wrong: maybe the player obtained 7 heads in a row with a fair coin by chance. Seven heads in a row do occur sometimes, and maybe we happened to observe one of those times. In the same way, we might have been wrong when we rejected the idea that the sample from Prunepit U. represented the SAT population where $\mu$ is 500. The sampling distribution clearly shows that sample means in the region of rejection do occur sometimes by chance when the sample does represent the SAT population where $\mu$ is 500. Maybe our Prunepit sample produced one of those means. In the same way, anytime we reject the idea that a sample represents a particular population, we may be wrong.

We can also be wrong in another way. Say that we obtained a sample of SAT scores having a sample mean of 500! This sample certainly appears to represent the population of scores where $\mu$ is 500. Using the above procedures, we would compute a *z*-score of 0.0, so we would retain this idea. But it is possible that this sample actually represents some other population. Perhaps, for example, the sample is a very poor, unrepresentative sample from the population having a $\mu$ of 700! Simply by the luck of the draw, maybe our sample contains too many low scores, so that, coincidentally, it appears to represent the population where $\mu$ is 500. In the same way, anytime we retain the idea that a sample represents a particular population, we may be wrong.

Thus, regardless of which population we decide our sample represents, we have not proven anything, and there is always the possibility that we have made an incorrect decision. In the next chapter we shall discuss these errors and their probabilities. For now, recognize that even though such errors are possible, they are not likely. By incorporating probability into our decision making, we can be confident that we have made the correct decision. Thus, in the final analysis, inferential statistical procedures help us to be more confident that a sample represents a particular population.

### *FINALLY*

The decision-making process discussed in this chapter is the essence of all inferential statistics. As we shall see in the remaining chapters, the basic question we address is "Did chance produce an unrepresentative sample from a particular raw score population?" To answer this question, we create a sampling distribution based on that particular population. Then we compute a statistic, such as a $z$-score, to describe the results of our study. If the $z$-score lies beyond the critical value, then the $z$-score and the corresponding sample data fall in the region of rejection. Any sample in the region of rejection is, by definition, too unlikely for us to accept as having occurred by chance when we sample the raw score population reflected in the sampling distribution. Therefore, we reject the idea that chance produced an unrepresentative sample from this raw score population, and we conclude that the sample represents some other population that is more likely to produce such data.

## CHAPTER SUMMARY

*1.* *Probability,* or *p,* is a mathematical statement indicating the likelihood of an event when random chance is operating. The probability of an event is its relative frequency in the population and thus is the expected relative frequency of the event in any random sample.

*2.* When computing the probability of equally likely events, we determine the number of outcomes that can satisfy the event out of the total number of possible outcomes that can occur.

*3.* The probability that we are correct when we predict a chance event is equal to the probability that the event will occur. The probability that we are incorrect when we predict a chance event is equal to the probability that the event will not occur.

*4.* Events are *independent events* if the probability of one event is not influenced by the occurrence of the other events. Events are *dependent events* if the probability of one event is influenced by the occurrence of the other events. *Sampling with replacement* involves replacing a sample in the population before another sample is selected. *Sampling without replacement* involves *not* replacing one sample in the population before another sample is selected.

5.  A *theoretical probability distribution* is a theoretical model of the relative frequencies of all possible events in a population when random chance is operating.

6.  The standard normal curve model is a theoretical probability distribution that can be applied to any normal raw score distribution. Raw scores can be transformed into $z$-scores, and then the proportion of the area under the curve is the probability of randomly selecting those $z$-scores. This is also the probability of selecting the corresponding raw scores from the underlying raw score distribution.

7.  The standard normal curve model can also be applied to a sampling distribution. Sample means can be transformed into $z$-scores, and then the proportion of the area under the curve is the probability of randomly selecting those $z$-scores. This is also the probability of selecting the corresponding sample means from the underlying raw score population.

8.  The probability of randomly selecting a particular sample mean is the same as the probability of randomly selecting a sample of subjects whose scores produce that sample mean.

9.  All inferential statistical procedures involve deciding whether a sample represents a particular population by determining the probability of obtaining the sample from that population. If the sample is likely to occur when the particular population is sampled, then we decide that it may represent that population. If the sample is unlikely to occur when the particular population is sampled, then we decide that it does not represent that population and that it instead represents some other population.

10. The *region of rejection* is an area in the extreme tail or tails of a sampling distribution. Any $z$-score and corresponding sample mean that fall in the region of rejection are, by definition, too unlikely for us to accept as having occurred by random chance when we sample from the raw score population reflected by the sampling distribution.

11. The edge of the region of rejection closest to the mean of the sampling distribution is at the *critical value*. In order for a sample to fall in the

region of rejection, the sample's $z$-score must fall beyond the critical value.

12. The size of the region of rejection is determined by our criterion. The *criterion* is the probability that defines a sample as too unlikely. We usually use the criterion of .05. This produces a region of rejection that constitutes the extreme .05 of the sampling distribution.

## USING THE COMPUTER

The computer program will not compute a probability for random events such as coin tosses or playing cards. It will, however, compute a $z$-score for a sample mean, in routine **5**, if you know the mean and true standard deviation of the population. This is done as part of the inferential statistical procedure known as the $z$-test. Then you can decide whether your sample mean is representative of the population mean by comparing your $z$-score to the critical value.

## PRACTICE PROBLEMS

(Answers are provided for odd-numbered problems.)

1. (a) What does a probability convey about a random event in a sample? (b) What is the probability of a random event based on?
2. What is the difference between an empirical probability distribution and a theoretical probability distribution?
3. We often decide that a highly unlikely event will not occur. What risk do we run with this decision?
4. (a) When are events independent? (b) When are they dependent?
5. A couple with eight children, all girls, decides to have one more baby, because the next one is bound to be a boy! Is this reasoning accurate?
6. How does sampling without replacement affect the probability of events, compared to sampling with replacement?
7. What is the probability of randomly selecting the following?
   a. $z = +2.03$ or above
   b. $z = -2.8$ or above
   c. $z$ between $-1.5$ and $+1.5$
   d. $z$ beyond $\pm 1.72$
8. For a distribution where $\overline{X} = 43$ and $S_x = 8$, what is the probability of randomly selecting the following?
   a. a score of 27 or below
   b. a score of 51 or above

c. a score between 42 and 44
d. a score below 33 or above 49
9. What is the region of rejection, and what is it used for?
10. What is the critical value of $z$, and what is it used for?
11. The mean of a population of raw scores is 18 ($\sigma_x = 12$). What is the probability of randomly selecting a sample of 30 scores having a mean above 24?
12. The mean of a population of raw scores is 50 ($\sigma_x = 18$). What is the probability of randomly selecting a sample of 40 scores having a mean below 46?
13. Suppose that for the data in problem 11, you obtained a sample mean equal to 24. Using the .05 criterion with the region of rejection in both tails of the sampling distribution, should you consider the sample to be representative of the population for which $\mu = 18$? Why?
14. Suppose that for the data in problem 12, you obtained a sample mean of 46. Using the .05 criterion with the region of rejection in both tails of the distribution, should you consider the sample to be representative of the population for which $\mu = 50$? Why?

## SUMMARY OF FORMULAS

The formula for computing the probability of any event is

$$p(\text{event}) = \frac{\text{number of outcomes that satisfy event}}{\text{total number of possible outcomes}}$$

# 10

# Overview of Statistical Hypothesis Testing: The z-Test

In Chapter 9 we saw how to decide whether a sample is representative of a particular raw score population: the farther into a tail of the sampling distribution the sample mean lies, the less likely it is to occur. A sample mean that falls in the region of rejection occurs so infrequently that we reject the idea that our sample represents the underlying raw score population. Instead, we assume that it represents some other population in which the sample mean is more likely to occur.

If you understand the above review, then you understand the basics of inferential statistical procedures. In this chapter we simply put these procedures in a research context and present the statistical language and symbols used to describe them.

## MORE STATISTICAL NOTATION

Five new symbols will be used in stating mathematical relationships.

1. The symbol for *greater than* is >. We read from left to right, so, for example, $A > B$ means that $A$ is greater than $B$. (The large opening in the symbol > is always on the side of the larger quantity, and the symbol points toward the smaller quantity.)

2. The symbol for *less than* is <. The notation $B < A$ means that $B$ is less than $A$. (Again the symbol points toward the smaller quantity.)

3. The symbol for *greater than or equal to* is ≥. The notation $B \geq A$ indicates that $B$ is greater than or equal to $A$.

4. The symbol for *less than or equal to* is ≤. The notation $B \leq A$ indicates that $B$ is less than or equal to $A$.

5. The symbol for *not equal to* is ≠. The notation $A \neq B$ means that $A$ is different from $B$.

## THE ROLE OF INFERENTIAL STATISTICS IN RESEARCH

As we saw at the end of the previous chapter, a random sample may be more or less representative of a population. Just by the luck of the draw, the sample may contain too many high scores or too many low scores relative to the population. Because the sample is not perfectly representative of the population from which it is selected, the sample mean does not equal the mean of the population.

We have a shorthand term for describing when random chance produces an unrepresentative sample. We say that the sample reflects sampling error. **Sampling error** results when random chance produces a sample statistic (such as $\overline{X}$) that is not equal to the population parameter it represents (such as μ). Because of the luck of the draw, the sample is in error to some degree in representing the population.

> *STAT ALERT* Sampling error is the result of chance factors which produce a sample statistic that is different from the population parameter it represents.

There is always the possibility of sampling error in any sample. Whenever a sample mean is different from a particular population mean, it may be because either (1) the sample poorly represents that population of scores or (2) the sample represents some other population. This creates a dilemma for a researcher, who is trying to infer that a relationship exists in nature. Recall that in an experiment, we change the conditions of the independent variable in hopes of seeing scores on the dependent variable change in a consistent fashion. We want to infer that we would find this relationship in the population: if we measured the entire population, we would find a different population of scores located around a different value of μ under each condition. But here is where sampling error raises its ugly little head. Even though we obtain a different sample mean for each condition, perhaps we are being misled by sampling error. Maybe the samples are all more or less representative of the same population, so that if we tested everyone in the population under each condition, we would find the same population of scores, having the same μ, in each condition. Thus, perhaps there is no relationship in the population. Or perhaps there is a relationship in the population, but because of sampling error, it is different from the relationship represented by our sample data.

To deal with the possibility of sampling error, we apply inferential statistics. **Inferential statistics** are the procedures we use to decide whether our sample data represent a particular relationship in the population. Using the process we discussed in the previous chapter, we decide whether our samples are likely to represent populations that form a particular relationship or whether they are likely to represent populations that do not form the relationship.

There are two types of inferential statistics: parametric and nonparametric. **Parametric statistics** are procedures that require certain assumptions about the parameters of the raw score populations represented by the sample data. Recall that parameters describe the characteristics of a population, so parametric procedures are used when we can assume the population has certain characteristics. In essence, the assumptions of a procedure are the rules for using it, so think of them as a checklist for selecting the procedure to use in a particular study. There are specific assumptions for each procedure, but one assumption is common to all parametric procedures: regardless of the population of raw scores that a sample represents, we assume the population forms a normal distribution. Usually, the data are continuous interval or ratio scores most appropriately described by the mean. This chapter and Chapters 11 through 14 discuss the most common parametric procedures.

On the other hand, as the name implies, **nonparametric statistics** are inferential procedures that do not require such stringent assumptions about the parameters of the populations represented by the sample data. Usually these procedures are used when we have nominal or ordinal scores or when we have a skewed interval or ratio distribution most appropriately described by the median or mode. Chapter 15 presents the most common nonparametric procedures.

We choose nonparametric procedures if our data clearly violate the assumptions of parametric procedures. However, we can use a parametric procedure if our data come close to meeting the assumptions. This is because parametric procedures are robust. With a **robust procedure,** if we do not meet the assumptions of the procedure perfectly, we will have only a negligible amount of error in the inferences we draw. So, for example, if our data represent a population that is approximately normally distributed, we can still use a parametric procedure.

In the remainder of this book, we will become immersed in the details of inferential statistics. However, do not lose sight of the fact that in every procedure we ultimately decide whether our data represent a relationship in the population. A study is *never* finished until we have performed the appropriate inferential procedure and made that decision.

In this chapter we will discuss one parametric procedure so that you can see the general format and terminology used in all inferential procedures.

# SETTING UP INFERENTIAL STATISTICAL PROCEDURES

It is not appropriate to think about our statistical analysis only after we have collected our data. There are several decisions that we should make beforehand, for two reasons. First, the fact that we are performing a study indicates that we have some idea about how nature operates. To fairly test this idea, we must state it clearly before collecting the data. Second, we want to check that the data we plan on collecting will be "analyzable." It is possible to collect data and then find out that there are no appropriate statistical procedures we can apply.

In setting up a study, we do four things before collecting any data. First, we create our experimental hypotheses, which describe the relationship that the experiment either will or will not demonstrate. Then we design the experiment to test the experimental hypotheses. Then we translate the experimental hypotheses into statistical hypotheses, which can be tested using inferential statistics. Finally, we select and set up the appropriate statistical procedure. Once we have accomplished these steps, we collect the data, perform the analysis, and draw conclusions about the study.

## Creating the Experimental Hypotheses

Whenever we conduct research, we have some idea of how it should turn out. We formally express this expectation in the form of two experimental hypotheses. **Experimental hypotheses** describe the predicted relationship we may or may not find in our experiment. One experimental hypothesis states that we will demonstrate the predicted relationship (manipulation of the independent variable will work as expected), and the other experimental hypothesis states that we will not demonstrate the predicted relationship (manipulation of the independent variable will not work as expected). These two hypotheses are important because they help us to precisely define the purpose of a study, they force us to decide how we will recognize whether or not the study works, and they form the basis for setting up our statistical analysis.

We state our hypotheses in terms of the predicted relationship. For statistical purposes, we describe a predicted relationship in one of two ways. The simplest prediction is that there is some kind of relationship, but we are not sure whether scores will increase or decrease as we change the independent variable. The other, more complicated prediction states not only that there will be a relationship, but also the direction in which the scores will change. We may predict that as we change the independent variable, the dependent scores will increase, or we may predict that the scores will decrease.

In the following discussion we will examine a study in which we merely predict some kind of a relationship. Say that we are researchers interested in intelligence as measured by the intelligence quotient, or IQ. We have developed a new IQ pill that we believe will affect IQ, but we are not sure whether the pill will make people smarter or whether it will make them dumber. In any case, we hypothesize that there is a relationship such that the more of the pill a subject consumes, the more his or her IQ will change. Thus, the amount of the pill is our independent variable, and the subject's IQ is our dependent variable. Our two experimental hypotheses are

1. We will demonstrate that the pill works by either increasing or decreasing IQ scores.
2. We will not demonstrate that the pill works, and IQ scores will not change.

Once we understand the nature of the relationship our study is supposed to demonstrate, we design the study.

## Designing a Single-Sample Experiment

Although there are many ways we could design our IQ pill study, we will choose the simplest approach: a single-sample experiment. We will randomly select one sample of subjects and give each subject one pill. After waiting for the pill to work, we will give the subjects a standard IQ test. Our sample will represent the population of IQ scores of all subjects when they have taken one of our pills, and the sample $\overline{X}$ will represent that population's $\mu$.

To demonstrate a relationship, we must demonstrate that *different* amounts of the pill produce *different* populations of IQ scores, having different $\mu$'s. Therefore, we must compare the population represented by our sample to some other population receiving some other amount of the pill. (To perform any single-sample experiment, we must already know the population mean under some other condition of the independent variable.) One amount of the pill is zero, or no amount. The IQ test we are using has been given over the years to many subjects who have not taken our IQ pill, and this population of IQ scores has a $\mu$ of 100. We will compare this population without the pill to the population with the pill represented by our sample. If we find that the population represented by our sample has a different $\mu$ than the population without the pill, then we have demonstrated a relationship in the population.

## Creating the Statistical Hypotheses

Statistical hypotheses are translations of experimental hypotheses. They allow us to rephrase our experimental hypotheses in such a way that we can apply statistical procedures to them. **Statistical hypotheses** are statements that describe the population parameters our sample data will represent if the predicted relationship exists or does not exist. There are always two statistical hypotheses, the alternative hypothesis and the null hypothesis.

**The alternative hypothesis**  Although we can create the two statistical hypotheses in either order, it is often easier to first create the alternative hypothesis, because it corresponds to the experimental hypothesis that the experiment *does* work as predicted. The *alternative hypothesis* describes the population parameters that the sample data will represent if the predicted relationship exists. The alternative hypothesis is always the hypothesis of a difference; it says that changing the independent variable produces the predicted difference in the population of scores.

If our IQ pill works as predicted, we will find one of two outcomes. Figure 10.1 shows the change in the population if the pill increases IQ scores. The amount of overlap merely indicates how much the pill increases scores. If there is overlap, then the highest scores in the population without the pill are among the lowest scores in the population with the pill. If there is no overlap, then the pill increases scores to such a degree that there are no scores in common.

To summarize the relationship in Figure 10.1, we use $\mu$. We do not know how much IQ scores will increase, so we do not know the value of $\mu$ with the pill. But we do know that if the pill increases IQ, then the $\mu$ of the population with the pill will be *greater* than 100, the $\mu$ of the population without the pill.

On the other hand, Figure 10.2 shows the change in the population if the pill decreases IQ scores. Here, the $\mu$ of the population with the pill is *less* than 100, the $\mu$ of the population without the pill.

**FIGURE 10.1**   Relationship in the Population If the IQ Pill Increases IQ Scores

*As the amount of the pill is changed from 0 pills to 1 pill, the IQ scores in the population tend to increase in a consistent fashion.*

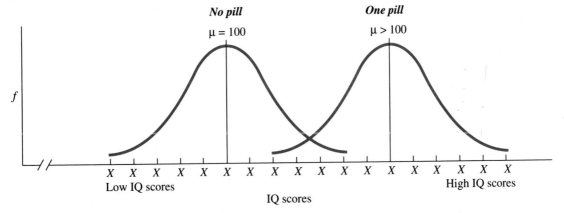

**FIGURE 10.2**   Relationship in the Population If the IQ Pill Decreases IQ Scores

*As the amount of the pill is changed from 0 pills to 1 pill, the IQ scores in the population tend to decrease in a consistent fashion.*

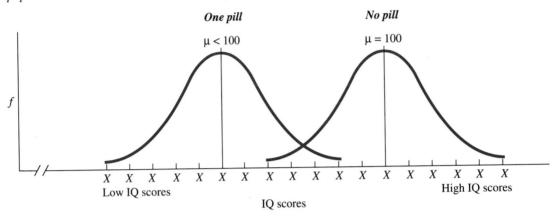

The alternative hypothesis provides a shorthand way of communicating all of the above. If the pill works as predicted, then the population with the pill will have a $\mu$ that is either greater than or less than 100. In other words, the population mean with the pill will *not equal* 100.

The symbol for the alternative hypothesis is $H_a$. (The *H* stands for hypothesis, and the a stands for alternative.) For our IQ pill experiment, we would write the alternative hypothesis as

$$H_a: \mu \neq 100$$

$H_a$ implies that our sample mean represents a population mean not equal to 100, in which case we have demonstrated the predicted relationship. Thus, we interpret $H_a$ as stating that our experiment worked as predicted.

**The null hypothesis**   The statistical hypothesis corresponding to the experimental hypothesis that the experiment does *not* work as predicted is the null hypothesis. The **null hypothesis** describes the population parameters that the sample data will represent if the predicted relationship does *not* exist. The null hypothesis is the hypothesis of "no difference": it says that changing the independent variable does *not* produce the predicted difference in the population of scores.

If our IQ pill does not work, then it will be as if the pill were not present. The population of IQ scores without the pill has a $\mu$ of 100. Therefore, if the pill does not work, then after everyone has taken the pill, the population of IQ scores will be unchanged and $\mu$ will still be 100. If we measured the

**FIGURE 10.3** Population of Scores If the IQ Pill Does Not Affect IQ Scores

*Here there is no relationship.*

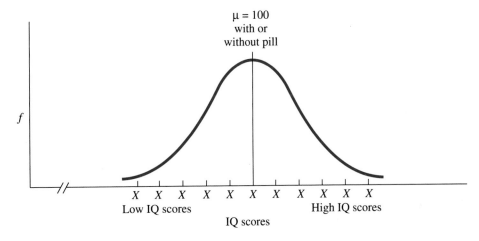

population with and without the pill, we would have one population of scores, located at the $\mu$ of 100, as shown in Figure 10.3.

The null hypothesis is a shorthand way of writing the above. The symbol for the null hypothesis is $H_0$. (The subscript is 0 because *null* means zero, as in zero relationship.) We write the null hypothesis for our IQ pill study as

$H_0$: $\mu = 100$

$H_0$ implies that our sample mean represents a population mean equal to 100, in which case we have not demonstrated the predicted relationship. Thus, we interpret $H_0$ as implying that our experiment did not work as predicted.

The final step prior to collecting data is to select and set up the appropriate statistical procedure. However, we will violate the order of things and go directly to our data so that you can understand what it is we are setting up.

## The Logic of Statistical Hypothesis Testing

The statistical hypotheses for our IQ pill study are

$H_0$: $\mu = 100$

$H_a$: $\mu \neq 100$

Notice that, together, $H_0$ and $H_a$ always include all possibilities: our sample mean represents either a $\mu$ equal to 100 or a $\mu$ not equal to 100. We use inferential procedures to test (choose between) these two statistical hypotheses.

To see why we need statistical hypothesis testing, say that we randomly selected a sample of 36 subjects, gave them the IQ pill, and then measured their IQ. We found that the mean of our sample of IQ scores was 105. Can we conclude that the IQ pill works?

We want to say this: People who have not taken this IQ pill have a mean IQ of 100. If the pill did not work, then our sample mean should have been 100. However, our sample mean was 105. This suggests that the pill does work, raising IQ scores about 5 points. If the pill does this for the sample, we assume that it would do this for the population. Therefore, we expect that the population that received the pill would have a μ of 105. Our results appear to be consistent with our alternative hypothesis, $H_a$: μ ≠ 100, which states that our sample represents a population mean not equal to 100. It seems that if we were to measure everyone in the population with and without the pill, we would have the distributions shown previously in Figure 10.1, with the population that received the pill located at a μ of 105. Conclusion: we have demonstrated that our IQ pill works. In nature there is a relationship such that increasing the amount of the pill from 0 to 1 pill is associated with increasing IQ scores.

But hold on! Not so fast! Remember sampling error? We just assumed that our sample is *perfectly* representative of the population it represents. We said that if the pill did not work we *should* have obtained a sample mean of 100. What we should have said is "If the pill did not work *and there was no sampling error,* the sample mean should have been 100." But what if there *was* sampling error? Maybe we obtained a mean of 105 not because the pill works, but because we inaccurately represented the situation where the pill does *not* work. Maybe the pill does nothing, but we happened to select a smarter-than-average sample. Maybe the null hypothesis is the correct hypothesis: even though it does not look like it, maybe our sample represents the population where μ is 100. Maybe we have not demonstrated that the pill works.

Strange, isn't it? We conducted this research because we did not know whether the pill works. Now, after we have conducted the research, we *still* don't know whether the pill works! The truth is that we can never *know* whether our IQ pill works based on the results of one study. Whether our sample mean is 105, 1050, or 105,000, it is still possible that the null hypothesis is true: the pill doesn't work, the sample actually represents the population where μ is 100, and the sample mean merely reflects sampling error. In any study, the null hypothesis steadfastly maintains that the sample data reflect sampling error and do not represent the predicted relationship.

> **STAT ALERT** The null hypothesis always includes the idea that if our sample statistic is different from the parameters described by $H_0$, it is because of sampling error.

To know for certain whether our pill actually works, we would have to give it to the entire population and see whether $\mu$ was 100 or 105. We cannot do that. Instead, the best we can do is to use our study to increase our *confidence* that the pill works. Before we tested the pill, our confidence that the pill works was based solely on our confidence that we had derived the correct formula for the magic ingredients in the pill. We conducted empirical research to increase our confidence that the pill works. But now we see that the null hypothesis says that chance sampling error gave the impression that the pill works. If we can reject the null hypothesis, then we can be even more confident that the pill works. From this perspective, statistical hypothesis testing is merely a slight detour we take—a tool we use—to increase our confidence that we have demonstrated a relationship.

So first we must make a decision about that pesky sampling error. In statistical hypothesis testing, the hypothesis that we actually test is the null hypothesis: we test the idea that we have sampling error in representing the population for which $\mu$ is 100 and the pill does not work. If the null hypothesis and sampling error can reasonably explain our results, then we will *not* accept the hypothesis that the pill works. After all, it makes no sense to believe that the IQ pill works if our results can be easily explained by sampling error from the population of IQ scores *without* the pill. As scientists trying to describe nature, we want to be very careful not to conclude that we have demonstrated a relationship when actually our results are due to chance factors. Therefore, we won't buy that the pill works unless we are convinced that the results are *not* due to sampling error. Only if the null hypothesis fails the test do we accept the alternative hypothesis (that the pill works). By testing and eliminating the null hypothesis, we can have greater confidence that the data actually demonstrate that the pill works and that there is a relationship in nature.

Although we cannot determine whether the null hypothesis is true, we can determine how *likely* it is that a sample mean of 105 will occur when the sample represents the population where $\mu$ is 100. If such a mean is too unlikely, then we reject $H_0$ and reject the idea that, because of sampling error, our sample poorly represents the population where $\mu$ is 100. If this sounds familiar, it's because this is the procedure we discussed in the previous chapter. In fact, all parametric and nonparametric inferential statistics involve the same logic: we test our null hypothesis by determining the probability of obtaining our sample data from the population described by the null hypothesis.

Which particular inferential procedure we use depends on the design of our experiment and the characteristics of our dependent variable. In other words, our study must meet the assumptions of the procedure. Our IQ pill study meets the assumptions of the parametric inferential test known as the *z*-test.

## TESTING STATISTICAL HYPOTHESES WHEN $\sigma_X$ IS KNOWN: THE z-TEST

You already know how to perform the z-test. The **z-test** is the procedure for computing a z-score for a sample mean on the sampling distribution of means discussed in previous chapters. The formula for the z-test is the formula we used in Chapter 6 and again in Chapter 9 (and we will see it again in a moment). The assumptions of the z-test are as follows:

1. We have randomly selected one sample.
2. The dependent variable is at least approximately normally distributed in the population, it involves an interval or ratio scale, and the mean is the appropriate measure of central tendency.
3. We know the mean of the population of raw scores under some other condition of the independent variable.
4. We know the standard deviation ($\sigma_X$) of the *population* described by the null hypothesis. It is *not* estimated using the sample.

We can use the z-test for our IQ pill study because we have one sample of IQ scores, such scores are from an interval variable, and the population of IQ scores is normally distributed. Most importantly, we know $\sigma_X$ for the population. Say that from our reading of the literature on IQ testing, we know that in the population where $\mu$ is 100, the standard deviation, $\sigma_X$, is 15.

> **STAT ALERT** The z-test is used only if the raw score population's $\sigma_X$ is *known*.

Now that we have chosen our statistical procedure, we can set up our sampling distribution.

### Setting Up the Sampling Distribution of Means for a Two-Tailed Test

In our IQ pill study, $H_0$ is that the sample represents the population where $\mu$ is 100 (and $\sigma_X$ is 15). To test this $H_0$, we will examine the sampling distribution created from the raw score population where $\mu$ is 100 and $\sigma_X$ is 15. One way of creating the sampling distribution of means would be to again hire our bored statistician (she's getting very bored, but she's a good sport). Using our $N$ of 36, she would infinitely sample the raw score population of IQ scores where $\mu$ is 100. She would then create a frequency distribution of the different values of sample means she obtained. An easier way to create the sampling distribution is to apply the central limit theorem. The central limit theorem tells us that the means will be normally distributed and that the mean of the sampling distribution will equal the $\mu$ of the raw score population, 100. Recall that this is the value of $\mu$ in our null hypothesis, $H_0: \mu = 100$.

>    ***STAT ALERT*** The mean of the sampling distribution always equals the value described by $H_0$.

We call this sampling distribution the null, or $H_0$, sampling distribution because it describes the situation *when null is true:* it describes random samples from a population where $\mu$ *is* 100 and any sample mean not equal to 100 occurs solely because of sampling error—the luck of the draw that determined who was selected to be in that particular sample. (To any information you obtain from a sampling distribution, add the phrase "when null is true.")

Recall that those means that we consider "too unlikely" are located in the extreme tail of the sampling distribution, the area we call the region of rejection. The next step before we collect our data is to identify the size and location of the region of rejection.

**Choosing alpha: the size of the region of rejection**    Recall from Chapter 9 that the criterion is the probability we use to define sample means that are "too unlikely" to represent the underlying raw score population. The criterion is also the theoretical size of the region of rejection. Here is a new symbol: the symbol for our criterion and the theoretical size of our rejection region is $\alpha$, the Greek letter **alpha**. Psychologists usually set their criterion at .05, so in code they say $\alpha = .05$.

**Locating the region of rejection in the two-tailed test**    In the previous chapter we saw that the region of rejection can be located in both tails of the distribution or in only one tail. Which arrangement we use depends entirely on our statistical hypotheses—in particular, our alternative hypothesis. According to the alternative hypothesis in our IQ study, our sample mean represents either a $\mu$ larger than 100 or a $\mu$ smaller than 100, because we predicted that the pill would make people either smarter or dumber. Thus, our prediction is that our sample mean will be either larger than 100 or smaller than 100 and, in either case, too unlikely to represent the population for which $\mu = 100$. Therefore, as shown in Figure 10.4, we place part of the region of rejection in the tail above $\mu = 100$ and part of it in the tail below $\mu = 100$.

Because we have placed the region of rejection in the two tails of the distribution, we are testing our null hypothesis with a two-tailed test. A **two-tailed test** is used to test statistical hypotheses in which we predict that there

**FIGURE 10.4**   Sampling Distribution of IQ Means for a Two-Tailed Test

*There is a region of rejection in each tail of the distribution, marked by the critical values of ±1.96.*

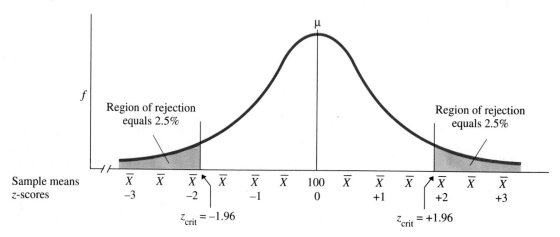

is some kind of relationship, but we do not predict whether scores increase or decrease.

> **STAT ALERT**  A two-tailed test is used whenever we do *not* predict the direction in which scores will change.

You have a two-tailed test whenever your null hypothesis simply states that the population parameter equals some value and your alternative hypothesis states that the population parameter does not equal that value.

**Determining the critical value**  Once we have decided that we have a two-tailed test, we identify the *critical value of z*. In code, we abbreviate the critical value of *z* as $z_{crit}$.

As shown in Figure 10.4, $z_{crit}$ demarcates the region of rejection. When we set $\alpha = .05$ and place one-half of the region of rejection in each tail, each half contains the extreme 2.5% of the distribution. From the *z*-tables we see that a *z*-score of 1.96 demarcates the extreme 2.5% of the curve. Since either +1.96 or −1.96 demarcates a part of our region of rejection, $z_{crit}$ is ±1.96.

Now our test of $H_0$ boils down to this: if the *z*-score for our sample lies beyond ±1.96, then our sample mean lies in the region of rejection. The final step for our IQ pill data is to compute the *z*-score for our sample.

## PERFORMING THE z-TEST

Here is some more code. Since the z-score we compute is the z-score we obtain from our sample data, we will identify this z-score as *z obtained*, which we abbreviate as $z_{obt}$.

As we saw in previous chapters,

*THE COMPUTATIONAL FORMULA FOR THE z-TEST IS*

$$z_{obt} = \frac{\overline{X} - \mu}{\sigma_{\overline{X}}}$$

$\overline{X}$ is the value of our sample mean. $\mu$ is the mean of the sampling distribution when $H_0$ is true: it is the $\mu$ of the raw score population that $H_0$ says the sample represents. $\sigma_{\overline{X}}$ is the standard error of the mean, which is computed as

$$\sigma_{\overline{X}} = \frac{\sigma_X}{\sqrt{N}}$$

where $N$ is the $N$ of our sample and $\sigma_X$ is the true population standard deviation ($\sigma_X$ is *not* estimated from the sample data).

We first find the standard error of the mean, $\sigma_{\overline{X}}$. For our IQ pill study, the population standard deviation, $\sigma_X$, is 15, and the sample $N$ is 36. Putting these values into the formula for $\sigma_{\overline{X}}$ gives

$$\sigma_{\overline{X}} = \frac{\sigma_X}{\sqrt{N}} = \frac{15}{\sqrt{36}} = \frac{15}{6} = 2.5$$

Recall that the standard error of the mean is the standard deviation of the sampling distribution. So, when $N = 36$ and $\sigma_X = 15$, our sampling distribution of means has a "standard deviation" equal to 2.5.

Now we compute the z-score for our sample mean of 105 by putting the appropriate values into the formula for $z_{obt}$:

$$z_{obt} = \frac{\overline{X} - \mu}{\sigma_{\overline{X}}} = \frac{105 - 100}{2.5} = \frac{+5}{2.5} = +2.0$$

On the sampling distribution from the population where $\mu = 100$ (and $\sigma_{\overline{X}} = 2.5$), our sample mean of 105 has a z-score of +2.0.

In essence, this is what we have done: We want to know whether a mean of 105 is frequent and thus likely when representing the population where $\mu$ is 100. We cannot evaluate such a mean directly, but we can evaluate z-scores.

Therefore, we have transformed the mean into a z-score, and we have computed another sample statistic. The larger the difference between a sample mean and $\mu$, the larger the absolute value of $z_{obt}$. We know that our $z_{obt}$ of $+2.0$ is rather large and tends to describe a rather infrequent and unlikely sample mean. To confirm our suspicions, we compare $z_{obt}$ to $z_{crit}$.

### Interpreting $z_{obt}$: Rejecting $H_0$

Our $H_0$ implies that the pill does not work and that our sample represents the population where $\mu$ is 100. If we are to believe that $H_0$ is true, then a mean of 105 should be likely to occur when sampling from the population where $\mu$ is 100. Thus, the $H_0$ sampling distribution should show that a mean of 105 would occur relatively frequently for our bored statistician. However, looking at the sampling distribution in Figure 10.5, we see just the opposite.

The location of our $z_{obt}$ of $+2.0$ tells us that the bored statistician would hardly ever obtain a sample mean of 105 when she was drawing samples that *did* represent the population where $\mu$ is 100 (when $N = 36$ and $\sigma_X = 15$). This makes it difficult to believe that *our* sample mean of 105 represents the population where $\mu$ is 100. In fact, because our $z_{obt}$ of $+2.0$ is beyond the $z_{crit}$ of $\pm 1.96$, our sample is in the region of rejection. Therefore, we will conclude that our mean of 105 is "too unlikely" to accept as representing the population where $\mu = 100$. In essence, the idea that our sample is merely a poor representation of the population where $\mu = 100$ is not reasonable: samples

**FIGURE 10.5**   Sampling Distribution of IQ Means

*The sample mean of 105 is located at $z_{obt} = +2.0$.*

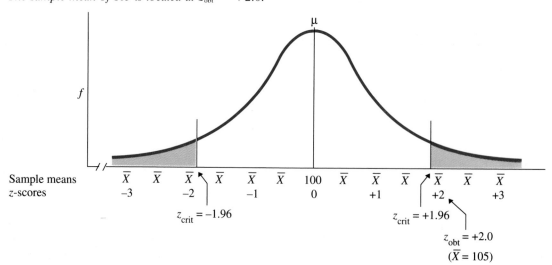

are seldom *that* poor at representing this population. Because random chance is too unlikely to produce such a sample from the population where $\mu = 100$, we reject the idea that our sample represents this population.

We have just rejected the null hypothesis. $H_0$ states that our sample represents the population where $\mu$ is 100, and we have found that this is not a reasonable hypothesis. Whenever our sample mean falls in the region of rejection, we say that we "reject $H_0$." If we reject $H_0$, then we are left with $H_a$. Thus, when we reject $H_0$, we also say that we "accept $H_a$." Here $H_a$ is $\mu \neq 100$, so we accept the idea that our sample represents a population where $\mu$ is not 100. In essence, since we have decided that our sample is unlikely to represent the population where $\mu$ is 100, we conclude that it is likely to represent a population where $\mu$ is not 100.

> **STAT ALERT** When a sample statistic falls beyond the critical value, the sample statistic lies in the region of rejection on the $H_0$ sampling distribution. This indicates that the statistic is too unlikely to accept as representing the parameter described by $H_0$, so we reject $H_0$ and accept $H_a$.

**Reporting significant results**   The shorthand way of communicating that we have rejected $H_0$ and accepted $H_a$ is to use the term *significant*. (Statistical hypothesis testing is sometimes called significance testing.) *Significant* does *not* mean important or impressive: when we say that our results are **significant,** we mean that our results are too unlikely to accept as being due to chance sampling error from the population where there is not the predicted relationship.

> **STAT ALERT** Whenever we use the term *significant*, we mean that we have rejected the null hypothesis.

We use the term *significant* in several ways. In our IQ pill study, we might say that our pill produced a "significant difference" in IQ scores. This indicates that the difference between our sample mean and the $\mu$ found without the pill is too large to accept as occurring by chance if our data represent that $\mu$. Or we might say that we obtained a "significant z": our sample mean has too large a z-score to accept as occurring by chance if the sample represents the $\mu$ described by $H_0$. Or finally, we can say that there is a "significant effect of our IQ pill": we have decided that the change in IQ scores reflected by our sample mean is not caused by chance sampling error, so presumably it is an effect caused by changing the conditions of the independent variable.

It is very important to remember that we decide either yes, we reject $H_0$, or no, we do not reject $H_0$. All z-scores in the region of rejection are treated the same, so one $z_{obt}$ cannot be "more significant" than another. Likewise, there is no such thing as "very significant" or "highly significant." (That's like saying "very yes" or "highly yes.") If $z_{obt}$ is beyond $z_{crit}$, regardless of how far it is beyond, we completely and fully reject $H_0$ and our results are simply significant, period!

Recognize that whether we have a significant result depends solely on how we define "too unlikely." *Significant* implicitly means that *given* our $\alpha$ and therefore the size of our region of rejection, we have decided that our data are too unlikely to represent the situation described by our null hypothesis. Because our decision depends on our criterion, anytime we use the word *significant*, we also report our value of $\alpha$. In reporting the results of any significant statistical test, we indicate the statistic we computed, the obtained value, and the $\alpha$ we used. Thus, to report our significant $z_{obt}$ of $+2.0$, we would write

$$z_{obt} = +2.0, \quad p < .05$$

Notice that instead of indicating that $\alpha$ equals .05, we indicate that the probability, $p$, is less than .05, or $p < .05$. We shall discuss the reason for this shortly.

**Interpreting significant results**   In accepting $H_a$, we also accept the corresponding experimental hypothesis that the experiment works as predicted: apparently, our IQ pill study has demonstrated that the pill works. However, there are three very important restrictions on how far we can go in claiming that the pill works.

First, we did not *prove* that the pill works, because we did not *prove* that $H_0$ is false. Statistics don't prove anything! All we have "proven" is that a sample of 36 scores is unlikely to produce a mean of 105 if the scores represent the population where $\mu = 100$ and $\sigma_X$ is 15. However, as the sampling distribution plainly shows, unrepresentative means of 105 *do* occur sometimes for samples representing this population. Maybe the pill did not work, and our sample was simply unrepresentative. There is *always* that possibility.

Second, by accepting $H_a$, we are only accepting the hypothesis that our sample mean represents a $\mu$ not equal to 100. We have not proven that the pill produced these scores. We have simply obtained data consistent with the idea that the pill works. We have been assuming that the higher IQ scores were produced by the pill, but they could have been caused by many other things (cheating on the IQ test, sunspots, who knows?). If we have performed a good experiment and can eliminate such factors, then we can *argue* that it is our pill that produced higher IQ scores.

Finally, assuming that the pill increased IQ scores and produced the mean of 105, then it is logical to assume that if we gave the pill to everyone in the population, the resulting $\mu$ would be 105. However, even if the pill works, the $\mu$ might not be *exactly* 105, because our sample may reflect (you guessed it) sampling error! Our sample may accurately indicate that the pill influences IQ, but it may not be perfectly representative of how the pill influences scores. If we gave the pill to the population, we might find a $\mu$ of 104, or 106, or *any* other value. However, since a sample mean of 105 is most likely when the population $\mu$ is around 105, we would conclude that the $\mu$ resulting from our pill is probably *around* 105.

Bearing these qualifications in mind, we can return to the sample mean of 105 and interpret it the way we wanted to about 10 pages back: it looks as if our pill increases IQ scores by about 5 points. But now, because we know that our sample mean is *significantly* different from a $\mu$ of 100, we are confident that we are not being misled by sampling error and that our sample does represent the population of higher IQ scores that would occur with the pill. Therefore, we are more confident that a relationship exists in the population and that we have discovered something about how nature operates. Ultimately, whenever we use the term *significant* to describe our results, we claim that the relationship found in the experiment represents a relationship found in nature. (But stay tuned, because we could be wrong.)

## Interpreting $z_{obt}$: Retaining $H_0$

For the sake of illustration, let's say that our IQ pill produced a sample mean of 99. Should we conclude that the pill decreases IQ scores, or should we conclude that our sample reflects sampling error from the population where $\mu$ is 100 and there is no pill? Using the z-test, we compute the z-score for the sample as

$$z_{obt} = \frac{\overline{X} - \mu}{\sigma_{\overline{X}}} = \frac{99 - 100}{2.5} = \frac{-1.0}{2.5} = -.40$$

Now our sample mean has a $z_{obt}$ of $-.40$. We again examine the sampling distribution, shown in Figure 10.6.

The $z_{obt}$ of $-.40$ is *not* beyond the $z_{crit}$ of $\pm 1.96$, so the sample does not lie in the region of rejection on our $H_0$ sampling distribution where $\mu$ is 100 (and $N = 36$ and $\sigma_{\overline{X}} = 2.5$). As the figure shows, when the bored statistician drew samples from this population, drawing a mean of 99 was a rather common, likely event. Thus, *our* sample mean of 99 is not too unlikely to accept as occurring by chance sampling error when the sample represents the population where $\mu$ is 100. Therefore, the null hypothesis—that our sample is merely a poor representation of a population where $\mu$ is 100—is a reasonable hypothesis. Given this situation, we certainly have no reason to think that $H_0$ is *not* true. In the language of statistics, we say that we have "failed to reject $H_0$" or we "retain $H_0$." Sampling error from the population where $\mu$ is 100 can explain these results just fine, thank you, so we will not reject this explanation.

**FIGURE 10.6** Sampling Distribution of IQ Means

*Our sample mean of 99 has a $z_{obt}$ of $-.40$.*

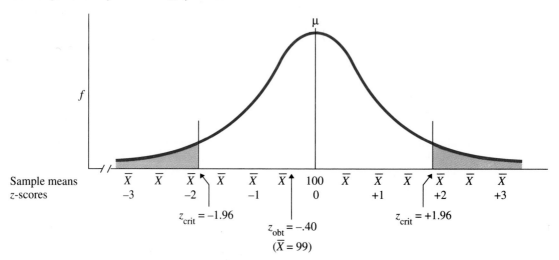

**STAT ALERT** We retain $H_0$ whenever $z_{obt}$ does not lie beyond $z_{crit}$ and thus does not lie in the region of rejection.

The shorthand way to communicate all of this is to say that we have *nonsignificant* results (note that we don't say *insignificant*). **Nonsignificant** means that our results are *not* too unlikely to accept as resulting from sampling error. *Nonsignificant* implies that the differences reflected by our results were likely to have occurred by chance if our data represent no difference in the population. Because we do not have *convincing* evidence of a relationship, we play it safe and conclude that we have not demonstrated a relationship.

When we decide that a result is not significant, we again report the $\alpha$ level used in making the decision. Thus, to report our nonsignificant $z_{obt}$ when $\alpha = .05$, we would write

$$z_{obt} = -0.40, \quad p > .05$$

Notice that with nonsignificant results, we indicate that $p$ is greater than .05.

**Interpreting nonsignificant results**  When we retain $H_0$, we also retain the corresponding experimental hypothesis that our experiment did not work as expected (we cannot yet become rich and famous). However, we have not proven that our *pill* does not work. Remember, we phrased our experimental hypothesis in terms of what our experiment demonstrates. Our *experiment* did not work, because it failed to demonstrate the predicted relationship. The only thing we are sure of is that we have failed to find convincing evidence that the pill works. Since we are likely to obtain a sample with a mean of 99 without the IQ pill, why should we think the pill works?

Recognize that failing to find evidence for something is not the same as proving that it is not there. For example, if you look outside on a cloudy night and do not see the moon, you have not proven that the moon is not there. You have simply failed to see it. You don't know if it is there (behind the clouds) or not there (below the horizon). In the same way, we have failed to obtain a sample mean that convincingly shows us that the pill works. Maybe, in fact, the pill does not work. Or maybe the pill does work, but it changes scores by so little that we do not see that it works. Or maybe the pill changes IQ scores greatly, but we don't see the change because we have so much sampling error in representing the different population $\mu$ that would be created. We simply don't know if the pill works or not.

Thus, when we do not reject $H_0$, all that we can say is that we have failed to find a significant difference, and thus we have failed to demonstrate the predicted relationship in the population.

> **STAT ALERT** When we retain $H_0$, we do not know if the predicted relationship exists in the population or not.

Because of the various reasons that we might obtain nonsignificant results, we cannot design a study that is intended to show that no relationship exists. For example, we could not do a study to demonstrate that the pill does not work.

## Summary of Statistical Hypothesis Testing

The steps and logic we have discussed above are used in all inferential procedures, so it is worthwhile to review them. In any research project, we do the following:

1. Create the experimental hypotheses predicting the relationship the study will or will not demonstrate.
2. Design a study to demonstrate the predicted relationship with the sample data.
3. Create the null hypothesis ($H_0$), which describes the value of the population parameter that the sample statistic represents if the predicted relationship does *not* exist. This value is also the mean of the sampling distribution.
4. Create the alternative hypothesis ($H_a$), which describes the value of the population parameter that the sample statistic represents if the predicted relationship *does* exist.

5. Select the value of $\alpha$, which determines the size of the region of rejection.

6. Select the appropriate parametric or nonparametric procedure by matching the assumptions of the procedure to the study.

7. Collect the data, and compute the obtained value of the inferential statistic. This is analogous to finding a z-score for the sample data on the sampling distribution.

8. Set up the sampling distribution, and, based on $\alpha$ and the way the test is set up, determine the critical value.

9. Compare the obtained value to the critical value.

10. If the obtained value lies beyond the critical value in the region of rejection, reject $H_0$, accept $H_a$, and describe the results as significant. Significant results provide greater confidence that your sample data represent the predicted relationship in the population and do not reflect mere sampling error in representing no such relationship. Then describe the relationship in the population based on the sample data.

11. If the obtained value does not lie beyond the critical value in the region of rejection, do not reject $H_0$ and describe the results as nonsignificant. Nonsignificant results imply that you cannot eliminate the possibility that the data reflect sampling error, so you have failed to find convincing evidence that the sample represents the predicted relationship. Do *not* draw any conclusions about the possible relationship in the population.

## THE ONE-TAILED TEST OF STATISTICAL HYPOTHESES

In some experiments we predict that scores will only increase or only decrease. In such situations we perform a one-tailed test. A **one-tailed test** is used when we predict the *direction* in which scores will change. For a one-tailed test, we set up our statistical hypotheses and the sampling distribution differently than for a two-tailed test.

### The One-Tailed Test for Increasing Scores

Say that we have developed a "smart" pill, and we want to perform a single-sample experiment. Our experimental hypotheses are (1) we will demonstrate that the pill makes subjects smarter by increasing IQ scores or (2) we will not demonstrate that the pill makes subjects smarter.

Our alternative hypothesis again follows the experimental hypothesis that the experiment works as predicted. Since the population without the pill has a $\mu$ of 100, if the smart pill worked and we gave it to everyone, it would *increase* IQ scores, so the population $\mu$ would be greater than 100. In symbols, our alternative hypothesis is

$H_a$: $\mu > 100$

$H_a$ implies that our sample mean represents the *larger* population $\mu$ that would occur if the pill worked as predicted.

Our null hypothesis again implies that the experiment does not work as predicted. Since we supposedly have a smart pill, the pill does not work if it either leaves IQ scores unchanged or decreases IQ scores (making subjects dumber). Therefore, if the smart pill did not work as predicted, the population would have a $\mu$ either equal to 100 or less than 100. Our null hypothesis is

$H_0$: $\mu \leq 100$

$H_0$ implies that our sample mean represents one of these populations.

We again test $H_0$ by examining the sampling distribution that describes sample means we obtain when $H_0$ is true. Of the infinite number of populations having a $\mu$ less than or equal to 100, there is only one population we know, and that is the population without the pill, which has a $\mu$ equal to 100. However, if we are unlikely to obtain a sample from a population where $\mu$ equals 100, then we are even less likely to obtain a sample from a population where $\mu$ is less than 100. Therefore, we test $H_0$: $\mu \leq 100$ by testing whether the sample represents the raw score population where $\mu$ is 100.

> **STAT ALERT** In a one-tailed test, the null hypothesis always includes a population parameter equal to some value. In testing $H_0$, we test whether the sample data represent that population.

We again set $\alpha = .05$. However, because we have a one-tailed test, we place our region of rejection in only *one tail* of the sampling distribution. For us to reject $H_0$, our sample mean must fall in the region of rejection in the *upper* tail of the distribution. This is because the sample mean must be significantly *larger* than 100 for us to be convinced that the smart pill works as predicted. Therefore, we place the entire region in the upper tail of the distribution, to form the sampling distribution shown in Figure 10.7.

As in the previous chapter, the region of rejection in the upper tail of the distribution that constitutes 5% of the curve is marked by a $z_{crit}$ of $+1.645$. The $z_{crit}$ is only *plus* 1.645 so that we will reject $H_0$ only when the sample mean is greater than 100. (However, notice that we have a *smaller* critical value than with the two-tailed test, and the edge of the region of rejection is closer to $\mu$.)

Say that we test our smart pill on a sample of 36 subjects and find $\overline{X} = 106.58$. We still base our sampling distribution on the population of IQ scores where $\mu = 100$ and $\sigma_X = 15$, so using the previous formula for the z-test, we

**FIGURE 10.7**   Sampling Distribution of IQ Means for a One-Tailed Test of Whether Scores
Increase

*The region of rejection is entirely in the upper tail.*

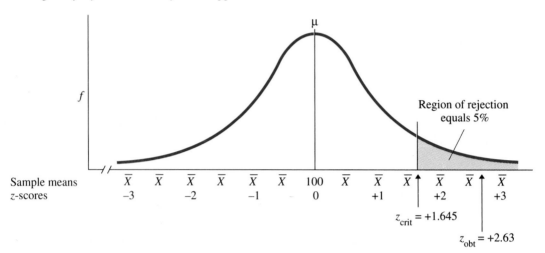

find that the sample mean has a z-score of $(106.58 - 100)/2.5$, which is $+2.63$.
As shown above, since this $z_{obt}$ is beyond our $z_{crit}$, our sample mean is among
those sample means that occur only 5% of the time when samples do represent
the population where $\mu$ is 100. Thus, we conclude that our sample mean is too
unlikely to accept as representing the population where $\mu$ is 100. Further, if
our sample is too unlikely to represent the population where $\mu$ is 100, then
our sample is far too unlikely to represent a population where $\mu$ is less than
100. Therefore, we reject the null hypothesis, $H_0$: $\mu \leq 100$, and accept the
alternative hypothesis, $H_a$: $\mu > 100$. We are now confident that our results do
not reflect sampling error, but rather represent the predicted relationship where
the smart pill works. We conclude that the pill produces a significant increase
in IQ scores, and we describe our sample mean and the relationship it represents
(with all of the cautions and qualifications we discussed above for interpreting
significant results).

   If our $z_{obt}$ did not lie in the region of rejection, we would retain $H_0$ and we
would have no evidence as to whether the smart pill works or not.

## The One-Tailed Test for Decreasing Scores

We can also arrange a one-tailed test using the lower tail. Say that we created
a pill to lower IQ scores. If we gave this pill to the entire population, we would
expect to find a population $\mu$ *less than* 100. On the other hand, if the pill did
not work, it would produce the same population as no pill (with $\mu = 100$) or

it would make subjects smarter (with $\mu > 100$). Thus, the hypotheses we would be testing are

Pill does not work:   $H_0$: $\mu \geq 100$

Pill works:              $H_a$: $\mu < 100$

We again test our null hypothesis, using the sampling distribution from the raw score population where $\mu$ is 100. If our pill lowers IQ, then the sample mean should be less than 100. For us to reject $H_0$, our sample must fall in the region of rejection in the *lower* tail of the distribution. Therefore, we place the entire region in the lower tail of the distribution, to form the sampling distribution in Figure 10.8. With $\alpha = .05$, our $z_{crit}$ is now *minus* 1.645. If our sample produces a *negative* $z_{obt}$ beyond $-1.645$ (for example, $z_{obt} = -1.69$), then we reject the idea that our sample mean represents a $\mu$ equal to or greater than 100. If we reject $H_0$, we accept $H_a$ (that the sample represents a $\mu$ less than 100). This significant result would then increase our confidence that we had demonstrated a relationship in nature where the pill works to lower IQ scores. If our $z_{obt}$ did not fall in the region of rejection (for example, $z_{obt} = -1.25$), we would not reject $H_0$ and would have no evidence as to whether the pill works or not.

### Choosing One-Tailed Versus Two-Tailed Tests

Look again at the sampling distributions for the one-tailed tests, and notice that there is no region of rejection in one of the tails of each distribution. This

**FIGURE 10.8**  Sampling Distribution of IQ Means for a One-Tailed Test of Whether Scores Decrease

*The region of rejection is in the lower tail.*

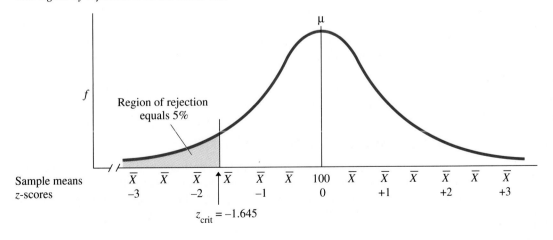

means that if our pills work in the opposite way from the way we predict, regardless of how well they work, we *cannot* reject $H_0$. If our smart pill produces a mean that is below 100, having a negative *z*-score, then the smart pill does not increase scores as predicted. Likewise, if our pill to lower IQ produces a mean above 100, then the pill does not decrease scores as predicted. In either case, we would retain $H_0$ and the corresponding experimental hypothesis that we have not demonstrated that the pill works *as predicted*.

> ***STAT ALERT***  In a one-tailed test, $z_{obt}$ is significant only if it lies beyond $z_{crit}$ *and* has the same sign as $z_{crit}$.

You cannot switch the region of rejection and the sign of $z_{crit}$ after the results are in. If you predict that the pill will increase IQ but it actually appears to decrease IQ, you can't switch and say, "Oh, I meant to say it decreased scores." You make the bet that the pill works in a particular way, and you either win or lose that bet. (Likewise, you can't switch between a one-tailed and a two-tailed test after the fact.) Statistical hypothesis testing is based on testing random chance, and switching after the results are in does not produce a fair and accurate test. Because of this, a one-tailed test should be used *only* if, before the experiment, you have a convincing reason for predicting the *direction* in which the independent variable will change scores. Otherwise, use two-tailed tests. They are safer because they allow you to determine whether an independent variable works, even if you cannot accurately predict whether it will work by increasing or decreasing scores.

> ***STAT ALERT***  Unless you have a specific prediction regarding the direction in which scores will change, you should use a two-tailed test.

## ERRORS IN STATISTICAL DECISION MAKING

There is one other major issue that we must consider when performing statistical hypothesis testing, and it involves our potential errors. The errors we will discuss are not errors in our calculations, but rather errors in our decisions: whether we conclude that our sample data do or do not represent the predicted relationship in the population, we may be wrong.

### Type I Errors: Rejecting $H_0$ When $H_0$ Is True

In previous examples where we rejected $H_0$ and claimed that our various pills worked, it is still possible that our sample was an infrequent, unrepresentative sample from the population where $\mu$ is 100. That is, it is possible that our sample so poorly represented the situation that we thought the pill would work when in fact it does not. If so, then we made a Type I error. A **Type I error** is defined as rejecting $H_0$ when $H_0$ is true. In a Type I error, we have so much sampling error that we are fooled into thinking that the predicted relationship exists when it does not.

Anytime we reject $H_0$, there is some probability that we made a Type I error. The probability of making a Type I error is the probability that we have rejected a true $H_0$. We determine this probability based on the size of the region of rejection, so, to use the lingo, it is $\alpha$ that determines the probability of a Type I error.

Figure 10.9 shows the region of rejection in a one-tailed test when $\alpha$ is .05. By definition, a Type I error can occur only when $H_0$ is true. As the sampling distribution shows, sample means that are in the region of rejection occur 5% of the time when $H_0$ is true. But we *always* reject $H_0$ when our sample mean falls in the region of rejection. The result is that sample means that cause us to reject $H_0$ occur 5% of the time when $H_0$ is true. Therefore, 5% of the time when $H_0$ is true and sampling error did produce our sample mean, we will reject $H_0$. In other words, 5% of the time when $H_0$ is true, we will make a Type I error. Thus, the relative frequency of Type I errors is .05. Since relative frequency equals probability, the theoretical probability of a Type I error is .05 anytime we reject $H_0$. (For a two-tailed test, when $\alpha$ is .05, the total region of rejection is still .05, so again the theoretical probability of making a Type I error is .05.)

Although the theoretical probability of a Type I error equals $\alpha$, the actual

**FIGURE 10.9**  Sampling Distribution of Sample Means Showing That 5% of All Sample Means Fall in the Region of Rejection When $H_0$ Is True

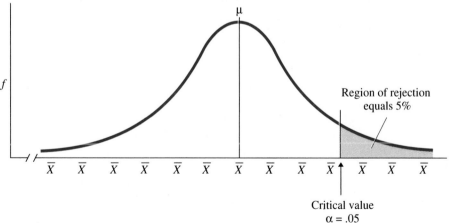

probability of a Type I error is slightly less than $\alpha$. This is because in figuring the size of the region of rejection, we include the critical value: in Figure 10.9, 5% of the curve is at or above $+1.645$. Yet for us to reject $H_0$, the $z_{\text{obt}}$ must be *larger* than the critical value. We cannot determine the precise area under the curve for the infinitely small point located at 1.64500, so we can't remove it from our 5%. All that we can say is that when $\alpha$ is .05, any $z_{\text{obt}}$ that allows us to reject $H_0$ falls in a region of rejection that is slightly less than 5% of the curve. Since the actual area of the region of rejection is less than $\alpha$, the actual probability of a Type I error is slightly less than $\alpha$.

Thus, in any of our previous examples when we rejected $H_0$, the probability that we made a Type I error was slightly less than .05. This is why we reported our significant result as $z_{\text{obt}} = +2.0$, $p < .05$. Think of $p < .05$ as a shortened form of $p(\text{Type I error}) < .05$. This indicates that our $\alpha$ was .05, and the probability is slightly less than .05 that we made a Type I error by calling this result significant when we shouldn't have. It is very important to always report $\alpha$ in this way, so that you communicate the probability that you have made a Type I error.

On the other hand, we reported our nonsignificant result as $z_{\text{obt}} = -.40$, $p > .05$. Here, $p > .05$ communicates that the reason we did not call this result significant is because if we did, then the probability that we made a Type I error would be greater than our $\alpha$ of .05.

We typically set $\alpha$ at .05 because .05 is an acceptably low probability of making a Type I error. Usually we do not set $\alpha$ larger than .05, because then we are too likely to conclude that a relationship exists when it does not. This may not sound like a big deal, but the next time you fly in an airplane, consider the possibility that the designer's belief that the wings will stay on may actually be a Type I error. A 5% chance is scary enough—we certainly do not want more than a 5% chance that the wings will fall off.

Recall that our study must meet the assumptions of our statistical procedure. This is because if we violate the assumptions of the procedure, then the actual probability of a Type I error will be *greater* than our $\alpha$. Luckily, as mentioned previously, parametric tests are robust. This means that if we violate their assumptions somewhat, the error in estimating the probability of a Type I error is negligible: the actual probability of a Type I error will be close to our $\alpha$. For example, if we set $\alpha$ at .05 and violate the assumptions of a parametric test somewhat, then the actual probability of a Type I error will be a number close to .05, such as .051. However, if we greatly violate the assumptions, we may think that $\alpha$ is .05 when in fact it is much larger, such as .20!

Sometimes we want to reduce the probability of making a Type I error even further, and then we usually set alpha at .01. For example, we might have set alpha at .01 if our smart pill had some dangerous side-effects. We would be concerned about subjecting the public to these side-effects, especially if the pill does not work. When $\alpha$ is .01, the region of rejection is in the extreme

1% of the sampling distribution, so we have a larger absolute critical value than when $\alpha$ is .05. This means that our $z_{obt}$ must be larger in order for us to reject $H_0$. Intuitively, it takes even more to convince us that the pill works, and thus there is a lower probability that we will make an error. Statistically, since we will reject $H_0$ only 1% of the time when $H_0$ is true, the probability of a Type I error is now $p < .01$.

Remember, use of the term *significant* is an all or nothing matter: a result is *not* "more" significant when $\alpha = .01$ than when $\alpha = .05$. If $z_{obt}$ falls in the region of rejection that we have used to define *significant,* then the result is significant, period! The *only* difference is that when $\alpha = .01$, there is a smaller probability that we have decided incorrectly and made a Type I error.

**Avoiding Type I errors**   If we *retain* $H_0$ when $H_0$ is true, we avoid making a Type I error by making the correct decision: we conclude that we have no evidence that the pill works, and it doesn't. Since $\alpha$ is the theoretical probability of making a Type I error, $1 - \alpha$ is the probability of avoiding a Type I error. In other words, if 5% of the time we obtain samples in the region of rejection when $H_0$ is true, then 95% of the time we obtain samples that are not in the region of rejection when $H_0$ is true. Thus, 95% of the time when $H_0$ is true, we will not reject $H_0$ and so will avoid a Type I error. (The other 5% of the time when $H_0$ is true, we will incorrectly decide to reject $H_0$ and make a Type I error.)

> **STAT ALERT**   We make a Type I error when we reject $H_0$ and $H_0$ is true. The theoretical probability of a Type I error is equal to $\alpha$. We do not make a Type I error when we do not reject $H_0$ and $H_0$ is true. The theoretical probability of correctly retaining $H_0$ is equal to $1 - \alpha$.

## Type II Errors: Retaining $H_0$ When $H_0$ Is False

In addition to Type I errors, it is possible to make a totally different kind of error. This error can occur when we *retain* $H_0$, and it is called a Type II error. A **Type II error** is retaining $H_0$ when $H_0$ is false (and $H_a$ is true). With a Type II error, we conclude that we have no evidence for the predicted relationship in the population, when, in fact, the relationship exists.

Anytime we discuss Type II errors, it is a given that $H_0$ is false and $H_a$ is true. We make a Type II error because our sample mean is so close to the mean of the population described by $H_0$ that we conclude that the sample reflects sampling error from that population. We might have made a Type II error in our previous example when we obtained a sample mean of 99 and did not reject $H_0$. Perhaps the $\mu$ of the population with the pill would be 99, and our sample represents this $\mu$. Or perhaps our pill would increase IQ scores greatly, say to a $\mu$ of 115, but we obtained a very unrepresentative sample with a mean of 99. In either case, because our sample mean of 99 was so close to 100 (the population $\mu$ without the pill), we retained $H_0$ and maybe made a Type II error.

The computation of the probability of Type II errors is beyond the scope of this discussion, but you should know that the symbol for the theoretical probability of a Type II error is $\beta$, the Greek letter **beta.** Whenever we retain $H_0$, $\beta$ is the probability that we have made a Type II error.

**Avoiding Type II errors**   We can potentially make a Type II error only when $H_0$ is false. If we reject $H_0$ when $H_0$ is false, we have avoided a Type II error and made a correct decision: for example, we conclude that the IQ pill works, and the pill does work. If $\beta$ is the probability of making a Type II error, then $1 - \beta$ is the probability of avoiding a Type II error. Thus, anytime we reject $H_0$, the probability is $1 - \beta$ that we have made a correct decision and rejected a false $H_0$.

> **STAT ALERT**   We make a Type II error when we retain $H_0$ and $H_0$ is false. The theoretical probability of Type II errors is equal to $\beta$. We do not make a Type II error when we reject $H_0$ and $H_0$ is false. The theoretical probability of correctly rejecting $H_0$ is equal to $1 - \beta$.

### Comparing Type I and Type II Errors

There is no doubt that Type I and Type II errors are two of the most confusing inventions ever devised. To better understand them and their probabilities, look at Table 10.1. The first row describes the situation when $H_0$ is true. If we

**TABLE 10.1**   Possible Results of Rejecting or Retaining $H_0$

|  |  | *Our decision* | |
|---|---|---|---|
|  |  | *We reject $H_0$* *(claim $H_a$ is true)* | *We retain $H_0$* *(claim $H_0$ may be true)* |
| *The truth about $H_0$* | $H_0$ is true *($H_a$ is false: no relationship exists)* | We make a Type I error *($p = \alpha$)* | We are correct, avoiding a Type I error *($p = 1 - \alpha$)* |
|  | $H_0$ is false *($H_a$ is true: a relationship exists)* | We are correct, avoiding a Type II error *($p = 1 - \beta$)* | We make a Type II error *($p = \beta$)* |

reject $H_0$ when $H_0$ is true, we make a Type I error, and the probability of this is $\alpha$. If we retain $H_0$ when $H_0$ is true, we avoid a Type I error by making a correct decision, and the probability of this is $1 - \alpha$. The second row describes the situation when $H_0$ is false. If we retain $H_0$ when $H_0$ is false, we make a Type II error, and the probability of this is $\beta$. If we reject $H_0$ when $H_0$ is false, we avoid a Type II error by making a correct decision, and the probability of this is $1 - \beta$.

In any experiment, the results of our hypothesis testing procedures will place us in one of the two columns. Anytime we reject $H_0$, either we make a Type I error or we make the correct decision and avoid a Type II error. Anytime we retain $H_0$, either we make a Type II error or we make the correct decision and avoid a Type I error.

Statistical procedures are designed to minimize the probability of Type I errors because they are the more serious for science: a Type I error means that we conclude that an independent variable works when really it does not. Basing scientific "facts" on what are actually Type I errors can cause untold damage. On the other hand, Type II errors are also important. In order for us to accurately learn about nature, we must avoid making Type II errors and conclude that an independent variable works when it really does.

## Power

Of the various outcomes in Table 10.1, the ideal situation is to reject $H_0$ when $H_0$ is false: our results lead us to conclude that our pill works, and the truth is that the pill does work. Not only have we avoided making an error, but we have also learned something about nature and our study has paid off (it's nice to be right). Thus, the goal of any scientific research is to reject $H_0$ when $H_0$ is false. This ability is so important that it has a special name: power. The **power** of a statistical test is the probability that we will reject a false $H_0$. Because this rejection avoids a Type II error, power equals $1 - \beta$. Think of power as it is used with microscopes: the more powerful a microscope, the better we can detect fine differences when they exist. The more powerful a statistical test, the better we can detect fine differences in a relationship, so we are more likely to conclude that one is present when it is.

The question of whether we have sufficient power arises anytime we retain $H_0$. Previously, when we failed to conclude that our pill produced significant differences when the sample mean was 99, maybe the problem was that we did not have much power. Maybe the probability was not high that we would reject $H_0$ *even if the predicted relationship existed*. So that we can have confidence in our decision to retain $H_0$, we want to maximize our power. Then the probability of avoiding a Type II error will be high (and the probability of making a Type II error will be low).

We cannot do anything to alter the probability that $H_0$ is false and that a relationship exists in the population. However, we can do things to increase the probability that we will reject $H_0$ when it is false. The logic behind maximizing power is this: when $H_0$ is false, we "should" reject it. In other words, when $H_0$ is false, our results "should" be significant. Thus, we maximize our power by maximizing the probability that our results will be significant. (If it sounds as if we are cheating by trying to rig the decision to reject $H_0$, remember: by setting $\alpha$ at .05 or less, we control the probability of making the *wrong* decision when $H_0$ is true. At the same time, by maximizing power, we maximize the probability of making the *correct* decision when $H_0$ is false.)

As we have seen, our results are significant if our $z_{obt}$ is larger than our $z_{crit}$. Therefore, we maximize power by maximizing the size of our obtained value relative to the critical value. This increases the probability that our results will be significant and thus increases the probability of rejecting $H_0$ when $H_0$ is false.

> **STAT ALERT**  The larger our obtained value, the more likely it is to be significant and thus the greater the power.

There are several things we can do to maximize power. At the beginning of this chapter, I said that we use nonparametric procedures only if we cannot use parametric procedures. This is because parametric tests are more powerful than nonparametric tests: if we analyze data using a parametric test, we are more likely to reject $H_0$ when it is false than if we analyze the same data using a nonparametric test.

Likewise, a one-tailed test is more powerful than a two-tailed test. This is because the $z_{crit}$ for a one-tailed test is smaller (closer to the mean of the sampling distribution) than the $z_{crit}$ for a two-tailed test. Previously, we used a $z_{crit}$ of 1.645 for a one-tailed test and 1.96 for a two-tailed test. All other things being equal, our $z_{obt}$ is more likely to be beyond 1.645 than beyond 1.96. Thus, we are more likely to conclude that our results are significant with a one-tailed test than with a two-tailed test. (With $\alpha = .05$ for both, the probability that we will incorrectly call the result significant is the same.) Of course, remember that we can reject $H_0$ only if our $z_{obt}$ has the same sign as $z_{crit}$.

As we shall see in later chapters, there are also ways to design and conduct research so as to maximize the power of statistical procedures.

## FINALLY

Conceptually, all statistical hypothesis testing procedures follow the logic described here: $H_0$ is the hypothesis that says our data represent the populations we would find if the predicted relationship did not exist; $H_a$ says that our data represent the predicted relationship. We then compute something like a $z$-score for our experiment's results on the sampling distribution when $H_0$ is true. If our $z$-score is larger than the critical value, it is unlikely that the results represent the populations described by $H_0$, so we reject $H_0$ and accept $H_a$. That's it! That's inferential statistics (well, not quite).

Each of the following chapters will describe procedures for testing statistical hypotheses from different kinds of experiments using different kinds of sampling distributions. In each, we will discuss the specific calculations we perform. However, the calculations should not be your primary concern. (After all, that's why they invented computers.) What a computer cannot do is tell you *why* you perform the calculations or what the answer *means*. It can never decide whether a result is significant or how you should treat the result. So your major goal should be to understand what the concepts mean and the logic of each procedure.

---

## CHAPTER SUMMARY

1. *Sampling error* occurs when random chance produces a sample statistic that is not equal to the population parameter it represents.

2. *Inferential statistics* are procedures that allow us to decide whether sample data represent a particular relationship in the population.

3. *Parametric statistics* are inferential procedures in which we make assumptions about the parameters of the raw score populations our data represent. They are usually performed when it is appropriate to compute the mean.

4. *Nonparametric statistics* are inferential procedures that do not require such stringent assumptions about the population parameters represented by our sample. They are usually performed when it is appropriate to compute the median or mode.

5. The *alternative hypothesis*, $H_a$, is the statistical hypothesis that describes the population $\mu$'s we would find if an experiment were performed on the entire population and the predicted relationship existed. $H_a$ implies that the sample mean represents one of these $\mu$'s.

6. The *null hypothesis*, $H_0$, is the statistical hypothesis that describes the population $\mu$'s we would find if the experiment were performed on the entire population and the predicted relationship did not exist. $H_0$ implies that the sample mean represents one of these $\mu$'s.

7. When we predict that changing the independent variable will change scores, but do not predict the direction in which the scores will change, we perform a *two-tailed test*. When we do predict the direction of the relationship, we perform a *one-tailed test*.

8. *Alpha*, $\alpha$, is the theoretical size of the region of rejection on the sampling distribution. Typically we set $\alpha$ at .05 and then determine the appropriate critical value for the one- or two-tailed test.

9. The *z-test* is the parametric procedure for testing the statistical hypotheses from a single-sample experiment if (a) the population of raw scores is normally distributed and contains interval or ratio scores, and (b) the standard deviation of the raw score population, $\sigma_X$, is *known*. The value of $z_{obt}$ indicates the location of the sample mean on the sampling distribution of means when $H_0$ is true.

10. If $z_{obt}$ lies beyond $z_{crit}$, then the corresponding sample mean lies in the region of rejection. This indicates that such a sample mean is unlikely to occur when samples are randomly selected from the population described by $H_0$. Therefore, we reject the idea that our sample represents such a population, so we *reject $H_0$* and *accept $H_a$*. This is called a *significant* result and is taken as evidence that the predicted relationship exists in the population.

11. If $z_{obt}$ does not lie beyond $z_{crit}$, then the corresponding sample mean is *not* located in the region of rejection. This indicates that such a sample mean is likely to occur when randomly sampling the population described by $H_0$. Therefore, we *fail to reject*, or *retain*, $H_0$. This is called a *nonsignificant* result and is taken as a failure to obtain evidence that the predicted relationship exists in the population.

12. A *Type I error* occurs when we reject a true $H_0$. The theoretical probability of a Type I error is equal to $\alpha$. If a result is significant, the probability that we have made a Type I error is $p < \alpha$. The theoretical probability of avoiding a Type I error by retaining a true $H_0$ is $1 - \alpha$.

13. A *Type II error* occurs when we retain a false $H_0$. The theoretical probability of making a Type II error is $\beta$. The theoretical probability of avoiding a Type II error by rejecting a false $H_0$ is $1 - \beta$.

14. When we reject $H_0$, either we have committed a Type I error or we have avoided a Type II error. When we retain $H_0$, either we have committed a Type II error or we have avoided a Type I error.

*15.* The *power* of a statistical test is the probability of rejecting a false $H_0$, and it equals $1 - \beta$. A powerful statistic has a high probability of detecting a relationship when one exists. When used appropriately, parametric procedures are more powerful than nonparametric procedures, and one-tailed tests are more powerful than two-tailed tests. The manner in which a study is designed and conducted also influences power.

## USING THE COMPUTER

In the computer program, you can perform the entire $z$-test using routine **5**. You do not have to determine the critical value, because the computer does it for you. However, note that this information is for a two-tailed test *only*. For a one-tailed test, you must obtain $z_{crit}$ from the $z$-tables and compare it to $z_{obt}$ as discussed in this chapter.

## PRACTICE PROBLEMS

(Answers are provided for odd-numbered problems.)

*1.* (a) What is sampling error? (b) Why does the possibility of sampling error present a problem to researchers?

*2.* What are inferential statistics used for?

*3.* (a) When are parametric statistics used, and when are nonparametric statistics used? (b) Why do researchers prefer parametric procedures?

*4.* What are experimental hypotheses?

*5.* What do $H_0$ and $H_a$ communicate?

*6.* What does $\alpha$ stand for?

*7.* What does the term *significant* mean?

*8.* How does the significance or nonsignificance of a result depend on the size of $\alpha$?

*9.* A researcher predicts that listening to music while taking a test is beneficial. He obtains a sample mean of 54.63 when 49 subjects take a test while listening to music. The mean of the population of students who have taken this test without music is 50 ($\sigma_X = 12$).

  *a.* Should he use a one-tailed or two-tailed test, and why?

  *b.* What are $H_0$ and $H_a$ for this study?

  *c.* Compute $z_{obt}$.

  *d.* With $\alpha = .05$, what is $z_{crit}$?

  *e.* Does the researcher have evidence of a relationship in the population? What is the relationship?

10. A researcher wonders whether attending a private high school leads to higher or lower performance on a test of social skills. A random sample of 100 students from a private school produces a mean score of 71.30 on the test, and the national mean score for students from public schools is 75.62 ($\sigma_X = 28.0$).
    a. Should she use a one-tailed or two-tailed test, and why?
    b. What are $H_0$ and $H_a$ for this study?
    c. Compute $z_{obt}$.
    d. With $\alpha = .05$, what is $z_{crit}$?
    e. What should the researcher conclude about this relationship in the population?

11. (a) What is the probability that the researcher in problem 9 made a Type I error, and what would the error be in terms of the independent and dependent variables? (b) What is the probability that the researcher in problem 9 made a Type II error, and what would the error be in terms of the independent and dependent variables?

12. (a) What is the probability that the researcher in problem 10 made a Type I error? Explain what the error would be in terms of the independent and dependent variables. (b) What is the probability that the researcher in problem 10 made a Type II error? Explain what the error would be in terms of the independent and dependent variables.

13. (a) What is power? (b) Why do we want to maximize power?

## SUMMARY OF FORMULAS

1. *The computational formula for the z-test is*

$$z_{obt} = \frac{\overline{X} - \mu}{\sigma_{\overline{X}}}$$

where $\overline{X}$ is the value of our sample mean and $\mu$ is the mean of the sampling distribution when $H_0$ is true (the $\mu$ of the raw score population described by $H_0$).

2. *The computational formula for the standard error of the mean, $\sigma_{\overline{X}}$, is*

$$\sigma_{\overline{X}} = \frac{\sigma_X}{\sqrt{N}}$$

where $N$ is the $N$ of our sample and $\sigma_X$ is the *known* population standard deviation.

# Significance Testing of a Single Sample Mean or a Correlation Coefficient: The *t*-Test

Statistical hypothesis testing is second nature to behavioral researchers. Different statistical procedures are used in different types of experiments, so an important part of learning statistics is learning *when* (and how) to use each procedure. Remember, though, that we are always computing a statistic that summarizes the location of our sample data on a sampling distribution when $H_0$ is true and the predicted relationship does not exist. The larger the value of the statistic, the less likely that $H_0$ is true for our study. A significant statistic indicates that our results are too unlikely to occur unless they represent the predicted relationship.

This chapter introduces a procedure known as the *t*-test. Like the *z*-test, the *t*-test is used for significance testing of a single sample mean. The approach is similar to that of the *z*-test, so be sure you are familiar with the logic and terminology of the *z*-test before proceeding. The *t*-test forms the basis for understanding significance testing of a sample correlation coefficient, so it is also a good idea to review $r$, $r_s$, and $r_{pb}$, discussed in Chapter 7. Finally, this chapter introduces the confidence interval, a new procedure for describing a population $\mu$.

## MORE STATISTICAL NOTATION

Officially the *t*-test is known as Student's *t*-test (although it was developed by a statistician named W. S. Gosset). The answer we obtain when we perform the *t*-test is symbolized by $t_{obt}$. The critical value of $t$ is symbolized by $t_{crit}$. (Do not confuse *t*-tests—with a lowercase *t*—with *T*-scores—with a capital *T*—which we met in Chapter 6: *t* has nothing to do with *T*-scores.)

Recall from Chapter 5 that $s_X$ stands for the *estimated* standard deviation of a raw score population computed from our sample. If we do not find the square root in the formula for $s_X$, we have computed $s_X^2$, the *estimated* population variance. We compute $s_X$ and $s_X^2$ using the formula that divides by $N - 1$, and we call $N - 1$ the degrees of freedom or *df*.

## UNDERSTANDING THE *t*-TEST FOR A SINGLE SAMPLE MEAN

In Chapter 10 an assumption of the *z*-test was that we know the true standard deviation of the raw score population, $\sigma_X$, so we can compute the true standard error of the mean, $\sigma_{\bar{X}}$, which is the standard deviation of the sampling distribution of means. Then $z_{\text{obt}}$ is a *z*-score indicating the location of our sample mean on the sampling distribution of means. However, I have a confession: in most research we do *not* know the standard deviation of the raw score population, so we seldom perform the *z*-test. Instead, we estimate $\sigma_X$ by computing $s_X$. Then we use this estimated population standard deviation to compute an *estimate* of the standard error of the mean. With this estimated standard error of the mean, we again compute something *like* a *z*-score to locate our sample mean on the sampling distribution of means. However, because this location is based on an estimate of the standard error, we have not computed a *z*-score and performed the *z*-test. Instead we have computed $t_{\text{obt}}$ and performed the single-sample *t*-test. The **single-sample *t*-test** is the parametric procedure used to test the null hypothesis from a single-sample experiment when the standard deviation of the raw score population must be estimated.

Here is an example of an experiment that calls for the *t*-test. Some people cram just prior to taking a test. Presumably, this is so that they take the test before anything leaks out. To study this suicidal strategy, say that we randomly select a sample of subjects who have not read Chapter 12 in this book. We allow those students one hour to cram, and then we give them a test on the chapter. We assume that the resulting sample of test scores represents the population of test scores for crammers in statistics. To demonstrate a relationship, we compare the population represented by our sample to some other population. From research by the book's author (me), we determine that for the population of students who do not cram for Chapter 12, the $\mu$ of scores on the same test is 75. Therefore, in our study, we will compare the $\mu$ of the population of crammers represented by our sample to the $\mu$ of 75 for the population of noncrammers. Thus, our independent variable is the presence or absence of cramming, and our dependent variable is test scores.

Some students maintain that cramming is a good way to study, actually improving their grades. We are open-minded, so our experimental hypotheses will not predict the direction in which cramming will change test grades. Therefore, we have the two-tailed experimental hypotheses that (1) the experiment will demonstrate that cramming either increases or decreases grades or (2) the experiment will not demonstrate that cramming affects grades.

The null hypothesis always indicates that the experiment does not demonstrate the predicted relationship, so here it will indicate that cramming has no effect on grades. If cramming has no effect on grades, $\mu$ should be the same for crammers as for noncrammers: 75. Thus, our null hypothesis is

$$H_0: \mu = 75$$

$H_0$ implies that our sample of crammers represents the population where $\mu = 75$.

The alternative hypothesis always indicates that the experiment demonstrates the predicted relationship, so here it will indicate that cramming does affect grades. If cramming affects grades, the population $\mu$ of crammers should be different from that of noncrammers, so it should not be equal to 75. Therefore, the alternative hypothesis is

$$H_a: \mu \neq 75$$

$H_a$ implies that our sample represents a population where $\mu \neq 75$.

Our next step is to select and set up the appropriate statistical test. First, we choose alpha: we think $\alpha = .05$ is acceptable (of course). Second, we determine that our study meets the assumptions of the single-sample *t*-test.

## The Assumptions of the Single-Sample *t*-Test

To perform the single sample *t*-test, we should be able to assume the following:

1. We have one random sample of interval or ratio scores.
2. The raw score population forms a normal distribution for which the mean is the appropriate measure of central tendency.
3. The standard deviation of the raw score population is estimated by $s_X$ computed from our sample. (Regardless of which population of raw scores the sample represents, $s_X$ is an estimate of that population's $\sigma_X$.)

If our data reasonably meet these assumptions, we can perform the *t*-test. Because the *t*-test is a parametric test, it is robust, producing minimal error if we violate these assumptions somewhat. This is especially true if $N$ is at least 30.

In our cramming study, we have a single-sample experiment measuring ratio scores, we can assume that the distribution of test scores is reasonably normal, it is appropriate to summarize the scores using a mean, and we can estimate the population standard deviation by computing $s_X$. Everything looks good, so we collect the data.

### The Logic of the Single-Sample *t*-Test

Say that we test nine cramming subjects. (As we shall see, for maximum power, we never collect so few scores in an actual experiment.) First, we compute the sample mean, which turns out to be $\overline{X} = 65.67$. If cramming makes no difference in scores, then the sample mean should be 75, representing the $\mu$ of the population of scores without cramming. However, our sample mean is 65.67, so it looks as if your parents were right, and cramming for an exam results in lower grades than not cramming. Thus, we might conclude that we have demonstrated a relationship in which increasing the amount of cramming results in lower grades.

But hold on! We must always consider sampling error. Maybe cramming has no effect on grades and we are being misled by sampling error: maybe our sample represents the population of noncrammers, but by chance we selected subjects who just happened to have low scores on the exam. If so, then our sample poorly represents the population where $\mu = 75$. Maybe our null hypothesis is true and the study did not demonstrate a relationship.

To be confident in our conclusions about the effect of cramming, we will first test this null hypothesis by performing the *t*-test. We use exactly the same logic as in the *z*-test: $H_0$ says that our mean of 65.67 is different from the $\mu$ of 75 because of sampling error. By computing $t_{obt}$, we determine the location of our sample mean on the sampling distribution of means that occur when the sample does represent the population described by $H_0$. This allows us to determine the likelihood of obtaining our sample mean through sampling error if $H_0$ is true and the sample represents a $\mu$ of 75. If our $t_{obt}$ is beyond our $t_{crit}$, our sample mean lies in the region of rejection, so we will reject the idea that our sample represents the population described by $H_0$.

As we shall see, the only differences between the *z*-test and the *t*-test are that $t_{obt}$ is not calculated in the same way as $z_{obt}$ and the value of $t_{crit}$ is obtained from the *t*-distribution instead of from the *z*-distribution.

---

## CALCULATING THE SINGLE-SAMPLE *t*-TEST

Let's first look at the definitional formulas for computing $t_{obt}$ and then see how they produce the computational formulas. The computation of $t_{obt}$ consists of three steps.

First, using the scores in the sample, we find the estimated standard deviation of the raw score population, $s_X$, with the formula

$$s_X = \sqrt{\frac{\Sigma X^2 - \dfrac{(\Sigma X)^2}{N}}{N - 1}}$$

Then, with $s_X$, we compute the estimated standard error of the mean. The symbol for the **estimated standard error of the mean** is $s_{\overline{X}}$. (The $s$ stands for an estimate of the standard deviation, and the subscript $\overline{X}$ indicates that it is for a distribution of means.) Previously we computed the true standard error of the mean for the $z$-test by dividing the true standard deviation ($\sigma_X$) by the square root of $N$:

$$\sigma_{\overline{X}} = \frac{\sigma_X}{\sqrt{N}}$$

For the $t$-test, we compute the estimated standard error by dividing the estimated standard deviation by the square root of $N$. Thus,

> **THE DEFINITIONAL FORMULA FOR THE ESTIMATED STANDARD ERROR OF THE MEAN IS**
>
> $$s_{\overline{X}} = \frac{s_X}{\sqrt{N}}$$

Notice the similarity between the preceding formulas for $\sigma_{\overline{X}}$ and $s_{\overline{X}}$. The only difference is whether we divide into $\sigma_X$ or $s_X$.

Finally, we compute $t_{\text{obt}}$. For the $z$-test, we computed $z_{\text{obt}}$ using the formula

$$z_{\text{obt}} = \frac{\overline{X} - \mu}{\sigma_{\overline{X}}}$$

Similarly,

> **THE DEFINITIONAL FORMULA FOR THE $t$-TEST FOR A SINGLE SAMPLE MEAN IS**
>
> $$t_{\text{obt}} = \frac{\overline{X} - \mu}{s_{\overline{X}}}$$

$\overline{X}$ is the sample mean, $\mu$ is the mean of the $H_0$ sampling distribution (which also equals the value of $\mu$ described in the null hypothesis), and $s_{\overline{X}}$ is the estimated standard error of the mean.

Notice the similarity between the formulas for $z_{obt}$ and $t_{obt}$. The $z_{obt}$ indicates the distance of the sample mean from the $\mu$ of the sampling distribution, measured in units called the standard error of the mean. The $t_{obt}$ measures this distance in estimated standard error units.

## Computational Formulas for the Single-Sample *t*-Test

We can compute $t_{obt}$ through the three steps given above, or we can use one of the following computational formulas. First, we can replace the symbol $s_{\bar{X}}$ with a formula for computing $s_{\bar{X}}$ and rewrite our definitional formula for $t_{obt}$ as

$$t_{obt} = \frac{\bar{X} - \mu}{\dfrac{s_X}{\sqrt{N}}}$$

This simply shows the computation of $s_{\bar{X}}$ in the denominator of the *t*-test by dividing $s_X$ by the square root of $N$.

To shorten the computations, we will not take the square root when computing the standard deviation, $s_X$. Instead, we will replace the standard deviation with the estimated variance, $s_X^2$, and then take the square root of the entire denominator. Thus, we have the following two formulas.

> **THE COMPUTATIONAL FORMULAS FOR THE SINGLE SAMPLE *t*-TEST ARE**
>
> $$t_{obt} = \frac{\bar{X} - \mu}{\sqrt{\dfrac{s_X^2}{N}}} \qquad \text{and} \qquad t_{obt} = \frac{\bar{X} - \mu}{\sqrt{(s_X^2)\left(\dfrac{1}{N}\right)}}$$

We can use either of these formulas. The formula on the left computes $s_{\bar{X}}$ by dividing $s_X^2$ by $N$, and the formula on the right computes $s_{\bar{X}}$ by multiplying $s_X^2$ times the quantity $1/N$. With either formula, you first perform all operations inside of the square root sign and then find the square root. Remember, the final number obtained in the denominator of any of these formulas is still the estimated standard error, $s_{\bar{X}}$. Then, dividing $s_{\bar{X}}$ into the difference found in the numerator gives $t_{obt}$.

For our cramming study, say that we obtained the data in Table 11.1. First we compute $\Sigma X$, $\Sigma X^2$, and $(\Sigma X)^2$ so that we can compute $s_X^2$. Substituting our values from Table 11.1 into the formula for $s_X^2$, we have

$$s_X^2 = \frac{\Sigma X^2 - \dfrac{(\Sigma X)^2}{N}}{N - 1} = \frac{39289 - \dfrac{349281}{9}}{9 - 1} = 60.00$$

**TABLE 11.1** Grades of Nine Subjects Who Crammed for the Exam

| Subject | Grades (X) | X² |
|---------|-----------|-----|
| 1 | 50 | 2500 |
| 2 | 75 | 5625 |
| 3 | 65 | 4225 |
| 4 | 72 | 5184 |
| 5 | 68 | 4624 |
| 6 | 65 | 4225 |
| 7 | 73 | 5329 |
| 8 | 59 | 3481 |
| 9 | 64 | 4096 |
| $N = 9$ | $\Sigma X = 591$ | $\Sigma X^2 = 39289$ |
| | $(\Sigma X)^2 = 349281$ | |
| | $\overline{X} = 65.67$ | |

Thus, we estimate that the variance of the population of test grades represented by our sample is 60.

Now we compute $t_{\text{obt}}$ for our mean of 65.67 when the population $\mu$ is 75, $s_X^2$ is 60, and $N$ is 9. Filling in a computational formula, we have

$$t_{\text{obt}} = \frac{\overline{X} - \mu}{\sqrt{(s_X^2)\left(\dfrac{1}{N}\right)}} = \frac{65.67 - 75}{\sqrt{(60)\left(\dfrac{1}{9}\right)}}$$

In the denominator, 1/9 is .11, which multiplied times 60 is 6.667. So we have

$$t_{\text{obt}} = \frac{65.67 - 75}{\sqrt{6.667}} = \frac{-9.33}{2.582} = -3.61$$

The square root of 6.667 is 2.582. Since the denominator in this formula is the estimated standard error of the mean, $s_{\overline{X}}$ is 2.582. Dividing $-9.33$ by 2.582, we arrive at a $t_{\text{obt}}$ of $-3.61$.

Thus, our sample mean produced a $t_{\text{obt}}$ of $-3.61$ on the sampling distribution of means where $\mu = 75$. This is very similar to having a *z*-score of $-3.61$. According to $H_0$, if our sample is perfectly representative of the population where $\mu$ is 75, then the sample mean "should" be 75, producing a $t_{\text{obt}}$ equal to 0.0. The question now is "Is our $t_{\text{obt}}$ of $-3.61$ (and the underlying difference between our mean and $\mu$) significant? That is, is it reasonable to expect chance sampling error to produce such a result if our sample represents the population $\mu$ of 75?" To answer this question, we must compare our $t_{\text{obt}}$ to the appropriate $t_{\text{crit}}$, and for that we must examine the *t*-distribution.

## THE *t*-DISTRIBUTION

In previous chapters we described the sampling distribution of means using *z*-scores, because the *z*-distribution provides us with a model of the probability of obtaining a particular sample mean from a particular raw score population when $\sigma_X$ is known. Now, the *t*-distribution is our model of the probability of obtaining a sample mean from a particular raw score population when $\sigma_X$ is *estimated*. Think of the *t*-distribution in the following way. One last time, we hire our very persistent (and by now *very* bored) statistician. She infinitely draws samples of the same size *N* from the raw score population where $\mu$ is 75. For each sample, she computes $\overline{X}$, $s_X$, $s_{\overline{X}}$, and $t_{obt}$. She then plots the frequency of the different means, as well as the values of $t_{obt}$. Thus, the **t-distribution** is the distribution of all possible values of *t* computed for random sample means having the same *N* that are selected from the raw score population described by $H_0$. You can envision a *t*-distribution as shown in Figure 11.1.

The values of *t* are analogous to *z*-scores. A sample mean equal to $\mu$ has a *t* equal to zero. Means greater than $\mu$ have positive values of *t*. Means less than $\mu$ have negative values of *t*. The larger the absolute value of $t_{obt}$, the farther it and the corresponding sample mean are from the $\mu$ of the distribution. Therefore, the larger the *t*, the lower the relative frequency and thus the lower the probability of obtaining the sample mean by chance when the sample represents the underlying raw score population.

Our $t_{obt}$ locates our sample mean on this model, telling us the probability of obtaining such a mean when $H_0$ is true. To complete the *t*-test, we find $t_{crit}$ and create the region of rejection. If our $t_{obt}$ is beyond $t_{crit}$, then our sample mean is too unlikely to accept as representing the population described by $H_0$.

There is one important novelty here: there are actually *many* versions of the *t*-distribution, each having a slightly different shape. The shape of a particular *t*-distribution depends on the *N* of the samples represented in the *t*-distribution.

**FIGURE 11.1**    Example of a *t*-Distribution of Random Sample Means

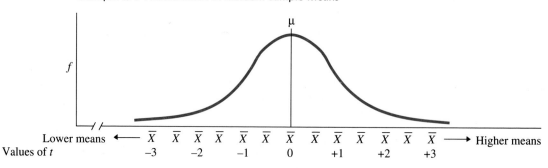

If the bored statistician selects small samples, the *t*-distribution will be only a rough approximation to the standard normal curve. This is because $s_X$ often contains large sampling error, so it is often a very rough estimate of $\sigma_X$. Further, the statistician will often obtain a different value of $s_X$ for each sample, and inconsistency in $s_X$ over all samples will produce a *t*-distribution that is only a rough approximation to a normal curve. However, if she selects larger samples, the *t*-distribution will conform more closely to the true normal curve. A larger sample tends to more accurately represent the population, so $s_X$ is closer to the one true value of $\sigma_X$. As we saw with the *z*-test, consistently using the true value of $\sigma_X$ produces a sampling distribution that closely conforms to the true normal *z*-distribution. Therefore, as the sample size increases, each *t*-distribution is a successively closer approximation to the true normal curve.

The fact that there are differently shaped *t*-distributions is important for one reason: when we set up the region of rejection, we want it to contain precisely that portion of the curve defined by our $\alpha$. If $\alpha = .05$, then we want to mark off precisely the extreme 5% of the curve. On distributions that are shaped differently, we mark off that 5% at different locations. Since the size of the region of rejection is marked off by the critical value, *with differently shaped t-distributions we have different critical values.* For example, Figure 11.2 shows a one-tailed region of rejection in two *t*-distributions. Say that the extreme 5% of Distribution A is beyond a $t_{crit}$ of $+2.5$. If we use $+2.5$ as $t_{crit}$ on Distribution B, the region of rejection will contain *more* than 5% of the distribution. Conversely, the $t_{crit}$ marking off 5% of Distribution B will mark off *less* than 5% of Distribution A. (The same problem also exists for a two-tailed test.)

This issue is important because not only is $\alpha$ the size of the region of rejection,

**FIGURE 11.2** Comparison of Two *t*-Distributions Based on Different Sample *N*s

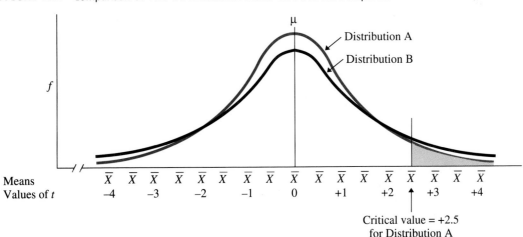

it is also the theoretical probability of a Type I error (rejecting $H_0$ when $H_0$ is true). Unless we use the correct $t_{crit}$ from the *t*-distribution for our $N$, the probability of a Type I error in our experiment will not equal our $\alpha$ (and that's not supposed to happen!). Thus, there is only one version of the *t*-distribution that we should use when testing a particular $t_{obt}$: the one that our bored statistician would have created by using the same $N$ as in our sample.

## The Degrees of Freedom

To identify the appropriate *t*-distribution for our study, we do not use $N$. Instead, the shape of a particular *t*-distribution is determined by the size of $N - 1$, what we call the degrees of freedom, or *df*, of the sample. Since we compute $s_X$ using $N - 1$, it is the *df* that determines how consistently $s_X$ estimates the true $\sigma_X$. The larger the *df*, the closer the value of $s_X$ in each sample is to $\sigma_X$, so the closer the *t*-distribution is to forming a normal curve.

It does not take a tremendously large *df*, however, to produce a truly normal *t*-distribution. When *df* is greater than 120, the *t*-distribution is virtually identical to the standard normal curve. For each value of *df* between 1 and 120, we have a differently shaped *t*-distribution. Therefore, for samples having a *df* between 1 and 120, we determine our critical value by first identifying the appropriate sampling distribution using the particular *df* that we have in our sample. Only then will $t_{crit}$ accurately mark off the region of rejection so that the true theoretical probability of a Type I error is equal to our $\alpha$.

> **STAT ALERT**  The appropriate $t_{crit}$ for the single-sample *t*-test comes from the *t*-distribution that has *df* equal to $N - 1$, where $N$ is the number of scores in the sample.

## The *t*-Tables

The good news is that we can obtain critical values from Table 2 in Appendix D, entitled "Critical Values of *t*." Take a look at these *t*-tables: there are separate tables for two-tailed and one-tailed tests. Identify the appropriate column for your value of $\alpha$, and find the value of $t_{crit}$ in the row opposite the *df* of your sample. For example, in our cramming study, $N$ is 9, so *df* is $N - 1 = 8$. For a two-tailed test with $\alpha = .05$ and $df = 8$, $t_{crit}$ is 2.306.

As usual, the table contains no positive or negative signs. In a one-tailed test, you must decide whether $t_{crit}$ is positive or negative. Also, notice that the table uses the symbol for infinity ($\infty$) for *df* greater than 120. This means that when a sample has a *df* greater than 120, measuring the sample is virtually as good as measuring the population. Then the *t*-distribution matches the standard normal curve, and the critical values are those we saw with the *z*-test.

## Using the *t*-Tables

If you peruse the *t*-tables (a little light reading), you will *not* find a critical value for every *df* between 1 and 120. When the *df* of your sample does not appear in the table, there are two approaches you can take.

First, remember that all we need to know is whether or not $t_{obt}$ lies beyond $t_{crit}$. Often we can determine this by examining the critical values for the *df* above and below the *df* of our sample. For example, say that we perform a one-tailed *t*-test at α = .05 with 49 *df*. The *t*-tables only give $t_{crit}$ for 40 *df* (+1.684) and for 60 *df* (+1.671). Since 49 *df* lies between 40 *df* and 60 *df*, the critical value we seek lies between +1.671 and +1.684, as shown in Figure 11.3.

Notice that as the *df increases*, the absolute size of $t_{crit}$ *decreases*. Therefore, the $t_{crit}$ at 49 *df* is *smaller* than the $t_{crit}$ at 40 *df*. If $t_{obt}$ is far enough from μ to be beyond the $t_{crit}$ of +1.684 for only 40 *df*, then $t_{obt}$ is also beyond the $t_{crit}$ for 49 *df* and it is significant. On the other hand, the $t_{crit}$ for 49 *df* is *larger* than the $t_{crit}$ for 60 *df*. If $t_{obt}$ is *not* far enough from μ to be beyond the $t_{crit}$ of +1.671 for 60 *df*, then $t_{obt}$ is also not beyond the $t_{crit}$ for 49 *df*, and it is not significant. In the same way we can evaluate any obtained value that falls outside of the bracketing critical values given in the tables.

If $t_{obt}$ falls *between* the bracketing values of $t_{crit}$ in the table, then you should use the interpolation procedure described in Appendix A.

**FIGURE 11.3**  One *t*-Distribution Showing the Location of Three Values of $t_{crit}$

*The $t_{crit}$ of +1.684 is for 40 df (dashed line), the $t_{crit}$ of +1.671 is for 60 df (dotted line), and the $t_{crit}$ for 49 df (solid line) is between them.*

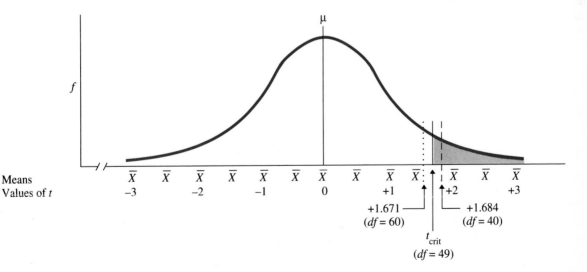

## INTERPRETING THE SINGLE-SAMPLE *t*-TEST

Remember our cramming experiment? Our purpose is to decide whether cramming results in a different population of test scores than does not cramming. Once we have our values of $t_{obt}$ and $t_{crit}$, the single-sample *t*-test is identical to the *z*-test.

In the cramming study, $t_{obt}$ is $-3.61$ and the two-tailed $t_{crit}$ is $\pm 2.306$. With this information, we envision the sampling distribution shown in Figure 11.4. Remember, this is the sampling distribution when $H_0$ is true and the samples *do* represent the population where $\mu$ is 75 (and $s_{\bar{X}}^2$ and $N = 9$). $H_0$ implies that because of sampling error, our sample mean of 65.67 poorly represents this $\mu$. But, as the *t*-distribution shows, sampling error seldom produces a mean *that* poor at representing this $\mu$. In fact, our $t_{obt}$ lies beyond the $t_{crit}$, so our $t_{obt}$ is in the region of rejection. Thus, when $\alpha$ is .05, a $t_{obt}$ of $-3.61$ and a $\bar{X}$ of 65.67 are too unlikely to accept as occurring by chance when $H_0$ is true. Therefore, we reject $H_0$, rejecting the idea that our sample represents the population where $\mu$ is 75. We report the results of our *t*-test as

$$t(8) = -3.61, \quad p < .05$$

This statement communicates four facts:

1. We performed the *t*-test.
2. We had 8 degrees of freedom.
3. Our $t_{obt}$ is $-3.61$.
4. We judged this $t_{obt}$ to be significant, with the probability less than .05 that we made a Type I error (rejected a true $H_0$).

**FIGURE 11.4**   Two-Tailed *t*-Distribution for *df* = 8 When $H_0$ Is True and $\mu$ = 75

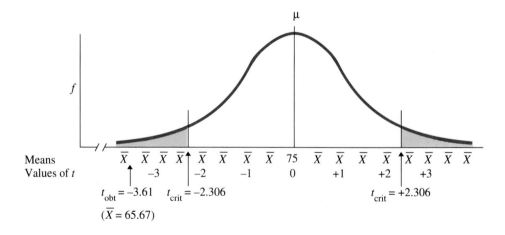

[In fact, from the *t*-tables, when $\alpha$ is .01, $t_{crit}$ is $\pm 3.355$. Since our $t_{obt}$ is $-3.61$, it would be significant if we had used the .01 level of significance. Some researchers advocate reporting the smallest value of $\alpha$ at which results are significant (as long as it's less than .05). Instead of saying $p < .05$, we gain more information by reporting that $p < .01$, because now we know that the probability of a Type I error is not in the neighborhood of .04, .03, or .02.]

Thus, we conclude that our sample mean of 65.67 is significantly different from the population mean of 75. In other words, we accept our alternative hypothesis that our sample mean represents a $\mu$ that is not equal to 75. Since a sample mean of 65.67 is most likely to occur when the sample represents the population where $\mu$ is 65.67, our best estimate is that our sample represents a population of scores for crammers located at around 65.67. Since we expect one population of scores for crammers located at around 65.67 and a different population of scores for noncrammers located at a $\mu$ of 75, we conclude that our results demonstrate a relationship in the population between the independent variable (the presence or absence of cramming) and the dependent variable (test scores). We can have confidence in this conclusion, because the probability is less than .05 that we have made a Type I error.

Of course, if our $t_{obt}$ were a number that did not fall beyond our $t_{crit}$ (for example, $t_{obt} = +1.32$), then it would not lie in the region of rejection and we would not reject $H_0$. We would conclude that our sample was likely to represent the population where $\mu$ is 75, so we would not have convincing evidence for a relationship between cramming and test scores. We would report such a nonsignificant result as $t(8) = +1.32, p > .05$.

## Testing One-Tailed Hypotheses in the Single-Sample *t*-Test

If we decide to predict that cramming only *increases* test scores, then $H_a$ is that the sample represents a population $\mu$ greater than 75, or $H_a$: $\mu > 75$. $H_0$ is that the study does not work and the sample represents a population $\mu$ less than or equal to 75, or $H_0$: $\mu \leq 75$. We obtain the one-tailed $t_{crit}$ from the *t*-tables for our *df* and $\alpha$. For us to conclude that the sample represents the predicted population where cramming increases scores, the sample mean must be significantly *larger* than 75. Thus, we place all of the region of rejection in the upper tail of the sampling distribution, as shown in the left-hand graph in Figure 11.5. For $t_{obt}$ to be significant, it must be positive and beyond $t_{crit}$. If it is, then our mean is too unlikely to represent a $\mu$ equal to 75, and even less likely to represent a $\mu$ less than 75. Therefore, we reject $H_0$ and accept $H_a$ that the sample mean represents a $\mu$ greater than 75.

If we decide to predict that cramming *decreases* scores, we use the sampling distribution on the right in Figure 11.5. Now $H_a$ is that the sample mean represents a cramming $\mu$ that is less than 75. $H_0$ is that the sample mean represents a $\mu$ greater than or equal to 75. Since we predict a sample mean less

**FIGURE 11.5**   $H_0$ Sampling Distributions of *t* for a One-Tailed Test

*On the left, we predict an increase in scores. On the right, we predict a decrease in scores.*

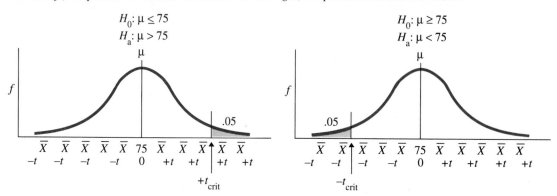

than 75, to be significant $t_{obt}$ must be negative and beyond $-t_{crit}$. If it is, our mean is too unlikely to represent a $\mu$ equal to 75, and even less likely to represent a $\mu$ greater than 75. Therefore, we reject $H_0$ and accept $H_a$ that the sample mean represents a $\mu$ less than 75.

In any of the above examples, if we reject $H_0$, then we conclude that our sample mean represents a $\mu$ that is different from the one described by $H_0$. The next important step is to estimate the numerical value of that population $\mu$. We estimate a population $\mu$ by computing a confidence interval.

## ESTIMATING THE POPULATION $\mu$ BY COMPUTING A CONFIDENCE INTERVAL

There are two ways to estimate a population $\mu$. When we say that the population $\mu$ is equal to the sample mean, we are performing **point estimation.** Earlier we estimated that the $\mu$ of the population of crammers is located on the dependent variable of test grades at the *point* identified as 65.67. However, no one really believes that if we actually tested the entire population, $\mu$ would be *exactly* 65.67. The problem with point estimation is that it is extremely vulnerable to sampling error. Cramming may lower test grades, as our study suggests, but the sample probably does not *perfectly* represent the population of crammers. Realistically, therefore, we expect the population $\mu$ of crammers to be *around* 65.67.

   The other way to estimate a population $\mu$ is to include the possibility of sampling error and perform **interval estimation.** With interval estimation, we specify an interval, or range, of values within which we estimate the population parameter falls. You often encounter such intervals in real life, and they are usually phrased in terms of "plus or minus" some amount. For example, on the evening news when Dan Blather reports that a sample survey showed that 45% of the voters support the president, he may also report that there is plus or minus 3% error. What he means is that the surveyors have created an interval around 45%. They expect that if they asked the entire population, the $\mu$ would be within $\pm 3\%$ of 45%. In other words, they believe that between 42% and 48% of all voters in the population actually support the president.

   We perform interval estimation by creating a confidence interval. Confidence intervals can be used to describe various population parameters, but the most common is the confidence interval for a single population $\mu$. The **confidence interval for a single population $\mu$** describes an interval containing values of $\mu$, any one of which our sample mean is likely to represent. Above, we said that our sample mean of crammers probably represents a $\mu$ *around* 65.67. A confidence interval is our way of statistically defining "around." As shown in the following diagram, by creating a confidence interval, we identify those values of $\mu$ around 65.67 that our sample mean is likely to represent.

$$\mu_{low} \quad \cdots \quad \mu \quad \mu \quad \mu \quad \mu \quad 65.67 \quad \mu \quad \mu \quad \mu \quad \mu \quad \cdots \quad \mu_{high}$$

values of $\mu$, one of which is likely to be
represented by our sample mean

The symbol $\mu_{low}$ stands for the lowest value of $\mu$ that our sample mean is likely to represent, and $\mu_{high}$ stands for the highest value of $\mu$ that the mean is likely to represent. When we compute these two values of $\mu$, we have the confidence interval.

   How do we know if a sample mean is likely to represent a particular value of $\mu$? It depends on sampling error. For example, intuitively we know that sampling error is too unlikely to produce a sample mean of 65.67 if the sample represents a population $\mu$ of 500. In other words, 65.67 is significantly different from 500. On the other hand, sampling error is likely to produce a sample mean of 65.67 if the sample represents a population $\mu$ of 65 or 66. In other words, a mean of 65.67 is not significantly different from these $\mu$'s. Thus, a sample mean is likely to represent a particular value of $\mu$ if the sample mean is *not* significantly different from that $\mu$. The logic behind computing a confidence interval is simply to compute the highest and lowest values of $\mu$ that are not significantly different from our sample mean. All values of $\mu$ between these two values are also not significantly different from the sample mean, so it is likely that the sample mean represents one of them.

*STAT ALERT* A confidence interval contains the values between the highest and lowest values of $\mu$ that are not significantly different from our sample mean.

### Computing the Confidence Interval for a Single $\mu$

Since the *t*-test was appropriate for testing the significance of our sample mean in our hypothesis testing, the *t*-test also forms the basis for computing a confidence interval. However, previously we set up our *t*-test to compare the one value of $\mu$ described by $H_0$ to any possible sample mean we might obtain. Now we set it up to compare the one value of our sample mean to any possible $\mu$. Then we find the highest and lowest possible values of $\mu$ that are not significantly different from our sample mean.

Recall that a sample mean differs significantly from $\mu$ if $t_{\text{obt}}$ is *beyond* $t_{\text{crit}}$. Therefore, the most a sample mean can differ from $\mu$ and still not differ significantly is the amount it differs when $t_{\text{obt}}$ *equals* $t_{\text{crit}}$. We can state this using our formula for the *t*-test:

$$t_{\text{obt}} = \frac{\overline{X} - \mu}{s_{\overline{X}}} = t_{\text{crit}}$$

To find the largest and smallest values of $\mu$ that do not differ significantly from our sample mean, we simply determine the values of $\mu$ that we can put into this formula, with our sample mean and our $s_{\overline{X}}$, so that $t_{\text{obt}}$ equals $t_{\text{crit}}$. Since we want to describe values above and below our sample mean, we use the two-tailed value of $t_{\text{crit}}$. Thus, we want to find the value of $\mu$ that produces a $-t_{\text{obt}}$ equal to $-t_{\text{crit}}$. Rearranging the above formula, we have the formula for finding this value of $\mu$:

$$\mu = (s_{\overline{X}})(+t_{\text{crit}}) + \overline{X}$$

We also want to find the value of $\mu$ that produces a $+t_{\text{obt}}$ equal to $+t_{\text{crit}}$. The formula for finding this value of $\mu$ is

$$\mu = (s_{\overline{X}})(-t_{\text{crit}}) + \overline{X}$$

Since our sample mean represents a $\mu$ *between* these two values of $\mu$, we put the above formulas together in one formula.

*THE COMPUTATIONAL FORMULA FOR A CONFIDENCE INTERVAL FOR A SINGLE SAMPLE MEAN IS*

$$(s_{\overline{X}})(-t_{\text{crit}}) + \overline{X} \leq \mu \leq (s_{\overline{X}})(+t_{\text{crit}}) + \overline{X}$$

The symbol $\mu$ stands for the unknown value represented by our sample mean. We replace the other symbols with the values of $\overline{X}$ and $s_{\overline{X}}$ (the standard error of the mean) we computed from the sample data. We find the two-tailed value of $t_{\text{crit}}$ in the $t$-tables at our $\alpha$ for $df = N - 1$, where $N$ is the sample $N$.

> **STAT ALERT**　In computing a confidence interval, use the two-tailed critical value, even if you have performed one-tailed hypothesis testing.

We can use the above formula to compute the confidence interval for our cramming study. There, $\overline{X} = 65.67$ and $s_{\overline{X}} = 2.582$. The two-tailed $t_{\text{crit}}$ for $df = 8$ and $\alpha = .05$ is $\pm 2.306$. Filling in the above formula for the confidence interval, we have

$$(2.582)(-2.306) + 65.67 \leq \mu \leq (2.582)(+2.306) + 65.67$$

Multiplying 2.582 times $-2.306$ and times $+2.306$ gives $-5.954$ and $+5.954$, respectively. Rewriting the formula, we have

$$-5.954 + 65.67 \leq \mu \leq +5.954 + 65.67$$

Since adding $-5.954$ is the same as subtracting 5.954, the formula at this point tells us that our sample mean represents a $\mu$ that is greater than or equal to the quantity $65.67 - 5.954$, but less than or equal to the quantity $65.67 + 5.954$. In other words, our mean represents a $\mu$ of 65.67, plus or minus 5.954.

After adding $\pm 5.954$ to 65.67, we have

$$59.72 \leq \mu \leq 71.62$$

This is the finished confidence interval for the $\mu$ represented in our cramming study. We can now return to our previous diagram of the confidence interval and replace the symbols $\mu_{\text{low}}$ and $\mu_{\text{high}}$ with the numbers 59.72 and 71.62, respectively.

$$59.72 \quad \ldots \quad \mu \quad \mu \quad \mu \quad \mu \quad 65.67 \quad \mu \quad \mu \quad \mu \quad \mu \quad \ldots \quad 71.62$$

values of $\mu$, one of which is likely to be
represented by our sample mean

As shown, the confidence interval says that our sample mean probably represents a $\mu$ greater than or equal to 59.72, but less than or equal to 71.62.

## Confidence Intervals and the Size of Alpha

Why do we call this a "confidence" interval? We defined this interval using $\alpha = .05$, so .05 is the theoretical probability of making a Type I error. Thus, 5% of the time the interval will be in error and will not contain the $\mu$

represented by our $\overline{X}$. However, recall that the quantity $1 - \alpha$ is the probability of avoiding a Type I error. Thus, $1 - .05$, or 95%, of the time the interval will contain the $\mu$ represented by our $\overline{X}$. Therefore, the probability is .95 that the interval contains the $\mu$. Recall that probability is our way of expressing our confidence in an event. In our cramming study, we are 95% confident that the interval between 59.72 and 71.62 contains the $\mu$ represented by our sample mean.

> **STAT ALERT**  The amount of confidence we have that a confidence interval contains the $\mu$ represented by our sample mean is always equal to the quantity $1 - \alpha$ multiplied times 100.

The smaller our $\alpha$, the smaller the probability of an error, so the greater our confidence. Had we set $\alpha$ equal to .01 in our cramming study, we would have $1 - .01(100)$, or a 99% confidence interval. With $\alpha = .01$ and $df = 8$, our $t_{\text{crit}}$ would be $\pm 3.355$, and the 99% confidence interval based on the sample mean of 65.67 would be

$$57.01 \leq \mu \leq 74.33$$

When we compare our 95% confidence interval to our 99% confidence interval, we see that the 99% confidence interval spans a wider range of values of $\mu$:

95% confidence interval     59.72 . . . $\mu$ $\mu$ $\mu$ $\mu$ 65.67 $\mu$ $\mu$ $\mu$ $\mu$ . . . 71.62

99% confidence interval     57.01 . . . $\mu$ $\mu$ $\mu$ $\mu$ $\mu$ 65.67 $\mu$ $\mu$ $\mu$ $\mu$ $\mu$ . . . 74.33

values of $\mu$, one of which is likely to be<br>
represented by our sample mean

Logically, the larger the range of values within the interval, the greater our confidence that the interval contains the $\mu$ represented by the sample mean. (Think of a confidence interval as a fishing net. The larger the net, the more confident we are that we will catch the $\mu$ represented by the sample mean.) There is, however, an inevitable tradeoff: when we increase confidence by including a wider range of possible values of $\mu$, we less precisely identify the specific value of $\mu$ represented by our sample. Usually we compromise between sufficient confidence and sufficient precision by using $\alpha = .05$ and creating the 95% confidence interval.

Thus, we conclude our single-sample *t*-test by saying, with 95% confidence, that our sample of crammers represents a $\mu$ between 59.72 and 71.62. Since the center of the interval is at 65.67, we have defined how our mean represents a $\mu$ of *around* 65.67. But notice how much more information we provide by computing the confidence interval rather than merely saying that $\mu$ is somewhere around 65.67. Therefore, anytime you wish to describe a population $\mu$ represented by a sample mean, you should compute a confidence interval.[1]

## SIGNIFICANCE TESTS FOR CORRELATION COEFFICIENTS

It's time to shift mental gears. Remember the correlation coefficient described in Chapter 7? This statistic describes the strength and direction of a linear relationship formed by pairs of $X$ and $Y$ scores. A coefficient of 0 indicates no relationship. The larger the coefficient (the closer to $\pm 1.0$), the stronger the relationship. For example, say we studied the relationship between cramming and test scores using a correlation. For a sample of 25 subjects, we measured their test scores and how crammed their studying was. Using the formula given in Chapter 7, say we then computed a Pearson correlation coefficient of $r = -.45$. This indicates that the more a subject crammed, the lower his or her test score.

Remember, though, that a correlation coefficient is a sample statistic that describes the relationship found in the sample. Ultimately we want to describe the relationship in the population. Therefore, we use the sample coefficient to estimate the population parameter we would find if we computed the correlation for the entire population. Recall that the population correlation coefficient is called rho and its symbol is $\rho$. Thus, for our cramming study, we want to conclude that if we measured the entire population and computed the correlation, $\rho$ would equal $-.45$.

But hold on, there is a problem here: that's right, it's sampling error. The problem of sampling error applies to *all* sample statistics. Thus, even though our sample $r$ suggests a relationship, it is possible that, because of sampling error, the sample actually poorly represents either no relationship or a different relationship in the population. Regardless of the value of any sample correlation coefficient we compute, before we can be confident that the relationship exists in the population, we must answer the question "Is the sample correlation coefficient statistically significant?"

> **STAT ALERT** We never accept that a sample correlation coefficient demonstrates a relationship until we decide that it is significant.

---

[1]We can also compute a confidence interval when performing the $z$-test. In such a situation we use the formula given above, except that we use the critical values of $z$ from the $z$-tables. If $\alpha = .05$, then $z_{crit} = \pm 1.96$. If $\alpha = .01$, then $z_{crit} = \pm 2.575$.

## Statistical Hypotheses for the Correlation Coefficient

As usual, we should create our experimental and statistical hypotheses before we collect the data. We then perform either a one-tailed or a two-tailed test, depending on our hypotheses. We use a two-tailed test if we do not predict the direction of the relationship. For example, in our cramming study, we might have the experimental hypothesis that the study works by demonstrating either (1) that the more students cram, the higher their grades (a positive correlation) or (2) that the more students cram, the lower their grades (a negative correlation). Our other experimental hypothesis is that the study does not work and does not demonstrate any relationship.

The null hypothesis implies that the predicted relationship does not occur in the population. If there is neither a positive nor a negative relationship, then there is zero correlation. Most of the time, behavioral researchers test a null hypothesis involving zero correlation in the population. Therefore, in this book,

*THE TWO-TAILED NULL HYPOTHESIS FOR SIGNIFICANCE TESTING OF A CORRELATION COEFFICIENT IS ALWAYS*

$$H_0: \ \rho = 0$$

$H_0$ implies that the sample $r$ represents a $\rho$ equal to zero. If $r$ does not equal zero, the difference is written off as sampling error. We can understand how such sampling error can occur by examining the hypothetical scatterplot in Figure 11.6, for a population when $H_0$ is true and $\rho$ is 0. Recall that a circular scatterplot reflects zero correlation, while a slanting elliptical scatterplot reflects an $r$ not equal to zero. The null hypothesis implies that if our sample $r$ does not equal zero, it is because by chance we have selected an elliptical sample scatterplot from the circular population plot shown. Thus, our sample $r$ may not equal 0, but this is because it is a poor representation of the population where $\rho$ equals 0.

On the other hand, the alternative hypothesis always implies that the predicted relationship does occur in the population. If we predict that there is either a positive or a negative relationship, we predict that $\rho$ does *not* equal zero.

*THE TWO-TAILED ALTERNATIVE HYPOTHESIS FOR SIGNIFICANCE TESTING OF A CORRELATION COEFFICIENT IS ALWAYS*

$$H_a : \rho \neq 0$$

**FIGURE 11.6** Scatterplot of a Population When $\rho = 0$

*Scatterplots of random samples are found within the population scatterplot.*

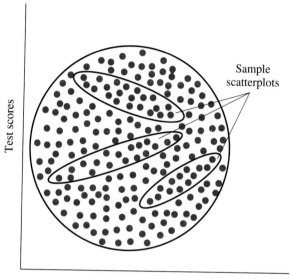

$H_a$ implies that our sample represents a population where $\rho$ is not zero and thus represents a relationship in the population. We assume that the scatterplot for the population would be similar to the scatterplot for the sample.

As usual, we test our data by testing $H_0$. Here we test whether our sample correlation is likely to be a poor representation of a population $\rho$ of zero. If our sample $r$ is too unlikely to be accepted as representing $\rho = 0$, then we reject $H_0$ and accept $H_a$ (that the sample represents a population where $\rho$ is not equal to zero).

Recall from Chapter 7 that we may compute one of three types of correlation coefficients: the Pearson $r$, the Spearman $r_s$, and the point-biserial $r_{pb}$. The logic and format of the above statistical hypotheses are used regardless of the type of correlation coefficient we compute (we merely change the subscripts). In the following sections we shall discuss the particulars of statistical hypothesis testing for each type of correlation coefficient.

## The Significance Test for the Pearson *r*

As usual, before we collect any data, we should make sure our study meets the assumptions of our statistical procedure. *The assumptions for hypothesis testing of the Pearson correlation coefficient are as follows:*

*1.* We have a random sample of *X*-*Y* pairs, and each variable is an interval or ratio variable.

2. The *Y* scores and the *X* scores in the sample each represent a normal distribution. Further, they represent a bivariate normal distribution. This means that the *Y* scores at each value of *X* form a normal distribution and that the *X* scores at each value of *Y* form a normal distribution. (If *N* is larger than 25, however, violating this assumption is of little consequence.)

*3.* For the procedures discussed here, we are testing the null hypothesis that the population correlation is zero. (When $H_0$ states that ρ is some value other than 0.0, a different statistical procedure from the one presented here is used.)

Our cramming correlation meets the above assumptions, so we set α at .05 and test our *r* of $-$.45. To do that, we set up the sampling distribution.

**The sampling distribution of *r***    As with previous procedures, we test $H_0$ by examining the $H_0$ sampling distribution. Here the $H_0$ sampling distribution of *r* shows the values of *r* that occur when we randomly sample the population where ρ is 0. Our bored statistician has quit, but by now you could create the sampling distribution yourself. Using the same *N* as in our study, you would select an infinite number of samples of *X*-*Y* pairs from the population where ρ = 0. For each sample, you would compute *r*. If you then plotted the frequency of the various values of *r*, you would have the sampling distribution of *r*. The **sampling distribution of a correlation coefficient** is a frequency distribution showing all possible values of the coefficient that can occur when samples of size *N* are drawn from a population where ρ is zero. Such a sampling distribution is shown in Figure 11.7.

The only novelty here is that, instead of plotting different sample means along the horizontal axis, we have plotted the different values of *r*. As shown, when $H_0$ is true and ρ is 0, the most frequent sample *r* will equal zero, so the mean of the sampling distribution is 0. However, because of sampling error, sometimes the sample *r* will not equal zero. The larger the *r* (whether positive or negative), the less frequently it occurs, and thus the less likely it is to occur when the sample represents a population where ρ is zero.

To test our sample *r*, we could determine how far the sample *r* was from the mean of the sampling distribution by using a variation of the formula for $t_{obt}$. Luckily, all that is not necessary. We can use our obtained value of *r* to directly locate our sample on the sampling distribution. This is because the value of *r* already indicates how far *r* is from the mean of the distribution, which is at zero. (An *r* = $-$.45, for example, is a distance of .45 below 0.) Therefore, we test $H_0$ by directly examining the value of our obtained sample *r*. The symbol for our obtained *r* is $r_{obt}$. To determine whether $r_{obt}$ lies in the

**FIGURE 11.7** Distribution of Random Sample *r*'s When ρ = 0

*It is an approximately normal distribution, with values of r plotted along the X axis.*

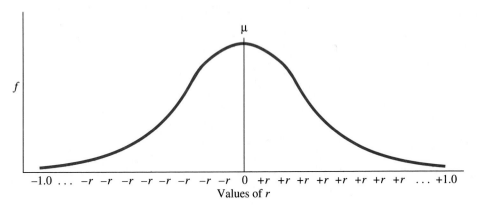

region of rejection, we simply compare it to the critical value of *r*, which we identify as $r_{crit}$.

**Determining the significance of the Pearson *r*** As with the *t*-distribution, the shape of the sampling distribution of *r* is slightly different for each *df*, so there is a different value of $r_{crit}$ for each *df*. Table 3 in Appendix D gives the critical values of the Pearson correlation coefficient. To use these *r*-tables, we first need the appropriate degrees of freedom. *But,* here's a new one: with the Pearson correlation coefficient, the degrees of freedom equals $N - 2$, where *N* is the number of pairs of scores in the sample.

> ***STAT ALERT*** In significance testing of *r*, the degrees of freedom equals $N - 2$, where *N* is the number of pairs of scores.

To find $r_{crit}$, enter Table 3 for a one- or a two-tailed test at the appropriate α and *df*. For our cramming correlation, *N* was 25, so $df = 23$. For a two-tailed test with α = .05 and $df = 23$, $r_{crit}$ is ±.396. Armed with this information, we set up the sampling distribution as in Figure 11.8. Since our $r_{obt}$ of − .45 is beyond the $r_{crit}$ of ±.396, $r_{obt}$ is in the region of rejection. Looking at the sampling distribution, we see that when samples *do* represent the population where ρ is 0, we seldom have an $r_{obt}$ that falls in the region of rejection. Thus, it is too unlikely that our sample poorly represents the population where ρ = 0, because samples are seldom *that* poor. Therefore, we reject the hypothesis that the $r_{obt}$ from our cramming study represents the population ρ of 0, and we conclude that our $r_{obt}$ is significantly different from 0.

**FIGURE 11.8**   *H*₀ Sampling Distribution of *r* When *H*₀: ρ = 0.0

*For the two-tailed test, there is a region of rejection for positive values of r$_{obt}$ and for negative values of r$_{obt}$.*

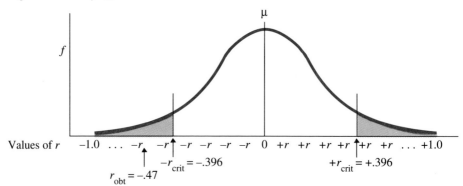

As usual, α is the theoretical probability of making a Type I error. As the sampling distribution shows, the values of *r* in the region of rejection do occur when *H*₀ is true and ρ is 0. Since α = .05, over the long run we will obtain values of *r*$_{obt}$ that cause us to erroneously reject *H*₀ a total of 5% of the time. Thus, the probability that we have made a Type I error this time is slightly less than .05. We report our significant *r*$_{obt}$ as

$$r(23) = -.45, \quad p < .05$$

(Note the *df* in parentheses.)

By rejecting *H*₀, we accept *H*ₐ (that our sample represents a population where the correlation coefficient is not 0). Remember, though, that we have not proven anything. Our correlation does not prove that changes in cramming cause test scores to change. In fact, we have not even proven that there is a relationship in nature (we may have made a Type I error). Instead, because we have a significant *r*$_{obt}$, we have become more confident that our *r*$_{obt}$ does not merely reflect some quirk of sampling error, but rather represents a "real" relationship in the population.

Since the sample *r*$_{obt}$ is −.45, our best estimate is that if we performed this study on the population, we would compute a ρ equal to −.45. However, recognizing that our sample may contain sampling error, we expect that ρ is probably *around* −.45. (We could more precisely identify the value of ρ by computing a confidence interval. This interval would describe the values of ρ that our *r*$_{obt}$ is likely to represent. However, confidence intervals for ρ are computed using a very different procedure from the one we discussed previously.)

In Chapter 8 we saw that we can further describe a relationship by computing the linear regression equation and *r*². When *r*$_{obt}$ is significant, the regression equation and *r*² provide valuable additional information about the relationship.

For our cramming correlation, for example, we can now compute the linear regression equation that will allow us to predict test scores if we know subjects' cramming scores. Computing $r^2$, we find that $-.45^2$ equals $.20$. Recall that this is the proportion of variance in the $Y$ variable that is accounted for by the $X$ variable in our sample data. (It is only a rough estimate of the variance accounted for in the population.) This value tells us that if we use subjects' cramming scores and this relationship, we will be, on average, approximately $.20$, or 20%, more accurate in predicting their test scores than if we do not use their cramming scores. Thus, when we are finished examining our $r_{obt}$, we are confident that we are describing a relationship in nature, we can use the relationship to predict scores, and we can say how well we will predict them.

Of course, if $r_{obt}$ does not lie beyond $r_{crit}$, then we retain $H_0$ and conclude that our sample may represent a population where $\rho = 0$. As usual, we have not proven that there is not a relationship in the population—we have simply failed to convincingly demonstrate that there is one. Therefore, we cannot make any claims about a relationship that may or may not exist in the population. Further, we do not describe the relationship by performing regression analysis or computing $r^2$. Because we have not eliminated the possibility that our correlation may simply reflect sampling error, we are not confident that we even have a relationship to describe. We report nonsignificant results as above, except that $p > .05$.

Finally, remember that the term *significant* does *not* indicate that we have an important relationship. In saying that $r_{obt}$ is significant, we are merely saying that our $r_{obt}$ is unlikely to occur by chance when $\rho$ is 0. We determine a relationship's importance by computing $r^2$. For example, we might find that an $r_{obt}$ of $+.10$ is significant. However, this $r_{obt}$ is *not* very important statistically. Since $+.10^2$ is $.01$, this relationship accounts for only 1% of the variance. Thus, we have demonstrated a relationship that is very unlikely to occur through sampling error, but we have also demonstrated an unimportant and not very useful relationship.

**One-tailed tests of r**  If our experimental hypothesis predicted only a positive correlation or only a negative correlation, we would perform a one-tailed test and have either of the following:

THE ONE-TAILED HYPOTHESES FOR SIGNIFICANCE TESTING OF A CORRELATION
COEFFICIENT ARE

| *Predicting positive correlation* | *Predicting negative correlation* |
|---|---|
| $H_0$: $\rho \leq 0$ | $H_0$: $\rho \geq 0$ |
| $H_a$: $\rho > 0$ | $H_a$: $\rho < 0$ |

If we predict a positive correlation, $H_a$ is that our sample represents a $\rho$ greater than zero and $H_0$ is that our sample represents a $\rho$ less than or equal to 0. If we predict a negative relationship, $H_a$ is that our sample represents a $\rho$ less than 0 and $H_0$ is that our sample represents a $\rho$ greater than or equal to 0.

We again test each $H_0$ by testing whether our sample represents a population where there is zero relationship, so we again examine the sampling distribution for $\rho = 0$. From the *r*-tables, we find the one-tailed critical value for our *df* and $\alpha$, and we set up one of the sampling distributions shown in Figure 11.9.

If we predict a positive correlation, we use the left-hand sampling distribution. Our $r_{obt}$ is significant if it is positive and falls beyond the positive $r_{crit}$ marking the region of rejection in the upper tail of the sampling distribution. If it does, $r_{obt}$ is unlikely to represent a $\rho$ equal to 0, and even less likely to represent a $\rho$ less than 0. Then we reject $H_0$ and accept $H_a$ (that the sample represents a $\rho$ greater than 0).

Conversely, if we predict a negative correlation, we use the right-hand sampling distribution in Figure 11.9. Here, $r_{obt}$ is significant if it is negative and falls beyond the negative $r_{crit}$ marking the region of rejection in the lower tail of the distribution. If it does, $r_{obt}$ is unlikely to represent a $\rho$ equal to or greater than 0, so we reject $H_0$ and accept $H_a$.

If $r_{obt}$ is not beyond the appropriate $r_{crit}$, then $r_{obt}$ is not significant, we do not reject $H_0$, and we conclude that the study failed to demonstrate the predicted relationship.

## Significance Testing of the Spearman $r_s$ and the Point-Biserial $r_{pb}$

Recall that the Spearman $r_s$ describes the relationship between two sets of rank-ordered scores, and the point-biserial correlation coefficient, $r_{pb}$, describes the relationship between one interval or ratio variable and one dichotomous variable. These correlations describe relationships in our *sample,* but—that's right—perhaps they merely reflect sampling error. Perhaps if we computed the correlation in the population, we would find that our $r_s$ actually represents a population correlation, symbolized by $\rho_s$, that is 0. Likewise, perhaps our $r_{pb}$ actually represents a population correlation, symbolized by $\rho_{pb}$, that is 0. Therefore, before we can conclude that either of these sample correlations represents a relationship in nature, we must perform the appropriate hypothesis testing.

To test each sample correlation coefficient, we perform the following steps:

1. Set alpha: how about .05?
2. Consider the assumptions of the test. The Spearman $r_s$ assumes that we have a random sample of pairs of *ranked* (or ordinal) scores. The point-biserial $r_{pb}$ assumes that we have random scores from one dichotomous

**FIGURE 11.9**   $H_0$ Sampling Distribution of $r$ Where $\rho = 0$ for One-Tailed Test

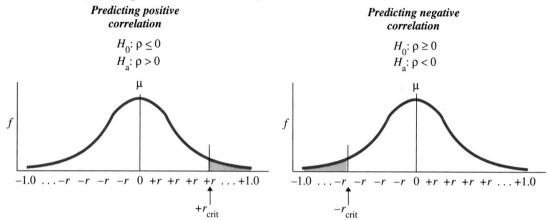

variable and one interval or ratio variable. (Note: Because of the type of data involved and the lack of parametric assumptions, technically the statistical hypothesis testing procedures for $r_s$ and $r_{pb}$ are nonparametric procedures. But since they are otherwise the same as for $r$, we discuss them here.)

3. Create the statistical hypotheses. We can test either one- or two-tailed hypotheses, as we did with the Pearson $r$, except now we are testing $\rho_s$ or $\rho_{pb}$.

The only new aspect in testing $r_s$ or $r_{pb}$ is how we conceptualize their respective sampling distributions.

**Significance testing of $r_s$**   For significance testing of $r_s$, we have a new family of differently shaped sampling distributions and a different table of critical values. Table 4 in Appendix D, entitled "Critical Values of the Spearman Rank-Order Correlation Coefficient," contains the critical values of $r_s$ for one- and two-tailed tests for $\alpha$ levels of .05 and .01. We obtain the critical value from this table in the same manner as we did from previous tables, except that we use $N$, *not* degrees of freedom.

> **STAT ALERT**   The critical value of $r_s$ is obtained using $N$, the number of pairs of scores in the sample.[2]

---

[2]Table 4 contains critical values for $N$ up to 30. When $N$ is greater than 30, transform $r_s$ to a z-score using the formula $z_{obt} = (r_s)(\sqrt{N-1})$. For $\alpha = .05$, the two-tailed $z_{crit} = \pm 1.96$ and the one-tailed $z_{crit} = 1.645$.

As an example, in Chapter 7 we correlated the nine rankings of each of two observers and found that $r_s = +.85$. Is this value significant? We performed this correlation assuming the observers' rankings would agree, so we were predicting a positive correlation. Therefore, we have a one-tailed test with the hypotheses $H_0$: $\rho_s \leq 0$ and $H_a$: $\rho_s > 0$. From Table 4, with $\alpha = .05$ and $N = 9$, the critical value for the one-tailed test is $+.600$. We can envision the $H_0$ sampling distribution of $r_s$ when $N = 9$ as shown in Figure 11.10.

The larger the value of our obtained $r_s$ (whether positive or negative), the less likely it is to occur when $H_0$ is true and the population $\rho_s$ is 0.0. We interpret a significant $r_s$ (or a nonsignificant one) in the same way we have interpreted previous statistics. In our example, the obtained $r_s$ or $+.85$ is beyond the critical value of $+.600$, so we reject $H_0$ (that our sample represents $\rho_s \leq 0.0$). An $r_s$ of $+.85$ is too unlikely to represent the population where $\rho_s$ is zero or less than zero, so we accept $H_a$ (that $\rho_s > 0$). We have a significant $r_s$, and we estimate that the value of the correlation in the population of such rankings, $\rho_s$, is around $+.85$. We report our results as

$$r_s(9) = +.85, \quad p < .05$$

(Note that the $N$ of the sample is given in parentheses.)

If, instead, we predicted either a positive or a negative $r_s$, we would set up the corresponding two-tailed test using the appropriate two-tailed critical value.

**Significance testing of $r_{pb}$**  We test $r_{pb}$ using the same logic as above. The $H_0$ sampling distributions of $r_{pb}$ are identical to the distributions for the Pearson $r$, so critical values of $r_{pb}$ are obtained from Table 3 in Appendix D, Critical Values of the Pearson Correlation Coefficient. Again we use degrees of freedom, which equals $N - 2$.

> **STAT ALERT**  The critical value of $r_{pb}$ is found in Table 3 for *df* equal to $N - 2$, where $N$ is the number of pairs of scores.

**FIGURE 11.10**  One-Tailed $H_0$ Sampling Distribution of Values of $r_s$ When $H_0$ Is $\rho_s = 0.0$

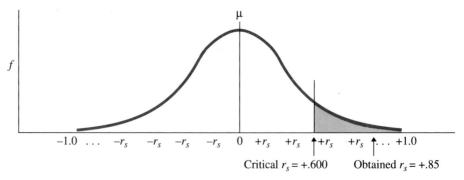

**FIGURE 11.11**   $H_0$ Sampling Distribution of $r_{pb}$ When $H_0$ Is $\rho_{pb} = 0.0$

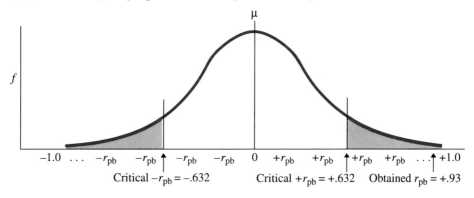

As an example, in Chapter 7 we computed the $r_{pb}$ between subjects' scores on a dichotomous variable (whether they were male or female) and their scores on a personality test. We obtained $r_{pb} = +.93$, with $N = 10$. Say we perform a two-tailed test with the hypotheses $H_0$: $\rho_{pb} = 0$ and $H_a$: $\rho_{pb} \neq 0$. From Table 3, with $\alpha = .05$ and $df = 8$, the critical value for the two-tailed test is $\pm.632$. We can envision the sampling distribution of $r_{pb}$ as shown in Figure 11.11. Our obtained $r_{pb}$ of $+.93$ is beyond the critical value, so it is in the region of rejection. Thus, we reject $H_0$ and conclude that our sample represents the population where $\rho_{pb}$ does not equal zero. We estimate that the $\rho_{pb}$ between gender and personality scores in the population is around $+.93$. We report our results as

$$r_{pb}(8) = +.93, \quad p < .05$$

If we had predicted only a positive or only a negative correlation, then we would perform a one-tailed test. Remember, though, as discussed in Chapter 7, *we* determine whether $r_{pb}$ is positive or negative by how we arrange the categories of the dichotomous variable. Therefore, one-tailed tests of $r_{pb}$ must be consistent with how we arrange the computation of $r_{pb}$.

## MAXIMIZING THE POWER OF A STATISTICAL TEST

In Chapter 10 we discussed the *power* of a statistical procedure, which is the probability of *not* committing a Type II error. We avoid this error by rejecting $H_0$ when $H_0$ is false and concluding that the data represent a relationship that actually does exist. Recall that we maximize the power of a statistical procedure by maximizing the probability that we will obtain significant results. To do that, we make various decisions about how we conduct a study, each of which translates into maximizing the absolute size of the obtained statistic relative to the critical value. The larger the obtained value, the more likely it is to fall beyond the critical value and thus the more likely it is to be significant, causing us to reject $H_0$ when it is false.[3]

The following sections discuss how researchers maximize power in the *t*-test and in correlations. (These principles also apply to the *z*-test and to other inferential procedures we will discuss.)

## Maximizing Power in the *t*-Test

To maximize power, we want to maximize the size of $t_{\text{obt}}$ relative to $t_{\text{crit}}$. Looking at the formula

$$t_{\text{obt}} = \frac{\overline{X} - \mu}{\frac{s_X}{\sqrt{N}}}$$

we see that there are three aspects of a study that increase power.

1. *The greater the differences produced by changing the independent variable, the greater the power.* Remember our cramming study? The greater the difference between the sample mean for crammers and the $\mu$ of 75 for noncrammers, the greater our power. Conceptually, the larger the difference between scores with cramming and scores without cramming, the less likely we are to erroneously accept that the difference is due to sampling error. Mathematically, in the above formula, a larger difference between $\overline{X}$ and $\mu$ produces a larger numerator. All other things ($N$ and $s_X$) being equal, dividing into a larger numerator results in a larger $t_{\text{obt}}$. Therefore, in conducting research, we want to select conditions of the independent variable that are likely to produce a large difference between $\overline{X}$ and $\mu$.

2. *The smaller the variability of the raw scores, the greater the power.* The *t*-test measures the difference between $\overline{X}$ and $\mu$ relative to the standard error of the mean, $s_{\overline{X}}$. The size of the standard error is determined by the variability (the standard deviation or variance) of the raw scores. Conceptually, the smaller the raw score variability, the more easily we can detect a relationship. For example, if every student who crammed obtained a score of exactly 65 on the test and those who did not cram consistently scored exactly 75, we could more easily detect the relationship because it would be a clearer, more consistent one. Mathematically, in the above formula, the smaller the variability of the raw scores, $s_X$,

---

[3]More advanced textbooks give computational procedures for determining the amount of power that is present in a given study.

the smaller the denominator. Dividing by a smaller denominator produces a larger $t_{obt}$. Therefore, in conducting research, we want to test our subjects and measure their scores in a way that minimizes the variability of the scores within a sample.

3. *For small samples, the greater the N, the greater the power.* Conceptually, the larger the $N$, the more accurately we will represent the true situation in the population and the less likely we are to make any type of error. Mathematically, the size of $N$ influences the results in two ways. First, in the above formula we divide $s_X$ by $\sqrt{N}$. Dividing $s_X$ by a larger number produces a smaller final denominator in the $t$-test, which results in a larger $t_{obt}$. Second, a larger $N$ produces a larger $df$. The larger the $df$, the smaller the absolute value of $t_{crit}$. The smaller $t_{crit}$, the more likely $t_{obt}$ is to lie beyond it, so the more likely $t_{obt}$ is to be significant. Therefore, in research, we select as large an $N$ as we can.

Notice that we are discussing *small* samples. Generally, an $N$ of at least 30 is needed for minimal power, and increasing $N$ up to 121 adds substantially to the power. However, an $N$ such as 500 is generally not substantially more powerful than an $N$ of, say, 450.

## Maximizing Power in the Correlation Coefficient

To maximize power when testing a correlation coefficient, we focus on three factors.

1. *The larger the absolute size of the correlation coefficient, the greater the power.* Recall that a correlation coefficient describes the extent to which one value of $Y$ is consistently paired with one and only one value of $X$. Therefore, in conducting research, we want to measure subjects in ways that maximize the consistency with which subjects scoring a particular $X$ all score at or close to the same $Y$ score. This maximizes the size of the correlation coefficient so that we are less likely to erroneously conclude that the sample represents zero correlation in the population. Mathematically, a larger obtained correlation coefficient is more likely to fall beyond the critical value and be significant.

2. *Avoiding the restriction of range problem maximizes power.* One way to obtain a large correlation coefficient is to avoid the restriction of range problem. Recall from Chapter 7 that restriction of range occurs when we have a small range of scores on either the $X$ or the $Y$ variable. A restricted range produces a sample correlation that is *artificially* small, smaller than it would be without a restricted range. For greatest power, we want the most accurate reflection of the relationship that may exist, so we want to avoid restriction of range.

3. *Increasing the N of small samples maximizes power.* As with the *t*-test, the larger the sample *N*, the greater the probability that we will accurately represent the population and avoid any error. In addition, with larger *N* and thus larger *df*, the critical value is smaller, and thus a given coefficient is more likely to be significant.

### FINALLY

Hopefully, you found this chapter rather boring—not because it *is* boring, but because, for each statistic, we performed virtually the same operations. In significance testing of *any* statistic, we ultimately do and say the same things. In all cases, if the obtained statistic is out there far enough in the $H_0$ sampling distribution, it is too unlikely to accept as occurring when $H_0$ is true, so we reject the hypothesis that $H_0$ is true. Since $H_0$ implies that the sample does not represent the predicted relationship, by rejecting $H_0$ we become more confident that the data do represent the predicted relationship, with the probability of a Type I error equal to $p < \alpha$.

## CHAPTER SUMMARY

*1.* The *t*-test is used to test the significance of a single sample mean when (a) there is one random sample of interval or ratio data, (b) the raw score population is a normal distribution for which the mean is the appropriate measure of central tendency, and (c) the standard deviation of the raw score population is estimated by computing $s_X$ using the sample data.

*2.* A *t*-distribution is a theoretical sampling distribution of all possible values of *t* when a raw score population is infinitely randomly sampled using a particular *N*. The shape of a *t*-distribution is determined by the *degrees of freedom,* or *df*. The appropriate *t*-distribution for a single-sample *t*-test is the distribution identified by $N - 1$ degrees of freedom.

*3.* In *point estimation,* the value of the population parameter is assumed to equal the value of the corresponding sample statistic. Because the sample statistic probably contains sampling error, any point estimate is likely to be incorrect.

*4.* In *interval estimation,* the value of a population parameter is assumed to lie within a specified interval. Interval estimation is performed by computing a confidence interval. The *confidence interval for a single popula-*

*tion* $\mu$ describes an interval containing values of $\mu$, any one of which our sample mean is likely to represent. The interval is computed by determining the highest and lowest values of $\mu$ that are not significantly different from the sample mean. Our confidence that the interval contains the value of $\mu$ represented by the sample is equal to $(1 - \alpha)100$.

5. The *sampling distribution of a correlation coefficient* is a frequency distribution showing all possible values of the coefficient that occur when samples of size $N$ are drawn from a population where the correlation coefficient is zero.

6. Significance testing of the Pearson $r$ assumes that (a) we have a random sample of pairs of scores from two interval or ratio variables and (b) the $Y$ scores are normally distributed at each value of $X$ and the $X$ scores are normally distributed at each value of $Y$.

7. Significance testing of the *Spearman* $r_s$ assumes that $r_s$ is computed from a random sample of pairs of ranked-order (ordinal) scores.

8. Significance testing of the *point-biserial* $r_{pb}$ assumes that $r_{pb}$ is computed from a random sample of pairs of scores where one score is from a dichotomous variable and one score is from an interval or ratio variable.

9. Anything that increases the probability of rejecting $H_0$ increases the *power* of a statistical test. Therefore, anything that increases the size of the obtained value relative to the critical value increases power.

10. We maximize the power of the *t*-test by (a) creating large differences when changing the conditions of the independent variable, (b) minimizing the variability of the scores in a sample, and (c) increasing the $N$ of small samples.

11. We maximize the power of a correlation coefficient by (a) maximizing the size of the correlation coefficient, (b) avoiding the restriction of range problem, and (c) increasing the $N$ of small samples.

## USING THE COMPUTER

In the computer program, routine **5** performs the single-sample *t*-test. Based on your sample data, the program computes the sample mean and the estimated population standard deviation and variance as well as *df* and $t_{obt}$. You do not have to determine the critical value, because the computer does it for you. From your $t_{obt}$, the computer reports that $p$ equals some value. This value reflects the smallest size of the criterion (the size of $\alpha$ and the region of rejection) that you could select and still reject $H_0$. Since we usually require that $\alpha$ be no larger than .05, your results are significant only if the computer indicates that $p$ equals .05 or a value *less than* .05. Then, the computer's value of $p$ is the probability that you have made a Type I error. However, note that this information is for a two-tailed test *only*. For a one-tailed test, divide the reported $p$ by 2. If the answer equals or is less than .05, your $t_{obt}$ is significant. In addition, the program computes the 95% confidence interval ($\alpha = .05$) for the $\mu$ represented by your sample mean.

Use routine **4** (Correlation and Regression) to test the significance of $r$, $r_s$, or $r_{pb}$. In addition to computing these statistics, the program also provides $df$ and indicates that $p$ equals some value, which is the minimum value of $\alpha$ for the correlation to be significantly different from zero in a two-tailed test.

## PRACTICE PROBLEMS

(Answers are provided for odd-numbered problems.)

*1.* What determines whether we perform the $z$-test or the $t$-test?

*2.* What is $s_{\bar{x}}$ and what does it communicate?

*3.* (a) Why must we obtain different values of $t_{crit}$ when samples have different $N$'s? (b) What must we compute prior to finding $t_{crit}$?

*4.* (a) What does a confidence interval for a single $\mu$ tell us? (b) Why is using confidence intervals a better approach than using point estimates?

*5.* You wish to determine whether this textbook is beneficial or detrimental to students learning statistics. On a national statistics exam, $\mu = 68.5$ for students who have used other textbooks. A random sample of students who have used this book have the following scores:

  64  69  92  77  71  99  82  74  69  88

  *a.* What are $H_0$ and $H_a$ for this study?
  *b.* Compute $t_{obt}$.
  *c.* With $\alpha = .05$, what is $t_{crit}$?
  *d.* What do you conclude about the use of this book?
  *e.* Compute the confidence interval for $\mu$.

*6.* A researcher predicts that smoking cigarettes decreases a person's sense of smell. On a standard test of olfactory sensitivity, the $\mu$ for nonsmokers is 18.4. By giving this test to a random sample of subjects who smoke a pack a day, the researcher obtains the following scores:

  16  14  19  17  16  18  17  15  18  19  12  14

  *a.* What are $H_0$ and $H_a$ for this study?
  *b.* Compute $t_{obt}$.
  *c.* With $\alpha = .05$, what is $t_{crit}$?

   *d.* What should the researcher conclude about this relationship?

   *e.* Compute the confidence interval for $\mu$.

7. When seeking to determine whether or not there is a relationship between two variables, a researcher obtains $r = +.38$ based on 30 subjects.

   *a.* What are $H_0$ and $H_a$ for this study?

   *b.* With $\alpha = .05$, what is $r_{crit}$?

   *c.* What should the researcher conclude about this relationship?

8. A researcher believes that there is a negative linear relationship between two rank-ordered variables. She obtains an $r_s$ of $-.46$ based on 25 subjects.

   *a.* What are $H_0$ and $H_a$ for this study?

   *b.* With $\alpha = .05$, what is the critical value of $r_s$?

   *c.* What should the researcher conclude about this relationship?

9. A researcher computes an $r_{pb}$ of $+.69$ for a sample of 8 subjects. The researcher asks if there is likely to be a positive relationship in the population.

   *a.* What'are $H_0$ and $H_a$ for this study?

   *b.* With $\alpha = .05$, what is the critical value of $r_{pb}$?

   *c.* What should the researcher conclude about this relationship?

10. (a) What is the obvious factor that might produce a low degree of power in the study in problem 9? (b) What does this mean for the conclusions of the study?

11. (a) You compute a nonsignificant $t_{obt}$. What three aspects of your study may have produced insufficient power? (b) What does this mean for your conclusions?

## *SUMMARY OF FORMULAS*

*1. The definitional formula for the single sample t-test is*

$$t_{obt} = \frac{\overline{X} - \mu}{s_{\overline{X}}}$$

The value of $s_{\overline{X}}$ is computed as

$$s_{\overline{X}} = \frac{s_X}{\sqrt{N}}$$

and $s_X$ is computed as

$$s_X = \sqrt{\frac{\Sigma X^2 - \dfrac{(\Sigma X)^2}{N}}{N - 1}}$$

2. *The computational formulas for the single sample t-test are*

$$t_{\text{obt}} = \frac{\overline{X} - \mu}{\sqrt{\dfrac{s_X^2}{N}}} \quad \text{and} \quad t_{\text{obt}} = \frac{\overline{X} - \mu}{\sqrt{(s_X^2)\left(\dfrac{1}{N}\right)}}$$

where $s_X^2$ is the estimated variance computed for the sample.

*Values of $t_{\text{crit}}$ are found in Table 2 of Appendix D, "Critical Values of t," for df = N − 1.*

3. *The computational formula for a confidence interval for a single population $\mu$ is*

$$(s_{\overline{X}})\,(-t_{\text{crit}}) + \overline{X} \le \mu \le (s_{\overline{X}})\,(+t_{\text{crit}}) + \overline{X}$$

where $t_{\text{crit}}$ is the two-tailed value for $df = N - 1$ and $\overline{X}$ and $s_{\overline{X}}$ are computed using the sample data.

4. *To test the significance of a correlation coefficient,* compare the obtained correlation coefficient to the critical value.
   a. *Critical values of r are found in Table 3, for df = N − 2, where N is* the number of pairs of scores in the sample.
   b. *Critical values of $r_s$ are found in Table 4, for N, the number of pairs* in the sample.
   c. *Critical values of $r_{pb}$ are found in Table 3, for df = N − 2, where N* is the number of pairs in the sample.

# Significance Testing of Two Sample Means: The *t*-Test

So far we've limited our discussions to statistical procedures for a single-sample experiment. In this chapter we discuss the major parametric statistical procedures for a two-sample experiment. These procedures center around the two-sample *t*-test. As the name implies, this test is the same as the single-sample *t*-test we saw in Chapter 11, except for the changes brought on by the fact that we have two samples.

In addition, this chapter shows how to describe the relationship found in a two-sample experiment using the point-biserial correlation coefficient ($r_{pb}$). In case you missed it, $r_{pb}$ is discussed in Chapter 7. Also, it would be a good idea to review linear regression and the idea of the "proportion of variance accounted for," discussed in Chapter 8.

## MORE STATISTICAL NOTATION

It is time to pay very close attention to subscripts. We will compute the mean of each of our two samples, identifying one as $\overline{X}_1$ and the other as $\overline{X}_2$. Likewise, we will compute an estimate of the variance of the raw score population represented by each sample, identifying the variance from one sample as $s_1^2$ and the variance from the other sample as $s_2^2$. Recall that we compute the estimated population variance using the general formula

$$s_X^2 = \frac{\Sigma X^2 - \dfrac{(\Sigma X)^2}{N}}{N - 1}$$

Finally, instead of using $N$ to indicate the number of scores in a sample, we will use the lowercase $n$ with a subscript to indicate the number of scores in each sample. Thus, $n_1$ is the number of scores in Sample 1, and $n_2$ is the number of scores in Sample 2.

## UNDERSTANDING THE TWO-SAMPLE EXPERIMENT

To perform the single-sample experiments discussed in previous chapters, we must already know the value of $\mu$ of the population of raw scores under one condition of our independent variable. However, usually behavioral researchers study variables for which they do not know any values of $\mu$ ahead of time. Then they may design a two-sample experiment. In a two-sample experiment, we measure subjects' scores under two conditions of the independent variable. Condition 1 produces a sample mean $\overline{X}_1$ that represents $\mu_1$, the population $\mu$ we would find if we tested everyone in the population under Condition 1. Condition 2 produces a sample mean $\overline{X}_2$ that represents $\mu_2$, the population $\mu$ we would find if we tested everyone in the population under Condition 2. For statistical purposes, the specific values of $\mu_1$ and $\mu_2$ are not that important. What *is* important is that $\mu_1$ and $\mu_2$ are *different* from each other. If the sample means represent a different population for each condition, then our experiment has demonstrated a relationship in nature: as we change the conditions of the independent variable, the scores in the population change in a consistent fashion.

Of course, the problem is that even though we may have different sample means, the relationship may not exist in the population. If we could test the entire population, we might find the same population of scores under each condition of our independent variable. Thus, it is possible that our different sample means poorly represent the same population $\mu$ and we are being misled by sampling error. After all, if we drew two random samples from one population, we would hardly expect both sample means to equal the population $\mu$. Therefore, before we make any conclusions about our experiment, we perform hypothesis testing to determine whether the difference between our sample means is likely to merely reflect sampling error.

To perform hypothesis tests for two sample means, we perform the two-sample *t*-test. However, as we shall see, there are two distinctly different ways that we can create our samples, so there are two very different versions of the *t*-test, one for independent samples and one for related samples.

> **STAT ALERT** There are two versions of the two-sample *t*-test, depending on the nature of our samples.

First we will discuss the *t*-test for independent samples.

## THE *t*-TEST FOR TWO INDEPENDENT SAMPLES

The **t-test for independent samples** is the parametric procedure used for significance testing when we have sample means from two *independent* samples. Two samples are independent when we randomly select and assign a subject to a sample, without regard to who else has been selected for either sample. Then the samples are composed of independent events, which, as we saw in Chapter 9, means that the probability of a particular score's occurring in one sample is not influenced by a particular score's occurring in the other sample.

Here is a study that calls for the independent samples *t*-test. We wish to study the effects of hypnosis on memory. We know that hypnosis tends to help people recall past events, but we want to determine how well people recall an event when they are mildly hypnotized compared to when they are deeply hypnotized. We will randomly select two samples of subjects, who will each read a story containing 25 details. Later, one sample will be mildly hypnotized and then recall the story, while the other sample will be deeply hypnotized and then recall the story. Each subject's score will be the number of details that he or she recalls from the story. Thus, the conditions of our independent variable are mild and deep hypnosis, and our dependent variable is the number of details subjects recall.

By now you know the routine: (1) we check the assumptions of the statistical procedure and create our statistical hypotheses, (2) we set up and perform the statistical test, and (3) if our results are significant, we describe the relationship we have demonstrated.

### Assumptions of the *t*-Test for Two Independent Samples

In addition to requiring independent samples, the independent samples *t*-test assumes the following.

1. The two random samples of scores measure an interval or ratio variable.

2. The population of raw scores represented by each sample forms a normal distribution, and the mean is the appropriate measure of central tendency. (If each sample $n$ is greater than 30, the populations need only form roughly normal distributions.)

3. We do not know the variance of any raw score population and must estimate it from the sample data.

*4.* The populations represented by our samples have homogeneous variance. **Homogeneity of variance** means that if we could compute the variance of the populations represented by our samples, the value of $\sigma_X^2$ in one population would equal the value of $\sigma_X^2$ in the other population. (Although it is not required that each sample have the same *n*, the more the *n*'s differ from each other, the more important it is to have homogeneity of variance.[1])

Our hypnosis study meets the above assumptions, because we will randomly assign subjects to either condition, and recall scores are ratio scores that we think form approximately normal distributions with homogeneous variance.

Now we derive our statistical hypotheses.

## Statistical Hypotheses for the *t*-Test for Two Independent Samples

Depending on our experimental hypotheses, we may have a one- or a two-tailed test. For our hypnosis study, say that we do not predict whether deep hypnosis will produce higher or lower recall scores. This is a two-tailed test because we do not predict the direction of the relationship: we merely predict that the sample means from the conditions of mild and deep hypnosis represent different populations of recall scores having different values of $\mu$. Therefore, our experimental hypotheses are that the experiment either does or does not demonstrate a relationship between degree of hypnosis and recall.

First, we can write our alternative hypothesis. Because we do not predict which of the two $\mu$'s (and corresponding $\overline{X}$'s) will be larger, the predicted relationship exists if one population mean ($\mu_1$) is larger or smaller than the other ($\mu_2$)—in other words, if $\mu_1$ does not equal $\mu_2$. We could state the alternative hypothesis as $H_a$: $\mu_1 \neq \mu_2$, but there is a better way to do it. If the two $\mu$'s are not equal, then their *difference* is not equal to zero. Thus, the two-tailed alternative hypothesis for our study is

$$H_a: \mu_1 - \mu_2 \neq 0$$

$H_a$ implies that the means from our two conditions each represent a different population of recall scores, having a different $\mu$.

Of course, we must also deal with our old nemesis, the null hypothesis. Perhaps there is no relationship, so if we tested the entire population under the two conditions, we would not find two different values of $\mu$. Any difference in our sample means may be due to sampling error, and the means may actually represent the same population $\mu$. We can call it $\mu_1$ or $\mu_2$, it doesn't matter,

---

[1]The next chapter introduces a test for determining whether we can assume homogeneity of variance.

because $\mu_1$ *equals* $\mu_2$. We could state our null hypothesis as $H_0$: $\mu_1 = \mu_2$, but again there is a better way to do it. If the two $\mu$'s are equal, then their difference is zero. Thus, our two-tailed null hypothesis is

$$H_0: \mu_1 - \mu_2 = 0$$

$H_0$ implies that both sample means represent the same population of recall scores, having the same $\mu$.

Notice that we derived these hypotheses without specifying the value of either $\mu$, so we have the same hypotheses regardless of the dependent variable we are measuring. Therefore, the above hypotheses are the two-tailed hypotheses for *any* independent samples *t*-test when $H_0$ states that there is zero difference between the $\mu$'s.

As usual, we test our null hypothesis. To see how this is done let's jump ahead and say that our hypnosis study produced the sample means in Table 12.1. We can summarize our results by looking at the *difference* between these means. Apparently, changing the condition of the independent variable from mild hypnosis to deep hypnosis results in a difference in mean recall scores of 3 points. However, $H_0$ says that these sample means represent the same population $\mu$. We always test $H_0$ by finding the probability of obtaining our results when $H_0$ is true. Here we will determine the probability of obtaining a *difference* of 3 when both sample means actually represent the same population $\mu$. $H_0$ says that if it weren't for sampling error, the difference between the sample means would be zero. To test $H_0$, we determine whether a difference of 3 is significantly different from zero. If it is, then there is a significant difference *between* the two sample means: sampling error is too unlikely to produce such different sample means if they represent the same population $\mu$. Then we can be confident that the sample means represent two different $\mu$'s.

> **STAT ALERT** In the independent-samples *t*-test, we always test whether the difference between $\overline{X}_1$ and $\overline{X}_2$ is significantly different from the difference between $\mu_1$ and $\mu_2$ described by $H_0$.

As usual, to test $H_0$ we need a sampling distribution.

**TABLE 12.1** Sample Means from Hypnosis Study

| Degree of hypnosis | Mean number of details recalled |
|---|---|
| Mild hypnosis | 20 |
| Deep hypnosis | 23 |

### The Sampling Distribution When $H_0$ Is $\mu_1 - \mu_2 = 0$

Any sampling distribution is the distribution of sample statistics when $H_0$ is true. Here we can think of creating our sampling distribution as follows. Using the same $n$'s as in our study, we select *two* random samples at a time from one raw score population. We compute the two sample means and arbitrarily subtract one from the other. The result is the *difference between the means,* which we symbolize by $\overline{X}_1 - \overline{X}_2$. We do this an infinite number of times and plot a frequency distribution of all the differences. We then have the **sampling distribution of differences between the means,** which is the distribution of all possible differences between two means when they are drawn from the raw score populations described by $H_0$. We can picture the sampling distribution of differences between the means as shown in Figure 12.1.

This distribution is just like any other sampling distribution except that we have plotted the *differences* between two sample means along the $X$ axis, each labeled $\overline{X}_1 - \overline{X}_2$. As usual, the mean of the sampling distribution is the value stated in $H_0$, and here $H_0$ is $\mu_1 - \mu_2 = 0$. The mean of the distribution is zero because most often each sample mean will equal the raw score population $\mu$, in which case the difference between the means will be zero. However, sometimes by chance both sample means will not equal $\mu$ or each other. Depending on whether $\overline{X}_1$ or $\overline{X}_2$ is larger, the difference will be greater than zero (positive) or less than zero (negative). The larger the absolute difference between the means, the farther into either tail of the distribution the difference falls, so the less likely such a difference is to occur when $H_0$ is true.

**FIGURE 12.1**    Sampling Distribution of Differences Between Means When $H_0$: $\mu_1 - \mu_2 = 0$

*The mean of this distribution is zero. Larger positive differences are to the right, and larger negative differences are to the left.*

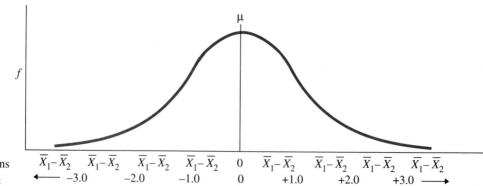

To test $H_0$, we simply determine where the difference between our sample means lies on this sampling distribution. Our model of the sampling distribution of differences between the means is the *t*-distribution. We will locate the difference between our means on the sampling distribution by computing $t_{obt}$. As shown in Figure 12.1, the larger the absolute value of $\pm t_{obt}$, the less likely it is that the corresponding difference between the means occurs when $H_0$ is true. To determine if $t_{obt}$ is significant, we compare it to $t_{crit}$, which is found in Table 2 in Appendix D. We again obtain $t_{crit}$ using degrees of freedom, but we have two samples, so we compute *df* differently: now degrees of freedom equals $(n_1 - 1) + (n_2 - 1)$.

> **STAT ALERT**  Critical values of $t$ for the independent samples *t*-test have $df = (n_1 - 1) + (n_2 - 1)$.

Another way of expressing *df* is $(n_1 + n_2) - 2$.

For our hypnosis study, say that we tested 17 subjects under deep hypnosis and 15 subjects under mild hypnosis. Thus, $n_1 = 17$ and $n_2 = 15$, so *df* equals $(17 - 1) + (15 - 1)$, which is 30. As usual, we set alpha at .05, and the *t*-tables show that for a two-tailed test, $t_{crit}$ is $\pm 2.042$.

Of course, we must compute $t_{obt}$.

## Computing the *t*-Test for Two Independent Samples

We have arbitrarily labeled the deep hypnosis condition as Sample 1, so its mean, variance, and *n* are $\overline{X}_1$, $s_1^2$, and $n_1$, respectively. Likewise, for the mild hypnosis condition, we have $\overline{X}_2$, $s_2^2$, and $n_2$. (Note: If $s_1^2$ does not equal $s_2^2$, this does not necessarily violate our assumption about homogeneity of variance in the *population:* the samples may contain some sampling error in representing the same $\sigma_X^2$.)

In the previous chapter we computed $t_{obt}$ by performing three steps: we computed the estimated variance of the raw score population, then we computed the estimated standard error of the sampling distribution, and then we computed $t_{obt}$. In performing the two-sample *t*-test, we complete the same three steps.

**Estimating the population variance**  First we compute $s_X^2$ for each sample, using the formula given at the beginning of the chapter. Each $s_X^2$ estimates the population variance, but each estimate may contain sampling error. Therefore, we obtain the best estimate of the population variance by computing a weighted average of the two values of $s_X^2$. Each variance is weighted based on the size of *df* in the sample. The weighted average of the sample variances is called the *pooled variance* (we pool our resources). The symbol for the pooled variance is $s_{pool}^2$.

THE COMPUTATIONAL FORMULA FOR THE POOLED VARIANCE IS

$$s_{pool}^2 = \frac{(n_1 - 1)s_1^2 + (n_2 - 1)s_2^2}{(n_1 - 1) + (n_2 - 1)}$$

This formula says that we multiply the $s_X^2$ from a sample times $n - 1$ for that sample, then add the results together and divide by the sum of $(n_1 - 1) + (n_2 - 1)$.

As shown in Table 12.2, for our hypnosis study $s_1^2$ is 9.0 and $n_1$ is 17; $s_2^2$ is 7.5 and $n_2$ is 15. Filling in the above formula, we have

$$s_{pool}^2 = \frac{(17 - 1)9.0 + (15 - 1)7.5}{(17 - 1) + (15 - 1)}$$

In the numerator, 16 times 9 is 144, and 14 times 7.5 is 105. In the denominator, 16 plus 14 is 30. Now we have

$$s_{pool}^2 = \frac{144 + 105}{30} = \frac{249}{30} = 8.30$$

We have $s_{pool}^2 = 8.30$. Thus, we estimate that the variance of any of the populations of recall scores represented by our samples is 8.30.

With the value of $s_{pool}^2$, we can compute the standard error of the sampling distribution.

**Computing the standard error of the difference**   The standard error of the sampling distribution of differences between the means is called the standard error of the difference. The **standard error of the difference** is the standard deviation of the sampling distribution of differences between the means, indicating how spread out the values of $\overline{X}_1 - \overline{X}_2$ are when the distribution is created using samples having our $n$ and our value of $s_{pool}^2$. The symbol for the

**TABLE 12.2**   Data from the Hypnosis Study

|  | Sample 1: subjects under deep hypnosis | Sample 2: subjects under mild hypnosis |
|---|---|---|
| Mean details recalled | $\overline{X}_1 = 23$ | $\overline{X}_2 = 20$ |
| Number of subjects | $n_1 = 17$ | $n_2 = 15$ |
| Sample variance | $s_1^2 = 9.0$ | $s_2^2 = 7.5$ |

standard error of the difference is $s_{\overline{X}_1 - \overline{X}_2}$. (The subscript $\overline{X}_1 - \overline{X}_2$ indicates that this is the standard error for the differences between pairs of means.)

In the previous chapter we saw that for the single-sample *t*-test, a formula for the standard error of the mean was

$$s_{\overline{X}} = \sqrt{(s_X^2)\left(\frac{1}{N}\right)}$$

The formula for the standard error of the difference is very similar.

---

**THE DEFINITIONAL FORMULA FOR THE STANDARD ERROR OF THE DIFFERENCE IS**

$$s_{\overline{X}_1 - \overline{X}_2} = \sqrt{(s_{\text{pool}}^2)\left(\frac{1}{n_1} + \frac{1}{n_2}\right)}$$

---

To compute $s_{\overline{X}_1 - \overline{X}_2}$, it is easiest if you first reduce the fractions $1/n_1$ and $1/n_2$ to decimals; then add them together and multiply the sum times $s_{\text{pool}}^2$. Then find the square root.

For our hypnosis study, we computed $s_{\text{pool}}^2$ as 8.30, and $n_1$ is 17 and $n_2$ is 15. Filling in the above formula, we have

$$s_{\overline{X}_1 - \overline{X}_2} = \sqrt{8.30\left(\frac{1}{17} + \frac{1}{15}\right)}$$

Since 1/17 is .059 and 1/15 is .067, their sum is .126. Multiplying 8.3 times .126, we have

$$s_{\overline{X}_1 - \overline{X}_2} = \sqrt{8.3(.126)} = \sqrt{1.046} = 1.02$$

Thus, with *n*'s of 17 and 15 and $s_{\text{pool}}^2 = 8.30$, the standard error of the difference, $s_{\overline{X}_1 - \overline{X}_2}$, equals 1.02.

Note that we can take the above definitional formula for $s_{\overline{X}_1 - \overline{X}_2}$ and replace the symbol for $s_{\text{pool}}^2$ with the formula for $s_{\text{pool}}^2$. Then,

---

**THE COMPUTATIONAL FORMULA FOR THE STANDARD ERROR OF THE DIFFERENCE IS**

$$s_{\overline{X}_1 - \overline{X}_2} = \sqrt{\left(\frac{(n_1 - 1)s_1^2 + (n_2 - 1)s_2^2}{(n_1 - 1) + (n_2 - 1)}\right)\left(\frac{1}{n_1} + \frac{1}{n_2}\right)}$$

In the left-hand parentheses we compute $s_{pool}^2$, and by multiplying it times the right-hand parentheses and then taking the square root, we compute $s_{\overline{X}_1 - \overline{X}_2}$.

Now that we have determined the standard error of the difference, we can finally compute $t_{obt}$.

**Computing $t_{obt}$ for two independent samples**   After all is said and done, we are still computing a variation of a *z*-score. In previous chapters we found how far the result of our study ($\overline{X}$) was from the mean of the $H_0$ sampling distribution ($\mu$), measured in standard error units. In general, this formula is

$$t_{obt} = \frac{(\text{result of the study}) - (\text{mean of } H_0 \text{ sampling distribution})}{\text{standard error}}$$

Now we will perform the same computation, but here the "result of the study" is the *difference* between the two sample means. So in place of "result of the study" in the formula, we put the quantity $\overline{X}_1 - \overline{X}_2$. Also, now the mean of the $H_0$ sampling distribution is the *difference* between $\mu_1$ and $\mu_2$ described by $H_0$. Thus, we replace "mean of $H_0$ sampling distribution" in the formula with the quantity $\mu_1 - \mu_2$. Finally, we replace "standard error" with $s_{\overline{X}_1 - \overline{X}_2}$. Putting this all together we have our formula.

---

**THE DEFINITIONAL FORMULA FOR THE INDEPENDENT-SAMPLES *t*-TEST IS**

$$t_{obt} = \frac{(\overline{X}_1 - \overline{X}_2) - (\mu_1 - \mu_2)}{s_{\overline{X}_1 - \overline{X}_2}}$$

---

$\overline{X}_1$ and $\overline{X}_2$ are our sample means, $s_{\overline{X}_1 - \overline{X}_2}$ is computed as shown above, and the value of $\mu_1 - \mu_2$ is the difference specified by the null hypothesis. The reason we write $H_0$ as $\mu_1 - \mu_2 = 0$ is so that it directly tells us the mean of the sampling distribution and thus the value of $\mu_1 - \mu_2$ to put in the above formula. (Later this becomes important when $\mu_1 - \mu_2$ is not zero.)

Now we can compute $t_{obt}$ for our hypnosis study. Our sample means were 23 and 20, the difference between $\mu_1$ and $\mu_2$ specified by our $H_0$ is 0, and we computed $s_{\overline{X}_1 - \overline{X}_2}$ to be 1.02. Putting these values into the above formula, we have

$$t_{obt} = \frac{(23 - 20) - 0}{1.02}$$

Subtracting $23 - 20$, we have a difference of $+3$, so

$$t_{obt} = \frac{(+3) - 0}{1.02} = \frac{+3}{1.02} = +2.94$$

Our $t_{obt}$ is $+2.94$. The $t_{obt}$ is like a $z$-score, telling us how far our sample mean difference $(\overline{X}_1 - \overline{X}_2)$ lies from the mean of the $H_0$ sampling distribution $(\mu_1 - \mu_2)$, measured in units of the standard error of the difference. Thus, the difference of $+3$ between our sample means is located at something like a $z$-score of $+2.94$ on the sampling distribution of differences when $H_0$ is true and both samples represent the same population $\mu$ (and $df = 30$ and $s_{\overline{X}_1 - \overline{X}_2} = 1.02$).

**Computational formula for $t_{obt}$ for two independent samples**   We can save a little paper by combining the steps of computing $s^2_{pool}$, $s_{\overline{X}_1 - \overline{X}_2}$, and $t_{obt}$ into one formula.

THE COMPUTATIONAL FORMULA FOR THE *t*-TEST FOR INDEPENDENT SAMPLES IS

$$t_{obt} = \frac{(\overline{X}_1 - \overline{X}_2) - (\mu_1 - \mu_2)}{\sqrt{\left(\dfrac{(n_1 - 1)s^2_1 + (n_2 - 1)s^2_2}{(n_1 - 1) + (n_2 - 1)}\right)\left(\dfrac{1}{n_1} + \dfrac{1}{n_2}\right)}}$$

The numerator is the same as in the definitional formula for $t_{obt}$. In the denominator, however, we have replaced the symbol for the standard error, $s_{\overline{X}_1 - \overline{X}_2}$, with its computational formula. The operations within the left-hand parentheses are those we saw in computing $s^2_{pool}$. We perform the operations in the right-hand parentheses and multiply the answer times $s^2_{pool}$. After we take the square root, the answer is $s_{\overline{X}_1 - \overline{X}_2}$. Then dividing the denominator into the numerator produces $t_{obt}$.

For our hypnosis study, substituting the data into the above formula, we have

$$t_{obt} = \frac{(23 - 20) - 0}{\sqrt{\left(\dfrac{(17 - 1)9.0 + (15 - 1)7.5}{(17 - 1) + (15 - 1)}\right)\left(\dfrac{1}{17} + \dfrac{1}{15}\right)}}$$

In the left-hand parentheses of the denominator, we again find an $s^2_{pool}$ of 8.3, and in the right-hand parentheses, we again compute .126, so we have

$$t_{obt} = \frac{+3}{\sqrt{(8.3)(.126)}} = \frac{+3}{1.02} = +2.94$$

Thus, again we find that $t_{obt} = +2.94$. Note that since the denominator in the *t*-test is the standard error of the difference, $s_{\overline{X}_1 - \overline{X}_2}$ is again 1.02.

## Interpreting $t_{obt}$ in the Independent Samples *t*-Test

To interpret $t_{obt}$, we compare it to the $t_{crit}$ found in the *t*-tables. As we saw, our hypnosis study has $df = 30$, so $t_{crit}$ is $\pm 2.042$. Figure 12.2 locates these values on our sampling distribution of differences.

Although $H_0$ says that the difference between our sample means is merely a poor representation of no difference between $\mu_1$ and $\mu_2$, the location of our $t_{obt}$ on the sampling distribution shows that samples such as ours are seldom *that* poor at representing no difference. As you can see, sample means that differ from each other by $+3$ are relatively infrequent on this sampling distribution. In fact, our $t_{obt}$ lies beyond $t_{crit}$, so it—and the corresponding difference of $+3$—is in the region of rejection. Therefore, we reject $H_0$ and conclude that the difference between our two sample means is too unlikely to accept as occurring by chance if the sample means represent the same population $\mu$. In other words, the difference between our means is significantly different from zero. We communicate our results as

$$t_{obt}(30) = +2.94, \quad p < .05$$

As usual, *df* is reported in parentheses, and because $\alpha = .05$, the probability is less than .05 that we have made a Type I error (rejected a true $H_0$).

We can now accept the alternative hypothesis, which says that $\mu_1 - \mu_2 \neq 0$: the difference between our sample means represents a difference between two population $\mu$'s that is not zero. Now we work backwards from this difference to the individual populations of recall scores. Since the mean for deep hypnosis ($\overline{X} = 23$) is larger than the mean for mild hypnosis ($\overline{X} = 20$), we

**FIGURE 12.2**   $H_0$ Sampling Distribution of Differences Between Means When $\mu_1 - \mu_2 = 0$

*The $t_{obt}$ shows the location of $\overline{X}_1 - \overline{X}_2 = +3.0$.*

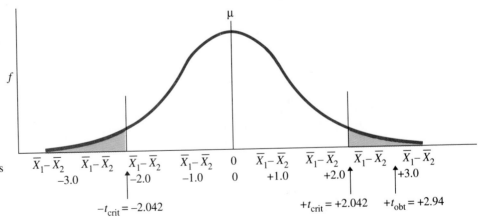

conclude that deep hypnosis leads to significantly higher recall scores than mild hypnosis. Thus, we have evidence of a relationship where increasing the degree of hypnosis is associated with populations having higher $\mu$'s.

If our $t_{\text{obt}}$ were not beyond $t_{\text{crit}}$, we would not reject $H_0$. We would not have convincing evidence that the difference between our sample means was anything other than sampling error, so we could not say that there was a relationship between degree of hypnosis and recall scores.

Since we did find a significant difference, we now describe the relationship. From the previous chapter you already know that we could compute a confidence interval for the $\mu$ that is likely to be represented by each of our sample means. However, there is another way to describe the populations represented by our samples. Since we found a significant difference of $+3$ between our sample means, we expect that if we performed this experiment on the entire population, we would find that the $\mu$ for deep hypnosis differed from the $\mu$ for mild hypnosis by $+3$. Of course, our samples may contain a little sampling error, so the actual difference between the $\mu$'s is probably *around* $+3$. We can create a confidence interval to more specifically define this difference.

## Confidence Interval for the Difference Between Two $\mu$'s

As you know, a confidence interval describes a range of population values, any one of which is likely to be represented by our sample. The **confidence interval for the difference between two $\mu$'s** describes a range of *differences* between two population $\mu$'s, any one of which is likely to be represented by the *difference* between our two sample means. To compute the interval, we find the largest and smallest values of the quantity $\mu_1 - \mu_2$ that are not significantly different from the difference between our sample means $(\overline{X}_1 - \overline{X}_2)$.

> **THE COMPUTATIONAL FORMULA FOR THE CONFIDENCE INTERVAL FOR THE DIFFERENCE BETWEEN TWO POPULATION $\mu$'S IS**
>
> $$(s_{\overline{X}_1 - \overline{X}_2})(-t_{\text{crit}}) + (\overline{X}_1 - \overline{X}_2) \leq \mu_1 - \mu_2 \leq (s_{\overline{X}_1 - \overline{X}_2})(+t_{\text{crit}}) + (\overline{X}_1 - \overline{X}_2)$$

Here $\mu_1 - \mu_2$ stands for the unknown difference we are estimating, $t_{\text{crit}}$ is the two-tailed value found for the appropriate $\alpha$ at $df = (n_1 - 1) + (n_2 - 1)$, and the values of $s_{\overline{X}_1 - \overline{X}_2}$ and $(\overline{X}_1 - \overline{X}_2)$ are computed in the *t*-test from the sample data.

In our hypnosis study, the two-tailed $t_{\text{crit}}$ for $df = 30$ and $\alpha = .05$ is $\pm 2.042$. We computed that $s_{\overline{X}_1 - \overline{X}_2}$ is 1.02 and $\overline{X}_1 - \overline{X}_2$ is $+3$. Filling in the above formula, we have

$$(1.02)(-2.042) + (+3) \leq \mu_1 - \mu_2 \leq (1.02)(+2.042) + (+3)$$

Multiplying 1.02 times $\pm 2.042$ gives

$$-2.083 + (+3) \leq \mu_1 - \mu_2 \leq +2.083 + (+3)$$

At this point, we see that the difference between our sample means is likely to represent a difference between the $\mu$'s of $+3$, plus or minus 2.083. By adding and subtracting 2.083 from $+3$, we obtain the final confidence interval:

$$.092 \leq \mu_1 - \mu_2 \leq 5.08$$

Because we used the .05 alpha level, we created the 95% confidence interval. It indicates that, if we were to perform this experiment on the entire population of subjects, we are 95% confident that the interval of .092 to 5.08 contains the difference we would find between the $\mu$s under mild and deep hypnosis. In essence, if someone asked us how big a difference mild versus deep hypnosis makes for everyone in recalling the story, our answer would be that we are 95% confident that the difference in number of details recalled is, on average, between .092 and 5.08.

## Performing One-Tailed Tests on Independent Samples

We could have performed our hypnosis study using a one-tailed test if we had predicted the direction of the difference between the two conditions. Say that we predicted a positive relationship where the greater the degree of hypnosis, the higher the recall scores. Everything we have discussed above applies to the one-tailed test, but beware: one-tailed tests can produce serious confusion! This is because we *arbitrarily* call one mean $\overline{X}_1$ and one mean $\overline{X}_2$ and then we subtract $\overline{X}_1 - \overline{X}_2$. How we assign the subscripts determines whether we have a positive or a negative difference, and thus whether we have a positive or a negative $t_{\mathrm{obt}}$. As you know, the sign of $t_{\mathrm{obt}}$ is very important in a one-tailed test.

To prevent confusion, it is helpful to use more meaningful subscripts than 1 and 2. For example, we can use the subscript d for the deep hypnosis condition and m for the mild hypnosis condition. Then there are two important steps. First, we must decide which sample $\overline{X}$ and corresponding population $\mu$ we expect to be larger and carefully formulate our hypotheses. If we think that the $\mu$ for mild hypnosis ($\mu_m$) is *smaller* than the $\mu$ for deep hypnosis ($\mu_d$), then if we subtract the smaller $\mu_m$ from the larger $\mu_d$, we predict a difference that is greater than zero. Our alternative hypothesis would then be written as $H_a$: $\mu_d - \mu_m > 0$ (and $H_0$ as $\mu_d - \mu_m \leq 0$). The second important step is to subtract the sample means in the *same* way that we subtract the $\mu$'s in our hypotheses. If we subtract $\mu_d - \mu_m$, then we must subtract $\overline{X}_d - \overline{X}_m$. If our means represent the predicted relationship, then subtracting the smaller $\overline{X}_m$

from the larger $\overline{X}_d$ should yield a difference that is also positive, producing a positive $t_{obt}$. For us to reject $H_0$, our $t_{obt}$ must lie beyond our $t_{crit}$, so $t_{crit}$ must be a *positive* number. Therefore, as shown on the left-hand graph in Figure 12.3, we place the region of rejection in the positive tail of the sampling distribution.

One-tailed tests are confusing because we could have reversed how we stated $H_a$, expressing it as $H_a$: $\mu_m - \mu_d < 0$. This again predicts a larger $\mu_d$, but now subtracting the larger $\mu_d$ from the smaller $\mu_m$ produces a difference that is less than zero. Subtracting the sample means this way, we predict that the difference will be negative, producing a negative $t_{obt}$. Therefore, we place the region of rejection in the negative tail of the distribution, and we have a negative $t_{crit}$, as shown in the right-hand graph in Figure 12.3.

You must pay attention and think through each step. If you subtract the sample means in the opposite way from the way you subtract the $\mu$'s, the sign of your $t_{obt}$ will be the opposite of what it should be for testing your $H_0$. Then you may erroneously conclude that there is not a significant difference when there is, or vice versa.

## Testing Hypotheses About Nonzero Differences

Regardless of whether we have used a one- or two-tailed test, so far we have tested $H_0$: $\mu_1 - \mu_2 = 0$, which says that there is no difference between the populations. Looking at $H_0$ from another perspective, we can interpret it as saying that there is a difference between $\mu_1$ and $\mu_2$ and that difference equals 0. Therefore, using the same procedure, we can test any $H_0$ that says that the difference between the two populations equals any amount.

**FIGURE 12.3**   Sampling Distribution for One-Tailed Independent Samples *t*-Test

*Above each figure is the appropriate $H_a$, along with the appropriate way to subtract the sample means to obtain the predicted $t_{obt}$.*

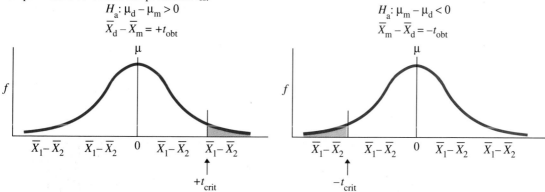

For example, here's a new experiment. Say that on a test of flying ability, the population of Navy pilots differs from the population of Marine pilots by 10 points. However, recently the Navy developed a new training method that has been used with all its pilots. To test the effectiveness of this method, we randomly select a sample of Navy pilots and compare their flying ability to the flying ability of a sample of Marine pilots. Now we want to test whether our samples represent populations that still differ by 10 points. In a two-tailed test, our null hypothesis is that the training program has no effect, so with or without it, the difference between Navy and Marine pilots should still be 10. Thus, we have $H_0 = \mu_1 - \mu_2 = 10$. On the other hand, our alternative hypothesis is that the training program has an effect, so the difference will no longer be 10. Thus, we have $H_a$: $\mu_1 - \mu_2 \neq 10$.

In the $t$-test for this study, we do everything we did previously, except wherever we said that the quantity $\mu_1 - \mu_2$ was zero, we now say that $\mu_1 - \mu_2$ is 10. Now we have a sampling distribution of differences created when the $\mu$'s of the two populations differ by 10, so the mean of the sampling distribution is 10. Our $t_{obt}$ indicates where the difference between our sample means is located on this sampling distribution. Comparing $t_{obt}$ to $t_{crit}$ indicates whether the difference between our sample means is significantly different from 10. If it is, then we conclude that with the training, the populations of Navy and Marine pilots would no longer differ by 10, but rather by the difference represented by our samples.

## Power and the Independent Samples $t$-Test

Remember *power*—the probability of *not* making a Type II error, or the probability of rejecting $H_0$ when $H_0$ is false? As we saw previously, researchers maximize their statistical power by maximizing the size of $t_{obt}$ relative to $t_{crit}$. Looking at the formula

$$t_{obt} = \frac{(\overline{X}_1 - \overline{X}_2) - (\mu_1 - \mu_2)}{\sqrt{\left(\dfrac{(n_1 - 1)s_1^2 + (n_2 - 1)s_2^2}{(n_1 - 1) + (n_2 - 1)}\right)\left(\dfrac{1}{n_1} + \dfrac{1}{n_2}\right)}}$$

we see that anything that increases the size of the numerator or decreases the size of the denominator produces a larger $t_{obt}$. To maximize the size of $t_{obt}$, we design a study in which we

1. *Maximize the difference produced by the two conditions.* This produces a larger value of $(\overline{X}_1 - \overline{X}_2)$, so the numerator of the $t$-test is larger. To maximize the difference produced by the conditions, we select two very different conditions of the independent variable that are likely to produce relatively large differences between the means. For example, in the

hypnosis study, we select a deep level of hypnosis that is *much* deeper than the mild level of hypnosis. Then, if the predicted relationship exists in nature, we are likely to see a large difference in recall scores.

2. *Minimize the variability of the raw scores,* $s_1^2$ *and* $s_2^2$. This produces a smaller $s_{\text{pool}}^2$ and thus a smaller $s_{\bar{X}_1 - \bar{X}_2}$, so the denominator of the *t*-test is smaller. To minimize the variability of the scores in each sample, we design and conduct the experiment so that all of the subjects in a sample are treated and tested in a consistent manner. Thus, for example, we want all subjects in the hypnosis experiment to study the story they will recall for the same length of time, to pay attention to the same degree, to have the same familiarity with the story, to answer the same questions, and so on. Then none of the subjects will be inadvertently disadvantaged relative to other subjects, so they will all score relatively consistently within a sample.

3. *Maximize the sample n's.* This also results in a smaller value of $s_{\bar{X}_1 - \bar{X}_2}$ in the denominator. In addition, larger *n*'s give a larger *df*, resulting in a smaller value of $t_{\text{crit}}$. Therefore, within reason, whenever we can easily test a few more subjects per group, we should do so.

All of the above will increase the probability that we will reject $H_0$ when it is false, so they increase our power.

## THE *t*-TEST FOR RELATED SAMPLES

Now we will discuss the other version of the *t*-test for two samples. This version is used when, instead of performing experiments containing two independent samples, we perform experiments containing two related samples. The **t-test for related samples** is the parametric procedure used for significance testing when we have two sample means from two related samples. Two samples are *related* when we pair each score in one sample with a particular score in the other sample. There are two general types of research designs that produce related samples: matched samples designs and repeated measures designs.

In a *matched samples design,* we match each subject in one sample with a subject in the other sample. For example, say that we want to measure how well subjects in two samples shoot baskets, where one sample uses a standard basketball and the other uses a new type of basketball with handles. Ideally, we want the subjects in one sample to be the same height as those in the other sample. If they are not, then differences in shooting baskets may be due to the differences in height instead of the different balls. One way to create two samples containing subjects that are the same height is to form matching pairs of subjects who are the same height and then assign each member of the pair to one condition. Thus, if we select two subjects who are six feet tall, one subject is assigned to one condition and the other subject is assigned to the other condition. Likewise, a four-foot subject in one condition is matched with a four-footer in the other condition, and so on. Now any differences in basket shooting between the two samples will not be due to differences in height. In the same way, we may match subjects using any relevant variable, such as weight, age, physical ability, or the school they attend. (We may also rely on natural pairs to match our subjects. For example, we might study pairs of identical twins, placing one member of a pair in each condition.)

The ultimate form of matching is to match each subject with himself or herself. This is the other way we produce related samples, called repeated measures. In a **repeated measures design,** we repeatedly measure the same subjects under all conditions of an independent variable. For example, we might first measure a sample of subjects when they were using the standard basketball, and then measure the same subjects again when they were using the new basketball. Here, although we have one sample of subjects, we again have two samples of scores.

What makes matched and repeated measures samples related is the fact that each score in one sample is related to the paired score in the other sample. Related samples are also called *dependent samples.* As we saw in Chapter 9, two events are dependent when the probability of one event is influenced by the occurrence of the other event. Related samples are dependent because the probability that one score in a pair is a particular value is influenced by the value of the paired score. For example, if a four-foot-tall male scored close to 0 in one sample, the probability is high that the other matching four-footer also scored close to 0. This is not the case when we have independent samples, as in our hypnosis study. There, the fact that a subject scored 0 in the mild hypnosis condition did not influence the probability of any subject's scoring a 0 in the deep hypnosis condition.

In the previous *t*-test for independent samples, our sampling distribution described the probability of obtaining a particular difference between two means from independent samples of scores. With related samples, we must compute this probability differently, so we create our sampling distribution differently and we compute $t_{\text{obt}}$ differently.

### Assumptions of the *t*-Test for Related Samples

Except for requiring related samples, the assumptions of the *t*-test for related samples are the same as those for the *t*-test for independent samples: (1) the dependent variable involves an interval or ratio scale, (2) the population represented by either sample forms a normal distribution, (3) the variance of the raw score populations is estimated by $s_X^2$, and (4) the populations represented by our samples have homogeneous variance. Because related samples form pairs of scores, the *n* in each sample must be equal.

If the data meet the assumptions, then it's onward and upwards: (1) we create our statistical hypotheses, (2) we set up and perform the statistical test, and (3) if our results are significant, we describe the relationship we have demonstrated.

## The Logic of Hypotheses Testing in the Related Samples *t*-Test

Let's say that we are interested in phobias (irrational fears of objects or events). We have a new therapy we want to test on spider-phobics—people who are frightened by big, black, hairy, spiders (which doesn't sound all that irrational). From the membership of the local phobia club, we randomly select a decidedly unpowerful *N* of five spider-phobics, and we test our therapy using repeated measures of two conditions: before therapy and after therapy. Before therapy we will measure each subject's fear response to a picture of a spider. We will measure a subject's fear by measuring heart rate, breathing rate, perspiration, etc., and then compute a "fear" score between 0 (no fear) and 20 (holy terror!). After providing the therapy, we will again measure the subject's fear response to the picture. (Anytime we have a before-and-after, or pre-test/post-test, design such as this, we use the *t*-test for related samples.) Our study meets the assumptions of the related samples *t*-test, and we set alpha at .05.

Obviously, we expect to demonstrate that the therapy will decrease subjects' fear of spiders, so our hypotheses are one-tailed: (1) the experiment will demonstrate a relationship in which the population $\mu$ for scores after therapy is lower than the $\mu$ for scores before therapy or (2) the experiment will not work, either showing no difference between the $\mu$'s for before and after scores or showing that the $\mu$ for scores after therapy is larger than the $\mu$ for scores before therapy. So far, it sounds as if we are testing the same type of hypotheses we had in the independent samples *t*-test. However, instead of directly comparing the means from our samples to determine the population $\mu$'s they represent, we must first transform our data. Then we test our hypotheses using these transformed scores.

We transform the raw scores in related samples by finding the *difference scores*. A difference score is the difference between the two raw scores in a pair, and the symbol for a difference score is *D*. Say that for our phobia study we collected the data shown in Table 12.3. We find each difference score by arbitrarily subtracting each subject's after score from the corresponding before score. (We could subtract the before scores from the after scores, but we must subtract all scores in the same way.)

Now we summarize the sample of difference scores by computing the mean difference score. The symbol for the mean difference is $\overline{D}$. We add the positive

**TABLE 12.3**   Scores for the Before-Therapy and After-Therapy Conditions

*Each D equals (before − after).*

| Subject | Before therapy | − | After therapy | = | Difference, D |
|---------|---------------|---|--------------|---|---------------|
| 1 (Dorcas) | 11 | − | 8 | = | +3 |
| 2 (Biff) | 16 | − | 11 | = | +5 |
| 3 (Millie) | 20 | − | 15 | = | +5 |
| 4 (Binky) | 17 | − | 11 | = | +6 |
| 5 (Slug) | 10 | − | 11 | = | −1 |
| | | | | | $\Sigma D = 18$ |

and negative differences to find the sum of the differences, symbolized by $\Sigma D$ (in Table 12.3, $\Sigma D = 18$). Then we divide this amount by $N$, the number of difference scores. For our phobia data, the mean difference, $\overline{D}$, equals 18/5, which is $+3.6$. This indicates that before scores were, on average, 3.6 points higher than after scores.

Now here is the strange part: forget about the before and after scores for the moment, and consider only the difference scores. From a statistical standpoint, we have *one* sample mean ($\overline{D}$) from *one* random sample of difference scores. As we saw in the previous chapter, when we have one sample mean, we perform the single-sample *t*-test! The fact that we have difference scores in no way violates the *t*-test, so we will create our statistical hypotheses and then test them in virtually the same way as we did with the single-sample *t*-test.

> **STAT ALERT**   The *t*-test for two related samples is performed by conducting the single-sample *t*-test on the sample of difference scores.

## Statistical Hypotheses for the Related Samples *t*-Test

Now we can create our statistical hypotheses. Our sample of difference scores represents the population of difference scores that would result if we could measure the population of raw scores under each of our conditions and then subtract the scores in one population from the corresponding scores in the other population. The population of difference scores has some $\mu$ that we identify as $\mu_D$. To create our statistical hypotheses, we simply determine the predicted values of $\mu_D$ in $H_0$ and $H_a$.

In our one-tailed phobia study, we predict that the population of scores after therapy will contain lower fear scores than the population of scores before therapy. If we subtract the after scores from the before scores, as we did in our sample, then we should have a population of difference scores containing positive numbers. The resulting $\mu_D$ should also be a positive number. Our alternative hypothesis always implies that the predicted relationship exists, so here we state it as

$H_a$: $\mu_D > 0$

$H_a$ implies that our sample $\overline{D}$ represents a population of differences having a $\mu_D$ greater than zero, and thus demonstrates that after scores are lower than before scores in the population.

On the other hand, according to the null hypothesis, there are two ways we may fail to demonstrate the predicted relationship. First, the therapy may do nothing to fear scores, so that the population of before scores contains the same scores as the population of after scores. If we subtract the after scores from the before scores, the population of difference scores will have a $\mu_D$ of zero. Note that every difference need not equal zero. Because of random physiological or psychological factors, all subjects may not produce the same fear score on two observations, and thus their difference scores may not be zero. On average, however, the positive and negative differences will cancel out to produce a $\mu_D$ of zero. Second, the therapy may increase fear scores, so that subtracting larger after scores from smaller before scores produces a population of difference scores consisting of negative numbers, with a $\mu_D$ that is less than zero. Thus, given the way we are subtracting to find our difference scores, our null hypothesis is

$H_0$: $\mu_D \leq 0$

$H_0$ implies that our sample $\overline{D}$ represents such a population $\mu_D$, thus demonstrating that the predicted relationship between therapy and fear scores does not exist.

As usual, we test $H_0$ by testing whether our sample mean represents the $\mu$ that is equal to the value described by $H_0$. Here, $H_0$ says that our sample mean represents the population of difference scores where $\mu_D$ equals zero. If the sample perfectly represents this population, then $\overline{D}$ "should" equal zero. However, because of those chance fluctuations in fear scores, all of the difference scores in our sample may not equal zero, so neither will $\overline{D}$. Thus, $H_0$ says that $\overline{D}$ represents a population where $\mu_D$ is zero, and if $\overline{D}$ is not zero, it is because of sampling error.

To test $H_0$, we determine whether our sample mean of $+3.6$ is likely to occur through sampling error when the sample represents a $\mu_D$ equal to zero. To do this, we examine the sampling distribution of means, which here is the sampling distribution of $\overline{D}$. This is the frequency distribution of the different values of $\overline{D}$ that occur when $H_0$ is true and the sample mean represents a $\mu_D$ equal to zero. We simply locate our $\overline{D}$ on this sampling distribution by computing $t_{obt}$.

## Computing the *t*-Test for Related Samples

To see how to compute $t_{obt}$, we will use the data from our phobia study, presented in Table 12.4. Note that we need $N$, $\Sigma D$, $\overline{D}$, and $\Sigma D^2$.

Computing $t_{obt}$ here is identical to computing the single-sample *t*-test discussed in Chapter 11, except that we have changed the symbols from $X$ to $D$. Thus, to compute the $t_{obt}$ for related samples, we perform the following three steps.

The first step is to find $s_D^2$, which is the estimated variance of the population of difference scores.

---

**THE FORMULA FOR $s_D^2$ IS**

$$s_D^2 = \frac{\Sigma D^2 - \dfrac{(\Sigma D)^2}{N}}{N - 1}$$

---

For our phobia study, we fill in this formula using the data in Table 12.4.

$$s_D^2 = \frac{\Sigma D^2 - \dfrac{(\Sigma D)^2}{N}}{N - 1} = \frac{96 - \dfrac{(18)^2}{5}}{4} = 7.80$$

The second step is to find $s_{\overline{D}}$, which is the **standard error of the mean difference,** or the "standard deviation" of the sampling distribution of $\overline{D}$.

**TABLE 12.4**  Summary of Data from Phobia Study

| Subject | *Before therapy* | − | *After therapy* | = | *Difference, D* | $D^2$ |
|---------|------------------|---|-----------------|---|-----------------|-------|
| 1 | 11 | | 8 | | +3 | 9 |
| 2 | 16 | | 11 | | +5 | 25 |
| 3 | 20 | | 15 | | +5 | 25 |
| 4 | 17 | | 11 | | +6 | 36 |
| 5 | 10 | | 11 | | −1 | 1 |
| | $\overline{X} = 14.80$ | | $\overline{X} = 11.20$ | | $\Sigma D = +18$ | $\Sigma D^2 = 96$ |
| $N = 5$ | | | | | $\overline{D} = +3.6$ | |

> **THE FORMULA FOR THE STANDARD ERROR OF THE MEAN DIFFERENCE, $s_{\overline{D}}$, IS**
>
> $$s_{\overline{D}} = \sqrt{(s_D^2)\left(\frac{1}{N}\right)}$$

For our phobia study, with $s_D^2 = 7.80$ and $N = 5$, we have

$$s_{\overline{D}} = \sqrt{(s_D^2)\left(\frac{1}{N}\right)} = \sqrt{(7.80)\left(\frac{1}{5}\right)} = \sqrt{1.56} = 1.25$$

The third step is to find $t_{obt}$.

> **THE DEFINITIONAL FORMULA FOR THE *t*-TEST FOR RELATED SAMPLES IS**
>
> $$t_{obt} = \frac{\overline{D} - \mu_D}{s_{\overline{D}}}$$

For our phobia study, $\overline{D}$ is $+3.6$, $s_{\overline{D}}$ is 1.25, and $H_0$ says that $\mu_D$ equals 0. Putting these values into the above formula, we have

$$t_{obt} = \frac{\overline{D} - \mu_D}{s_{\overline{D}}} = \frac{+3.6 - 0}{1.25} = +2.88$$

This tells us that our sample $\overline{D}$ of $+3.6$ is located at a $t_{obt}$ of $+2.88$ on the sampling distribution of $\overline{D}$ where $\mu_D = 0$ (and $N = 5$ and $s_{\overline{D}} = 1.25$).

**Computational formula for the related samples *t*-test**  We can combine the above steps of computing $s_{\overline{D}}$ and $t_{obt}$ into one formula.

> **THE COMPUTATIONAL FORMULA FOR THE *t*-TEST FOR RELATED SAMPLES IS**
>
> $$t_{obt} = \frac{\overline{D} - \mu_D}{\sqrt{(s_D^2)\left(\frac{1}{N}\right)}}$$

The numerator is the same as we saw in the definitional formula. The denominator simply contains the formula for the standard error of the mean difference, $s_{\overline{D}}$.

**Combined formula for $t_{obt}$ in the related samples *t*-test**   When we are testing an $H_0$ that contains $\mu_D = 0$, then $\mu_D$ is always zero in the above formulas for $t_{obt}$, so the numerator always equals the value of $\overline{D}$. Using this fact, we have combined all computations into one combined formula for $t_{obt}$.

> **STAT ALERT**   We can use the combined formula only when our one- or two-tailed null hypothesis includes $\mu_D = 0$.

THE COMBINED FORMULA FOR $t_{obt}$ WHEN $\mu_D = 0$ IS

$$t_{obt} = \frac{\Sigma D}{\sqrt{[N(\Sigma D^2) - (\Sigma D)^2]\left(\dfrac{1}{N-1}\right)}}$$

Putting the data for our phobia study into the above formula, we have

$$t_{obt} = \frac{+18}{\sqrt{[5(96) - (18)^2]\left(\dfrac{1}{5-1}\right)}}$$

In the left-hand bracket of the denominator, 5 times 96 is 480 and $18^2$ is 324. Subtracting 324 from 480 gives 156. In the right-hand parentheses, 1/4 is .25. Thus, we have

$$t_{obt} = \frac{+18}{\sqrt{(156)(.25)}} = \frac{+18}{\sqrt{39.00}} = \frac{+18}{6.245} = +2.88$$

So $t_{obt}$ is again $+2.88$.

> **STAT ALERT**   Usually the final answer in the denominator of the *t*-test is the standard error. However, when we use the combined formula above, the final answer is *not* $s_{\overline{D}}$. You must compute $s_{\overline{D}}$ using the formula given previously.

## Interpreting $t_{obt}$ in the Related Samples *t*-Test

To interpret $t_{obt}$, we compare it to $t_{crit}$. We find $t_{crit}$ in the *t*-tables (Table 2 in Appendix D) for $df = N - 1$, where $N$ is the number of difference scores. For our phobia study, with $\alpha = .05$ and $df = 4$, the one-tailed value of $t_{crit}$ is $+2.132$. Our $t_{crit}$ is positive, because we predicted that therapy works to decrease fear. When we subtract the after scores from the before scores, we should obtain a positive value of $\overline{D}$, producing a positive $t_{obt}$.

Figure 12.4 shows our completed sampling distribution. This is another sampling distribution of means, except that each mean is a mean of difference scores. The mean of the distribution is zero, and the values of $\overline{D}$ that are farther from zero (whether positive or negative) are less likely to occur when $H_0$ is true and the sample actually represents a $\mu_D$ of zero. As shown, our $t_{obt}$ of $+2.88$ is in the region of rejection, so sampling error is too unlikely to produce our $\overline{D}$ of $+3.60$ when the sample actually represents a $\mu_D$ of zero (and even less likely when the sample represents a $\mu_D$ less than zero). Therefore, we reject the null hypothesis that our sample represents $\mu_D \le 0$. Our results are significant, and we report them as

$$t_{obt}(4) = +2.88, \quad p < .05$$

By rejecting $H_0$, we accept $H_a$ (that our sample represents a $\mu_D$ that is greater than zero). We would see such a population of difference scores if the population of before-therapy scores contained scores that were larger than those in the population of after-therapy scores. Therefore, we conclude that we have demonstrated a significant difference between the before and after scores that

**FIGURE 12.4**  One-Tailed Sampling Distribution of Random $\overline{D}$s When $\mu_D = 0$

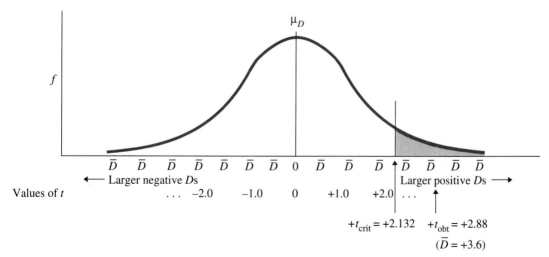

represents a relationship in the population, so we are confident that our therapy works. (If $t_{obt}$ had not been beyond $t_{crit}$, then we would retain $H_0$ and we would not have convincing evidence that our therapy reduces fear scores.)

Way back in Table 12.4, we computed the mean of the before scores as 14.80 and the mean of the after scores as 11.20. Our best estimate is that if we measured the fear scores of all subjects in the population, before therapy the $\mu$ would be around 14.80, and after therapy the $\mu$ would be around 11.20. However, because our sample means are from related samples, we *cannot* use the formula from the previous chapter to compute a confidence interval for each $\mu$. Instead, we can only deal with $\mu_D$. Since our sample mean, $\overline{D}$, is $+3.60$, it probably represents a population of difference scores where $\mu_D$ is "around" $+3.60$. We now compute a confidence interval to describe this $\mu_D$.

## Computing the Confidence Interval for $\mu_D$

The confidence interval for $\mu_D$ describes a range of values of $\mu_D$, one of which our sample mean difference is likely to represent. We compute the interval by computing the highest and lowest values of $\mu_D$ that are not significantly different from $\overline{D}$.

THE COMPUTATIONAL FORMULA FOR THE CONFIDENCE INTERVAL FOR $\mu_D$ OF THE POPULATION OF DIFFERENCE SCORES IS

$$(s_{\overline{D}})(-t_{crit}) + \overline{D} \le \mu_D \le (s_{\overline{D}})(+t_{crit}) + \overline{D}$$

The value of $t_{crit}$ is the two-tailed value for $df = N - 1$, where $N$ is the number of difference scores, $s_{\overline{D}}$ is standard error of the mean difference as computed above, and $\overline{D}$ is the mean of our difference scores.

To compute the confidence interval for our phobia study, we have $s_{\overline{D}} = 1.25$ and $\overline{D} = +3.60$, and with $\alpha = .05$ and $df = 4$, the two-tailed $t_{crit}$ is $\pm 2.776$. Filling in the above formula, we have

$$(1.25)(-2.776) + 3.60 \le \mu_D \le (1.25)(+2.776) + 3.60$$

which becomes

$$0.13 \le \mu_D \le 7.07$$

Thus, we are 95% confident that our sample mean of $+3.60$ represents a population $\mu_D$ within this interval. In other words, if we performed this study on the entire population, we would expect the average difference in before and after scores to be between 0.13 and 7.07.

## Testing Other Hypotheses with the Related Samples *t*-Test

In the preceding study we could have reversed how we computed the difference scores, subtracting the predicted larger before scores from the predicted smaller after scores. Then, if the study did not work as predicted, we would expect a $\overline{D}$ of zero or greater, representing a $\mu_D \geq 0$. If the study worked, we would expect a negative $\overline{D}$, representing a $\mu_D$ less than zero. Therefore, our hypotheses would be

$$H_0: \mu_D \geq 0$$
$$H_a: \mu_D < 0$$

In an experiment where we do not predict which sample of raw scores will produce the higher scores, we have two-tailed hypotheses: our sample of difference scores either does or does not reflect differences between the populations for our two conditions. If the populations of raw scores do not differ, then $\mu_D$ is equal to zero. If the populations of raw scores differ, then $\mu_D$ is not equal to zero. Therefore, the two-tailed hypotheses are

$$H_0: \mu_D = 0$$
$$H_a: \mu_D \neq 0$$

Finally, we can also test an $H_0$ that the populations differ by some amount other than zero. For example, previously we discussed a study where Navy and Marine pilots differed by 10 points in flying ability. Suppose we want to perform a related samples study in which we match each Navy pilot with a Marine pilot who has had the same amount of flying experience. Our null hypothesis is that the training does not work, so the two samples still represent populations that differ by 10. When we subtract the two populations, the population of differences has a $\mu_D$ equal to 10, so our $H_0$ is $\mu_D = 10$. Our alternative hypothesis is that the training alters the difference between the two raw score populations so that, when we subtract the two populations, the difference is not 10. Thus we have $H_a: \mu_D \neq 10$.

To test any of the above null hypotheses, we select the appropriate $t_{crit}$ and then calculate and test $t_{obt}$ using the same procedure we used in the phobia study.

## Power and the Related Samples *t*-Test

With the related samples *t*-test, we are again concerned about maximizing power. As before, our goal is to maximize the size of $t_{obt}$. Looking at the formula

$$t_{obt} = \frac{\overline{D} - \mu_D}{\sqrt{(s_D^2)\left(\dfrac{1}{N}\right)}}$$

we see that to maximize power here, we want to (1) maximize the differences between the scores in the two samples, producing a large difference between $\overline{D}$ and $\mu_D$, (2) minimize the variability of the differences scores, producing a small $s_D^2$, and (3) maximize the size of $N$. Each of these increases the size of $t_{obt}$ relative to $t_{crit}$ and thus increases the probability that we will reject $H_0$ when $H_0$ is false.

In addition, recognize that a related samples design is intrinsically more powerful than an independent samples design. For example, say we re-analyzed our phobia study, violating the assumptions and treating the two samples as independent samples of fear scores. Comparing the two procedures, we would find that the variability of the original fear scores was larger than the variability of the difference scores. We eliminate some of the variability between the raw scores by transforming them to *D*s. For example, Table 12.5 presents the scores of Subjects 2 and 3 (from Table 12.4). Although there is variability (differences) in their before scores and in their after scores, there is no variability in their difference scores. As we have seen, reducing variability in scores is one way to produce a larger $t_{obt}$, so the $t_{obt}$ for related samples will be larger than the $t_{obt}$ for independent samples. A larger $t_{obt}$ is more likely to be significant, so the *t*-test for related samples is more powerful.

## DESCRIBING THE RELATIONSHIP IN A TWO-SAMPLE EXPERIMENT

By this time you understand how to determine whether results are significant. The fact that $t_{obt}$ is significant is not the end of the story, however, because this tells us nothing about the relationship. Therefore, in addition to computing the appropriate confidence interval, we also describe the relationship by graphing the results, computing the correlation coefficient, and computing the proportion of variance accounted for.

**TABLE 12.5** Scores of Subjects 2 and 3 from Phobia Study

| Subject | Before therapy | − | After therapy | = | Difference, D |
|---|---|---|---|---|---|
| 2 | 16 | | 11 | | +5 |
| 3 | 20 | | 15 | | +5 |

## Graphing the Results of a Two-Sample Experiment

As you know, we graph experimental results by plotting the mean of each condition on the $Y$ axis and the conditions of the independent variable on the $X$ axis. Thus, we would plot the results of our hypnosis study as shown in the left-hand graph in Figure 12.5 and the results of our phobia study as shown in the right-hand graph. (Note that for the phobia study, we plot the mean of the original raw fear scores from the before and after conditions, and not the $D$'s.) Such slanting lines indicate a relationship in the samples. Because the sample means are significantly different, we expect that if we measured and then plotted the population $\mu$'s, we would obtain similar graphs.

As we saw in Chapters 7 and 8, another way to summarize data is through correlation and regression. Thus, we could plot the scatterplot for each study, using the condition under which each subject was tested as the $X$ score and the subject's score on the dependent variable as the $Y$ score. Recall that a linear regression line is the straight line that summarizes a scatterplot. When there are only two values of $X$, the regression line connects the means of $Y$ at each $X$. Therefore, if we used the procedures in Chapter 8 to compute and plot the linear regression line for each experiment, we would again have these line graphs.

The regression equation allows us to predict a subject's $Y$ score if we know the corresponding $X$ score. The predicted $Y$ score is the value of $Y$ lying on the regression line at that $X$. Since each line graph is the same as a regression line, not surprisingly our best prediction of a subject's $Y$ score in a particular condition is the mean of that condition. Thus, for example, using the relationship found in our hypnosis study, we would predict the mean score of 20 for

**FIGURE 12.5** Line Graphs of the Results of the Hypnosis Study and the Phobia Study

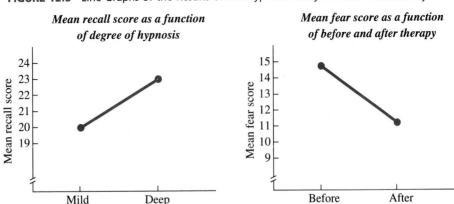

each subject in the mild hypnosis condition and the mean score of 23 for each subject in the deep hypnosis condition.

Recall that a correlation coefficient describes the strength of a relationship, indicating how consistently one value of $Y$ is associated with one and only one value of $X$. In an experiment, if we correlate the scores on the dependent variable with the conditions of the independent variable, we describe how consistently subjects scored at or close to the mean score for each condition of the independent variable. Thus, a correlation coefficient will tell us how consistently close subjects' recall scores were to the mean score of 20 under mild hypnosis and to the mean score of 23 under deep hypnosis.

This is the point at which significance testing of means converges with significance testing of a correlation coefficient. Because our previous values of $t_{obt}$ were significant, we know that if we computed correlation coefficients to describe our experiments, they too would be significant. A significant relationship is a significant relationship, regardless of whether it is summarized using means or a correlation coefficient. The advantage of a correlation coefficient is that it describes how strong, or how consistent, the relationship is. Thus, whenever we obtain significant results by testing means, we also describe the strength of the relationship by computing the appropriate correlation coefficient.

## Describing the Strength of the Relationship in a Two-Sample Experiment Using $r_{pb}$

The point-biserial correlation coefficient ($r_{pb}$) is appropriate for describing a two-sample experiment: the conditions of the independent variable are a dichotomous variable (consisting of two categories), and scores on the dependent variable are a continuous interval or ratio variable. We could compute $r_{pb}$ using the formula in Chapter 7, but instead we can compute $r_{pb}$ directly from our $t_{obt}$.

*THE FORMULA FOR COMPUTING $r_{pb}$ FROM $t_{obt}$ IS*

$$r_{pb} = \sqrt{\frac{(t_{obt})^2}{(t_{obt})^2 + df}}$$

Although this formula can be used for either independent or related samples, there is one important distinction:

**For independent samples, $df = (n_1 - 1) + (n_2 - 1)$, where each $n$ is the number of scores in a sample.**

**For related samples, $df = N - 1$, where $N$ is the number of difference scores.**

In our hypnosis study, we found $t_{obt} = +2.94$ with $df = 30$, so

$$r_{pb} = \sqrt{\frac{(2.94)^2}{(2.94)^2 + 30}} = \sqrt{\frac{8.64}{8.64 + 30}} = \sqrt{\frac{8.64}{38.64}} = \sqrt{.224} = .47$$

Thus, the relationship between recall scores and degree of hypnosis can be summarized as $r_{pb} = .47$. Likewise, for our phobia study, with $t_{obt} = +2.88$ and $df = 4$, the relationship between fear scores and before or after therapy can be summarized as $r_{pb} = .82$.

Notice that the final step in the formula for computing $r_{pb}$ is taking the square root, so our answer will always be positive. Depending on the data, we decide whether $r_{pb}$ is positive or negative. Looking back at our graphs, we see that our hypnosis study produced a positive relationship, so $r_{pb} = +.47$. Our phobia study produced a negative relationship, so $r_{pb} = -.82$. Although both describe significant relationships, the $r_{pb}$ of $-.82$ for the phobia study indicates that there we demonstrated a stronger, more consistent relationship than in the hypnosis study (where $r_{pb}$ was only $+.47$).

Recall that the most direct way to evaluate a relationship is to compute the proportion of variance accounted for.

## Describing the Proportion of Variance Accounted For in a Two-Sample Experiment

We saw in Chapter 8 that we compute the "proportion of variance in $Y$ scores that is accounted for by the $X$ variable" by squaring the correlation coefficient. Thus, to compute the proportion of variance accounted for in a two-sample experiment, we compute the squared value of $r_{pb}$ (in the formula, simply don't find the square root). The resulting value essentially indicates how much more accurately we can predict scores when we know the condition under which subjects were tested than when we predict each subject's score using the overall mean of all scores. For our hypnosis study, squaring $r_{pb}$ gives $(.47)^2$, or .22. Thus, we are, on average, 22% closer to predicting subjects' actual recall scores when we use the mean score of each hypnosis condition to predict their scores, rather than using the overall mean recall score of the experiment. Likewise, in the phobia study, $r_{pb}^2 = (.82)^2$, or .67, so we can account for 67% of the variance in fear scores by knowing whether or not subjects have undergone the therapy.

Recall that the goal of science is to explain variability: to understand why one score or behavior is different from another. When an experiment demonstrates a significant relationship, our explanation is that the independent variable has an *effect* on the dependent variable. That is, we argue that by changing the conditions of the independent variable, we "cause" scores on the dependent variable to change. The word "cause" is in quotes because remember, we never *prove* that changing the independent variable causes the scores to change (a change in some other unknown variable may actually have caused subjects' scores to change). Thus, we explain the variability in our recall scores, for example, as being "caused" by changing the degree of hypnosis. For this reason, in an experiment, the proportion of variance accounted for is also called the effect size. The **effect size** indicates how consistently differences in the dependent scores are "caused" by changes in the independent variable. The larger the effect size, the more consistently the raw scores for each condition are located at or close to the mean score for that condition, so the more consistent the effect of the independent variable.

A scientifically important variable is one that has a very consistent effect and thus explains a large proportion of variability. For example, say that a given degree of hypnosis would cause everyone to have the same recall score. Increase the degree of hypnosis, and every recall score would increase by the same amount. There would be no differences in $Y$ scores except when $X$ changed, so there would be no variability in $Y$ scores not associated with changes in $X$. In this hypothetical case, $r_{pb}$ would equal $+1.0$, so 100% of the variance in $Y$ would be explained by, or accounted for by, changes in $X$. Here, degree of hypnosis is the *only* variable that influences recall scores, so it is a very important variable.

On the other hand, we actually found that $r_{pb}$ was only $+.47$. Now, at one degree of hypnosis we get more or less the same recall scores, but the $Y$ scores are different when $X$ has not changed. Here there is variability in $Y$ scores that is *not* associated with changes in $X$: only 22% of the variance in recall scores is accounted for by changes in degree of hypnosis. Now there must be *other* variables that also cause recall scores to change, so the variable of degree of hypnosis is only somewhat important in determining variability in recall scores.

Recognize that although a large effect size indicates an important relationship in a statistical sense, it does not indicate importance in a practical sense: statistics will never tell you if you have performed a silly study. In the real world, our conclusion that memory was improved by deep hypnosis has little practical importance. (To improve my memory, I should walk around under deep hypnosis all the time?) Statistical importance addresses a different issue: if you want to understand how nature works when it comes to hypnosis and memory, *then* this relationship is relevant and important. It is relevant because our results were significant, so we are confident that it is a relationship found in nature. It is important to the extent that degree of hypnosis has an influence on recall scores that accounts for 22% of the differences in recall scores.

## FINALLY

You should compute the effect size whenever you have significant results in an experiment. This is the only way to determine whether the relationship is important or is much ado about nothing. Effect size is not always reported in psychological research, although it should be. Great, elaborate experiments are often performed to study what are actually very minor variables. Researchers often forget the old adage "Things that are not worth doing are not worth doing well!" If you use $r_{pb}^2$—or other measures you will learn about—you will know whether a variable is worth studying, and you will be on the cutting edge of statistical sophistication (and that's not bad).

## CHAPTER SUMMARY

1. Two samples are *independent* when we randomly select subjects and assign them to samples without regard to who else has been selected for either sample.

2. The *t*-test for independent samples assumes that (a) the two random, independent samples of scores measure an interval or ratio variable, (b) the population of raw scores represented by each sample forms a normal distribution for which it is appropriate to compute the mean, and (c) the populations represented by the samples have homogeneous variance.

3. *Homogeneity of variance* means that if we could compute the variance of the populations represented by our samples, the value of $\sigma_X^2$ in one population would equal the value of $\sigma_X^2$ in the other population.

4. A significant $t_{obt}$ from the independent samples *t*-test indicates that the difference between our sample means, $\overline{X}_1 - \overline{X}_2$, is significantly different from, and thus unlikely to represent, the difference between $\mu_1$ and $\mu_2$ described by $H_0$. Therefore, the results are assumed to represent the predicted relationship in the population.

5. The *confidence interval for* $\mu_1 - \mu_2$ contains a range of differences between two population $\mu$'s, one of which is the difference that is likely to be represented by the difference between our independent sample means.

6. Two samples are *related samples* when each score in the sample is paired with a particular score in the other condition. We pair the scores either by *matching* each subject in one condition with a subject in the other

condition or by *repeated measures* of the same subjects under both
conditions.

**6.** In performing the *t*-test for related samples, we first find the difference
between the two scores in each pair. Then we perform the *t*-test for a
single sample, using the difference scores. A significant $t_{obt}$ indicates that
the mean of the difference scores, $\overline{D}$, is significantly different from the
$\mu_D$ described by $H_0$. This implies that the means of the raw scores in
each condition differ significantly and thus represent a relationship in the
population.

**7.** The *confidence interval for* $\mu_D$ contains a range of values of $\mu_D$, one of
which is likely to be represented by the sample mean, $\overline{D}$, from our
related samples.

**8.** The power of the two-sample *t*-test increases with (a) larger differences
in scores between the conditions, (b) smaller variability of scores within
each condition with independent samples and smaller variability in the
difference scores with related samples, and (c) larger *N*. All other things
being equal, the *t*-test for related samples is more powerful than the
*t*-test for independent samples.

**9.** We describe the strength of a significant relationship between the independent and dependent variables in a two-sample experiment by computing the *point-biserial correlation coefficient,* $r_{pb}$.

**10.** The squared point-biserial coefficient, $r_{pb}^2$, measures the *proportion of
variance* in the dependent scores that is accounted for, or explained, by
changing the conditions of the independent variable. The proportion of
variance accounted for is also referred to as the *effect size*. The larger
the effect size, the more consistently the dependent scores change as we
change the conditions of the independent variable.

## USING THE COMPUTER

Using routine **6** of the computer program, you can perform the independent
samples *t*-test or the related samples *t*-test. In each, the program computes the
mean and standard deviation from each sample, presents a graph of the sample
means, and calculates the appropriate $t_{obt}$. As usual, the given value of *p* is the
minimum $\alpha$ that you could use for $t_{obt}$ to be significant in a two-tailed test. The
program also computes the 95% confidence interval ($\alpha = .05$) for the difference

between two population $\mu$'s in the independent samples test, and the 95% confidence interval for $\mu_D$ in the related samples test. Finally, the program computes the proportion of variance accounted for in the relationship by finding $r_{pb}^2$.

---

## PRACTICE PROBLEMS

(Answers are provided for odd-numbered problems.)

1. When do we use a two-sample $t$-test?
2. (a) When do we use the independent samples $t$-test? (b) When do we use the related samples $t$-test?
3. What is homogeneity of variance?
4. What is $s_{\bar{X}_1 - \bar{X}_2}$ and what is $s_{\bar{D}}$?
5. What does a confidence interval for the difference between two $\mu$'s indicate?
6. What does the confidence interval for $\mu_D$ indicate?
7. In an experiment, a researcher seeks to demonstrate a relationship between hot or cold baths (the independent variable) and amount of relaxation (the dependent variable). He obtains the following relaxation scores:

    Sample 1 (hot):   $\bar{X} = 43$, $s_X^2 = 22.79$, $N = 15$
    Sample 2 (cold):   $\bar{X} = 39$, $s_X^2 = 24.6$, $N = 15$

    a. What are $H_0$ and $H_a$ for this study?
    b. Compute $t_{obt}$.
    c. With $\alpha = .05$, what is $t_{crit}$?
    d. What should the researcher conclude about this relationship?
    e. Compute the confidence interval for the difference between the $\mu$'s.

8. A researcher investigates whether a period of time feels longer when people are bored than when they are not bored. The researcher obtains the following estimates of the time period (in minutes):

    Sample 1 (bored):       $\bar{X} = 14.5$, $s_X^2 = 10.22$, $N = 28$
    Sample 2 (not bored):   $\bar{X} = 9.0$, $s_X^2 = 14.6$, $N = 34$

    a. What are $H_0$ and $H_a$ for this study?
    b. Compute $t_{obt}$.
    c. With $\alpha = .05$, what is $t_{crit}$?
    d. What should the researcher conclude about this relationship?
    e. Compute the confidence interval for the difference between the $\mu$'s.

9. A researcher investigates whether children exhibit a higher number of aggressive acts after watching a violent television show. The numbers of aggressive acts for the same ten subjects before and after watching the show are as follows:

| Sample 1 (After) | Sample 2 (Before) |
|:---:|:---:|
| 5 | 4 |
| 6 | 6 |
| 4 | 3 |
| 4 | 2 |
| 7 | 4 |
| 3 | 1 |
| 2 | 0 |
| 1 | 0 |
| 4 | 5 |
| 3 | 2 |

  *a.* What are $H_0$ and $H_a$ for this study?
  *b.* Compute $t_{obt}$.
  *c.* With $\alpha = .05$, what is $t_{crit}$?
  *d.* What should the researcher conclude about this relationship?
  *e.* Compute the confidence interval for $\mu_D$.
*10.* You investigate whether the older or younger male in pairs of brothers tends to be more extroverted. You obtain the following extroversion scores:

| Sample 1 (Younger) | Sample 2 (Older) |
|:---:|:---:|
| 10 | 18 |
| 11 | 17 |
| 18 | 19 |
| 12 | 16 |
| 15 | 15 |
| 13 | 19 |
| 19 | 13 |
| 15 | 20 |

  *a.* What are $H_0$ and $H_a$ for this study?
  *b.* Compute $t_{obt}$.
  *c.* With $\alpha = .05$, what is $t_{crit}$?
  *d.* What should you conclude about this relationship?
*11.* (a) For problem 9, compute the effect size. (b) What does this indicate about that relationship?
*12.* What do you conclude about the effect size in problem 10?

## *SUMMARY OF FORMULAS*

*1. Formulas for independent samples*

    **A.** *The computational formula for the t-test for independent samples is*

$$t_{obt} = \frac{(\overline{X}_1 - \overline{X}_2) - (\mu_1 - \mu_2)}{\sqrt{\left(\dfrac{(n_1 - 1)s_1^2 + (n_2 - 1)s_2^2}{(n_1 - 1) + (n_2 - 1)}\right)\left(\dfrac{1}{n_1} + \dfrac{1}{n_2}\right)}}$$

Values of $t_{crit}$ are found in Table 2 for $df = (n_1 - 1) + (n_2 - 1)$.

In the formula, $(\overline{X}_1 - \overline{X}_2)$ is the difference between the sample means, $(\mu_1 - \mu_2)$ is the difference described in $H_0$, $s_1^2$ and $n_1$ are from one sample, and $s_2^2$ and $n_2$ are from the other sample. Values of $s_1^2$ and $s_2^2$ are found using the formula

$$s_X^2 = \frac{\Sigma X^2 - \dfrac{(\Sigma X)^2}{N}}{N - 1}$$

    **B.** *The computational formula for the confidence interval for the difference between two population $\mu$'s is*

$$(s_{\overline{X}_1 - \overline{X}_2})(-t_{crit}) + (\overline{X}_1 - \overline{X}_2) \leq \mu_1 - \mu_2 \leq (s_{\overline{X}_1 - \overline{X}_2})(+t_{crit}) + (\overline{X}_1 - \overline{X}_2)$$

where $t_{crit}$ is the two-tailed value for $df = (n_1 + n_2) - 2$, the quantity $(\overline{X}_1 - \overline{X}_2)$ is the difference between the sample means, and $s_{\overline{X}_1 - \overline{X}_2}$ is the standard error of the difference found using the formula

$$s_{\overline{X}_1 - \overline{X}_2} = \sqrt{\left(\frac{(n_1 - 1)s_1^2 + (n_2 - 1)s_2^2}{(n_1 - 1) + (n_2 - 1)}\right)\left(\frac{1}{n_1} + \frac{1}{n_2}\right)}$$

*2. Formulas for related samples*

    **A.** *The computational formula for the t-test for related samples is*

$$t_{obt} = \frac{\overline{D} - \mu_D}{\sqrt{(s_D^2)\left(\dfrac{1}{N}\right)}}$$

Values of $t_{crit}$ are found in Table 2 for $df = N - 1$, where $N$ is the number of difference scores.

In the formula, $\overline{D}$ is the mean of the difference scores, $\mu_D$ is the value described by $H_0$, and $s_D^2$ is the variance of the difference scores, found using the formula

$$s_D^2 = \frac{\Sigma D^2 - \dfrac{(\Sigma D)^2}{N}}{N - 1}$$

where $D$ is each difference score and $N$ is the number of difference scores.

**B.** *The combined formula for the t-test for related samples when* $\mu_D = 0$ *is*

$$t_{\text{obt}} = \frac{\Sigma D}{\sqrt{[N(\Sigma D^2) - (\Sigma D)^2]\left(\dfrac{1}{N - 1}\right)}}$$

Values of $t_{\text{crit}}$ are found in Table 2 for $df = N - 1$, where $N$ is the number of difference scores.

**C.** *The computational formula for the confidence interval for* $\mu_D$ *is*

$$(s_{\overline{D}})(-t_{\text{crit}}) + \overline{D} \leq \mu_D \leq (s_{\overline{D}})(+t_{\text{crit}}) + \overline{D}$$

$t_{\text{crit}}$ is the two-tailed value for $df = N - 1$, where $N$ is the number of difference scores, and $s_{\overline{D}}$ is the standard error of the mean difference, found using the formula

$$s_{\overline{D}} = \sqrt{(s_D^2)\left(\frac{1}{N}\right)}$$

where $s_D^2$ is the variance of difference scores and $N$ is the number of difference scores.

**3.** *The formula for computing* $r_{pb}$ *from* $t_{obt}$ *is*

$$r_{pb} = \sqrt{\frac{(t_{\text{obt}})^2}{(t_{\text{obt}})^2 + df}}$$

With independent samples, $df = (n_1 - 1) + (n_2 - 1)$, where each $n$ is the number of scores in a sample. With related samples, $df = N - 1$, where $N$ is the number of difference scores.

**4.** *The proportion of variance accounted for* in a two-sample experiment equals the squared value of $r_{pb}$, or $r_{pb}^2$.

# 13

## One-Way Analysis of Variance: Testing the Significance of Two or More Sample Means

You may have noticed that each new procedure we discuss involves a more complex experiment than the previous one (it's a plot!). In the last chapter we saw how to analyze a two-sample experiment involving two conditions of an independent variable. However, researchers often conduct experiments involving more than two conditions. The parametric procedure used in such experiments is called *analysis of variance*. Analysis of variance is perhaps *the* most common inferential statistical procedure because it can be used with many different experimental designs: it can be applied to independent samples or to repeated measures samples, to any number of conditions of an independent variable, and to any number of independent variables.

In this chapter we will discuss analysis of variance for one independent variable. At first glance, analysis of variance appears to be very different from previous procedures. This is because analysis of variance is calculated differently and has its own language. However, ultimately the logic of hypothesis testing for this procedure is very similar to that for previous procedures we have discussed.

### MORE STATISTICAL NOTATION

There are several new terms used in analysis of variance. First, analysis of variance is abbreviated as **ANOVA**. Second, a **one-way ANOVA** is performed when only one independent variable is involved in the experiment. Third, an independent variable is called a **factor.** Thus, an experiment with one independent variable has one factor (and calls for a one-way ANOVA).

We identify a factor in terms of whether we have independent samples or repeated measures. As in the previous chapter, we have independent samples when we randomly select subjects and assign them to one condition without regard to who has been selected for any other condition. In ANOVA, an independent variable that is studied using independent samples in all conditions is called a **between-subjects** factor. When an independent variable is studied by repeatedly measuring the same subjects under all conditions, we have a **repeated measures** factor. (Throughout this chapter we shall discuss the between-subjects, one-way ANOVA.)

Finally, each condition of the independent variable, or factor, is called a **level.** It is important to know the number of levels in a factor, and the symbol for the number of levels in a factor is $k$. These conditions, or levels, of an independent variable are also called **treatments.** When the different conditions of the independent variable produce significant differences in scores, we call this the *treatment effect* of the factor.

To illustrate all of these terms, let's say we are interested in how subjects' performance on a task is influenced by how difficult they perceive the task to be (the perceived difficulty of the task). We will select three random samples containing five subjects each and provide them with the same easy math problems. However, to influence their perceptions, we will tell subjects in Sample 1 that the problems are easy, subjects in Sample 2 that the problems are of medium difficulty, and subjects in Sample 3 that the problems are difficult. Thus, we have three conditions of easy, medium, and difficult for our independent variable of perceived difficulty. In other words, we will need to use a one-way ANOVA with the three *levels* of easy, medium, and difficult for our *factor* of perceived difficulty. Subjects will be randomly assigned to and tested under only one condition, and we will not in any way match subjects, so this is a one-way, between-subjects design. Our dependent measure will be the number of problems that subjects correctly solve within an allotted time. Thus, we are seeking to demonstrate a treatment effect on scores by telling subjects the problems are either easy, of medium difficulty, or difficult.

A good way to see the layout of a one-way ANOVA is to diagram it as shown in Table 13.1. Each column is a level of the factor, containing the scores of the subjects tested under that condition. (Here they are symbolized by $X$, but they will be the number of problems solved by a subject.) The symbol $n$ stands for the number of scores in each level, and here there are five scores per level. The mean of each level is the mean of the scores from that condition. We again identify the $n$ and $\overline{X}$ for each level using a subscript. Thus, $\overline{X}_1$ and $n_1$ are the mean and $n$ from level 1, the easy condition. Since there are three levels in this factor, $k = 3$. (Notice that the general format is to label the factor as factor A, with levels $A_1$, $A_2$, and $A_3$.)

**TABLE 13.1** Diagram of a Study Having
Three Levels of One Factor

*Factor A: independent variable of
perceived difficulty*

| Level $A_1$:<br>easy | Level $A_2$:<br>medium | Level $A_3$:<br>difficult | |
|:---:|:---:|:---:|:---|
| | | | ← *Conditions*<br>*k* = 3 |
| X | X | X | |
| X | X | X | |
| X | X | X | |
| X | X | X | |
| X | X | X | |

| $\overline{X}_1$ | $\overline{X}_2$ | $\overline{X}_3$ | Overall $\overline{X}$ |
|:---:|:---:|:---:|:---|
| $n_1 = 5$ | $n_2 = 5$ | $n_3 = 5$ | $N = 15$ |

The total number of scores in the experiment is symbolized by $N$, and here $N = 15$. Further, the overall mean of all scores in the experiment will be the mean of all 15 scores.

## AN OVERVIEW OF ANOVA

As with all experiments, the purpose of the above study is to demonstrate a relationship between the independent variable and the dependent variable. The only difference from previous studies is that now we have three samples of subjects. Ideally we will find a different sample mean for each condition. Then we want to conclude that if we tested the entire population under each level of the factor (each level of difficulty), we would find three different populations of scores located at three different $\mu$'s. But there is the usual problem: differences between the sample means may reflect sampling error, in which case we would actually find the same population of scores, having the same $\mu$, for each level of difficulty. Therefore, as usual, before we can conclude that a relationship exists, we must eliminate the idea that the differences between our sample means reflect sampling error. **Analysis of variance** is the parametric statistical procedure for determining whether significant differences exist in an experiment containing two or more sample means. (When there are only two levels of the independent variable, we can perform either the two-sample $t$-test or ANOVA.)

## Why Perform ANOVA? Experiment-wise Error Rate

You might think that we could use the independent samples $t$-test to determine whether there are significant differences between any two of our three means above. We might perform multiple $t$-tests, testing whether $\overline{X}_1$ differs from $\overline{X}_2$, then whether $\overline{X}_2$ differs from $\overline{X}_3$, and finally whether $\overline{X}_1$ differs from $\overline{X}_3$. However, we cannot use this approach because of the probability of making a Type I error (rejecting a true $H_0$). With $\alpha = .05$, the theoretical probability of a Type I error in a *single* $t$-test is .05. However, we can make a Type I error when comparing $\overline{X}_1$ to $\overline{X}_2$, or when comparing $\overline{X}_2$ to $\overline{X}_3$, or when comparing $\overline{X}_1$ to $\overline{X}_3$. Therefore, the *overall* probability of a Type I error in at least one of the three $t$-tests is considerably greater than .05.

This overall probability of making a Type I error is called the experiment-wide or experiment-wise error rate. The **experiment-wise error rate** is the probability of making at least one Type I error in comparing all means in an experiment. When we compared only two means in an experiment, we could use the $t$-test because our experiment-wise error rate was equal to our $\alpha$. However, when there are more than two levels in a factor, we *must* perform ANOVA. Only then will the experiment-wise error rate after we have compared all sample means equal the alpha we choose.

As usual, before we proceed with a study, we must check that it meets the assumptions of our statistical procedure.

## Assumptions of the One-Way Between-Subjects ANOVA

In a one-way, between-subjects ANOVA, the experiment has only one independent variable, and all of the conditions contain independent samples. We assume that

1. Each condition contains a random sample of interval or ratio scores.
2. The population represented by the scores in each condition forms a normal distribution, and the mean is the appropriate measure of central tendency.
3. The variances of all populations represented in the study are homogeneous.

Like other parametric procedures, ANOVA is robust, so we can use it even if we do not have perfectly normal or homogeneous populations. Although the number of subjects in each condition ($n$) need not be equal, violations of the assumptions are less serious when all $n$'s are equal. Also, certain procedures are *much* easier to perform with equal $n$'s.

If the study meets the assumptions of ANOVA, we set alpha (usually at .05) and create our statistical hypotheses.

## Statistical Hypotheses of ANOVA

ANOVA never involves one-tailed hypotheses. ANOVA tests only two-tailed hypotheses. Our null hypothesis is that there are no differences between the populations represented by the conditions. Thus, for our perceived difficulty study with the three conditions of easy, medium, and difficult, we have

$$H_0: \mu_1 = \mu_2 = \mu_3$$

In general, when we perform ANOVA on a factor with $k$ levels, the null hypothesis is

$$H_0: \mu_1 = \mu_2 = \cdot \cdot \cdot = \mu_k$$

The "$. . . = \mu_k$" indicates that there are as many $\mu$'s as there are levels.

$H_0$ implies that our sample means for all conditions represent the same population mean, and therefore the sample means "should" be equal. If the means are not equal, it is because of sampling error in representing the one value of $\mu$.

You might think that the alternative hypothesis would be that the various $\mu$'s are not equal, or $\mu_1 \neq \mu_2 \neq \mu_3$. However, the study may demonstrate differences between *some* but not *all* conditions. Perhaps our data represent a difference between $\mu_1$ and $\mu_2$, but not between $\mu_1$ and $\mu_3$, or perhaps only $\mu_2$ and $\mu_3$ differ. To communicate this idea, we write our alternative hypothesis as

$$H_a: \text{not all } \mu\text{'s are equal}$$

$H_a$ implies that there is a relationship in the population involving at least two of our conditions: the population mean represented by one of the sample means is different from the population mean represented by at least one other sample mean.

As usual, we must test $H_0$, so in ANOVA, we always test whether all sample means are likely to represent the same population mean.

## The Order of Operations in ANOVA: The *F* Statistic and Post Hoc Comparisons

The statistic that forms the basis for ANOVA is called $F$. The **F statistic** simultaneously compares all sample means in a factor to determine whether two or more sample means represent different $\mu$'s. We will call the $F$ we obtain from our calculations $F_{obt}$. We compare $F_{obt}$ to the critical value of $F$, $F_{crit}$. When $F_{obt}$ is not significant, it indicates that there are no significant differences between any of our sample means and that all means are likely to represent the same $\mu$. When this occurs, the experiment has failed to demonstrate a relationship, we are finished with our statistical analyses, and it's back to the drawing board.

However, when $F_{obt}$ is significant, it indicates that *at least two* sample means are likely to represent different $\mu$'s. Maybe more than two means are significantly different, or maybe all of them are. Further, $F_{obt}$ does not indicate *which* specific means differ significantly. Thus, for example, if $F_{obt}$ for our perceived difficulty study is significant, then all we know is that there is at least one significant difference somewhere between the means of the easy, medium, and difficult levels.

Obviously, to understand the relationship between our independent variable and dependent variable, we must determine which levels differ significantly from which. Therefore, we must perform a second statistical procedure, called *post hoc* comparisons. **Post hoc comparisons,** like *t*-tests, compare every possible pair of sample means from a factor, to determine which means differ significantly from each other. Thus, if $F_{obt}$ for our perceived difficulty study is significant, we will perform *post hoc* comparisons to compare the means from easy and medium, easy and difficult, and medium and difficult. The results of these comparisons will indicate which means differ significantly from each other.

Note that we perform *post hoc* comparisons *only* when $F_{obt}$ is significant (*post hoc* means "after the fact," which here is after $F_{obt}$ is significant). By finding a significant $F_{obt}$ and then performing *post hoc* comparisons, we ensure that the experiment-wise probability of a Type I error in all of the significant differences together is less than .05.

> **STAT ALERT**  If $F_{obt}$ is significant, we perform *post hoc* comparisons to determine which specific means differ significantly.

There is one exception to this rule. When there are only two levels in the factor, the significant difference indicated by $F_{obt}$ must be between the only two means in the study, so it is unnecessary to perform *post hoc* comparisons.

In later sections we shall see how to perform *post hoc* comparisons. Our first procedure, though, is to compute $F_{obt}$. As we shall see, $F_{obt}$ is ultimately like a *z*-score that locates our results on a sampling distribution when $H_0$ is true. However, the computation of $F_{obt}$ is unlike anything we have encountered. Therefore, in the following sections we shall discuss the statistical basis for ANOVA and the logic of its computation. The remainder of this chapter will then deal with getting through these computations, so hold on . . . here we go.

## COMPONENTS OF THE *F* STATISTIC

Analysis of variance does just that: it analyzes variance. Recall that computing variance is simply a way to measure the *differences* between "scores." (As you read the following, keep saying to yourself: "Variance is differences.") ANOVA involves partitioning the variance. That is, we take the total variability of the scores in an experiment and break it up, or partition it, in terms of its source. As we shall see, there are two potential sources of variance. First, scores may differ from each other even when subjects are in the same condition. We call this variability the variance *within groups*. Second, scores may differ from each other because they are from different conditions. We call this variability the variance *between groups*. Thus, in a one-way ANOVA, we partition the variance as shown in this diagram:

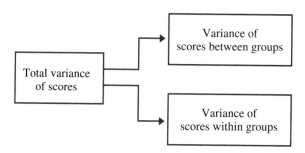

Using our sample data, we compute estimates of the value each of these variances would have in the population. But we do not *call* each an estimated variance. Instead, we call each a **mean square,** for the *mean squared* deviation, which is variance. The symbol for a mean square is *MS*. Because we estimate the variance within groups and the variance between groups, we compute two mean squares: the mean square within groups and the mean square between groups.

## The Mean Square Within Groups

The **mean square within groups** is an estimate of the variability of scores as measured by differences within the conditions of our experiment. The symbol for the mean square within groups is $MS_{wn}$. The word *within* says it all: think of $MS_{wn}$ as the "average variability" of the scores within, or inside, each condition around the mean of that condition. Table 13.2 illustrates how to conceptualize the computation of $MS_{wn}$. You can think of $MS_{wn}$ in this way: we find the squared differences between the scores in level 1 and $\overline{X}_1$, then between the scores in level 2 and $\overline{X}_2$, and then between the scores in level 3 and $X_3$. Then we sum these squared differences for each group, and we "average" the sums. The $MS_{wn}$ is the "average" variability of the scores in each condition around the mean of that condition.

Since we compare the scores in each condition with the mean for that condition, $MS_{wn}$ reflects the inherent variability between subjects' scores that

**TABLE 13.2**   How to Conceptualize the
Computation of $MS_{wn}$

*Factor A*

| *Level A₁* | *Level A₂* | *Level A₃* |
|:---:|:---:|:---:|
| X | X | X |
| X | X | X |
| X | X | X |
| X | X | X |
| X | X | X |
| $\overline{X}_1$ | $\overline{X}_2$ | $\overline{X}_3$ |

arises from individual differences (or from other random factors) when subjects are all treated the same. We saw in Chapter 5 that such variance is also called error. By estimating the inherent variability in the population, $MS_{wn}$ estimates the **error variance,** which is symbolized by $\sigma^2_{error}$. (For this reason, $MS_{wn}$ is also known as the *error term.*) In symbols,

| *Sample* | *Estimates* | *Population* |
|:---|:---:|:---|
| $MS_{wn}$ | $\rightarrow$ | $\sigma^2_{error}$ |

Because we assume homogeneity of variance, we assume that $MS_{wn}$ is an estimate of the error variance found in any of the populations represented by our samples. Thus, for example, an $MS_{wn}$ equal to 4 indicates that the variance of the scores in any of the populations represented by our samples is 4.

> **STAT ALERT**   The $MS_{wn}$ is an estimate of the error variance, the inherent variability within any population represented by our samples.

## The Mean Square Between Groups

The other variance we compute in ANOVA is the mean square between groups. Here, the word *between* says it all. The **mean square between groups** is an estimate of the variability in scores that occurs *between* the levels in a factor. The mean square between groups is symbolized by $MS_{bn}$. We can conceptualize the computation of $MS_{bn}$ as shown in Table 13.3. We summarize the scores in each level by computing the mean of that level, and then we determine how much it deviates from the overall mean of all scores in the experiment. In the same way that the deviations of raw scores around their mean describe how different the scores are from each other, the $MS_{bn}$ indicates how different the

**TABLE 13.3**  How to Conceptualize
the Computation of $MS_{bn}$

|  | *Factor A* |  |
| :---: | :---: | :---: |
| *Level $A_1$* | *Level $A_2$* | *Level $A_3$* |
| X | X | X |
| X | X | X |
| X | X | X |
| X | X | X |
| X | X | X |
| $\overline{X}_1$ | $\overline{X}_2$ | $\overline{X}_3$ |

Overall $\overline{X}$

sample means are from each other. *Thus, $MS_{bn}$ is our way of measuring how much the means in a factor differ from each other.*

The key to understanding ANOVA is to understand what $MS_{bn}$ represents. Sample means can differ from each other for two reasons, and therefore $MS_{bn}$ contains estimates of *two* forms of variance in the population. The first reason sample means differ from each other is the same reason raw scores differ from each other: error variance. If scores inherently vary, or differ, to a certain extent, then sample means composed of such scores should also differ to that extent. In other words, some of the variability reflected in $MS_{bn}$ is due to error variance. Therefore, $MS_{bn}$ contains another estimate of the error variance, $\sigma^2_{error}$.

The second reason sample means may differ from each other is *treatment effects:* "treating" subjects with the different conditions of our independent variable may raise or lower scores and therefore produce different means. In other words, our sample means may differ from each other because they represent different populations, having different values of $\mu$. Differences in scores resulting from our treatment are called treatment variance, which we symbolize by $\sigma^2_{treat}$. *Treatment variance* reflects differences between scores that occur because the scores are from different populations. The $MS_{bn}$ also contains an estimate of the treatment variance in the populations.

Thus, the two components of the $MS_{bn}$ are estimates of error variance (differences among the scores within any population) *and* treatment variance (differences among the scores because of differences between the populations). In symbols,

| *Sample* | *Estimates* | *Population* |
| :--- | :---: | :--- |
| $MS_{bn}$ | $\rightarrow$ | $\sigma^2_{error} + \sigma^2_{treat}$ |

***STAT ALERT*** The $MS_{bn}$ contains estimates of both error variance ($\sigma^2_{error}$), which measures differences in each population, and treatment variance ($\sigma^2_{treat}$), which measures differences between the populations.

Thus, for example, say that when $MS_{wn}$ equals 4, we compute that $MS_{bn}$ equals 10. We can think of $MS_{bn}$ as indicating that, in addition to an error variance of 4, there is an "average difference" of 6 between the populations.

It's nice to think of $MS_{bn}$ and $MS_{wn}$ as breaking down like this, but, of course, the problem of sampling error makes the issue much more complicated.

## Comparing the Mean Squares: The Logic of the *F*-Ratio

For our purposes, we are not interested in directly comparing the actual values of $MS_{bn}$ and $MS_{wn}$. Instead, in computing $F_{obt}$, we are interested in their ratio, called the *F*-ratio. The **F-ratio** is the mean square between groups divided by the mean square within groups.

---

*THE COMPUTATIONAL FORMULA FOR THE F-RATIO IS*

$$F_{obt} = \frac{MS_{bn}}{MS_{wn}}$$

---

***STAT ALERT*** In the *F*-ratio, $MS_{bn}$ is always on top!

We can conceptualize what the *F*-ratio represents as follows:

$$F_{obt} = \frac{MS_{bn}}{MS_{wn}} \quad \overset{Sample \quad Estimates}{\begin{matrix} \rightarrow \\ \rightarrow \end{matrix}} \quad \overset{Population}{\frac{\sigma^2_{error} + \sigma^2_{treat}}{\sigma^2_{error}}}$$

The $MS_{bn}$ represents the inherent differences between scores in any population ($\sigma^2_{error}$) *plus* whatever differences there are between the populations represented by our samples ($\sigma^2_{treat}$). This value is divided by the $MS_{wn}$, which is only an estimate of the error variance in the populations ($\sigma^2_{error}$).

Now we can understand what the *F*-ratio tells us about our null hypothesis, $H_0: \mu_1 = \mu_2 = \cdots = \mu_k$. If $H_0$ is true and all conditions represent the same population, then there are zero differences due to treatment. Instead, differences between the sample means totally reflect the inherent variability of scores that occurs naturally in the one population. Thus, when $H_0$ is true, $MS_{bn}$ contains solely $\sigma^2_{error}$, and the $\sigma^2_{treat}$ component of $MS_{bn}$ equals zero. In symbols, when $H_0$ is true, we have

$$F_{\text{obt}} = \frac{\overset{\textit{Sample}}{MS_{\text{bn}}}}{MS_{\text{wn}}} \quad \begin{array}{c} \textit{Estimates} \\ \rightarrow \\ \rightarrow \end{array} \quad \frac{\overset{\textit{Population}}{\sigma^2_{\text{error}} + 0}}{\sigma^2_{\text{error}}}$$

Both mean squares are merely estimates of the one value of $\sigma^2_{\text{error}}$. If our data are perfectly representative of the situation when $H_0$ is true, then the mean square between groups should *equal* the mean square within groups. When two numbers are equal, their ratio equals 1. *Therefore, when $H_0$ is true and all conditions perfectly represent one population, the F-ratio should equal 1.*

On the other hand, $H_a$ says that not all $\mu$'s are equal. If $H_a$ is true, then at least two conditions represent different populations and there are differences between at least two of our means that are due to treatment. Therefore, when $H_a$ is true, the $\sigma^2_{\text{treat}}$ component of $MS_{\text{bn}}$ does not equal zero, so we have

$$F_{\text{obt}} = \frac{\overset{\textit{Sample}}{MS_{\text{bn}}}}{MS_{\text{wn}}} \quad \begin{array}{c} \textit{Estimates} \\ \rightarrow \\ \rightarrow \end{array} \quad \frac{\overset{\textit{Population}}{\sigma^2_{\text{error}} + \text{some amount of } \sigma^2_{\text{treat}}}}{\sigma^2_{\text{error}}}$$

Here $MS_{\text{bn}}$ contains error variance *plus* some amount of treatment variance, so $MS_{\text{bn}}$ will be *larger* than $MS_{\text{wn}}$, which contains only error variance. Placing a larger number in the numerator of the *F*-ratio produces an $F_{\text{obt}}$ greater than 1. *Thus, when $H_a$ is true, $MS_{\text{bn}}$ is larger than $MS_{\text{an}}$ and $F_{\text{obt}}$ is greater than 1.* The larger the differences in the populations represented by our sample means, the larger the $\sigma^2_{\text{treat}}$ component, and thus the larger $MS_{\text{bn}}$ will be. Regardless of the effect of the independent variable, however, we assume homogeneous variance, so the size of $MS_{\text{wn}}$ remains constant. Therefore, the larger the differences between means, the larger $F_{\text{obt}}$ will be.

Recognize that regardless of whether we have a positive, negative, or curvilinear relationship, $MS_{\text{bn}}$ reflects only differences between the means. Therefore, any relationship produces an $MS_{\text{bn}}$ larger than $MS_{\text{wn}}$, and $F_{\text{obt}}$ is greater than 1.0. (This is why we have only two-tailed hypotheses in ANOVA.) An $F_{\text{obt}}$ between 0 and 1 is possible, but it occurs when the denominator of the *F*-ratio, $MS_{\text{wn}}$, is larger than the numerator, $MS_{\text{bn}}$. Here we assume that $MS_{\text{bn}}$ and $MS_{\text{wn}}$ are merely poor estimates of $\sigma^2_{\text{error}}$ and therefore are not equal. $F_{\text{obt}}$ cannot be less than zero, because the mean squares are variances—squared numbers—and therefore cannot be negative numbers.

Thus, on the one hand, $F_{\text{obt}}$ should equal 1.0 if the means represent the same $\mu$. On the other hand, $F_{\text{obt}}$ should be greater than 1.0 if the means represent two or more different $\mu$'s. But hold on! There is one other reason $F_{\text{obt}}$ might be greater than 1.0, and that is (here we go again) sampling error! When $H_0$ is true, $F_{\text{obt}}$ "should" equal 1.0 *if* the mean squares are perfectly representative. *But,* through sampling error, we may obtain different sample means that poorly represent the one population mean. Then the variability between the sample means will be greater than the inherent variability of the raw scores. This in turn will produce an $MS_{bn}$ that is larger than $MS_{wn}$, so $F_{obt}$ will be larger than 1.0, simply because of sampling error.

This all boils down to the same old problem of significance testing. An $F_{obt}$ greater than 1.0 may accurately reflect the situation where two or more conditions of the independent variable represent different populations of raw scores (and there is a treatment effect). Or, because of sampling error, an $F_{obt}$ greater than 1.0 may inaccurately reflect the situation where all conditions represent the same population (and there only *appears* to be a treatment effect).

Therefore, whenever we obtain an $F_{obt}$ greater than 1.0, we must test $H_0$: we determine the probability of obtaining such an $F_{obt}$ if $H_0$ is true and all sample means represent one $\mu$. To do this, we examine the $F$-distribution.

## The *F*-Distribution

The **F-distribution** is the $H_0$ sampling distribution showing the various values of $F$ that occur when $H_0$ is true and all conditions represent one population $\mu$. We could create a sampling distribution in the following way: Using the same number of levels ($k$) as in our study and using the same $n$'s as in our study, we randomly sample one raw score population repeatedly. Each time, we compute $MS_{bn}$ and $MS_{wn}$, form the $F$-ratio, and compute $F_{obt}$. After doing this an infinite number of times, we plot the various values of $F_{obt}$. The resulting distribution can be envisioned as shown in Figure 13.1. This is more or less the same old $H_0$ sampling distribution, except that now the $X$ axis shows the values of $F$ that occur when $H_0$ is true and all sample means *do* represent the

**FIGURE 13.1** Sampling Distribution of F When $H_0$ Is True

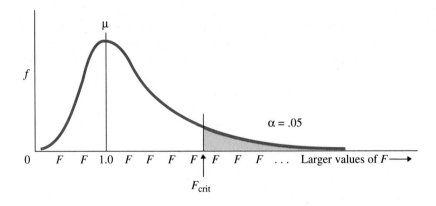

same $\mu$. The *F*-distribution is not a normal distribution, because there is no limit to how large $F_{obt}$ can be, but it cannot be less than zero. The mean of the distribution is 1.0 because, most often, $MS_{bn}$ will equal $MS_{wn}$ and *F* will equal 1.0. We are concerned with the tail, which shows that sometimes the means are unrepresentative, producing an $MS_{bn}$ that is larger than $MS_{wn}$, which results in an *F* greater than 1.0. However, as shown, the larger the *F*, the farther it is from the mean of the *F*-distribution and the less likely it is to occur when $H_0$ is true.

Since the $F_{obt}$ we compute in a study can reflect a relationship in the population only when it is greater than 1.0, we place the entire region of rejection in the upper tail of the *F*-distribution. (With ANOVA, we always have two-tailed hypotheses, yet we test them using a one-tailed test!) If our $F_{obt}$ is larger than $F_{crit}$, then $F_{obt}$—and the differences between the sample means that produced it—is too unlikely for us to accept as having occurred by chance when $H_0$ is true and all conditions of the factor represent the same population. Therefore, we reject $H_0$ and have a significant $F_{obt}$. This tells us that at least two of our sample means differ significantly from each other, so we are confident that they represent at least two different population $\mu$'s.

Like the *t*-distribution, the *F*-distribution consists of a family of curves. Each *F*-distribution has a slightly different shape depending on the degrees of freedom in the data, and thus there is a different value of $F_{crit}$ for each *df*. However, there are *two* values of *df* that determine the shape of each *F*-distribution: the *df* for the mean square between groups and the *df* for the mean square within groups. The symbol for the *df* between groups is $df_{bn}$, and the symbol for the *df* within groups is $df_{wn}$. We use both $df_{bn}$ and $df_{wn}$ when finding $F_{crit}$.

To obtain $F_{crit}$, turn to Table 5 in Appendix D, entitled "Critical Values of *F*." Across the top of these *F*-tables, the columns are labeled "*df* between groups," and along the left-hand side, the rows are labeled "*df* within groups." We locate the appropriate column and row using the *df*'s from our study. The critical values of *F* in light type are for $\alpha = .05$, and the values in dark type are for $\alpha = .01$. For example, say we eventually determine that $df_{bn} = 2$ and $df_{wn} = 12$. Then for $\alpha = .05$, the $F_{crit}$ is 3.88.

> **STAT ALERT**   Be careful to keep your "withins" and "betweens" straight: $df_{bn} = 2$ and $df_{wn} = 12$ is very different from $df_{bn} = 12$ and $df_{wn} = 2$.

Do not be overwhelmed by all the details of ANOVA. Buried in here is the simple idea that the larger the differences between our sample means for the conditions of the independent variable, the larger the $MS_{bn}$ and thus the larger the $F_{obt}$. If the $F_{obt}$ is larger than $F_{crit}$, then the $F_{obt}$ (and the corresponding differences between our means) is too unlikely to occur if our means represent the same population $\mu$. Therefore, we can reject $H_0$ and confidently conclude that at least two of our means represent two different $\mu$'s.

## COMPUTING THE *F*-RATIO

When we computed the estimated variance in Chapter 5, we called the quantity $\Sigma(X - \overline{X})^2$ the sum of the squared deviations. In ANOVA, we shorten this to the **sum of squares.** The symbol for the sum of squares is *SS*. Thus, in the numerator of the following formula for variance, we replace the sum of the squared deviations with *SS:*

$$s_{\overline{X}}^2 = \frac{\Sigma(X - \overline{X})^2}{N - 1} = \frac{SS}{df} = MS$$

In the denominator, $N - 1$ is the degrees of freedom, so we replace $N - 1$ with *df*. Since variance is called a mean square in ANOVA, the fraction formed by the sum of squares (*SS*) divided by the degrees of freedom (*df*) is the general formula for a mean square.

Adding our subscripts, we compute the mean square between groups ($MS_{bn}$) by computing the sum of squares between groups ($SS_{bn}$) and then dividing by the degrees of freedom between groups ($df_{bn}$). Likewise, we compute the mean square within groups ($MS_{wn}$) by computing the sum of squares within groups ($SS_{wn}$) and then dividing by the degrees of freedom within groups ($df_{wn}$). Once we have $MS_{bn}$ and $MS_{wn}$, we compute $F_{obt}$.

If all this strikes you as the most confusing thing ever devised by humans, you will find creating an ANOVA summary table very useful. The general format of the summary table for a one-way ANOVA is as follows:

Summary Table of One-Way ANOVA

| *Source* | *Sum of squares* | *df* | *Mean square* | *F* |
|----------|------------------|------|---------------|-----|
| Between  | $SS_{bn}$        | $df_{bn}$ | $MS_{bn}$ | $F_{obt}$ |
| Within   | $SS_{wn}$        | $df_{wn}$ | $MS_{wn}$ | |
| Total    | $SS_{tot}$       | $df_{tot}$ | | |

The source column indicates how we computed each component. Eventually we will fill in the values in the other columns. Notice that as we do, the computations become built in. Dividing $SS_{bn}$ by $df_{bn}$ produces the $MS_{bn}$. Dividing $SS_{wn}$ by $df_{wn}$ produces the $MS_{wn}$. Finally, the fraction formed by putting $MS_{bn}$ "over" $MS_{wn}$ produces $F_{obt}$. [Along the way, we will also compute the total sum of squares ($SS_{tot}$) and the total *df* ($df_{tot}$).] The $F_{obt}$ is always placed in the row labeled "Between." (In place of the word "Between," we can use the name of the factor or independent variable. Also, in place of the word "Within," you will sometimes see "Error.")

## Computational Formulas for the One-Way Between-Subjects ANOVA

To provide some example data to work with, say that we actually performed our study of the effects of perceived difficulty: we told three samples of five subjects each that some math problems were easy, of medium difficulty, or difficult, and we measured the number of problems they correctly solved. The data are presented in Table 13.4.

As shown in the table, the first step in performing ANOVA is to compute $\Sigma X$, $\Sigma X^2$, and $\overline{X}$ for each level. By adding the $\Sigma X$ from each level, we compute the total $\Sigma X$, and by adding the $\Sigma X^2$ from each level, we compute the total $\Sigma X^2$. Then, as shown in the following sections, we compute the sum of squares, the degrees of freedom, the mean squares, and then $F_{\text{obt}}$. So that you do not get lost, as you complete each step, fill in the results in the ANOVA summary table created above. (There *will* be a test later.)

**Computing the sums of squares**  The first task is to compute the sum of squares. We do this in three steps.

Step 1 is to compute the total sum of squares $(SS_{\text{tot}})$.

---

*THE COMPUTATIONAL FORMULA FOR $SS_{\text{tot}}$ IS*

$$SS_{\text{tot}} = \Sigma X^2_{\text{tot}} - \left( \frac{(\Sigma X_{\text{tot}})^2}{N} \right)$$

---

**TABLE 13.4**  Data from Perceived Difficulty Experiment

*Factor A: perceived difficulty*

| Level $A_1$: easy | Level $A_2$: medium | Level $A_3$: difficult | |
|:---:|:---:|:---:|:---:|
| 9 | 4 | 1 | |
| 12 | 6 | 3 | |
| 4 | 8 | 4 | |
| 8 | 2 | 5 | |
| 7 | 10 | 2 | *Totals* |
| $\Sigma X = 40$ | $\Sigma X = 30$ | $\Sigma X = 15$ | $\Sigma X = 85$ |
| $\Sigma X^2 = 354$ | $\Sigma X^2 = 220$ | $\Sigma X^2 = 55$ | $\Sigma X^2 = 629$ |
| $n_1 = 5$ | $n_2 = 5$ | $n_3 = 5$ | $N = 15$ |
| $\overline{X}_1 = 8$ | $\overline{X}_2 = 6$ | $\overline{X}_3 = 3$ | $k = 3$ |

Here we treat the entire experiment as if it were one big sample. Thus, $\Sigma X_{tot}$ is the sum of all $X$s, and $\Sigma X_{tot}^2$ is the sum of all squared $X$s. $N$ is the total $N$ in the study.

Using the data from Table 13.4, we have $\Sigma X_{tot}^2 = 629$, $\Sigma X_{tot} = 85$, and $N = 15$, so

$$SS_{tot} = 629 - \frac{(85)^2}{15}$$

$$= 629 - \frac{7225}{15}$$

$$= 629 - 481.67$$

Thus, $SS_{tot} = 147.33$.

Step 2 is to compute the sum of squares between groups ($SS_{bn}$).

---

**THE COMPUTATIONAL FORMULA FOR $SS_{bn}$ IS**

$$SS_{bn} = \Sigma \left( \frac{(\text{sum of scores in the column})^2}{n \text{ of scores in the column}} \right) - \left( \frac{(\Sigma X_{tot})^2}{N} \right)$$

---

When we diagram the study, each column represents a level of the factor. Thus, the formula says to find the $\Sigma X$ for each level, square $\Sigma X$, and then divide by the $n$ for the level. After doing this for all levels, we add the results together and subtract the quantity $(\Sigma X_{tot})^2/N$. From Table 13.4, we have

$$SS_{bn} = \left( \frac{(40)^2}{5} + \frac{(30)^2}{5} + \frac{(15)^2}{5} \right) - \left( \frac{(85)^2}{15} \right)$$

so

$$SS_{bn} = (320 + 180 + 45) - 481.67$$

and

$$SS_{bn} = 545 - 481.67$$

Thus, we have $SS_{bn} = 63.33$.

Finally, compute the sum of squares within groups ($SS_{wn}$). It was relatively painless to directly compute $SS_{tot}$ and $SS_{bn}$ above, but it is not so painless to directly compute $SS_{wn}$. Instead, we use a shortcut. Mathematically, $SS_{tot}$ equals $SS_{bn}$ plus $SS_{wn}$. Therefore, the total minus the between leaves the within.

> **THE COMPUTATIONAL FORMULA FOR $SS_{wn}$ IS**
>
> $$SS_{wn} = SS_{tot} - SS_{bn}$$

In our example, $SS_{tot}$ is 147.33 and $SS_{bn}$ is 63.33, so

$$SS_{wn} = 147.33 - 63.33 = 84.00$$

and $SS_{wn} = 84.00$. (Now that's painless.)

Filling in the first column of our ANOVA summary table, we have

Summary Table of One-Way ANOVA

| *Source* | *Sum of squares* | *df* | *Mean square* | *F* |
|----------|------------------|------|---------------|-----|
| Between | 63.33 | $df_{bn}$ | $MS_{bn}$ | $F_{obt}$ |
| Within | 84.00 | $df_{wn}$ | $MS_{wn}$ | |
| Total | 147.33 | $df_{tot}$ | | |

As a double check, make sure that the total equals the sum of the between plus the within. Here, $63.33 + 84.00 = 147.33$.

Now we compute the degrees of freedom.

**Computing the degrees of freedom**   We compute $df_{bn}$, $df_{wn}$, and $df_{tot}$.

1. *The degrees of freedom between groups equals $k - 1$,* where *k* is the number of levels in the factor. In our example, there are three levels in the factor of perceived difficulty (easy, medium, and difficult), so $k = 3$. Thus, $df_{bn} = 2$.

2. *The degrees of freedom within groups equals $N - k$,* where *N* is the total *N* of the study and *k* is the number of levels in the factor. In our example, the total *N* is 15 scores and *k* equals 3, so $df_{wn}$ equals $15 - 3$, or 12.

3. *The degrees of freedom total equals $N - 1$,* where *N* is the total *N* in the experiment. In our example, we have a total of 15 scores, so $df_{tot} = 15 - 1 = 14$.

The $df_{tot}$ is useful because it equals the sum of the $df_{bn}$ plus the $df_{wn}$. Thus, to check our work in the example, we find that $df_{bn} + df_{wn} = 2 + 12$, which equals 14, our $df_{tot}$.

After *SS* and *df* are recorded, our summary table is as shown on the next page.

Summary Table of One-Way ANOVA

| Source | Sum of squares | df | Mean square | F |
|--------|---------------|-----|-------------|-----|
| Between | 63.33 | 2 | $MS_{bn}$ | $F_{obt}$ |
| Within | 84.00 | 12 | $MS_{wn}$ | |
| Total | 147.33 | 14 | | |

Now we find each mean square.

**Computing the mean squares**   To compute the mean squares, we work directly from our summary table. Any mean square equals the appropriate sum of squares divided by the corresponding *df*.

*THE COMPUTATIONAL FORMULA FOR MS$_{bn}$ IS*

$$MS_{bn} = \frac{SS_{bn}}{df_{bn}}$$

From the above summary table for our example, we see that

$$MS_{bn} = \frac{63.33}{2} = 31.67$$

so $MS_{bn}$ is 31.67.

*THE COMPUTATIONAL FORMULA FOR MS$_{wn}$ IS*

$$MS_{wn} = \frac{SS_{wn}}{df_{wn}}$$

For our example,

$$MS_{wn} = \frac{84}{12} = 7.00$$

so $MS_{wn}$ is 7.00.

Notice that we do *not* compute the mean square for $SS_{tot}$.
Placing these values in the summary table, we have

Summary Table of One-Way ANOVA

| Source | Sum of squares | df | Mean square | F |
|--------|----------------|-----|-------------|---|
| Between | 63.33 | 2 | 31.67 | $F_{obt}$ |
| Within | 84.00 | 12 | 7.00 | |
| Total | 147.33 | 14 | | |

**Computing the $F_{obt}$** Last but not least, we compute $F_{obt}$.

THE COMPUTATIONAL FORMULA FOR F IS

$$F_{obt} = \frac{MS_{bn}}{MS_{wn}}$$

In our example, $MS_{bn}$ is 31.67 and $MS_{wn}$ is 7.0, so

$$F_{obt} = \frac{MS_{bn}}{MS_{wn}} = \frac{31.67}{7.00} = 4.52$$

Thus $F_{obt}$ is 4.52.

Now we have the completed ANOVA summary table:

Summary Table of One-Way ANOVA

| Source | Sum of squares | df | Mean square | F |
|--------|----------------|-----|-------------|---|
| Between | 63.33 | 2 | 31.67 | 4.52 |
| Within | 84.00 | 12 | 7.00 | |
| Total | 147.33 | 14 | | |

## Interpreting $F_{obt}$ in a One-Way ANOVA

To interpret $F_{obt}$, we must have $F_{crit}$, so we turn to the F-tables in Table 5. In our example, $df_{bn}$ is 2 and $df_{wn}$ is 12. With $\alpha = .05$, $F_{crit}$ is 3.88.

Thus, our $F_{obt}$ is 4.52 and our $F_{crit}$ is 3.88. Lo and behold, as shown in Figure 13.2, we have a significant $F_{obt}$. The null hypothesis ($H_0$: $\mu_1 = \mu_2 = \mu_3$) says that any differences between our sample means are due to sampling error and that all means poorly represent one population mean. However, our $F_{obt}$ is out there in the region of rejection, and such an $F_{obt}$ tells us that such differences

**FIGURE 13.2**   Sampling Distribution of $F$ When $H_0$ Is True for $df_{bn} = 2$ and $df_{wn} = 12$

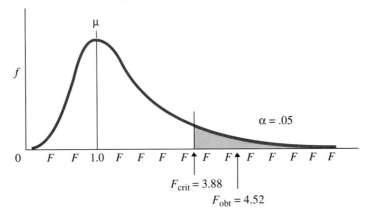

between $\overline{X}$s hardly ever happen when $H_0$ is true. Because $F_{obt}$ is larger than $F_{crit}$, we reject $H_0$: we conclude that the differences between our sample means are too unlikely to accept as having occurred by chance when all means represent one population mean. That is, we conclude that our $F_{obt}$ is significant and that the factor of perceived difficulty does produce a significant difference in mean performance scores. We report our results as

$$F_{obt}(2, 12) = 4.52, \quad p < .05$$

Notice that in the parentheses we report $df_{bn}$ and then $df_{wn}$. (Get in the habit of saying the $df_{bn}$ first and the $df_{wn}$ second.) Since $\alpha = .05$, the probability that we have incorrectly rejected $H_0$ (made a Type I error) is $p < .05$.

Of course, had $F_{obt}$ been less than $F_{crit}$, then the corresponding differences between our means would *not* be too unlikely to accept as occurring by chance when $H_0$ is true, so we would not reject $H_0$.

Since we reject $H_0$ and accept $H_a$, we return to the means from the levels of our factor:

*Perceived difficulty*

| Easy | Medium | Difficult |
|------|--------|-----------|
| $\overline{X}_1 = 8$ | $\overline{X}_2 = 6$ | $\overline{X}_3 = 3$ |

We are confident that these means represent a relationship in the population: changing the level of perceived difficulty would produce different populations of performance scores, having different $\mu$'s. However, we do not know whether *every* sample mean represents a different $\mu$. Remember: a significant $F_{obt}$ merely indicates that there is at least one significant difference between two of these means. Now we must determine which specific means differ significantly, and to do that we perform *post hoc* comparisons.

## PERFORMING POST HOC COMPARISONS

Statisticians have developed a variety of *post hoc* procedures which differ in how likely they are to produce Type I or Type II errors. We shall discuss two procedures that are generally considered to have acceptably low error rates. Depending on whether or not our $n$'s are equal, we compute either Fisher's protected $t$-test or Tukey's *HSD* test.

### Fisher's Protected *t*-Test

If the $n$'s in all levels are *not* equal, then we compare all pairs of means using Fisher's protected $t$-test.

*THE COMPUTATIONAL FORMULA FOR THE PROTECTED t-TEST IS*

$$t_{\text{obt}} = \frac{\overline{X}_1 - \overline{X}_2}{\sqrt{MS_{\text{wn}}\left(\dfrac{1}{n_1} + \dfrac{1}{n_2}\right)}}$$

This is basically the formula for the independent samples $t$-test, except that we have replaced the pooled variance ($s_{\text{pool}}^2$) with the $MS_{\text{wn}}$ computed in our ANOVA. We are testing $H_0$: $\mu_1 - \mu_2 = 0$, where $\overline{X}_1$ and $\overline{X}_2$ are the means for any two levels of the factor and $n_1$ and $n_2$ are the corresponding $n$'s in those levels. The $t_{\text{crit}}$ is the two-tailed value found in Table 2 for $df = df_{\text{wn}} = N - k$.

Even when the $n$'s in all the conditions are equal, we can perform the protected $t$-test. Thus, for example, we can compare the mean from our easy level ($\overline{X} = 8.0$) to the mean from our difficult level ($\overline{X} = 3.0$). Each $n$ is 5, and from our ANOVA summary table we know that $MS_{\text{wn}}$ is 7.0. Filling in the formula, we have

$$t_{\text{obt}} = \frac{8.0 - 3.0}{\sqrt{7.0\left(\dfrac{1}{5} + \dfrac{1}{5}\right)}}$$

Reducing and then adding the fractions, we have

$$t_{obt} = \frac{+5.0}{\sqrt{7.0(.4)}}$$

which becomes

$$t_{obt} = \frac{+5.0}{\sqrt{2.8}} = \frac{+5.0}{1.67} = +2.99$$

We then compare our $t_{obt}$ to the two-tailed value of $t_{crit}$ found in the $t$-tables (Table 2). To find $t_{crit}$, we use the $df_{wn}$ as the degrees of freedom. For our example, with $\alpha = .05$ and $df_{wn} = 12$, $t_{crit}$ is $\pm 2.179$. Since our $t_{obt}$ of $+2.99$ is beyond the $t_{crit}$ of $\pm 2.179$, we conclude that the means from the easy and difficult levels differ significantly and that they do not represent the same $\mu$.

To complete our *post hoc* comparisons, we perform the protected $t$-test on all possible pairs of means in the factor. Thus, for example, after comparing the means from easy and difficult, we would perform the protected $t$-test comparing the means from easy and medium, and then the means from medium and difficult. When we are finished, because the $F_{obt}$ is significant, we have *protected* the experiment-wise error rate, so that the probability of a Type I error for all of these comparisons together is $p < .05$.

If a factor contains many levels, then the protected $t$-test becomes very tedious. If you think there has *got* to be a better way, you're right.

## Tukey's *HSD* Multiple Comparisons Test

The Tukey *HSD* multiple comparisons procedure is appropriate *only* if the $n$'s in all levels of the factor are equal. The *HSD* is a convoluted variation of the $t$-test in which we compute the minimum difference between two means that is required for the means to differ significantly (*HSD* stands for the Honestly Significant Difference). There are four steps in performing the *HSD* test.

Step 1 is to find $q_k$. The value of $q_k$ is a number found in Table 6 in Appendix D, entitled "Values of the Studentized Range Statistic, $q_k$." In the table, locate the column labeled with the $k$ corresponding to the number of means in the factor. Next, find the row labeled with the $df_{wn}$ used to compute our previous significant $F_{obt}$. Then find the value of $q_k$ for the appropriate $\alpha$. For our study above, $k = 3$, $df_{wn} = 12$, and $\alpha = .05$, so $q_k = 3.77$. By using the appropriate $q_k$ in our computations, we protect our experiment-wise error rate for the number of means we are comparing.

Step 2 is to compute the *HSD*.

*THE COMPUTATIONAL FORMULA FOR THE HSD IS*

$$HSD = (q_k)\left(\sqrt{\frac{MS_{wn}}{n}}\right)$$

$MS_{wn}$ is the denominator from our significant $F$-ratio, and $n$ is the number of scores in each level of the factor. To find HSD, divide $MS_{wn}$ by $n$, find the square root, and then multiply the answer times $q_k$.

In our example, $MS_{wn}$ was 7.0 and $n$ was 5, so

$$HSD = (q_k)\left(\sqrt{\frac{MS_{wn}}{n}}\right) = (3.77)\left(\sqrt{\frac{7.0}{5}}\right) = 4.46$$

Thus, our *HSD* is 4.46.

Step 3 is to determine the differences between all means. Simply subtract each mean from every other mean. Ignore whether differences are positive or negative (this is a two-tailed test of the $H_0$ that $\mu_1 - \mu_2 = 0$). For our perceived difficulty study, we can diagram the differences as shown below:

*Perceived difficulty*

| *Easy* | *Medium* | *Difficult* |
|--------|----------|-------------|
| $\overline{X}_1 = 8$ | $\overline{X}_2 = 6$ | $\overline{X}_3 = 3$ |

2.0 ——— 3.0
——— 5.0 ———
$HSD = 4.46$

On the line connecting any two samples is the absolute difference between their means.

Step 4 is to compare the differences between the means to the *HSD*. To complete the *post hoc* comparison, we simply compare each difference between two means to the value of *HSD*. If the absolute difference between the two means is *greater than* the *HSD*, then these means differ significantly. (It is as if we performed the protected *t*-test on these two means and $t_{obt}$ was significant.) If the absolute difference between the two means is less than or equal to the *HSD*, then it is *not* a significant difference (and would not produce a significant $t_{obt}$).

Above, our *HSD* was 4.46. Of our three means, the means from the easy level ($\overline{X}_1 = 8$) and the difficult level ($\overline{X}_3 = 3$) differ by more than 4.46, so they differ significantly. The mean from the medium level ($\overline{X}_2 = 6$) differs from the other means by less than 4.46, so it does not differ significantly from them.

Thus, our final conclusion about our perceived difficulty study is that we demonstrated a relationship between subjects' scores and perceived difficulty, but only for the easy and difficult conditions. If these two conditions were given to the population, we would expect to find two different populations of scores, having two different $\mu$'s. We cannot say anything about whether the medium level would produce a different population and $\mu$, because we failed to find that it produced a significant difference in our data.

## SUMMARY OF STEPS IN PERFORMING A ONE-WAY ANOVA

It has been a long haul, but here is everything we do when performing a one-way ANOVA:

1. Our null hypothesis is $H_0$: $\mu_1 = \mu_2 = \ldots = \mu_k$, and our alternative hypothesis is $H_a$: not all $\mu$'s are equal. We choose our alpha level, check the assumptions, and then collect the data.

2. We first compute the sum of squares between groups ($SS_{bn}$) and the sum of squares within groups ($SS_{wn}$). Then we compute the degrees of freedom between groups ($df_{bn}$) and the degrees of freedom within groups ($df_{wn}$). Dividing the $SS_{bn}$ by the $df_{bn}$ gives the mean square between groups ($MS_{bn}$), and dividing the $SS_{wn}$ by the $df_{wn}$ gives the mean square within groups ($MS_{wn}$). Finally, dividing the $MS_{bn}$ by the $MS_{wn}$ gives the $F_{obt}$.

3. We find $F_{crit}$ in Table 5, using the $df_{bn}$ and the $df_{wn}$. If the null hypothesis is true, $F_{obt}$ "should" equal 1. The larger the value of $F_{obt}$, the less likely it is that $H_0$ is true. If $F_{obt}$ is larger than $F_{crit}$, we have a significant $F_{obt}$. We conclude that the means in at least two conditions differ significantly, representing at least two different population $\mu$'s.

4. If $F_{obt}$ is significant and there are more than two levels of the factor, we determine which specific levels differ significantly by performing *post hoc* comparisons. We perform the protected *t*-test if the *n*'s in all levels of the factor are not equal, or the *HSD* procedure if all *n*'s are equal.

If you followed all of that, then congratulations, you are getting *good* at this stuff. Of course, all of this merely determines whether we have a relationship. Now we must describe that relationship.

## DESCRIBING THE RELATIONSHIP IN A ONE-WAY ANOVA

When $F_{obt}$ is significant, we conclude that our experiment represents a relationship in the population between at least some of the levels of the factor and the dependent variable. As we saw in previous chapters, we can describe this relationship further by computing a confidence interval for each $\mu$, by graphing the relationship, and by computing the proportion of variance accounted for.

### The Confidence Interval for Each Population $\mu$

In our example, the mean from the easy condition ($\overline{X} = 8.0$) differs significantly from the mean from the difficult condition ($\overline{X} = 3.0$). Therefore, we expect that the population means represented by these conditions would be "around" 8 and 3, respectively. As usual, to more clearly define "around," we compute a confidence interval for the $\mu$ represented by the sample mean from each condition. This confidence interval for a single $\mu$ is the same as the one we discussed in Chapter 11, except that here it is computed directly from the components of ANOVA.

*THE COMPUTATIONAL FORMULA FOR COMPUTING THE CONFIDENCE INTERVAL FOR A SINGLE $\mu$, USING THE RESULTS OF A BETWEEN-SUBJECTS ANOVA, IS*

$$\left(\sqrt{\frac{MS_{wn}}{n}}\right)(-t_{crit}) + \overline{X} \leq \mu \leq \left(\sqrt{\frac{MS_{wn}}{n}}\right)(+t_{crit}) + \overline{X}$$

The value of $t_{crit}$ is the two-tailed value found in the $t$-tables, using the appropriate $\alpha$ and using our $df_{wn}$ as the $df$. We find $MS_{wn}$ in our ANOVA, and $\overline{X}$ and $n$ are from the level we are describing.

For example, in our easy condition, $\overline{X} = 8.0$, we have $MS_{wn} = 7.0$, $df_{wn} = 12$, and $n = 5$. The two-tailed $t_{crit}$ (at $df = 12$ and $\alpha = .05$) is $\pm 2.179$. Placing these values in the above formula, we have

$$\left(\sqrt{\frac{7.0}{5}}\right)(-2.179) + 8.0 \leq \mu \leq \left(\sqrt{\frac{7.0}{5}}\right)(+2.179) + 8.0$$

Dividing 7.0 by 5 gives 1.4, and the square root of 1.4 is 1.183. Now we have

$$(1.183)(-2.179) + 8.0 \leq \mu \leq (1.183)(+2.179) + 8.0$$

Multiplying 1.183 times $\pm 2.179$ gives $\pm 2.578$, so we have

$$(-2.578) + 8.0 \leq \mu \leq (+2.578) + 8.0$$

Finally, after adding, we have

$$5.42 \leq \mu \leq 10.58$$

Since $\alpha = .05$, this is the 95% confidence interval: if we were to test the entire population of subjects under our easy condition, we are 95% confident that the population mean would be between 5.42 and 10.58.

We follow the same procedure to describe the $\mu$ from any other significant level of the factor.

## Graphing the Results in ANOVA

As usual, we graph our results with the dependent variable on the $Y$ axis and the independent variable (levels of the factor) on the $X$ axis. Then we plot the mean for each condition. Figure 13.3 shows the line graph for our perceived difficulty study. Note that even though the medium level of difficulty did not produce significant differences, we still include it in the graph.

## Eta Squared: The Proportion of Variance Accounted For in the Sample Data

We can describe the strength of the relationship in our data by computing a new correlation coefficient called eta (pronounced "ay-tah"). **Eta** is analogous to $r_{pb}$ except that eta can be used to describe any linear or nonlinear relationship containing two or more levels of a factor.

**FIGURE 13.3**   Mean Number of Problems Correctly Solved as a Function of Perceived Difficulty

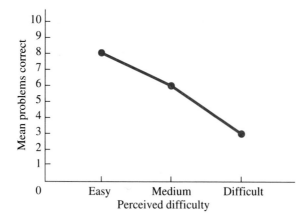

Previously we saw that we ultimately square the correlation coefficient to indicate the proportion of variance accounted for. Thus, **eta squared** indicates the proportion of variance in the dependent variable that is accounted for, or explained by, changing the levels of a factor. This is our way of measuring effect size in ANOVA. The symbol for eta squared is $\eta^2$. The larger the value of $\eta^2$, the more consistent the effect of the factor and thus the more important the factor is in explaining the differences in scores.

We compute $\eta^2$ directly from the components of our ANOVA.

---

*THE COMPUTATIONAL FORMULA FOR $\eta^2$ IS*

$$\eta^2 = \frac{SS_{bn}}{SS_{tot}}$$

---

The $SS_{bn}$ is a way of measuring the differences between the means from our various levels. The $SS_{tot}$ is a way of measuring the total differences between all scores in the experiment. Thus, $\eta^2$ reflects the proportion of the total differences in the scores that is associated with differences between the sample means. By computing $\eta^2$, we determine how consistently the differences in scores can be predicted using the means of the levels of our factor.

For example, from the ANOVA summary table for our study of perceived difficulty, we see that $SS_{bn}$ was 63.33 and $SS_{tot}$ was 147.33. So

$$\eta^2 = \frac{SS_{bn}}{SS_{tot}} = \frac{63.33}{147.33} = .43$$

This tells us that we are .43, or 43%, more accurate at predicting subjects' scores when we predict the mean score for the particular difficulty level subjects were tested under, rather than using the overall mean. Thus, 43% of all the variance in our scores is accounted for, or explained, as being the result of changing the levels of perceived difficulty.

Eta squared can be used with either equal or unequal $n$'s. However, eta squared is a *descriptive* statistic that only describes the effect size in our sample data. Usually, this is adequate. However, we can estimate the effect size in the *population* by computing omega squared.

## Omega Squared: The Proportion of Variance Accounted For in the Population

**Omega squared** is an estimate of the proportion of variance in the population that would be accounted for by our relationship. The symbol for omega squared is $\omega^2$. There are different formulas for omega squared, depending on the particular design of the experiment, but when we have a between-subjects factor with equal $n$'s in all levels of the factor,

THE COMPUTATIONAL FORMULA FOR $\omega^2$ IS

$$\omega^2 = \frac{SS_{bn} - (df_{bn})(MS_{wn})}{SS_{tot} + MS_{wn}}$$

Filling in this formula from the summary table of the one-way ANOVA for our perceived difficulty study, we have

$$\omega^2 = \frac{63.33 - (2)(7.0)}{147.33 + 7.0} = \frac{49.33}{154.33} = .32$$

Thus, if we conducted this study in the population, we would expect perceived difficulty to account for .32, or 32%, of the variance in performance scores.

## OTHER CONSIDERATIONS IN USING ANOVA

Before we leave the one-way ANOVA, there are three topics to consider: repeated measures, power, and homogeneity of variance.

### The Repeated Measures ANOVA

We sometimes conduct research that requires a one-way ANOVA for repeated measures (where we measure the same subjects under all the levels of a factor). A repeated measures $F_{obt}$ is conceptually identical to the $F_{obt}$ we have discussed in this chapter, except that with repeated measures we compute the denominator of the $F$-ratio differently. The computational formulas for a one-way, repeated measures ANOVA are presented in Appendix C. Because these computations are similar to those you will see in the next chapter, you'll understand them better if you read the next chapter first.

### Power and ANOVA

Recall that we always want to maximize our *power,* the probability of rejecting $H_0$ when $H_0$ is false. Here we do this by maximizing the size of $F_{obt}$. Looking at the $F$-ratio,

$$F_{obt} = \frac{MS_{bn}}{MS_{wn}}$$

we see that if we increase the relative size of the numerator or decrease the relative size of the denominator, the resulting $F_{obt}$ will be larger. Therefore, we attempt to increase the power of an ANOVA by designing an experiment that (1) maximizes the size of the differences between means, which increases the size of $MS_{bn}$, (2) minimizes the variability of scores within the conditions, which reduces the size of $MS_{wn}$, and (3) maximizes the $n$ of each condition, which increases $df_{wn}$ and thus also minimizes $MS_{wn}$. (A larger $df_{wn}$ also results in a smaller value of $F_{crit}$) Any of the above will increase the probability that $F_{obt}$ is significant, thereby giving us greater power to reject $H_0$ when it is false. The same considerations influence the power of our *post hoc* comparisons to detect differences between each pair of sample means.

## The Test for Homogeneity of Variance: The $F_{max}$ Test

Throughout our discussion of $t$-tests and ANOVA, we have assumed that our samples represent populations that have homogeneous, or equal, variance (the value of $\sigma_X^2$ is the same for each population). This is important because when we violate this assumption, the probability of a Type I error is greater than our $\alpha$. Therefore, if we are unsure that the data meet this assumption, we perform the homogeneity of variance test before we conduct $t$-tests or ANOVA. A **homogeneity of variance test** determines whether two estimated variances ($s_X^2$) are significantly different from each other. A significant difference between the values of $s_X^2$ for two samples indicates that they are likely to represent populations having different values of $\sigma_X^2$. Therefore, if our values of $s_X^2$ differ significantly, we cannot assume that the variances of our populations are homogeneous, and we should not perform the parametric procedure.

Although there are several tests of homogeneity, a simple version is Hartley's $F_{max}$ test. This test is used for independent samples when the $n$'s in all conditions are equal. To perform the $F_{max}$ test, first compute the estimated population variance ($s_X^2$) for each condition, using the formula you learned in Chapter 5. Then select the largest value of $s_X^2$ and the smallest value of $s_X^2$. As usual, the null hypothesis says there is no difference, so here $H_0$ says that the two sample variances represent the same value of $\sigma_X^2$. Then,

THE COMPUTATIONAL FORMULA FOR THE HOMOGENEITY OF VARIANCE TEST IS

$$F_{max} = \frac{\text{largest } s_X^2}{\text{smallest } s_X^2}$$

Critical values for $F_{max}$ are found in Table 7 in Appendix D, "Critical Values of the $F_{max}$ Test." In the table, columns across the top are labeled "$k$" for the number of levels or samples in the factor. The rows are labeled "$n - 1$," where $n$ is the number of scores in each sample.

The logic of the $F_{max}$ test is the same as the logic of the $F$-ratio. If both values of $s_X^2$ perfectly represent the same $\sigma_X^2$, then the two $s_X^2$'s should be equal, so $F_{max}$ should equal 1. If they are not equal, then $F_{max}$ will be larger than 1. The larger the $F_{max}$, the greater the difference between the largest and smallest $s_X^2$. If $F_{max}$ is significant, the difference between the two values of $s_X^2$ is significant.

For example, for our study of perceived difficulty, we obtain the following data from Table 13.4.

*Perceived difficulty*

| *Easy* | *Medium* | *Difficult* |
|---|---|---|
| $\Sigma X = 40$ | $\Sigma X = 30$ | $\Sigma X = 15$ |
| $\Sigma X^2 = 354$ | $\Sigma X^2 = 220$ | $\Sigma X^2 = 55$ |
| $n_1 = 5$ | $n_2 = 5$ | $n_3 = 5$ |
| $s_X^2 = 8.5$ | $s_X^2 = 10$ | $s_X^2 = 2.5$ |

After computing $s_X^2$ for each level, we see that the largest $s_X^2$ is 10 and the smallest $s_X^2$ is 2.5. Placing these numbers in the formula for $F_{max}$ gives

$$F_{max} = \frac{10}{2.5} = 4.0$$

With three levels in our factor, $k = 3$, and since $n$ is 5 in each condition, $n - 1$ is 4. From Table 7, the critical value of $F_{max}$ is 15.50. Since our obtained $F_{max}$ of 4.0 is less than the critical value of 15.50, the two variances are *not* significantly different. Therefore, we do not have evidence that the sample variances represent different population variances, so we can assume that our data meet the homogeneity of variance assumption, and it is acceptable to perform ANOVA.

## FINALLY

Be sure that you are comfortable with the logic and terminology of this chapter. When all is said and done, the $F$-ratio is a convoluted way to measure the differences between sample means and then to fit those differences to a sampling distribution. The larger the $F_{obt}$, the less likely that the differences between the sample means are the result of sampling error. A significant $F_{obt}$ indicates that the corresponding sample means are unlikely to represent one population mean. That's all there is to it.

There is one more type of procedure that you should be aware of. Everything in our discussions so far has involved *one* dependent variable, and the statistics we have performed are called *univariate statistics*. We can, however, measure subjects on two or more dependent variables in one experiment. Statistics for multiple dependent variables are called *multivariate statistics*. These include the multivariate *t*-test and the multivariate analysis of variance (MANOVA). Even though these are very complex procedures, the basic logic still holds: the larger the $t_{obt}$ or $F_{obt}$, the less likely it is that the samples represent the same population. (To discuss multivariates further would require another book.)

## CHAPTER SUMMARY

*1.* Analysis of variance, or *ANOVA,* has its own vocabulary. Below are the general terms we have used previously, along with the corresponding ANOVA terms.

| General term | = | ANOVA term |
|---|---|---|
| independent variable | = | factor |
| condition | = | level |
| sum of squared deviations | = | sum of squares ($SS$) |
| variance ($s_X^2$) | = | mean square ($MS$) |
| effect of independent variable | = | treatment effect |

*2.* A *one-way* analysis of variance tests for significant differences between the means from two or more levels of a factor. In a *between-subjects factor,* each independent sample is tested under only one level. In a *repeated measures factor,* the same subjects are tested under all levels of the factor.

*3.* The *experiment-wise error rate* is the probability that at least one Type I error will occur when all pairs of means in an experiment are compared. We perform ANOVA instead of multiple *t*-tests because with ANOVA the experiment-wise error rate will equal $\alpha$.

*4.* The *assumptions of the one-way, between-subjects ANOVA* are that (a) the scores in each condition are independent random samples, (b) each sample represents a normally distributed population of interval or ratio scores, and (c) all populations represented in the study have equal, or homogeneous, variance.

*5.* ANOVA tests two-tailed hypotheses. $H_0$ indicates that the mean of each condition represents the same population mean, so $H_0$ is $\mu_1 = \mu_2 = \mu_3$

$= \cdots = \mu_k$, where $k$ is the number of levels of the factor. $H_a$ indicates that the means from at least two of the conditions represent different population means, so $H_a$ is not all $\mu$'s are equal.

**6.** The *mean square within groups, $MS_{wn}$,* is an estimate of *error variance,* the inherent variability among scores *within* each population. The *mean square between groups, $MS_{bn}$,* is an estimate of the error variance plus the treatment variance. The *treatment variance* reflects differences in scores between the populations represented by the conditions of the independent variable.

**7.** $F_{obt}$ is computed using the *F-ratio,* which is the mean square between groups divided by the mean square within groups.

**8.** $F_{obt}$ may be greater than 1 because either (a) there is no treatment effect, but the sample means are not perfectly representative of this or (b) two or more sample means represent different population means.

**9.** The *F-distribution* is the sampling distribution of all values of $F_{obt}$ when $H_0$ is true. Values of $F_{crit}$ are found in the *F*-tables using $df_{bn}$ and $df_{wn}$.

**10.** The larger the value of $F_{obt}$, the less likely it is that the sample means from all levels represent one population mean. If the $F_{obt}$ is greater than $F_{crit}$, then the $F_{obt}$ is significant. Therefore, the corresponding differences between sample means are too unlikely to accept as having occurred by chance if all means actually represent the same population mean.

**11.** All of the levels in a factor may not produce significant differences. Therefore, if (a) $F_{obt}$ is significant and (b) there are more than two levels of the factor, we perform *post hoc comparisons* to determine which specific means differ significantly. When the *n*'s of all conditions are *not* equal, we perform *Fisher's protected t-test* on each pair of means. If all *n*'s are equal, then we perform *Tukey's HSD test.* Any two means that differ from each other by more than the *HSD* are significantly different.

**12.** When a significant relationship exists between the factor and the dependent scores, *eta squared* ($\eta^2$) describes the *effect size*—the *proportion of variance accounted for* by the factor in the sample data. *Omega squared* ($\omega^2$) estimates the proportion of variance accounted for in the population.

**13.** The *power* of ANOVA increases as we increase the differences between the conditions of the independent variable, decrease the variability of scores within each condition, or increase the *n* of small samples.

**14.** The $F_{max}$ *test* is a test of homogeneity of variance. It determines whether the variances from the levels in an experiment differ significantly. If they do not, then the data meet the assumption of homogeneity of variance.

## USING THE COMPUTER

The good news is that routine **7** in your computer program will perform the one-way, between-subjects ANOVA. From your data, it computes the $\overline{X}$ and $s_X$ of each level and presents a graph of the means. The program computes each *SS*, *MS*, and *df*, as well as $F_{obt}$, giving the minimum value of $p$ ($\alpha$) at which $F_{obt}$ is significant. The program also allows you to perform the Tukey *HSD* test, and it computes eta squared. To determine a confidence interval for the mean of a level, enter the data from that level into the one-sample $t$-test in routine **5**.

## PRACTICE PROBLEMS

(Answers are provided for odd-numbered problems.)

1. What does each of the following terms mean?
   a. ANOVA
   b. one-way
   c. factor
   d. level
   e. between subjects
   f. repeated measures
2. (a) What does $MS_{wn}$ estimate? (b) What does $MS_{bn}$ estimate?
3. (a) In a study comparing the effects of four conditions of the independent variable, what is $H_0$ for ANOVA? (b) What is $H_a$ for ANOVA in the same study?
4. Why should $F_{obt}$ equal 1.0 if the data represent the $H_0$ situation?
5. Why is $F_{obt}$ greater than 1.0 when the data represent the $H_a$ situation?
6. What does a significant $F_{obt}$ indicate about differences between the levels of a factor?
7. Why must we perform *post hoc* comparisons if $F_{obt}$ is significant?
8. When is Fisher's protected $t$-test performed and when is Tukey's *HSD* test performed?
9. Here are data from an experiment studying the effect of age level on creativity scores:

| Age 4 | Age 6 | Age 8 | Age 10 |
|-------|-------|-------|--------|
| 3     | 9     | 9     | 7      |
| 5     | 11    | 12    | 7      |
| 7     | 14    | 9     | 6      |
| 4     | 10    | 8     | 4      |
| 3     | 10    | 9     | 5      |

a. Compute $F_{obt}$ and create an ANOVA summary table.
b. With $\alpha = .05$, what do you conclude about $F_{obt}$?
c. Perform the appropriate *post hoc* comparisons.
d. What should you conclude about this relationship?
e. Statistically, how important is the relationship in this study?

10. In a study where $k = 3$, $n = 16$, and $\overline{X}_1 = 45.3$, $\overline{X}_2 = 16.9$, and $\overline{X}_3 = 8.2$, you compute the following sums of squares:

| Source | Sum of squares | df | Mean square | F |
|--------|---------------|-----|-------------|---|
| Between | 147.32 | ___ | ___ | ___ |
| Within | 862.99 | ___ | ___ | |
| Total | 1010.31 | ___ | | |

a. Complete the ANOVA summary table.
b. With $\alpha = .05$, what do you conclude about $F_{obt}$?
c. Perform the appropriate *post hoc* comparisons.
d. What should you conclude about this relationship?
e. What is the effect size in this study?

11. In problem 10, $s_X^2 = 43.68$ in level 1, $s_X^2 = 23.72$ in level 2, and $s_X^2 = 9.50$ in level 3. (a) With $\alpha = .05$, does this study meet the assumption of homogeneity of variance? (b) What does this indicate about the appropriateness of ANOVA?

12. What is the difference between $\eta^2$ and $\omega^2$?

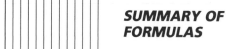

## SUMMARY OF FORMULAS

*1. The format for the summary table for a one-way ANOVA is as follows:*

Summary Table of One-Way ANOVA

| Source | Sum of squares | df | Mean square | F |
|--------|---------------|-----|-------------|---|
| Between | $SS_{bn}$ | $k - 1$ | $MS_{bn}$ | $F_{obt}$ |
| Within | $SS_{wn}$ | $N - k$ | $MS_{wn}$ | |
| Total | $SS_{tot}$ | $N - 1$ | | |

**2.** Computing the sum of squares

a. *The computational formula for $SS_{tot}$ is*

$$SS_{tot} = \Sigma X_{tot}^2 - \left( \frac{(\Sigma X_{tot})^2}{N} \right)$$

All scores in the experiment are included, and $N$ is the total number of scores.

b. *The computational formula for $SS_{bn}$ is*

$$SS_{bn} = \Sigma \left( \frac{(\text{sum of scores in the column})^2}{n \text{ of scores in the column}} \right) - \left( \frac{(\Sigma X_{tot})^2}{N} \right)$$

where each column contains the scores from one level of the factor.

c. *The computational formula for $SS_{wn}$ is*

$$SS_{wn} = SS_{tot} - SS_{bn}$$

**3.** Computing the mean square

a. *The computational formula for $MS_{bn}$ is*

$$MS_{bn} = \frac{SS_{bn}}{df_{bn}}$$

with $df_{bn} = k - 1$, where $k$ is the number of levels in the factor.

b. *The computational formula for $MS_{wn}$ is*

$$MS_{wn} = \frac{SS_{wn}}{df_{wn}}$$

with $df_{wn} = N - k$, where $N$ is the total $N$ of the study and $k$ is the number of levels in the factor.

**4.** *The computational formula for the F-ratio is*

$$F_{obt} = \frac{MS_{bn}}{MS_{wn}}$$

Critical values of $F$ are found in Table 5 in Appendix D for $df_{bn}$ and $df_{wn}$.

**5.** When $F_{obt}$ is significant and $k$ is greater than 2, *post hoc* comparisons must be performed.

a. *The computational formula for the protected t-test is*

$$t_{\text{obt}} = \frac{\overline{X}_1 - \overline{X}_2}{\sqrt{MS_{\text{wn}}\left(\dfrac{1}{n_1} + \dfrac{1}{n_2}\right)}}$$

Values of $t_{\text{crit}}$ are the two-tailed values found in the $t$-tables for $df = df_{\text{wn}} = N - k$.

b. *When the n's in all levels are equal, the computational formula for the HSD is*

$$HSD = (q_k)\left(\sqrt{\frac{MS_{\text{wn}}}{n}}\right)$$

Values of $q_k$ are found in Table 6 for $df_{\text{wn}}$ and $k$, where $k$ equals the number of levels of the factor.

6. *The computational formula for computing the confidence interval for a single* $\mu$, *using the results of a between-subjects ANOVA, is*

$$\left(\sqrt{\frac{MS_{\text{wn}}}{n}}\right)(-t_{\text{crit}}) + \overline{X} \leq \mu \leq \left(\sqrt{\frac{MS_{\text{wn}}}{n}}\right)(+t_{\text{crit}}) + \overline{X}$$

$\overline{X}$ and $n$ are from the level being described, and $t_{\text{crit}}$ is the two-tailed value of $t_{\text{crit}}$ at the appropriate $\alpha$ for $df_{\text{wn}}$.

7. *The computational formula for eta squared is*

$$\eta^2 = \frac{SS_{\text{bn}}}{SS_{\text{tot}}}$$

8. *The computational formula for omega squared, when the factor is a between-subjects factor and all n's are equal, is*

$$\omega^2 = \frac{SS_{\text{bn}} - (df_{\text{bn}})(MS_{\text{wn}})}{SS_{\text{tot}} + MS_{\text{wn}}}$$

9. *The computational formula for the* $F_{\text{max}}$ *test is*

$$F_{\text{max}} = \frac{\text{largest } s_X^2}{\text{smallest } s_X^2}$$

where each $s_X^2$ is computed using the scores in one level of the experiment. Critical values are found in Table 7, where $k$ is the number of levels in the factor and $n - 1$ is found using $n$, the number of scores in each level.

# 14

# Two-Way Analysis of Variance: Testing the Means from Two Independent Variables

In the previous chapter we saw that ANOVA simultaneously tests for significant differences between all means from one factor. The real beauty of ANOVA is it can be applied to even more complex experiments which contain more than one factor. We can change the conditions of as many independent variables as we wish and then examine the effect of each independent variable separately, as well as the effect of the combination of the variables.

When an experiment contains more than one factor, we perform a multi-factor ANOVA. To introduce you to multi-factor ANOVA, this chapter will discuss experiments containing two factors, which we analyze using a two-way ANOVA. This is like the ANOVA of the previous chapter, except that we compute several values of $F_{obt}$. Therefore, be forewarned that the procedure is rather involved (although it is more tedious than it is difficult). As you read this chapter, do not be concerned about memorizing all of the specific formulas. Rather, understand the overall steps involved, so that you can see why we perform the computations.

## MORE STATISTICAL NOTATION

A two-way ANOVA has two different independent variables, or factors. Each factor may contain any number of levels, so we use a code to describe the number of levels in each factor of a specific ANOVA. The generic format for describing a two-way ANOVA is to call one factor factor A and the other factor factor B. To describe a particular ANOVA, we use the number of levels in each factor. If, for example, factor A has two levels and factor B has two levels, we have a two by two ANOVA, which is written as $2 \times 2$. Or if one factor has four levels and the other factor has three levels, we have a $4 \times 3$ ANOVA, and so on.

To understand the code used in a two-way ANOVA, say that we conduct a study with two factors. Factor A is the number of smart pills we will give to subjects, and we will test two levels (1 and 2 pills). Factor B is the age of subjects, and we will test two levels (10- and 20-year-olds). A good way to visualize a two-way ANOVA is to draw a diagram that shows how we combine the levels of both factors. Table 14.1 shows the diagram of this $2 \times 2$ ANOVA.

Each column of the diagram is a level of factor A: number of pills. Each row is a level of Factor B: age. Each small square produced by the particular combination of a level of A with a level of B is called a **cell.** Thus, we have four cells, each containing a sample of subjects who are one age and are given one amount of our smart pill. For example, the highlighted cell contains the scores of a sample of 20-year-olds who receive one pill.

We identify the levels of factor A as $A_1$ and $A_2$ and the levels of factor B as $B_1$ and $B_2$. Sometimes it is useful to identify each cell using the levels of the two factors. For example, the cell formed by combining level 1 of factor A and level 1 of factor B is cell $A_1B_1$. We can identify the mean and $n$ from each cell in the same way, so, for example, in cell $A_1B_1$ we have $\overline{X}_{A_1B_1}$.

One final consideration: when we combine all levels of one factor with all levels of the other factor, we have a **complete factorial design.** The design below is a complete factorial, because all of our levels of drug dose are combined

**TABLE 14.1**   Diagram of a $2 \times 2$ ANOVA

|  |  | Factor A: number of pills | |
|---|---|---|---|
|  |  | Level $A_1$: 1 pill | Level $A_2$: 2 pills |
| Factor B: age | Level $B_1$: 10-year-olds | $X$ $X$ $X$ $\overline{X}_{A_1B_1}$ | $X$ $X$ $X$ $\overline{X}_{A_2B_1}$ |
|  | Level $B_2$: 20-year-olds | $X$ $X$ $X$ $\overline{X}_{A_1B_2}$ | $X$ $X$ $X$ $\overline{X}_{A_2B_2}$ |

scores

one of the four cells

with all of our levels of age. On the other hand, in an **incomplete factorial design,** all levels of the two factors are not combined. For example, if for some reason we did not collect data for 20-year-olds given one smart pill, we would have an incomplete factorial design. Incomplete factorial designs require elaborate procedures not discussed here.

In this chapter we will focus on the two-way factorial ANOVA in which both factors are between-subjects factors (we have independent samples in all cells of the experiment).

## OVERVIEW OF THE TWO-WAY ANOVA

As with all experiments, the purpose of a two-factor experiment is to determine whether there is a relationship between the independent variable and the dependent variable. The only difference from previous experiments is that now we have two independent variables.

Why would we want to combine two factors in one experiment? We could perform two separate studies, one testing the effect of factor A and one testing the effect of factor B. However, if we did, we would miss a potential third influence on scores, and that is the *combined* effect of factor A and factor B. This combined effect is called the *interaction effect.* The major reason for conducting experiments with more than one factor is so that we can examine the interaction effect. Later we will discuss interaction effects in detail, but for now, think of an interaction as the effect produced by the particular combination of the levels from the two factors. Thus, in the previous example, the interaction would indicate the combined influence on scores as we change both the age of subjects and the number of smart pills.

As usual, regardless of whether we are talking about each factor separately or their interaction, we want to conclude that our sample means indicate that if we tested the entire population under the various conditions in our experiment, we would find different populations of scores located at different $\mu$'s. But there is the usual problem: differences between the sample means may simply reflect sampling error, so we would actually find the same population, having the same $\mu$. Therefore, once again we must eliminate the idea that the differences between our sample means merely reflect sampling error. To do this, we perform ANOVA. As usual, we first set our alpha, usually $\alpha = .05$, and then check the assumptions.

### Assumptions of the Two-Way Between-Subjects ANOVA

We can perform the two-way, between-subjects ANOVA when we have a complete factorial design and we can assume that

*1.* All cells contain independent random samples of subjects.

*2.* The dependent variable measures interval or ratio scores.

*3.* The populations represented by the data are approximately normally distributed, and the mean is the appropriate measure of central tendency.

*4.* The represented populations all have homogeneous variance (all have equal $\sigma_X^2$). (We test whether the cells meet this assumption using the $F_{\max}$ test discussed in the previous chapter.)

If our experiment generally meets the assumptions, we perform the two-way ANOVA.

## Logic of the Two-Way ANOVA

Here is a semi-fascinating idea for a study. Have you ever noticed that television commercials are much louder than the programs themselves? Many advertisers seem to believe that increased volume creates increased viewer attention and so makes the commercial more persuasive. To test whether louder messages are more persuasive, we conduct an experiment. We play a recording of an advertising message at each of three volumes. (Volume is measured in decibels, but to simplify things we will refer to the three levels of volume as soft, medium, and loud.) We are also interested in the differences between how males and females are persuaded, so we have another factor: the gender of the listener. If, in one study, we examine both the volume of the message and the gender of the subjects hearing the message, we have a two-factor experiment involving three levels of volume and two levels of gender. We will test all conditions with independent samples, so we have a 3 × 2 between-subjects, factorial ANOVA. Our dependent variable is a persuasiveness score, indicating how persuasive a subject believes the message to be on a scale of 0 (not at all) to 25 (totally convincing).

Say we collect the scores and organize them as in Table 14.2. As usual, for simplicity we have a distinctly unpowerful $N$: nine males and nine females were randomly selected, and then three males and three females were randomly assigned to hear the message at each volume, so we have three persuasiveness scores per cell.

But now what? How do we make sense out of it all? To answer this question, stop and think about what the study is designed to investigate. We want to show the effects of (1) changing the levels of the factor of volume, (2) changing the levels of the factor of gender, and (3) changing the combination, or interaction, of the factors of volume and gender. As usual, we want to demonstrate that each of these has a significant effect. Since we want to view each of these effects one at a time, *the way to understand a two-way ANOVA is to treat it as if it contained three one-way ANOVAs.* Since you already understand a one-way ANOVA, the rest of this chapter simply provides a guide for computing the ANOVAs.

**TABLE 14.2** 3 × 2 ANOVA for the Factors of Volume of Message and Gender of Subject

|  |  | Factor A: volume | | |
|---|---|---|---|---|
|  |  | Level A₁: soft | Level A₂: medium | Level A₃: loud |
| Factor B: gender | Level B₁: male | 9<br>4<br>11 | 8<br>12<br>13 | 18<br>17<br>15 |
|  | Level B₂: female | 2<br>6<br>4 | 9<br>10<br>17 | 6<br>8<br>4 |

$$N = 18$$

Any two-way ANOVA breaks down into finding the main effects and the interaction effect.

**Main effects of factor A and factor B**   The **main effect** of a factor is the effect on the dependent scores of changing the levels of that factor while ignoring all other factors in the study. In our persuasiveness study, to find the main effect of factor A (volume), we simply ignore the levels of factor B (gender). Literally erase the horizontal line that separates the males and females in Table 14.2, and treat the experiment as if it were as follows:

*Factor A: volume*

| Level A₁: soft | Level A₂: medium | Level A₃: loud |
|---|---|---|
| 9 | 8 | 18 |
| 4 | 12 | 17 |
| 11 | 13 | 15 |
| 2 | 9 | 6 |
| 6 | 10 | 8 |
| 4 | 17 | 4 |

| $\overline{X}_{A_1} = 6$ | $\overline{X}_{A_2} = 11.5$ | $\overline{X}_{A_3} = 11.33$ |  |
|---|---|---|---|
| $n_{A_1} = 6$ | $n_{A_2} = 6$ | $n_{A_3} = 6$ | $N = 18$ |

We ignore the fact that we have some males and females in each condition: we simply have six subjects tested under each volume. In this diagram we have one factor, with three means from the three levels of volume, so $k = 3$, with $n = 6$ in each level.

In statistical terminology, we have collapsed across the factor of subject gender. **Collapsing** across a factor means averaging together all scores from all levels of the factor. When we collapse across one factor, we have the *main effect means* for the remaining factor. Thus, above we have the main effect means for the three levels of volume, $\overline{X}_{A_1} = 6$, $\overline{X}_{A_2} = 11.5$, and $\overline{X}_{A_3} = 11.33$.

Once we have collapsed, we find the main effect of changing the levels of factor A by performing a one-way ANOVA. We ask: Do these main effect means represent the different $\mu$'s that would be found if we tested the entire population under each of these three volumes? To answer this question, we first create our statistical hypotheses for factor A. The null hypothesis is

$$H_0: \mu_{A_1} = \mu_{A_2} = \mu_{A_3}$$

For our study, this says that changing volume has no effect, so the main effect means from the levels of volume represent the same population of persuasiveness scores. If we can reject $H_a$, then we will accept the alternative hypothesis, which is

$$H_a: \text{not all } \mu_A\text{'s are equal}$$

For our study, this says that at least two main effect means from our levels of volume represent different populations of persuasiveness scores, having different $\mu$'s.

We now follow the procedures of a one-way ANOVA. To test $H_0$, we compute an $F_{obt}$ called $F_A$. If $F_A$ is significant, it indicates that at least two of our main effect means differ significantly. Then we will describe this relationship by graphing the main effect means of factor A, performing *post hoc* comparisons to determine which of the specific means of factor A differ significantly, and determining the proportion of variance in dependent scores that is accounted for by changing the levels of factor A.

Once we have completed our analysis of the main effect of factor A, we move on to the main effect of factor B. To do this, we collapse across factor A (volume). Now we erase the vertical lines separating the levels of volume in our original diagram, obtaining this diagram of the main effect of factor B:

| Factor B: gender | Level $B_1$: male | 9 | 8 | 18 | $\overline{X}_{B_1} = 11.89$ |
| | | 4 | 12 | 17 | |
| | | 11 | 13 | 15 | $n_{B_1} = 9$ |
| | Level $B_2$: female | 2 | 9 | 6 | $\overline{X}_{B_2} = 7.33$ |
| | | 6 | 10 | 8 | |
| | | 4 | 17 | 4 | $n_{B_2} = 9$ |

$$N = 18$$

Now we simply have the persuasiveness scores of males and females, ignoring the fact that some of each heard the message at different volumes. In this diagram we have a one-factor, two-sample design (arranged horizontally instead of vertically). We treat this as a one-way ANOVA to see if there are significant differences between the main effect means of persuasiveness scores for males ($\overline{X}_{B_1} = 11.89$) and females ($\overline{X}_{B_2} = 7.33$). Notice that there are two levels of subject gender, so $k$ is now 2 and the $n$ of each level is 9, whereas for factor A, $k$ was 3 and $n$ was 6.

> **STAT ALERT**  In a two-way ANOVA, the values of $n$ and $k$ may be different for each factor.

Now we write our statistical hypotheses for the main effect of factor B. The null hypothesis is

$$H_0: \mu_{B_1} = \mu_{B_2}$$

For our study, this says that changing gender has no effect, so the sample mean for males represents the same population mean as the sample mean for females. If we can reject $H_0$, then we will accept the alternative hypothesis. The alternative hypothesis is

$$H_a: \text{not all } \mu_B\text{'s are equal}$$

For our study, this says that our sample means for males and females represent different populations of persuasiveness scores, having different $\mu$'s.

To test $H_0$ for factor B, we compute a separate $F_{obt}$, called $F_B$. If $F_B$ is significant, it indicates that the main effect means for factor B differ significantly. Then we graph the main effect means for factor B, perform the *post hoc* comparisons, and compute the proportion of variance accounted for by factor B.

**Interaction effects of factor A and factor B**  After we examine the main effects of factors A and B, we examine the interaction of the two factors. The interaction of two factors is called a two-way interaction. The **two-way interaction effect** is the effect of the combination of the levels of factor A with the levels of factor B. In our example, the interaction effect is the effect of each particular volume when combined with each particular subject gender. An interaction is identified as A $\times$ B. Our factor A has 3 levels and our factor B has 2 levels, so we have a $3 \times 2$ interaction.

Since we examine the combinations of the levels of both factors in an interaction, we do not collapse across, or ignore, either factor. Instead, we treat each *cell* in the study as a level of the interaction and we compare the sample means from each cell. We can draw the diagram of the interaction effect as shown on the next page.

A × B Interaction Effect

| Male soft | Male medium | Male loud |
|:---:|:---:|:---:|
| 9 | 8 | 18 |
| 4 | 12 | 17 |
| 11 | 13 | 15 |

| Female soft | Female medium | Female loud |
|:---:|:---:|:---:|
| 2 | 9 | 6 |
| 6 | 10 | 8 |
| 4 | 17 | 4 |

$\overline{X} = 8$    $\overline{X} = 11$    $\overline{X} = 16.67$    $\overline{X} = 4$    $\overline{X} = 12$    $\overline{X} = 6$    $N = 18$
$k = 6$
$n = 3$

These are the original six cells, containing three scores per subject, that we saw back in Table 14.2. We can think of this as a one-way ANOVA for the six levels of the interaction, so $k$ is now 6 and $n$ is now 3. However, examining an interaction is not as simple as saying that the cell means are significantly different. Here we are testing the extent to which the cell means differ *after* we have removed those differences that are attributable to the separate main effects of factor A and factor B. Thus, consistent differences between scores that are not due to changing the levels of factor A or factor B are due to changing the combinations of the levels of A and B.

Understanding and interpreting an interaction is difficult, because the levels of both independent variables are changing, as well as the dependent scores. To simplify the process, we look at the effect of changing the levels of factor A under *one* level of factor B. Then we see if the effect of factor A is *different* when we look at the other level of factor B. For example, the means are grouped in the above diagram so that on the left, we can see how the three means for males change as we change volume. On the right, we can see how the means for females change as we change volume. For males, each time we increase volume, the mean score also appears to increase. However, this is not the case for females: increasing volume from soft to medium apparently increases the mean, but increasing volume from medium to loud apparently *decreases* the mean.

Thus, there are three ways to define an interaction (take your pick). An interaction exists when

*1.* The effect of changing the levels of one factor is not consistent for each level of the other factor. Above, increasing volume does not have the same effect on male scores as on female scores.

*2.* The effect of changing the levels of one factor *depends on* the levels of the other factor. Above, whether increasing the volume increases persuasiveness scores depends on whether you are talking about males or females.

3. The relationship between one factor and the dependent variable changes as we change the levels of the other factor. For males, we have a positive linear relationship between volume and scores, but for females, we have a curvilinear relationship.

All of these statements describe the overall pattern we find when the particular combinations of the levels of the two factors produce different means. Conversely, of course, there may not be differences due to the particular combinations. Above, for example, if scores for females had increased in the same way scores for males increased, then there would be no interaction. When we do not have an interaction, we see that (1) the effect of changing one factor is the same for all levels of the other factor, (2) the effect of changing the levels of one factor does not depend on which level of the other variable we are talking about, or (3) we have the same relationship between the scores and one factor in each level of the other factor.

As with other effects, our data may appear to represent an interaction, but this may be an illusion created by sampling error. Therefore, we determine whether there is a significant interaction by performing ANOVA for the interaction. This ANOVA is similar to a one-way ANOVA for the six cell means. First, we create the statistical hypotheses for the $A \times B$ interaction. If the interaction of factors A and B has no effect on scores, then regardless of the particular combination of the levels of the two factors, all cell means represent the same population mean. Thus, $H_0$ is

$$H_0: \mu_{A_1B_1} = \mu_{A_2B_1} = \mu_{A_3B_1} = \cdots = \mu_{A_3B_2}$$

The alternative hypothesis for the interaction effect is

$$H_a: \text{not all interaction } \mu\text{'s are equal}$$

$H_a$ implies that at least two of our cell means represent different population means.

To test $H_0$ for the interaction, we compute yet another separate $F_{obt}$, called $F_{A \times B}$. If $F_{A \times B}$ is significant, it indicates that at least two of the cell means differ significantly in a way that produces a significant interaction. Therefore, we conclude that this interaction would be found in the population. Then we graph the interaction effect by graphing the cell means, we perform *post hoc* comparisons to determine which specific cell means differ significantly, and we compute the proportion of variance accounted for by the interaction.

## Overview of the Computations of the Two-Way ANOVA

In a two-way ANOVA, we compute three $F$s: one for the main effect of factor A, one for the main effect of factor B, and one for the interaction effect of $A \times B$. The logic and calculations for each of these are basically the same as for the one-way ANOVA, because any $F_{obt}$ is the ratio formed by dividing the mean square between groups ($MS_{bn}$) by the mean square within groups ($MS_{wn}$).

As with any ANOVA, we again partition, or break up, the total differences in scores (the total variance) into those differences that occur within groups (variance within) and those that occur between groups (variance between). The variance within groups is the $MS_{wn}$, and in a two-way ANOVA we compute $MS_{wn}$ by computing the "average" variability of the scores in each *cell*. All subjects in a cell are treated identically, so any differences among the scores are due to the inherent variability of scores. Thus, the $MS_{wn}$ is our estimate of the error variance in the population—the inherent variability within any of the raw score populations represented by our samples. This is our *one* estimate of the error variance, so we use it as the denominator in computing all three $F$ ratios.

We measure the variance between groups by computing the mean square between groups. This is our way of measuring the differences between our means, as an estimate of the treatment variance plus the error variance in the population. Thus, each $F$ estimates the following:

$$F_{obt} = \begin{array}{ccc} \textit{Sample} & \textit{Estimates} & \textit{Population} \\ \dfrac{MS_{bn}}{MS_{wn}} & \begin{array}{c} \rightarrow \\ \rightarrow \end{array} & \dfrac{\sigma_{error}^2 + \sigma_{treat}^2}{\sigma_{error}^2} \end{array}$$

However, since we have two factors and the interaction, we have three sources of between groups variance. We partition the between groups variance into (1) variance between groups due to factor A, (2) variance between groups due to factor B, and (3) variance between groups due to the interaction. We will compute a separate mean square between groups for each of these to estimate the treatment variance in the population each produces, and then we will compute the appropriate $F$ ratio.

Each mean square between groups is computed by dividing the appropriate sum of squares ($SS$) by the corresponding degrees of freedom ($df$). Table 14.3 shows the means from our persuasiveness study. First we collapse across factor B and examine the main effect means of factor A, volume ($\overline{X}_{A_1} = 6$, $\overline{X}_{A_2} = 11.5$, and $\overline{X}_{A_3} = 11.33$). We describe the differences between these means by computing the sum of squares between groups for factor A, $SS_A$, and then, dividing by the degrees of freedom for factor A, $df_A$, we have the mean square between groups for factor A, $MS_A$.

Likewise, for factor B, we collapse across factor A and examine the difference between the main effect means for factor B, gender ($\overline{X}_{B_1} = 11.89$ and $\overline{X}_{B_2} = 7.33$). We compute the sum of squares between groups for factor B, $SS_B$, and

**TABLE 14.3**  Summary of Means in Persuasiveness Study

|  |  | $A_1$: soft | $A_2$: medium | $A_3$: loud |  |
|---|---|---|---|---|---|
|  | $B_1$: male | $\overline{X} = 8$ | $\overline{X} = 11$ | $\overline{X} = 16.67$ | $\overline{X}_{male} = 11.89$ |
| **Factor B: gender** | $B_2$: female | $\overline{X} = 4$ | $\overline{X} = 12$ | $\overline{X} = 6$ | $\overline{X}_{fem} = 7.33$ |
|  |  | $\overline{X}_{soft} = 6$ | $\overline{X}_{med} = 11.5$ | $\overline{X}_{loud} = 11.33$ |  |

*Factor A: volume* (spanning header over $A_1$, $A_2$, $A_3$)

then, dividing by the degrees of freedom between groups for factor B, $df_B$, we find the mean square between groups for factor B, $MS_B$.

For the interaction, we do not collapse across either factor: we compare the differences between the six cell means that are not attributable to factor A or factor B. We compute the sum of squares between groups for A × B, $SS_{A \times B}$, and then, dividing by the degrees of freedom for A × B, $df_{A \times B}$, we have the mean square between groups for the interaction, $MS_{A \times B}$.

We also compute $MS_{wn}$ by computing $SS_{wn}$ and then dividing by $df_{wn}$. In the summary table in Table 14.4, we can see all of the components of the two-way ANOVA. To complete the summary table, for factor A we divide $MS_A$ by $MS_{wn}$ to produce $F_A$. For factor B, we divide $MS_B$ by $MS_{wn}$ to produce $F_B$. For the interaction, dividing $MS_{A \times B}$ by $MS_{wn}$ produces $F_{A \times B}$.

**TABLE 14.4**  Summary Table of Two-Way ANOVA

| Source | Sum of squares | df | Mean square | F |
|---|---|---|---|---|
| Between |  |  |  |  |
| Factor A (volume) | $SS_A$ | $df_A$ | $MS_A$ | $F_A$ |
| Factor B (gender) | $SS_B$ | $df_B$ | $MS_B$ | $F_B$ |
| Interaction (vol × gen) | $SS_{A \times B}$ | $df_{A \times B}$ | $MS_{A \times B}$ | $F_{A \times B}$ |
| Within | $SS_{wn}$ | $df_{wn}$ | $MS_{wn}$ |  |
| Total | $SS_{tot}$ | $df_{tot}$ |  |  |

Each $F_{obt}$ in a two-way ANOVA is tested in the same way we tested $F_{obt}$ in the previous chapter. $F_{obt}$ may be larger than 1.0 because (1) $H_0$ is true but the sample means do not perfectly represent one population $\mu$ or (2) $H_0$ is false and at least two sample means represent different values of $\mu$. The larger the value of $F_{obt}$, the less likely it is that $H_0$ is true. If any $F_{obt}$ is larger than $F_{crit}$, then $F_{obt}$ is significant and we reject the corresponding $H_0$.

## COMPUTING THE TWO-WAY ANOVA

Having a computer perform the calculations is the best way to perform the ANOVA. However, whether or not you use a computer program, you should first organize the data in each cell. Table 14.5 shows our persuasiveness scores for the factors of volume of message and gender of subject, as well as the various components we must compute.

To compute the components, first we compute $\Sigma X$ and $\Sigma X^2$ for each cell and

**TABLE 14.5**   Summary of Data for 3 × 2 ANOVA

|  |  | *Factor A: volume* | | | |
|---|---|---|---|---|---|
|  |  | $A_1$: soft | $A_2$: medium | $A_3$: loud | |
|  | $B_1$: male | 4<br>9<br>11<br>$\overline{X} = 8$<br>$\Sigma X = 24$<br>$\Sigma X^2 = 218$<br>$n = 3$ | 8<br>12<br>13<br>$\overline{X} = 11$<br>$\Sigma X = 33$<br>$\Sigma X^2 = 377$<br>$n = 3$ | 18<br>17<br>15<br>$\overline{X} = 16.67$<br>$\Sigma X = 50$<br>$\Sigma X^2 = 838$<br>$n = 3$ | $\overline{X}_{male} = 11.89$<br>$\Sigma X = 107$<br>$n = 9$ |
| *Factor B: gender* | $B_2$: female | 2<br>6<br>4<br>$\overline{X} = 4$<br>$\Sigma X = 12$<br>$\Sigma X^2 = 56$<br>$n = 3$ | 9<br>10<br>17<br>$\overline{X} = 12$<br>$\Sigma X = 36$<br>$\Sigma X^2 = 470$<br>$n = 3$ | 6<br>8<br>4<br>$\overline{X} = 6$<br>$\Sigma X = 18$<br>$\Sigma X^2 = 116$<br>$n = 3$ | $\overline{X}_{fem} = 7.33$<br>$\Sigma X = 66$<br>$n = 9$ |
|  |  | $\overline{X}_{soft} = 6$<br>$\Sigma X = 36$<br>$n = 6$ | $\overline{X}_{med} = 11.5$<br>$\Sigma X = 69$<br>$n = 6$ | $\overline{X}_{loud} = 11.33$<br>$\Sigma X = 68$<br>$n = 6$ | $\Sigma X_{tot} = 173$<br>$\Sigma X^2_{tot} = 2075$<br>$N = 18$ |

note the $n$ of each cell. Thus, for the male-soft cell, $\Sigma X = 4 + 9 + 11 = 24$, $\Sigma X^2 = 4^2 + 9^2 + 11^2 = 218$, and $n = 3$. We also compute the mean for each cell (for the male-soft cell, $\overline{X} = 24/3 = 8$). These are the means we will test in the interaction.

Now we collapse across factor B, gender, and look only at the three volumes. We compute $\Sigma X$ vertically for each column: the $\Sigma X$ in a column is the sum of the $\Sigma X$s from the cells in that column (for soft, $\Sigma X = 24 + 12$). We note the $n$ in each column (here $n = 6$) and compute the sample mean for each column ($\overline{X}_{\text{soft}} = 6$). These are the means we will test in the main effect of factor A.

Now we collapse across factor A, volume, and look only at males and females. We compute $\Sigma X$ horizontally for each row: the $\Sigma X$ in a row equals the sum of the $\Sigma X$s from the cells in that row (for males, $\Sigma X = 24 + 33 + 50 = 107$). We note the $n$ in each row (here $n = 9$) and compute the sample mean for each row ($\overline{X}_{\text{male}} = 11.89$). These are the means we will test in the main effect of factor B.

Finally, we compute the total $\Sigma X$, $\Sigma X_{\text{tot}}$, by adding the $\Sigma X$ from the three levels of factor A (the three column sums), so $\Sigma X_{\text{tot}} = 36 + 69 + 68 = 173$. Alternatively, we can add the $\Sigma X$ from the two levels of factor B (the two row sums). We also find the total $\Sigma X^2$, $\Sigma X_{\text{tot}}^2$, by adding the $\Sigma X^2$ from each cell, so $\Sigma X_{\text{tot}}^2 = 218 + 377 + 838 + 56 + 470 + 116 = 2075$. Note that the total $N$ is 18.

We use these components to compute all of our sums of squares and degrees of freedom. Then we compute the mean squares and, finally, each $F_{\text{obt}}$. You will see how this is done in the following sections. To keep track of your computations and prevent brain strain, fill in the ANOVA summary table as you go along.

## Computing the Sums of Squares

First we compute the various sums of squares. We do this in five steps.

Step 1 is to compute the total sum of squares, $SS_{\text{tot}}$.

*THE COMPUTATIONAL FORMULA FOR $SS_{\text{tot}}$ IS*

$$SS_{\text{tot}} = \Sigma X_{\text{tot}}^2 - \left( \frac{(\Sigma X_{\text{tot}})^2}{N} \right)$$

This equation says to divide $(\Sigma X_{\text{tot}})^2$ by $N$ and then subtract the answer from $\Sigma X_{\text{tot}}^2$.

For our persuasiveness study, in Table 14.5 we have $\Sigma X_{tot} = 173$, $\Sigma X^2_{tot} = 2075$, and $N = 18$. Filling in the above formula, we have

$$SS_{tot} = 2075 - \left(\frac{(173)^2}{18}\right)$$

Squaring 173, we have

$$SS_{tot} = 2075 - \left(\frac{29929}{18}\right)$$

Dividing gives

$$SS_{tot} = 2075 - 1662.72$$

so $SS_{tot} = 412.28$.

Note that the quantity $(\Sigma X_{tot})^2/N$ above is used in the computation of most of the other sums of squares. It is called the *correction* (here the correction equals 1662.72).

Step 2 is to compute the sum of squares for factor A. In our diagram of the two-way ANOVA, the levels of factor A form the columns.

> **THE COMPUTATIONAL FORMULA FOR THE SUM OF SQUARES BETWEEN GROUPS FOR COLUMN FACTOR A IS**
>
> $$SS_A = \Sigma\left(\frac{(\text{sum of scores in the column})^2}{n \text{ of scores in the column}}\right) - \left(\frac{(\Sigma X_{tot})^2}{N}\right)$$

This equation says to square the $\Sigma X$ for each column of factor A and divide by the $n$ in the column. After doing this for all levels, add the answers together and then subtract the correction.

In our example, from Table 14.5 we found that the three columns produced sums of 36, 69, and 68 and $n$ was 6. Filling in the above formula, we have

$$SS_A = \left(\frac{(36)^2}{6} + \frac{(69)^2}{6} + \frac{(68)^2}{6}\right) - \left(\frac{(173)^2}{18}\right)$$

$$SS_A = (216 + 793.5 + 770.67) - 1662.72$$

$$SS_A = 1780.17 - 1662.72$$

so $SS_A = 117.45$.

Step 3 is to compute the sum of squares between groups for factor B. In our diagram of the two-way ANOVA, the levels of factor B form the rows.

This equation says to square $\Sigma X$ for each level of factor B and divide by the $n$ in the level. After doing this for all levels, add the answers and then subtract the correction.

In our example, we found that the two rows produced sums of 107 and 66 and $n$ was 9. Filling in the above formula gives

$$SS_B = \left(\frac{(107)^2}{9} + \frac{(66)^2}{9}\right) - 1662.72$$

$$SS_B = 1756.11 - 1662.72$$

so $SS_B = 93.39$.

Step 4 is to compute the sum of squares between groups for the interaction, $SS_{A \times B}$. To do this, we first compute something called the overall sum of squares between groups, which we identify as $SS_{bn}$.

Here we find $(\Sigma X)^2$ for each cell, divide by the $n$ of the cell, add the answers from all cells together, and subtract the correction.

In our example, filling in the formula from Table 14.5, we have

$$SS_{bn} = \left(\frac{(24)^2}{3} + \frac{(33)^2}{3} + \frac{(50)^2}{3} + \frac{(12)^2}{3} + \frac{(36)^2}{3} + \frac{(18)^2}{3}\right) - 1662.72$$

$$SS_{bn} = 1976.33 - 1662.72$$

so $SS_{bn} = 313.61$.

The reason we compute $SS_{bn}$ is that it is equal to the sum of squares for factor A plus the sum of squares for factor B plus the sum of squares for the interaction. To find $SS_{A \times B}$, we subtract the sum of squares for both main effects from the overall $SS_{bn}$. Thus,

THE COMPUTATIONAL FORMULA FOR THE SUM OF SQUARES BETWEEN GROUPS FOR THE INTERACTION, $SS_{A \times B}$, IS

$$SS_{A \times B} = SS_{bn} - SS_A - SS_B$$

In our example,

$$SS_{A \times B} = 313.61 - 117.45 - 93.39$$

so $SS_{A \times B} = 102.77$.

Step 5 is to compute the sum of squares within groups, $SS_{wn}$. The sum of squares within groups plus the overall sum of squares between groups equals the total sum of squares. Therefore, when we subtract the overall $SS_{bn}$ in step 4 from the $SS_{tot}$ in step 1, we obtain the $SS_{wn}$.

THE COMPUTATIONAL FORMULA FOR THE SUM OF SQUARES WITHIN GROUPS, $SS_{wn}$, IS

$$SS_{wn} = SS_{tot} - SS_{bn}$$

In our example, we have $SS_{tot} = 412.28$ and $SS_{bn} = 313.61$, so

$$SS_{wn} = 412.28 - 313.61$$

Thus, $SS_{wn} = 98.67$.

Placing the various sums of squares in the ANOVA summary table, we have Table 14.6. Notice that we do not include the overall $SS_{bn}$.

**TABLE 14.6**  Summary Table of Two-Way ANOVA

| Source | Sum of squares | df | Mean square | F |
|--------|----------------|-----|-------------|---|
| Between | | | | |
| Factor A (volume) | 117.45 | $df_A$ | $MS_A$ | $F_A$ |
| Factor B (gender) | 93.39 | $df_B$ | $MS_B$ | $F_B$ |
| Interaction (vol × gen) | 102.77 | $df_{A \times B}$ | $MS_{A \times B}$ | $F_{A \times B}$ |
| Within | 98.67 | $df_{wn}$ | $MS_{wn}$ | |
| Total | 412.28 | $df_{tot}$ | | |

## Computing the Degrees of Freedom

Now we must determine the various values of $df$.

1. *The degrees of freedom between groups for factor A is $k_A - 1$, where $k_A$ is the number of levels in factor A. (In our example, $k_A$ is the three levels of volume, so $df_A = 2$.)*
2. *The degrees of freedom between groups for factor B is $k_B - 1$, where $k_B$ is the number of levels in factor B. (In our example, $k_B$ is the two levels of gender, so $df_B = 1$.)*
3. *The degrees of freedom between groups for the interaction is the df for factor A multiplied times the df for factor B. (In our example, $df_A = 2$ and $df_B = 1$, so $df_{A \times B} = 2$.)*
4. *The degrees of freedom within groups equals $N - k$, where $N$ is the total $N$ of the study and $k$ is the total number of cells in the study. (In our example, $N$ is 18 and we have six cells, so $df_{wn} = 18 - 6 = 12$.)*
5. *The degrees of freedom total equals $N - 1$, or the sum of the above degrees of freedom. (In our example, $df_{tot} = 17$.)*

## Computing the Mean Squares

It is easiest to perform the remainder of the computations by working directly from the summary table. So far, with the sums of squares and degrees of freedom we computed above, we have Table 14.7.

Now we compute the mean squares.

**TABLE 14.7**  Summary Table of Two-Way ANOVA

| Source | Sum of squares | df | Mean square | F |
|--------|----------------|-----|-------------|---|
| Between | | | | |
| Factor A (volume) | 117.45 | 2 | $MS_A$ | $F_A$ |
| Factor B (gender) | 93.39 | 1 | $MS_B$ | $F_B$ |
| Interaction (vol × gen) | 102.77 | 2 | $MS_{A \times B}$ | $F_{A \times B}$ |
| Within | 98.67 | 12 | $MS_{wn}$ | |
| Total | 412.28 | 17 | | |

THE COMPUTATIONAL FORMULA FOR THE MEAN SQUARE FOR FACTOR A IS

$$MS_A = \frac{SS_A}{df_A}$$

In our example,

$$MS_A = \frac{117.45}{2} = 58.73$$

THE COMPUTATIONAL FORMULA FOR THE MEAN SQUARE FOR FACTOR B IS

$$MS_B = \frac{SS_B}{df_B}$$

Thus, we have

$$MS_B = \frac{93.39}{1} = 93.39$$

THE COMPUTATIONAL FORMULA FOR THE MEAN SQUARE FOR THE INTERACTION IS

$$MS_{A \times B} = \frac{SS_{A \times B}}{df_{A \times B}}$$

Thus, we have

$$MS_{A \times B} = \frac{102.77}{2} = 51.39$$

THE COMPUTATIONAL FORMULA FOR THE MEAN SQUARE WITHIN GROUPS IS

$$MS_{wn} = \frac{SS_{wn}}{df_{wn}}$$

Thus, we have

$$MS_{wn} = \frac{98.67}{12} = 8.22$$

Putting these values in the summary table, we have Table 14.8.
    Finally, we compute the $F$s.

## Computing $F_{obt}$

Recall that to compute any $F$, we divide the $MS_{bn}$ by the $MS_{wn}$. Therefore,

*THE COMPUTATIONAL FORMULA FOR $F_A$ FOR THE MAIN EFFECT OF FACTOR A IS*

$$F_A = \frac{MS_A}{MS_{wn}}$$

Thus, we have

$$F_A = \frac{58.73}{8.22} = 7.14$$

*THE COMPUTATIONAL FORMULA FOR $F_B$ FOR THE MAIN EFFECT OF FACTOR B IS*

$$F_B = \frac{MS_B}{MS_{wn}}$$

**TABLE 14.8**  Summary Table of Two-Way ANOVA

| Source | Sum of squares | df | Mean square | F |
|--------|----------------|----|-------------|----|
| Between | | | | |
| Factor A (volume) | 117.45 | 2 | 58.73 | $F_A$ |
| Factor B (gender) | 93.39 | 1 | 93.39 | $F_B$ |
| Interaction (vol × gen) | 102.77 | 2 | 51.39 | $F_{A \times B}$ |
| Within | 98.67 | 12 | 8.22 | |
| Total | 412.28 | 17 | | |

Thus, we have

$$F_B = \frac{93.39}{8.22} = 11.36$$

**THE COMPUTATIONAL FORMULA FOR $F_{A \times B}$ FOR THE INTERACTION EFFECT IS**

$$F_{A \times B} = \frac{MS_{A \times B}}{MS_{wn}}$$

Thus, we have

$$F_{A \times B} = \frac{51.39}{8.22} = 6.25$$

And now, the completed summary table is shown in Table 14.9.

## Interpreting Each $F_{obt}$

Once we have completed the summary table, we determine whether each $F_{obt}$ is significant in the same way we did in the previous chapter: we compare each $F_{obt}$ to the appropriate value of $F_{crit}$. To find each $F_{crit}$ in the $F$-tables (Table 5 in Appendix D), we need the $df_{bn}$ and the $df_{wn}$ used in computing each $F_{obt}$.

1. To find $F_{crit}$ for testing $F_A$, we use $df_A$ as the $df$ between groups and $df_{wn}$. In our example, $df_A = 2$ and $df_{wn} = 12$. So, for $\alpha = .05$, the $F_{crit}$ for 2 and 12 $df$ is 3.88.

**TABLE 14.9**   Summary Table of Two-Way ANOVA

| Source | Sum of squares | df | Mean square | F |
|--------|----------------|-----|-------------|---|
| Between | | | | |
| Factor A (volume) | 117.45 | 2 | 58.73 | 7.14 |
| Factor B (gender) | 93.39 | 1 | 93.39 | 11.36 |
| Interaction (vol × gen) | 102.77 | 2 | 51.39 | 6.25 |
| Within | 98.67 | 12 | 8.22 | |
| Total | 412.28 | 17 | | |

2. To find $F_{crit}$ for testing $F_B$, we use $df_B$ as the $df$ between groups and $df_{wn}$. In our example, $df_B = 1$ and $df_{wn} = 12$. So, at $\alpha = .05$, the $F_{crit}$ for 1 and 12 $df$ is 4.75.

3. To find $F_{crit}$ for the interaction, we use $df_{A \times B}$ as the $df$ between groups and $df_{wn}$. In our example, $df_{A \times B} = 2$ and $df_{wn} = 12$. Thus, at $\alpha = .05$, the $F_{crit}$ for 2 and 12 $df$ is 3.88.

Note that since the $df$ for factor B is different from the $df$ for factor A, the $F_{crit}$ for factor B is different from the $F_{crit}$ for factor A.

> **STAT ALERT** Each $F_{crit}$ in the two-way ANOVA will be different if the degrees of freedom between groups are different.

Thus, we end up comparing our values of $F_{obt}$ from our ANOVA summary table with our values of $F_{crit}$, as follows:

|  | $F_{obt}$ | $F_{crit}$ |
|---|---|---|
| Main effect of volume (A) | 7.14 | 3.88 |
| Main effect of gender (B) | 11.36 | 4.75 |
| Interaction (A × B) | 6.25 | 3.88 |

By now, you can do this with your eyes closed: Imagine a sampling distribution with a region of rejection and $F_{crit}$ in the positive tail. (If you can't imagine this, look back in Chapter 13 at Figure 13.1.) Since our obtained $F_A$ of 7.14 is larger than the $F_{crit}$, $F_A$ falls in the region of rejection. Therefore, we conclude that differences between the means for the levels of factor A are significant: changing the volume of a message produces significant differences in persuasiveness scores. However, remember that a significant $F_{obt}$ only indicates that, somewhere in the factor, at least two of the means differ significantly. Therefore, since $\alpha = .05$, we are confident that changing volume results in at least two different population means. We report our results as

$$F_A(2, 12) = 7.14, \quad p < .05$$

Likewise, our $F_B$ is significant, so we conclude that the males and females in our study represent different populations of scores. We report this result as

$$F_B(1, 12) = 11.36, \quad p < .05$$

Finally, our $F_{A \times B}$ of 6.25 is significant, so we conclude that the specific combinations of the levels of our factors produce means that represent an interaction in the population. We report this interaction effect as

$$F_{A \times B}(2, 12) = 6.25, \quad p < .05$$

This indicates that the effect of changing the volume on the population *depends on* whether it is a population of males or a population of females. Or, we can say that the difference between the male and female populations of scores *depends on* whether a message is played at the soft, medium, or loud level.

> **STAT ALERT**  A significant two-way interaction indicates that as we change the levels of one factor, we change the relationship found in the population between the other factor and the dependent scores.

Note: It is just a coincidence of the particular data in our example that all three values of $F_{obt}$ were significant. Whether any one $F_{obt}$ is significant does not influence whether any other $F_{obt}$ is significant. With different data, any combination of the main effects and/or the interaction may or may not be significant.

At this point we have completed our ANOVA. However, we are a long way from being finished with our analysis. Because each significant $F_{obt}$ indicates only that a difference exists somewhere among the means we tested, we now must examine those means.

## INTERPRETING THE TWO-WAY EXPERIMENT

To understand and interpret the results of a two-way ANOVA, we must examine each significant main effect and interaction by graphing the means and performing the *post hoc* comparisons on those means.

First we want to look at each effect by graphing it.

### Graphing the Effects

To interpret our persuasiveness study, we again look at the various means shown in Table 14.10.

**Graphing main effects**  We graph the main effect of factor A by plotting the main effect means from each level of factor A (the column means across the bottom of Table 14.10). We graph the main effects of factor B separately by plotting the main effect means from each level of factor B (the row means at the right of Table 14.10). As usual, we plot the dependent variable along the $Y$ axis and the levels of each factor along the $X$ axis. Figure 14.1 shows the resulting graphs of the main effects in our persuasiveness study. Note that since

**TABLE 14.10** Summary of Means for Persuasiveness Study

|  |  | *Factor A: volume* | | | |
|---|---|---|---|---|---|
|  |  | $A_1:$ soft | $A_2:$ medium | $A_3:$ loud |  |
| **Factor B: gender** | $B_1:$ male | $\overline{X} = 8$ | $\overline{X} = 11$ | $\overline{X} = 16.67$ | $\overline{X}_{male} = 11.89$ |
|  | $B_2:$ female | $\overline{X} = 4$ | $\overline{X} = 12$ | $\overline{X} = 6$ | $\overline{X}_{fem} = 7.33$ |

$$\overline{X}_{soft} = 6 \qquad \overline{X}_{med} = 11.5 \qquad \overline{X}_{loud} = 11.33$$

volume is measured in decibels, the $X$ axis of the volume factor should be labeled in decibels. Also note that we graph the main effect of our gender variable as a bar graph because, as discussed in Chapter 4, this is how we graph means from a nominal independent variable.

The graphs reflect the same differences we see by comparing the means in Table 14.10 above. In the right-hand graph, we see that males scored higher than females. In the left-hand graph, the slanting line between soft and medium volume suggests a large (possibly significant) difference between those means.

**FIGURE 14.1** Graphs Showing Main Effects of Volume and Gender

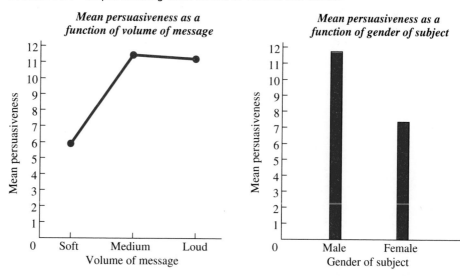

However, the line between medium and loud volume is close to horizontal and the means are close to equal, so there may not be a significant difference here. To specifically determine which means differ significantly, we perform *post hoc* comparisons. But first we will graph our significant interaction.

**Graphing the interaction effect**   An interaction can be a beast to interpret, so always graph it! To graph the interaction, we plot all cell means on a *single* graph. As usual, we place the dependent variable along the $Y$ axis. However, we have two independent variables (here volume and subject gender), but only one $X$ axis. To solve this problem, we place the levels of one factor along the $X$ axis. We show the second factor by drawing on the graph a separate line connecting the means for each level of the second factor. Since we must use one line on the graph for each level of the second factor, we typically place the factor with more levels on the $X$ axis so that there are as few lines as possible. Thus, for our persuasiveness study, we label the $X$ axis with the three volume levels. Then, plotting the cell means from Table 14.10 above, we connect the three means for males with one line and the three means for females with a different line. The graph of the interaction between volume and subject gender is shown in Figure 14.2.

**FIGURE 14.2**   Graph of Interaction, Showing Mean Persuasiveness as a Function of Volume of Message and Subject Gender

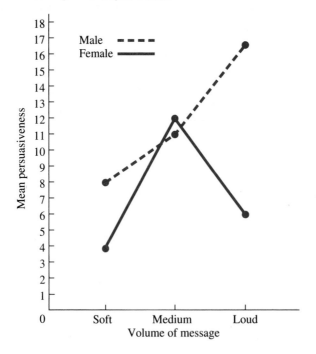

The way to read the graph is to look at one line at a time. Thus, for males (the dashed line), as we increased volume, mean persuasiveness scores increased. However, for females (the solid line), as we increased volume, persuasiveness scores first increased but then decreased. Thus, the effect of increasing volume was not the same for males as for females. Instead, the effect of increasing volume on persuasiveness scores *depends* on whether the subjects are male or female. There is a positive linear relationship between scores and increasing volume for males and a nonlinear relationship between scores and increasing volume for females.

Of course, if the interaction were not significant, then we would have no reason to believe that changing the volume had different effects on males and females, regardless of what our graph suggested. Further, we do not know which of these cell means actually differ significantly, because we haven't performed the *post hoc* comparisons yet.

Before we get to the *post hoc* tests, however, note one final aspect of an interaction. An interaction can produce an infinite variety of different graphs, but the key is that *a significant interaction will produce a graph on which the lines are not parallel*. When the lines are not parallel, each line depicts a *different* relationship. Conversely, a nonsignificant interaction will produce a graph on which the lines are basically parallel, with each line depicting basically the same relationship. For example, say that our data had produced one of the two graphs in Figure 14.3. On the left-hand graph, we have the ultimate in nonparallel lines. Here, as we change the levels of A, the mean scores either increase or decrease, *depending* on the level of B we are talking about. Therefore, this graph depicts an interaction. However, in the right-hand graph, the lines are parallel. Here, as we change the levels of A, the scores increase, regardless of which level of factor B we examine. Therefore, this graph does not depict an interaction. (The fact that, *overall*, the scores are higher in $B_1$ than in $B_2$ is the main effect produced by changing the levels of factor B.)

**FIGURE 14.3** Two Graphs Showing When an Interaction Is and Is Not Present

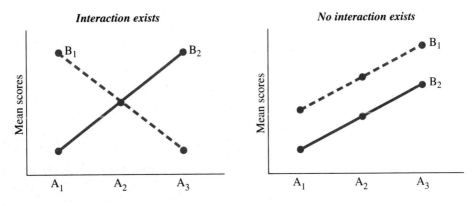

Think of significance testing of the interaction $F_{A \times B}$ as testing whether the lines are significantly different from parallel. When an interaction is *not* significant, the lines on the graph are not significantly different from parallel, so they may represent parallel lines that would be found if we graphed the means of the populations. Conversely, when an interaction is significant, somewhere in the graph the lines *do* differ significantly from parallel. Thus, if we graphed the means of the populations, the lines probably would not be parallel, and there would be an interaction in the population.

## Performing the Post Hoc Comparisons

As usual, we perform *post hoc* comparisons on the means from any *significant* $F_{obt}$. If we have unequal $n$'s between the levels of a factor, we perform Fisher's protected *t*-test, as described in the previous chapter. If the $n$'s in all levels of a factor are equal, we perform Tukey's *HSD* procedure. However, recognize that the *post hoc* comparisons for an interaction effect are computed differently from those for a main effect.

**Performing Tukey's *HSD* for main effects**   We perform the *post hoc* comparisons on *each* significant main effect, as if it were a one-way ANOVA. We compare all of the column means in factor A, then we compare all of the row means in factor B.

Recall that the computational formula for the *HSD* is

$$HSD = (q_k) \left( \sqrt{\frac{MS_{wn}}{n}} \right)$$

where $MS_{wn}$ is the denominator of the $F_{obt}$, $q_k$ is found in Table 6 for $df_{wn}$ and $k$ (where $k$ is the number of levels in the factor), and $n$ is the number of scores in a level. *But,* tread carefully here: for each factor, there may be a different value of $n$ and $k$! In our persuasiveness study, six scores went into each mean for a level of volume, but nine scores went into each mean for a level of subject gender. *The n is always the number of scores used to compute each mean you are comparing.* Also, since $q_k$ depends on $k$, different factors having different numbers of levels will have different values of $q_k$.

> **STAT ALERT**   We must compute a different *HSD* for each main effect when their $k$'s or $n$'s are different.

In our persuasiveness study, for the volume factor we have three means for the main effect, so $k = 3$, and the $n$ of each mean is 6. In our ANOVA we found $MS_{wn} = 8.22$ and $df_{wn} = 12$. From Table 6, for $\alpha = .05$, we find $q_k =$

3.77. Placing these values in the above formula gives

$$HSD = (q_k)\left(\sqrt{\frac{MS_{wn}}{n}}\right) = (3.77)\left(\sqrt{\frac{8.22}{6}}\right) = 4.41$$

Thus, the *HSD* for factor A is 4.41.
  Finding the differences between all pairs of means, we have

*Factor A: volume*

| $A_1$:<br>soft | $A_2$:<br>medium | $A_3$:<br>loud |
|---|---|---|
| $\overline{X} = 6$ | $\overline{X} = 11.5$ | $\overline{X} = 11.33$ |

5.50          0.17
5.33

*HSD* = 4.41

In the middle of each line connecting two means is the absolute difference between them. The mean for soft volume differs from the means for medium and loud by more than the *HSD* of 4.41. Thus, soft volume produces a significant difference from the other volumes. Since the means for medium and loud volume differ by less than 4.41, these conditions do *not* differ significantly.
  Since factor B (subject gender) contains only two levels, we do not perform *post hoc* comparisons (it must be that the mean for males differs significantly from the mean for females). If, however, there were more than two levels in a significant factor B, we would compute the appropriate *HSD* for the *n* and *k* in that factor and compare the factor B main effect means.

**Performing Tukey's *HSD* for the interaction**  In performing *post hoc* comparisons on a significant interaction, we compare the cell means. However, we do *not* compare every cell mean to every other cell mean. Look again at the diagram of the interaction in Table 14.11. If we compare cells that are diagonally positioned, we are comparing apples to oranges. For example, if we compare the mean for males at the soft volume to the mean for females at the loud volume, we do not know what produced the difference in scores, because the two cells differ in terms of subject gender *and* volume. We have a confused, or confounded, comparison. A **confounded comparison** occurs when two cells differ along more than one factor. In performing *post hoc* comparisons of an interaction, we perform only **unconfounded comparisons,** in which two cells

**TABLE 14.11**  *Summary of Interaction Means for Persuasiveness Study*

| | | *Factor A: volume* | | |
|---|---|---|---|---|
| | | $A_1$: soft | $A_2$: medium | $A_3$: loud |
| **Factor B: gender** | $B_1$: male | $\overline{X} = 8$ | $\overline{X} = 11$ | $\overline{X} = 16.67$ |
| | $B_2$: female | $\overline{X} = 4$ | $\overline{X} = 12$ | $\overline{X} = 6$ |

differ along only one factor. Therefore, we compare only cell means within the same column or within the same row.

When we have equal $n$'s in all cells, we can compare the means in the interaction using a slight variation of the Tukey *HSD*.[1] Previously when we computed the *HSD*, we found $q_k$ in Table 6 using $k$, the number of means being compared. To compute the *HSD* for an interaction, we must first determine the *adjusted k*. This $k$ adjusts for the number of unconfounded comparisons we can make out of all the cell means in our interaction. We obtain our adjusted $k$ from Table 14.12. In the left-hand column, locate the design of the study you are examining. The numbers must correspond to the numbers of the levels in the factors of your ANOVA, but do not be concerned about the order of the numbers. For example, we called our persuasiveness study a 3 $\times$ 2 study, so we look at the row labeled "2 $\times$ 3." Reading across that row, as a double check we confirm that the middle column contains the total number of cell means in the interaction (yup, we have 6). In the right-hand column is the adjusted value of $k$ (for our example, it is 5).

The adjusted value of $k$ is the value of $k$ we use in obtaining $q_k$ from Table 6. Thus, for our persuasiveness study, we find that, with $\alpha = .05$, $df_{wn} = 12$, and adjusted $k = 5$, our $q_k = 4.51$. Now we compute the *HSD* using the same old formula we used previously. Our $MS_{wn}$ is 8.22, and $n$ is 3, the number of scores in each *cell*. We have

$$HSD = (q_k)\left(\sqrt{\frac{MS_{wn}}{n}}\right) = (4.51)\left(\sqrt{\frac{8.22}{3}}\right) = 7.47$$

Thus, the *HSD* for our interaction is 7.47.

Now we determine the differences between all cell means within each column and between all cell means within each row. To see these differences, we can

---

[1]Adapted from D.V. Cicchetti (1972), Extension of Multiple Range Tests to Interaction Tables in the Analysis of Variance, *Psychological Bulletin, 77,* 405–408.

**TABLE 14.12** Values of Adjusted $k$

| Design of study | Number of cell means in study | Adjusted value of $k$ |
|---|---|---|
| 2 × 2 | 4 | 3 |
| 2 × 3 | 6 | 5 |
| 2 × 4 | 8 | 6 |
| 3 × 3 | 9 | 7 |
| 3 × 4 | 12 | 8 |
| 4 × 4 | 16 | 10 |
| 4 × 5 | 20 | 12 |

arrange our interaction means as shown in Table 14.13. In the middle of each line connecting two cells is the absolute difference between the two means.

Any difference between two means that is larger than our HSD of 7.47 is a significant difference. We have only three significant differences here, (1) between the mean for females at the soft volume and the mean for females at the medium volume, (2) between the mean for males at the soft volume and the mean for males at the loud volume, and (3) between the mean for males at the loud volume and the mean for females at the loud volume.

## Interpreting the Overall Results of the Experiment

There is no *one* way to interpret all experiments, because the data in each experiment indicate something different. Our goal is to come up with a complete, honest, and simplified description of the results of the study. We do that

**TABLE 14.13** Table of Interaction Means

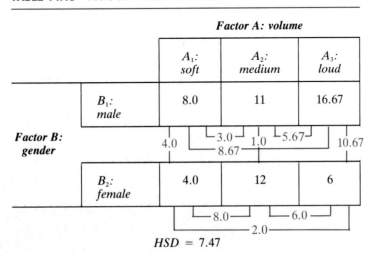

*HSD* = 7.47

by looking at the significant *post hoc* comparisons within all significant main effects and interaction effects.

We can summarize the differences we found in the persuasiveness study using the diagram in Table 14.14. Outside of the diagram are the main effect means. Each line connecting two means indicates that they differ significantly. Inside the diagram, each line connecting two cell means indicates a significant difference within the interaction.

Both of the main effects and the interaction produced significant values of $F_{obt}$. However, recognize that often our conclusions about significant main effects must be qualified (or are downright untrue) given a significant interaction. For example, there is a significant difference between the main effect means of males and females. If there were not a significant interaction, we could conclude that, overall, males score higher than females. However, our interaction contradicts the overall pattern suggested by the main effect, so we *cannot* make an overall, general conclusion about differences between males and females. When we look at the cell means of the interaction, we see that gender differences *depend* on the volume: only in the loud condition is there a significant difference between males and females. (This difference is so large that it produces an overall mean for males that is larger than the overall mean for females.)

Likewise, the interpretation of the effect of changing volume rests on the interaction. We cannot make an overall conclusion based on the main effect, which showed that soft volume was significantly different from both the medium and loud volumes. The interaction indicates that increasing the volume from soft to medium produced a significant difference only in females, and increasing the volume from soft to loud produced a significant difference only in males.

**TABLE 14.14**  Summary of Significant Differences in Our Persuasiveness Study

*Each line connects two means that differ significantly.*

|  |  | Factor A: volume | | | |
|---|---|---|---|---|---|
|  |  | Level $A_1$: soft | Level $A_2$: medium | Level $A_3$: loud |  |
| Factor B: gender | Level $B_1$: male | 8.0 | 11 | 16.67 | $\overline{X} = 11.89$ |
|  | Level $B_2$: female | 4.0 | 12 | 6 | $\overline{X} = 7.33$ |

$\overline{X}_{soft} = 6$   $\overline{X}_{med} = 11.5$   $\overline{X}_{loud} = 11.33$

As the above example illustrates, we usually must limit our interpretation of a study to the interaction when it is significant. When the interaction is not significant, then we focus on any significant main effects.

> ***STAT ALERT***  The primary interpretation of a two-way ANOVA rests on the interpretation of the significant interaction.

Thus, we conclude that increasing volume beyond soft does tend to increase persuasiveness scores in the population, but this occurs for females with medium volume and for males with loud volume. Further, we conclude that differences in persuasiveness scores between males and females do occur in the population, but only if the volume of the message is loud.

Remember experiment-wise error, the probability of a Type I error some-where in our conclusions? Well, after all of the above shenanigans, we have protected our experiment-wise error, so that for all of these conclusions to-gether, the probability of a Type I error is still $p < .05$. Also, remember power—the probability of not making a Type II error? All that we said in previous chapters about power applies to the two-way ANOVA as well. Thus, for any of the differences that are not significant, we must be concerned about whether we have maximized our power by maximizing the difference between the means, minimizing the variability within each cell, and having a large enough $n$.

To round out our analysis of an experiment, we should consider two addi-tional procedures: computing the proportion of variance accounted for and computing confidence intervals.

## Describing the Proportion of Variance Accounted For: Eta Squared

Remember that eta squared ($\eta^2$) describes the proportion of variance in the dependent scores that is accounted for by an independent variable. We compute a separate eta squared for each *significant* main and interaction effect. The formula for eta squared is

$$\eta^2 = \frac{\text{sum of squares for the effect}}{SS_{tot}}$$

To compute each eta squared, we divide the sum of squares for the effect, either $SS_A$, $SS_B$, or $SS_{A \times B}$, by $SS_{tot}$. For example, in our persuasiveness study, for factor A (volume), $SS_A$ was 117.45 and $SS_{tot}$ was 412.28. Therefore, we have

$$\eta_A^2 = \frac{SS_A}{SS_{tot}} = \frac{117.45}{412.28} = .28$$

Thus, if we predict subjects' scores using the main effect mean of the volume they were tested under, we can account for .28, or 28%, of the total variance in persuasiveness scores in our data. Following the same procedure for the gender factor, we have an $SS_B$ of 93.39, so $\eta_B^2$ is .23: using the main effect mean for each subject's gender, we can account for an additional 23% of the variance in scores. Finally, for the interaction of volume and gender, $SS_{A \times B}$ is 102.77, so $\eta_{A \times B}^2$ is .25: using the mean of the cell that subjects were in to predict their scores, we can account for an additional 25% of the variance in scores.

Recall that eta squared is a measure of our effect size. Since each of the above effects has about the same size, they are all of equal importance in explaining differences in persuasiveness scores in our experiment. However, suppose that one effect accounted for only .01, or 1%, of the total variance. Such a small $\eta^2$ indicates that this relationship is very inconsistent. Therefore, it is not a very useful or informative relationship, and we are better served by emphasizing the other, larger significant effects. In essence, eta squared tells us that this effect was not a big deal in our experiment, so we should not make a big deal out of it in our interpretation.

Usually we are content to describe the effect size in our sample data by computing eta squared. However, we can also estimate the effect size in the population by computing omega squared ($\omega^2$) for each factor or interaction (using the formula presented in Chapter 13).

### Confidence Intervals for a Single $\mu$

We can compute the confidence interval for the population $\mu$ that is represented by the mean of a level from a main effect or cell from the interaction. We use the formula presented in the previous chapter, which was

$$\left( \sqrt{\frac{MS_{wn}}{n}} \right)(-t_{crit}) + \overline{X} \leq \mu \leq \left( \sqrt{\frac{MS_{wn}}{n}} \right)(+t_{crit}) + \overline{X}$$

where $t_{crit}$ is the two-tailed value at the appropriate $\alpha$ with $df = df_{wn}$, $MS_{wn}$ is from our ANOVA summary table, $\overline{X}$ is the mean for the level or a cell we are describing, and $n$ is the number of scores that the mean is based on.

## SUMMARY OF THE STEPS IN PERFORMING A TWO-WAY ANOVA

Everything we have discussed in this chapter is summarized in the following steps for performing a two-way ANOVA:

1. Design the experiment, check the assumptions, and collect the data.

2. Compute the sums of squares between groups for each main effect and for the interaction, and compute the sum of squares within groups. Dividing each sum of squares by the appropriate *df* produces the mean square between groups for each main effect and the interaction, as well as the mean square within groups. Dividing each mean square between groups by the mean square within groups produces an $F_{obt}$

3. Find $F_{crit}$ in Table 5, using the *df* between groups for each factor or interaction and the $df_{wn}$. If the $F_{obt}$ is larger than $F_{crit}$, then there is a significant difference between two or more of the means for that factor or interaction.

4. Graph the main effects by plotting the mean of each level of a factor, with the dependent variable on the *Y* axis and the levels of the factor on the *X* axis. Graph the interaction by plotting the cell means. Place the levels of one factor on the *X* axis, and in the body of the graph use a separate line to connect the means from each level of the other factor.

5. Perform *post hoc* comparisons for each significant main effect or interaction.

6. Based on significant main and/or interaction effects and the specific means from cells and levels that differ significantly, develop an overall conclusion regarding the relationships demonstrated by the study.

7. Compute eta squared to describe the proportion of variance in dependent scores accounted for by each significant main effect or interaction in the experiment.

8. Compute the confidence interval for the value of $\mu$ represented by the mean in any relevant level or cell.

Congratulations, you are getting *very* good at this stuff.

---

## A WORD ON REPEATED MEASURES AND MIXED DESIGNS

Recall that experiments with a repeated measures factor measure the same subjects repeatedly under all levels of the factor. When both factors are repeated measures factors, we perform a two-way, repeated measures ANOVA. If a study has a mix of one repeated measures factor and one between-subjects factor, we perform a mixed design ANOVA. Although the computations for repeated measures and mixed designs are different from those for the between-subjects design discussed here, the logic is the same: the individual factors and the interaction are each treated as a one-way ANOVA, and a significant $F_{obt}$ indicates that at least two of the corresponding means differ significantly.

## FINALLY

Technically there is no limit to the number of factors we can have in an ANOVA. There is, however, a practical limit to how many factors we can *interpret,* especially when we try to interpret the interaction. Say that we add a third factor—the sex of the speaker of the message—to our previous two-way persuasiveness study. We then have a three-way ($3 \times 2 \times 2$) ANOVA in which we compute an $F_{obt}$ for the main effect of each factor: A (volume), B (subject gender) and C (speaker gender). We also have an $F_{obt}$ for each of three two-way interactions (A $\times$ B, A $\times$ C, and B $\times$ C). In addition, we have an $F_{obt}$ for a three-way interaction (A $\times$ B $\times$ C)! If it's significant, it indicates that the interaction between volume and subject gender changes, depending on the sex of the speaker.

If this sounds very complicated, it's because it *is* very complicated. Further, to graph a $3 \times 2 \times 2$ interaction, you would have to draw at least four lines on *one* graph! Three-way interactions are very difficult to interpret, and interactions containing four or more factors tend to be practically impossible to interpret. Therefore, unless you have a very good reason for including many factors in one study, it is best to limit a study to two or, at most, three factors. You may not learn about many variables at once, but what you do learn you will understand.

## CHAPTER SUMMARY

*1.* In a two-way, between-subjects ANOVA, there are two independent variables, and all of the conditions of both factors contain independent samples. In a *complete factorial design,* each level of one factor is combined with all levels of the other factor. Each *cell* is formed by a particular combination of a level from each factor. In ANOVA, we examine the *main effects* of manipulating each variable separately, as well as the *interaction effect* of manipulating both variables simultaneously.

*2.* The *assumptions* of the two-way ANOVA are that (a) each cell is a random sample of interval or ratio scores, (b) the populations represented in the study are normally distributed, and (c) the variances of all populations are homogeneous.

*3.* We perform a two-way ANOVA as three one-way ANOVAs, computing an $F_{obt}$ for each main effect and for the interaction. For the means in each main effect, we *collapse across* the levels of the other factor. For the interaction, we do not collapse: we examine all cell means in the experiment.

*4.* A significant $F_{obt}$ for a main effect indicates that at least two main effect means from the factor represent significant differences in scores. We graph the effect of the factor by plotting the mean score for each level.

**5.** A significant $F_{obt}$ for an interaction indicates that the effect of changing the levels of one factor is not the same for each level of the other factor. In other words, the effect of changing the levels of one factor *depends on* which level of the other factor you examine. Therefore, the relationship between one factor and the dependent variable changes as we change the levels of the other factor. When graphed, an interaction produces *nonparallel lines*.

**6.** We perform *post hoc comparisons* on each significant effect having more than two levels, to determine which specific means differ significantly. In performing *post hoc* comparisons on the interaction, we make only *unconfounded* comparisons. The means from two cells are unconfounded if the cells differ along only one factor. Two means are *confounded* if the cells differ along more than one factor.

**7.** We draw conclusions from a two-way ANOVA by considering the significant main and interaction effects and which levels or cells differ significantly. Usually, we cannot draw conclusions about the main effects when the interaction is significant.

**8.** *Eta squared* is computed to describe the effect size of each significant main effect and interaction. A confidence interval can be computed for the $\mu$ represented by any $\overline{X}$ in the study.

---

## USING THE COMPUTER

Thankfully, the computer program performs the two-way, between-subjects ANOVA for you in routine **8**. For each main effect, it computes the $\overline{X}$ and $s_X$ of each level, presents a graph of the means, and calculates $F_{obt}$ and the minimum value of $p(\alpha)$ at which $F_{obt}$ is significant. The program also computes each cell mean (and $s_X$) for the interaction, graphs the interaction, and computes the interaction $F_{obt}$ (with its $p$ value). For each main effect and interaction, the program also performs the Tukey *HSD* test and computes eta squared. To compute a confidence interval for the mean of a level or cell, enter the data from that level or cell into the one-sample $t$-test in routine **5**.

---

## PRACTICE PROBLEMS

(Answers are provided for odd-numbered problems.)

*1.* Identify the following terms:

    *a.* two-way

b. factorial

c. cell

d. two-way, between-subjects design

2. What is meant by a main effect?

3. What is meant by a two-way interaction effect?

4. Describe how a two-way ANOVA consists of three one-way ANOVAs.

5. For a 2 × 2 ANOVA, what are (a) the statistical hypotheses for factor A, (b) the statistical hypotheses for factor B, and (c) the statistical hypotheses for A × B?

6. What does it mean to collapse across a factor?

7. The following table shows the main effect and cell means from a study:

**Factor A**

|  |  | Level $A_1$ | Level $A_2$ |  |
|---|---|---|---|---|
| **Factor B** | Level $B_1$ | 14 | 23 | 18.5 |
|  | Level $B_2$ | 25 | 12 | 18.5 |
|  |  | 19.5 | 17.5 |  |

a. Describe the graph of the interaction means.

b. Why is (or is not) this an interaction?

c. Why does the interaction prohibit making conclusions based on main effects?

8. What is meant by a confounded comparison and an unconfounded comparison?

9. A study compared males and females tested either early or late in the day. Here are the data:

**Factor A**

|  |  | Level $A_1$: males | Level $A_2$: females |
|---|---|---|---|
| **Factor B** | Level $B_1$: early | 6<br>11<br>9<br>10<br>9 | 8<br>14<br>17<br>16<br>19 |
|  | Level $B_2$: late | 8<br>10<br>9<br>7<br>10 | 4<br>6<br>5<br>5<br>7 |

a. Using $\alpha$ = .05, perform an ANOVA.

b. Compute the main effect means and interaction means.

c. Perform the appropriate *post hoc* comparisons.

d. What do you conclude about the relationships this study demonstrates?

e. Compute the effect size where appropriate.

10. With two levels of A and four levels of B, we compute the following sums of squares ($n$ = 5 and $N$ = 40):

| Source | Sum of squares | df | Mean square | F |
|---|---|---|---|---|
| Between | | | | |
| Factor A | 8.42 | ___ | ___ | ___ |
| Factor B | 76.79 | ___ | ___ | ___ |
| Interaction | 23.71 | ___ | ___ | ___ |
| Within | 110.72 | ___ | ___ | |
| Total | 219.64 | ___ | | |

a. Complete the ANOVA summary table.

b. With $\alpha$ = .05, what do you conclude about each $F_{obt}$?

c. Compute the appropriate values of *HSD*.

d. For the levels of factor B, the means are $\overline{X}_1$ = 18.36, $\overline{X}_2$ = 20.02, $\overline{X}_3$ = 24.6, and $\overline{X}_4$ = 27.3. What should you conclude about the main effect of B?

e. What is the effect size of factor B?

## SUMMARY OF FORMULAS

The general format for the summary table for a two-way between-subjects ANOVA is

Summary Table of Two-Way ANOVA

| Source | Sum of squares | df | Mean square | F |
|---|---|---|---|---|
| Between | | | | |
| Factor A | $SS_A$ | $df_A$ | $MS_A$ | $F_A$ |
| Factor B | $SS_B$ | $df_B$ | $MS_B$ | $F_B$ |
| Interaction | $SS_{A \times B}$ | $df_{A \times B}$ | $MS_{A \times B}$ | $F_{A \times B}$ |
| Within | $SS_{wn}$ | $df_{wn}$ | $MS_{wn}$ | |
| Total | $SS_{tot}$ | $df_{tot}$ | | |

*1.* Computing the sums of squares
   a. *The computational formula for $SS_{tot}$ is*

$$SS_{tot} = \Sigma X_{tot}^2 - \left( \frac{(\Sigma X_{tot})^2}{N} \right)$$

   b. *The computational formula for the sum of squares between groups for the column factor A is*

$$SS_A = \Sigma \left( \frac{(\text{sum of scores in the column})^2}{n \text{ of scores in the column}} \right) - \left( \frac{(\Sigma X_{tot})^2}{N} \right)$$

   c. *The computational formula for the sum of squares between groups for the row factor B is*

$$SS_B = \Sigma \left( \frac{(\text{sum of scores in the row})^2}{n \text{ of scores in the row}} \right) - \left( \frac{(\Sigma X_{tot})^2}{N} \right)$$

   d. *The computational formula for the sum of squares between groups for the interaction, $SS_{A \times B}$, is*

$$SS_{A \times B} = SS_{bn} - SS_A - SS_B$$

   where $SS_{bn}$ is found using the formula

$$SS_{bn} = \Sigma \left( \frac{(\text{sum of scores in the cell})^2}{n \text{ of scores in the cell}} \right) - \left( \frac{(\Sigma X_{tot})^2}{N} \right)$$

   e. *The computational formula for the sum of squares within groups, $SS_{wn}$, is*

$$SS_{wn} = SS_{tot} - SS_{bn}$$

*2.* Computing the degrees of freedom
   a. The degrees of freedom between groups for factor A, $df_A$, equals $k_A - 1$, where $k_A$ is the number of levels in factor A.
   b. The degrees of freedom between groups for factor B, $df_B$, equals $k_B - 1$, where $k_B$ is the number of levels in factor B.
   c. The degrees of freedom between groups for the interaction, $df_{A \times B}$, equals $df_A$ multiplied times $df_B$.
   d. The degrees of freedom within groups equals $N - k$, where $N$ is the total $N$ of the study and $k$ is the total number of cells in the study.

*3.* Computing the mean square
   a. *The formula for $MS_A$ is*

$$MS_A = \frac{SS_A}{df_A}$$

b. *The formula for $MS_B$ is*

$$MS_B = \frac{SS_B}{df_B}$$

c. *The formula for $MS_{A \times B}$ is*

$$MS_{A \times B} = \frac{SS_{A \times B}}{df_{A \times B}}$$

d. *The formula for $MS_{wn}$ is*

$$MS_{wn} = \frac{SS_{wn}}{df_{wn}}$$

**4.** Computing $F_{obt}$
   a. *The formula for $F_A$ is*

$$F_A = \frac{MS_A}{MS_{wn}}$$

   b. *The formula for $F_B$ is*

$$F_B = \frac{MS_B}{MS_{wn}}$$

   c. *The formula for $F_{A \times B}$ is*

$$F_{A \times B} = \frac{MS_{A \times B}}{MS_{wn}}$$

**5.** The critical values of $F$ are found in Table 5 of Appendix D.
   a. To find $F_{crit}$ to test $F_A$, use $df_A$ and $df_{wn}$.
   b. To find $F_{crit}$ to test $F_B$, use $df_B$ and $df_{wn}$.
   c. To find $F_{crit}$ to test $F_{A \times B}$, use $df_{A \times B}$ and $df_{wn}$.

**6.** Performing Tukey's *HSD post hoc* comparisons
   a. *For each significant main effect, the computational formula for the HSD is*

$$HSD = (q_k) \left( \sqrt{\frac{MS_{wn}}{n}} \right)$$

where $q_k$ is found in Table 6 for $k$ equal to the number of levels in the factor, $MS_{wn}$ is the denominator of $F_{obt}$, and $n$ is the number of scores used to compute each mean in the factor. Any means that differ by an amount that is greater than the value of *HSD* are significantly different.

b. *For a significant interaction, the HSD is computed as follows.*
  (1) Enter the following table for the design (or number of cells), and obtain the adjusted value of $k$.

Values of Adjusted $k$

| Design of study | Number of cell means in study | Adjusted value of k |
|---|---|---|
| 2 × 2 | 4 | 3 |
| 2 × 3 | 6 | 5 |
| 2 × 4 | 8 | 6 |
| 3 × 3 | 9 | 7 |
| 3 × 4 | 12 | 8 |
| 4 × 4 | 16 | 10 |
| 4 × 5 | 20 | 12 |

  (2) Enter Table 6 for the value of $q_k$, using the adjusted $k$ and $df_{wn}$ at the appropriate $\alpha$.
  (3) Compute the value of *HSD* as described in step 6.a, above.
  (4) Any unconfounded cell means that differ by an amount that is greater than the value of *HSD* are significantly different.

7. *The computational formula for eta squared is*

$$\eta^2 = \frac{\text{sum of squares for the effect}}{SS_{tot}}$$

When $\eta^2$ is computed for factor A, factor B, or the A × B interaction, the sum of squares for the effect is $SS_A$, $SS_B$, or $SS_{A \times B}$, respectively.

8. *The computational formula for computing the confidence interval for a single* $\mu$, *using the results of a between-subjects ANOVA, is*

$$\left( \sqrt{\frac{MS_{wn}}{n}} \right)(-t_{crit}) + \overline{X} \leq \mu \leq \left( \sqrt{\frac{MS_{wn}}{n}} \right)(+t_{crit}) + \overline{X}$$

where $t_{crit}$ is the two-tailed value at the appropriate $\alpha$ with $df = df_{wn}$, $MS_{wn}$ is from the ANOVA, and $\overline{X}$ and $n$ are from the level or cell being described.

# 15

# Nonparametric Procedures for Frequency Data and Ranked Data

Throughout the preceding chapters we performed parametric inferential statistics in which we assumed that our samples represented raw score populations that were normally distributed, that all population variances were homogeneous, and that the dependent variable was from an interval or ratio variable. These assumptions are necessary for our various sampling distributions to be appropriate. However, we cannot insist on using a parametric procedure if we seriously violate its assumptions. If we use a parametric test under such conditions, the actual probability of a Type I error will be substantially larger than our alpha level. Therefore, in such instances we turn to nonparametric procedures.

As the name implies, nonparametric procedures do not require that we make such assumptions about the parameters of the populations represented by our samples. In particular, we do not need to assume that the populations form a normal distribution or any particularly shaped distribution. For this reason, nonparametric procedures are also called *distribution-free procedures*. We use nonparametric statistics when we have scores from very skewed or otherwise nonnormal distributions, when the samples have significantly heterogeneous variances, or when our scores are from an ordinal (ranked) or nominal (categorical) variable.

Nonparametric procedures are still inferential statistics that we use to decide whether the differences between our samples represent differences we would find in the populations. Therefore, the concepts of $H_0$ and $H_a$, sampling distributions, Type I and Type II errors, alpha levels, critical values, and power all apply. Nonparametric procedures are never our first choice, because they are less powerful than parametric procedures, but sometimes we must use them.

In this chapter we will first discuss the most common nonparametric procedure, chi square, which is used when we have frequency data. Then we will discuss the nonparametric procedures that are analogous to *t*-tests and ANOVAs, except that they are used for rank-ordered scores or for interval or ratio data that violate the assumptions of *t*-tests or ANOVAs.

## CHI SQUARE PROCEDURES

Up to now, a score has measured the *amount* of a dependent variable that a subject demonstrates, and we have summarized the scores using the mean. However, sometimes researchers study scores that do not indicate an amount, but rather indicate the *category* that a subject falls in. We summarize these data by indicating the *number* of subjects who give a certain response: how many answer yes, no, or maybe to a question; how many indicate that they are male or female; how many claim to vote Republican, Democratic, or Communist; how many say that they were or were not abused children; and so on. In the above cases, each variable is a nominal, or categorical, variable, and our data consist of the total number, or *frequency,* of subjects falling in each category.

For example, we might find that out of 100 subjects, 40 say yes to a particular question and 60 say no. These numbers indicate how the *frequencies are distributed* across our categories of yes/no. As usual, we want to draw inferences about what we would find in the population: If we were to ask the entire population this question, can we infer that 40% of the population would say yes and 60% would say no? Or would the frequencies be distributed in a different manner? To make inferences about the frequencies that would be found in the population, we perform the procedure called chi square (pronounced "kigh square"). The **chi square procedure** is the nonparametric inferential procedure for testing whether the frequencies in each category in our samples represent certain frequencies in the population.

> STAT ALERT Whenever your data consist of the number of subjects in each category, the chi square procedure is the procedure to use.

The symbol for the chi square statistic is $\chi^2$. Theoretically, there is no limit to the number of categories, or levels, we may have in a variable and no limit to the number of variables we may have. We describe a chi square design in the same way we described ANOVAs: when a study has only one variable, we use the one-way chi square; when a study has two variables, we use the two-way chi square; and so on.

## ONE-WAY CHI SQUARE: THE GOODNESS OF FIT TEST

We use the one-way chi square when our data consist of the frequencies with which subjects belong to the different categories of *one* variable. As usual, we are examining a relationship, but here the relationship is between the different categories and the frequency with which subjects fall in each category. We are asking, "As we change the categories, do the frequencies with which subjects fall in the categories change in a consistent fashion?"

Here is a study that calls for a one-way chi square. Scientists believe that being right-handed or left-handed is related to brain organization and function. Interestingly, many of history's great geniuses were left-handed. To explore the relationship between the frequencies of left- and right-handedness in geniuses, say that we randomly select a sample of 50 geniuses using an IQ test. Then we ask them whether they are left- or right-handed (ambidextrous is not an option). The total numbers of left- and right-handers are the frequencies in the two categories. We can summarize our results as shown in the following diagram.

*Handedness*

| *Left-handers* | *Right-handers* |
|:---:|:---:|
| $f_o = 10$ | $f_o = 40$ |

$$k = 2$$
$$N = \text{total } f_o = 50$$

Each cell contains the frequency with which subjects fall in that category. We call this value the *observed frequency,* symbolized by $f_o$. The sum of the $f_o$'s from all categories must equal $N$, the total number of subjects in the study. Notice that the symbol $k$ again stands for the number of categories, or levels, in a one-way chi square, and here $k = 2$.

The results of the above study seem pretty straightforward: 10 of our 50 subjects, or 20%, are left-handers, and 40, or 80%, are right-handers. Because this is a random sample, we want to argue that the same distribution of 20% left-handers and 80% right-handers would occur in the population of all geniuses. But, of course, there is the usual problem: sampling error. Maybe, by luck, the subjects in our sample are unrepresentative, so if we could examine the population of all geniuses, we would not find this distribution of right- and left-handers. Maybe our results poorly represent some other distribution. As usual, this is our null hypothesis, implying that we are being misled by sampling error.

The question is "What is that 'other distribution' of frequencies that our sample poorly represents?" To answer this question, we create a *model* of the distribution of the frequencies we expect to find in the population when $H_0$ is true. Recall that $H_0$ always implies that our study did not work—that it failed to demonstrate the predicted relationship. Therefore, our $H_0$ model describes the distribution of frequencies we would find in the population if there is not the predicted relationship.

You'll notice that the title of this section is "The Goodness of Fit Test." In testing our $H_0$ model of the distribution of frequencies in the population, we test how "good" the "fit" is between our data and that model. Thus, goodness of fit is merely another way of saying that we determine whether our sample data are likely to represent the distribution of frequencies in the population that is described by $H_0$.

## Creating the Statistical Hypotheses for $\chi^2$

Usually, researchers test the $H_0$ model that there is no difference between the frequencies in the categories in the population. This, of course, means that $H_0$ states that there is no relationship in the population. For our handedness study, say that we want to test the $H_0$ model that there is no difference between the frequencies of left- and right-handers in the population of geniuses (even though there are more right-handers than left-handers in the general population). Therefore, our $H_0$ model is that the frequencies of left- and right-handed geniuses in the population are equal. There is no conventional way to write our hypotheses in symbols, so we simply write $H_0$ as

$H_0$: all frequencies in the population are equal

$H_0$ implies that if the observed frequencies ($f_o$) in our sample are not equal, it is because of sampling error.

Our alternative hypothesis always implies that the study did demonstrate the predicted relationship. Here, our $H_a$ is

$H_a$: all frequencies in the population are not equal

$H_a$ implies that our observed frequencies represent different frequencies of left- and right-handers in the population of geniuses.

The one-way $\chi^2$ only tests two-tailed hypotheses.

### Computing the Expected Frequencies, $f_e$

To compute the $\chi^2$ statistic, we must translate our $H_0$ model into a specific expected frequency for each category. The **expected frequency** is the frequency we expect in a category if the sample data perfectly represent the distribution of frequencies in the population described by the null hypothesis. The symbol for the expected frequency is $f_e$.

In our study, $H_0$ is that the frequencies of left- and right-handedness are equal in the population of geniuses. If our sample perfectly represents this population, then out of the 50 subjects in our study, 25 should be right-handed and 25 should be left-handed. Thus, when $H_0$ is true, the expected frequency in each category is $f_e = 25$.

For future reference, notice that $f_e$ is actually based on a probability. If the frequencies in the population are equal, then the probability of someone's being left-handed equals the probability of someone's being right-handed. With only two possible categories, the probability of someone's falling in either category is .5. Since probability is the same as relative frequency, we expect .5 of all geniuses to be left-handed and .5 of all geniuses to be right-handed. Therefore, out of the 50 geniuses in our study, we expect to have a frequency of (.5)(50), or 25, in each category. *Thus, the expected frequency in a category is equal to the probability of someone's falling in that category multiplied times the N of the study.*

Whenever our $H_0$ is that the frequencies in the categories are equal, the expected frequency for each category can be computed as the total $N$ in the study divided by the number of categories. Thus,

> *THE COMPUTATIONAL FORMULA FOR EACH EXPECTED FREQUENCY, $f_e$, IN TESTING AN $H_0$ OF NO DIFFERENCE IS*
>
> $$f_e \text{ in each category} = \frac{N}{k}$$

Thus, in our handedness study, with an $N$ of 50 and $k = 2$,

$$f_e \text{ in each category} = \frac{50}{2} = 25$$

Note: Sometimes $f_e$ may contain a decimal. (For example, if we included a third category for ambidextrous, then $k$ would be 3, and for 50 subjects, each $f_e$ would be 16.67.)

As in any statistical test, we must check the assumptions of the test. Now that you understand expected frequencies, we can check the assumptions of $\chi^2$.

## Assumptions of the One-Way Chi Square

The assumptions of the one-way $\chi^2$ are as follows:

1. The independent variable is a categorical, or nominal, variable with two or more categories.
2. The dependent variable is the frequency (the number) of subjects belonging to each category.
3. Each subject is measured only once and can be in one and only one category.
4. Category membership is independent: the fact that a particular subject falls in one category does not influence the probability of any other subject's falling in any category.
5. The computations are based on the responses of all subjects in the study. (That is, we would not count only the number of right-handers. Or, in a different study, if we counted the number of subjects who agreed with some statement, we would also include a separate category for those subjects who disagreed with the statement.)
6. So that our data meet certain theoretical considerations, the $f_e$ in any category should equal at least 5. When there are only two categories for a variable, the $f_e$ in each category should be at least 10.

## Computing $\chi^2$

If the sample perfectly represents the situation where there are no differences in handedness in the population, then we expect to find 25 subjects in each category. In other words, when $H_0$ is true, our $f_o$ "should" equal our $f_e$. Any difference between $f_o$ and $f_e$ is chalked up to sampling error. Of course, the greater the difference between the observed frequency and the expected frequency, the less likely it is that the difference is due to sampling error. Therefore, the greater the difference between $f_o$ and $f_e$, the less likely it is that $H_0$ is true and our sample represents an equal distribution of frequencies in the population.

The $\chi^2$ is a way to measure the overall differences between $f_o$ and $f_e$ in the categories in our study. We compute an obtained $\chi^2$, which we'll call $\chi^2_{obt}$.

THE COMPUTATIONAL FORMULA FOR THE OBTAINED CHI SQUARE, $\chi^2_{\text{obt}}$, IS

$$\chi^2_{\text{obt}} = \Sigma\left(\frac{(f_o - f_e)^2}{f_e}\right)$$

(Critical values of $\chi^2$ are found in Table 7 of Appendix D for $df = k - 1$.) In English, this equation tells you to find the difference between $f_o$ and $f_e$ in each category and square that difference. Then divide each squared difference by the $f_e$ for that category. After doing this for all categories, sum the quantities, and the answer is $\chi^2_{\text{obt}}$. (Note that because each difference is squared, $\chi^2$ can never be a negative number.)

For our handedness study, we have the frequencies

**Handedness**

| Left-handers | Right-handers |
|:---:|:---:|
| $f_o = 10$ $f_e = 25$ | $f_o = 40$ $f_e = 25$ |

Filling in the formula, we have

$$\chi^2_{\text{obt}} = \Sigma\left(\frac{(f_o - f_e)^2}{f_e}\right) = \left(\frac{(10 - 25)^2}{25}\right) + \left(\frac{(40 - 25)^2}{25}\right)$$

After subtracting, we have

$$\chi^2_{\text{obt}} = \left(\frac{(-15)^2}{25}\right) + \left(\frac{(15)^2}{25}\right)$$

Squaring then gives

$$\chi^2_{\text{obt}} = \left(\frac{225}{25}\right) + \left(\frac{225}{25}\right)$$

After dividing, we have

$$\chi^2_{\text{obt}} = 9 + 9 = 18.0$$

so $\chi^2_{\text{obt}} = 18.0$.

## Interpreting $\chi^2$

As always, to interpret our obtained statistic we must determine its location on the sampling distribution when $H_0$ is true. The $H_0$ sampling distribution of $\chi^2$ contains all possible values of $\chi^2$ when $H_0$ is true (the observed frequencies represent the model described by $H_0$). Thus, for our handedness study, our $\chi^2$-distribution is the distribution of all possible values of $\chi^2$ when there are two categories and the frequencies in the two categories in the population are equal. Envision the $\chi^2$-distribution as shown in Figure 15.1.

Even though the $\chi^2$-distribution is not at all normal, it is used in the same way as previous sampling distributions. When the data perfectly represent the $H_0$ model so that each $f_o$ equals the corresponding $f_e$, $\chi^2$ is zero. The larger the value of $\chi^2$, the larger the differences between the expected and observed frequencies and the less frequently they occur when $H_0$ is true and the observed frequencies do represent our $H_0$ model. Therefore, the larger the $\chi^2_{obt}$, the less likely it is that our data represent the population frequencies described by $H_0$. With chi square, we have two-tailed hypotheses but one region of rejection. If $\chi^2_{obt}$ is larger than the critical value, then it is in the region of rejection and it occurs less than 5% of the time when $H_0$ is true. Then $\chi^2$ is significant, because the observed frequencies are so different from the expected frequencies that the observed frequencies are too unlikely to accept as representing the distribution of frequencies in the population described by $H_0$.

To determine if our $\chi^2_{obt}$ is significant, we compare it to the critical value, symbolized by $\chi^2_{crit}$. As with previous statistics, the $\chi^2$-distribution changes shape

**FIGURE 15.1**   Sampling Distribution of $\chi^2$ When $H_0$ Is True

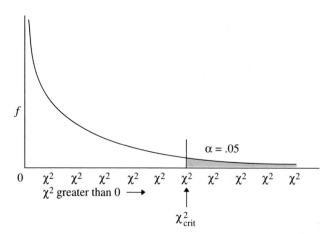

as the degrees of freedom changes, so to find the appropriate value of $\chi^2_{crit}$ for our particular study, we must first have the degrees of freedom.

> **In a one-way $\chi^2$, the degrees of freedom is equal to $k - 1$, where $k$ is the number of categories.**

To determine the critical value of $\chi^2$, we turn to Table 8 in Appendix D, entitled "Critical Values of Chi Square." Then for the appropriate degrees of freedom $(k - 1)$ and $\alpha$, we locate the critical value of $\chi^2$. For our handedness study, $k = 2$, so $df = 1$, and with $\alpha = .05$, our $\chi^2_{crit} = 3.84$.

Since our $\chi^2_{obt}$ of 18.0 is larger than the $\chi^2_{crit}$ of 3.84, our results lie in the region of rejection and are significant: we reject the $H_0$ that each $f_o$ represents an equal frequency in the population. We report our results as

$$\chi^2(1) = 18.0, \quad p < .05$$

Notice the $df$ in parentheses.

By rejecting $H_0$, we accept the $H_a$ that our observed frequencies represent frequencies in the population that are not equal. Therefore, we are confident that the relative frequency of left- and right-handers in the population is not equal. In fact, as in our samples, we would expect to find about 20% left-handers and 80% right-handers in the population of geniuses. We conclude that we have evidence of a relationship between the categories of handedness and the frequency with which geniuses fall in each.

If our $\chi^2_{obt}$ had not been significant, we would have failed to reject $H_0$. As usual, failing to reject $H_0$ does not prove that it is true. Therefore, we would *not* be able to say that the distribution of left- and right-handed geniuses in the population was equal. We would simply remain unconvinced that the distribution was unequal.

## Other Uses of the Goodness of Fit Test

In addition to testing an $H_0$ that the frequencies in all categories are distributed equally, we can also test the goodness of fit to other $H_0$ models, which say that the frequencies are distributed in some other way. For example, we know that only about 10% of the general population is left-handed. Therefore, we might wish to determine whether the distribution of handedness in our sample of geniuses fits this model of the distribution of handedness in the general population.

The null hypothesis is still that our data fit our $H_0$ model, so we can state our $H_0$ as

$H_0$: 10% left-handed, 90% right-handed

For simplicity, we can write our $H_a$ as

$H_a$: not $H_0$

$H_a$ implies that our observed frequencies represent a population that does not fit the $H_0$ model, so the population of geniuses is not 10% left-handed and 90% right-handed.

As usual, we compute our values of $f_e$ based on $H_0$, but now the new model is that 10% of the population is left-handed and 90% is right-handed. If $H_0$ is true and our sample is perfectly representative of the general population, then we expect left-handed geniuses to occur 10% of the time. For the 50 geniuses in our study, 10% is 5, so our expected frequency for left-handers is $f_e = 5$. We expect right-handed geniuses to occur 90% of the time, and 90% of 50 is 45, so our expected frequency for right-handers is $f_e = 45$. As usual, according to $H_0$, any differences between the observed and expected frequencies are due to sampling error in representing this model.

We should *not* perform two $\chi^2$ procedures on the same data, but for the sake of illustration, we will compare our previous handedness frequencies and our new expected frequencies. We have

*Handedness*

| *Left-handers* | *Right-handers* |
|---|---|
| $f_o = 10$ <br> $f_e = 5$ | $f_o = 40$ <br> $f_e = 45$ |

$$k = 2$$
$$\text{Total } f_o = 50$$

We compute $\chi^2$ using the same formula we used in the previous section. Putting these values in our formula, we have

$$\chi^2_{obt} = \Sigma\left(\frac{(f_o - f_e)^2}{f_e}\right) = \left(\frac{(10 - 5)^2}{5}\right) + \left(\frac{(40 - 45)^2}{45}\right)$$

(Notice that we now have a different value of $f_e$ in each fraction.) Working through the formula, we have

$$\chi^2_{obt} = 5.0 + .56$$

so $\chi^2_{obt} = 5.56$.

With $\alpha = .05$ and $k = 2$, the critical value of $\chi^2$ for $df = 1$ is again 3.84. Because the $\chi^2_{obt}$ of 5.56 is larger than the $\chi^2_{crit}$ of 3.84, our results fall in the region of rejection. Therefore, we reject $H_0$ and conclude that the observed frequencies are significantly different from what we would expect if handedness in the population of geniuses was distributed as it is in the general population. Instead, our best guess is that the population of geniuses would be distributed as in our sample data, with 20% left-handers and 80% right-handers.

If our $\chi^2_{obt}$ had not been significant, we would have failed to reject $H_0$ and would simply remain unconvinced that handedness is distributed differently in geniuses than in the general population.

### Additional Procedures in a One-Way Chi Square

As usual, a graph is a useful way to summarize data, especially if there are more than two categories. We label the $Y$ axis with the frequencies and the $X$ axis with the levels or categories, and then we plot the $f_o$ in each category. Figure 15.2 shows the results of our handedness study. Notice that handedness is a categorical, or nominal, variable, and as we saw way back in Chapter 3, we plot frequencies from a nominal variable using a bar graph.

Notably, unlike ANOVA, the one-way chi square usually is not followed by *post hoc* comparisons. A significant $\chi^2_{obt}$ indicates that, across the categories of the variable, the frequencies are distributed in a manner that is significantly different from that described by $H_0$. We use the observed frequency in each category to estimate the frequencies that would be found in the population. Likewise, we do not compute such measures as eta squared.

## THE TWO-WAY CHI SQUARE: THE TEST OF INDEPENDENCE

We use the *two-way* chi square procedure when our data consist of the frequencies with which subjects belong to the categories in each of *two* variables. This is similar to the complete factorial design we saw in the previous chapter. Depending on the number of categories in each variable, the design can be

**FIGURE 15.2**　Frequencies of Left- and Right-Handed Geniuses

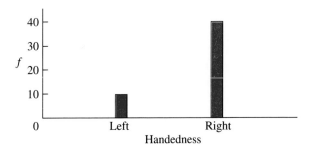

$2 \times 2, 2 \times 3, 4 \times 3$, and so on. The procedures for computing $\chi^2$ are the same regardless of the design.

The assumptions of the two-way chi square are the same as for the one-way chi square. If an $f_e$ is less than 5, we cannot compute $\chi^2$. Instead, we perform Fisher's exact test.[1]

### Logic of the Two-Way Chi Square

Here is a study that calls for a two-way chi square. Some psychologists claim that they have identified two personality types: Type A and Type B. A Type A personality tends to be a very pressured, frantic individual who never seems to have enough time. A Type B personality tends not to be so time pressured, being more relaxed and mellow. A controversy has developed over whether people with Type A personalities are less healthy, especially when it comes to the big one—having heart attacks. Say that we enter this controversy by randomly selecting a sample of 80 people. Using the appropriate personality test, we determine how many are Type A and how many Type B. We then count the frequency with which Type A and Type B subjects have had heart attacks. We must also count the frequency with which Type A and Type B subjects have *not* had heart attacks (see item 5 in the assumptions of the one-way chi square). Therefore, we have two categorical variables: personality type (A or B) and subject's health (heart attack or no heart attack). We can diagram this study as shown below.

|  | | *Personality type* | |
|---|---|---|---|
|  |  | *Type A* | *Type B* |
| *Subject's health* | *Heart attack* | $f_o$ | $f_o$ |
|  | *No heart attack* | $f_o$ | $f_o$ |

Understand that although this looks like a two-way ANOVA, there is one very important difference between a two-way ANOVA and a two-way chi square. ANOVA tests the main effects and the interaction of the two variables, but chi square tests only the interaction. Recall that an interaction indicates that the relationship between one factor and the scores *depends* on which level

---

[1]Described in S. Siegel and N. J. Castellan (1988), *Nonparametric Statistics for the Behavioral Sciences,* 2nd ed. (New York: McGraw Hill).

of the other factor we examine. In the same way, *the two-way* $\chi^2$ *determines whether the distribution of the frequencies in the categories of one variable depends on which category of the other variable we examine.* That is, the two-way $\chi^2$ is a *test of independence.* We compute $\chi^2$ to determine whether the frequency of subjects in a particular category of one variable is independent of the frequency of subjects in a particular category of the other variable. Thus, in our study, we will test whether the frequencies for having or not having a heart attack are independent of the frequencies for being Type A or Type B.

To understand this idea of independence, consider the following ideal example of data when the two variables are independent.

|  |  | *Personality type* | |
| --- | --- | --- | --- |
|  |  | *Type A* | *Type B* |
| *Subject's health* | *Heart attack* | $f_o = 20$ | $f_o = 20$ |
|  | *No heart attack* | $f_o = 20$ | $f_o = 20$ |

Here, the frequency of subjects' having or not having a heart attack does not depend on the frequency of subjects' being Type A or Type B. Thus, the two variables are independent.

Another way to view the two-way $\chi^2$ is as a test of whether a correlation exists between the two variables. When the variables are independent, there is no correlation. Then, using the categories from one variable does not help us to accurately predict the frequencies for the other variable. Above, using Type A or Type B does not help us predict how frequently subjects have or do not have a heart attack (and using the categories of heart attack and no heart attack does not help us predict the frequency of each personality type).

On the other hand, below is an ideal example of data when the two variables are not independent: they are dependent.

|  |  | *Personality type* | |
| --- | --- | --- | --- |
|  |  | *Type A* | *Type B* |
| *Subject's health* | *Heart attack* | $f_o = 40$ | $f_o = 0$ |
|  | *No heart attack* | $f_o = 0$ | $f_o = 40$ |

Here, the frequency of a heart attack or no heart attack *depends* on personality type. Thus, a correlation exists, because whether subjects are Type A or Type B is a very good predictor of whether they have or have not had a heart attack (and vice versa).

As usual, our goal is to describe the population. The null hypothesis always says that there is zero correlation, so the null hypothesis in the two-way $\chi^2$ always says that the variables are independent in the population. If, in the sample data, the variables appear to be dependent and correlated, $H_0$ says that this is due to sampling error. The alternative hypothesis is that the variables are dependent. Therefore, a significant $\chi^2_{obt}$ indicates that we can be confident that our data represent two variables that are dependent. A nonsignificant $\chi^2_{obt}$ indicates that the two variables may be independent.

STAT ALERT  A significant two-way $\chi^2$ indicates that the sample data are likely to represent two variables that are dependent in the population.

## Computing the Expected Frequencies in the Two-Way Chi Square

As usual, our expected frequencies are based on our model of the population described by $H_0$, so here we compute the $f_e$ in each category based on the idea that the variables are independent. To see how we do this, say that we actually obtained the following data in our heart attack study.

|  | | *Personality type* | | |
| --- | --- | --- | --- | --- |
| | | *Type A* | *Type B* | |
| *Subject's health* | *Heart attack* | $f_o = 25$ | $f_o = 10$ | row total = 35 |
| | *No heart attack* | $f_o = 5$ | $f_o = 40$ | row total = 45 |
| | | column total = 30 | column total = 50 | total = 80 / N = 80 |

Notice that, after recording the $f_o$ for each cell, we compute the total of the observed frequencies in each column and in each row. Also, we compute the total of all frequencies, which equals $N$. (To check your work, note that the sum of the row totals should equal the sum of the column totals, which equals $N$.)

Now we can compute the expected frequency for each cell. As with the one-way $\chi^2$, the expected frequency is based on the probability of a subject's being located in the cell. First let's compute the probability of a subject's being in the top left-hand cell of heart attack and Type A. Out of a total of 80 subjects in the study, 35 reported having had a heart attack (the row total). Thus, the probability of someone's reporting a heart attack is 35/80, or .438. Similarly, the probability of a subject's being Type A is 30 (the column total) out of 80, or 30/80, which is .375. We want to know the probability of a subject's being Type A *and* reporting a heart attack. Whenever we want to determine the probability of having event A and event B occur simultaneously, we *multiply* the probability of event A times the probability of event B (an explanation of this multiplication rule for independent events is given in Appendix B.) Thus, the probability of a subject's reporting a heart attack *and* being Type A is equal to the probability of reporting a heart attack multiplied times the probability of being Type A, (.438)(.375), which is .164. Thus, the probability of someone's falling in the cell for a heart attack and Type A is .164, if the two variables are independent.

Since probability is the same as relative frequency, we expect .164 of our subjects to fall in this cell if the variables are independent. This means that out of our 80 subjects, we expect .164 times 80, or 13.125 subjects to be in this cell. Therefore, our expected frequency for this cell is $f_e = 13.125$.

Luckily, there is a shortcut formula for calculating each $f_e$. Above, we multiplied 35/80 times 30/80 and then multiplied the answer times 80. The 35 is the total $f_o$ of the *row* that contains the cell, 30 is the total $f_o$ of the *column* that contains the cell, and 80 is the total $N$ of the study. Using these components, we can construct a formula.

*THE COMPUTATIONAL FORMULA FOR COMPUTING THE EXPECTED FREQUENCY IN A CELL OF A TWO-WAY CHI SQUARE IS*

$$f_e = \frac{(\text{cell's row total } f_o)\,(\text{cell's column total } f_o)}{N}$$

To find $f_e$ for a cell, we multiply the total observed frequencies for the row containing the cell times the total observed frequencies for the column containing the cell, and then we divide by the $N$ of the study.

Table 15.1 shows the finished diagram for our study, giving the computed $f_e$ for each cell. To check your work, confirm that the sum of the $f_e$'s in each column or row equals the column or row total.

If $H_0$ is true and the variables are independent, then each observed frequency should equal each corresponding expected frequency. $H_0$ implies that any difference between $f_o$ and $f_e$ is merely due to sampling error. However, the

**TABLE 15.1**   Diagram Containing $f_o$ and $f_e$ for Each Cell

*Each $f_e$ equals the row total times the column total, divided by N.*

|  |  | **Personality type** |  |  |
|---|---|---|---|---|
|  |  | *Type A* | *Type B* |  |
| *Subject's health* | *Heart attack* | $f_o = 25$ $f_e = 13.125$ (35)(30)/80 | $f_o = 10$ $f_e = 21.875$ (35)(50)/80 | row total = 35 |
|  | *No heart attack* | $f_o = 5$ $f_e = 16.875$ (45)(30)/80 | $f_o = 40$ $f_e = 28.125$ (45)(50)/80 | row total = 45 |
|  |  | column total = 30 | column total = 50 | total = 80 |

greater the value of $\chi^2_{obt}$, the greater the difference between $f_o$ and $f_e$, so the less likely it is that the data poorly represent variables that are independent.

## Computing the Two-Way Chi Square

We compute the $\chi^2_{obt}$ for the two-way $\chi^2$ using the same formula we used in the one-way design, which is

$$\chi^2_{obt} = \Sigma\left(\frac{(f_o - f_e)^2}{f_e}\right)$$

Using the data in Table 15.1 from our heart attack study, we have

$$\chi^2_{obt} = \left(\frac{(25 - 13.125)^2}{13.125}\right) + \left(\frac{(10 - 21.875)^2}{21.875}\right)$$
$$+ \left(\frac{(5 - 16.875)^2}{16.875}\right) + \left(\frac{(40 - 28.125)^2}{28.125}\right)$$

As before, in the numerator of each fraction is the observed frequency minus the expected frequency for a cell, and in the denominator is the expected frequency for that cell. Solving each fraction gives

$$\chi^2_{obt} = 10.74 + 6.45 + 8.36 + 5.01$$

so $\chi^2_{obt} = 30.56$.

Although this is a rather large value, such answers are possible. (If you get one, however, it's a good idea to triple-check your computations.)

To evaluate our $\chi^2_{obt}$, we need to find the appropriate $\chi^2_{crit}$, so first we must determine the degrees of freedom.

> **THE DEGREES OF FREEDOM IN A TWO-WAY CHI SQUARE IS**
>
> $$df = (\text{number of rows} - 1)(\text{number of columns} - 1)$$

For our study, $df$ is $(2 - 1)(2 - 1)$, or 1. We again find the critical value of $\chi^2$ in Table 8. At $\alpha = .05$ and $df = 1$, the $\chi^2_{crit}$ is 3.84.

Since our $\chi^2_{obt}$ of 30.56 is larger than the $\chi^2_{crit}$ of 3.84, our obtained $\chi^2$ is significant. When the two-way $\chi^2_{obt}$ is significant, the observed frequencies are too unlikely to accept as poorly representing frequencies for variables that are independent. Therefore, we reject our $H_0$ that the variables are independent and accept the alternative hypothesis: we are confident that the sample represents frequencies for two variables that are dependent in the population. In other words, we conclude that there is a significant correlation such that the frequency of having or not having a heart attack depends on the frequency of being Type A or Type B (and vice versa). We report our results as

$$\chi^2(1) = 30.56, \quad p < .05$$

If our $\chi^2_{obt}$ had not been larger than the critical value, we would not have rejected $H_0$. Therefore, we could not say whether or not these variables are independent.

## Additional Procedures in the Two-Way Chi Square

When we find a significant two-way $\chi^2_{obt}$, there are two procedures we can apply to further describe our data: we can graph the data, and we can describe the strength of the relationship.

**Graphing the two-way chi square**   We graph the data of a two-way chi square by creating a bar graph. Frequency is plotted along the $Y$ axis, and one of the category variables is plotted along the $X$ axis. The other category variable is indicated within the body of the graph. Figure 15.3 shows such a bar graph for our heart attack study.

If you drew a straight line connecting the tops of the filled bars for heart attacks and another line connecting the tops of the open bars for no heart attacks, you would have the nonparallel lines of an interaction, which we discussed in the previous chapter. The graph here is interpreted in the same way as the graph of a two-way interaction.

**FIGURE 15.3**   Frequency of Heart Attacks and Personality Type

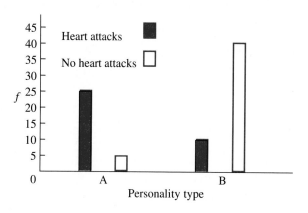

**Describing the relationship in a two-way chi square**   A significant two-way chi square indicates that there is a significant relationship, or correlation, between the two variables. If we have performed a 2 × 2 chi square (and it is significant), we describe the strength of the relationship by computing a new correlation coefficient known as the **phi coefficient.** The symbol for the phi coefficient is ɸ, and its value can be between 0 and +1.0. You can think of phi as comparing our actual data to the ideal situation when the variables are perfectly dependent, or correlated. The larger the value of phi, the closer our data come to fitting this ideal situation.

*THE COMPUTATIONAL FORMULA FOR THE PHI COEFFICIENT IS*

$$\phi = \sqrt{\frac{\chi^2_{obt}}{N}}$$

$N$ equals the total number of subjects in the study.

For our heart attack study, $\chi^2_{obt}$ was 30.56 and $N$ was 80, so ɸ is

$$\phi = \sqrt{\frac{\chi^2_{obt}}{N}} = \sqrt{\frac{30.56}{80}} = \sqrt{.382} = .62$$

Thus, on a scale of 0 to +1.0, where +1.0 indicates that the variables are perfectly dependent, we found a correlation of .62 between the frequency of heart attacks and the frequency of personality types.

If we did not take the square root in the above formula, we would have $\phi^2$

(phi squared). This is analogous to $r^2$ or $\eta^2$, indicating how much more accurately we can predict scores by using the relationship. In our study above, $\phi^2$ = .38, so we can be 38% more accurate in predicting the frequency of heart attacks/no heart attacks when we know personality type (or vice versa).

If we have performed a two-way chi square that is *not* 2 × 2 (and it is significant), we do *not* compute the phi coefficient. Instead, we compute the **contingency coefficient,** symbolized by $C$.

---

*THE COMPUTATIONAL FORMULA FOR THE CONTINGENCY COEFFICIENT, C, IS*

$$C = \sqrt{\frac{\chi^2_{obt}}{N + \chi^2_{obt}}}$$

---

$N$ is the number of subjects in the study.

We interpret $C$ in the same way we interpret $\phi$. Likewise, $C^2$ is analogous to $\phi^2$.

Finally, when one of the variables in a significant two-way $\chi^2$ contains more than two categories, we can perform advanced procedures that are somewhat analogous to *post hoc* comparisons.[2]

## NONPARAMETRIC PROCEDURES FOR RANKED DATA

In addition to chi square, there are several other nonparametric procedures you should be aware of. We perform these procedures when we have rank-ordered (ordinal) scores, where subjects' scores are 1st, 2nd, 3rd, and so on. We obtain ranked scores in a study either because we have measured ranked scores or because we have measured interval or ratio scores that violate the assumptions of parametric procedures. Then we transform the scores by assigning them ranks (the highest raw score is ranked 1, the next highest score is ranked 2, and so on). Either way, we then compute one of the following nonparametric inferential statistics to determine whether there are significant differences in the ranked scores for the different conditions of our independent variable.

[2]Described in S. Siegel and N. J. Castellan (1988), *Nonparametric Statistics for the Behavioral Sciences,* 2nd ed. (New York: McGraw Hill).

## The Logic of Nonparametric Procedures for Ranked Data

Instead of computing the mean of each condition in the experiment, as we did with $t$ or $F$, with nonparametric procedures we add the ranked scores in each condition and then examine these sums of ranks. Our symbol for a sum of ranks is $\Sigma R$. We will compare the observed sum of ranks to an expected sum of ranks. To see the logic of this, say we have the following ranked scores:

| Group 1 | Group 2 |
|---|---|
| 1 | 2 |
| 4 | 3 |
| 5 | 6 |
| 8 | 7 |
| $\Sigma R = 18$ | $\Sigma R = 18$ |

Here there is no difference between the groups, with each group containing both high and low ranks. When the high and low ranks are distributed equally between the two groups, the sums of ranks are equal (here $\Sigma R$ is 18 in each group). Since there is no difference between these two samples, they may represent the same distribution of ranks in their respective populations. That is, in each population there may be both low ranks and high ranks. Our null hypothesis always states that the populations from our conditions are the same, so here $H_0$ is that we have the same distribution of ranks in each population. Notice that, for our data to be consistent with $H_0$, we *expect* the sum of the four ranks in each group to equal 18. In the same way, for every study, we have an expected sum of ranks for each group when $H_0$ is true.

But now look at the following two groups of ranked scores:

| Group 1 | Group 2 |
|---|---|
| 1 | 5 |
| 2 | 6 |
| 3 | 7 |
| 4 | 8 |
| $\Sigma R = 10$ | $\Sigma R = 26$ |

Group 1 contains all of the low ranks, and Group 2 contains all of the high ranks. Because these samples are different, they may represent two different populations. Our alternative hypothesis is always that the populations represented by our samples are different, so here $H_a$ says that the distribution of ranks in each population is different, one containing predominantly low ranks and the other containing predominantly high ranks. When our data is consistent with $H_a$ (that the two samples represent different populations of ranks) the sum of ranks in each sample is different from the expected sum of ranks when $H_0$ is true. (Here, each $\Sigma R$ is not equal to 18.)

As usual, the problem is that there is another reason that each observed sum of ranks may not equal the expected sum of ranks. It may be that $H_0$ is true and the groups represent the same distribution of ranks in the population, but our data reflect sampling error. However, the larger the difference between the expected and observed sum of ranks, the less likely it is that this difference is due to sampling error, and the more likely it is that each sample represents a different distribution of ranks in the population.

Therefore, in each of the following procedures, we compute a statistic that measures the difference between the expected and the observed sum of ranks. If the statistic is a certain size, then we reject $H_0$ and accept $H_a$: we are confident that the reason the observed sum of ranks is different from the expected sum of ranks is that the samples represent different distributions of ranks in the population. (If the ranks reflect underlying interval or ratio scores, a significant difference in ranks indicates that the raw score populations are also different.)

In all of the following procedures, we compute the expected sum of ranks when $H_0$ is true. The symbol for the expected sum of ranks is $\Sigma R_{exp}$. The value of $\Sigma R_{exp}$ is based on the number of ranks in the study and the $n$ in each group. If there are equal $n$'s, then $\Sigma R_{exp}$ is the same for each group. If the $n$'s are not equal, then $\Sigma R_{exp}$ will not be the same for each group. (In some procedures you will not actually see $\Sigma R_{exp}$, because it is built into the calculations.) Finally, in all of these procedures, we handle tied ranks as described in Chapter 7.

## Choices Among the Nonparametric Procedures

Each of the parametric procedures found in previous chapters has a corresponding nonparametric procedure for ranked data. Your first task is to know which nonparametric procedure to choose for the type of research design you are testing. Table 15.2 shows the name of the nonparametric version of each parametric procedure we have previously discussed. We consider these nonparametric tests in the following sections.

## Tests for Two Independent Samples: The Mann-Whitney *U* Test and the Rank Sums Test

There are two nonparametric procedures that are analogous to the *t*-test for two independent samples: the Mann-Whitney *U* test and the rank sums test. Both are used to test for significant differences between ranked scores measured

**TABLE 15.2** Parametric Procedures and Their Nonparametric Counterparts

| Type of design | Parametric test | Nonparametric test |
|---|---|---|
| Two independent samples | Independent samples $t$-test | Mann-Whitney $U$ or rank sums test for independent samples |
| Two related samples | Related samples $t$-test | Wilcoxon $T$ test for related samples |
| Three or more independent samples | Between-subjects ANOVA (*Post hoc* test: protected $t$-test) | Kruskal-Wallis $H$ test for independent samples (*Post hoc* test: rank sums test) |
| Three or more repeated measures samples | Repeated measures ANOVA (*Post hoc* test: Tukey's *HSD*) | Friedman $\chi^2$ test for repeated measures (*Post hoc* test: Nemenyi's test) |

under two conditions of an independent variable. Which test we use depends on the $n$ in each condition.

**The Mann-Whitney $U$ test for independent samples**  The Mann-Whitney test is appropriate when the $n$ in each condition is equal to or less than 20 and we have two independent samples of ranks. For example, say we measure the reaction times of two groups of subjects to certain symbols. For one group the symbols are printed in black ink, and for the other group the symbols are printed in red ink. We wish to know whether there is a significant difference between reaction times for each colored symbol. However, a raw score population of reaction times tends to be highly positively skewed, so we cannot perform the $t$-test. Therefore, we convert the reaction time scores to ranks. Say that our $n$ in each condition is 5 (but we can perform this procedure when the $n$'s are not equal). Table 15.3 gives the reaction times (measured in milliseconds) and their corresponding ranks from our study.

To perform the Mann-Whitney $U$ test, we do the following.

1. *Assign ranks to all scores in the experiment.* As shown in Table 15.3, assign the rank of 1 to the lowest score in the experiment, regardless of which group it is in. Assign the rank of 2 to the second lowest score in the experiment, and so on. Now we will ignore the original scores and perform the analysis on the ranks.

2. *Compute the sum of the ranks for each group.* Compute $\Sigma R$ for each group, and note its $n$, the number of scores in the group.

**TABLE 15.3**  Ranked Data from Two Independent Samples

| Red symbols | | Black symbols | |
|---|---|---|---|
| Reaction time | Ranked score | Reaction time | Ranked score |
| 540 | 2 | 760 | 7 |
| 480 | 1 | 890 | 8 |
| 600 | 5 | 1105 | 10 |
| 590 | 3 | 595 | 4 |
| 605 | 6 | 940 | 9 |
| | $\Sigma R = 17$ | | $\Sigma R = 38$ |
| | $n = 5$ | | $n = 5$ |

3. *Compute two versions of the Mann-Whitney U.* First, compute $U_1$ for Group 1, using the formula

$$U_1 = (n_1)(n_2) + \frac{n_1(n_1 + 1)}{2} - \Sigma R_1$$

where $n_1$ is the $n$ of Group 1, $n_2$ is the $n$ of the other group, and $\Sigma R_1$ is the sum of ranks from Group 1. We'll call the red symbol group Group 1, so filling in the above formula using the values from Table 15.3, we have

$$U_1 = (5)(5) + \frac{5(5 + 1)}{2} - 17 = 40 - 17 = 23.0$$

Now, compute $U_2$ for Group 2, using the formula

$$U_2 = (n_1)(n_2) + \frac{n_2(n_2 + 1)}{2} - \Sigma R_2$$

Here, the numerator of the fraction involves $n_2$ instead of $n_1$, and we use the sum of ranks from Group 2, $\Sigma R_2$.

We call the black symbol group Group 2, so filling in the formula using Table 15.3, we have

$$U_2 = (5)(5) + \frac{5(5 + 1)}{2} - 38 = 40 - 38 = 2.0$$

4. *Determine the Mann-Whitney $U_{obt}$.* In a two-tailed test, the value of $U_{obt}$ equals the *smaller* of $U_1$ or $U_2$. In our example, $U_1 = 23.0$ and $U_2 = 2.0$, so $U_{obt} = 2.0$. In a one-tailed test, we predict that one of the

groups has the largest sum of ranks. The corresponding value of $U_1$ or $U_2$ from that group becomes our $U_{obt}$.

5. *Find the critical value of U in Table 9, entitled "Critical Values of Mann-Whitney U."* There are two parts to Table 9, one for a two-tailed test and one for a one-tailed test. Choose the appropriate part of the table. Then, using $n_1$ across the top of the table and $n_2$ along the left-hand side of the table, locate $U_{crit}$. For our example, with a two-tailed test and $n_1 = 5$ and $n_2 = 5$, $U_{crit}$ is 2.0.

6. *Compare $U_{obt}$ to $U_{crit}$.* WATCH OUT! This is a biggie! Unlike any statistic we have yet discussed, the $U_{obt}$ is significant if it is *equal to or less than $U_{crit}$.* (This is because the *smaller* the $U_{obt}$, the more likely it is that the group represents a distribution of ranks that is different from the distribution represented by the other group.)

**STAT ALERT**   The Mann-Whitney $U_{obt}$ is significant if it is *less than or equal to* the critical value of U.

In our example, $U_{obt} = 2.0$ and $U_{crit} = 2.0$, so our results are significant. Therefore, we conclude that the distribution of ranked scores represented by one sample is significantly different from the distribution represented by the other sample. Since the ranks reflect reaction time scores, we conclude that the populations of reaction time scores for subjects who see red and black symbols are different. With $\alpha = .05$, the probability that we have made a Type I error is $p < .05$. (To describe the effect size, compute eta squared, as shown in the following section.)

**The rank sums test for independent samples**   The rank sums test is used to test two independent samples of ranks when the *n* in either condition is *greater* than 20. To illustrate how this statistic is calculated, however, we'll violate this rule and use our previous ranked scores from our reaction time study.

To perform the rank sums test, we do the following.

1. *Assign ranks to the scores in the experiment.* As shown in Table 15.3, rank-order all scores in the experiment.

2. *Choose one group and compute the sum of the ranks.* Compute $\Sigma R$ for one group, and note *n*, the number of scores in the group.

3. *Compute the expected sum of ranks, $\Sigma R_{exp}$, for the chosen group.* Use the formula

$$\Sigma R_{exp} = \frac{n(N + 1)}{2}$$

where $n$ is the $n$ of the chosen group and $N$ is the total $N$ of the study. We'll compute $\Sigma R_{\text{exp}}$ for the red symbol group, which had $\Sigma R = 17$ and $n = 5$ ($N$ is 10). Filling in the formula, we have

$$\Sigma R_{\text{exp}} = \frac{n_1(N + 1)}{2} = \frac{5(10 + 1)}{2} = \frac{55}{2} = 27.5$$

Thus, 27.5 is the expected sum of ranks for the red symbol group if the null hypothesis is true.

4. *Compute the rank sums statistic, symbolized by $z_{\text{obt}}$. Use the formula*

$$z_{\text{obt}} = \frac{\Sigma R - \Sigma R_{\text{exp}}}{\sqrt{\dfrac{(n_1)(n_2)(N + 1)}{12}}}$$

where $\Sigma R$ is the sum of the ranks for the chosen group, $\Sigma R_{\text{exp}}$ is the expected sum of ranks for the chosen group, $n_1$ and $n_2$ are the $n$'s of the two groups, and $N$ is the total $N$ of the study.

For our example, we have

$$z_{\text{obt}} = \frac{\Sigma R - \Sigma R_{\text{exp}}}{\sqrt{\dfrac{(n_1)(n_2)(N + 1)}{12}}} = \frac{17 - 27.5}{\sqrt{\dfrac{(5)(5)(10 + 1)}{12}}}$$

$$= \frac{-10.5}{\sqrt{22.92}} = \frac{-10.5}{4.79} = -2.19$$

Thus, $z_{\text{obt}} = -2.19$.

5. *Find the critical value of z in the z-tables (Table 1).* For the appropriate alpha level, determine the critical value of $z$. At $\alpha = .05$, the two-tailed $z_{\text{crit}} = \pm 1.96$. (If we had predicted that the sum of ranks of the chosen group would be either only greater than or only less than the expected sum of ranks, then we would use the one-tailed value of either $+1.645$ or $-1.645$.)

6. *Compare $z_{\text{obt}}$ to $z_{\text{crit}}$.* If the absolute value of $z_{\text{obt}}$ is larger than the corresponding $z_{\text{crit}}$, there is a significant difference between the two samples. In our example, $z_{\text{obt}} = -2.19$ and $z_{\text{crit}} = \pm 1.96$. Therefore, we conclude that the distribution of ranked scores represented by one sample is significantly different from the distribution represented by the other sample. Since the ranks reflect reaction time scores, we conclude that the populations of reaction time scores for subjects who see red and black symbols are different ($p < .05$).

7. *Describe a significant relationship using eta squared.* Here eta squared is analogous to $r_{pb}^2$ which we discussed in Chapter 12. To compute eta squared, use the formula

$$\eta^2 = \frac{(z_{obt})^2}{N - 1}$$

where $z_{obt}$ is computed in the above rank sums test and $N$ is the total number of subjects. In our example, $z_{obt}$ is $-2.19$ and $N$ is 10, so we have $(2.19)^2/9$, or .53. Thus, the color of the symbols accounts for approximately .53 of the variance, or differences, in the ranks. Since the ranks reflect reaction time scores, *approximately 53%* of the differences in reaction time scores are associated with the color of the symbol.

## The Wilcoxon *T* Test for Related Samples

The Wilcoxon test is analogous to the related samples *t*-test for ranked data. Recall that we have related samples when we match samples or when we have repeated measures. For example, say we perform a study similar to the above reaction time study, but this time we measure the reaction times of the *same* subjects to both the red and black symbols. Table 15.4 gives the data we might obtain.

To determine whether the two samples of scores represent different populations of ranks, we compute the Wilcoxon $T_{obt}$ as follows. (This $T_{obt}$ is not the $t_{obt}$ from Chapters 11 and 12:)

**TABLE 15.4**   Data for the Wilcoxon Test for Two Related Samples

| Subject | Reaction time to red symbols | Reaction time to black symbols | Difference, D | Ranked scores | R_ | R_+ |
|---|---|---|---|---|---|---|
| 1 | 540 | 760 | −220 | 6 | 6 | |
| 2 | 580 | 710 | −130 | 4 | 4 | |
| 3 | 600 | 1105 | −505 | 9 | 9 | |
| 4 | 680 | 880 | −200 | 5 | 5 | |
| 5 | 430 | 500 | −70 | 3 | 3 | |
| 6 | 740 | 990 | −250 | 7 | 7 | |
| 7 | 600 | 1050 | −450 | 8 | 8 | |
| 8 | 690 | 640 | +50 | 2 | | 2 |
| 9 | 605 | 595 | +10 | 1 | | 1 |
| 10 | 520 | 520 | 0 | | | |
| | | | $N = 9$ | | $\Sigma R = 42$ | $\Sigma R = 3$ |

1. *Determine the difference score, D, for each pair of scores.* For each pair of scores, subtract the score in one condition from the score in the other. It makes no difference which score is subtracted from which, but subtract the scores the same way for all pairs. Record the difference scores.

2. *Determine the N of the difference scores, but ignore all difference scores equal to zero.* The $N$ is the total number of nonzero difference scores. In our study, there is one difference of zero (for subject 10), so even though there were ten subjects, $N = 9$.

3. *Assign ranks to the nonzero difference scores.* Ignore the sign ($+$ or $-$) of each difference. Assign the rank of 1 to the smallest difference, the rank of 2 to the second smallest difference, and so on. Record ranked scores in a column.

4. *Separate the ranks, using the sign of the difference scores.* Create two columns of ranks, labeled "$R_-$" and "$R_+$." The $R_-$ column contains the ranks you assigned to negative differences in step 3 above. The $R_+$ column contains the ranks you assigned to positive differences.

5. *Compute the sums of ranks for the positive and negative difference scores.* Compute $\Sigma R$ for the column labeled "$R_+$." Then compute $\Sigma R$ for the column labeled "$R_-$."

6. *Determine the Wilcoxon $T_{obt}$.* In the two-tailed test, the Wilcoxon $T_{obt}$ is equal to the *smallest* $\Sigma R$. In our example, the smallest $\Sigma R$ equals 3, so $T_{obt} = 3$. In the one-tailed test, we predict whether most differences are positive or negative, depending on our experimental hypotheses. Thus, we predict whether $R_+$ or $R_-$ contains the smaller $\Sigma R$. The $\Sigma R$ that we predict will be the smallest is our value of $T_{obt}$. (In our study, say we predicted that red symbols would produce the largest reaction time scores. Given the way we subtracted, we would predict that $\Sigma R$ for the $R_-$ column would be smaller, so our $T_{obt}$ would be 42.)

7. *Find the critical value of T in Table 10, entitled "Critical Values of the Wilcoxon T."* Find $T_{crit}$ for the appropriate level of alpha and $N$, the number of nonzero difference scores. In our study, $N = 9$, so for $\alpha = .05$, $T_{crit}$ is 5.0.

8. *Compare $T_{obt}$ to $T_{crit}$.* Again, watch out: the Wilcoxon $T$ is significant if it is *equal to or less than* $T_{crit}$. The critical value is the largest value that our smallest $\Sigma R$ can be and still reflect a significant difference.

**STAT ALERT**  The Wilcoxon $T_{obt}$ is significant if it is *less than or equal to* the critical value of $T$.

In the above example, for our two-tailed test, the $T_{obt}$ of 3.0 is less than the $T_{crit}$ of 6.0, so we have a significant difference. Therefore, we conclude that each sample represents a different distribution of ranks and thus a different population of reaction time scores ($p < .05$). (There is no recognized way to compute $\eta^2$ for this procedure.)

## The Kruskal-Wallis *H* Test for Independent Samples

The Kruskal-Wallis *H* test is analogous to a between-subjects, one-way ANOVA for ranks. It assumes that the study involves one independent variable and that there are *three* or more independent samples with at least five subjects in each sample. The null hypothesis states that all conditions represent the same distribution of ranks in the population.

As an example, consider a study that explores the relationship between the independent variable of a golfer's height and the dependent variable of the distance he or she hits the ball. We will test three groups of novice golfers, classified on the factor of height as either short, medium, or tall. We will measure the distance each subject drives the ball in meters. However, say that, using the $F_{max}$ test discussed in Chapter 13, we have determined that we cannot assume that the distance scores have homogeneous variance, so we dare not use the parametric ANOVA. Instead, we rank the scores and perform the Kruskal-Wallis *H* test. Our data are shown in Table 15.5.

Now we test the null hypothesis that all conditions represent the same distribution of ranks in the population. To compute the Kruskal-Wallis *H*, we do the following.

**TABLE 15.5**  Data for the Kruskal-Wallis *H* Test

|  | *Height* |  |  |  |  |
|---|---|---|---|---|---|
| *Short* | | *Medium* | | *Tall* | |
| *Score* | *Rank* | *Score* | *Rank* | *Score* | *Rank* |
| 10 | 2 | 24 | 3 | 68 | 14 |
| 28 | 6 | 27 | 5 | 71 | 15 |
| 26 | 4 | 35 | 7 | 57 | 10 |
| 39 | 8 | 44 | 9 | 60 | 12 |
| 6 | 1 | 58 | 11 | 62 | 13 |
| | $\Sigma R_1 = 21$ | | $\Sigma R_2 = 35$ | | $\Sigma R_3 = 64$ |
| | $n_1 = 5$ | | $n_2 = 5$ | | $n_3 = 5$ |

$N = 15$

1. *Assign ranks, using all scores in the experiment.* Assign the rank of 1 to the lowest score in the experiment, the rank of 2 to the second lowest score in the experiment, and so on.

2. *Compute the sum of the ranks in each condition.* Compute the sum of the ranks, $\Sigma R$, in each column. Also note the $n$ in each condition.

3. *Compute the sum of squares between groups, $SS_{bn}$.* Use the formula

$$SS_{bn} = \frac{(\Sigma R_1)^2}{n_1} + \frac{(\Sigma R_2)^2}{n_2} + \cdots + \frac{(\Sigma R_k)^2}{n_k}$$

This equation says that, for each level, we square the sum of the ranks and then divide that quantity by the $n$ in the level. (There may be a different $n$ in each level.) After doing this for all $k$ levels in the factor, we add the amounts together.

For our example, we have from Table 15.5

$$SS_{bn} = \frac{(21)^2}{5} + \frac{(35)^2}{5} + \frac{(64)^2}{5} = 88.2 + 245 + 819.2$$

so $SS_{bn} = 1152.4$.

4. *Compute the $H_{obt}$.* Use the formula

$$H_{obt} = \left(\frac{12}{N(N + 1)}\right)(SS_{bn}) - 3(N + 1)$$

where $N$ is the total $N$ of the study. Divide 12 by $N(N + 1)$ and multiply the answer times the $SS_{bn}$. Then subtract $3(N + 1)$. (Note that $H_{obt}$ cannot be a negative number.)

In our example, we have

$$H_{obt} = \left(\frac{12}{15(15 + 1)}\right)(1152.4) - 3(15 + 1) = (.05)(1152.4) - 48$$

$$= 57.62 - 48$$

Thus, the answer is $H_{obt} = 9.62$.

5. *Find the critical value of H in the $\chi^2$-tables (Table 8).* Values of $H$ have the same sampling distribution as $\chi^2$. The degrees of freedom is

$$df = k - 1$$

where $k$ is the number of levels in the factor.

In our example, $k$ is 3, so $df = 2$. In the $\chi^2$-tables for $\alpha = .05$ and $df = 2$, $\chi^2_{crit}$ is 5.99.

6. *Compare the obtained value of H to the critical value of $\chi^2$. If $H_{obt}$ is larger* than the critical value found in the $\chi^2$-tables, then $H_{obt}$ is significant. For our study of golfers, the $H_{obt}$ of 9.62 is larger than the $\chi^2_{crit}$ of 5.99, so it is significant. This means that at least two of our samples represent different populations of ranks. Because the distance the subjects hit the ball underlies each rank, we conclude that at least two of the populations of distances for short, medium, and tall golfers are not the same ($p < .05$).

7. *Perform post hoc comparisons using the rank sums test.* When $H_{obt}$ is significant, we determine which specific conditions differ by performing the rank sums test on all pairs of conditions. This is analogous to Fisher's protected *t*-test, discussed in Chapter 13, and it is used regardless of the *n* in each group. To perform the procedure, treat the two conditions being compared as if they comprised the entire study, then follow the procedure described previously for the rank sums test.

   **STAT ALERT**   When performing the rank sums test as a *post hoc* test for $H_{obt}$, re-rank the scores in the two conditions being compared, using only those scores.

   In our example, comparing the ranks of short and medium-height golfers produces a $z_{obt} = 1.36$, comparing short and tall golfers produces a $z_{obt} = 2.62$, and comparing medium-height and tall golfers produces a $z_{obt} = 2.40$. With $\alpha = .05$, from the *z*-tables we find a $z_{crit}$ of $\pm 1.96$. Therefore, the scores of short and medium-height subjects are not significantly different, but they both differ significantly from the scores of tall subjects. We conclude that our tall golfers represent one population of distances that is different from the population for short and medium-height golfers.

8. *Describe a significant relationship using eta squared.* Use the formula

$$\eta^2 = \frac{H_{obt}}{N - 1}$$

   where $H_{obt}$ is the value computed in the Kruskal-Wallis test and $N$ is the total number of subjects. In our study, we have $H_{obt} = 9.62$ and $N = 15$. Substituting into the above formula, we have $\eta^2 = 9.62/14$, or .69. Therefore, the variable of player's height accounts for approximately .69 of the variance in the distance scores.

## The Friedman $\chi^2$ Test for Repeated Measures

The Friedman $\chi^2$ test is analogous to a one-way, repeated measures ANOVA for ranks. It assumes that the study involves one independent variable, or factor, and that the same subjects are repeatedly measured under *three* or more conditions. If there are only three levels of the factor, there must be at least ten subjects in the study. If there are only four levels of the factor, there must be at least five subjects.

As an example, consider a study in which the scores we collect are already ranked. The three levels of our independent variable are the teaching styles of Dr. Highman, Dr. Shyman, and Dr. Whyman. We obtain a random sample of students who have taken courses from all three instructors, and each student rank-orders the three instructors. Table 15.6 gives the data for our study.

Now we test the null hypothesis that all conditions represent the same distribution of ranks in the population. To perform the Friedman $\chi^2$ test, follow these steps.

1. *Assign ranks within the scores of each subject.* If the scores are not already ranks, assign the rank of 1 to the lowest score received by Subject 1, assign the rank of 2 to the second lowest score received by Subject 1, and so on. Repeat the process for each subject.

2. *Compute the sum of the ranks, $\Sigma R$, in each condition.* Find the sum of the ranks in each column.

3. *Compute the sum of squares between groups, $SS_{bn}$.* Use the formula

$$SS_{bn} = (\Sigma R_1)^2 + (\Sigma R_2)^2 + \cdots + (\Sigma R_k)^2$$

Square the sum of the ranks in each of the $k$ conditions, and then add the squared sums together. In our example, we have

**TABLE 15.6**  Data for the Friedman Test

| Subject | Rankings for three instructors | | |
| | Dr. Highman | Dr. Shyman | Dr. Whyman |
| --- | --- | --- | --- |
| 1 | 1 | 2 | 3 |
| 2 | 1 | 3 | 2 |
| 3 | 1 | 2 | 3 |
| 4 | 1 | 3 | 2 |
| 5 | 2 | 1 | 3 |
| 6 | 1 | 3 | 2 |
| 7 | 1 | 2 | 3 |
| 8 | 1 | 3 | 2 |
| 9 | 1 | 3 | 2 |
| 10 | 2 | 1 | 3 |
| $N = 10$ | $\Sigma R_1 = 12$ | $\Sigma R_2 = 23$ | $\Sigma R_3 = 25$ |

$$SS_{bn} = (12)^2 + (23)^2 + (25)^2$$

so $SS_{bn} = 1298$.

4. *Compute the Friedman $\chi^2$ statistic.* Use the formula

$$\chi^2_{obt} = \left(\frac{12}{(k)(N)(k + 1)}\right)(SS_{bn}) - 3(N)(k + 1)$$

where $N$ is the number of subjects and $k$ is the number of levels of the factor. First divide 12 by the quantity $(k)(N)(k + 1)$. Then multiply this number times $SS_{bn}$. Then subtract the quantity $3(N)(k + 1)$. ($\chi^2$ cannot be a negative number.)

In our example,

$$\chi^2_{obt} = \left(\frac{12}{(3)(10)(3 + 1)}\right)(1298) - 3(10)(3 + 1)$$

$$= (.10)(1298) - 120 = 129.8 - 120$$

And the survey says, $\chi^2_{obt} = 9.80$.

5. *Find the critical value of $\chi^2$ in the $\chi^2$-tables (Table 8).* The degrees of freedom is

$$df = k - 1$$

where $k$ is the number of levels in the factor.

For our example, $k = 3$, so for $df = 2$ and $\alpha = .05$, the critical value is 5.99.

6. *Compare $\chi^2_{crit}$ to the critical value of $\chi^2$.* If $\chi^2_{obt}$ is larger than $\chi^2_{crit}$, the results are significant. For our example, our $\chi^2_{obt}$ of 9.80 is larger than the $\chi^2_{crit}$ of 5.99, so our results are significant. Thus, we conclude that at least two of the samples represent different populations ($p < .05$).

7. *When the Friedman $\chi^2$ is significant, perform post hoc comparisons using Nemenyi's procedure.* This procedure is analogous to Tukey's *HSD* procedure, which we saw in Chapter 13. We compute one value that is the *critical difference.* Any two conditions that differ by more than this critical difference are significantly different. To perform Nemenyi's procedure, follow these steps.

   a. *Compute the critical difference.* Use the formula

$$\text{Critical difference} = \sqrt{\left(\frac{k(k + 1)}{6(N)}\right)(\chi^2_{crit})}$$

where $k$ is the number of levels of the factor, $N$ is the number of subjects, and $\chi^2_{crit}$ is the critical value used to test the Friedman $\chi^2$. To compute the critical difference, multiply $k$ times $k + 1$, and then divide by $6(N)$. Multiply this number times $\chi^2_{crit}$, and then find the square root.

In our example, $\chi^2_{crit} = 5.99$, $k = 3$, and $N = 10$. We have

$$\text{Critical difference} = \sqrt{\left(\frac{k(k + 1)}{6(N)}\right)(\chi^2_{crit})} = \sqrt{\left(\frac{3(3 + 1)}{6(10)}\right)(5.99)}$$

$$\text{Critical difference} = \sqrt{(.2)(5.99)} = \sqrt{1.198} = 1.09$$

so our critical difference is $\pm 1.09$.

b. *Compute the mean rank for each condition.* For each condition, divide the sum of ranks ($\Sigma R$) by the number of subjects. In our example, the sums of ranks are 12, 23, and 25 in the three conditions, and $N$ is 10. Therefore, the mean sums of ranks are 1.2, 2.3, and 2.5 for Highman, Shyman, and Whyman, respectively.

c. *Compute the differences between all pairs of mean ranks.* Subtract each mean rank from the other mean ranks. Any absolute difference between two mean ranks that is greater than the critical difference indicates that the two conditions differ significantly. In our example, the differences between the mean ranks for Dr. Highman and the other two instructors are 1.10 and 1.30, respectively, and the difference between Shyman and Whyman is .20. Our critical difference is 1.09, so only Dr. Highman's ranking are significantly different from those of the other two instructors. Thus, we conclude that if the entire population were to rank the three instructors, Dr. Highman would be ranked superior to the other two instructors.

8. *Describe a significant relationship using eta squared.* Use the formula

$$\eta^2 = \frac{\chi^2_{obt}}{(N)(k) - 1}$$

where $\chi^2_{obt}$ is the value computed in the Friedman $\chi^2$ test, $N$ is the number of subjects, and $k$ is the number of levels of the factor. For our example, we have

$$\eta^2 = \frac{\chi^2_{obt}}{(N)(k) - 1} = \frac{9.80}{(10)(3) - 1} = \frac{9.80}{30 - 1} = .34$$

Thus, our instructor variable accounts for .34 of the variability, or differences, in rankings.

### FINALLY

Congratulations! If you are reading this, you have read an entire statistics book, and that is an accomplishment! You should be proud of the sophisticated level of your knowledge. You are now familiar with the vast majority of statistical procedures used in psychology and other behavioral sciences. Although you may encounter more complicated research designs, after this experience with introductory statistics you will find that there really is nothing new under the sun.

## CHAPTER SUMMARY

1. *Nonparametric procedures* are applied when our data do not meet the assumptions of parametric procedures.

2. *Chi square,* $\chi^2$, is used when we have one or more categorical variables and the data are the frequencies with which subjects fall in a category. Chi square assumes that (a) any subject falls in only one category, (b) the probability of a subject's falling in a particular category is independent of any other subject's falling in a particular category, (c) the responses of all subjects are included in the study, and (d) the $f_e$ in any category is at least 5.

3. The *one-way* $\chi^2$ is a goodness of fit test that determines whether the observed frequencies fit the model of the expected frequencies described by $H_0$. The larger the $\chi^2$, the larger the overall differences between the observed and expected frequencies. A significant $\chi^2$ indicates that the observed frequencies are unlikely to represent the distribution of frequencies in the population described by $H_0$.

4. In the *two-way* $\chi^2$, $H_0$ states that the frequencies in the categories of the two variables are independent. The $\chi^2$ describes the differences between the observed frequencies and the expected frequencies if $H_0$ is true and the variables are independent. A significant $\chi^2$ indicates that the observed frequencies are unlikely to represent variables that are independent in the population. Instead, we conclude that the two variables are dependent, or correlated.

5. In a significant 2 × 2 chi square, the strength of the relationship is described by the *phi correlation coefficient,* $\phi$. In a significant two-way chi square that is not 2 × 2, the strength of the relationship is described by the *contingency coefficient, C.* The larger these coefficients are, the closer the data are to forming a relationship where the variables are perfectly dependent, or correlated.

**6.** There are two nonparametric versions of the independent samples *t*-test for ranks. The *Mann-Whitney U test* is performed when the *n* in each condition is less than 20. The *rank sums test* is performed when the *n* in either condition is greater than 20.

**7.** The *Wilcoxon T test* is the nonparametric equivalent of the related samples *t*-test for ranks.

**8.** The *Kruskal-Wallis H test* is the nonparametric equivalent of the one-way, between-subjects ANOVA for ranks. The rank sums test is used as the *post hoc* test to identify the specific conditions that differ from each other.

**9.** The *Friedman $\chi^2$ test* is the nonparametric equivalent of the one-way, repeated measures ANOVA for ranks. *Nemenyi's test* is used as the *post hoc* test to identify the specific conditions that differ from each other.

**10.** *Eta squared* describes the relationship found in experiments using ranked data.

---

## USING THE COMPUTER

The one-way and two-way chi square procedures are performed by routine **9** of the computer program. For the one-way procedures, you must provide the values of $f_e$, but for the two-way procedures, they are computed for you. Then you are given a graph of the results, $\chi^2_{obt}$, and the minimum *p* value ($\alpha$) at which it is significant. For the two-way chi square, the program will compute the appropriate value of either the phi coefficient or the contingency coefficient.

The program also performs the nonparametric procedures for ranked scores discussed in this chapter. You can enter ranked scores or nonranked interval or ratio scores, which the program will rank. Routine **10** performs the Mann-Whitney *U* test or the rank sums test, and routine **11** performs the Wilcoxon *T* test. Routine **12** performs the Kruskal-Wallis *H* test, and routine **13** performs the Friedman $\chi^2$ test. Like past procedures, the program either computes the minimum value of *p* ($\alpha$) at which the obtained value is significant or reports the critical value at $\alpha = .05$.

---

## PRACTICE PROBLEMS

(Answers are provided for odd-numbered problems.)

*1.* When do we perform nonparametric inferential procedures?
*2.* When do we perform chi square?

3. What is a one-way chi square used for?
4. What is a two-way chi square used for?
5. In the general population, the distribution of political party affiliation is 30% Republican, 55% Democratic, and 15% other. We wish to determine whether this distribution is also found among the elderly. In a sample of 100 senior citizens, we find 18 Republicans, 64 Democrats, and 18 other.
   a. What are $H_0$ and $H_a$?
   b. What is $f_e$ for each group?
   c. Compute $\chi^2_{obt}$.
   d. With $\alpha = .05$, is party affiliation in the population of senior citizens different from that in the general population?
6. A survey finds that, given the choice, 34 females prefer males much taller than themselves, and 55 females prefer males only slightly taller than themselves.
   a. What are $H_0$ and $H_a$ for this survey?
   b. With $\alpha = .05$, what is the preference of females in the population?
7. A study similar to that of problem 5 determines the frequency of political party affiliation for male and female senior citizens. The following data are obtained:

|          | *Republican* | *Democrat* | *Other* |
|----------|--------------|------------|---------|
| *Male*   | 18           | 43         | 14      |
| *Female* | 39           | 23         | 18      |

   a. What are $H_0$ and $H_a$?
   b. What is $f_e$ in each cell?
   c. Compute $\chi^2_{obt}$.
   d. With $\alpha = .05$, what should we conclude about the relationship between gender and party affiliation in the population of senior citizens?
   e. How consistent is the relationship between gender and party affiliation in these data?
8. The following data reflect the frequency with which subjects voted in the last election and were satisfied with the officials elected:

|          |       | *Satisfied* |       |
|----------|-------|-------------|-------|
|          |       | *yes*       | *no*  |
| *Vote*   | *yes* | 48          | 35    |
|          | *no*  | 33          | 52    |

    *a.* What are $H_0$ and $H_a$?
    *b.* What is $f_e$ in each cell?
    *c.* Compute $\chi^2_{obt}$.
    *d.* With $\alpha = .05$, what should we conclude about the correlation coefficient?
    *e.* How consistent is the relationship for these data?
9. What is the nonparametric version for each of the following?
    *a.* one-way, between-subjects ANOVA
    *b.* independent samples *t*-test ($n \le 20$)
    *c.* related samples *t*-test
    *d.* independent samples *t*-test ($n > 20$)
    *e.* one-way, repeated measures ANOVA
    *f.* Fisher's protected *t*-test
    *g.* Tukey's *HSD* test
10. Perform the two-tailed Mann-Whitney *U* test on the following interval data ($\alpha = .05$).

| Sample 1 | Sample 2 |
|----------|----------|
| 43 | 51 |
| 52 | 58 |
| 65 | 72 |
| 23 | 81 |
| 31 | 92 |
| 36 | 64 |

*11.* Perform the two-tailed Wilcoxon *T* test on the following interval data ($\alpha = .05$).

| Sample 1 | Sample 2 |
|----------|----------|
| 14 | 36 |
| 18 | 31 |
| 20 | 19 |
| 28 | 48 |
| 3 | 10 |
| 34 | 49 |
| 20 | 20 |
| 24 | 29 |

## SUMMARY OF FORMULAS

**A.** Summary of chi square formulas

   **1.** *The computational formula for chi square is*

$$\chi^2_{obt} = \Sigma\left(\frac{(f_o - f_e)^2}{f_e}\right)$$

   where $f_o$ is the observed frequency in a cell and $f_e$ is the expected frequency in a cell.

   a. Computing expected frequency

   (1) *In a one-way chi square, the expected frequency in a category is equal to the probability of someone's falling in that category multiplied times the N of the study. In testing an $H_0$ of no difference, the computational formula for each expected frequency is*

$$f_e \text{ in each category} = \frac{N}{k}$$

   where $N$ is the total $N$ in the study and $k$ is the number of categories.

   (2) *In a two-way chi square, the computational formula for finding the expected frequency in each cell is*

$$f_e = \frac{(\text{cell's row total } f_o)(\text{cell's column total } f_o)}{N}$$

   b. *Critical values of $\chi^2$ are found in Table 8.*

   (1) In a one-way chi square, the degrees of freedom is

$$df = k - 1$$

   where $k$ is the number of categories in the variable.

   (2) In a two-way chi square, the degrees of freedom is

$$df = (\text{number of rows} - 1)(\text{number of columns} - 1)$$

   **2.** *The computational formula for the phi coefficient is*

$$\phi = \sqrt{\frac{\chi^2_{obt}}{N}}$$

   where $N$ is the total number of subjects in the study.

**3.** *The computational formula for the contingency coefficient, C, is*

$$C = \sqrt{\frac{\chi^2_{obt}}{N + \chi^2_{obt}}}$$

where $N$ is the total number of subjects in the study.

**B.** Summary of nonparametric formulas

    **1.** Formulas for two independent samples

        **a.** *The computational formula for the Mann-Whitney U Test for independent samples is*

$$U_1 = (n_1)(n_2) + \frac{n_1(n_1 + 1)}{2} - \Sigma R_1$$

and

$$U_2 = (n_1)(n_2) + \frac{n_2(n_2 + 1)}{2} - \Sigma R_2$$

This test is used when $N$ is equal to or less than 20. Here $n_1$ and $n_2$ are the $n$'s of the groups. After ranks are assigned based on all scores, $\Sigma R_1$ is the sum of ranks in Group 1, and $\Sigma R_2$ is the sum of ranks in Group 2.

           In a two-tailed test, the value of $U_{obt}$ equals the *smaller* of $U_1$ or $U_2$. In a one-tailed test, the value of $U_1$ or $U_2$ from the group predicted to have the largest sum of ranks is $U_{obt}$. Critical values of $U$ are found in Table 9. (Note that $U$ is significant if it is equal to or less than the critical value.)

        **b.** *The computational formula for the rank sums test for independent samples is*

$$z_{obt} = \frac{\Sigma R - \Sigma R_{exp}}{\sqrt{\dfrac{(n_1)(n_2)(N + 1)}{12}}}$$

This test is used when either $n$ is greater than 20. Here $n_1$ and $n_2$ are the $n$'s of the two groups, and $N$ is the total $N$. After ranks are assigned based on all scores, $\Sigma R$ is the sum of the ranks for the chosen group. $\Sigma R_{exp}$ is the expected sum of ranks for the chosen group, found using the formula

$$\Sigma R_{exp} = \frac{n(N + 1)}{2}$$

where $n$ is the $n$ of the chosen group. Critical values of $z$ are found in Table 1.

c. *Eta squared is computed using the formula*

$$\eta^2 = \frac{(z_{obt})^2}{N - 1}$$

2. *For related samples, the computational formula for the Wilcoxon T is*

$$T_{obt} = \Sigma R$$

After the difference scores are found and assigned ranks, in the two-tailed test, $\Sigma R$ is the smaller of the sum of ranks for the positive difference scores or the sum of ranks for the negative difference scores. In the one-tailed test, $\Sigma R$ is the sum of ranks that is predicted to be the smallest. Critical values of $T$ are found in Table 10, where $N$ is the number of nonzero difference scores. (Note that $T$ is significant if it is equal to or less than the critical value.)

3. *For three or more independent samples, the computational formula for the Kruskal-Wallis H test is*

$$H_{obt} = \left(\frac{12}{N(N + 1)}\right)(SS_{bn}) - 3(N + 1)$$

where $N$ is the number of subjects in the study. After ranks are assigned using all scores, $SS_{bn}$ is found using the formula

$$SS_{bn} = \frac{(\Sigma R_1)^2}{n_1} + \frac{(\Sigma R_2)^2}{n_2} + \cdots + \frac{(\Sigma R_k)^2}{n_k}$$

where each $n$ is the number of scores in a level, each $\Sigma R$ is the sum of ranks for that level, and $k$ is the number of levels of the factor. Critical values of $H$ are found in Table 8 for $df = k - 1$, where $k$ is the number of levels in the factor.
a. When $H_{obt}$ is significant, *post hoc* comparisons are performed using the rank sums test, regardless of the size of $n$.
b. Eta squared is computed using the formula

$$\eta^2 = \frac{H_{obt}}{N - 1}$$

4. *For three or more repeated measures samples, the computational formula for the Friedman $\chi^2$ test is*

$$\chi^2_{obt} = \left(\frac{12}{(k)(N)(k + 1)}\right)(SS_{bn}) - 3(N)(k + 1)$$

where $N$ is the number of subjects and $k$ is the number of levels of the factor. After ranks are assigned within the scores of each subject, $SS_{bn}$ is found using the formula

$$SS_{bn} = (\Sigma R_1)^2 + (\Sigma R_2)^2 + \cdots + (\Sigma R_k)^2$$

where each $(\Sigma R)^2$ is the squared sum of ranks for a level. Critical values of $\chi^2$ are found in Table 8 for $df = k - 1$, where $k$ is the number of levels in the factor.

a. When the Friedman $\chi^2$ is significant, *post hoc* comparisons are performed using Nemenyi's procedure.

(1) Compute the critical difference using the formula

$$\text{Critical difference} = \sqrt{\left(\frac{k(k + 1)}{6(N)}\right)(\chi^2_{\text{crit}})}$$

where $k$ is the number of levels of the factor and $N$ is the number of subjects. $\chi^2_{\text{crit}}$ is the critical value of $\chi^2$ for the appropriate $\alpha$ at $df = k - 1$.

(2) Compute the mean rank in each condition as $\Sigma R/n$.

(3) Any two mean ranks that differ by more than the critical difference are significantly different.

b. Eta squared is found using the formula

$$\eta^2 = \frac{\chi^2_{\text{obt}}}{(N)(k) - 1}$$

# Interpolation

## INTERPOLATING FROM THE *z*-TABLES

In essence, interpolation is a procedure for reading between the lines of a table. We interpolate when we must find an exact proportion that is not shown in the *z*-table or when we seek a proportion for a *z*-score that has three decimal places. In any interpolation, carry all computations to four decimal places.

### Finding an Unknown *z*-Score

Say that we seek a target *z*-score that corresponds to a target proportion of exactly .45 (.4500) of the curve between the mean and *z*. To interpolate, enter the *z*-tables and identify the two bracketing proportions—the closest proportions above and below the target proportion. Note their corresponding *z*-scores. For .4500, the bracketing proportions are .4505 at $z = 1.6500$ and .4495 at $z = 1.6400$. Arrange the values this way:

|  | *Known* proportion under curve | *Unknown* *z*-score |
|---|---|---|
| Upper bracket | .4505 | 1.6500 |
| Target | .4500 | ? |
| Lower bracket | .4495 | 1.6400 |

Notice the labels. We seek the "unknown" target $z$-score which corresponds to the "known" target proportion of .4500. The known target proportion is bracketed by .4505 and .4495. The unknown target $z$-score is bracketed by 1.6500 and 1.6400.

Interpolation is actually quite simple. If you look at the above table, you can see that the target proportion of .4500 is a number that is halfway between .4495 and .4505. That is, the difference between the lower known proportion and our target proportion is one-half of the difference between the two known proportions. We assume that the $z$-score corresponding to .4500 is also halfway between the two bracketing $z$-scores of 1.6400 and 1.6500. The difference between the two bracketing $z$-scores is .010, and one-half of that is .005. Thus, to go to halfway between 1.6400 and 1.6500, we add .005 to 1.6400. Our answer is that a $z$-score of 1.6450 corresponds to .4500 of the curve between the mean and $z$.

Since the answer will not always be as obvious as in this example, use the following steps.

> *Step 1.* Determine the difference between the upper known bracket and the lower known bracket. In the above example, .4505 − .4495 = .0010. This is the total distance between the two known proportions.
>
> *Step 2.* Determine the difference between the known target and the lower known bracket. Above, .4500 − .4495 = .0005.
>
> *Step 3.* Form a fraction, with the answer from step 2 as the numerator and the answer from step 1 as the denominator. Above, the fraction is .0005/.0010, which equals .5. This tells us that .4500 is one-half of the distance from .4495 to .4505.
>
> *Step 4.* Find the difference between the two brackets in the unknown column. Above, 1.6500 − 1.6400 = .010. This is the total distance between the two $z$-scores that bracket the unknown target $z$-score.
>
> *Step 5.* Multiply the proportion found in step 3 by the answer found in step 4. Above, (.5)(.010) = .005. This tells us that the unknown target $z$-score, lying .5 of the distance from 1.640 to 1.650, is .005 larger than the lower bracketing $z$-score.
>
> *Step 6.* Add the answer in step 5 to the lower bracketing score. Above, .005 + 1.640 = 1.645. This is our unknown target $z$-score. Thus, .4500 of the normal curve lies between the mean and $z$ = 1.645.

## Finding an Unknown Proportion

We can also apply the above steps to find an unknown proportion for a known three-decimal-place $z$-score. For example, say we have a known target $z$ of

1.382. What is the corresponding proportion between the mean and this $z$? From the $z$-table, we see that the upper and lower known brackets around our target $z$-score are 1.390 and 1.380. We arrange the $z$-scores and corresponding proportions as shown below.

|  | *Known* <br> *z-score* | *Unknown* <br> *proportion under curve* |
|---|---|---|
| Upper bracket | 1.390 | .4177 |
| Target | 1.382 | ? |
| Lower bracket | 1.380 | .4162 |

Here the $z$-scores are in the "known" column and the proportions are in the "unknown" column. To find the target proportion, use the above steps.

*Step 1:* $1.390 - 1.380 = .010$

This is the total difference between the known bracketing $z$-scores.

*Step 2:* $1.382 - 1.380 = .002$

This is the distance between the lower known bracketing $z$-score and the target $z$-score.

*Step 3:* $\dfrac{.002}{.010} = .20$

This is the proportion of the distance that the target $z$-score lies from the lower bracket. A $z$ of 1.382 is .20 of the distance from 1.380 to 1.390.

*Step 4:* $.4177 - .4162 = .0015$

This tells us that .0015 is the total distance between the brackets of .4177 and .4162 in the unknown column.

Since our known target $z$-score is .20 of the distance from the lower bracketing $z$-score to the higher bracketing $z$-score, the proportion we seek is .20 of the distance from the lower bracketing proportion to the upper bracketing proportion.

*Step 5:* $(0.20)(0.0015) = .0003$

This tells us that .20 of the distance separating the bracketing proportions in the unknown column is .0003.

*Step 6:* $.4162 + .0003 = .4165$

Increasing the lower proportion in the unknown column by .0003 takes us to the point corresponding to .20 of the distance between the bracketing proportions. This point is .4165, which is the proportion that corresponds to the *z*-score of 1.382.

---

## INTERPOLATING CRITICAL VALUES

In conducting inferential statistical procedures, sometimes we must interpolate between tabled critical values. We apply the same steps described above, except that now we use tabled degrees of freedom and critical values.

For example, say that we are performing a *t*-test and we seek the critical value corresponding to 35 *df* (with $\alpha$ = .05, two-tailed test). The *t*-tables have values only for 30 *df* and 40 *df*. We obtain the following:

|  | *Known df* | *Unknown critical value* |
|---|---|---|
| Upper bracket | 30 | 2.042 |
| Target | 35 | ? |
| Lower bracket | 40 | 2.021 |

Logically, since 35 *df* is halfway between 30 *df* and 40 *df*, we know that the critical value for 35 *df* must be halfway between 2.042 and 2.021.

To find the unknown target critical value, follow the steps described for *z*-scores.

*Step 1:*   $40 - 30 = 10$

This is the total difference between the known bracketing *df*'s.

*Step 2:*   $35 - 30 = 5$

This is the distance between the upper bracketing *df* and our target *df*.

*Step 3:*   $\dfrac{5}{10} = .50$

This is the proportion of the distance that our target *df* lies from the upper known bracket. The *df* of 35 is .50 of the distance from 30 to 40.

*Step 4:*   $2.042 - 2.021 = .021$

This tells us that .021 is the total distance between the bracketing critical values of 2.042 and 2.021 in the unknown column.

Since our *df* of 35 is .50 of the distance between the bracketing *df*'s, the critical value we seek is .50 of the distance between 2.042 and 2.021, or .50 of .021.

*Step 5:*   $(.50)(.021) = .0105$

This tells us that .50 of the distance separating the bracketing critical values is .0105. Since critical values decrease as *df* increases and we are going from 30 *df* to 35 *df*, we *subtract* .0105 from the larger value, 2.042.

*Step 6:*   $2.042 - .0105 = 2.0315$

Thus, $t = 2.0315$ is the critical value associated with 35 *df* at $\alpha = .05$ for a two-tailed test.

  The same logic can be applied to find critical values for any of the other statistical procedures.

# Additional Formulas for Computing Probability

## THE MULTIPLICATION RULE

Sometimes we are "satisfied" only if several events occur. We use the multiplication rule when the word "and" links the events that all must occur in order for us to be satisfied. *The following multiplication rule can be used only with independent events.* (For dependent events, a different, more complex rule is needed.)

> **THE MULTIPLICATION RULE IS**
>
> $$p(\text{A and B}) = p(\text{A}) \times p(\text{B})$$

The multiplication rule states that the probability of several independent events is equal to the probabilities of the individual events *multiplied* together. (When you say "and," think "multiply.") Thus, the probability that we will be satisfied by having both A and B occur is equal to the probability of A multiplied times the probability of B. (If there were three events, then all three probabilities would be multiplied together, and so on.)

We may use the multiplication rule when describing a *series* of independent events. Say that we want to know the probability of obtaining 3 heads on 3 coin tosses. We can restate the problem as the probability of obtaining a head *and* then a head *and* then a head. Thus, by the multiplication rule, the probability of 3 heads is

$$p(\text{head}) \times p(\text{head}) \times p(\text{head}) = .5 \times .5 \times .5 = .125$$

The answer we obtain is the same one we would find by forming the ratio of the number of sequences of heads and tails that would satisfy us to the number of possible sequences we could obtain when tossing 3 coins. The multiplication rule simply provides a shorter, less complicated route.

We may also use the multiplication rule if we are satisfied when two or more independent events occur *simultaneously*. For example, the probability of drawing the king of hearts can be restated as the probability of drawing a king *and* a heart simultaneously. Since there are 4 kings, the probability of drawing a king is 4/52, or .0769. Since there are 13 hearts, the probability of drawing a heart is 13/52, or .25. Thus, the probability of drawing a king and a heart is (.0769 × .25), so $p(\text{king and heart}) = .0192$. (As a check on our answer, there is 1 king of hearts in 52 cards, so the probability of drawing the king of hearts is 1/52, which is again .0192. Amazing!)

## THE ADDITION RULE

Sometimes we are satisfied by any *one* of a number of outcomes that may occur in one sample. We use the addition rule when the word "or" links the events that will satisfy us. For example, if we will be satisfied by either A *or* B, then we seek $p(\text{A or B})$. However, there are two versions of the addition rule, depending on whether we are describing mutually exclusive or mutually inclusive events. **Mutually exclusive events** are events that cannot occur together: the occurrence of one event prohibits, or excludes, the occurrence of another. Head and tail, for example, are mutually exclusive on any *one* flip of a coin. Conversely, **mutually inclusive events** are events that can occur together. For example, drawing a king from a deck is mutually inclusive with drawing a heart, since we can draw the king of hearts.

> *THE ADDITION RULE FOR MUTUALLY EXCLUSIVE EVENTS IS*
>
> $$p(\text{A or B}) = p(\text{A}) + p(\text{B})$$

This formula says that the probability of being satisfied by having either A or B occur is equal to the probability of A plus the probability of B. (For mutually exclusive events, when you say "or," think "add.") For example, the probability of randomly drawing a queen or a king is found by adding the probability of a king (which is 4/52, or .0769) and the probability of a queen (which is also .0769). Thus, $p$(king or queen) = .0769 + .0769, so $p$(king or queen) = .1538. In essence, we have found that there are a total of 8 cards out of 52 that can satisfy us with a king or a queen, and 8/52 corresponds to a $p$ of .1538.

When events are mutually *inclusive,* we may obtain A, we may obtain B, or we may obtain A and B simultaneously. To see how this can play havoc with our computations, say that we seek the probability of randomly drawing either a king *or* a heart in one draw. We *might* think that since there are 4 kings and there are 13 hearts, there are a total of 17 cards that will satisfy us—right? Wrong! If you count the cards in a deck that will satisfy us, you will find only 16, not 17. The problem is that we counted the king of hearts twice, once as a king and once as a heart. To correct this, we must subtract the "extra" king of hearts.

*THE ADDITION RULE FOR MUTUALLY INCLUSIVE EVENTS IS*

$$p(A \text{ or } B) = p(A) + p(B) - [p(A) \times p(B)]$$

This version of the addition rule states that the probability of obtaining any one of several mutually inclusive events is equal to the sum of the probabilities of the individual events *minus* the probability of those events' occurring simultaneously (minus the probability of A and B). We compute the probability of A and B using the multiplication rule, where $p(A \text{ and } B) = p(A) \times p(B)$. The probability of a king is 4/52, or .0769, and the probability of a heart is 13/52, or .25. Since we have counted the king of hearts both as a king and as a heart, we then subtract the extra king of hearts: the probability of a king and a heart is 1/52, or .0192. Therefore, altogether we have

$$p(\text{king or heart}) = .0769 + .25 - .0192 = .3077$$

This is equivalent to finding the ratio of the number of outcomes that satisfy the event to the total number of possible outcomes. There are 16 out of 52 outcomes that can satisfy king or heart, and 16/52 corresponds to $p$ = .3077.

For fun, we can combine the addition and multiplication rules. For example, what is the probability of drawing either the jack of diamonds *or* the king of spades on one draw, *and* then drawing either the 5 *or* the 6 of diamonds on a second draw? In symbols, we have

$$p[(A \text{ or } B) \text{ and } (C \text{ or } D)]$$

Because these events are all mutually exclusive, we have

$$p[(A \text{ or } B) \text{ and } (C \text{ or } D)] = [p(A) + p(B)] \times [p(C) + p(D)]$$

If we are sampling with replacement, the answer is .00148. If we are sampling without replacement, the answer is .00151. (Come on, try it.)

## THE BINOMIAL EXPANSION

In Chapter 9 we computed the probability of obtaining 7 heads in 7 coin tosses. In doing so, we listed all of the possible sequences of heads and tails that might occur, and then we counted the number of outcomes that would satisfy us. We could use the same technique to determine the probability of obtaining 1 head in 3 coin tosses. If we list all of the possible sequences of head and tails we might obtain with 3 tosses, we have

| | | | | | |
|---|---|---|---|---|---|
| head | head | head | tail | tail | tail |
| head | head | tail | tail | tail | head |
| head | tail | head | head | tail | tail |
| tail | head | head | tail | head | tail |

There are a total of 8 possible combinations we might obtain, 3 of which contain 1 head. Thus, the probability of obtaining 1 head in 3 tosses is 3/8, or .375.

Instead of listing all of the possible outcomes and then counting those that satisfy us, we can use a mathematical formula, called the *binomial expansion,* for computing such probabilities. A "binomial" situation exists when one of only two possible outcomes occurs on each occasion and the two outcomes are mutually exclusive. Then the binomial expansion can be used to compute the probability of obtaining a certain number of one of the outcomes in some total number of tries. In statistical terms, we find the probability of a certain *combination* of N events taken r at a time. Since either a head or a tail occurs on each toss of the coin, the binomial expansion can be used to determine the probability of obtaining some number of heads in a certain number of tosses. We will use the symbol $p_C$ to stand for the probability of the particular combination that satisfies us.

*THE FORMULA FOR THE BINOMIAL EXPANSION IS*

$$p_C = \left(\frac{N!}{r!(N-r)!}\right)(p^r)(q^{N-r})$$

$N$ stands for the total number of tries or occasions, and $r$ stands for the number of events that satisfy us. Thus, to find the probability of obtaining 1 head in 3 tries, we use $N = 3$ and $r = 1$. The symbol $p$ stands for the probability of the desired event, and we raise it to the $r$ power (multiply it times itself $r$ times). Here heads is the desired event, so $p = .5$. Since $r = 1$, we have $.5^1$. The symbol $q$ stands for the probability of the event that is not desired, and it is raised to the $N - r$ power. Tails is the undesirable event, so $q = .5$. Since $N - r$ equals 2, we have $.5^2$. Thus, filling in the binomial expansion, we have

$$p_C = \left(\frac{3!}{1!(3 - 1)!}\right)(.5^1)(.5^2)$$

The exclamation point (!) is the symbol for *factorial,* meaning that you multiply the number times all whole numbers less than it down to 1. Thus, 3! equals 3 times 2 times 1, for an answer of 6. The quantity 1! is (1)(1), or 1, and the quantity $(3 - 1)!$ is (2)!, which is (2)(1), or 2. Now the formula becomes

$$p_C = \left(\frac{6}{1(2)}\right)(.5^1)(.5^2)$$

Any number raised to the first power is that number, so $.5^1$ equals .5. (In a different problem, if you had to raise $p$ or $q$ to the zero power, the answer would be 1.) Since $.5^2$ is .25, we have

$$p_C = \left(\frac{6}{1(2)}\right)(.5)(.25)$$

Multiplying 1 times 2 yields 2, divided into 6 is 3. Multiplying .5 times .25 gives .125, so we have

$$p_C = 3(.125)$$

and $p_C = .375$. Thus, the probability of obtaining 1 head in 3 coin tosses is, as we found initially, equal to .375. Notice that this is not the probability of obtaining at least 1 head. Rather, it is the probability of obtaining precisely 1 head (and 2 tails) in 3 coin tosses.

We can also use the binomial expansion when we can classify various events as either "yes" or "no." For example, say we are playing with dice, and we want to determine the probability of showing a two on 4 out of 6 rolls of one die. The desired event of a two is the "yes." We want it to happen 4 times, so $r = 4$. Its probability on any single roll is $p$, which equals 1/6, or .167. Showing any other number on the die is a "no," and the probability of any other number on 1 roll of the die is $q$, which equals 5/6, or .83. Thus, filling in the binomial expansion, we have

$$p_C = \left(\frac{N!}{r!(N-r)!}\right)(p^r)(q^{N - r}) = \frac{6!}{4!(6 - 4)!}(.167^4)(.83^2)$$

which becomes

$$p_C = \left(\frac{720}{24(2)}\right)(.00078)(.689)$$

which equals

$$p_C = \left(\frac{720}{48}\right)(.00054)$$

Thus,

$$p_C = 15(.00054) = .0081$$

so the probability of rolling a die 6 times and showing a two on 4 of the rolls equals .0081.

# One-Way Repeated Measures Analysis of Variance

A one-way ANOVA for repeated measures is similar to a two-way ANOVA, which is discussed in Chapter 14, so read that chapter first.

## ASSUMPTIONS OF THE REPEATED MEASURES ANOVA

In a repeated measures ANOVA, the same subjects are measured repeatedly under all levels of one factor, and there must be an equal number of scores in each condition. The other assumptions of the repeated measures ANOVA are the same as those for the between-subjects ANOVA: (1) subjects are randomly selected and the dependent variable is a ratio or interval variable, (2) the populations of scores represented by the conditions are normally distributed and the mean is the appropriate measure of central tendency, and (3) the population variances are equal or homogeneous.

## LOGIC OF THE ONE-WAY REPEATED MEASURES $F$-RATIO

Let's look at an example of a repeated measures study. Say our factor has three levels. First we test five subjects under level $A_1$, then we test the same five subjects under level $A_2$, and then again under level $A_3$. The design of this study would be diagramed as follows.

*Factor A*

| | Level $A_1$ | Level $A_2$ | Level $A_3$ |
|---|---|---|---|
| *1* | X | X | X |
| *2* | X | X | X |
| *3* | X | X | X |
| *4* | X | X | X |
| *5* | X | X | X |
| | $\overline{X}_{A_1}$ | $\overline{X}_{A_2}$ | $\overline{X}_{A_3}$ |

*Subjects* appears to the left of the subject numbers.

We find the mean of each column of scores under factor A. As usual, we are testing whether the means from the different levels of the factor represent different population $\mu$'s. Therefore, the hypotheses are the same as in a between-subjects design.

$$H_0: \mu_1 = \mu_2 = \mu_3$$

$H_a$: not all $\mu$'s are equal

Although this is a one-way ANOVA, we can view it as a two-way ANOVA, with factor A as one factor and the different subjects as a second factor, here with five levels. Then factor A is the independent variable we are interested in, factor B is the subjects factor, and the interaction is between subjects and factor A.

## ELEMENTS OF THE REPEATED MEASURES ANOVA

Previously when computing $F_{obt}$, we needed a mean square within groups ($MS_{wn}$). This was our estimate of the error variance ($\sigma^2_{error}$), the inherent variability of any of the populations being represented. We computed $MS_{wn}$ using the differences between the scores in each cell and the mean of the cell. However, as you can see from the above diagram, each cell contains only one score, because there is only one subject. Therefore, the mean of each cell *is* the score in the cell, and the differences within a cell are always zero. Obviously, we cannot compute $MS_{wn}$ in the usual way.

However, in a repeated measures ANOVA, the mean square for the interaction between factor A and the subjects (abbreviated $MS_{A \times subs}$) does reflect the inherent variability of scores. An interaction indicates that the effect of one factor changes across the levels of the other factor. It is because of the inherent variability, or differences, between subjects that the effect of factor

A changes across the different subjects. Therefore, $MS_{A \times subs}$ is our estimate of error variance ($\sigma^2_{error}$), and it is used as the denominator of the repeated measures $F$-ratio.

As usual, $MS_A$ describes the difference between the means in factor A, and it is our estimate of variability due to error plus variability due to treatment. Thus, the $F$-ratio for a repeated measures factor is

| *Sample* | *Estimates* | *Population* |
|---|---|---|
| $F_{obt} = \dfrac{MS_A}{MS_{A \times subs}}$ | $\rightarrow$ <br> $\rightarrow$ | $\dfrac{\sigma^2_{error} + \sigma^2_{treat}}{\sigma^2_{error}}$ |

As usual, if the data represent the situation where $H_0$ is true and all $\mu$'s are equal, then both the numerator and the denominator will contain only $\sigma^2_{error}$, so $F_{obt}$ will equal 1.0. However, the larger the $F_{obt}$, the less likely it is that the differences between the means merely reflect sampling error in representing one population $\mu$. If $F_{obt}$ is significant, then at least two of the means from factor A represent different values of $\mu$.

## COMPUTING THE ONE-WAY REPEATED MEASURES ANOVA

Say we have tested the same five subjects under three levels of factor A and obtained these data:

**Factor A**

| Subjects | Level $A_1$ | Level $A_2$ | Level $A_3$ | |
|---|---|---|---|---|
| 1 | 4 | 9 | 1 | $\Sigma X_{sub} = 14$ |
| 2 | 6 | 12 | 3 | $\Sigma X_{sub} = 21$ |
| 3 | 8 | 4 | 4 | $\Sigma X_{sub} = 16$ |
| 4 | 2 | 8 | 5 | $\Sigma X_{sub} = 15$ |
| 5 | 10 | 7 | 2 | $\Sigma X_{sub} = 19$ |

Total:

| | | | |
|---|---|---|---|
| $\Sigma X = 30$ | $\Sigma X = 40$ | $\Sigma X = 15$ | $\Sigma X_{tot} = 30 + 40 + 15 = 85$ |
| $\Sigma X^2 = 220$ | $\Sigma X^2 = 354$ | $\Sigma X^2 = 55$ | $\Sigma X^2_{tot} = 220 + 354 + 55 = 629$ |
| $n_1 = 5$ | $n_2 = 5$ | $n_3 = 5$ | $N = 15$ |
| $\overline{X}_1 = 6$ | $\overline{X}_2 = 8$ | $\overline{X}_3 = 3$ | $k = 3$ |

The first step is to compute the $\Sigma X$, the $\overline{X}$, and the $\Sigma X^2$ for each level of factor A (each column). Then compute $\Sigma X_{tot}$ and $\Sigma X^2_{tot}$. Also compute $\Sigma X_{sub}$, which is the $\Sigma X$ for each subject's scores (each horizontal row). Notice that the $n$'s and $N$ are based on the number of *scores*, not the number of subjects.

Then follow these steps.

Step 1 is to compute the total sum of squares ($SS_{tot}$).

THE COMPUTATIONAL FORMULA FOR $SS_{tot}$ IS

$$SS_{tot} = \Sigma X^2_{tot} - \left( \frac{(\Sigma X_{tot})^2}{N} \right)$$

Filling in this formula from our example data, we have

$$SS_{tot} = 629 - \left( \frac{85^2}{15} \right)$$

$$SS_{tot} = 629 - 481.67$$

so

$$SS_{tot} = 147.33$$

Note that we call the quantity $(\Sigma X)^2/N$ the *correction* in the following computations. (Here the correction is 481.67.)

Step 2 is to compute the sum of squares for factor A, $SS_A$.

THE COMPUTATIONAL FORMULA FOR THE SUM OF SQUARES BETWEEN GROUPS FOR FACTOR A IS

$$SS_A = \Sigma \left( \frac{(\text{sum of scores in the column})^2}{n \text{ of scores in the column}} \right) - \left( \frac{(\Sigma X_{tot})^2}{N} \right)$$

This formula says to take the sum of $X$ in each level (column) of factor A, square the sum, and divide by the $n$ of the level. After doing this for all levels, add the results together and subtract the correction.

In our example, we have

$$SS_A = \left( \frac{(30)^2}{5} + \frac{(40)^2}{5} + \frac{(15)^2}{5} \right) - 481.67$$

so

$$SS_A = 545 - 481.67$$

Thus,

$$SS_A = 63.33$$

Step 3 is to find the sum of squares for subjects, $SS_{subs}$.

---

**THE COMPUTATIONAL FORMULA FOR THE SUM OF SQUARES FOR SUBJECTS, $SS_{subs}$, IS**

$$SS_{subs} = \frac{(\Sigma X_{sub1})^2 + (\Sigma X_{sub2})^2 + \cdots + (\Sigma X_n)^2}{k} - \frac{(\Sigma X_{tot})^2}{N}$$

---

This says to take $\Sigma X_{sub}$, the sum for each subject, and square it. Then add the squared sums together. Next divide by $k$, where $k$ is the number of levels of factor A. Finally, subtract the correction.

In our example, we have

$$SS_{subs} = \frac{(14)^2 + (21)^2 + (16)^2 + (15)^2 + (19)^2}{3} - 481.67$$

so

$$SS_{subs} = 493 - 481.67$$

Thus,

$$SS_{subs} = 11.33$$

Step 4 is to find the sum of squares for the interaction, $SS_{A \times subs}$. To do this, subtract the sums of squares for the other factors from the total.

---

**THE COMPUTATIONAL FORMULA FOR THE INTERACTION OF FACTOR A BY SUBJECTS, $SS_{A \times subs}$, IS**

$$SS_{A \times subs} = SS_{tot} - SS_A - SS_{subs}$$

---

In our example,

$$SS_{A \times subs} = 147.33 - 63.33 - 11.33$$

so

$$SS_{A \times subs} = 72.67$$

Step 5 is to determine the degrees of freedom.

THE DEGREES OF FREEDOM BETWEEN GROUPS FOR FACTOR A IS

$$df_A = k_A - 1$$

$k_A$ is the number of levels of factor A. (In the example, there are three levels, so $df_A$ is 2.)

THE DEGREES OF FREEDOM FOR THE INTERACTION IS

$$df_{A \times subs} = (k_A - 1)(k_{subs} - 1)$$

$k_A$ is the number of levels of factor A, and $k_{subs}$ is the number of subjects. In the example, there are three levels of factor A and 5 subjects, so $df_{A \times subs} = (2)(4) = 8$.

Compute $df_{subs}$ and $df_{tot}$ to check the above $df$. The $df_{subs} = k_{subs} - 1$, where $k_{subs}$ is the number of subjects. The $df_{tot} = N - 1$, where $N$ is the total number of *scores* in the experiment. The $df_{tot}$ is equal to the sum of all the other $df$'s.

Step 6 is to place the sum of squares and the $df$'s in the summary table. For our example, we have the following table.

Summary Table of One-Way Repeated Measures ANOVA

| Source | Sum of squares | df | Mean square | F |
|---|---|---|---|---|
| Subjects | 11.33 | 4 | | |
| Factor A | 63.33 | 2 | $MS_A$ | $F_A$ |
| Interaction | | | | |
| (A × subjects) | 72.67 | 8 | $MS_{A \times subs}$ | |
| Total | 147.33 | 14 | | |

Since we have only one factor of interest here (factor A), we will find only the $F_{obt}$ for factor A.

Step 7 is to find the mean squares for factor A and the interaction.

THE MEAN SQUARE FOR FACTOR A, $MS_A$, EQUALS

$$MS_A = \frac{SS_A}{df_A}$$

In our example,

$$MS_A = \frac{SS_A}{df_A} = \frac{63.33}{2} = 31.67$$

---

**THE MEAN SQUARE FOR THE INTERACTION BETWEEN FACTOR A AND SUBJECTS, $MS_{A \cdot subs}$, IS**

$$MS_{A \times subs} = \frac{SS_{A \times subs}}{df_{A \times subs}}$$

---

In our example,

$$MS_{A \times subs} = \frac{SS_{A \times subs}}{df_{A \times subs}} = \frac{72.67}{8} = 9.08$$

Step 8 is to find $F_{obt}$.

---

**THE COMPUTATIONAL FORMULA FOR THE REPEATED MEASURES F-RATIO IS**

$$F_{obt} = \frac{MS_A}{MS_{A \times subs}}$$

---

In our example,

$$F_{obt} = \frac{MS_A}{MS_{A \times subs}} = \frac{31.67}{9.09} = 3.49$$

Step 9 is to find the critical value of $F$ in Table 5 of Appendix D. Use $df_A$ as the degrees of freedom between groups and $df_{A \times subs}$ as the degrees of freedom within groups. In the example, for $\alpha = .05$, $df_A = 2$, and $df_{A \times subs} = 8$, the $F_{crit}$ is 4.46.

---

## INTERPRETING THE REPEATED MEASURES *F*

At this point, we interpret the repeated measures $F_{obt}$ in exactly the same way we would a between-subjects $F_{obt}$. Since $F_{obt}$ in the above example is *not* larger than $F_{crit}$, it is not significant. Thus, we do not have evidence that the means from at least two of our levels of factor A represent different populations of scores. Had $F_{obt}$ been significant, it would indicate that at least two of the cell means differ significantly. Then, for *post hoc* comparisons, graphing, eta squared, and confidence intervals, we would follow the procedures discussed in Chapter 13. However, in any of those formulas, in place of the term $MS_{wn}$ we would use the above $MS_{A \times subs}$.

Note that in discussing the related samples or repeated measures *t*-test in Chapter 12, we said that it is more powerful than the independent samples *t*-test, because the variability in the scores is less. For the same reason, the repeated measures ANOVA is more powerful than a between-subjects ANOVA for the same data. In the repeated measures ANOVA, we delete some of the variability in the raw scores by separating (and then ignoring) the sum of squares for the subjects factor. By removing the differences due to subjects from our calculations, we obtain an $MS_{A \times subs}$ that is smaller than the $MS_{wn}$ we would compute in a between-subjects ANOVA. Therefore, we obtain a larger $F_{obt}$, which is more likely to be significant, so we have greater power. The results in the above example were not significant because of the relatively small $N$, given the amount of variability in the scores. However, this design was still more powerful—more likely to produce significant results—than a comparable between-subjects design.

# D

# Statistical Tables

## Table 1 Proportions of Area Under the Standard Normal Curve: The z-Tables

Column (A) lists z-score values. Column (B) lists the proportion of the area between the mean and the z-score value. Column (C) lists the proportion of the area beyond the z-score. *Note:* Because the normal distribution is symmetrical, areas for negative z-scores are the same as those for positive z-scores.

| (A) | (B) | (C) | (A) | (B) | (C) | (A) | (B) | (C) |
|---|---|---|---|---|---|---|---|---|
| | Area between | Area | | Area between | Area | | Area between | Area |
| z | mean and z | beyond z | z | mean and z | beyond z | z | mean and z | beyond z |
| 0.00 | .0000 | .5000 | 0.30 | .1179 | .3821 | 0.60 | .2257 | .2743 |
| 0.01 | .0040 | .4960 | 0.31 | .1217 | .3783 | 0.61 | .2291 | .2709 |
| 0.02 | .0080 | .4920 | 0.32 | .1255 | .3745 | 0.62 | .2324 | .2676 |
| 0.03 | .0120 | .4880 | 0.33 | .1293 | .3707 | 0.63 | .2357 | .2643 |
| 0.04 | .0160 | .4840 | 0.34 | .1331 | .3669 | 0.64 | .2389 | .2611 |
| 0.05 | .0199 | .4801 | 0.35 | .1368 | .3632 | 0.65 | .2422 | .2578 |
| 0.06 | .0239 | .4761 | 0.36 | .1406 | .3594 | 0.66 | .2454 | .2546 |
| 0.07 | .0279 | .4721 | 0.37 | .1443 | .3557 | 0.67 | .2486 | .2514 |
| 0.08 | .0319 | .4681 | 0.38 | .1480 | .3520 | 0.68 | .2517 | .2483 |
| 0.09 | .0359 | .4641 | 0.39 | .1517 | .3483 | 0.69 | .2549 | .2451 |
| 0.10 | .0398 | .4602 | 0.40 | .1554 | .3446 | 0.70 | .2580 | .2420 |
| 0.11 | .0438 | .4562 | 0.41 | .1591 | .3409 | 0.71 | .2611 | .2389 |
| 0.12 | .0478 | .4522 | 0.42 | .1628 | .3372 | 0.72 | .2642 | .2358 |
| 0.13 | .0517 | .4483 | 0.43 | .1664 | .3336 | 0.73 | .2673 | .2327 |
| 0.14 | .0557 | .4443 | 0.44 | .1700 | .3300 | 0.74 | .2704 | .2296 |
| 0.15 | .0596 | .4404 | 0.45 | .1736 | .3264 | 0.75 | .2734 | .2266 |
| 0.16 | .0636 | .4364 | 0.46 | .1772 | .3228 | 0.76 | .2764 | .2236 |
| 0.17 | .0675 | .4325 | 0.47 | .1808 | .3192 | 0.77 | .2794 | .2206 |
| 0.18 | .0714 | .4286 | 0.48 | .1844 | .3156 | 0.78 | .2823 | .2177 |
| 0.19 | .0753 | .4247 | 0.49 | .1879 | .3121 | 0.79 | .2852 | .2148 |
| 0.20 | .0793 | .4207 | 0.50 | .1915 | .3085 | 0.80 | .2881 | .2119 |
| 0.21 | .0832 | .4168 | 0.51 | .1950 | .3050 | 0.81 | .2910 | .2090 |
| 0.22 | .0871 | .4129 | 0.52 | .1985 | .3015 | 0.82 | .2939 | .2061 |
| 0.23 | .0910 | .4090 | 0.53 | .2019 | .2981 | 0.83 | .2967 | .2033 |
| 0.24 | .0948 | .4052 | 0.54 | .2054 | .2946 | 0.84 | .2995 | .2005 |
| 0.25 | .0987 | .4013 | 0.55 | .2088 | .2912 | 0.85 | .3023 | .1977 |
| 0.26 | .1026 | .3974 | 0.56 | .2123 | .2877 | 0.86 | .3051 | .1949 |
| 0.27 | .1064 | .3936 | 0.57 | .2157 | .2843 | 0.87 | .3078 | .1922 |
| 0.28 | .1103 | .3897 | 0.58 | .2190 | .2810 | 0.88 | .3106 | .1894 |
| 0.29 | .1141 | .3859 | 0.59 | .2224 | .2776 | 0.89 | .3133 | .1867 |

## Table 1 (cont.)   Proportions of Area Under the Standard Normal Curve: The z-Tables

| (A) z | (B) Area between mean and z | (C) Area beyond z | (A) z | (B) Area between mean and z | (C) Area beyond z | (A) z | (B) Area between mean and z | (C) Area beyond z |
|---|---|---|---|---|---|---|---|---|
| 0.90 | .3159 | .1841 | 1.25 | .3944 | .1056 | 1.60 | .4452 | .0548 |
| 0.91 | .3186 | .1814 | 1.26 | .3962 | .1038 | 1.61 | .4463 | .0537 |
| 0.92 | .3212 | .1788 | 1.27 | .3980 | .1020 | 1.62 | .4474 | .0526 |
| 0.93 | .3238 | .1762 | 1.28 | .3997 | .1003 | 1.63 | .4484 | .0516 |
| 0.94 | .3264 | .1736 | 1.29 | .4015 | .0985 | 1.64 | .4495 | .0505 |
| 0.95 | .3289 | .1711 | 1.30 | .4032 | .0968 | 1.65 | .4505 | .0495 |
| 0.96 | .3315 | .1685 | 1.31 | .4049 | .0951 | 1.66 | .4515 | .0485 |
| 0.97 | .3340 | .1660 | 1.32 | .4066 | .0934 | 1.67 | .4525 | .0475 |
| 0.98 | .3365 | .1635 | 1.33 | .4082 | .0918 | 1.68 | .4535 | .0465 |
| 0.99 | .3389 | .1611 | 1.34 | .4099 | .0901 | 1.69 | .4545 | .0455 |
| 1.00 | .3413 | .1587 | 1.35 | .4115 | .0885 | 1.70 | .4554 | .0446 |
| 1.01 | .3438 | .1562 | 1.36 | .4131 | .0869 | 1.71 | .4564 | .0436 |
| 1.02 | .3461 | .1539 | 1.37 | .4147 | .0853 | 1.72 | .4573 | .0427 |
| 1.03 | .3485 | .1515 | 1.38 | .4162 | .0838 | 1.73 | .4582 | .0418 |
| 1.04 | .3508 | .1492 | 1.39 | .4177 | .0823 | 1.74 | .4591 | .0409 |
| 1.05 | .3531 | .1469 | 1.40 | .4192 | .0808 | 1.75 | .4599 | .0401 |
| 1.06 | .3554 | .1446 | 1.41 | .4207 | .0793 | 1.76 | .4608 | .0392 |
| 1.07 | .3577 | .1423 | 1.42 | .4222 | .0778 | 1.77 | .4616 | .0384 |
| 1.08 | .3599 | .1401 | 1.43 | .4236 | .0764 | 1.78 | .4625 | .0375 |
| 1.09 | .3621 | .1379 | 1.44 | .4251 | .0749 | 1.79 | .4633 | .0367 |
| 1.10 | .3643 | .1357 | 1.45 | .4265 | .0735 | 1.80 | .4641 | .0359 |
| 1.11 | .3665 | .1335 | 1.46 | .4279 | .0721 | 1.81 | .4649 | .0351 |
| 1.12 | .3686 | .1314 | 1.47 | .4292 | .0708 | 1.82 | .4656 | .0344 |
| 1.13 | .3708 | .1292 | 1.48 | .4306 | .0694 | 1.83 | .4664 | .0336 |
| 1.14 | .3729 | .1271 | 1.49 | .4319 | .0681 | 1.84 | .4671 | .0329 |
| 1.15 | .3749 | .1251 | 1.50 | .4332 | .0668 | 1.85 | .4678 | .0322 |
| 1.16 | .3770 | .1230 | 1.51 | .4345 | .0655 | 1.86 | .4686 | .0314 |
| 1.17 | .3790 | .1210 | 1.52 | .4357 | .0643 | 1.87 | .4693 | .0307 |
| 1.18 | .3810 | .1190 | 1.53 | .4370 | .0630 | 1.88 | .4699 | .0301 |
| 1.19 | .3830 | .1170 | 1.54 | .4382 | .0618 | 1.89 | .4706 | .0294 |
| 1.20 | .3849 | .1151 | 1.55 | .4394 | .0606 | 1.90 | .4713 | .0287 |
| 1.21 | .3869 | .1131 | 1.56 | .4406 | .0594 | 1.91 | .4719 | .0281 |
| 1.22 | .3888 | .1112 | 1.57 | .4418 | .0582 | 1.92 | .4726 | .0274 |
| 1.23 | .3907 | .1093 | 1.58 | .4429 | .0571 | 1.93 | .4732 | .0268 |
| 1.24 | .3925 | .1075 | 1.59 | .4441 | .0559 | 1.94 | .4738 | .0262 |

## Table 1 (cont.)   Proportions of Area Under the Standard Normal Curve: The z-Tables

| (A) z | (B) Area between mean and z | (C) Area beyond z | (A) z | (B) Area between mean and z | (C) Area beyond z | (A) z | (B) Area between mean and z | (C) Area beyond z |
|---|---|---|---|---|---|---|---|---|
| 1.95 | .4744 | .0256 | 2.30 | .4893 | .0107 | 2.65 | .4960 | .0040 |
| 1.96 | .4750 | .0250 | 2.31 | .4896 | .0104 | 2.66 | .4961 | .0039 |
| 1.97 | .4756 | .0244 | 2.32 | .4898 | .0102 | 2.67 | .4962 | .0038 |
| 1.98 | .4761 | .0239 | 2.33 | .4901 | .0099 | 2.68 | .4963 | .0037 |
| 1.99 | .4767 | .0233 | 2.34 | .4904 | .0096 | 2.69 | .4964 | .0036 |
| 2.00 | .4772 | .0228 | 2.35 | .4906 | .0094 | 2.70 | .4965 | .0035 |
| 2.01 | .4778 | .0222 | 2.36 | .4909 | .0091 | 2.71 | .4966 | .0034 |
| 2.02 | .4783 | .0217 | 2.37 | .4911 | .0089 | 2.72 | .4967 | .0033 |
| 2.03 | .4788 | .0212 | 2.38 | .4913 | .0087 | 2.73 | .4968 | .0032 |
| 2.04 | .4793 | .0207 | 2.39 | .4916 | .0084 | 2.74 | .4969 | .0031 |
| 2.05 | .4798 | .0202 | 2.40 | .4918 | .0082 | 2.75 | .4970 | .0030 |
| 2.06 | .4803 | .0197 | 2.41 | .4920 | .0080 | 2.76 | .4971 | .0029 |
| 2.07 | .4808 | .0192 | 2.42 | .4922 | .0078 | 2.77 | .4972 | .0028 |
| 2.08 | .4812 | .0188 | 2.43 | .4925 | .0075 | 2.78 | .4973 | .0027 |
| 2.09 | .4817 | .0183 | 2.44 | .4927 | .0073 | 2.79 | .4974 | .0026 |
| 2.10 | .4821 | .0179 | 2.45 | .4929 | .0071 | 2.80 | .4974 | .0026 |
| 2.11 | .4826 | .0174 | 2.46 | .4931 | .0069 | 2.81 | .4975 | .0025 |
| 2.12 | .4830 | .0170 | 2.47 | .4932 | .0068 | 2.82 | .4976 | .0024 |
| 2.13 | .4834 | .0166 | 2.48 | .4934 | .0066 | 2.83 | .4977 | .0023 |
| 2.14 | .4838 | .0162 | 2.49 | .4936 | .0064 | 2.84 | .4977 | .0023 |
| 2.15 | .4842 | .0158 | 2.50 | .4938 | .0062 | 2.85 | .4978 | .0022 |
| 2.16 | .4846 | .0154 | 2.51 | .4940 | .0060 | 2.86 | .4979 | .0021 |
| 2.17 | .4850 | .0150 | 2.52 | .4941 | .0059 | 2.87 | .4979 | .0021 |
| 2.18 | .4854 | .0146 | 2.53 | .4943 | .0057 | 2.88 | .4980 | .0020 |
| 2.19 | .4857 | .0143 | 2.54 | .4945 | .0055 | 2.89 | .4981 | .0019 |
| 2.20 | .4861 | .0139 | 2.55 | .4946 | .0054 | 2.90 | .4981 | .0019 |
| 2.21 | .4864 | .0136 | 2.56 | .4948 | .0052 | 2.91 | .4982 | .0018 |
| 2.22 | .4868 | .0132 | 2.57 | .4949 | .0051 | 2.92 | .4982 | .0018 |
| 2.23 | .4871 | .0129 | 2.58 | .4951 | .0049 | 2.93 | .4983 | .0017 |
| 2.24 | .4875 | .0125 | 2.59 | .4952 | .0048 | 2.94 | .4984 | .0016 |
| 2.25 | .4878 | .0122 | 2.60 | .4953 | .0047 | 2.95 | .4984 | .0016 |
| 2.26 | .4881 | .0119 | 2.61 | .4955 | .0045 | 2.96 | .4985 | .0015 |
| 2.27 | .4884 | .0116 | 2.62 | .4956 | .0044 | 2.97 | .4985 | .0015 |
| 2.28 | .4887 | .0113 | 2.63 | .4957 | .0043 | 2.98 | .4986 | .0014 |
| 2.29 | .4890 | .0110 | 2.64 | .4959 | .0041 | 2.99 | .4986 | .0014 |

## Table 1 (cont.)   Proportions of Area Under the Standard Normal Curve: The z-Tables

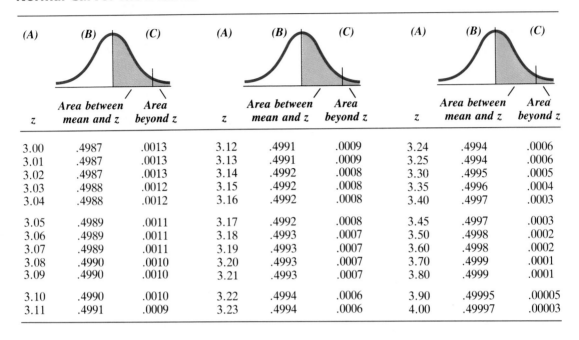

| (A) z | (B) Area between mean and z | (C) Area beyond z | (A) z | (B) Area between mean and z | (C) Area beyond z | (A) z | (B) Area between mean and z | (C) Area beyond z |
|---|---|---|---|---|---|---|---|---|
| 3.00 | .4987 | .0013 | 3.12 | .4991 | .0009 | 3.24 | .4994 | .0006 |
| 3.01 | .4987 | .0013 | 3.13 | .4991 | .0009 | 3.25 | .4994 | .0006 |
| 3.02 | .4987 | .0013 | 3.14 | .4992 | .0008 | 3.30 | .4995 | .0005 |
| 3.03 | .4988 | .0012 | 3.15 | .4992 | .0008 | 3.35 | .4996 | .0004 |
| 3.04 | .4988 | .0012 | 3.16 | .4992 | .0008 | 3.40 | .4997 | .0003 |
| 3.05 | .4989 | .0011 | 3.17 | .4992 | .0008 | 3.45 | .4997 | .0003 |
| 3.06 | .4989 | .0011 | 3.18 | .4993 | .0007 | 3.50 | .4998 | .0002 |
| 3.07 | .4989 | .0011 | 3.19 | .4993 | .0007 | 3.60 | .4998 | .0002 |
| 3.08 | .4990 | .0010 | 3.20 | .4993 | .0007 | 3.70 | .4999 | .0001 |
| 3.09 | .4990 | .0010 | 3.21 | .4993 | .0007 | 3.80 | .4999 | .0001 |
| 3.10 | .4990 | .0010 | 3.22 | .4994 | .0006 | 3.90 | .49995 | .00005 |
| 3.11 | .4991 | .0009 | 3.23 | .4994 | .0006 | 4.00 | .49997 | .00003 |

# Table 2  Critical Values of $t$: The $t$-Tables

*Note:* Values of $-t_{crit}$ = values of $+t_{crit}$.

| Two-Tailed Test | One-Tailed Test |
|---|---|
| 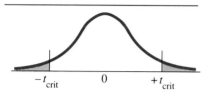 | 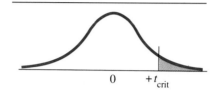 |

| | *Level of significance* | | | | *Level of significance* | |
|---|---|---|---|---|---|---|
| *df* | $\alpha = .05$ | $\alpha = .01$ | | *df* | $\alpha = .05$ | $\alpha = .01$ |
| 1 | 12.706 | 63.657 | | 1 | 6.314 | 31.821 |
| 2 | 4.303 | 9.925 | | 2 | 2.920 | 6.965 |
| 3 | 3.182 | 5.841 | | 3 | 2.353 | 4.541 |
| 4 | 2.776 | 4.604 | | 4 | 2.132 | 3.747 |
| 5 | 2.571 | 4.032 | | 5 | 2.015 | 3.365 |
| 6 | 2.447 | 3.707 | | 6 | 1.943 | 3.143 |
| 7 | 2.365 | 3.499 | | 7 | 1.895 | 2.998 |
| 8 | 2.306 | 3.355 | | 8 | 1.860 | 2.896 |
| 9 | 2.262 | 3.250 | | 9 | 1.833 | 2.821 |
| 10 | 2.228 | 3.169 | | 10 | 1.812 | 2.764 |
| 11 | 2.201 | 3.106 | | 11 | 1.796 | 2.718 |
| 12 | 2.179 | 3.055 | | 12 | 1.782 | 2.681 |
| 13 | 2.160 | 3.012 | | 13 | 1.771 | 2.650 |
| 14 | 2.145 | 2.977 | | 14 | 1.761 | 2.624 |
| 15 | 2.131 | 2.947 | | 15 | 1.753 | 2.602 |
| 16 | 2.120 | 2.921 | | 16 | 1.746 | 2.583 |
| 17 | 2.110 | 2.898 | | 17 | 1.740 | 2.567 |
| 18 | 2.101 | 2.878 | | 18 | 1.734 | 2.552 |
| 19 | 2.093 | 2.861 | | 19 | 1.729 | 2.539 |
| 20 | 2.086 | 2.845 | | 20 | 1.725 | 2.528 |
| 21 | 2.080 | 2.831 | | 21 | 1.721 | 2.518 |
| 22 | 2.074 | 2.819 | | 22 | 1.717 | 2.508 |
| 23 | 2.069 | 2.807 | | 23 | 1.714 | 2.500 |
| 24 | 2.064 | 2.797 | | 24 | 1.711 | 2.492 |
| 25 | 2.060 | 2.787 | | 25 | 1.708 | 2.485 |
| 26 | 2.056 | 2.779 | | 26 | 1.706 | 2.479 |
| 27 | 2.052 | 2.771 | | 27 | 1.703 | 2.473 |
| 28 | 2.048 | 2.763 | | 28 | 1.701 | 2.467 |
| 29 | 2.045 | 2.756 | | 29 | 1.699 | 2.462 |
| 30 | 2.042 | 2.750 | | 30 | 1.697 | 2.457 |
| 40 | 2.021 | 2.704 | | 40 | 1.684 | 2.423 |
| 60 | 2.000 | 2.660 | | 60 | 1.671 | 2.390 |
| 120 | 1.980 | 2.617 | | 120 | 1.658 | 2.358 |
| $\infty$ | 1.960 | 2.576 | | $\infty$ | 1.645 | 2.326 |

From Table 12 of E. Pearson and H. Hartley, *Biometrika Tables for Statisticians*, Vol 1, 3rd ed. Cambridge: Cambridge University Press, 1966. Reprinted with permission of the Biometrika trustees.

# Table 3 Critical Values of the Pearson Correlation Coefficient: The *r*-Tables

| Two-Tailed Test | One-Tailed Test |
|---|---|
| | |

| *df (no. of pairs − 2)* | Level of significance $\alpha = .05$ | Level of significance $\alpha = .01$ | *df (no. of pairs − 2)* | Level of significance $\alpha = .05$ | Level of significance $\alpha = .01$ |
|---|---|---|---|---|---|
| 1 | .997 | .9999 | 1 | .988 | .9995 |
| 2 | .950 | .990 | 2 | .900 | .980 |
| 3 | .878 | .959 | 3 | .805 | .934 |
| 4 | .811 | .917 | 4 | .729 | .882 |
| 5 | .754 | .874 | 5 | .669 | .833 |
| 6 | .707 | .834 | 6 | .622 | .789 |
| 7 | .666 | .798 | 7 | .582 | .750 |
| 8 | .632 | .765 | 8 | .549 | .716 |
| 9 | .602 | .735 | 9 | .521 | .685 |
| 10 | .576 | .708 | 10 | .497 | .658 |
| 11 | .553 | .684 | 11 | .476 | .634 |
| 12 | .532 | .661 | 12 | .458 | .612 |
| 13 | .514 | .641 | 13 | .441 | .592 |
| 14 | .497 | .623 | 14 | .426 | .574 |
| 15 | .482 | .606 | 15 | .412 | .558 |
| 16 | .468 | .590 | 16 | .400 | .542 |
| 17 | .456 | .575 | 17 | .389 | .528 |
| 18 | .444 | .561 | 18 | .378 | .516 |
| 19 | .433 | .549 | 19 | .369 | .503 |
| 20 | .423 | .537 | 20 | .360 | .492 |
| 21 | .413 | .526 | 21 | .352 | .482 |
| 22 | .404 | .515 | 22 | .344 | .472 |
| 23 | .396 | .505 | 23 | .337 | .462 |
| 24 | .388 | .496 | 24 | .330 | .453 |
| 25 | .381 | .487 | 25 | .323 | .445 |
| 26 | .374 | .479 | 26 | .317 | .437 |
| 27 | .367 | .471 | 27 | .311 | .430 |
| 28 | .361 | .463 | 28 | .306 | .423 |
| 29 | .355 | .456 | 29 | .301 | .416 |
| 30 | .349 | .449 | 30 | .296 | .409 |
| 35 | .325 | .418 | 35 | .275 | .381 |
| 40 | .304 | .393 | 40 | .257 | .358 |
| 45 | .288 | .372 | 45 | .243 | .338 |
| 50 | .273 | .354 | 50 | .231 | .322 |
| 60 | .250 | .325 | 60 | .211 | .295 |
| 70 | .232 | .302 | 70 | .195 | .274 |
| 80 | .217 | .283 | 80 | .183 | .256 |
| 90 | .205 | .267 | 90 | .173 | .242 |
| 100 | .195 | .254 | 100 | .164 | .230 |

From Table VI of R. A. Fisher and F. Yates, *Statistical Tables for Biological, Agricultural and Medical Research*, 6th ed. London: Longman Group Ltd., 1974 (previously published by Oliver and Boyd Ltd., Edinburgh).

### Table 4   Critical Values of the Spearman Rank-Order Correlation Coefficient: The $r_s$-Tables

*Note:* To interpolate the critical value for an $N$ not given, find the critical values for the $N$ above and below your $N$, add them together, and then divide the sum by 2.

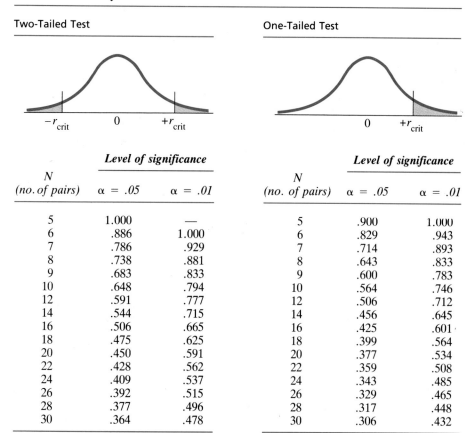

| | Two-Tailed Test | | | One-Tailed Test | |
|---|---|---|---|---|---|
| | **Level of significance** | | | **Level of significance** | |
| *N (no. of pairs)* | $\alpha = .05$ | $\alpha = .01$ | *N (no. of pairs)* | $\alpha = .05$ | $\alpha = .01$ |
| 5 | 1.000 | — | 5 | .900 | 1.000 |
| 6 | .886 | 1.000 | 6 | .829 | .943 |
| 7 | .786 | .929 | 7 | .714 | .893 |
| 8 | .738 | .881 | 8 | .643 | .833 |
| 9 | .683 | .833 | 9 | .600 | .783 |
| 10 | .648 | .794 | 10 | .564 | .746 |
| 12 | .591 | .777 | 12 | .506 | .712 |
| 14 | .544 | .715 | 14 | .456 | .645 |
| 16 | .506 | .665 | 16 | .425 | .601 |
| 18 | .475 | .625 | 18 | .399 | .564 |
| 20 | .450 | .591 | 20 | .377 | .534 |
| 22 | .428 | .562 | 22 | .359 | .508 |
| 24 | .409 | .537 | 24 | .343 | .485 |
| 26 | .392 | .515 | 26 | .329 | .465 |
| 28 | .377 | .496 | 28 | .317 | .448 |
| 30 | .364 | .478 | 30 | .306 | .432 |

From E. G. Olds (1949), The 5 Percent Significance Levels of Sums of Squares of Rank Differences and a Correction, *Ann. Math. Statist.,* **20,** 117–118, and E. G. Olds (1938), Distribution of Sums of Squares of Rank Differences for Small Numbers of Individuals, *Ann. Math. Statist.,* **9,** 133–148. Reprinted with permission of the Institute of Mathematical Statistics.

## Table 5   Critical Values of *F*: The *F*-Tables

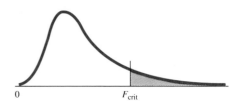

$0$                    $F_{crit}$

Critical values for $\alpha = .05$ are in light numbers.
Critical values for $\alpha = .01$ are in **dark numbers.**

| Degrees of freedom within groups (degrees of freedom in denominator of F ratio) | α | Degrees of freedom between groups (degrees of freedom in numerator of F ratio) | | | | | | | | | |
|---|---|---|---|---|---|---|---|---|---|---|---|
| | | *1* | *2* | *3* | *4* | *5* | *6* | *7* | *8* | *9* | *10* |
| 1 | .05 | 161 | 200 | 216 | 225 | 230 | 234 | 237 | 239 | 241 | 242 |
| | **.01** | **4,052** | **4,999** | **5,403** | **5,625** | **5,764** | **5,859** | **5,928** | **5,981** | **6,022** | **6,056** |
| 2 | .05 | 18.51 | 19.00 | 19.16 | 19.25 | 19.30 | 19.33 | 19.36 | 19.37 | 19.38 | 19.39 |
| | **.01** | **98.49** | **99.00** | **99.17** | **99.25** | **99.30** | **99.33** | **99.34** | **99.36** | **99.38** | **99.40** |
| 3 | .05 | 10.13 | 9.55 | 9.28 | 9.12 | 9.01 | 8.94 | 8.88 | 8.84 | 8.81 | 8.78 |
| | **.01** | **34.12** | **30.82** | **29.46** | **28.71** | **28.24** | **27.91** | **27.67** | **27.49** | **27.34** | **27.23** |
| 4 | .05 | 7.71 | 6.94 | 6.59 | 6.39 | 6.26 | 6.16 | 6.09 | 6.04 | 6.00 | 5.96 |
| | **.01** | **21.20** | **18.00** | **16.69** | **15.98** | **15.52** | **15.21** | **14.98** | **14.80** | **14.66** | **14.54** |
| 5 | .05 | 6.61 | 5.79 | 5.41 | 5.19 | 5.05 | 4.95 | 4.88 | 4.82 | 4.78 | 4.74 |
| | **.01** | **16.26** | **13.27** | **12.06** | **11.39** | **10.97** | **10.67** | **10.45** | **10.27** | **10.15** | **10.05** |
| 6 | .05 | 5.99 | 5.14 | 4.76 | 4.53 | 4.39 | 4.28 | 4.21 | 4.15 | 4.10 | 4.06 |
| | **.01** | **13.74** | **10.92** | **9.78** | **9.15** | **8.75** | **8.47** | **8.26** | **8.10** | **7.98** | **7.87** |
| 7 | .05 | 5.59 | 4.47 | 4.35 | 4.12 | 3.97 | 3.87 | 3.79 | 3.73 | 3.68 | 3.63 |
| | **.01** | **12.25** | **9.55** | **8.45** | **7.85** | **7.46** | **7.19** | **7.00** | **6.84** | **6.71** | **6.62** |
| 8 | .05 | 5.32 | 4.46 | 4.07 | 3.84 | 3.69 | 3.58 | 3.50 | 3.44 | 3.39 | 3.34 |
| | **.01** | **11.26** | **8.65** | **7.59** | **7.01** | **6.63** | **6.37** | **6.19** | **6.03** | **5.91** | **5.82** |
| 9 | .05 | 5.12 | 4.26 | 3.86 | 3.63 | 3.48 | 3.37 | 3.29 | 3.23 | 3.18 | 3.13 |
| | **.01** | **10.56** | **8.02** | **6.99** | **6.42** | **6.06** | **5.80** | **5.62** | **5.47** | **5.35** | **5.26** |
| 10 | .05 | 4.96 | 4.10 | 3.71 | 3.48 | 3.33 | 3.22 | 3.14 | 3.07 | 3.02 | 2.97 |
| | **.01** | **10.04** | **7.56** | **6.55** | **5.99** | **5.64** | **5.39** | **5.21** | **5.06** | **4.95** | **4.85** |
| 11 | .05 | 4.84 | 3.98 | 3.59 | 3.36 | 3.20 | 3.09 | 3.01 | 2.95 | 2.90 | 2.86 |
| | **.01** | **9.65** | **7.20** | **6.22** | **5.67** | **5.32** | **5.07** | **4.88** | **4.74** | **4.63** | **4.54** |
| 12 | .05 | 4.75 | 3.88 | 3.49 | 3.26 | 3.11 | 3.00 | 2.92 | 2.85 | 2.80 | 2.76 |
| | **.01** | **9.33** | **6.93** | **5.95** | **5.41** | **5.06** | **4.82** | **4.65** | **4.50** | **4.39** | **4.30** |
| 13 | .05 | 4.67 | 3.80 | 3.41 | 3.18 | 3.02 | 2.92 | 2.84 | 2.77 | 2.72 | 2.67 |
| | **.01** | **9.07** | **6.70** | **5.74** | **5.20** | **4.86** | **4.62** | **4.44** | **4.30** | **4.19** | **4.10** |

**Degrees of freedom between groups**
*(degrees of freedom in numerator of F ratio)*

| 11 | 12 | 14 | 16 | 20 | 24 | 30 | 40 | 50 | 75 | 100 | 200 | 500 | ∞ |
|---|---|---|---|---|---|---|---|---|---|---|---|---|---|
| 243 | 244 | 245 | 246 | 248 | 249 | 250 | 251 | 252 | 253 | 253 | 254 | 254 | 254 |
| **6,082** | **6,106** | **6,142** | **6,169** | **6,208** | **6,234** | **6,258** | **6,286** | **6,302** | **6,323** | **6,334** | **6,352** | **6,361** | **6,366** |
| 19.40 | 19.41 | 19.42 | 19.43 | 19.44 | 19.45 | 19.46 | 19.47 | 19.47 | 19.48 | 19.49 | 19.49 | 19.50 | 19.50 |
| **99.41** | **99.42** | **99.43** | **99.44** | **99.45** | **99.46** | **99.47** | **99.48** | **99.48** | **99.49** | **99.49** | **99.49** | **99.50** | **99.50** |
| 8.76 | 8.74 | 8.71 | 8.69 | 8.66 | 8.64 | 8.62 | 8.60 | 8.58 | 8.57 | 8.56 | 8.54 | 8.54 | 8.53 |
| **27.13** | **27.05** | **26.92** | **26.83** | **26.69** | **26.60** | **26.50** | **26.41** | **26.35** | **26.27** | **26.23** | **26.18** | **26.14** | **26.12** |
| 5.93 | 5.91 | 5.87 | 5.84 | 5.80 | 5.77 | 5.74 | 5.71 | 5.70 | 5.68 | 5.66 | 5.65 | 5.64 | 5.63 |
| **14.45** | **14.37** | **14.24** | **14.15** | **14.02** | **13.93** | **13.83** | **13.74** | **13.69** | **13.61** | **13.57** | **13.52** | **13.48** | **13.46** |
| 4.70 | 4.68 | 4.64 | 4.60 | 4.56 | 4.53 | 4.50 | 4.46 | 4.44 | 4.42 | 4.40 | 4.38 | 4.37 | 4.36 |
| **9.96** | **9.89** | **9.77** | **9.68** | **9.55** | **9.47** | **9.38** | **9.29** | **9.24** | **9.17** | **9.13** | **9.07** | **9.04** | **9.02** |
| 4.03 | 4.00 | 3.96 | 3.92 | 3.87 | 3.84 | 3.81 | 3.77 | 3.75 | 3.72 | 3.71 | 3.69 | 3.68 | 3.67 |
| **7.79** | **7.72** | **7.60** | **7.52** | **7.39** | **7.31** | **7.23** | **7.14** | **7.09** | **7.02** | **6.99** | **6.94** | **6.90** | **6.88** |
| 3.60 | 3.57 | 3.52 | 3.49 | 3.44 | 3.41 | 3.38 | 3.34 | 3.32 | 3.29 | 3.28 | 3.25 | 3.24 | 3.23 |
| **6.54** | **6.47** | **6.35** | **6.27** | **6.15** | **6.07** | **5.98** | **5.90** | **5.85** | **5.78** | **5.75** | **5.70** | **5.67** | **5.65** |
| 3.31 | 3.28 | 3.23 | 3.20 | 3.15 | 3.12 | 3.08 | 3.05 | 3.03 | 3.00 | 2.98 | 2.96 | 2.94 | 2.93 |
| **5.74** | **5.67** | **5.56** | **5.48** | **5.36** | **5.28** | **5.20** | **5.11** | **5.06** | **5.00** | **4.96** | **4.91** | **4.88** | **4.86** |
| 3.10 | 3.07 | 3.02 | 2.98 | 2.93 | 2.90 | 2.86 | 2.82 | 2.80 | 2.77 | 2.76 | 2.73 | 2.72 | 2.71 |
| **5.18** | **5.11** | **5.00** | **4.92** | **4.80** | **4.73** | **4.64** | **4.56** | **4.51** | **4.45** | **4.41** | **4.36** | **4.33** | **4.31** |
| 2.94 | 2.91 | 2.86 | 2.82 | 2.77 | 2.74 | 2.70 | 2.67 | 2.64 | 2.61 | 2.59 | 2.56 | 2.55 | 2.54 |
| **4.78** | **4.71** | **4.60** | **4.52** | **4.41** | **4.33** | **4.25** | **4.17** | **4.12** | **4.05** | **4.01** | **3.96** | **3.93** | **3.91** |
| 2.82 | 2.79 | 2.74 | 2.70 | 2.65 | 2.61 | 2.57 | 2.53 | 2.50 | 2.47 | 2.45 | 2.42 | 2.41 | 2.40 |
| **4.46** | **4.40** | **4.29** | **4.21** | **4.10** | **4.02** | **3.94** | **3.86** | **3.80** | **3.74** | **3.70** | **3.66** | **3.62** | **3.60** |
| 2.72 | 2.69 | 2.64 | 2.60 | 2.54 | 2.50 | 2.46 | 2.42 | 2.40 | 2.36 | 2.35 | 2.32 | 2.31 | 2.30 |
| **4.22** | **4.16** | **4.05** | **3.98** | **3.86** | **3.78** | **3.70** | **3.61** | **3.56** | **3.49** | **3.46** | **3.41** | **3.38** | **3.36** |
| 2.63 | 2.60 | 2.55 | 2.51 | 2.46 | 2.42 | 2.38 | 2.34 | 2.32 | 2.28 | 2.26 | 2.24 | 2.22 | 2.21 |
| **4.02** | **3.96** | **3.85** | **3.78** | **3.67** | **3.59** | **3.51** | **3.42** | **3.37** | **3.30** | **3.27** | **3.21** | **3.18** | **3.16** |

## Table 5   (cont.)   Critical Values of *F*: The *F*-Tables

| Degrees of freedom within groups (degrees of freedom in denominator of F ratio) | α | \multicolumn{10}{c}{Degrees of freedom between groups (degrees of freedom in numerator of F ratio)} |
|---|---|---|---|---|---|---|---|---|---|---|---|
| | | 1 | 2 | 3 | 4 | 5 | 6 | 7 | 8 | 9 | 10 |
| 14 | .05 | 4.60 | 3.74 | 3.34 | 3.11 | 2.96 | 2.85 | 2.77 | 2.70 | 2.65 | 2.60 |
|    | .01 | 8.86 | 6.51 | 5.56 | 5.03 | 4.69 | 4.46 | 4.28 | 4.14 | 4.03 | 3.94 |
| 15 | .05 | 4.54 | 3.68 | 3.29 | 3.06 | 2.90 | 2.79 | 2.70 | 2.64 | 2.59 | 2.55 |
|    | .01 | 8.68 | 6.36 | 5.42 | 4.89 | 4.56 | 4.32 | 4.14 | 4.00 | 3.89 | 3.80 |
| 16 | .05 | 4.49 | 3.63 | 3.24 | 3.01 | 2.85 | 2.74 | 2.66 | 2.59 | 2.54 | 2.49 |
|    | .01 | 8.53 | 6.23 | 5.29 | 4.77 | 4.44 | 4.20 | 4.03 | 3.89 | 3.78 | 3.69 |
| 17 | .05 | 4.45 | 3.59 | 3.20 | 2.96 | 2.81 | 2.70 | 2.62 | 2.55 | 2.50 | 2.45 |
|    | .01 | 8.40 | 6.11 | 5.18 | 4.67 | 4.34 | 4.10 | 3.93 | 3.79 | 3.68 | 3.59 |
| 18 | .05 | 4.41 | 3.55 | 3.16 | 2.93 | 2.77 | 2.66 | 2.58 | 2.51 | 2.46 | 2.41 |
|    | .01 | 8.28 | 6.01 | 5.09 | 4.58 | 4.25 | 4.01 | 3.85 | 3.71 | 3.60 | 3.51 |
| 19 | .05 | 4.38 | 3.52 | 3.13 | 2.90 | 2.74 | 2.63 | 2.55 | 2.48 | 2.43 | 2.38 |
|    | .01 | 8.18 | 5.93 | 5.01 | 4.50 | 4.17 | 3.94 | 3.77 | 3.63 | 3.52 | 3.43 |
| 20 | .05 | 4.35 | 3.49 | 3.10 | 2.87 | 2.71 | 2.60 | 2.52 | 2.45 | 2.40 | 2.35 |
|    | .01 | 8.10 | 5.85 | 4.94 | 4.43 | 4.10 | 3.87 | 3.71 | 3.56 | 3.45 | 3.37 |
| 21 | .05 | 4.32 | 3.47 | 3.07 | 2.84 | 2.68 | 2.57 | 2.49 | 2.42 | 2.37 | 2.32 |
|    | .01 | 8.02 | 5.78 | 4.87 | 4.37 | 4.04 | 3.81 | 3.65 | 3.51 | 3.40 | 3.31 |
| 22 | .05 | 4.30 | 3.44 | 3.05 | 2.82 | 2.66 | 2.55 | 2.47 | 2.40 | 2.35 | 2.30 |
|    | .01 | 7.94 | 5.72 | 4.82 | 4.31 | 3.99 | 3.76 | 3.59 | 3.45 | 3.35 | 3.26 |
| 23 | .05 | 4.28 | 3.42 | 3.03 | 2.80 | 2.64 | 2.53 | 2.45 | 2.38 | 2.32 | 2.28 |
|    | .01 | 7.88 | 5.66 | 4.76 | 4.26 | 3.94 | 3.71 | 3.54 | 3.41 | 3.30 | 3.21 |
| 24 | .05 | 4.26 | 3.40 | 3.01 | 2.78 | 2.62 | 2.51 | 2.43 | 2.36 | 2.30 | 2.26 |
|    | .01 | 7.82 | 5.61 | 4.72 | 4.22 | 3.90 | 3.67 | 3.50 | 3.36 | 3.25 | 3.17 |
| 25 | .05 | 4.24 | 3.38 | 2.99 | 2.76 | 2.60 | 2.49 | 2.41 | 2.34 | 2.28 | 2.24 |
|    | .01 | 7.77 | 5.57 | 4.68 | 4.18 | 3.86 | 3.63 | 3.46 | 3.32 | 3.21 | 3.13 |
| 26 | .05 | 4.22 | 3.37 | 2.98 | 2.74 | 2.59 | 2.47 | 2.39 | 2.32 | 2.27 | 2.22 |
|    | .01 | 7.72 | 5.53 | 4.64 | 4.14 | 3.82 | 3.59 | 3.42 | 3.29 | 3.17 | 3.09 |
| 27 | .05 | 4.21 | 3.35 | 2.96 | 2.73 | 2.57 | 2.46 | 2.37 | 2.30 | 2.25 | 2.20 |
|    | .01 | 7.68 | 5.49 | 4.60 | 4.11 | 3.79 | 3.56 | 3.39 | 3.26 | 3.14 | 3.06 |
| 28 | .05 | 4.20 | 3.34 | 2.95 | 2.71 | 2.56 | 2.44 | 2.36 | 2.29 | 2.24 | 2.19 |
|    | .01 | 7.64 | 5.45 | 4.57 | 4.07 | 3.76 | 3.53 | 3.36 | 3.23 | 3.11 | 3.03 |
| 29 | .05 | 4.18 | 3.33 | 2.93 | 2.70 | 2.54 | 2.43 | 2.35 | 2.28 | 2.22 | 2.18 |
|    | .01 | 7.60 | 5.42 | 4.54 | 4.04 | 3.73 | 3.50 | 3.33 | 3.20 | 3.08 | 3.00 |

### Degrees of freedom between groups
#### (degrees of freedom in numerator of F ratio)

| 11 | 12 | 14 | 16 | 20 | 24 | 30 | 40 | 50 | 75 | 100 | 200 | 500 | ∞ |
|---|---|---|---|---|---|---|---|---|---|---|---|---|---|
| 2.56 | 2.53 | 2.48 | 2.44 | 2.39 | 2.35 | 2.31 | 2.27 | 2.24 | 2.21 | 2.19 | 2.16 | 2.14 | 2.13 |
| **3.86** | **3.80** | **3.70** | **3.62** | **3.51** | **3.43** | **3.34** | **3.26** | **3.21** | **3.14** | **3.11** | **3.06** | **3.02** | **3.00** |
| 2.51 | 2.48 | 2.43 | 2.39 | 2.33 | 2.29 | 2.25 | 2.21 | 2.18 | 2.15 | 2.12 | 2.10 | 2.08 | 2.07 |
| **3.73** | **3.67** | **3.56** | **3.48** | **3.36** | **3.29** | **3.20** | **3.12** | **3.07** | **3.00** | **2.97** | **2.92** | **2.89** | **2.87** |
| 2.45 | 2.42 | 2.37 | 2.33 | 2.28 | 2.24 | 2.20 | 2.16 | 2.13 | 2.09 | 2.07 | 2.04 | 2.02 | 2.01 |
| **3.61** | **3.55** | **3.45** | **3.37** | **3.25** | **3.18** | **3.10** | **3.01** | **2.96** | **2.89** | **2.86** | **2.80** | **2.77** | **2.75** |
| 2.41 | 2.38 | 2.33 | 2.29 | 2.23 | 2.19 | 2.15 | 2.11 | 2.08 | 2.04 | 2.02 | 1.99 | 1.97 | 1.96 |
| **3.52** | **3.45** | **3.35** | **3.27** | **3.16** | **3.08** | **3.00** | **2.92** | **2.86** | **2.79** | **2.76** | **2.70** | **2.67** | **2.65** |
| 2.37 | 2.34 | 2.29 | 2.25 | 2.19 | 2.15 | 2.11 | 2.07 | 2.04 | 2.00 | 1.98 | 1.95 | 1.93 | 1.92 |
| **3.44** | **3.37** | **3.27** | **3.19** | **3.07** | **3.00** | **2.91** | **2.83** | **2.78** | **2.71** | **2.68** | **2.62** | **2.59** | **2.57** |
| 2.34 | 2.31 | 2.26 | 2.21 | 2.15 | 2.11 | 2.07 | 2.02 | 2.00 | 1.96 | 1.94 | 1.91 | 1.90 | 1.88 |
| **3.36** | **3.30** | **3.19** | **3.12** | **3.00** | **2.92** | **2.84** | **2.76** | **2.70** | **2.63** | **2.60** | **2.54** | **2.51** | **2.49** |
| 2:31 | 2.28 | 2.23 | 2.18 | 2.12 | 2.08 | 2.04 | 1.99 | 1.96 | 1.92 | 1.90 | 1.87 | 1.85 | 1.84 |
| **3.30** | **3.23** | **3.13** | **3.05** | **2.94** | **2.86** | **2.77** | **2.69** | **2.63** | **2.56** | **2.53** | **2.47** | **2.44** | **2.42** |
| 2.28 | 2.25 | 2.20 | 2.15 | 2.09 | 2.05 | 2.00 | 1.96 | 1.93 | 1.89 | 1.87 | 1.84 | 1.82 | 1.81 |
| **3.24** | **3.17** | **3.07** | **2.99** | **2.88** | **2.80** | **2.72** | **2.63** | **2.58** | **2.51** | **2.47** | **2.42** | **2.38** | **2.36** |
| 2.26 | 2.23 | 2.18 | 2.13 | 2.07 | 2.03 | 1.98 | 1.93 | 1.91 | 1.87 | 1.84 | 1.81 | 1.80 | 1.78 |
| **3.18** | **3.12** | **3.02** | **2.94** | **2.83** | **2.75** | **2.67** | **2.58** | **2.53** | **2.46** | **2.42** | **2.37** | **2.33** | **2.31** |
| 2.24 | 2.20 | 2.14 | 2.10 | 2.04 | 2.00 | 1.96 | 1.91 | 1.88 | 1.84 | 1.82 | 1.79 | 1.77 | 1.76 |
| **3.14** | **3.07** | **2.97** | **2.89** | **2.78** | **2.70** | **2.62** | **2.53** | **2.48** | **2.41** | **2.37** | **2.32** | **2.28** | **2.26** |
| 2.22 | 2.18 | 2.13 | 2.09 | 2.02 | 1.98 | 1.94 | 1.89 | 1.86 | 1.82 | 1.80 | 1.76 | 1.74 | 1.73 |
| **3.09** | **3.03** | **2.93** | **2.85** | **2.74** | **2.66** | **2.58** | **2.49** | **2.44** | **2.36** | **2.33** | **2.27** | **2.23** | **2.21** |
| 2.20 | 2.16 | 2.11 | 2.06 | 2.00 | 1.96 | 1.92 | 1.87 | 1.84 | 1.80 | 1.77 | 1.74 | 1.72 | 1.71 |
| **3.05** | **2.99** | **2.89** | **2.81** | **2.70** | **2.62** | **2.54** | **2.45** | **2.40** | **2.32** | **2.29** | **2.23** | **2.19** | **2.17** |
| 2.18 | 2.15 | 2.10 | 2.05 | 1.99 | 1.95 | 1.90 | 1.85 | 1.82 | 1.78 | 1.76 | 1.72 | 1.70 | 1.69 |
| **3.02** | **2.96** | **2.86** | **2.77** | **2.66** | **2.58** | **2.50** | **2.41** | **2.36** | **2.28** | **2.25** | **2.19** | **2.15** | **2.13** |
| 2.16 | 2.13 | 2.08 | 2.03 | 1.97 | 1.93 | 1.88 | 1.84 | 1.80 | 1.76 | 1.74 | 1.71 | 1.68 | 1.67 |
| **2.98** | **2.93** | **2.83** | **2.74** | **2.63** | **2.55** | **2.47** | **2.38** | **2.33** | **2.25** | **2.21** | **2.16** | **2.12** | **2.10** |
| 2.15 | 2.12 | 2.06 | 2.02 | 1.96 | 1.91 | 1.87 | 1.81 | 1.78 | 1.75 | 1.72 | 1.69 | 1.67 | 1.65 |
| **2.95** | **2.90** | **2.80** | **2.71** | **2.60** | **2.52** | **2.44** | **2.35** | **2.30** | **2.22** | **2.18** | **2.13** | **2.09** | **2.06** |
| 2.14 | 2.10 | 2.05 | 2.00 | 1.94 | 1.90 | 1.85 | 1.80 | 1.77 | 1.73 | 1.71 | 1.68 | 1.65 | 1.64 |
| **2.92** | **2.87** | **2.77** | **2.68** | **2.57** | **2.49** | **2.41** | **2.32** | **2.27** | **2.19** | **2.15** | **2.10** | **2.06** | **2.03** |

## Table 5 (cont.) Critical Values of *F*: The *F*-Tables

| Degrees of freedom within groups (degrees of freedom in denominator of F ratio) | α | \multicolumn{10}{c}{Degrees of freedom between groups (degrees of freedom in numerator of F ratio)} |
|---|---|---|---|---|---|---|---|---|---|---|---|
| | | 1 | 2 | 3 | 4 | 5 | 6 | 7 | 8 | 9 | 10 |
| 30 | .05 | 4.17 | 3.32 | 2.92 | 2.69 | 2.53 | 2.42 | 2.34 | 2.27 | 2.21 | 2.16 |
| | **.01** | **7.56** | **5.39** | **4.51** | **4.02** | **3.70** | **3.47** | **3.30** | **3.17** | **3.06** | **2.98** |
| 32 | .05 | 4.15 | 3.30 | 2.90 | 2.67 | 2.51 | 2.40 | 2.32 | 2.25 | 2.19 | 2.14 |
| | **.01** | **7.50** | **5.34** | **4.46** | **3.97** | **3.66** | **3.42** | **3.25** | **3.12** | **3.01** | **2.94** |
| 34 | .05 | 4.13 | 3.28 | 2.88 | 2.65 | 2.49 | 2.38 | 2.30 | 2.23 | 2.17 | 2.12 |
| | **.01** | **7.44** | **5.29** | **4.42** | **3.93** | **3.61** | **3.38** | **3.21** | **3.08** | **2.97** | **2.89** |
| 36 | .05 | 4.11 | 3.26 | 2.86 | 2.63 | 2.48 | 2.36 | 2.28 | 2.21 | 2.15 | 2.10 |
| | **.01** | **7.39** | **5.25** | **4.38** | **3.89** | **3.58** | **3.35** | **3.18** | **3.04** | **2.94** | **2.86** |
| 38 | .05 | 4.10 | 3.25 | 2.85 | 2.62 | 2.46 | 2.35 | 2.26 | 2.19 | 2.14 | 2.09 |
| | **.01** | **7.35** | **5.21** | **4.34** | **3.86** | **3.54** | **3.32** | **3.15** | **3.02** | **2.91** | **2.82** |
| 40 | .05 | 4.08 | 3.23 | 2.84 | 2.61 | 2.45 | 2.34 | 2.25 | 2.18 | 2.12 | 2.07 |
| | **.01** | **7.31** | **5.18** | **4.31** | **3.83** | **3.51** | **3.29** | **3.12** | **2.99** | **2.88** | **2.80** |
| 42 | .05 | 4.07 | 3.22 | 2.83 | 2.59 | 2.44 | 2.32 | 2.24 | 2.17 | 2.11 | 2.06 |
| | **.01** | **7.27** | **5.15** | **4.29** | **3.80** | **3.49** | **3.26** | **3.10** | **2.96** | **2.86** | **2.77** |
| 44 | .05 | 4.06 | 3.21 | 2.82 | 2.58 | 2.43 | 2.31 | 2.23 | 2.16 | 2.10 | 2.05 |
| | **.01** | **7.24** | **5.12** | **4.26** | **3.78** | **3.46** | **3.24** | **3.07** | **2.94** | **2.84** | **2.75** |
| 46 | .05 | 4.05 | 3.20 | 2.81 | 2.57 | 2.42 | 2.30 | 2.22 | 2.14 | 2.09 | 2.04 |
| | **.01** | **7.21** | **5.10** | **4.24** | **3.76** | **3.44** | **3.22** | **3.05** | **2.92** | **2.82** | **2.73** |
| 48 | .05 | 4.04 | 3.19 | 2.80 | 2.56 | 2.41 | 2.30 | 2.21 | 2.14 | 2.08 | 2.03 |
| | **.01** | **7.19** | **5.08** | **4.22** | **3.74** | **3.42** | **3.20** | **3.04** | **2.90** | **2.80** | **2.71** |
| 50 | .05 | 4.03 | 3.18 | 2.79 | 2.56 | 2.40 | 2.29 | 2.20 | 2.13 | 2.07 | 2.02 |
| | **.01** | **7.17** | **5.06** | **4.20** | **3.72** | **3.41** | **3.18** | **3.02** | **2.88** | **2.78** | **2.70** |
| 55 | .05 | 4.02 | 3.17 | 2.78 | 2.54 | 2.38 | 2.27 | 2.18 | 2.11 | 2.05 | 2.00 |
| | **.01** | **7.12** | **5.01** | **4.16** | **3.68** | **3.37** | **3.15** | **2.98** | **2.85** | **2.75** | **2.66** |
| 60 | .05 | 4.00 | 3.15 | 2.76 | 2.52 | 2.37 | 2.25 | 2.17 | 2.10 | 2.04 | 1.99 |
| | **.01** | **7.08** | **4.98** | **4.13** | **3.65** | **3.34** | **3.12** | **2.95** | **2.82** | **2.72** | **2.63** |
| 65 | .05 | 3.99 | 3.14 | 2.75 | 2.51 | 2.36 | 2.24 | 2.15 | 2.08 | 2.02 | 1.98 |
| | **.01** | **7.04** | **4.95** | **4.10** | **3.62** | **3.31** | **3.09** | **2.93** | **2.79** | **2.70** | **2.61** |
| 70 | .05 | 3.98 | 3.13 | 2.74 | 2.50 | 2.35 | 2.23 | 2.14 | 2.07 | 2.01 | 1.97 |
| | **.01** | **7.01** | **4.92** | **4.08** | **3.60** | **3.29** | **3.07** | **2.91** | **2.77** | **2.67** | **2.59** |
| 80 | .05 | 3.96 | 3.11 | 2.72 | 2.48 | 2.33 | 2.21 | 2.12 | 2.05 | 1.99 | 1.95 |
| | **.01** | **6.96** | **4.88** | **4.04** | **3.56** | **3.25** | **3.04** | **2.87** | **2.74** | **2.64** | **2.55** |

| | | | | | *Degrees of freedom between groups* | | | | | | | | |
| | | | | | *(degrees of freedom in numerator of F ratio)* | | | | | | | | |

| *11* | *12* | *14* | *16* | *20* | *24* | *30* | *40* | *50* | *75* | *100* | *200* | *500* | *∞* |
|---|---|---|---|---|---|---|---|---|---|---|---|---|---|
| 2.12 | 2.09 | 2.04 | 1.99 | 1.93 | 1.89 | 1.84 | 1.79 | 1.76 | 1.72 | 1.69 | 1.66 | 1.64 | 1.62 |
| **2.90** | **2.84** | **2.74** | **2.66** | **2.55** | **2.47** | **2.38** | **2.29** | **2.24** | **2.16** | **2.13** | **2.07** | **2.03** | **2.01** |
| 2.10 | 2.07 | 2.02 | 1.97 | 1.91 | 1.86 | 1.82 | 1.76 | 1.74 | 1.69 | 1.67 | 1.64 | 1.61 | 1.59 |
| **2.86** | **2.80** | **2.70** | **2.62** | **2.51** | **2.42** | **2.34** | **2.25** | **2.20** | **2.12** | **2.08** | **2.02** | **1.98** | **1.96** |
| 2.08 | 2.05 | 2.00 | 1.95 | 1.89 | 1.84 | 1.80 | 1.74 | 1.71 | 1.67 | 1.64 | 1.61 | 1.59 | 1.57 |
| **2.82** | **2.76** | **2.66** | **2.58** | **2.47** | **2.38** | **2.30** | **2.21** | **2.15** | **2.08** | **2.04** | **1.98** | **1.94** | **1.91** |
| 2.06 | 2.03 | 1.98 | 1.93 | 1.87 | 1.82 | 1.78 | 1.72 | 1.69 | 1.65 | 1.62 | 1.59 | 1.56 | 1.55 |
| **2.78** | **2.72** | **2.62** | **2.54** | **2.43** | **2.35** | **2.26** | **2.17** | **2.12** | **2.04** | **2.00** | **1.94** | **1.90** | **1.87** |
| 2.05 | 2.02 | 1.96 | 1.92 | 1.85 | 1.80 | 1.76 | 1.71 | 1.67 | 1.63 | 1.60 | 1.57 | 1.54 | 1.53 |
| **2.75** | **2.69** | **2.59** | **2.51** | **2.40** | **2.32** | **2.22** | **2.14** | **2.08** | **2.00** | **1.97** | **1.90** | **1.86** | **1.84** |
| 2.04 | 2.00 | 1.95 | 1.90 | 1.84 | 1.79 | 1.74 | 1.69 | 1.66 | 1.61 | 1.59 | 1.55 | 1.53 | 1.51 |
| **2.73** | **2.66** | **2.56** | **2.49** | **2.37** | **2.29** | **2.20** | **2.11** | **2.05** | **1.97** | **1.94** | **1.88** | **1.84** | **1.81** |
| 2.02 | 1.99 | 1.94 | 1.89 | 1.82 | 1.78 | 1.73 | 1.68 | 1.64 | 1.60 | 1.57 | 1.54 | 1.51 | 1.49 |
| **2.70** | **2.64** | **2.54** | **2.46** | **2.35** | **2.26** | **2.17** | **2.08** | **2.02** | **1.94** | **1.91** | **1.85** | **1.80** | **1.78** |
| 2.01 | 1.98 | 1.92 | 1.88 | 1.81 | 1.76 | 1.72 | 1.66 | 1.63 | 1.58 | 1.56 | 1.52 | 1.50 | 1.48 |
| **2.68** | **2.62** | **2.52** | **2.44** | **2.32** | **2.24** | **2.15** | **2.06** | **2.00** | **1.92** | **1.88** | **1.82** | **1.78** | **1.75** |
| 2.00 | 1.97 | 1.91 | 1.87 | 1.80 | 1.75 | 1.71 | 1.65 | 1.62 | 1.57 | 1.54 | 1.51 | 1.48 | 1.46 |
| **2.66** | **2.60** | **2.50** | **2.42** | **2.30** | **2.22** | **2.13** | **2.04** | **1.98** | **1.90** | **1.86** | **1.80** | **1.76** | **1.72** |
| 1.99 | 1.96 | 1.90 | 1.86 | 1.79 | 1.74 | 1.70 | 1.64 | 1.61 | 1.56 | 1.53 | 1.50 | 1.47 | 1.45 |
| **2.64** | **2.58** | **2.48** | **2.40** | **2.28** | **2.20** | **2.11** | **2.02** | **1.96** | **1.88** | **1.84** | **1.78** | **1.73** | **1.70** |
| 1.98 | 1.95 | 1.90 | 1.85 | 1.78 | 1.74 | 1.69 | 1.63 | 1.60 | 1.55 | 1.52 | 1.48 | 1.46 | 1.44 |
| **2.62** | **2.56** | **2.46** | **2.39** | **2.26** | **2.18** | **2.10** | **2.00** | **1.94** | **1.86** | **1.82** | **1.76** | **1.71** | **1.68** |
| 1.97 | 1.93 | 1.88 | 1.83 | 1.76 | 1.72 | 1.67 | 1.61 | 1.58 | 1.52 | 1.50 | 1.46 | 1.43 | 1.41 |
| **2.59** | **2.53** | **2.43** | **2.35** | **2.23** | **2.15** | **2.06** | **1.96** | **1.90** | **1.82** | **1.78** | **1.71** | **1.66** | **1.64** |
| 1.95 | 1.92 | 1.86 | 1.81 | 1.75 | 1.70 | 1.65 | 1.59 | 1.56 | 1.50 | 1.48 | 1.44 | 1.41 | 1.39 |
| **2.56** | **2.50** | **2.40** | **2.32** | **2.20** | **2.12** | **2.03** | **1.93** | **1.87** | **1.79** | **1.74** | **1.68** | **1.63** | **1.60** |
| 1.94 | 1.90 | 1.85 | 1.80 | 1.73 | 1.68 | 1.63 | 1.57 | 1.54 | 1.49 | 1.46 | 1.42 | 1.39 | 1.37 |
| **2.54** | **2.47** | **2.37** | **2.30** | **2.18** | **2.09** | **2.00** | **1.90** | **1.84** | **1.76** | **1.71** | **1.64** | **1.60** | **1.56** |
| 1.93 | 1.89 | 1.84 | 1.79 | 1.72 | 1.67 | 1.62 | 1.56 | 1.53 | 1.47 | 1.45 | 1.40 | 1.37 | 1.35 |
| **2.51** | **2.45** | **2.35** | **2.28** | **2.15** | **2.07** | **1.98** | **1.88** | **1.82** | **1.74** | **1.69** | **1.62** | **1.56** | **1.53** |
| 1.91 | 1.88 | 1.82 | 1.77 | 1.70 | 1.65 | 1.60 | 1.54 | 1.51 | 1.45 | 1.42 | 1.38 | 1.35 | 1.32 |
| **2.48** | **2.41** | **2.32** | **2.24** | **2.11** | **2.03** | **1.94** | **1.84** | **1.78** | **1.70** | **1.65** | **1.57** | **1.52** | **1.49** |

## Table 5   (cont.)   Critical Values of *F*: The *F*-Tables

| Degrees of freedom within groups (degrees of freedom in denominator of F ratio) | α | Degrees of freedom between groups (degrees of freedom in numerator of F ratio) | | | | | | | | | |
|---|---|---|---|---|---|---|---|---|---|---|---|
| | | *1* | *2* | *3* | *4* | *5* | *6* | *7* | *8* | *9* | *10* |
| 100 | .05 | 3.94 | 3.09 | 2.70 | 2.46 | 2.30 | 2.19 | 2.10 | 2.03 | 1.97 | 1.92 |
| | **.01** | **6.90** | **4.82** | **3.98** | **3.51** | **3.20** | **2.99** | **2.82** | **2.69** | **2.59** | **2.51** |
| 125 | .05 | 3.92 | 3.07 | 2.68 | 2.44 | 2.29 | 2.17 | 2.08 | 2.01 | 1.95 | 1.90 |
| | **.01** | **6.84** | **4.78** | **3.94** | **3.47** | **3.17** | **2.95** | **2.79** | **2.65** | **2.56** | **2.47** |
| 150 | .05 | 3.91 | 3.06 | 2.67 | 2.43 | 2.27 | 2.16 | 2.07 | 2.00 | 1.94 | 1.89 |
| | **.01** | **6.81** | **4.75** | **3.91** | **3.44** | **3.14** | **2.92** | **2.76** | **2.62** | **2.53** | **2.44** |
| 200 | .05 | 3.89 | 3.04 | 2.65 | 2.41 | 2.26 | 2.14 | 2.05 | 1.98 | 1.92 | 1.87 |
| | **.01** | **6.76** | **4.71** | **3.88** | **3.41** | **3.11** | **2.90** | **2.73** | **2.60** | **2.50** | **2.41** |
| 400 | .05 | 3.86 | 3.02 | 2.62 | 2.39 | 2.23 | 2.12 | 2.03 | 1.96 | 1.90 | 1.85 |
| | **.01** | **6.70** | **4.66** | **3.83** | **3.36** | **3.06** | **2.85** | **2.69** | **2.55** | **2.46** | **2.37** |
| 1000 | .05 | 3.85 | 3.00 | 2.61 | 2.38 | 2.22 | 2.10 | 2.02 | 1.95 | 1.89 | 1.84 |
| | **.01** | **6.66** | **4.62** | **3.80** | **3.34** | **3.04** | **2.82** | **2.66** | **2.53** | **2.43** | **2.34** |
| ∞ | .05 | 3.84 | 2.99 | 2.60 | 2.37 | 2.21 | 2.09 | 2.01 | 1.94 | 1.88 | 1.83 |
| | **.01** | **6.64** | **4.60** | **3.78** | **3.32** | **3.02** | **2.80** | **2.64** | **2.51** | **2.41** | **2.32** |

| | | | | ***Degrees of freedom between groups*** | | | | | | | | | |
| | | | | ***(degrees of freedom in numerator of F ratio)*** | | | | | | | | | |
| *11* | *12* | *14* | *16* | *20* | *24* | *30* | *40* | *50* | *75* | *100* | *200* | *500* | *∞* |
|------|------|------|------|------|------|------|------|------|------|------|------|------|------|
| 1.88 | 1.85 | 1.79 | 1.75 | 1.68 | 1.63 | 1.57 | 1.51 | 1.48 | 1.42 | 1.39 | 1.34 | 1.30 | 1.28 |
| **2.43** | **2.36** | **2.26** | **2.19** | **2.06** | **1.98** | **1.89** | **1.79** | **1.73** | **1.64** | **1.59** | **1.51** | **1.46** | **1.43** |
| 1.86 | 1.83 | 1.77 | 1.72 | 1.65 | 1.60 | 1.55 | 1.49 | 1.45 | 1.39 | 1.36 | 1.31 | 1.27 | 1.25 |
| **2.40** | **2.33** | **2.23** | **2.15** | **2.03** | **1.94** | **1.85** | **1.75** | **1.68** | **1.59** | **1.54** | **1.46** | **1.40** | **1.37** |
| 1.85 | 1.82 | 1.76 | 1.71 | 1.64 | 1.59 | 1.54 | 1.47 | 1.44 | 1.37 | 1.34 | 1.29 | 1.25 | 1.22 |
| **2.37** | **2.30** | **2.20** | **2.12** | **2.00** | **1.91** | **1.83** | **1.72** | **1.66** | **1.56** | **1.51** | **1.43** | **1.37** | **1.33** |
| 1.83 | 1.80 | 1.74 | 1.69 | 1.62 | 1.57 | 1.52 | 1.45 | 1.42 | 1.35 | 1.32 | 1.26 | 1.22 | 1.19 |
| **2.34** | **2.28** | **2.17** | **2.09** | **1.97** | **1.88** | **1.79** | **1.69** | **1.62** | **1.53** | **1.48** | **1.39** | **1.33** | **1.28** |
| 1.81 | 1.78 | 1.72 | 1.67 | 1.60 | 1.54 | 1.49 | 1.42 | 1.38 | 1.32 | 1.28 | 1.22 | 1.16 | 1.13 |
| **2.29** | **2.23** | **2.12** | **2.04** | **1.92** | **1.84** | **1.74** | **1.64** | **1.57** | **1.47** | **1.42** | **1.32** | **1.24** | **1.19** |
| 1.80 | 1.76 | 1.70 | 1.65 | 1.58 | 1.53 | 1.47 | 1.41 | 1.36 | 1.30 | 1.26 | 1.19 | 1.13 | 1.08 |
| **2.26** | **2.20** | **2.09** | **2.01** | **1.89** | **1.81** | **1.71** | **1.61** | **1.54** | **1.44** | **1.38** | **1.28** | **1.19** | **1.11** |
| 1.79 | 1.75 | 1.69 | 1.64 | 1.57 | 1.52 | 1.46 | 1.40 | 1.35 | 1.38 | 1.24 | 1.17 | 1.11 | 1.00 |
| **2.24** | **2.18** | **2.07** | **1.99** | **1.87** | **1.79** | **1.69** | **1.59** | **1.52** | **1.41** | **1.36** | **1.25** | **1.15** | **1.00** |

## Table 6    Values of the Studentized Range Statistic, $q_k$

For a one-way ANOVA, or a comparison of the means from a main effect, the value of $k$ is the number of means in the factor.

To compare the means from an interaction, find the appropriate design (or number of cell means) in the table below and obtain the adjusted value of $k$. Then find the value of $q_k$, using the adjusted value of $k$ and $df_{wn}$ at the appropriate $\alpha$.

Values of Adjusted $k$

| Design of study | Number of cell means in study | Adjusted value of k |
|---|---|---|
| 2 × 2 | 4 | 3 |
| 2 × 3 | 6 | 5 |
| 2 × 4 | 8 | 6 |
| 3 × 3 | 9 | 7 |
| 3 × 4 | 12 | 8 |
| 4 × 4 | 16 | 10 |
| 4 × 5 | 20 | 12 |

Values of $q_k$ for $\alpha = .05$ are light numbers and for $\alpha = .01$ are **dark numbers.**

| Degrees of freedom within groups (degrees of freedom in denominator of F ratio) | α | \(k = \text{number of means being compared}\) | | | | | | | | | | |
|---|---|---|---|---|---|---|---|---|---|---|---|---|
| | | 2 | 3 | 4 | 5 | 6 | 7 | 8 | 9 | 10 | 11 | 12 |
| 1 | .05 | 18.0 | 27.0 | 32.8 | 37.1 | 40.4 | 43.1 | 45.4 | 47.4 | 49.1 | 50.6 | 52.0 |
| | .01 | **90.0** | **135** | **164** | **186** | **202** | **216** | **227** | **237** | **246** | **253** | **260** |
| 2 | .05 | 6.09 | 8.3 | 9.8 | 10.9 | 11.7 | 12.4 | 13.0 | 13.5 | 14.0 | 14.4 | 14.7 |
| | .01 | **14.0** | **19.0** | **22.3** | **24.7** | **26.6** | **28.2** | **29.5** | **30.7** | **31.7** | **32.6** | **33.4** |
| 3 | .05 | 4.50 | 5.91 | 6.82 | 7.50 | 8.04 | 8.48 | 8.85 | 9.18 | 9.46 | 9.72 | 9.95 |
| | .01 | **8.26** | **10.6** | **12.2** | **13.3** | **14.2** | **15.0** | **15.6** | **16.2** | **16.7** | **17.1** | **17.5** |
| 4 | .05 | 3.93 | 5.04 | 5.76 | 6.29 | 6.71 | 7.05 | 7.35 | 7.60 | 7.83 | 8.03 | 8.21 |
| | .01 | **6.51** | **8.12** | **9.17** | **9.96** | **10.6** | **11.1** | **11.5** | **11.9** | **12.3** | **12.6** | **12.8** |
| 5 | .05 | 3.64 | 4.60 | 5.22 | 5.67 | 6.03 | 6.33 | 6.58 | 6.80 | 6.99 | 7.17 | 7.32 |
| | .01 | **5.70** | **6.97** | **7.80** | **8.42** | **8.91** | **9.32** | **9.67** | **9.97** | **10.2** | **10.5** | **10.7** |
| 6 | .05 | 3.46 | 4.34 | 4.90 | 5.31 | 5.63 | 5.89 | 6.12 | 6.32 | 6.49 | 6.65 | 6.79 |
| | .01 | **5.24** | **6.33** | **7.03** | **7.56** | **7.97** | **8.32** | **8.61** | **8.87** | **9.10** | **9.30** | **9.49** |

# Table 6 (cont.)  Values of the Studentized Range Statistic, $q_k$

| Degrees of freedom within groups (degrees of freedom in denominator of F ratio) | α | 2 | 3 | 4 | 5 | 6 | 7 | 8 | 9 | 10 | 11 | 12 |
|---|---|---|---|---|---|---|---|---|---|---|---|---|
| 7 | .05 | 3.34 | 4.16 | 4.69 | 5.06 | 5.36 | 5.61 | 5.82 | 6.00 | 6.16 | 6.30 | 6.43 |
|   | .01 | 4.95 | 5.92 | 6.54 | 7.01 | 7.37 | 7.68 | 7.94 | 8.17 | 8.37 | 8.55 | 8.71 |
| 8 | .05 | 3.26 | 4.04 | 4.53 | 4.89 | 5.17 | 5.40 | 5.60 | 5.77 | 5.92 | 6.05 | 6.18 |
|   | .01 | 4.74 | 5.63 | 6.20 | 6.63 | 6.96 | 7.24 | 7.47 | 7.68 | 7.87 | 8.03 | 8.18 |
| 9 | .05 | 3.20 | 3.95 | 4.42 | 4.76 | 5.02 | 5.24 | 5.43 | 5.60 | 5.74 | 5.87 | 5.98 |
|   | .01 | 4.60 | 5.43 | 5.96 | 6.35 | 6.66 | 6.91 | 7.13 | 7.32 | 7.49 | 7.65 | 7.78 |
| 10 | .05 | 3.15 | 3.88 | 4.33 | 4.65 | 4.91 | 5.12 | 5.30 | 5.46 | 5.60 | 5.72 | 5.83 |
|    | .01 | 4.48 | 5.27 | 5.77 | 6.14 | 6.43 | 6.67 | 6.87 | 7.05 | 7.21 | 7.36 | 7.48 |
| 11 | .05 | 3.11 | 3.82 | 4.26 | 4.57 | 4.82 | 5.03 | 5.20 | 5.35 | 5.49 | 5.61 | 5.71 |
|    | .01 | 4.39 | 5.14 | 5.62 | 5.97 | 6.25 | 6.48 | 6.67 | 6.84 | 6.99 | 7.13 | 7.26 |
| 12 | .05 | 3.08 | 3.77 | 4.20 | 4.51 | 4.75 | 4.95 | 5.12 | 5.27 | 5.40 | 5.51 | 5.62 |
|    | .01 | 4.32 | 5.04 | 5.50 | 5.84 | 6.10 | 6.32 | 6.51 | 6.67 | 6.81 | 6.94 | 7.06 |
| 13 | .05 | 3.06 | 3.73 | 4.15 | 4.45 | 4.69 | 4.88 | 5.05 | 5.19 | 5.32 | 5.43 | 5.53 |
|    | .01 | 4.26 | 4.96 | 5.40 | 5.73 | 5.98 | 6.19 | 6.37 | 6.53 | 6.67 | 6.79 | 6.90 |
| 14 | .05 | 3.03 | 3.70 | 4.11 | 4.41 | 4.64 | 4.83 | 4.99 | 5.13 | 5.25 | 5.36 | 5.46 |
|    | .01 | 4.21 | 4.89 | 5.32 | 5.63 | 5.88 | 6.08 | 6.26 | 6.41 | 6.54 | 6.66 | 6.77 |
| 16 | .05 | 3.00 | 3.65 | 4.05 | 4.33 | 4.56 | 4.74 | 4.90 | 5.03 | 5.15 | 5.26 | 5.35 |
|    | .01 | 4.13 | 4.78 | 5.19 | 5.49 | 5.72 | 5.92 | 6.08 | 6.22 | 6.35 | 6.46 | 6.56 |
| 18 | .05 | 2.97 | 3.61 | 4.00 | 4.28 | 4.49 | 4.67 | 4.82 | 4.96 | 5.07 | 5.17 | 5.27 |
|    | .01 | 4.07 | 4.70 | 5.09 | 5.38 | 5.60 | 5.79 | 5.94 | 6.08 | 6.20 | 6.31 | 6.41 |
| 20 | .05 | 2.95 | 3.58 | 3.96 | 4.23 | 4.45 | 4.62 | 4.77 | 4.90 | 5.01 | 5.11 | 5.20 |
|    | .01 | 4.02 | 4.64 | 5.02 | 5.29 | 5.51 | 5.69 | 5.84 | 5.97 | 6.09 | 6.19 | 6.29 |
| 24 | .05 | 2.92 | 3.53 | 3.90 | 4.17 | 4.37 | 4.54 | 4.68 | 4.81 | 4.92 | 5.01 | 5.10 |
|    | .01 | 3.96 | 4.54 | 4.91 | 5.17 | 5.37 | 5.54 | 5.69 | 5.81 | 5.92 | 6.02 | 6.11 |
| 30 | .05 | 2.89 | 3.49 | 3.84 | 4.10 | 4.30 | 4.46 | 4.60 | 4.72 | 4.83 | 4.92 | 5.00 |
|    | .01 | 3.89 | 4.45 | 4.80 | 5.05 | 5.24 | 5.40 | 5.54 | 5.56 | 5.76 | 5.85 | 5.93 |
| 40 | .05 | 2.86 | 3.44 | 3.79 | 4.04 | 4.23 | 4.39 | 4.52 | 4.63 | 4.74 | 4.82 | 4.91 |
|    | .01 | 3.82 | 4.37 | 4.70 | 4.93 | 5.11 | 5.27 | 5.39 | 5.50 | 5.60 | 5.69 | 5.77 |
| 60 | .05 | 2.83 | 3.40 | 3.74 | 3.98 | 4.16 | 4.31 | 4.44 | 4.55 | 4.65 | 4.73 | 4.81 |
|    | .01 | 3.76 | 4.28 | 4.60 | 4.82 | 4.99 | 5.13 | 5.25 | 5.36 | 5.45 | 5.53 | 5.60 |
| 120 | .05 | 2.80 | 3.36 | 3.69 | 3.92 | 4.10 | 4.24 | 4.36 | 4.48 | 4.56 | 4.64 | 4.72 |
|     | .01 | 3.70 | 4.20 | 4.50 | 4.71 | 4.87 | 5.01 | 5.12 | 5.21 | 5.30 | 5.38 | 5.44 |
| ∞ | .05 | 2.77 | 3.31 | 3.63 | 3.86 | 4.03 | 4.17 | 4.29 | 4.39 | 4.47 | 4.55 | 4.62 |
|   | .01 | 3.64 | 4.12 | 4.40 | 4.60 | 4.76 | 4.88 | 4.99 | 5.08 | 5.16 | 5.23 | 5.29 |

*k = number of means being compared*

From B. J. Winer, *Statistical Principles in Experimental Design*, McGraw-Hill, 1962; abridged from H. L. Harter, D. S. Clemm, and E. H. Guthrie, The probability integrals of the range and of the studentized range, WADC Tech. Rep. 58–484, Vol. 2, 1959, Wright Air Development Center, Table II.2, pp. 243–281. Reproduced with permission of McGraw-Hill, Inc.

## Table 7   Critical Values of the $F_{max}$ Test

Critical values for $\alpha = .05$ are light numbers and for $\alpha = .01$ are **dark numbers**.

*Note:* $n$ = number of scores in each condition or cell.

| $n-1$ | $\alpha$ | \multicolumn{11}{c}{$k$ = number of samples} |
|---|---|---|---|---|---|---|---|---|---|---|---|---|

| $n-1$ | $\alpha$ | 2 | 3 | 4 | 5 | 6 | 7 | 8 | 9 | 10 | 11 | 12 |
|---|---|---|---|---|---|---|---|---|---|---|---|---|
| 4 | .05 | 9.60 | 15.5 | 20.6 | 25.2 | 29.5 | 33.6 | 37.5 | 41.4 | 44.6 | 48.0 | 51.4 |
|   | **.01** | **23.2** | **37.** | **49.** | **59.** | **69.** | **79.** | **89.** | **97.** | **106.** | **113.** | **120.** |
| 5 | .05 | 7.15 | 10.8 | 13.7 | 16.3 | 18.7 | 20.8 | 22.9 | 24.7 | 26.5 | 28.2 | 29.9 |
|   | **.01** | **14.9** | **22.** | **28.** | **33.** | **38.** | **42.** | **46.** | **50.** | **54.** | **57.** | **60.** |
| 6 | .05 | 5.82 | 8.38 | 10.4 | 12.1 | 13.7 | 15.0 | 16.3 | 17.5 | 18.6 | 19.7 | 20.7 |
|   | **.01** | **11.1** | **15.5** | **19.1** | **22.** | **25.** | **27.** | **30.** | **32.** | **34.** | **36.** | **37.** |
| 7 | .05 | 4.99 | 6.94 | 8.44 | 9.70 | 10.8 | 11.8 | 12.7 | 13.5 | 14.3 | 15.1 | 15.8 |
|   | **.01** | **8.89** | **12.1** | **14.5** | **16.5** | **18.4** | **20.** | **22.** | **23.** | **24.** | **26.** | **27.** |
| 8 | .05 | 4.43 | 6.00 | 7.18 | 8.12 | 9.03 | 9.78 | 10.5 | 11.1 | 11.7 | 12.2 | 12.7 |
|   | **.01** | **7.50** | **9.9** | **11.7** | **13.2** | **14.5** | **15.8** | **16.9** | **17.9** | **18.9** | **19.8** | **21.** |
| 9 | .05 | 4.03 | 5.34 | 6.31 | 7.11 | 7.80 | 8.41 | 8.95 | 9.45 | 9.91 | 10.3 | 10.7 |
|   | **.01** | **6.54** | **8.5** | **9.9** | **11.1** | **12.1** | **13.1** | **13.9** | **14.7** | **15.3** | **16.0** | **16.6** |
| 10 | .05 | 3.72 | 4.85 | 5.67 | 6.34 | 6.92 | 7.42 | 7.87 | 8.28 | 8.66 | 9.01 | 9.34 |
|   | **.01** | **5.85** | **7.4** | **8.6** | **9.6** | **10.4** | **11.1** | **11.8** | **12.4** | **12.9** | **13.4** | **13.9** |
| 12 | .05 | 3.28 | 4.16 | 4.79 | 5.30 | 5.72 | 6.09 | 6.42 | 6.72 | 7.00 | 7.25 | 7.48 |
|   | **.01** | **4.91** | **6.1** | **6.9** | **7.6** | **8.2** | **8.7** | **9.1** | **9.5** | **9.9** | **10.2** | **10.6** |
| 15 | .05 | 2.86 | 3.54 | 4.01 | 4.37 | 4.68 | 4.95 | 5.19 | 5.40 | 5.59 | 5.77 | 5.93 |
|   | **.01** | **4.07** | **4.9** | **5.5** | **6.0** | **6.4** | **6.7** | **7.1** | **7.3** | **7.5** | **7.8** | **8.0** |
| 20 | .05 | 2.46 | 2.95 | 3.29 | 3.54 | 3.76 | 3.94 | 4.10 | 4.24 | 4.37 | 4.49 | 4.59 |
|   | **.01** | **3.32** | **3.8** | **4.3** | **4.6** | **4.9** | **5.1** | **5.3** | **5.5** | **5.6** | **5.8** | **5.9** |
| 30 | .05 | 2.07 | 2.40 | 2.61 | 2.78 | 2.91 | 3.02 | 3.12 | 3.21 | 3.29 | 3.36 | 3.39 |
|   | **.01** | **2.63** | **3.0** | **3.3** | **3.4** | **3.6** | **3.7** | **3.8** | **3.9** | **4.0** | **4.1** | **4.2** |
| 60 | .05 | 1.67 | 1.85 | 1.96 | 2.04 | 2.11 | 2.17 | 2.22 | 2.26 | 2.30 | 2.33 | 2.36 |
|   | **.01** | **1.96** | **2.2** | **2.3** | **2.4** | **2.4** | **2.5** | **2.5** | **2.6** | **2.6** | **2.7** | **2.7** |

From Table 31 of E. Pearson and H. Hartley, *Biometrika Tables for Statisticians*, 3rd ed. Cambridge: Cambridge University Press, 1966. Reprinted with permission of the Biometrika trustees.

## Table 8   Critical Values of Chi Square: The $\chi^2$-Tables

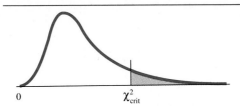

0          $\chi^2_{crit}$

| df | *Level of significance* | |
|---|---|---|
|  | $\alpha = .05$ | $\alpha = .01$ |
| 1 | 3.84 | 6.64 |
| 2 | 5.99 | 9.21 |
| 3 | 7.81 | 11.34 |
| 4 | 9.49 | 13.28 |
| 5 | 11.07 | 15.09 |
| 6 | 12.59 | 16.81 |
| 7 | 14.07 | 18.48 |
| 8 | 15.51 | 20.09 |
| 9 | 16.92 | 21.67 |
| 10 | 18.31 | 23.21 |
| 11 | 19.68 | 24.72 |
| 12 | 21.03 | 26.22 |
| 13 | 22.36 | 27.69 |
| 14 | 23.68 | 29.14 |
| 15 | 25.00 | 30.58 |
| 16 | 26.30 | 32.00 |
| 17 | 27.59 | 33.41 |
| 18 | 28.87 | 34.80 |
| 19 | 30.14 | 36.19 |
| 20 | 31.41 | 37.57 |
| 21 | 32.67 | 38.93 |
| 22 | 33.92 | 40.29 |
| 23 | 35.17 | 41.64 |
| 24 | 36.42 | 42.98 |
| 25 | 37.65 | 44.31 |
| 26 | 38.88 | 45.64 |
| 27 | 40.11 | 46.96 |
| 28 | 41.34 | 48.28 |
| 29 | 42.56 | 49.59 |
| 30 | 43.77 | 50.89 |
| 40 | 55.76 | 63.69 |
| 50 | 67.50 | 76.15 |
| 60 | 79.08 | 88.38 |
| 70 | 90.53 | 100.42 |

From Table IV of R. A. Fisher and F. Yates, *Statistical Tables for Biological, Agricultural and Medical Research*, 6th ed. London: Longman Group Ltd., 1974 (previously published by Oliver and Boyd, Edinburgh).

## Table 9   Critical Values of the Mann-Whitney *U*

To be significant, the $U_{obt}$ must be equal to or be *less than* the critical value. (Dashes in the table indicate that no decision is possible.) Critical values for $\alpha = .05$ are light numbers and for $\alpha = .01$ are **dark numbers.**

Two-Tailed Test

| $n_2$ (no. of scores in Group 2) | $\alpha$ | $n_1$ (no. of scores in Group 1) | | | | | | | | |
|---|---|---|---|---|---|---|---|---|---|---|
| | | 1 | 2 | 3 | 4 | 5 | 6 | 7 | 8 | 9 |
| 1 | .05 | — | — | — | — | — | — | — | — | — |
| | **.01** | **—** | **—** | **—** | **—** | **—** | **—** | **—** | **—** | **—** |
| 2 | .05 | — | — | — | — | — | — | — | 0 | 0 |
| | **.01** | **—** | **—** | **—** | **—** | **—** | **—** | **—** | **—** | **—** |
| 3 | .05 | — | — | — | — | 0 | 1 | 1 | 2 | 2 |
| | **.01** | **—** | **—** | **—** | **—** | **—** | **—** | **—** | **—** | **0** |
| 4 | .05 | — | — | — | 0 | 1 | 2 | 3 | 4 | 4 |
| | **.01** | **—** | **—** | **—** | **—** | **—** | **0** | **0** | **1** | **1** |
| 5 | .05 | — | — | 0 | 1 | 2 | 3 | 5 | 6 | 7 |
| | **.01** | **—** | **—** | **—** | **—** | **0** | **1** | **1** | **2** | **3** |
| 6 | .05 | — | — | 1 | 2 | 3 | 5 | 6 | 8 | 10 |
| | **.01** | **—** | **—** | **—** | **0** | **1** | **2** | **3** | **4** | **5** |
| 7 | .05 | — | — | 1 | 3 | 5 | 6 | 8 | 10 | 12 |
| | **.01** | **—** | **—** | **—** | **0** | **1** | **3** | **4** | **6** | **7** |
| 8 | .05 | — | 0 | 2 | 4 | 6 | 8 | 10 | 13 | 15 |
| | **.01** | **—** | **—** | **—** | **1** | **2** | **4** | **6** | **7** | **9** |
| 9 | .05 | — | 0 | 2 | 4 | 7 | 10 | 12 | 15 | 17 |
| | **.01** | **—** | **—** | **0** | **1** | **3** | **5** | **7** | **9** | **11** |
| 10 | .05 | — | 0 | 3 | 5 | 8 | 11 | 14 | 17 | 20 |
| | **.01** | **—** | **—** | **0** | **2** | **4** | **6** | **9** | **11** | **13** |
| 11 | .05 | — | 0 | 3 | 6 | 9 | 13 | 16 | 19 | 23 |
| | **.01** | **—** | **—** | **0** | **2** | **5** | **7** | **10** | **13** | **16** |
| 12 | .05 | — | 1 | 4 | 7 | 11 | 14 | 18 | 22 | 26 |
| | **.01** | **—** | **—** | **1** | **3** | **6** | **9** | **12** | **15** | **18** |
| 13 | .05 | — | 1 | 4 | 8 | 12 | 16 | 20 | 24 | 28 |
| | **.01** | **—** | **—** | **1** | **3** | **7** | **10** | **13** | **17** | **20** |
| 14 | .05 | — | 1 | 5 | 9 | 13 | 17 | 22 | 26 | 31 |
| | **.01** | **—** | **—** | **1** | **4** | **7** | **11** | **15** | **18** | **22** |
| 15 | .05 | — | 1 | 5 | 10 | 14 | 19 | 24 | 29 | 34 |
| | **.01** | **—** | **—** | **2** | **5** | **8** | **12** | **16** | **20** | **24** |
| 16 | .05 | — | 1 | 6 | 11 | 15 | 21 | 26 | 31 | 37 |
| | **.01** | **—** | **—** | **2** | **5** | **9** | **13** | **18** | **22** | **27** |
| 17 | .05 | — | 2 | 6 | 11 | 17 | 22 | 28 | 34 | 39 |
| | **.01** | **—** | **—** | **2** | **6** | **10** | **15** | **19** | **24** | **29** |
| 18 | .05 | — | 2 | 7 | 12 | 18 | 24 | 30 | 36 | 42 |
| | **.01** | **—** | **—** | **2** | **6** | **11** | **16** | **21** | **26** | **31** |
| 19 | .05 | — | 2 | 7 | 13 | 19 | 25 | 32 | 38 | 45 |
| | **.01** | **—** | **0** | **3** | **7** | **12** | **17** | **22** | **28** | **33** |
| 20 | .05 | — | 2 | 8 | 13 | 20 | 27 | 34 | 41 | 48 |
| | **.01** | **—** | **0** | **3** | **8** | **13** | **18** | **24** | **30** | **36** |

| | $n_1$ (no. of scores in Group 1) | | | | | | | | | |
|---|---|---|---|---|---|---|---|---|---|---|
| *10* | *11* | *12* | *13* | *14* | *15* | *16* | *17* | *18* | *19* | *20* |
| — | — | — | — | — | — | — | — | — | — | — |
| — | — | — | — | — | — | — | — | — | — | — |
| 0 | 0 | 1 | 1 | 1 | 1 | 1 | 2 | 2 | 2 | 2 |
| — | — | — | — | — | — | — | — | — | **0** | **0** |
| 3 | 3 | 4 | 4 | 5 | 5 | 6 | 6 | 7 | 7 | 8 |
| **0** | **0** | **1** | **1** | **1** | **2** | **2** | **2** | **2** | **3** | **3** |
| 5 | 6 | 7 | 8 | 9 | 10 | 11 | 11 | 12 | 13 | 13 |
| **2** | **2** | **3** | **3** | **4** | **5** | **5** | **6** | **6** | **7** | **8** |
| 8 | 9 | 11 | 12 | 13 | 14 | 15 | 17 | 18 | 19 | 20 |
| **4** | **5** | **6** | **7** | **7** | **8** | **9** | **10** | **11** | **12** | **13** |
| 11 | 13 | 14 | 16 | 17 | 19 | 21 | 22 | 24 | 25 | 27 |
| **6** | **7** | **9** | **10** | **11** | **12** | **13** | **15** | **16** | **17** | **18** |
| 14 | 16 | 18 | 20 | 22 | 24 | 26 | 28 | 30 | 32 | 34 |
| **9** | **10** | **12** | **13** | **15** | **16** | **18** | **19** | **21** | **22** | **24** |
| 17 | 19 | 22 | 24 | 26 | 29 | 31 | 34 | 36 | 38 | 41 |
| **11** | **13** | **15** | **17** | **18** | **20** | **22** | **24** | **26** | **28** | **30** |
| 20 | 23 | 26 | 28 | 31 | 34 | 37 | 39 | 42 | 45 | 48 |
| **13** | **16** | **18** | **20** | **22** | **24** | **27** | **29** | **31** | **33** | **36** |
| 23 | 26 | 29 | 33 | 36 | 39 | 42 | 45 | 48 | 52 | 55 |
| **16** | **18** | **21** | **24** | **26** | **29** | **31** | **34** | **37** | **39** | **42** |
| 26 | 30 | 33 | 37 | 40 | 44 | 47 | 51 | 55 | 58 | 62 |
| **18** | **21** | **24** | **27** | **30** | **33** | **36** | **39** | **42** | **45** | **48** |
| 29 | 33 | 37 | 41 | 45 | 49 | 53 | 57 | 61 | 65 | 69 |
| **21** | **24** | **27** | **31** | **34** | **37** | **41** | **44** | **47** | **51** | **54** |
| 33 | 37 | 41 | 45 | 50 | 54 | 59 | 63 | 67 | 72 | 76 |
| **24** | **27** | **31** | **34** | **38** | **42** | **45** | **49** | **53** | **56** | **60** |
| 36 | 40 | 45 | 50 | 55 | 59 | 64 | 67 | 74 | 78 | 83 |
| **26** | **30** | **34** | **38** | **42** | **46** | **50** | **54** | **58** | **63** | **67** |
| 39 | 44 | 49 | 54 | 59 | 64 | 70 | 75 | 80 | 85 | 90 |
| **29** | **33** | **37** | **42** | **46** | **51** | **55** | **60** | **64** | **69** | **73** |
| 42 | 47 | 53 | 59 | 64 | 70 | 75 | 81 | 86 | 92 | 98 |
| **31** | **36** | **41** | **45** | **50** | **55** | **60** | **65** | **70** | **74** | **79** |
| 45 | 51 | 57 | 63 | 67 | 75 | 81 | 87 | 93 | 99 | 105 |
| **34** | **39** | **44** | **49** | **54** | **60** | **65** | **70** | **75** | **81** | **86** |
| 48 | 55 | 61 | 67 | 74 | 80 | 86 | 93 | 99 | 106 | 112 |
| **37** | **42** | **47** | **53** | **58** | **64** | **70** | **75** | **81** | **87** | **92** |
| 52 | 58 | 65 | 72 | 78 | 85 | 92 | 99 | 106 | 113 | 119 |
| **39** | **45** | **51** | **56** | **63** | **69** | **74** | **81** | **87** | **93** | **99** |
| 55 | 62 | 69 | 76 | 83 | 90 | 98 | 105 | 112 | 119 | 127 |
| **42** | **48** | **54** | **60** | **67** | **73** | **79** | **86** | **92** | **99** | **105** |

One-Tailed Test

| $n_2$ (no. of scores in Group 2) | $\alpha$ | $n_1$ (no. of scores in Group 1) | | | | | | | | |
|---|---|---|---|---|---|---|---|---|---|---|
| | | 1 | 2 | 3 | 4 | 5 | 6 | 7 | 8 | 9 |
| 1 | .05 | — | — | — | — | — | — | — | — | — |
| | **.01** | — | — | — | — | — | — | — | — | — |
| 2 | .05 | — | — | — | — | 0 | 0 | 0 | 1 | 1 |
| | **.01** | — | — | — | — | — | — | — | — | — |
| 3 | .05 | — | — | 0 | 0 | 1 | 2 | 2 | 3 | 3 |
| | **.01** | — | — | — | — | — | — | **0** | **0** | **1** |
| 4 | .05 | — | — | 0 | 1 | 2 | 3 | 4 | 5 | 6 |
| | **.01** | — | — | — | — | **0** | **1** | **1** | **2** | **3** |
| 5 | .05 | — | 0 | 1 | 2 | 4 | 5 | 6 | 8 | 9 |
| | **.01** | — | — | — | **0** | **1** | **2** | **3** | **4** | **5** |
| 6 | .05 | — | 0 | 2 | 3 | 5 | 7 | 8 | 10 | 12 |
| | **.01** | — | — | — | **1** | **2** | **3** | **4** | **6** | **7** |
| 7 | .05 | — | 0 | 2 | 4 | 6 | 8 | 11 | 13 | 15 |
| | **.01** | — | — | **0** | **1** | **3** | **4** | **6** | **7** | **9** |
| 8 | .05 | — | 1 | 3 | 5 | 8 | 10 | 13 | 15 | 18 |
| | **.01** | — | — | **0** | **2** | **4** | **6** | **7** | **9** | **11** |
| 9 | .05 | — | 1 | 3 | 6 | 9 | 12 | 15 | 18 | 21 |
| | **.01** | — | — | **1** | **3** | **5** | **7** | **9** | **11** | **14** |
| 10 | .05 | — | 1 | 4 | 7 | 11 | 14 | 17 | 20 | 24 |
| | **.01** | — | — | **1** | **3** | **6** | **8** | **11** | **13** | **16** |
| 11 | .05 | — | 1 | 5 | 8 | 12 | 16 | 19 | 23 | 27 |
| | **.01** | — | — | **1** | **4** | **7** | **9** | **12** | **15** | **18** |
| 12 | .05 | — | 2 | 5 | 9 | 13 | 17 | 21 | 26 | 30 |
| | **.01** | — | — | **2** | **5** | **8** | **11** | **14** | **17** | **21** |
| 13 | .05 | — | 2 | 6 | 10 | 15 | 19 | 24 | 28 | 33 |
| | **.01** | — | **0** | **2** | **5** | **9** | **12** | **16** | **20** | **23** |
| 14 | .05 | — | 2 | 7 | 11 | 16 | 21 | 26 | 31 | 36 |
| | **.01** | — | **0** | **2** | **6** | **10** | **13** | **17** | **22** | **26** |
| 15 | .05 | — | 3 | 7 | 12 | 18 | 23 | 28 | 33 | 39 |
| | **.01** | — | **0** | **3** | **7** | **11** | **15** | **19** | **24** | **28** |
| 16 | .05 | — | 3 | 8 | 14 | 19 | 25 | 30 | 36 | 42 |
| | **.01** | — | **0** | **3** | **7** | **12** | **16** | **21** | **26** | **31** |
| 17 | .05 | — | 3 | 9 | 15 | 20 | 26 | 33 | 39 | 45 |
| | **.01** | — | **0** | **4** | **8** | **13** | **18** | **23** | **28** | **33** |
| 18 | .05 | — | 4 | 9 | 16 | 22 | 28 | 35 | 41 | 48 |
| | **.01** | — | **0** | **4** | **9** | **14** | **19** | **24** | **30** | **36** |
| 19 | .05 | 0 | 4 | 10 | 17 | 23 | 30 | 37 | 44 | 51 |
| | **.01** | — | **1** | **4** | **9** | **15** | **20** | **26** | **32** | **38** |
| 20 | .05 | 0 | 4 | 11 | 18 | 25 | 32 | 39 | 47 | 54 |
| | **.01** | — | **1** | **5** | **10** | **16** | **22** | **28** | **34** | **40** |

| $n_1$ (no. of scores in Group 1) | | | | | | | | | | |
|---|---|---|---|---|---|---|---|---|---|---|
| 10 | 11 | 12 | 13 | 14 | 15 | 16 | 17 | 18 | 19 | 20 |
| — | — | — | — | — | — | — | — | — | 0 | 0 |
| — | — | — | — | — | — | — | — | — | — | — |
| 1 | 1 | 2 | 2 | 2 | 3 | 3 | 3 | 4 | 4 | 4 |
| — | — | — | **0** | **0** | **0** | **0** | **0** | **0** | **1** | **1** |
| 4 | 5 | 5 | 6 | 7 | 7 | 8 | 9 | 9 | 10 | 11 |
| **1** | **1** | **2** | **2** | **2** | **3** | **3** | **4** | **4** | **4** | **5** |
| 7 | 8 | 9 | 10 | 11 | 12 | 14 | 15 | 16 | 17 | 18 |
| **3** | **4** | **5** | **5** | **6** | **7** | **7** | **8** | **9** | **9** | **10** |
| 11 | 12 | 13 | 15 | 16 | 18 | 19 | 20 | 22 | 23 | 25 |
| **6** | **7** | **8** | **9** | **10** | **11** | **12** | **13** | **14** | **15** | **16** |
| 14 | 16 | 17 | 19 | 21 | 23 | 25 | 26 | 28 | 30 | 32 |
| **8** | **9** | **11** | **12** | **13** | **15** | **16** | **18** | **19** | **20** | **22** |
| 17 | 19 | 21 | 24 | 26 | 28 | 30 | 33 | 35 | 37 | 39 |
| **11** | **12** | **14** | **16** | **17** | **19** | **21** | **23** | **24** | **26** | **28** |
| 20 | 23 | 26 | 28 | 31 | 33 | 36 | 39 | 41 | 44 | 47 |
| **13** | **15** | **17** | **20** | **22** | **24** | **26** | **28** | **30** | **32** | **34** |
| 24 | 27 | 30 | 33 | 36 | 39 | 42 | 45 | 48 | 51 | 54 |
| **16** | **18** | **21** | **23** | **26** | **28** | **31** | **33** | **36** | **38** | **40** |
| 27 | 31 | 34 | 37 | 41 | 44 | 48 | 51 | 55 | 58 | 62 |
| **19** | **22** | **24** | **27** | **30** | **33** | **36** | **38** | **41** | **44** | **47** |
| 31 | 34 | 38 | 42 | 46 | 50 | 54 | 57 | 61 | 65 | 69 |
| **22** | **25** | **28** | **31** | **34** | **37** | **41** | **44** | **47** | **50** | **53** |
| 34 | 38 | 42 | 47 | 51 | 55 | 60 | 64 | 68 | 72 | 77 |
| **24** | **28** | **31** | **35** | **38** | **42** | **46** | **49** | **53** | **56** | **60** |
| 37 | 42 | 47 | 51 | 56 | 61 | 65 | 70 | 75 | 80 | 84 |
| **27** | **31** | **35** | **39** | **43** | **47** | **51** | **55** | **59** | **63** | **67** |
| 41 | 46 | 51 | 56 | 61 | 66 | 71 | 77 | 82 | 87 | 92 |
| **30** | **34** | **38** | **43** | **47** | **51** | **56** | **60** | **65** | **69** | **73** |
| 44 | 50 | 55 | 61 | 66 | 72 | 77 | 83 | 88 | 94 | 100 |
| **33** | **37** | **42** | **47** | **51** | **56** | **61** | **66** | **70** | **75** | **80** |
| 48 | 54 | 60 | 65 | 71 | 77 | 83 | 89 | 95 | 101 | 107 |
| **36** | **41** | **46** | **51** | **56** | **61** | **66** | **71** | **76** | **82** | **87** |
| 51 | 57 | 64 | 70 | 77 | 83 | 89 | 96 | 102 | 109 | 115 |
| **38** | **44** | **49** | **55** | **60** | **66** | **71** | **77** | **82** | **88** | **93** |
| 55 | 61 | 68 | 75 | 82 | 88 | 95 | 102 | 109 | 116 | 123 |
| **41** | **47** | **53** | **59** | **65** | **70** | **76** | **82** | **88** | **94** | **100** |
| 58 | 65 | 72 | 80 | 87 | 94 | 101 | 109 | 116 | 123 | 130 |
| **44** | **50** | **56** | **63** | **69** | **75** | **82** | **88** | **94** | **101** | **107** |
| 62 | 69 | 77 | 84 | 92 | 100 | 107 | 115 | 123 | 130 | 138 |
| **47** | **53** | **60** | **67** | **73** | **80** | **87** | **93** | **100** | **107** | **114** |

From the *Bulletin of the Institute of Educational Research*, 1, No. 2, Indiana University, with permission of the publishers.

## Table 10   Critical Values of the Wilcoxon *T*

To be significant, the $T_{obt}$ must be equal to or *less than* the critical value. (Dashes in the table indicate that no decision can be made.) In the table, $N$ is the number of nonzero differences that occurred when $T_{obt}$ was calculated.

Two-Tailed Test

| N | α = .05 | α = .01 | N | α = .05 | α = .01 |
|---|---------|---------|---|---------|---------|
| 5 | — | — | 28 | 116 | 91 |
| 6 | 0 | — | 29 | 126 | 100 |
| 7 | 2 | — | 30 | 137 | 109 |
| 8 | 3 | 0 | 31 | 147 | 118 |
| 9 | 5 | 1 | 32 | 159 | 128 |
| 10 | 8 | 3 | 33 | 170 | 138 |
| 11 | 10 | 5 | 34 | 182 | 148 |
| 12 | 13 | 7 | 35 | 195 | 159 |
| 13 | 17 | 9 | 36 | 208 | 171 |
| 14 | 21 | 12 | 37 | 221 | 182 |
| 15 | 25 | 15 | 38 | 235 | 194 |
| 16 | 29 | 19 | 39 | 249 | 207 |
| 17 | 34 | 23 | 40 | 264 | 220 |
| 18 | 40 | 27 | 41 | 279 | 233 |
| 19 | 46 | 32 | 42 | 294 | 247 |
| 20 | 52 | 37 | 43 | 310 | 261 |
| 21 | 58 | 42 | 44 | 327 | 276 |
| 22 | 65 | 48 | 45 | 343 | 291 |
| 23 | 73 | 54 | 46 | 361 | 307 |
| 24 | 81 | 61 | 47 | 378 | 322 |
| 25 | 89 | 68 | 48 | 396 | 339 |
| 26 | 98 | 75 | 49 | 415 | 355 |
| 27 | 107 | 83 | 50 | 434 | 373 |

## Table 10 (cont.) Critical Values of the Wilcoxon *T*

One-Tailed Test

| N | α = .05 | α = .01 | N | α = .05 | α = .01 |
|---|---------|---------|---|---------|---------|
| 5 | 0 | — | 28 | 130 | 101 |
| 6 | 2 | — | 29 | 140 | 110 |
| 7 | 3 | 0 | 30 | 151 | 120 |
| 8 | 5 | 1 | 31 | 163 | 130 |
| 9 | 8 | 3 | 32 | 175 | 140 |
| 10 | 10 | 5 | 33 | 187 | 151 |
| 11 | 13 | 7 | 34 | 200 | 162 |
| 12 | 17 | 9 | 35 | 213 | 173 |
| 13 | 21 | 12 | 36 | 227 | 185 |
| 14 | 25 | 15 | 37 | 241 | 198 |
| 15 | 30 | 19 | 38 | 256 | 211 |
| 16 | 35 | 23 | 39 | 271 | 224 |
| 17 | 41 | 27 | 40 | 286 | 238 |
| 18 | 47 | 32 | 41 | 302 | 252 |
| 19 | 53 | 37 | 42 | 319 | 266 |
| 20 | 60 | 43 | 43 | 336 | 281 |
| 21 | 67 | 49 | 44 | 353 | 296 |
| 22 | 75 | 55 | 45 | 371 | 312 |
| 23 | 83 | 62 | 46 | 389 | 328 |
| 24 | 91 | 69 | 47 | 407 | 345 |
| 25 | 100 | 76 | 48 | 426 | 362 |
| 26 | 110 | 84 | 49 | 446 | 379 |
| 27 | 119 | 92 | 50 | 466 | 397 |

From F. Wilcoxon and R. A. Wilcox, *Some Rapid Approximate Statistical Procedures*. New York: Lederle Laboratories, 1964. Reproduced with the permission of the American Cyanamid Company.

# Answers to Practice Problems

**Chapter 1**

1. Researchers use statistics to organize, summarize, and communicate data and to draw conclusions about what the data indicate.
3. A transformation is a systematic mathematical procedure for converting a set of scores into different scores.
5. A proportion is computed by dividing the score by the highest possible score.
7. To transform a percent to a proportion, divide the percent by 100.
9. A data point is the dot on a graph representing a pair of $X$ and $Y$ scores.
11. *a.* 13.75    *b.* 10.04    *c.* 10.05    *d.* .08
    *e.* 1.00
13. $Q = (8 + -2)(64 + 4) = (6)(68) = 408$
15. $D = (-3.25)(3) = -9.75$

**Chapter 2**

1. A relationship exists between variables when certain scores on one variable are associated with certain scores on another variable, and as the scores on one variable change, the scores on the other variable tend to change in a consistent fashion.
3. The condition is the specific amount or category of the independent variable under which subjects are measured.
5. Random sampling is a method of selecting a sample whereby (1) every score in the population has an equal chance of being selected for a sample and (2) every possible sample has an equal chance of being selected.
7. The purpose of descriptive statistics is to organize, summarize, and describe the characteristics of a sample of scores.
9. A statistic is a number that describes a characteristic of a sample of scores. A parameter is a number that describes a characteristic of a population of scores.
11. Samples A and D
13. First we describe the relationship in the sample by computing statistics, and then we use the statistics to estimate the corresponding population parameters we would expect to find if we examined the relationship in the population.

## Chapter 3

*1.* $N$ stands for the number of scores in a sample.
*3.* A bar graph is used with nominal or ordinal data.
*5.* A polygon is used with a wide range of interval or ratio scores.
*7.* A positively skewed distribution is nonsymmetrical, containing extreme high scores which have relatively low frequency, but not containing extreme low scores which have low frequency.
*9.* A bimodal distribution is a symmetrical distribution that has two areas where there are relatively high frequency scores.
*11.* A proportion of the area under the normal curve reflects the relative frequency of the scores in that part of the curve.
*13.* A percentile indicates the percent of all scores at or below a particular score.
*15.*

| Score | f | rel. f | cf |
|-------|---|--------|----|
| 53 | 1 | .05 | 18 |
| 52 | 3 | .17 | 17 |
| 51 | 2 | .11 | 14 |
| 50 | 5 | .28 | 12 |
| 49 | 4 | .22 | 7 |
| 48 | 0 | .00 | 3 |
| 47 | 3 | .17 | 3 |

*17.* The score at the 50th percentile is

$$\text{score} = 49.5 + \left(\frac{9-7}{5}\right)(1) = 49.90$$

## Chapter 4

*1.* A measure of central tendency indicates where on a variable most of the scores in a distribution tend to be located.
*3.* The median is the score at the 50th percentile

(50% of the scores are below the median). It is used with ordinal scores or with highly skewed interval or ratio scores.
*5.* $\Sigma X = 460$, $N = 20$, $\overline{X} = 23.00$
*7.* A deviation conveys whether a score is above or below the mean and how far the score is from the mean.
*9.* The mean is the center of the distribution, so over the long run, over- and underestimates will cancel out and equal zero.
*11. a.* We use a bar graph when the independent variable is a nominal or ordinal variable. We use a line graph when the independent variable is an interval or ratio variable.
 *b.* The dependent variable is plotted on the $Y$ axis, and the independent variable is plotted on the $X$ axis.

## Chapter 5

*1.* Measures of variability communicate how different or spread out the scores are.
*3.* The variance is the average of the squared deviations of scores around the mean. The standard deviation is the square root of the variance.
*5. a.* Since $\overline{X} = 5.00$, we assume $\mu = 5.00$. Since $N - 1 = 19$, $s_X^2 = (668 - 500)/19 = 8.84$; $s_X = \sqrt{8.84} = 2.97$.
 *b.* Between 2.03 (5.00 − 2.97) and 7.97 (5.00 + 2.97).
*7.* Sample 2. We will predict the mean for all scores. Since $S_X$ is smaller in Sample 2 than in Sample 1 (5 versus 20), the scores are closer to $\overline{X}$, so there will be less error, or greater accuracy.
*9.* $S_X^2$ is used to describe a sample's variance; $s_X^2$ is used to estimate the population's variance based on the sample.
*11.* We measure "average error" using variance, so her error will be $S_X^2 = 36$.
*13.* She is computing the proportion of variance accounted for.

## Chapter 6

1. A $z$-score indicates the distance, measured in standard deviation units, that a score is above or below the mean.
3. A $z$-distribution is the distribution that results when a distribution is transformed from raw scores to $z$-scores.
5. $\Sigma X = 103$, $\Sigma X^2 = 931$, and $N = 12$, so $S_X = 1.98$ and $\overline{X} = 8.58$.
   a. For $X = 10$, $z = (10 - 8.58)/1.98 = +.72$.
   b. For $X = 6$, $z = (6 - 8.58)/1.98 = -1.30$.
7. a. $z = +1.0$     b. $z = -2.8$
   c. $z = -.70$     d. $z = -2.0$
9. a. .4706     b. .0107     c. .8914     d. .05
11. Convert each score to a $z$-score. According to Group A, your car scores $z = (92 - 80)/4 = +3$; according to Group B, your car scores $z = (40 - 35)/2 = +2.5$. Both groups rate your car very high relative to other cars in their study (in both cases its percentile is above 98%), so buy the car.
13. $\sigma_{\overline{X}}$ is the standard error of the mean; it tells us the standard deviation, or spread, of the sample means in a sampling distribution.
15. Convert $\overline{X}$ to a $z$-score. First, $\sigma_{\overline{X}}$ equals $6/\sqrt{50}$, or .849. Then $z = (18 - 19.4)/.849 = -1.65$. From the $z$-tables, .0495 of the curve is below this score. Out of 1000 samples, you would expect $(.0495)(1000) = 49.5$ sample means to be below 18.

## Chapter 7

1. In correlational research, we don't necessarily know which variable occurred first, nor have we controlled or eliminated any other variables that might potentially cause scores to change.
3. A coefficient describes (1) whether the relationship is a positive or negative linear relationship and (2) the strength of the relationship (the extent to which the relationship forms a perfect linear relationship).

5. a. The scatterplot forms a narrower ellipse.
   b. The variability of $Y$s at each $X$ decreases.
   c. The $Y$ scores are closer to the regression line.
   d. Our accuracy in predicting $Y$ increases.
7. a. $r$     b. $r_s$     c. $r_{pb}$     d. $r_s$ (after the liquid-consumed scores are transformed to rank-order scores)
9. When a small range of $X$ and/or $Y$ scores is measured, the coefficient underestimates the actual strength of the relationship that would be found with unrestricted data.
11. a. $\Sigma X = 49$, $\Sigma X^2 = 371$, $(\Sigma X)^2 = 2401$, $\Sigma Y = 31$, $\Sigma Y^2 = 171$, $(\Sigma Y)^2 = 961$, $\Sigma XY = 188$, and $N = 7$, so $r = (1316 - 1519)/\sqrt{(196)(236)} = -.94$.
   b. This is a highly consistent negative linear relationship for which the scatterplot is very close to forming a straight line.
13. a. After ties are resolved, the data are

| Subject | X | Y |
|---------|---|---|
| 1 | 2 | 3 |
| 2 | 9 | 7.5 |
| 3 | 1 | 2 |
| 4 | 5 | 7.5 |
| 5 | 3 | 1 |
| 6 | 7 | 9 |
| 7 | 4 | 4 |
| 8 | 6 | 5 |
| 9 | 8 | 6 |

   b. $\Sigma D^2 = 23.5$ and $N = 9$, so $r_s = 1 - (141/720) = +.80$.
   c. The rankings tend to form a very consistent positive linear relationship.
15. a. $\overline{Y}_2 = 6.5$, $\overline{Y}_1 = 7.167$, $S_Y = 2.468$, $p = .40$, and $q = .60$, so $r_{pb} = (-.270)(.490) = -.13$.
   b. These data tend to form a rather inconsistent negative linear relationship.

## Chapter 8

1. The linear regression line is the line that summarizes a scatterplot by, on average, passing through the center of the $Y$ scores at each $X$.

3. $Y'$ is the symbol for the predicted $Y$ score for an $X$, computed from the linear regression equation.

5. The $Y$-intercept indicates the value of $Y$ where the regression line crosses the $Y$ axis.

7. *a.* The standard error of the estimate is a standard deviation, indicating the "average" amount that the $Y$ scores at each $X$ deviate from their corresponding values of $Y'$.

   *b.* It indicates the "average" amount that the actual scores differ from the predicted $Y'$ scores, so it is the "average" error.

9. *a.* $S_{Y'}$ is inversely related to the absolute value of $r$.

   *b.* $S_{Y'}$ is at its maximum (equal to $S_Y$) when $r = 0$, because when there is no relationship the amount that the $Y$ scores deviate from the $Y'$ scores equals the overall spread in the data.

   *c.* $S_{Y'}$ is at its minimum (equal to 0) when $r = \pm 1.0$, because when there is a perfect linear relationship there are no differences between $Y$ scores and the corresponding $Y'$ scores.

11. *a.* $r^2$ indicates the proportion of variance in $Y$ that is accounted for by the relationship with $X$.

    *b.* $r^2$ can be interpreted as the proportional improvement in accuracy when we use the relationship with $X$ to predict $Y$ scores rather than using the overall mean of $Y$.

13. *a.* $\Sigma X = 45$, $\Sigma X^2 = 259$, $(\Sigma X)^2 = 2025$, $\Sigma Y = 89$, $\Sigma Y^2 = 887$, $(\Sigma Y)^2 = 7921$, $\Sigma XY = 460$, and $N = 10$, so $r = (4600 - 4005)/\sqrt{(565)(949)} = +.81$.

    *b.* $b = (4600 - 4005)/565 = +1.05$ and $a = 8.9 - (1.05)(4.5) = 4.18$, so $Y' = (+1.05)X + 4.18$.

    *c.* $Y' = (+1.05)9 + 4.18 = 13.63$

15. *a.* The proportion of variance accounted for is $r^2 = .81^2 = .66$.

    *b.* The proportion of variance not accounted for is $1 - r^2 = 1 - .66 = .34$.

    *c.* This is a valuable relationship because it allows us to account for a relatively large proportion of the variance in $Y$ scores, improving our accuracy in predictions by $66\%$.

## Chapter 9

1. *a.* It is the expected relative frequency of the event.

   *b.* It is based on the relative frequency of the event in the population.

3. Unlikely events do occur, so the risk is that sooner or later the event will occur.

5. No; the sex of a child is an independent event, so the sex of previous children does not influence the probability that a child will be a boy or a girl.

7. *a.* $p = .0212$    *b.* $p = .9974$
   *c.* $p = .8864$    *d.* $p = .0854$

9. It is the area in the tail or tails of a sampling distribution containing the least likely or least representative sample means. It is used to define those means that are too unlikely to accept as representing the $\mu$ of the underlying raw score population.

11. Transform 24 to $z$: $\sigma_{\bar{X}} = 12/\sqrt{30} = 2.19$; $z = (24 - 18)/2.19 = +2.74$; $p = .0031$

13. No; with a $z = +2.74$, this mean falls beyond the critical value of $+1.96$. It is too unlikely to accept as being representative of this population $\mu$.

## Chapter 10

1. *a.* Sampling error is the difference between a sample statistic and the population parameter it represents; it occurs by luck in drawing that sample.

*b.* We never know whether a sample (1) poorly represents one population parameter because of sampling error or (2) represents some other population parameter.

3. *a.* Parametric statistics are used when we can make certain assumptions about our populations, including that they are normal, that they contain interval or ratio scores, and that the mean accurately describes them. Nonparametric procedures are used when we cannot make the above assumptions.

*b.* They are more powerful than nonparametric procedures.

5. $H_0$, the null hypothesis, indicates that the sample represents a population such that the predicted relationship does not exist. $H_a$, the alternative hypothesis, indicates that the sample represents a population such that the predicted relationship does exist.

7. It means that, using a certain $\alpha$, we have rejected the hypothesis that our results reflect only chance sampling error because they are considered too unlikely to occur by chance. Instead, we have accepted the hypothesis that the results represent a relationship in the population.

9. *a.* The term *beneficial* implies only higher scores, so he should use a one-tailed test.

*b.* $H_0$: $\mu \leq 50$, $H_a$: $\mu > 50$

*c.* $\sigma_{\overline{X}} = 12/\sqrt{49} = 1.71$;
$z_{obt} = (54.63 - 50)/1.71 = +2.71$

*d.* $z_{crit} = +1.645$

*e.* Since $z_{obt}$ is beyond $z_{crit}$, his results are significant: he has evidence of a relationship in the population, so changing from the condition of no music to the condition of music results in test scores' changing from a $\mu$ of 50 to a $\mu$ of around 54.63.

11. *a.* The probability of a Type I error is $p < .05$. The error is saying that music influences scores when really it does not.

*b.* By rejecting $H_0$, we have no chance of making a Type II error—saying that music does not influence scores when really it does.

13. *a.* Power is the probability of rejecting a false $H_0$—the probability of not making a Type II error.

*b.* So that we can detect relationships when they exist and learn something about nature.

## Chapter 11

1. We perform the *z*-test when the population $\sigma_X$ is known. We perform the *t*-test when $\sigma_X$ is estimated using the sample $s_X$.

3. *a.* Because different *N*s produce differently shaped *t*-distributions, a different $t_{crit}$ is needed to demarcate a region of rejection equal to $\alpha$.

*b.* The degrees of freedom, *df*

5. *a.* $H_0$: $\mu = 68.5$; $H_a$: $\mu \neq 68.5$

*b.* $s_X^2 = 130.5$; $s_{\overline{X}} = \sqrt{130.5/10} = 3.61$;
$t_{obt} = (78.5 - 68.5)/3.61 = +2.77$

*c.* With $df = 9$, $t_{crit} = \pm 2.262$.

*d.* Using this book rather than other books produces a significant improvement in exam scores: $t_{obt}(9) = 2.77, p < .05$.

*e.* $(3.61)(-2.262) + 78.5 \leq \mu \leq (3.61)(+2.262) + 78.5 = 70.33 \leq \mu \leq 86.67$

7. *a.* $H_0$: $\rho = 0$; $H_a$: $\rho \neq 0$

*b.* With $df = 28$, $r_{crit} = \pm.361$.

*c.* With $r_{obt}(28) = +.38, p < .05$, the correlation is significant, so he should conclude that the relationship exists in the population with a $\rho$ of approximately $+.38$.

9. *a.* $H_0$: $\rho_{pb} \leq 0$; $H_a$: $\rho_{pb} > 0$

*b.* With $df = 6$, $r_{crit} = +.707$.

*c.* With $r_{pb}(6) = +.69, p > .05$, the correlation is not significant, so he should conclude that the relationship may or may not exist in the population.

11. *a.* The condition of your independent variable may have produced a value of $\overline{X}$ that was too close to $\mu$, there may have been too much variability ($s_X^2$ was too large), and *N* was too small.

*b.* Even if the relationship exists in the population, the study was not likely to produce significant results.

## Chapter 12

1. When we have two sample means that may represent a difference in the population $\mu$'s and our data meet the parametric assumptions.

3. The variances of the populations represented by our samples are equal.

5. It indicates a range of differences between two $\mu$'s, one of which the difference between our sample means is likely to represent.

7. a. $H_0: \mu_1 - \mu_2 = 0; H_a: \mu_1 - \mu_2 \neq 0.$
   b. $s^2_{pool} = 23.695; s_{\overline{X}_1 - \overline{X}_2} = 1.78;$
      $t_{obt} = (43 - 39)/1.78 = +2.25.$
   c. With $df = (15 - 1) + (15 - 1) = 28,$
      $t_{crit} = \pm 2.048.$
   d. The results are significant: conclude that, in the population, hot baths (with $\mu$ about 43) produce different relaxation scores than cold baths (with $\mu$ about 39).
   e. $(1.78)(-2.048) + 4 \leq \mu_1 - \mu_2 \leq (1.78)(+2.048) + 4 = .36 \leq \mu_1 - \mu_2 \leq 7.65$

9. a. Subtracting before scores from after scores, we have $H_0: \mu_D \leq 0; H_a: \mu_D > 0.$
   b. $\overline{D} = 1.2, s^2_D = 1.289, s_{\overline{D}} = .359;$
      $t_{obt} = (1.2 - 0)/.359 = +3.343.$
   c. With $df = 9, t_{crit} = +1.833.$
   d. The results are significant: conclude that, in the population, children exhibit more aggressive acts after watching the show (with $\mu$ about 3.9, the $X_1$) than they do before the show (with $\mu$ about 2.7, the $\overline{X}_2$).
   e. $(.359)(-2.262) + 1.2 \leq \mu_D \leq (.359)(+2.262) + 1.2 = .39 \leq \mu_D \leq 2.01$

11. a. $r^2_{pb} = (3.343)^2/[(3.343)^2 + 9] = .55$
    b. Using the mean of the before or after condition, we are 55% more accurate in predicting subjects' aggressiveness scores than if we use the overall mean aggressiveness score in the study.

## Chapter 13

1. a. Analysis of variance
   b. The study contains one independent variable.
   c. Independent variable
   d. Condition of the independent variable
   e. All samples are independent.
   f. The same subjects are tested under all conditions of the independent variable.

3. a. $H_0: \mu_1 = \mu_2 = \mu_3 = \mu_4$
   b. $H_a:$ not all $\mu$'s are equal

5. Because the independent variable produces differences in scores between the conditions, $MS_{bn}$ is larger than $MS_{wn}$, with $MS_{bn}$ containing error variance plus treatment variance, so the $F$-ratio is greater than 1.0.

7. Because only through *post hoc* tests can we determine which specific means from our levels differ significantly.

9. a.

| Source | Sum of squares | df | Mean square | F |
|--------|----------------|----|-------------|----|
| Between | 134.80 | 3 | 44.93 | 17.08 |
| Within | 42.00 | 16 | 2.63 | |
| Total | 176.80 | 19 | | |

   b. With $df = 3$ and 16, $F_{crit} = 3.24$, so $F_{obt}$ is significant, $p < .05$.
   c. For $k = 4$ and $df_{wn} = 16$, $q_k = 4.05$, so $HSD = (4.05)(\sqrt{2.63/5}) = 2.94$: $\overline{X}_4 = 4.4, \overline{X}_6 = 10.8, \overline{X}_8 = 9.40, \overline{X}_{10} = 5.8.$
   d. This is an inverted U-shaped function, in which only ages 4 and 10 and ages 6 and 8 do not differ significantly.
   e. $\eta^2 = 134.8/176.8 = .76$: this relationship accounts for 76% of the variance, so it is relatively a very important relationship.

11. a. $F_{max} = 43.68/9.50 = 4.598$. With $k = 3$ and $n - 1 = 15$, the critical value is 3.54. These variances differ significantly, so do not assume homogeneity.
    b. Technically, we should not have performed ANOVA.

## Chapter 14

1. *a.* The study contains two independent variables.
   *b.* All levels of one factor are combined with all levels of the other factor.
   *c.* The combination of a level of factor A with a level of factor B
   *d.* All cells contain independent samples.
3. The combined effect of factor A and factor B, in which the effect of changing the levels of one factor is not consistent for each level of the other factor; the effect of one factor depends on the level of the other factor being examined.
5. *a.* $H_0$: $\mu_{A_1} = \mu_{A_2}$, $H_a$: not all $\mu_A$'s are equal
   *b.* $H_0$: $\mu_{B_1} = \mu_{B_2}$, $H_a$: not all $\mu_B$'s are equal
   *c.* $H_0$: $\mu_{A_1B_1} = \mu_{A_1B_2} = \mu_{A_2B_1} = \mu_{A_2B_2}$, $H_a$: not all interaction $\mu$'s are equal
7. *a.* With the levels of factor A on the $X$ axis, 14 and 23 are connected by one line, and 25 and 12 by another. The lines form an X.
   *b.* This is an interaction: changing from $A_1$ to $A_2$ increases scores under $B_1$, but decreases scores under $B_2$.
   *c.* Overall, A decreases scores; B has no effect. Neither of these is true for both levels of the other factor.
9. *a.*

| Source | Sum of squares | df | Mean square | F |
|---|---|---|---|---|
| Between groups | | | | |
| Factor A | 7.20 | 1 | 7.20 | 1.19 |
| Factor B | 115.20 | 1 | 115.20 | 19.04 |
| Interaction | 105.80 | 1 | 105.80 | 17.49 |
| Within groups | 96.80 | 16 | 6.05 | |
| Total | 325.00 | | | |

For each factor, $df = 1$ and 16, so $F_{crit} = 4.49$: factor B and the interaction are significant, $p < .05$.
   *b.* For factor A, $\overline{X}_1 = 8.9$, $\overline{X}_2 = 10.1$; for factor B, $\overline{X}_1 = 11.9$, $\overline{X}_2 = 7.1$; for the

interaction, $\overline{X}_{A_1B_1} = 9.0$, $\overline{X}_{A_1B_2} = 8.8$, $\overline{X}_{A_2B_1} = 14.8$, $\overline{X}_{A_2B_2} = 5.4$.
   *c.* Because A is not significant and B contains only two levels, such tests are unnecessary for the main effects. For A × B, adjusted $k = 3$, so $q_k = 3.65$, HSD = $(3.65)(\sqrt{6.05/5}) = 4.02$: the only significant differences are between males and females tested early, and between females tested early and females tested late.
   *d.* We can conclude only that a relationship exists between gender and test scores when testing is early, and early/late testing produces a relationship with test scores for females, $p < .05$.
   *e.* For B, $\eta^2 = 115.2/325 = .35$; for A × B, $\eta^2 = 105.8/325 = .33$.

## Chapter 15

1. When the scores are ordinal or nominal data, or when they are interval or ratio data that either are very skewed or do not have homogeneous population variances.
3. For testing whether the frequencies in each category in our samples represent our $H_0$ model of the distribution of frequencies in the population.
5. *a.* $H_0$: the frequencies in the elderly population are 30% Republican, 55% Democrat, and 15% other, $H_a$: the frequencies in the elderly population are not distributed this way
   *b.* Based on the general population, for Republicans, $f_e = (.30)(100) = 30$; for Democrats, $f_e = (.55)(100) = 55$; and for other, $f_e = (.15)(100) = 15$.
   *c.* $\chi^2_{obt} = 4.80 + 1.47 + .60 = 6.87$
   *d.* For $df = 2$, $\chi^2_{crit} = 5.99$, so the results are significant: party membership in the population of senior citizens is different from party membership in the general population and is distributed as in our samples, $p < .05$.
7. *a.* $H_0$: the frequencies of gender and political party affiliation are independent in the

population, $H_a$: the frequencies of gender and political party affiliation are dependent in the population

b. For males, Republican $f_e = (75)(57)/155 = 27.58$, Democrat $f_e = (75)(66)/155 = 31.94$, and other $f_e = (75)(32)/155 = 15.48$. For females, Republican $f_e = (80)(57)/155 = 29.42$, Democrat $f_e = (80)(66)/155 = 34.06$, and other $f_e = (80)(32)/155 = 16.52$.

c. $\chi^2_{obt} = 3.328 + 3.83 + .141 + 3.12 + 3.591 + .133 = 14.14$

d. With $df = 2$, $\chi^2_{crit} = 5.99$, so the results are significant: in the population, frequency of political party affiliation depends on gender, $p < .05$.

e. Compute $C = \sqrt{14.14/(155 + 14.14)} = .29$, indicating a somewhat consistent relationship.

9. a. Kruskal Wallis $H$-test
   b. Mann-Whitney $U$-test
   c. Wilcoxon $T$-test
   d. Rank sums test
   e. Friedman $\chi^2$ test
   f. Rank sums test
   g. Nemenyi's procedure

11. Sum of positive ranks $= 1$, sum of negative ranks $= 27$, $T_{obt} = 1$. $N = 7$, so $T_{crit} = 2$. The two samples of ranks, and the underlying interval scores, differ significantly, $p < .05$.

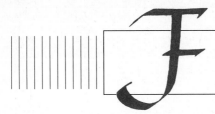

# Using HMSTAT

---

## HARDWARE AND SOFTWARE REQUIREMENTS

IBM® PC or compatible computer with 256K RAM

Two floppy disk drives *or* hard drive

Color or monochrome monitor

DOS 2.0 or higher

Dot-matrix printer (optional)

Blank floppy disk for making a copy

---

## HOW TO USE THIS PROGRAM: BRIEF INSTRUCTIONS

*1. Boot your computer.*

   *a.* If you are using a floppy disk system, turn on the computer with your DOS disk in drive A.

   *b.* If you are using a machine with a hard disk, DOS is probably already installed on drive C. Just turn on the computer.

*Note:* IBM is a registered trademark of International Business Machines Corporation.

2. *Back up your disk*. Make a copy of the program disk. Refer to your DOS manual for instructions on copying disks. Store the original disk in a safe place, and use the copy as your working disk.

3. *Start the program.*

   a. If your machine does not have DOS installed on a hard drive, the DOS disk must remain in drive A while you use the program.

      (1) Insert your working disk into drive B.

      (2) Type **B:** and press the Enter key.

      (3) Type **RUN** and press the Enter key.

      (4) Follow the on-screen prompts.

   b. If you are using a hard disk system, take the following steps to install the program in a new subdirectory called HMSTAT on your hard disk.

      *(1)* Insert the program disk in drive A.

      *(2)* Type **A:** and press the Enter key.

      *(3)* Type **HDCOPY** and press the Enter key.

   *Then, do the following to start the program from the hard disk.*

      *(1)* Type **C:** and press the Enter key.

      *(2)* To move to the HMSTAT subdirectory, type **CD\HMSTAT** and press the Enter key.

      *(3)* Type **RUN** and press the Enter key.

      *(4)* Follow the on-screen prompts.

# Glossary

**Alpha** The Greek letter $\alpha$, which symbolizes the criterion, the size of the region of rejection of a sampling distribution, and the theoretical probability of making a Type I error

**Alternative hypothesis** The statistical hypothesis describing the population parameters that the sample data represent if the predicted relationship does exist; symbolized by $H_a$

**Analysis of variance** The parametric procedure for determining whether significant differences exist in an experiment containing two or more sample means; abbreviated ANOVA

**ANOVA** Abbreviation of analysis of variance

**Bar graph** A graph in which a free-standing vertical bar is centered over each score on the $X$ axis; used with nominal or ordinal scores

**Beta** The Greek letter $\beta$, which symbolizes the theoretical probability of making a Type II error

**Between-subjects factor** A factor in ANOVA that is studied using independent samples in all levels

**Bimodal distribution** A symmetrical frequency polygon with two distinct humps where there are relatively high frequency scores and with center scores that technically have the same frequency

**Cell** In a two-way ANOVA, the combination of one level of one factor with one level of the other factor

**Central limit theorem** A statistical principle that defines the mean, standard deviation, and shape of a theoretical sampling distribution

$\chi^2$**-distribution** The sampling distribution of all possible values of $\chi^2$ that occur when the samples represent the distribution of frequencies described by the null hypothesis

**Chi square procedure** The nonparametric inferential procedure for testing whether the frequencies of category membership in the sample represent the predicted frequencies in the population

**Coefficient of alienation** The proportion of variance not accounted for by a relationship; computed by subtracting the squared correlation coefficient from 1

**Coefficient of determination** The proportion of variance accounted for by a relationship; computed by squaring the correlation coefficient

**Collapsing** In a two-way ANOVA, averaging together all scores from all levels of one factor in order to calculate the main effect means for the other factor

**Complete factorial design** A two-way ANOVA design in which all levels of one factor are combined with all levels of the other factor

**Condition** An amount or category of the independent variable that creates the specific situation under which subjects' scores on the dependent variable are measured

**Confidence interval for a single population $\mu$** A statistically defined range of values of $\mu$, any one of which is likely to be represented by the sample mean

**Confidence interval for the difference between two $\mu$'s** A statistically defined range of differences between two population $\mu$'s, any one of which is likely to be represented by the difference between the sample means

**Confounded comparison** In a two-way ANOVA, a comparison of two cells that differ along more than one factor

**Contingency coefficient** The statistic that describes the strength of the relationship in a two-way chi square when there are more than two categories for either variable; symbolized by $C$

**Continuous scale** A measurement scale that allows for fractional amounts of the variable being measured

**Correlational study** A procedure in which subjects' scores on two variables are simply measured, without manipulation of any variables, to determine whether there is a relationship

**Correlation coefficient** A number, computed from the pairs of $X$ scores and $Y$ scores in a set of data, that summarizes and describes the type of relationship present and the strength of that relationship

**Criterion** The probability that provides the basis for deciding whether a sample is too unlikely to have occurred by chance and thus is unrepresentative of a particular population

**Criterion variable** The variable in a relationship whose unknown scores are predicted through use of the known scores on the predictor variable

**Critical value** The value of the sample statistic that marks the edge of the region of rejection in a sampling distribution; values that fall beyond it fall in the region of rejection

**Cumulative frequency** The frequency of those scores at or below a particular score; symbolized by *cf*

**Cumulative frequency distribution** A distribution of scores organized to show the frequency of the scores at or below each score

**Curvilinear relationship** See *Nonlinear relationship*

**Degrees of freedom** The number of scores in a sample that are free to vary, and thus the number that is used to calculate an estimate of the population variability; symbolized by *df*

**Dependent events** Events for which the probability of one is influenced by the occurrence of the other

**Dependent variable** In an experiment, the variable that is measured under each condition of the independent variable

**Descriptive statistics** Procedures for organizing and summarizing data so that the important characteristics can be described and communicated

**Deviation** The distance that separates a score from the mean, and thus indicates how much the score differs from the man

**Dichotomous variable** A discrete variable that has only two possible amounts or categories

**Discrete scale** A measurement scale that allows for measurement only in whole-number amounts

**Distribution** An organized set of data

**Effect size** The proportion of variance accounted for in an experiment, which indicates how consistently differences in the dependent scores are "caused" by changes in the independent variable

**Empirical probability distribution** A probability distribution based on observations of the relative frequency of events

**Error variance** The inherent variability within a population, estimated in ANOVA by the mean square within groups

**Estimated standard error of the mean** An estimate of the standard deviation of the sampling distribution of means, used in calculating the single-sample *t*-test; symbolized by $s_{\overline{x}}$

**Eta** The correlation coefficient used to describe a linear or nonlinear relationship containing two or more levels of a factor; symbolized by $\eta$

**Eta squared** The proportion of variance in the dependent variable that is accounted for by changing the levels of a factor, and thus the measurement of effect size in the sample; symbolized by $\eta^2$

**Expected frequency** In chi square, the frequency expected in a category if the sample data perfectly represent the distribution of frequencies in the population described by the null hypothesis; symbolized by $f_e$

**Experiment** A research procedure in which one variable is actively changed or manipulated, the scores on another variable are measured, and all other variables are kept constant, to determine whether there is a relationship

**Experimental hypotheses** Two statements made before a study is begun, describing the predicted relationship that may or may not be demonstrated by the study

**Experiment-wise error rate** The probability of making at least one Type I error in comparing all means in an experiment

**Extreme scores** The scores that are relatively far above and below the middle score of any distribution

**Factor** In ANOVA, an independent variable

**F-distribution** The sampling distribution of all possible values of *F* that occur when the null hypothesis is true and all conditions represent one population $\mu$

**Fisher's protected *t*-test** The *post hoc* procedure performed with ANOVA to compare means from a factor in which all levels do not have equal $n$

***F*-ratio** In ANOVA, the ratio of the mean square between groups to the mean square within groups

**Frequency** The number of times each score occurs within a set of data; also called simple frequency; symbolized by $f$

**Frequency polygon** A graph that shows interval or ratio scores ($X$ axis) and their frequencies ($Y$ axis), using data points connected by straight lines

**Friedman $\chi^2$-test** The nonparametric version of the one-way repeated measures ANOVA for ranked scores

***F* statistic** In ANOVA, the statistic used to compare all sample means for a factor to determine whether two or more sample means represent different population means; equal to the $F$-ratio

**Grouped distribution** A distribution formed by combining different scores to make small groups whose total frequencies, relative frequencies, or cumulative frequencies can then be manageably reported

**Heterogeneity of variance** A characteristic of data describing populations represented by samples in a study that do not have the same variance

**Heteroscedasticity** An unequal spread of $Y$ scores around the regression line (that is, around the values of $Y'$)

**Histogram** A graph similar to a bar graph but with adjacent bars touching, used to plot the frequency distribution of a small range of interval or ratio scores

**Homogeneity of variance** A characteristic of data describing populations represented by samples in a study that have the same variance

**Homogeneity of variance test** A test performed before a *t*-test or ANOVA is conducted, to determine whether the estimated variances for two samples are significantly different from each other; also called the $F_{max}$ test

**Homoscedasticity** An equal spread of $Y$ scores around the regression line (that is, around the values of $Y'$)

**Incomplete factorial design** A two-way ANOVA design in which not all levels of the two factors are combined

**Independent events** Events for which the probability of one is not influenced by the occurrence of the other

**Independent samples** Samples created by selecting each subject for one sample, without regard to the subjects selected for any other sample

**Independent variable** In an experiment, a variable that is changed or manipulated by the experimenter; the variable hypothesized to cause a change in the other variable

**Individual differences** Variations in individuals' traits, backgrounds, genetic make-up, etc., that influence their behavior in a given situation and thus the strength of the relationship

**Inferential statistics** Procedures for determining whether sample data represent a particular relationship in the population

**Interval scale** A measurement scale in which each score indicates an actual amount and there is an equal unit of measurement between consecutive scores, but in which zero is simply another point on the scale (not zero amount)

**Kruskal-Wallis *H*-test** The nonparametric version of the one-way between-subjects ANOVA for ranked scores

**Level** In ANOVA, each condition of the factor (independent variable); also called treatment

**Linear regression** The procedure for describing the best-fitting straight line that summarizes a linear relationship

**Linear regression equation** The equation that defines the straight line summarizing a linear relationship by describing the value of $Y'$ at each $X$

**Linear regression line** The straight line that summarizes the scatterplot of a linear relationship by, on average, passing through the center of all $Y$ scores

**Linear relationship** A correlation between the $X$ scores and $Y$ scores in a set of data in which the $Y$ scores tend to change in only one direction as the $X$ scores increase, forming a slanted straight regression line on a scatterplot

**Line graph** A graph in which scores on an interval or ratio variable are plotted by connecting the data points with straight lines

**Main effect** In a two-way ANOVA, the effect on the dependent scores of changing the levels of one factor, while ignoring all other effects in the study

**Mann-Whitney *U* test** The nonparametric version of the independent samples *t*-test for ranked scores when $n$ is less than or equal to 20

**Mean** The score located at the mathematical center of a distribution

**Mean square** In ANOVA, an estimated population variance, symbolized by $MS$

**Mean square between groups** In ANOVA, the variability in scores that occurs between the levels in a factor or the cells in an interaction

**Mean square within groups** In ANOVA, the variability in scores that occurs in the conditions, or cells; also known as the error term

**Measure of central tendency** A score that summarizes the location of a distribution on a variable by indicating where the center of the distribution tends to be located

**Measures of variability** Measures that summarize and describe the extent to which scores in a distribution differ from one another

**Median** The score located at the 50th percentile; symbolized by Mdn; also called the median score

**Modal score** See *Mode*

**Mode** The most frequently occurring score in a sample; also called the modal score

**Negative linear relationship** A linear relationship in which the $Y$ scores tend to decrease as the $X$ scores increase

**Negatively skewed distribution** A frequency polygon with low frequency, extreme low scores but without corresponding low frequency, extreme high ones, so that its only pronounced tail is in the direction of the lower scores

**Nemenyi's procedure** The *post hoc* procedure performed with the Friedman $\chi^2$-test

**Nominal scale** A measurement scale in which each score is used simply for identification and does not indicate an amount

**Nonlinear relationship** A relationship in which the $Y$ scores change their direction of change as the $X$ scores change, forming a curved regression line; also called a curvilinear relationship

**Nonparametric statistics** Inferential procedures that do not require stringent assumptions about the parameters of the raw score population represented by the sample data; usually used with scores most appropriately described by the median or the mode

**Nonsignificant** Describes results that are considered likely to result from chance sampling error when the predicted relationship does not exist; it indicates failure to reject the null hypothesis

**Normal curve model** The most common model of how nature operates; it is based on the normal curve and describes a normal distribution of a population of scores

**Null hypothesis** The statistical hypothesis describing the population parameters that the sample data represent if the predicted relationship does not exist; symbolized by $H_0$

**Observed frequency** In chi square, the frequency with which subjects fall in a category of a variable; symbolized by $f_o$

**Omega squared** In ANOVA, an estimate of the proportion of variance in the population that would be accounted for by a relationship; symbolized by $\omega^2$

**One-tailed test** The test used to evaluate a statistical hypothesis that predicts that scores will only increase or only decrease (that is, the region of rejection falls in only one tail of the sampling distribution)

**One-way ANOVA** The analysis of variance performed when an experiment has only one independent variable

**One-way chi square** The chi square procedure performed in testing whether the sample frequencies of category membership along one variable represent the predicted distribution of frequencies in the population

**Ordinal scale** A measurement scale in which scores indicate only rank order or a relative amount

**Parameter** See *Population parameter*

**Parametric statistics** Inferential procedures that require certain assumptions about the parameters of the raw score population represented by the sample data; usually used with scores most appropriately described by the mean

**Pearson correlation coefficient** The correlation coefficient that describes the linear relationship between two interval or ratio variables; symbolized by $r$

**Percentile** A cumulative percentage; the percentage of all scores in the sample that are at or below a particular score

**Phi coefficient** The statistic that describes the strength of the relationship in a two-way chi square when there are only two categories for each variable; symbolized by $\phi$

**Point-biserial correlation coefficient** The correlation coefficient that describes the linear relationship between scores from one continuous interval or ratio variable and one dichotomous variable; symbolized by $r_{pb}$

**Pooled variance** The weighted average of the sample variances in a two-sample experiment; symbolized by $s^2_{pool}$

**Population** The infinitely large group of all possible scores that would be obtained if the behavior of every individual of interest in a particular situation could be measured

**Population parameter** A number that describes a characteristic of a population of scores, symbolized by a letter from the Greek alphabet; also called a parameter

**Positive linear relationship** A linear relationship in which the $Y$ scores tend to increase as the $X$ scores increase

**Positively skewed distribution** A frequency polygon with low frequency, extreme high scores but without corresponding low frequency, extreme low ones, so that its only pronounced tail is in the direction of the higher scores

**Post hoc comparisons** In ANOVA, statistical procedures used to compare all possible pairs of sample means in a significant effect, to determine which means differ significantly from each other

**Power** The probability that a statistical test will detect a true relationship and allow the rejection of a false null hypothesis

**Predicted Y score** In linear regression, the best description and prediction of the $Y$ scores at a particular $X$, based on the linear relationship summarized by the regression line; symbolized by $Y'$

**Predictor variable** The variable for which known scores in a relationship are used to predict unknown scores on another variable

**Probability** A mathematical statement indicating the likelihood that an event will occur when a particular population is randomly sampled; symbolized by $p$

**Probability distribution** The probability of every possible event in a population, derived from the relative frequency of every possible event in that popualtion

**Proportion of the area under the curve** The proportion of the total area beneath the normal curve at certain scores, which represents the relative frequency of those scores

**Proportion of variance accounted for** The proportion of the error in predicting scores that is eliminated when, instead of using the mean of $Y$, we use the relationship with the $X$ variable to predict $Y$ scores; the proportional improvement in predicting $Y$ scores thus achieved

**Random sampling** A method of selecting samples whereby all members of the population have the same chance of being selected for a sample and all samples have the same chance of being selected

**Range** The distance between the highest and lowest scores in a set of data

**Rank sums test** The nonparametric version of the independent samples $t$-test for ranked scores when $n$ is greater than 20; also the *post hoc* procedure performed with the Kruskal-Wallis $H$-test

**Ratio scale** A measurement scale in which each score indicates an actual amount, there is an equal unit of measurement, and there is a true zero (zero amount)

**Rectangular distribution** A symmetrical frequency polygon shaped like a rectangle; it has no discernible tails because its extreme scores do not have relatively low frequencies

**Region of rejection** That portion of a sampling distribution containing values considered too unlikely to occur by chance, found in the tail or tails of the distribution

**Regression line** The line drawn through the long dimension of a scatterplot that seems to best fit the center of the scatterplot, thereby visually summarizing the scatterplot and indicating the type of relationship that is present

**Related samples** Samples created by matching each subject in one sample with a subject in the other sample or by repeatedly measuring the same subject under all conditions; also called dependent samples

**Relationship** A correlation between two variables whereby a change in one variable is accompanied by a consistent change in the other

**Relative frequency** The proportion of time a score occurs in a distribution, which is equal to the proportion of the total number of scores that the score's simple frequency represents; symbolized by rel. $f$

**Relative frequency distribution** A distribution of scores, organized to show the proportion of time each score occurs in a set of data

**Relative standing** A description of a particular score derived from a systematic evaluation of the score using the characteristics of the sample or population in which it occurs

**Repeated measures design** A related samples research design in which the same subjects are measured repeatedly under all conditions of an independent variable

**Representative sample** A sample whose characteristics accurately reflect those of the population

**Research design** A description of the way in which a study is laid out so as to demonstrate a relationship

**Restriction of range** In correlation, improper limitation of the range of scores obtained on one or both variables, leading to an underestimate of the strength of the relationship between the two variables

**Robust procedure** A procedure that results in only a negligible amount of error in estimating the probability of a Type I error, even if the assumptions of the procedure are not perfectly met; describes parametric procedures

**Sample** A relatively small subset of a population, intended to represent the population; a subset of the complete group of scores found in any particular situation

**Sample statistic** A number that describes a characteristic of a sample of scores, symbolized by a letter from the English alphabet; also called a statistic

**Sampling distribution of a correlation coefficient** A frequency distribution showing all possible values of the coefficient that occur when samples of a particular size are drawn from a population whose correlation coefficient is zero

**Sampling distribution of differences between the means** A frequency distribution showing all possible differences between two means that occur when two independent samples of a particular size are drawn from the population of scores described by the null hypothesis

**Sampling distribution of mean differences** A frequency distribution showing all possible mean differences that occur when the difference scores from two related samples of a particular size are drawn from the population of difference scores described by the null hypothesis

**Sampling distribution of means** A frequency distribution showing all possible sample means that occur when samples of a particular size are drawn from the raw score population described by the null hypothesis

**Sampling error** The variation, due to random chance, between a sample statistic and the population parameter it represents

**Sampling without replacement** A sampling procedure in which previously selected samples are not returned to the population before additional samples are selected

**Sampling with replacement** A sampling procedure in which a previously selected sample is returned to the population before any additional samples are selected

**Scatterplot** A graph of the individual data points from a set of $X$-$Y$ pairs

**Semi-interquartile range** One-half of the distance between the scores at the 25th and 75th percentiles (the quartiles), used with the median to describe highly skewed distributions

**Significant** Describes results that are too unlikely to accept as resulting from chance sampling error when the predicted relationship does not exist; it indicates rejection of the null hypothesis

**Simple frequency distribution** A distribution of scores, organized to show the number of times each score occurs in a set of data

**Single-sample *t*-test** The parametric procedure used to test the null hypothesis for a single-sample experiment when the standard deviation of the raw score population must be estimated

**Skewed distribution** A frequency polygon similar in shape to a normal distribution except that it is not symmetrical and it has only one pronounced tail

**Slope** A number that indicates how much a linear regression line slants and in which direction it slants; used in computing predicted $Y$ scores; symbolized by $b$

**Spearman rank-order correlation coefficient** The correlation coefficient that describes the linear relationship between pairs of ranked scores; symbolized by $r_s$

**Squared sum of $X$** A result calculated by adding all scores and then squaring their sum; symbolized by $(\Sigma X)^2$

**Standard deviation** The statistic that communicates the average of the deviations of the scores from the mean in a set of data, computed by obtaining the square root of the variance

**Standard error of the difference** The standard deviation of the sampling distribution of differences between the means of independent samples in a two-sample experiment; symbolized by $s_{\bar{X}_1 - \bar{X}_2}$

**Standard error of the estimate** A standard deviation indicating the amount that the actual $Y$ scores in a sample differ from, or are spread out around, their corresponding $Y'$ scores; symbolized by $S_{Y'}$

**Standard error of the mean** The true standard deviation of the sampling distribution of means; used in the $z$-test; symbolized by $\sigma_{\bar{X}}$

**Standard error of the mean difference** The standard deviation of the sampling distribution of mean differences between related samples in a two-sample experiment; symbolized by $s_{\bar{D}}$

**Standard normal curve** A theoretical perfect normal curve, which serves as a model of the perfect normal $z$-distribution

**Standard scores** See *z-score*

**Statistic** See *Sample statistic*

**Statistical hypotheses** Two statements ($H_0$ and $H_a$) that describe the population parameters the sample statistics will represent if the predicted relationship exists or does not exist

**Strength of relationship** The extent to which one value of $Y$ within a relationship is consistently associated with one and only one value of $X$; also called the degree of association

**Subjects** The individuals who are measured in a sample

**Sum of squares** The sum of the squared deviations of a set of scores around a statistic

**Sum of the squared $X$s** A result calculated by squaring each score in a sample and adding the squared scores; symbolized by $\Sigma X^2$

**Sum of X** The sum of the scores in a sample; symbolized by $\Sigma X$

**Tail (of a distribution)** The far-left or far-right portion of a frequency polygon, containing the relatively low frequency, extreme scores

*t*-**distribution** The sampling distribution of all possible values of *t* that occur when samples of a particular size represent the raw score population(s) described by the null hypothesis

**Theoretical probability distribution** A probability distribution based on a theoretical model of the relative frequencies of events in a population

**Tied rank** The situation that occurs when two subjects in a sample receive the same rank-order score on a variable

**Total area under the curve** The area beneath the normal curve, which represents the total frequency of all scores

**Transformation** A systematic mathematical procedure for converting a set of scores into a different but equivalent set of scores

**Treatments** The conditions of the factor (independent variable); also called levels

**Treatment variance** In ANOVA, the variability between scores from different populations that would be created by the different levels of a factor

*t*-**test for independent samples** The parametric procedure used for significance testing of sample means from two independent samples

*t*-**test for related samples** The parametric procedure used for significance testing of sample means from two related samples

**Tukey's HSD test** The *post hoc* procedure performed with ANOVA to compare means from a factor in which all levels have equal *n*

**Two-tailed test** The test used to evaluate a statistical hypothesis that predicts a relationship but not whether scores will increase or decrease (that is, the region of rejection falls in both tails of the sampling distribution)

**Two-way chi square** The chi square procedure performed in testing whether, in the population, frequency of category membership on one variable is independent of frequency of category membership on the other variable

**Two-way interaction effect** In a two-way ANOVA, the effect of the combination of the levels of one factor with the levels of the other factor

**Type I error** A statistical decision-making error in which a large amount of sampling error causes rejection of the null hypothesis when the null hypothesis is true (that is, when the predicted relationship does not exist)

**Type II error** A statistical decision-making error in which the closeness of the sample statistic to the population parameter described by the null hypothesis causes the null hypothesis to be retained when it is false (that is, when the predicted relationship does exist)

**Type of relationship** The form of the correlation between the $X$ scores and the $Y$ scores in a set of data, determined by the overall direction in which the $Y$ scores change as the $X$ scores change

**Unconfounded comparisons** In a two-way ANOVA, comparisons between cells that differ along only one factor

**Unimodal distribution** A distribution whose frequency polygon has only one hump and thus has only one score qualifying as the mode

**Variable** Anything that, when measured, can produce two or more different scores

**Variance** A measure of the variability of the scores in a set of data, computed as the average of the squared deviations of the scores around the mean

**Wilcoxon *T* test** The nonparametric version of the related samples *t*-test for ranked scores

**Y-intercept** The value of $Y$ at the point where the linear regression line intercepts the $Y$ axis; used in computing predicted $Y$ scores; symbolized by $a$

**z-distribution** The distribution of *z*-scores produced by transforming all raw scores in a distribution into *z*-scores

**z-score** The statistic that describes the location of a raw score in terms of its distance from the mean when measured in standard deviation units; symbolized by $z$; also known as a standard score because it allows comparison of scores on different kinds of variables by equating, or standardizing, the distributions

**z-table** The table that gives the proportion of the total area under the standard normal curve for any two-decimal *z*-score

**z-test** The parametric procedure used to test the null hypothesis for a single-sample experiment when the true standard deviation of the raw score population is known

# Index

Catfulness

# Catfulness

## The Path to Inner Peace

This edition published in 2015 by Baker & Taylor UK Ltd,
Bicester, Oxfordshire

© Susanna Geoghegan Gift Publishing 2015

Compiled  *Michael Powell*
Illustrations  *Lorenzo Montatore*
Design  *Milestone Design*

ISBN  978-1-910562-04-8

Something important is spreading throughout
the world: more and more people are discovering the
amazing power of catfulness.

Inside this book, dozens of feisty felines reveal
the secret to living more catfully.

At home, at work, on the sofa or lying curled up on top
of a radiator, being catful is the way to be.

The first few moments
of the day are some of the
most important as they can
determine the mood for the
rest of the day.

*Daniel Willey*

Each place is the right
place – the place where
I now am can be
a sacred space.

**Ravi Ravindra**

# The Path to Inner Peace

# All happiness depends on a leisurely breakfast.

*John Gunther*

Seeking is endless.
It never comes to a
state of rest;
it never ceases.

**Sharon Salzberg**

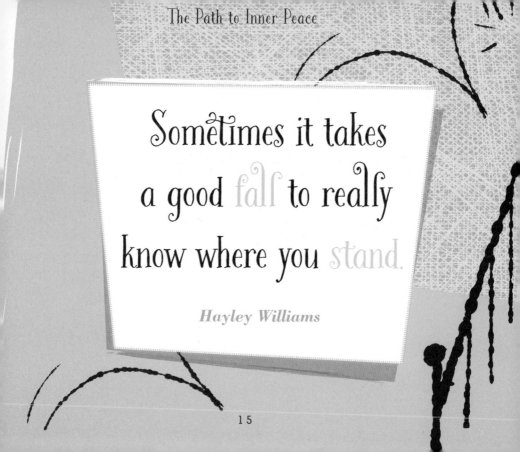

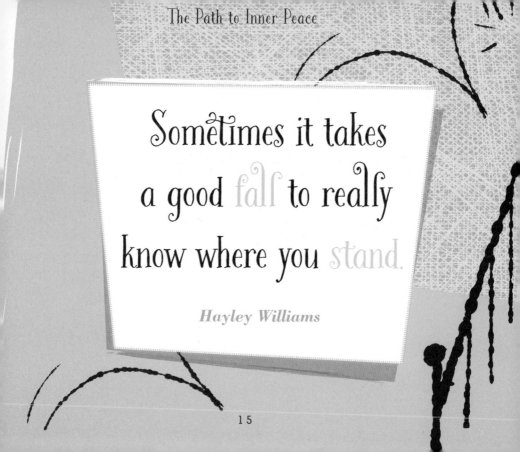

Sometimes it takes a good fall to really know where you stand.

*Hayley Williams*

# You settle for less, you get less.

**Brandi L. Bates**

Those not chasing their
dreams should stay
out of the way of
those who are.

**Tim Fargo**

# What greater gift than the love of a cat?

*Charles Dickens*

A fit, healthy body –
that is the best
fashion statement.

*Jess C. Scott*

There comes a time when you have to choose between turning the page and closing the book.

**Josh Jameson**

If you clean the floor
with love, you have
given the world
an invisible painting.

*Osho*

Earthly goods deceive the human heart into believing that they give it security and freedom from worry. But in truth, they are what cause anxiety.

**Dietrich Bonhoeffer**

# The Path to Inner Peace

All the art of living
lies in a fine mingling
of letting go and
holding on.

*Henry Ellis*

The present moment is filled
with joy and happiness.
If you are attentive,
you will see it.

**Thích Nhất Hạnh**

# The Path to Inner Peace

Replace fear of
the unknown with
curiosity.

*Danny Gokey*

Let one who seeks
not stop seeking until
that person finds.

*T. Scott McLeod*

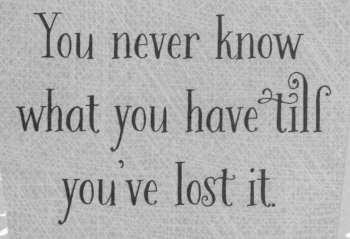

# You never know what you have till you've lost it.

**Alyson Noel**

# Turn off your mind, relax, and float downstream.

*John Lennon*

# The Path to Inner Peace

If you want to support others you have to stay upright yourself.

*Peter Høeg*

No matter how thoroughly you plan, no matter how much you think you know, you've never thought of everything.

**John Flanagan**

# The Path to Inner Peace

You rest now. Rest for longer than you are used to resting. Make a stillness around you, a field of peace. Your best work, the best time of your life will grow out of this peace.

*Peter Heller*

Giving connects two people,
the giver and the receiver, and
this connection gives birth to
a new sense of belonging.

*Deepak Chopra*

49

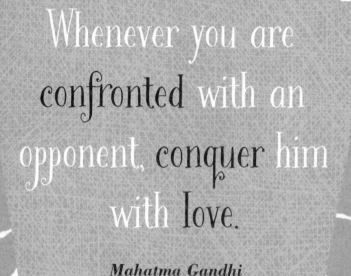

Whenever you are confronted with an opponent, conquer him with love.

**Mahatma Gandhi**

# Be an opener of doors.

**Ralph Waldo Emerson**

# The Path to Inner Peace

Sometimes your joy is the source of your smile, but sometimes your smile can be the source of your joy.

*Thích Nhất Hạnh*

Trust yourself,
you know more than
you think you do.

**Benjamin Spock**

# The Path to Inner Peace

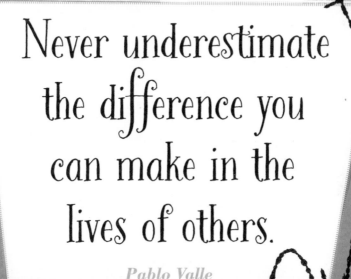

Never underestimate the difference you can make in the lives of others.

*Pablo Valle*

Do not dwell in the past,
do not dream of the future,
concentrate the mind on
the present moment.

**Buddha**

# The Path to Inner Peace

# Sometimes battles are unavoidable.

*Shannon A. Thompson*

But let there be spaces in your togetherness and let the winds of the heavens dance between you.

**Kahlil Gibran**

# The Path to Inner Peace

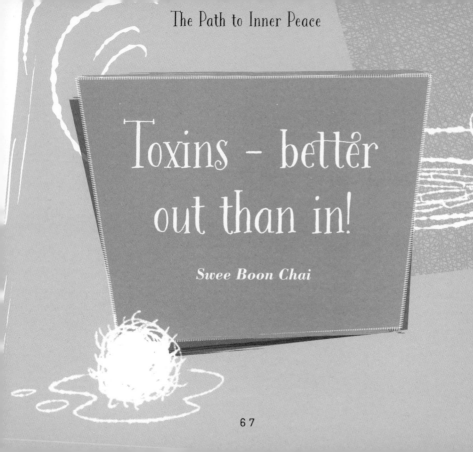

# Toxins – better out than in!

**Swee Boon Chai**

Don't be surprised by your greatness. Be surprised that no one expected it.

**Rebecca Maizel**

# The Path to Inner Peace

Retire to the centre
of your being,
which is calmness.

**Paramahansa Yogananda**

Don't believe everything
you think. Thoughts are
just that – thoughts.

**Allan Lokos**

Trees are sanctuaries.
Whoever knows how to speak
to them, whoever knows
how to listen to them,
can learn the truth.

**_Hermann Hesse_**

If a thing's worth
doing it's worth
doing together.

**Michael Bradley**

# The Path to Inner Peace

Behind every beautiful thing, there's some kind of pain.

**_Bob Dylan_**

There are no accidents . . .
there is only some purpose
that we haven't yet
understood.

**Deepak Chopra**

# The Path to Inner Peace

Collaboration, it turns out, is not a gift from the gods but a skill that requires effort and practice.

**Douglas B. Reeves**

# The first problem of communication is getting people's attention.

**Chip Heath**

# The Path to Inner Peace

# Rest and be thankful.

William Wordsworth

To make the right choices in life, you have to get in touch with your soul. To do this, you need to experience solitude, which most people are afraid of, because in the silence you hear the truth and know the solutions.

**Deepak Chopra**

# The Path to Inner Peace

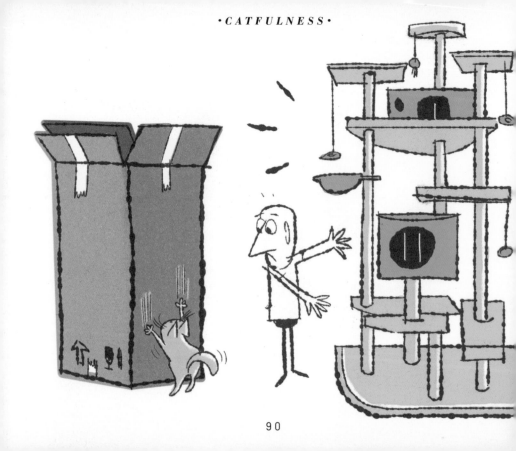

Sometimes, the simple things are more fun and meaningful than all the banquets in the world.

**E.A. Bucchianeri**

Whosoever is delighted
in solitude, is either a
wild beast or a god.

*Aristotle*

# The Path to Inner Peace

Cry. Forgive. Learn. Move on. Let your tears water the seeds of your future happiness.

**Steve Maraboli**

# THE STAIN AND SPOT REMOVER HANDBOOK

## How to Clean Your Home and Everything In It

### JEAN COOPER

GRAMERCY BOOKS
NEW YORK

*For Jennifer and Katherine, Bebbie and Marianne.*

This 2003 edition is published by Gramercy Books, an imprint of Random House Value Publishing, a division of Random House, Inc., New York, by arrangement with Storey Books.

Gramercy is a registered trademark and the colophon is a trademark of Random House, Inc.

Random House
New York • Toronto • London • Sydney • Auckland
www.randomhouse.com

Edited by Elizabeth McHale
Text design and production by Meredith Maker
Production assistance by Susan Bernier
Indexed by Northwind Editorial Services

Printed and bound in the Singapore

A catalog record for this title is available from the Library of Congress.

ISBN 0-517-22253-1

10 9 8 7 6 5 4 3 2 1

# Contents

# Introduction

A wide range of laundry aids are available these days: pre-wash enzyme-soaking compounds, spray-on stain and grime removers, soaps and detergents, water softeners, fabric softeners, starches and stiffeners. And along with that there are many fibers — and blends of fibers, natural and synthetic — that require special handling. Care instructions now come in most garments, but extra information is needed to treat fibers that have become stained.

Similarly, our homes present the same challenge — an infinite combination of surfaces that best serve our purposes when they are clean. To be efficient with your time, you need information on how to apply the minimum effort to caring for and cleaning your home and belongings, and at the same time receive the maximum return.

*The Stain and Spot Remover Handbook* will tell you exactly how to clean your home and everything in it. It will tell you how to remove stains from just about any surface or material. It will give you tips on how to brighten and revive dull finishes, how to remove rust, how to make your own furniture polish, how to launder fragile curtains, how to avoid cleaning disasters.

The first section gives general stain removal advice. The second section describes all the various stain-removing agents (in alphabetical order) that are useful around the house and in the laundry room. The next section tells you how to clean everything in your house: carpets, curtains, wicker, wood, sinks, appliances, and so on. The last section is the last word on stain removal — it lists specific stains alphabetically and describes various methods for successfully treating and removing the

**Organizing Your Care Labels**

It may simplify the laundering of fine washables if you remove the care label, but remember to first identify the garment it goes with. Care labels often become unreadable after washing and cleaning, so this will keep the instructions easy to read. Use push pins or small hooks to hang these in a handy place in the laundry room. A bulletin board or a square piece of cork would be good for this.

Hang the extra buttons or mending thread/darning yarn from the same hook as the garment care label. That way, you will have no problem finding these things when you need them later.

stain. In the appendix, the reader will find a handy reference for hazardous materials that — while they may save a garment or revive a valued item with their potency — must be disposed of with care.

This book gives you all the stain removal and cleaning suggestions that we could fit in these pages. Many of the methods are old-fashioned, tried and true, ranging from mild to those you would use with caution.

We continue to work toward finding environmentally friendly solutions for use in our homes and in our lives, and reducing polluted waste water and exposure to harmful chemicals, but ultimately the one place we can control our environment is in our home.

Some manufacturers are now producing an all-natural cleaning vinegar, which is twice the strength of cooking vinegar. In time, there will be more organic, non-toxic products available for use in our homes. Yet right now, in our kitchens and in our pantries, there are endless materials we can use that are mild, organic, and safe. With *The Stain and Spot Remover Handbook,* you can put those products to good use.

# Part One

# GENERAL STAIN REMOVAL ADVICE

There are a few important points to keep in mind when working with stains and spills.

➤ Most stains will be easy to remove if they are treated while fresh.

➤ *Always* remove as much of the spill as possible before you start treating the stain. Work as gently as you can. Wringing or rubbing can cause a stain to penetrate more deeply. Lift the spilled material off gently with a spoon or butter knife. The more you can remove before you start treating the stain, the less the fabric will absorb.

➤ Start at the outer edges of the stain and work toward the center to avoid spreading the stain. Always blot; never scrub.

➤ Read and follow all directions before you start to work on removing a stain.

➤ Work methodically and patiently when removing a stain.

➤ Avoid staining other parts of the garment by stretching the stained section over an absorbent pad. Use an old towel and fold it over several times to absorb the stain as it dissolves.

➤ *Always* test the stain removal agent on the garment or surface you want to use it on: Test it in an inconspicuous place, such as the tail of a shirt or blouse or an inside seam or hem. If it was safe, and especially if it removed the stain, make a note of it somewhere. You may need to remove something similar from the same item in the future.

➤ Try the simplest approach first. Cold, clean water is a solvent that can remove many stains quickly, easily, and safely. Consider the fibers you are treating. (Even water can damage some textiles. Always check the garment care label.) See the section in this book on the particular textile and also on the particular stain.

➤ Purchase expensive solvents if necessary in order to remove a stain. If the garment is a good one and the stain is difficult to remove, take it to a drycleaner and describe the cause of the stain and what treatment, if any, you have tried, and point out the label showing the type of fibers involved.

➤ If the origin of the stain is unknown, try to determine if it is a greasy or nongreasy mark. If it is a protein stain (e.g., blood, grass, or egg), soak it in cold water.

➤ Air-dry items you have treated to be sure that the stain is completely gone. Some stains are not easily seen when the fabric is wet, and a hot dryer could set the stain and make it more difficult to remove.

## GREASY STAINS

These can come from butter or margarine, oily foods, and automotive oil. Washable fabrics can be pre-treated by rubbing a little liquid detergent or drycleaning fluid directly on the spot. An old oil stain that has yellowed can be treated with bleach. For nonwashable fabrics, apply drycleaning fluid from the edges to the center of the stain. Allow the spot to dry completely before repeating. Another way to remove greasy stains from nonwashable fabrics is to use an absorbent substance, such as cornstarch, cornmeal, or chalk. Dust it on the greasy stain, wait until it looks caked, then brush it off gently.

## NONGREASY STAINS

Nongreasy stains include fruit juice, black coffee, tea, ink. Nongreasy stains on washable fabrics should be sponged with cool water as soon as possible. Then soak the fabric in cool water for a few hours or overnight. If the stain is persistent, rub some liquid detergent directly into the area, then rinse with cool water. As a last resort, you may want to try color-safe bleach, but always check the manufacturer's care label.

A nongreasy stain on nonwashable fabric can be sponged with cool water. You will want to flush the stain: Place a clean, absorbent cloth behind the stain and apply cool water with an eye dropper or spray bottle. Your chance of succeeding in removing a nongreasy stain this way is greatest if the stain is fresh.

### A Word of Caution

Never combine stain removal products, especially ammonia and chlorine bleach; it could generate dangerous fumes.

Treat flammable solvents with special care. Work in a well-ventilated room or on an outside patio. Do not smoke and do not work near a pilot light or open fire.

Air out rags or items thoroughly if they have been treated with a solvent-based product. Hang them outside where children and animals cannot get into them. Allow petroleum-based products to evaporate before putting the item of clothing through your washer.

Always dispose of used solvents or cleaning materials in accordance with your local hazardous waste regulations. (There is a hazardous waste chart at the end of this book. Use hazardous materials with caution and dispose of them properly.)

If water does not remove the stain on washable fabric, apply liquid detergent to the stained fabric and rinse the area with cool water. After you have rinsed the area and completely removed detergent residue, sponge the spot with rubbing alcohol.

## COMBINATION STAINS

When you have a combination of greasy and nongreasy stains (e.g., coffee with cream, lipstick), first deal with the nongreasy stain. With washable fabrics, first sponge the stain with cool water, then apply liquid detergent to the stain and rinse well. Let the fabric air dry, then deal with the greasy stain: Apply drycleaning fluid to the stain and allow it to dry. If the stain is not gone, reapply drycleaning fluid.

# Part Two

# STAIN REMOVAL AGENTS

## ABSORBENTS

Use clean white cloths to absorb spills on fabric. It is easier to see how much of the spill is being absorbed if the material is white. Tissues, blotting paper, and sponges are all good choices.

Blot and reblot fresh spills until no more stain can be absorbed. Avoid rubbing — this will spread the stain. When the spill is completely absorbed, treat the stain. (Part Four lists specific stains in alphabetical order.)

**Absorbent powders.** Absorbing agents include powdered starch, talcum powder, powdered chalk, cornstarch, and potato flour.

Sprinkle the powder over the damp spill. As the powder absorbs the spill and dries, brush it off or use the vacuum cleaner hose to remove it. Repeat until no more stain can be absorbed. Absorbent powders are good grease absorbers.

## ACETONE

Acetone is the basic ingredient in nail polish remover, but nail polish remover may contain other substances that can make a stain worse. A concentrated form of acetone can be used to remove stains such as ballpoint ink and household cement.

Spread the stained area over a pad, cover it with a few drops of acetone, and scrub gently with a butter knife. Discard the pad when it becomes discolored and repeat the process.

Rub the stained area with powdered detergent, then rinse under hard-running cold water. If the remainder of the stain does not wash out, wash it in color-safe bleach if the garment care label lists it as safe.

*Recommendations:* Flammable and poisonous. Do not use on acetate. Test before using on natural or synthetic fibers.

*Availability:* Drugstores

### ALCOHOL *(isopropyl alcohol, a 70 percent solution)*

Alcohol can be very helpful in removing some kinds of stains, but if you are working with acetate, acrylic, rayon, or vinyl, you will need to dilute the rubbing alcohol with water (1 part alcohol to 2 parts water). Denatured alcohol (a 90 percent solution) can also be used.

*Recommendations:* Flammable. May cause some dyes to fade; test an inconspicuous area of the garment first.

*Availability:* Grocery stores, drugstores

### AMMONIA

Ammonia is a colorless gas made up of nitrogen and hydrogen. It is easily absorbed by water. Sold in diluted form, it works well on many surfaces and materials as a deodorizer and cleanser. It is a good grease cutter, wax stripper, and soil remover. Ammonia can restore color altered by contact with acids.

*Recommendations:* Never mix ammonia and chlorine bleach; the combination produces toxic fumes. Do not use in a confined space; the fumes are strong.

May cause some dyes to fade, so test it on the fabric

**Ammonia — Cleaning Tips**
For washing windows, use ½ cup of ammonia in a gallon of water. To make oven cleaning easier, place a saucer of ammonia inside a cool oven overnight, then wipe out and clean the next day. **Note:** Do not use ammonia on a self-cleaning oven. Refer instead to the manufacturer's instructions.

first. Ammonia is generally not safe for use on silk or wool. If an article changes color as a result of the application of ammonia, quickly rinse the affected area with water that has a few drops of vinegar added to it; rinse thoroughly.
*Availability:* Grocery stores

## BAKING SODA *(sodium bicarbonate)*

Baking soda is a cheap, nonabrasive cleanser and deodorizer. It can be used as a mild scouring powder or mixed with water to create a paste for cleaning dirty surfaces.
*Availability:* Grocery stores

## BLEACHES. *See Ammonia, Chlorine Bleach, Hydrogen Peroxide, Lemon Juice, Powdered Bleaches, Sunlight, Vinegar*

Bleaching agents are helpful in treating stains and reducing the natural yellowing of fabrics. If bleaching is necessary, choose a type of bleach that suits the fabric.

## BORAX

Borax is used to remove fruit, tea, and coffee stains; to remove tannin from teapots and coffee makers; and to soften hard water. As a paste, it can be used to remove stains from carpets.

## CHLORINE BLEACH

Chlorine bleach can be used on white cottons, linens, and synthetic fabrics. It can remove stains but it does weaken fibers if it stays on fabrics for too long. Chlorine bleach should not be used on silk, wool, or fabrics that are exposed to sunlight. You must dilute chlorine bleach before adding it to the washer, and rinse articles thoroughly. Failure to do this can cause discoloration and can even leave holes in fabrics.
*Recommendations:* Wear rubber gloves and avoid inhaling the fumes. Never mix bleach with ammonia or any

**Chlorine Precautions**

☞ Do not use metal containers when soaking articles in bleach; use china, glass, porcelain, enamel, or plastic.

☞ Chlorine bleach is poisonous. Contact with skin or eyes can cause burns and irritation.

☞ Never mix bleach with any other cleaning materials except laundry detergent. Combining bleach with strong acids or alkalis can produce deadly gases.

ammonia-based cleaners. Use only in well-ventilated areas.

*Availability:* Grocery stores

## CITRIC ACID. *See also Lemon Juice*

Some stain removers on the market contain citric acid. The ones that also contain petroleum distillates are a combination of solvent and bleaching agent.

*Recommendation:* Always test the solution first. Use products with petroleum derivatives in well-ventilated area.

*Availability:* Grocery stores, drugstores

## DETERGENTS

Liquid and powdered detergents are often successful in removing fresh stains from washable clothing.

**Granular vs. Liquid Detergents**

Granular detergents generally remove mud and clay better than liquid detergents. Liquid detergents are preferable for cleaning greasy or oily stains. Some products may contain added enzymes or bleaching agents for stain removal.

Make a paste of powdered detergent and water or rub undiluted liquid dishwashing detergent directly onto the stain. Scrub the area between two fingers. Rinse by holding the stained area taut under cold running water. Then turn the fabric over and treat the reverse side.

If stain removal directions call for liquid laundry detergent to be applied directly to the stain, check the manufacturer's label. Not all liquid laundry detergents are safe to apply directly to fabric.

## DYE STRIPPERS

Dye strippers invariably entail the use of boiling water, which can damage crease-resistant and treated fabrics, woolens, and other materials. But for articles that can tolerate boiling water, dye strippers can be used effectively.
*Recommendations:* Follow manufacturer's directions.
*Availability:* Hardware stores

## EUCALYPTUS

Eucaluptus is widely cultivated for its gums, resins, and oil. It can be useful in cutting through some kinds of grease.
*Recommendations:* Test first in an inconspicuous area. Blot frequently as you work.
*Availability:* Drugstores

## FURNITURE POLISH

Read the labels carefully before purchasing a furniture polish to make sure the polish is the best for your purpose. Beeswax polishes preserve and enhance the finish on solid woods. They are excellent for use on light woods where the use of oily polishes would darken the grain. Oil-based polishes are good for dark woods. Apply sparingly on a slighly dampened cloth and polish with a dry duster.
*Recommendation:* Do not use oil-based polishes if a synthetic finish has been applied to the wood.
*Availability:* Grocery stores

## GLYCERIN

Glycerin is an ingredient in many solvents on the market today. Used alone, it is a weak solvent but a good pre-soaking agent for some stains.
*Availability:* Drugstores

## HOT WATER

Water that is 140° F or hotter, in general, provides the most soil removal and sanitizing, especially of white cottons, linens, and heavily soiled cottons that are colorfast.

*Recommendations:* Reduces the resilience of synthetic fibers; may cause some colors to run.

## HYDROGEN PEROXIDE

Hydrogen peroxide (3 percent strength) is a safe and handy stain remover. For white fabrics (except some rayons and white nylon), to 1 part of 3 percent peroxide add 3 parts of warm water, ¼ teaspoon of white vinegar, and 1 drop of ammonia. Soak stain for 10 minutes, then rinse well. Repeat as necessary.

*Recommendations:* Buy peroxide in small quantities to make sure it is fresh — it loses strength as it ages or if it is exposed to light. (Check the expiration date on the label.)

*Availability:* Grocery stores, drugstores

## KEROSENE

Kerosene has been used for years to remove hard-water stains in tubs and sinks, and for wiping down tiles.

*Recommendations:* Flammable and toxic; use with caution.

*Availability:* Hardware stores

## LEMON JUICE. *See also Citric Acid*

Lemon juice is a bleaching agent that is good for lightening ivory (such as ivory piano keys), removing some stains, and deodorizing.

## MOTHBALLS AND MOTHFLAKES

The special mothproofing process for blankets and garments employed by drycleaners is not available for domestic use. Synthetic fabrics are not vulnerable to moths; only woolen materials require mothproofing. But if thoroughly clean woolens are stored in pest-free surroundings, they will be protected. Mothballs and -flakes should never be in direct contact with woolens; enclose them in an old handkerchief or a cloth bag.

## NAVAL JELLY

Naval jelly removes rust stains instantly.
*Recommendations:* Wear gloves to protect the skin.
*Availability:* Hardware stores

## OXALIC ACID

Oxalic acid is a poisonous substance sold in crystal form. It is extremely useful for removing rust from metals.
*Recommendations:* Oxalic acid is poisonous and must be handled with care. Contact your local hazardous waste authority for proper disposal. Wear gloves and keep out of the reach of children and pets.
*Availability:* Can be special-ordered at drugstores

## PETROLEUM JELLY

Petroleum jelly can be used as a pre-solvent for difficult grease or oil stains, but after it dissolves the stain you will need to treat the remaining discoloration with an additional degreasing solution.

## POWDERED BLEACHES

Powdered bleaches are a good substitute when chlorine bleach cannot be used. When using powdered bleaches, make a paste with water and powder and apply to damp fabric. Rinse thoroughly with cool water any time you use a bleaching agent.

## POWDERS. *See Absorbents, Detergents, Scouring Powders*

## SCOURING POWDERS

Scouring powders come in many heavy-duty varieties: Some are good for rust spots on cast iron; others are good for sinks, bathtubs, and so on; and various softscrub cleaners are available for your fiberglass, Formica, and stainless steel surfaces.

## SOAP

Bar soap is sometimes called for in stain removal directions. Do not use bath soaps that contain added moisturizers, fragrances, dyes, or deodorants. These added ingredients can themselves sometimes cause stains.

### SOLVENTS. *See also Acetone*

Many cleaning products contain solvents. For example, turpentine is a solvent: It dissolves paint and grease. Water is also a solvent, but it is not a hazardous one. Most organic solvents are highly flammable and poisonous.

Common organic solvents are petroleum distillates, trichloroethane, mineral spirits, carbon tetrachloride, and methylene chloride. Many materials you might use in stain removal, such as nail polish removers, paint thinners, drycleaning fluids, and degreasers, contain almost 100 percent solvent.

If you want to know more about a particular solvent, contact the manufacturer of the product (your local library should be able to locate the address or telephone number). Your Cooperative Extension Service is also a good source of information. Contact local poison centers for information on health effects.

If you have applied a solvent to an item of clothing, place that item outdoors — away from children or pets — and allow the solvent to evaporate before washing the item.

Clothing treated with solvent-containing products should be completely dry before you wear them.

Some people are extremely sensitive to solvents such as petroleum distillates.

If it is necessary to buy a special solvent or if you are in doubt about your ability to treat a difficult stain, send the article to a drycleaner. The incorrect use of a solvent might damage the material and cause a worse stain than the original. Some solvents can remove dyes or finish from a material or actually damage the fabric.

Drycleaning fluids will remove most greasy stains. Apply in small amounts. Several light applications are more effective than one large one.

Work over an old folded towel. Place the stained side face down and work from the back of it so that the stain will be washed out of the fabric. Change the absorbent pad under the material as it becomes soiled so that loosened stain elements will not restain the fabric.

*Recommendations:* Use with caution; fumes are toxic and cumulative, particularly if the user has been drinking alcohol (alcohol can make solvents more toxic to the user). Some are flammable, so do not work near a fire or flame and do not smoke. Work in a well-ventilated area, and do not inhale the fumes.

**Solvent Precaution**
Avoid wearing contact lenses when using solvents because the vapors can get trapped between your eye and the lens.

**Disposing of Solvents**
Because they can be environmentally hazardous, use solvent-containing products conservatively. Used paint thinner can be strained and reused. Always follow your local solid waste authority's recommendations for disposing of unused cleaning solvents. (See Appendix for Hazardous Waste Disposal.)

## SUNLIGHT. *See Bleaches*

Sometimes bleaching can be achieved by natural means. For instance, fine lace, which could be weakened by commercial bleaches, can be bleached by sunlight. Carefully tack the lace to a sheet and suspend the sheet between three or four clotheslines overnight. Repeat if necessary.

To whiten a discolored article, dampen it and place it in strong sunlight. Gradually it should whiten.

***Recommendations:*** Some fibers may be weakened by sunlight.

## TURPENTINE

Turpentine is a solvent that is used as a thinner for oil-based paints. It is also very effective on paint and grease stains where the textile can tolerate turpentine.

## VINEGAR

White vinegar is a solution of 5 percent acetic acid. Dilute before using on cotton or linen. Vinegar can change the color of some dyes, so it should always be tested first.

## WASHING SODA *(sodium carbonate)*

Washing soda, or "sal soda," is sodium carbonate and can be used to help cut grease and soften water. Add it to your regular laundry: use 4 tablespoons (60 ml) to a load of wash, and cut back on the amount of detergent. Use more washing soda for heavily soiled clothes.

***Recommendations:*** Do not use on silk or wool.

***Availability:*** Grocery stores and drugstores

# Part Three

# CLEANING EVERYTHING IN YOUR HOUSE

## ACETATES

Acetate is used for curtains; for evening fabrics such as brocades, taffetas, and satin; and for lining materials. Do not allow acetates to become very dirty. Wash frequently in cool detergent suds. Swirl about in the water but do not rub, wring, or twist. Rinse well; press with a low-set iron while still slightly damp.

## ALUMINUM

Aluminum is widely used for cookware, and in different gauges it can be adapted for various uses. Heavy gauge saucepans with milled bases do not buckle with heat, and they rest flat on electric hot plates. Aluminum cake pans are easy to clean, and they are nonrusting.

This metal will stain easily, however, if it is exposed to any alkali, even to salt or soda; but contrary to popular belief, the stains are not harmful. They can be removed in a number of ways:

1. Scrub the utensil with well-soaped fine steel wool pads.
2. Boil apple peelings or citrus skins in the pan.
3. Add 2 teaspoons (10 ml) of cream of tartar per quart (liter) of cold water in a stained saucepan. Bring the water to boiling point and simmer for three minutes. Discard the water and polish with a soapy steel wool pad.

**Aluminum teapots.** The outside of an aluminum teapot can be polished with fine steel wool. Rinse under a running tap. Shake off the droplets of water that remain. Do not wipe dry.

To remove tannin stains from the inside of an aluminum teapot, fill it with boiling water and add ¼ cup (60 ml) borax. Let the solution stand in the pot until it is cold, then scrub the inside of the pot with a nylon brush. Do not use a pot scraper for this job; it could weaken thin aluminum and cause pinpricks, which will leak.

Push a pipe cleaner through tannin-clogged spout holes, working from the inside of the teapot and up the spout. Rinse well by forcing water from a running tap through the holes.

**Aluminum saucepans.** A burnt aluminum saucepan can be treated in several ways. Try to avoid chipping and scraping; the resultant scars will attract stains that will be difficult to remove later. Scrape out as much of the burnt food as possible with a wooden spoon or a firm plastic or rubber spatula. Then expose the dry pot to hot sunshine for at least a week, keeping it dry at night. Day by day some of the burnt food will flake off when nudged with a spatula. Then boil undiluted household bleach and a teaspoonful (5 ml) of borax in the pan, using an amount sufficient to cover the stain. Finally, polish the area with steel wool, and after rinsing thoroughly, return the pan to regular use. The remaining black flecks will gradually disappear. They are not detrimental to health.

Once badly burnt, an aluminum saucepan will easily burn again. Reconstitute it by rubbing the inside with unsalted fat, such as lard, and heat the pan very gently before using it.

Aluminum frying pans and the inside of deep-fry cookers often become very stained with burnt-on grease. There are commercial cleaners on the market, and these should be used according to instructions as they are highly corrosive.

## ANGORA

This is a wool made from rabbit fur or goat hair. Sometimes angora is blended with nylon, and this sheds less fluff than does pure angora.

Wash in lukewarm water with a well-whisked wool-washing liquid soap compound or mild soap flakes. Knead the garment under water. Do not rub or twist or lift it out of the water; the weight of the water can cause undue stretching. If possible, wash in a sink or tub so that the plug can be released to let out the washing and subsequent rinsing waters. Simply press the garment to extract the water. After rinsing, place the garment on a towel, mold it into shape, fold in the ends of the towel, and roll the garment in its folds. Dry flat on a sheet on the lawn, or over newspaper and a sheet on a clean cement surface, out of direct sunlight. Turn to dry the underside. Shake well when dry to raise the furry nap. Do not press. If wrinkles appear, simply hold a steaming iron just above the garment.

## APPLIANCES

Keep all booklets and warranties together in a plastic bag for easy reference. The date of purchase and the model number could be required in case of an insurance claim or if repairs are necessary.

Always switch off the electricity before attempting to clean an appliance. Cleaning with water can cause short circuits and prove life-threatening if the power is left on.

## BABY ITEMS

**Baby clothing.** Baby skin can become irritated by harsh detergents. Dissolve mild soap flakes well in lukewarm water before immersing baby garments. Rinse twice. Dry inside out in a semi-shaded area. Fine woolens will scorch in direct sunlight.

**Plastic and waterproof pants.** Wash frequently after rinsing or pre-soaking to remove traces of soiling or ammonia. Use lukewarm suds and soap flakes or very mild detergent. Dry inside out.

**Diapers.** Borax, long acclaimed as an excellent deodorizer and cleaner for baby (and geriatric) garments, is slightly cheaper than the soaking compounds. Borax or one of the compounds should be used as a soaking agent to counteract odor and traces of ammonia and to keep the diapers white.

An integral part of nursery equipment is a large plastic bucket with a lid. Once a day put 2 rounded tablespoons (30 ml) of your preferred soaking compound in the bottom of the bucket and add 7 quarts (liters) of cold water. Put in wet diapers as they are changed; dispose of heavy soiling before soaking other diapers. Leave for several hours or overnight.

Once a day empty the contents of the bucket into a tub and let the soaking water drain away. Flush the diapers with tap water and drain again. Now the diapers will be clean enough to be washed with other baby things such as sheets, pillowcases, and cotton undershirts that will withstand the use of hot water. Do not add woolens or drip-dry fabrics. Woolens will shrink in hot water and drip-dry garments will crease badly. Instead, these should be hand-washed in cool suds.

Use the hot-water cycle and soap flakes or a mild liquid detergent in the washing machine to wash the diapers and cotton articles. For economy's sake, use a cold-water rinse if the machine can be adjusted.

The two rinse cycles of the average automatic machine will adequately remove all traces of ammonia, soap, or detergent. Never use heavy-duty detergents to wash babywear. Residues can cause chafing and rashes.

If the water is hard, liquid detergent is preferable; and to dispel any traces (urine, soap, or detergent) use borax or fabric softener (occasionally, according to directions on the package) to make the diapers and garments soft and fluffy.

Dry the diapers in the sun whenever possible and fold them so they will be ready for use. Correctly laundered diapers prevent chafing and rashes, resulting in a more contented, comfortable baby.

**Bassinet and crib sheets, blankets, towels, and washrags.** Pre-soak to remove soil stains. Wash in water at a temperature suitable to the fabric. Use a very mild detergent or soap flakes. Thorough rinsing is necessary; ammonia in urine can react on traces of detergent and cause chafing and skin rashes.

**Hand-knitted baby clothes.** Hand-wash in lukewarm water using a mild soap powder or liquid. Rinse thoroughly. Roll in a towel to extract extra moisture. Dry in semi-shade out of direct sunlight to avoid yellowing.

To store baby clothing, wash and rinse well; dry thoroughly. Age and damp conditions can cause brown spots to appear; stains should be removed or they will become brown and impossible to treat.

**Baby toys.** Stuffed toys lose their pristine appearance after a few months of rough and tumble, and to keep them hygienic and attractive they must be cleaned or washed.

Not all fluffy toys are washable, however. Some have fillings that will swell and burst seams or disintegrate when immersed in water. It is important to check the care label on toys to see if they are washable, either by hand or in a machine, and whether machine drying is permitted.

When children become very attached to particular toys, it is often difficult to withdraw them even for a day for cleaning, let alone discard them because they are shabby.

Soft, stuffed pastel-colored and white toys that have been lightly soiled can be freshened by dusting them heavily with baby powder, powdered starch, or cornstarch. Work the powder into the pile with fingertips.

Roll the toys in the folds of a towel and leave them for several hours — overnight if the toys can be spared.

Have a freshly washed and dried clothes brush ready. Working outside, thoroughly brush the pile to remove the powder.

Wash and press any ribbon trimming, or apply new ribbon to give a cleaner look to much-handled fluffy toys.

If the care label so states, many toys, including some teddy bears, are washable in cool, mild detergent suds.

Rinse well, squeeze out as much water as possible, then run the toys through the spin cycle of the washing machine with two dry towels. The friction will fluff up the toy and drying can then be completed in open air.

**Safety Regulations**

Safety regulations are now quite strict regarding eyes, bells, and other such parts on stuffed toys, but it is advisable to test them from time to time, and certainly after the toys have been washed, to ensure that they have not loosened.

Use a piece of toweling with a good texture, or a toothbrush dipped in soapy water to brush and wipe soiled synthetic fur. Then wipe the fur with a damp cloth and dry again.

Plastic rattles, teethers, and similar toys, which often find themselves in babies' mouths, should be washed regularly in hot soapy water or in the dishwasher. Rinse thoroughly.

## BATHROOM FIXTURES

**Bathtub and sink.** Stains caused by spilled hair dyes, medicines, and cosmetics can often be removed by the application of a paste made of cream of tartar and peroxide. Smear it on heavily and let it dry for 3 hours. Rinse off, and repeat if necessary, using a fresh paste.

Put 10 tablespoons (150 ml) of cold water in a spray bottle. Add 1 tablespoon (15 ml) of acetic acid (vinegar) to the water. Spray about ½ square yard (0.5 square meter) at a time, beginning at the bottom and working upward. Leave the spray on for a minute. Wipe off with clean water. When the job is finished, wipe all over with clean water containing 1 tablespoon (15 ml) of washing soda to neutralize the acid.

A cracked bathroom sink can be patched until a replacement is possible. Work from the underside. Wash the length of the crack to remove traces of grease and soap. Then stretch a length of wide waterproof adhesive plaster along the length of the crack and smooth out all air bubbles.

Apply a coat of white paint and, when this dries, apply a second coat. Do not use the sink for 24 hours. Meanwhile use epoxy porcelain mender, obtainable at a hardware store, to fill in any chips on the inside of the sink.

Rust marks on a bathtub or sink can be rubbed hard with a cloth dipped in undiluted vinegar. Or wipe the rust marks off instantly with an application of naval jelly. It is available in some hardware stores, and it is worth the effort to acquire a bottle. Wear gloves to protect the skin.

**Bathroom tiles.** To clean the grouting around the tub and shower, use any thick emulsion cleaner as a temporary grout between tiles. Spread a few drops on with a fingertip and let it dry. Later, clean tiles to remove traces of dried emulsion.

**Bathroom mirrors.** To prevent a bathroom mirror from becoming clouded with steam, rub it all over with a cloth slightly dampened with glycerin.

The silver backing (which, by the way, is pure silver) can be affected by the use of and the method of application

**Keeping Sponges Fresh**
Loofahs and other natural sponges are excellent for removing scaly skin, but they tend to become slimy with soap unless they are cleaned regularly. First, rinse them under a running cold water tap, then soak them for an hour in cold vinegar water — 2 tablespoons (30 ml) per quart (liter).

of certain cleaners. Even the spray-on commercial window and glass cleaners, when applied to mirrors, should not be sprayed too liberally or be left on the surface for too long. It is safer to spray a soft cloth with the cleaner and apply that to the mirror.

A napless soft cloth wrung out of lukewarm liquid detergent suds will effectively clean mirrors. Or use ammonia water, 1 tablespoon (15 ml) to 1½ quarts (liters) of warm water. (See Mirrors)

**Bathroom scales.** These tend to rust with steam and dampness. Spray the metal parts with a rust inhibitor, or rub them lightly with petroleum jelly. Occasionally test the accuracy of the scales by weighing an article of marked weight, preferably one that weighs in excess of six or seven pounds. Adjust accordingly.

**Shower curtains.** These can be washed by hand or machine in warm suds. Warm water keeps plastic pliable.

Diluted bleach will remove most mold, mildew, and soap stains on shower curtains. The double benefit in soaking the curtain in the bathtub, of course, is that both will be cleaned. Stained white towels and other white cotton garments (not woolens, rayons, or silks) can be soaked at the same time.

**Shower heads.** These become clogged with mineral deposits after years of use. If possible, remove the head and scrub the inside with a ball of steel wool wrapped around a clothespin. If the head cannot be removed, scrub the underside with a sharp nylon brush or prick the holes with a darning needle. The removal of the shower head makes it possible to shake out loose grit that will reclog the holes.

## BED LINEN

**Sheets and pillowcases.** Mend tears and patch weak sections before washing in a machine. Wash in hot water with good laundry detergent. Dry in full sunshine and fold as you take it from the clothesline.

**Bedspreads.** Washable spreads should be laundered according to the instructions on the care label. Nylon, polyester, or polyester-blend fibers and cottons wash well, but rayons, silks, and acetates require drycleaning.

Chenille spreads are excellent for use on children's beds, and they are easily washed in a machine, using hot detergent suds. Rinse twice and double the bedspread over a line to dry, with the wrong side uppermost so that the tufts rub against each other in the breeze, thus raising their nap. Chenille quilts often have a lint problem when new, but this abates after a few launderings. After washing, when the quilt is on the bed, a very light application of hair spray or spray-on starch will help to control loose fibers that cause lint collection. Clean out the washing machine filter thoroughly after washing these spreads.

**Blankets.** Woolen blankets can be hand- or machine-washed if you use cold water and mild or wool-washing detergent. In machine washing, use the shortest possible cycle. Wash one blanket at a time in plenty of water and rinse well. Spin drying or mechanical wringing will ensure quicker drying; this is important for woolen blankets. Blankets made of synthetic fibers will not shrink, but to keep them soft and fluffy, use a very cool wash and mild detergent or soap flakes.

Some synthetic blankets will discolor if exposed to full sunlight, so choose a windy day and dry in semi-shade.

Dry blankets in an electric dryer on the low setting or over two clotheslines to permit the circulation of air between overhangs. Some woolen blankets become odorous when exposed to harsh sunlight, so dry these on a windy day in semi-shade also.

When blankets are dry, shake them vigorously to raise the nap. Press satin bindings with a very cool iron and store them in plastic bags or in new pillowcases, with moth deterrent if the blankets are made of wool. Synthetic blankets are mothproof.

## BOOKS

To remove grease spots from old book covers, use an art gum eraser or fresh white bread (ball it up like a gum eraser). Dust on talcum powder, leave it on for a few hours, and wipe clean.

To clean grease, mold, or mildew from cloth bindings, try a thin paste of cornstarch and a cleaning fluid (experiment first on a spot of the binding that doesn't show too much, as discoloration sometimes results).

## BRASS

The warmth and richness of well-polished brass adequately repays the time spent in maintaining its shine. Most homes have some brass objects. Ornaments can be cleaned, then clear-lacquered to maintain their glow and to cut down on work. The lacquer will last for months, depending on the amount of handling and the use the article receives, as well as climatic conditions. It is seldom worthwhile lacquering a brass tray that is regularly used because the surface will soon be abraded and the protective layer of lacquer will gradually flake off.

Church brasses are ideal candidates for lacquering. Some firms specialize in this type of lacquering. The only cleaning necessary is regular dusting with a soft cloth sprayed with silicone polish.

Many new brass articles are lacquered before they are sold, but thoroughly cleaned brass articles are easily sprayed at home. Purchase clear lacquer in an aerosol can for easy application, and follow the instructions on the label.

Neglected brass becomes almost black. If mild cleaners (such as brass polish, a cut lemon dipped in salt, or a mixture of vinegar and salt) prove ineffective, soak the item in a citric acid solution. Use a 1-ounce (25 g) packet of citric acid dissolved in 3½ quarts (liters) of hot (but not boiling) water in a nonmetal container. Use more solution if the article is large.

Soak for five minutes, then gently scrub etchings, ornamentation, or engravings with an old, soft toothbrush. Rinse under a running hot water tap, pat dry, and polish in the usual way.

This method of cleaning is ideal for Eastern brasses that are often deeply etched or inlaid.

An intermediate rubbing with a cloth dampened with cloudy ammonia will brighten unlacquered brass articles. The cloth will become quite black; check it frequently to ensure that you are polishing with a clean section of the cloth. Ammonia will also remove traces of polish embedded in etched brass objects. Do not immerse painted brassware.

When green or blue deposits build up on brass, a different treatment is necessary. Small, solid brass articles can be boiled in water containing washing soda: ½ cup (125 ml) soda to 1½ quarts (liters) water. Larger articles can be sponged with the solution. Small traces of deposits can often be rubbed off with a cloth dampened with vinegar or lemon juice sprinkled with salt. Rinse, wash, rinse again, dry, and polish.

Ornamental brass attached to canvas, leather, or to doors or cabinets requires careful cleaning if the base material is not to be stained by polish. Fine wood or cigarette ash can be used to polish the brass without damage to the base, or cardboard shields can be cut to slip under the brass ornament to be cleaned. After cleaning, apply clear lacquer.

The inside of brass cooking utensils must *not* be cleaned with polish. Instead, rub with vinegar or lemon juice and salt. If necessary, polish with a well-soaped pad of fine steel wool. Rinse under a running tap; wash in hot detergent suds, and rinse again. Keep these utensils thoroughly dry when not in use.

Commercial brass polishes are nonabrasive and will not cause scratches — providing the surface has first been dusted with a soft cloth to remove gritty deposits.

It is best to rub off the polish before it dries completely. Use a fresh cloth, for the cleaning pad will be black with metal deposits and grime.

## BRONZE

Items made of a combination of copper and tin need little maintenance. Dust with a slightly oily cloth or with silicone polish to preserve their soft luster.

Neglected bronze should be washed in hot detergent suds. Use a soft brush to remove dust and grime. Rinse and dry, and finish off with an oily cloth or with silicone cream.

### Candle Tips

☞ When setting new candles into candlesticks, dip the bases in hot water for a few seconds and push them firmly into position.

☞ Candles will burn longer if they are chilled in a refrigerator before being lit.

☞ Save candle ends to rub drawer runners and inside window frames to make windows and drawers run smoothly.

## CANDLESTICK HOLDERS

Clean candlestick holders with the appropriate polish: Silver should be cleaned with silver polish, brass with brass polish. Crystal and glass can be washed in water containing ammonia. Wipe lacquered metals with a damp cloth and spray with silicone wax.

Old candle wax can be removed from candlesticks more easily if the wax is warmed. Leave the sticks in hot sunlight, train a hair dryer on them, or dip them in hot water for a few minutes. Ease off the softened wax with a blunt knife.

## CARPETS

Act quickly when something has spilled on a carpet. Prompt attention and using correct solvents and cleaning methods is invariably more successful than belated attention by a professional carpet cleaner.

Don't panic! Use any dry colorfast absorbent material that is handy — a handkerchief, a cloth, tissues, or towels. The stain is more easily removed from these washable cloths than from the carpet. Do not rub; simply blot, using a series of fresh tissues or cloths until no more can be absorbed. Then treat the stain according to its nature.

**Emergency Care Kit for Carpets**

Keep these simple cleaning solutions handy:

- ☞ Powdered laundry detergent. Do not use liquid detergent.
- ☞ Tissues or clean absorbent dustrags. Old dish towels are excellent.
- ☞ A bottle of drycleaning solvent. This is flammable. Observe safety precautions.
- ☞ Paint thinner or acetone.
- ☞ Carpet-cleaning powder, which both cleans and deodorizes.
- ☞ An old clean toothbrush; borax; white vinegar; and household bleach.

For solid stains such as grease or food, use a kitchen spatula or pliable knife to scrape up as much as possible, then treat the remaining stain appropriately.

Note the telephone number of a reliable carpet-cleaning firm. Don't hesitate to call for help if the stain is a bad one.

Avoid excessive wetting. Water can *cause* a stain if it penetrates the backing and dissolves deep-down dirt.

Do not tread on a damp carpet. Dry the area as quickly as possible with a fan, creating cross-ventilation, or use a hand-held hair dryer on a low setting. *Never* use a radiator.

When the stain has been treated, smooth the treated area so that it will dry as it should.

**Bathroom carpets.** Light-colored, rubber-backed bathroom carpeting soon becomes soiled from frequent traffic.

Synthetic floor coverings can be shampooed in place or taken up and cleaned in the washing machine.

Some drycleaners will accept these rugs, but they should be washed, not drycleaned, because the cleaning fluids can damage the rubber backing.

Some bathroom-sized carpets will fit into a large domestic washing machine. First vacuum the carpet well while it is still on the floor, then spray the soiled area with a pre-wash spray to loosen stubborn stains.

Set the machine for a short cycle using a full-load cold water supply and a cold water detergent. Hot water is detrimental to the rubber backing. Put the detergent in the bottom of the machine, not over the rug, which should be rolled loosely with the rubber backing in and the pile out. Arrange the rug evenly in the machine so as not to unbalance the load.

When the wash cycle is completed, spread the rug, pile side up, over three lines. Rubber-backed rugs should not be exposed to dryer heat.

When the carpet is quite dry, re-lay it and spray it with fabric protector to keep it cleaner longer.

**Indoor-outdoor carpets.** This type of carpet is generally stain-, mildew-, and rot-resistant. It is available in a wide range of patterns and colors and is ideal for use in schools, around pools, and on patios. No underfelt is required because the carpet and tiles are foam-backed.

The carpet can be loose-laid and affixed with a special carpet tape, or the clean, dry floor can be covered with adhesive and the carpet affixed.

Regular cleaning will make the carpet last longer and look better. Vacuum, hose, or sweep the carpet frequently, particularly if it is exposed to tracked-on sand and dirt.

Allow felt-type carpets to dry before walking on them. The wet surface can easily scuff, particularly from rubber-soled shoes.

Blot up spills and stains as soon as they occur. Make up a jar of laundry detergent suds — 1 tablespoon (15 ml) to one cup (250 ml) of water — and use this to sponge spots. Remove the suds with a series of clean, damp cloths.

Greasy stains might require special treatment with a solvent, but do not use spot removers or ammoniated cleaners on carpets containing vinyl.

Dilute drycleaning fluid with an equal amount of cold water to remove greasy marks, then test the solution on an inconspicuous part of the carpet.

Indoor-outdoor carpet is susceptible to burns from cigarette ash, barbecue fires, and so on. Although some

## Carpet Cleaning with Foam and Powder Shampoo

There are several drycleaning powders on the market that absorb grease and grime in the carpet pile. Several hours after application, vacuum the powder; both powder and grime will lift away together.

Powder shampoo is an excellent stain absorber if it is applied as soon as spills have been blotted up. Work the powder into the stained area with a special appliance (often sold with the powder) or with a firm-bristled clean brush.

When vacuuming up the powder, work first across the pile and then in the opposite direction, slowly and methodically, so that no trace remains.

For regular cleaning, use about 1 oz. (25 g) per square yard (meter) — more if the area is deeply soiled. Leave it on for at least 20 minutes; several hours is preferable.

The use of shampoo powder avoids the problem of overwetting the carpet; and after vacuuming, the carpet can be walked on without having to wait for it to dry.

such fibers might not be dangerously flammable, they are sensitive to heat and will melt, leaving indelible stains.

**Woolen carpets.** Wool fibers have particularly good resilience. That is, having been walked upon, they bounce back. They do not burst into flame, but instead burn slowly with a telltale odor, which is an alarm itself. Provided spills are treated without delay, wool fibers are fairly resistant to most stains. Deeper stains usually respond to more concentrated treatment.

Woolen carpets need to be mothproofed to protect them against carpet beetles, silverfish, and moths.

Tests show that **nylon carpets** wear best of all. They soil easily but they can be cleaned without difficulty.

**Acrylic carpets** also wear well and maintain their appearance, despite heavy traffic. They soil quickly but are easy to clean. Choose a stippled or sculptured pattern to camouflage day-to-day soiling.

**Polypropylene carpeting** is a popular indoor-outdoor carpeting that is quite durable and easy to keep clean. It can safely be exposed to sparks from a barbecue fire or dropped cigarettes without danger of flaming; but be prepared for melted fibers, which are difficult to camouflage. The disadvantage of this type of carpet is its poor resilience.

**Viscose rayon carpets** have only a moderate resistance to wear and tear. They soil quickly, but care must be taken not to make them too damp while cleaning. Deal with stains promptly, blotting frequently, and there is a good chance you will succeed in removing them. These carpets are flammable.

**Carpet underlay.** Some carpets are lined with a heavy foam-rubber backing, which serves as its own underlay. Other carpets need a different form of underlay. There are several gradings of plastic foam, some more spongy than others, and an experienced salesperson will help you choose one that will suit both the type of carpet and its location.

Underfelts made of a mixture of wool, hair, and/or jute are still popular. Some are rubber-coated to make them more mothproof and less likely to absorb spills.

**New carpet on an old floor.** When old carpet and underlay have been taken up to be replaced by new, heed the following guidelines:

1. Vacuum the room thoroughly.
2. Damp mop the room using a good household cleaner in the water.
3. If a wool carpet is going down, shake powder pesticide around the perimeter of the room, particularly under warped or raised baseboards. If the old carpet was wool and if it appears to have been eaten by moths or carpet beetles, it is wise to have the room pestproofed. Synthetic carpets are not affected by beetles or moths.

Manufacturers usually mothproof woolen carpets before they leave the factory. Check to see if this is the case when purchasing woolen or wool-blend carpets.

## CASHMERE

This fabric requires careful hand laundering. Use very cool suds made with a

### Carpet Cleaning with Wet Shampoo

If you decide to wet shampoo the carpet yourself, first remove as much furniture as possible from the room. Slip plastic or cardboard discs under the legs of remaining furniture. Lift floor-length curtains out of the way and vacuum thoroughly. Read and follow all instructions. Use only the detergent or cleaner recommended for that particular machine. Provide cross-ventilation by opening doors and windows. After shampooing, smooth pile with a thoroughly clean nylon broom. When the carpet is dry — after several hours, depending on the type of cleaner and method of cleaning used — vacuum slowly and thoroughly to remove the dried detergent.

Never use the carpet until it is dry. Choose good dry weather when you wet shampoo, and let the carpet dry for 15–20 hours before walking on it.

You might find that the carpet pile soils quickly. This can be caused by a buildup of detergent, which attracts grime.

wool-washing detergent. Try to use a sink or tub with a plug so that the water can be released after washing and subsequent rinsings. Cashmere must not be wrung, but it can be spin-dried in your machine. Put a towel or other soft article of clothing into the machine to act as a buffer, or roll the wet garment in a large towel and press out excess water.

Cashmere will stretch with the weight of water, so when wet you should lift it with both hands. Dry inside out, pinned to a sheet hung like a hammock between three or four clotheslines or on a plastic drying rack. If a machine dryer is used, maintain a very low setting. Steam press when dry.

## CAST IRON

**Kettles** soon become corroded with a furrylike deposit on the inside. A "furry" kettle takes longer to boil, but the gritty deposits do not affect the taste of the water.

Treat an iron kettle by filling it with cold water. Add ¼ cup (60 ml) water softener and bring it slowly to a boil. Remove from heat. Let the solution remain until it is cold, then discard. Scrub out the kettle with a nylon brush; rinse out the loosened scale, and rinse again. Repeat if the kettle has been neglected.

A large seashell or smooth stone left in a kettle also helps to loosen the deposits, which are then poured out with the water.

## CHILDREN'S CLOTHING

Pre-treat or soak stained items before washing. Many stains will soak out. White and light-colored socks will need pre-soaking. Rub them with soap and soak, or slip them into an enzyme pre-wash solution for half an hour. Then they can be washed in the machine with other clothing.

Woolen and dark socks can be washed in a short cold water cycle with dark shorts and trousers, using a detergent designed for cold water machine washing.

## CHINA

To remove brown stains from old china, soak the china in a mild solution of bleach (5 percent) and water. Soak for several hours, then wash and rinse. If the stains return, repeat the process. Stubborn brown stains on old china can be removed with a solution of equal parts vinegar and salt.

**Think Prevention**
All clothing should be clean before it is stored. Mildew will attack food stains in damp or humid conditions, and the larvae of moths and silverfish can cause irreparable damage to woolens and many other fabrics that have been stored with stains.

## CHINTZ

Chintz usually has a permanent glaze but some fabrics are only lightly glazed, and this finish deteriorates when the material is washed. Drycleaning is preferable to maintain the characteristic surface gloss of this fabric.

If the glaze is permanent and the label states that the fabric is washable, do so by hand, not in a machine. Use hand-hot suds and mild detergent. Do not twist or rub the surface. Rinse in cold water and drip-dry until the article is just slightly damp. Iron on the right side with a cool iron.

## CHROME

Chrome will rust easily if the surface is eroded by soda, salt, or traces of food. For this reason, use only clean cloths when wiping chromed frames on furniture. Silicone wax can be used, but only on thoroughly clean chrome.

When rust occurs, dip very fine steel wool in the above cleaner and rub gently. Wipe off and spray with a rust inhibitor, available from hardware stores.

Chromium plate can be cleaned with spray-on silicone cream or with automobile polish. Wipe over grease-stained chrome with a cloth wrung out of hot detergent suds containing a few drops of ammonia. Dry well before applying polish.

Do not wipe chromed fittings with a dishcloth. Traces of grease and food will cause deterioration and eventually rust.

Chromium-plated parts of stools, chairs, highchairs, and desks often rust at joints. Rub gently with dry steel wool, and wipe clean with a dry cloth. Apply a thin coat of chrome polish.

## CONCRETE OR CEMENT FLOORS

These floors have a tendency to be dusty unless they are sealed with either clear or colored paving paint or cement sealer, both available at paint stores.

Paths, stairs, and outdoor patios of concrete often develop black or green mold during damp weather. To clean them, mix equal parts of household bleach and water. Apply and leave for three minutes. Kill the mold spores by scrubbing the area with a brush or broom.

Treat a small section at a time, then hose off the loosened mold. Be careful outdoors not to run bleach solution into the lawn or flowerbeds.

**Spilled milk** will leave a greasy mark on concrete. Hose it off with cold water, scrub the stain with hot water containing washing soda — ½ cup (125 ml) to ½ bucketful of water — then hose again.

To remove light oil stains from a cement floor in a garage, saturate half a dozen sheets of newspaper with water and press firmly over the oil stains. Weigh the papers down with bricks or boards. The drying sheets will act as a poultice and absorb most of the oil.

If no fire risk is involved, another method is to sprinkle a little gasoline over the stain and rub in dry cement powder. Cover with a sheet of plastic, leave for two hours, then sweep the cement.

## COPPER

Copper pots and pans will buckle if exposed to high heat. Because they will abrade easily, do not use harsh scrapers and cleaners.

To avoid scraping, simply soak the containers with hot detergent suds until the food loosens. Then use a nylon sponge or brush to remove stubborn traces.

Copper can be kept gleaming for a long period of time by using long-term copper polish, now available at most supermarkets.

Blue or green deposits develop quickly on not-quite-clean or not-quite-dry copper surfaces. This is a poisonous deposit, and it should not come into contact with food. The deposit should come off when you rub the item with a cloth dipped in a mixture of vinegar and salt.

Avoid the use of vinegar in any food to be cooked in a copper pan, and remove cooked food as soon as possible from a copper container.

## CURTAINS

Many ready-made, lined, synthetic curtains cannot be washed successfully. Although it may be expensive, drycleaning will keep them looking as good as new, whereas washing can cause permanent creasing.

Keep curtains cleaner longer by lightly vacuuming them to remove surface dust. Use the upholstery attachment on the end of the vacuum cleaner hose.

**Lace and light synthetic curtains** should be taken down, all hooks removed, shaken, then soaked in warm detergent suds for 15 minutes before they are hand-washed. Rinse twice. Drip-dry; the weight of the water will draw out creases. Do not dry these curtains in full sunlight. Rehang as soon as they cease to drip.

**Cotton and linen-type curtains** may shrink. A curtain rod inserted in the lower hem while the curtains are still slightly damp and rehung in their correct position will help them to drop a little, and its weight will draw out creases. Other curtains will need heavy ironing from top to bottom, not across the fabric.

It is advisable to test the dyes of any colored washable curtains being laundered for the first time. Never use hot water. Pre-soak in cold water with a handful of salt for 15 minutes. Drain that water, then pre-soak for five minutes in mild detergent. Wash in warm water, rinse twice in cold, and immediately hang the curtains to dry.

Long, hanging drapes can be laid across three or four clotheslines to drip-dry. Shorter curtains can be pegged to the clothesline without doubling the material. Others can be hung horizontally.

**Worn, threadbare curtains** should be handled very carefully. Fold them loosely and slip one (or two small light curtains) into an old pillowcase. Pre-soak the enclosed curtain for 15 minutes, occasionally swirling it in plenty of cool suds. Press out excess soaking water. Wash in the same way and rinse twice. Remove the still-folded curtain or curtains from the pillowcase and roll in a towel. Rehang light synthetic curtains to dry, or dry outdoors and iron if necessary, being careful not to put undue stress upon the worn fabric.

**Tears and holes** can be mended by dipping a large patch of similar material in raw starch. Lay the patch over the tear, cover it with brown paper, and press hard with a moderately hot iron until the patch adheres. This will last until the curtains are washed again, and the patch will be almost invisible in the hanging folds.

**Curtain fittings.** One way to brighten rusty metal curtain fittings is to boil them in a vinegar solution —

1 tablespoon (15 ml) to 1 cup (250 ml) water — for 15 minutes. Pat dry without rinsing.

Use plastic curtain fittings if rust is prevalent in a badly ventilated room or in seaside environments.

## DENIM AND JEANS

Few denims are fast-dyed; fading often is desirable in this fabric. If soaking is necessary, do so in cool water with an enzyme pre-wash compound; wash in cool suds either by hand or in a machine. Drip-drying makes them slightly stiffer. Press denim with a hot iron while still slightly damp.

**Identify Stains**

Help your drycleaner by pinning a note to the stains, advising the cleaner of their origin. Be specific rather than general. For instance, if a garment is stained with paint, try to state the brand name and the type of paint, as well as what treatment, if any, you have applied. Do this for all stains — food and drink spills, ink stains, and so on. This will save the cleaner unnecessary experimentation.

Denim garments that are too stiff to be worn comfortably can be relaxed by adding a fabric softener to the final rinse. Never add fabric softener if suds are present. This treatment can be applied once in three or four washes. Used too frequently, the softener will give the fabric a greasy feeling.

## DOWN COMFORTERS

These are best drycleaned, but not every cleaner will accept these heavy items. Careful home laundering is successful in an emergency, either by hand or in a machine, using the shortest cycle on a fully automatic washing machine. Usually a good airing, however, will freshen down or feathers, and the use of a new removable cover will improve the appearance of the comforter. Try to avoid washing.

**Feather eiderdowns** can tear and the feathers might clog drycleaning equipment or a washing machine, so an assessment of the strength and age of the covering must be made before a feather comforter is machine-washed.

If the corners are worn, reinforce them with corners of contrasting material finely stitched into place before washing the eiderdown.

Machine wash feather eiderdowns for not more than three minutes, interrupting the cycle if necessary. Use the greatest amount of *very cool water* and mild detergent suds. (Hot water will release oils contained in the feathers and cause an unpleasant odor.) Stains on the cover should be pre-treated. A paste made of borax and warm water can be rubbed into old tea and coffee stains. A pre-wash spray can be used on other stains before the cover is wet, or you can dampen the marks and rub in laundry soap. Scrub the stains gently with an old toothbrush.

Rinse for two minutes, interrupting the cycle if necessary, then spin dry. A very low-set electric dryer can be used, provided it is large enough for the eiderdown. Again, heat will cause an unpleasant odor.

If hand washing, use plenty of cool water in a large tub with a plug. Whisk detergent into the water before immersing the quilt. Push it up and down to rinse out dissolved grime. Remove the plug and press out excess water. Rinse twice in the same way. If a spin dryer or wringer is not available, remove further water by rolling the article in a large towel. Hang to dry in a breezy semi-shaded area. If possible, choose a windy day to wash an eiderdown. Use about a dozen clothespins to attach it to the line so that

**Redistributing Down**

To fluff up a down comforter or jacket, put it in the dryer with a clean tennis ball or a pair of clean canvas shoes. The friction will redistribute the feathers.

it can dry in an even thickness. Turn it several times while it is drying, and loosen clumps of feathers with your fingers.

Washing an old eiderdown might weaken the downproofing of the cover. Spray the surface lightly with spray-on starch or with a silicone-based fabric shield, which will also help to make the cover more grime-resistant.

## EMBROIDERED ARTICLES

These should be washed in hand-hot water with mild detergent. Rinse well; starch if necessary. Small articles can be rolled in a towel until it is time to iron them. Use a spray-on starch to restore their stiffness. Iron on the wrong side with the iron heated to suit the material.

New embroidery, which needs freshening after much handling and which is perhaps required for gift-giving or for display purposes, can be dipped in hot water containing 1 tablespoon (15 ml) borax. First ascertain color-fastness. Then push the article up and down in the water. Do not wring or crease. Spread it flat over a towel and cover it with another towel. Press to absorb the water. Then press on the wrong side over a thoroughly clean ironing sheet, using an iron heated to suit the material. Wrong-side pressing raises the embroidery on the right side. Borax will clean and restore a slight stiffness to the material.

To test for colorfastness, use sample threads spread on a white cloth and covered with a wet cloth. Press with a hot iron. If the cloths are stained with dye, do not use hot water; instead use cool water and add to it the borax dissolved in a little boiling water.

## FLAMEPROOFED FABRICS

Garments treated with flame retardants should be laundered according to instructions on the label. Do not boil or bleach these garments. As a general rule, wash in cool detergent suds and rinse well to remove traces of the suds.

*Note:* Flameproof does not mean fireproof. Fabrics will still burn and char, but they will not burst into flame.

## FLANNEL

Wash in a machine or by hand. Use cooler water for pajamas and other articles that have been made flame-resistant.

**Flannel sheets and pillowcases** provide sleeping comfort in cold weather, but the flannel nap can be irritating to people with respiratory problems.

Sometimes flannel poses a dust problem. New sheets have loose nap that sheds fluff and causes furniture to have a dusty appearance, but this problem will ease after several washings.

In the meantime, do not spin dry the sheets. Let them drip-dry. They will be slightly stiffer, but their warmth will not be affected. Shedding will be lessened.

## FURNITURE

Wood furniture is usually polished, waxed, lacquered, sealed, or finished in some way — so maintenance is cut to a minimum. Still, regular care and a little knowledge are necessary to keep furniture that is in daily use in good order.

This can be done by keeping it clean and suitably polished. Keep two points in mind:

1. Do not apply polish over a grimy surface. Polish can seal in traces of makeup, food, perspiration, and dirt, causing the surface to become dull and unattractive.

2. Do not use too much polish. A small amount well rubbed in produces far better results than an abundance applied lightly. Test by running your finger over the freshly polished surface; if it leaves a smeared mark the polish has been applied too liberally.

Daily dusting and frequent rubbing with soft cloths will keep polished furniture in excellent condition. As a rule, polish should not be applied every time you rub, unless the furniture has been exposed to heavy use.

Never be afraid to wipe the surface of furniture with a damp cloth to remove surface stickiness. A good cleaning solution for wood furniture can be made by adding 1 tablespoon (15 ml) of vinegar and ½ teaspoonful (2 ml) of liquid detergent to 1 quart (1 liter) of warm water.

Wipe the surface of the furniture methodically, changing the cloth or rinsing it well as it becomes grimy, to prevent redistribution of the dissolved grime.

Immediately follow this treatment with a brisk rub with a dry, soft duster, rubbing in the direction of the wood grain. Then the wood can be polished in the usual way: Spray the duster with polish; do not spray the furniture surface directly. The warmed duster ensures even distribution of the polish.

Silicone spray, again applied on the soft polishing cloth, is also good for highly lacquered finishes.

Surfaces that have always been oiled — teak, for instance — should be maintained with oil.

Do not change or mix polishes. They are often incompatible, and one used on top of another results in dinginess. In the case of waxed antiques, the solvent in another type of polish could reveal pit marks and scars that the original wax had camouflaged.

Extremely grimy furniture can be cleaned with very fine steel wool saturated with raw linseed oil. Rub lightly, wipe off with clean cloths, and polish as usual.

**Beeswax polishes.** These preserve and enhance solid woods. They are excellent for use on light woods such as pine or oak, where the use of oily polishes would darken the grain. This can be applied to wood, leather, stained wooden surfaces, iron, steel, and bronze. You will need 5 ounces (125 g) beeswax and 1¼ cups (325 ml) turpentine. Melt the beeswax in a pan and remove it from heat.

Carefully stir in the turpentine. (Remember, turpentine is flammable.)

A thicker paste wax is obtained by using less turpentine. A lighter-colored polish can be made by using purified beeswax instead of the yellow.

To make a creamy wax, you will need 3 ounces (75 g) white beeswax, 1 cup (250 ml) turpentine, and 1 cup (250 ml) hot water. Melt the beeswax in a clean pan and remove it from the heat. Stir in the turpentine and then the water. Add ½ teaspoon (5 ml) cloudy ammonia to emulsify the mixture. This wax is excellent for use on inlays and veneers.

**Recommendations:** Turpentine and kerosene are toxic and flammable. Always use with extreme caution, and store according to hazardous waste regulations. Store in a sealed container.

**Availabilty:** Beeswax can be purchased at crafts and health food stores.

**Oil-based furniture polishes**. These are appropriate for use on dark woods, such as cherry or mahogany. Apply sparingly on a slightly dampened cloth and polish with a dry duster. Oily polishes or raw linseed oil rubbed into the *underside* of antique tabletops "feed" the wood and help to prevent cracking, which can occur in dry climates. Do not use if a synthetic finish has been applied to the wood.

**Synthetic furniture finishes.** Cellulose and polyurethane finishes are found on many items of furniture. The glossy surfaces are hard and durable. Regular dusting and the occasional application of liquid silicone polish will maintain them well.

If the finish becomes sticky or dull, wipe it over with a sponge cloth wrung out of warm detergent suds containing 1 tablespoon (15 ml) vinegar. Wipe with a second clean damp cloth, then dry and polish in the usual way.

Care must be taken with the use of plastic items on polyurethane surfaces. Plastic reacts with the finish and causes erosion, which will require professional treatment to remedy. Heatproof mats should be underlined with cork or felt.

**White untreated wood furniture.** Scrub with cold water containing household bleach. Rub stains with a cut lemon sprinkled with salt. If that fails, mix equal parts of hydrogen peroxide and cloudy ammonia. Saturate a pad of cotton wool and leave it on the stain for several hours. Rinse well.

**Bamboo and cane furniture.** Vacuum with brush attachment to remove dust. Wipe over with a damp cloth and polish with silicone wax.

Very dirty and neglected pieces can be scrubbed gently with warm soapy water. If possible, work outside. A hose can be used to rinse off the suds, provided the spray is fine. Dry in indirect sunlight and polish with silicone wax.

The sagging woven cane seat of a chair or stool can be tightened. Work out of doors, and sponge the cane

**Stripping Paint from Wood Surfaces**

Follow instructions on the product's label. Work outdoors, over thick pads of newspaper.

High-gloss cellulose finish on solid wood furniture can be removed with a cellulose thinner.

Dark oak can be lightened by removing the stain with paint stripper, following manufacturer's directions. When the oak is dry, sand the surface evenly to remove the remaining stain. Then, treating a small area at a time, rub in warmed linseed oil applied with a soft duster. Repeat 2 or 3 times. Leave for 2 days until the oil is thoroughly absorbed, then polish with white wax or silicone cream.

**Hint:** It is difficult to successfully remove polyurethane or cellulose high-gloss finish from veneers. Often it is best to avoid lifting and buckling of the veneer by simply painting over the varnish with an attractive antique-type paint finish.

with a salt solution: 1 cup (250 ml) of salt in 1 cup (250 ml) of boiling water. Do not wet surrounding bentwood. Dry outdoors and do not sit in the seat for 24 hours.

**Carved furniture.** Carved furniture needs regular maintenance or dust will settle in the grooves. Vacuum regularly, using the brush attachment.

Use a clean paintbrush or old shaving brush dipped in furniture oil or silicone wax to keep carved wood clean and polished.

**Drawers.** Drawers that do not run smoothly should be examined for loose runners, nails, or screws. Drawers sometimes expand and stick during wet weather, but the wood will shrink again when the atmosphere is drier. In the meantime, rub the runners with candle wax, beeswax, or paste polish to make the drawers operate more smoothly.

**Ebony.** Wash with a cloth wrung out in vinegar water made of 1 tablespoon (15 ml) vinegar per 2 cups (500 ml) water. Polish with raw linseed oil. This treatment will keep ebony dark and shining.

**Enameled furniture.** Wipe over with a damp cloth once a week. Occasionally wipe with a cloth wrung out of warm mild detergent suds containing a teaspoonful (5 ml) of borax, or use a soft emulsion-type cleaner on a damp cloth. Remove traces of the suds and cleaner with a second damp cloth. Polish with silicone wax if the paint is dull.

**Gilt trimmings.** Often found on painted furniture, mirrors, and picture frames, these need regular dusting. If the gilt appears dull, brighten it by rubbing it very gently with a soft cloth sprinkled with mineral spirits. Spray silicone cream onto a clean duster and polish lightly.

**Inlaid furniture.** This requires careful handling to protect the thin inlays. Polishing cloths should be smooth and unfrayed; loose threads could lift the corners of the inlay. Use a light-colored wax polish rather than oil; the latter will darken lighter inlays and detract from the general appearance.

**Leather upholstery** enjoys a well-earned reputation for durability unmatched by other upholstery materials. Only minimal maintenance is needed — an occasional wipe with a piece of soft toweling or a sponge cloth wrung out of warm suds made with a wool-washing liquid or powder, or with a smudge of dishwashing soap or glycerin soap on the damp cloth.

Treat about one square yard (meter) at a time and go over the cleaned section with a second cloth wrung out of clear water. This will remove traces of dissolved grime and soap. Create a cross-breeze in the room so the damp leather will dry quickly. Never expose upholstery leather to strong sunlight.

This simple treatment two or three times a year, depending on what use the furniture has had, will keep the upholstery clean and shining.

**Marble surfaces.** Undiluted liquid detergent applied on a soft cloth will remove light stains from marbled surfaces. To remove other stains, rub with toothpaste, then rinse off. Rub with a cloth moistened with turpentine to restore the polish.

Badly discolored and neglected marble can be brightened by smearing heavily with a paste made of mild scouring powder and crushed washing soda (two parts soda to one part powder). Mix to a paste with boiling water and leave on the marble for 24 hours. Wipe off, then polish with turpentine or silicone wax. *Note:* Protect marble from acids — they will erode the surface.

**Wicker furniture.** Wickerwork is created by weaving or plaiting water reeds or osiers, and it benefits by being thoroughly wet down from time to time. However, this treatment is limited if wicker is combined with wood. First vacuum, using the brush attachment, to extract surface dust. Scrub with light detergent suds containing one tablespoon (15 ml) borax. Avoid overwetting. Rinse off with a textured cloth, lightly wrung out of clean

**Oxalic Acid**

This acid is poisonous and must be handled cautiously. Wear gloves.

Thoroughly hose out the bucket used for rinsing. Contact your local hazardous waste authority for proper disposal of the cloths and can that held this mixture.

water containing salt. Dry in a breezy place, out of direct sunlight. When the wickerwork is completely dry, spray with silicone furniture cream. Do not sit on wicker seats until they are completely dry; wet wicker will sag.

Wax stripper, the kind used for removing accumulated wax polish from floors, also can be used to remove wax from old furniture. Test on an inconspicuous section before proceeding.

Oxalic acid is also a good bleach to whiten stripped, stained furniture. Mix in the proportion of 1 ounce (25 g) to a full cup (250 ml) of warm water. Mix the solution in an old can using a stick. Stand the can on several sheets of newspaper as you work. Paint the acid on to the wood and let it dry. Then, still wearing gloves, rinse it off with plenty of cold water containing ½ cup (125 ml) of ammonia, which will neutralize the acid.

## FURS

Ideally, any fur garment should be professionally cleaned once a year before it is stored for the summer. Stains caused by cosmetics, drinks, and food spills provide attractive lures for moths, which can ruin a fur.

Furriers will clean and store fur garments if home facilities are inadequate. However, it is not always convenient or economical to store a fur. Storage at home means that the fur is readily accessible. Providing certain guidelines are followed, a fur can be adequately stored at home.

A dull, brittle fur needs professional cleaning, but a lustrous fur with an isolated stain can be treated at home. Lightly sponge a stain on a dark fur with drycleaning fluid.

Rub oven-heated bran (the edible kind, which is cleaner) into a light-colored fur. Work over an old sheet; roll up the fur and leave it for three days before shaking it out of doors and brushing it lightly with a clean clothes brush.

Sponge the lining with drycleaning fluid, particularly around the neckline where cosmetics and perspiration stains are most evident. Avoid overuse of the cleaner. It should not penetrate to the backing.

Store the fur on a well-padded hanger in a bag made of unbleached calico. This bag should be longer than the garment, so that paradichlorobenzene crystals (from a hardware store or drugstore) can be placed in the bottom of the bag where they will not come in contact with the fur. These crystals are an exellent moth deterrent, but they can cause discoloration if they come into direct contact with the fur over a long period. Use about 1 tablespoonful (15 ml) of crystals. Tie the bag firmly around the crook of the hanger.

The fur should be examined every six weeks for moths. Shake it well and air it in the shade, never in the sun. Place fresh crystals in the bag to compensate for evaporation of the original ones. Retie the bag tightly.

## GLASS

To clean discolored glass, soak in ammonia and water for several hours. Or, soak in vinegar with the contents of a tea bag, then wash and rinse. Badly discolored glass can be cleaned by soaking it in acetone for a few hours. Follow with a thorough wash and rinse.

To clean glass tabletops, try rubbing them with lemon juice. For scratches in glass tabletops, try rubbing some toothpaste on the scratch.

**Glass chandeliers.** To clean glass chandeliers, wipe the prisms with a soft cloth moistened with commercial window cleaner or with water containing 1 tablespoon (15 ml) ammonia. The use of ammoniated water helps to remove insect marks more easily.

If the prisms merely need dusting, brush them lightly with a feather duster; or slip on a pair of old cotton gloves, dampen them, and wipe over the crystals by hand.

If it is possible to take down the chandelier for cleaning, line a tub or sink with an old towel, and add warm water, detergent, and a tablespoon (15 ml) of ammonia. Wash and rinse carefully. Then spray with silicone wax.

Wipe the light bulbs and check the metal pieces attached to the pendants before rehanging.

## HAIRBRUSHES

Brushes are more easily cleaned if two are washed at the same time. Scrub one with the other to clean bases and bristles. Dip in soapy water containing 1 teaspoon (5 ml) ammonia to dissolve grease. Rinse well. Dry brushes on their sides to prevent distortion of the bristles.

Wash combs in the same solution, scrubbing the teeth with a nailbrush.

## HANDBAGS

**Evening bags.** Keep taffeta or satin linings clean by sponging lightly with drycleaning fluid. Air well before closing the bag.

Beaded bags should be treated with care: One broken thread and beads will be lost. Dust white-beaded bags with talcum powder and enclose the bag in a folded towel. Leave it there for 48 hours, then brush lightly to remove the powder.

**Leather bags** can be sponged with a cloth wrung out of warm water, then lightly rubbed with good quality soap. Wipe off the soapy deposits with two or three clean damp cloths. When the bag is dry, polish with leather polish or cream. Then leave the bag in the sun for half an hour so that the polish will be absorbed and it will not rub off onto clothing.

Brush or vacuum the lining to remove fluff and dust. Sponge soil marks with drycleaning fluid and air well before closing the bag.

Never store a leather handbag on or under a plastic handbag. The plastic bag will absorb dye from the leather bag and it will become permanently stained.

Leather bags might become moldy in wet humid weather, and stored bags should be examined frequently under these adverse climatic conditions.

Mildew can be removed from leather bags, belts, and shoes by wiping or brushing it off outdoors. Wipe the mildewed surface with a damp cloth. When dry, rub in petroleum jelly. Let the vaseline absorb before cleaning in the usual way.

Wipe with a damp cloth to remove light soil marks and perspiration, then spray with silicone wax and rub gently.

**Patent leather bags.** Buff to a shine with a little petroleum jelly or silicone spray.

**Plastic bags.** Sponge clean with a damp cloth lightly coated with a good quality household soap. Wipe off the soapy residue with several damp cloths; dry, then spray with silicone wax and buff to a glow.

**Suede bags** should be brushed frequently using a suede-cleaning brush. Grease marks, often caused by perspiring hands, can be sponged with drycleaning fluid.

Raise the flattened nap by rubbing lightly with fine sandpaper.

A light steaming will also raise a flattened nap. Hold the bag briefly over steam rising from boiling water in a shallow pan — the less water, the more steam. Prolonged steaming might dissolve adhesives. Dry, then use a sponge or a suede brush to raise the nap.

## HARDWOOD FLOORS

Hardwood floors, if well sealed, need little maintenance. Common sealants include varnish and polyurethane. For either type, damp mopping will remove grime;
dry mopping on a daily basis will get rid of dust and grit
that can get ground in and wear away the finish.

In time, even with care, traffic areas will show signs
of wear. Touch up these areas with the same type of sealant originally used on the floor. Because some sealants
are incompatible, it is not advisable to use one type on
top of another. And if a floor has had even one coat of
wax, it cannot be sealed successfully unless every trace
of wax has been removed, usually accomplished by
resanding the entire floor.

Sealant protects the boards from moisture, which
can cause warping and coarsen the grain.

Chairs and movable furniture should be fitted with
protective plastic glides to avoid damage to the seal.

## KITCHEN COUNTERTOPS

Countertops are durable and easy to maintain, but
care should be taken not to use them as cutting boards
or as a rest for hot pans. Always use a cutting board when
slicing anything. If the counter is used as a cutting
board even once, microscopic cuts or scratches result that
will collect traces of grime. These will dull the sheen
of the laminate. Always place some protection under
hot pots.

Always use a clean cloth or sponge when wiping the
kitchen countertops.

## KITCHEN SINK

**Enamel and porcelain-enamel sinks** are less durable
than stainless steel. Enamel will chip easily, so it is advisable to line the bottom of an enamel sink with a

plastic or rubber mat when washing up heavy ovenproof dishes and saucepans. An emulsion-type cleaner can be used to remove light stains that do not respond to powdered or liquid detergent. Severe stains will respond to soaking with diluted household bleach or to an application of a paste made by mixing cream of tartar with peroxide.

**Fiberglass sinks** are attractive, but they scratch easily. Care should be taken when washing cutlery or sharp household items. Keep fiberglass sinks shiny by wiping them with liquid detergent on a damp cloth. Rinse with hot water and wipe dry.

**Plastic sinks** are not intended for heavy use. They are light and ideal for use in recreational vehicles and small boats. They must be protected from scratches and burns caused by hot pots and dishes and cigarettes. Spilled chemicals will dull the surface, and cracks might be caused by dropped articles, such as cans of food from an above-sink cupboard. To clean plastic sinks, use metal polish.

**Stainless steel sinks** are very durable for family use and require little maintenance. To remove grease, use liquid detergent on a soft cloth. An emulsion cleaner may be used occasionally to restore the sheen. The use of powdered detergents can cause rainbow effects on stainless steel. If you use a powdered detergent, rinse completely and dry the stainless steel immediately.

## LACE

Because of its delicacy, lace should be handled carefully. The weight of water can cause tears. Valuable old lace can be washed in a large jar with a firm-fitting lid. Add mild detergent or soap flakes to warm water in the jar, tighten the lid, and shake until it is well mixed. Then immerse the lace and shake the jar for a minute or so. Rinse in the same way.

If the lace is very frail, tack it to a white cloth before washing it. After washing and rinsing, simply spread out the cloth and the lace to dry.

Never use bleach on old lace. Rain or dew will bleach it naturally. Tack the lace to a towel or sheet and peg the ends between two clotheslines, like a hammock. This will expose the lace to dew or rain in a safe, off-the-ground position.

Wash frail lace curtains inside a pillowcase after folding each one loosely. Thus protected, they can be pushed up and down in mild suds and rinsed in the same way after sudsy water has been pressed out.

Press lace on the wrong side so that the pattern will be raised. Every care should be taken not to dig the point of the iron into the fine threads. Lead with the back or the side of the iron to avoid this possibility.

## LAMB'S WOOL

Wash in very cool suds with wool-washing detergent or mild soap flakes. Dry inside out. Sweaters dry best on a plastic drying rack. Or slip the legs of a pair of pantyhose through the sleeves and peg the toes and waist of the pantyhose to the line.

## LAMPSHADES

Stitched, fabric-covered lampshades are washable. Swirl them around in tepid detergent suds, rinse under a running tap, pat with a towel to absorb excess water, and dry as quickly as possible.

Shades that are glued must not be wet; the adhesive will not withstand water. Instead, first dust them by brushing with a clean clothes brush, then wipe the shades on both sides with a piece of toweling moistened with drycleaning fluid. Change the position of the cloth frequently to prevent the redistribution of loosened grime.

Scorch marks caused by the heat of a light blub that is too large or too strong for a small shade cannot be removed. The material is weakened by heat, and treatment usually results in damage to the shade.

Parchment shades should be dusted regularly. Occasionally they can be wiped over with a barely damp cloth or rubbed with a slice of fairly fresh bread. Work over newspaper to catch the grimy crumbs as they fall.

Plastic and fiberglass shades can be washed in tepid detergent suds. Rinse well. After drying, rub lightly with a cloth dampened with spray-on silicone wax.

Collapsible balloon or pendant-shaped paper shades must not get wet. Dust them well; then, working over an old sheet, sprinkle them freely with powdered starch or talcum powder. Let the shades collapse, wrap them loosely in the sheet, and leave them for 24 hours. Dust again to remove traces of powder.

## LEATHER

Clean leather items or upholstery with a damp cloth and some saddle soap. Prevent leather from cracking by polishing occasionally with a solution of vinegar and linseed oil (1:2).

To remove white water spots from leather, cover the spots with a thick coat of petroleum jelly, and leave it in place for a few days. Wipe with a soft cloth. Petroleum jelly and hairspray will also remove ballpoint ink from leather.

## LINED GARMENTS

Follow the manufacturer's label. Many need to be drycleaned because laundering will distort the lining and interlining, causing the garment to lose its shape.

## LINEN

Pure linen is a natural fiber made from flax. Many linen fabrics contain blends of synthetic fibers. Soiled garments should be pre-soaked for 10 minutes in warm suds, then washed in hot suds and rinsed twice. Remove pure linen garments from the line or dryer while still slightly damp, and if a sheen is not desirable, press with a hot iron on the wrong side. Press on the right side if a sheen is preferred. Press synthetic linen combinations with a cooler iron; test on an inner seam if you are in doubt. Air well before storing in a closet.

## MARBLE

To remove stains and water marks from marble, use a cream-type silver polish. Or scrub with a paste of salt and lemon juice. For persistent stains, treat with hydrogen peroxide and a couple drops of ammonia. Pour the mixture on the stain, wait a few minutes, then wash and rinse the area.

It is important to remember not to rub marble surfaces too hard. Always try nonabrasive cleaners and approaches first. If possible, move the marble item into the sunlight.

Oil-based cleaners or waxes can cause discoloration of marble and should be avoided.

## MIRRORS

Make your own cleaning solution for mirrors: Mix 2 tablespoons (30 ml) of vinegar and 5 tablespoons (75 ml) of ammonia in 1 quart (1 liter) of water.

## MOHAIR

Hand wash in plenty of very cool suds using a wool-washing detergent or hair shampoo. Rinse twice. Hand-knitted mohair sweaters might stretch with the weight of water in them, so launder them by hand in a tub with a plug. Squeeze and knead to loosen grime. Remove the plug and press out surplus water. Add cold rinsing water and repeat. Avoid allowing the incoming water to hit the garment with force as the tub refills. Finally, roll the garment in a thick towel and press out as much water as possible. Dry flat, inside out, and turn the garment halfway through the drying time. Thick wads of newspaper spread over a clean cement surface or a dry lawn and weighted down can be used to keep drying garments clean and to speed the drying process. When dry, shake lightly to raise the pile.

## NETTED MATERIALS

Some mosquito nets act as a magnet to dirt particles, either in the air or in washing water. They tend to become dingy looking unless they are washed frequently and separately.

Shake the net, pre-soak it for 15 minutes in cool detergent suds, then launder it in cool detergent suds. Rinse three times. Dry in the shade. Sunlight will yellow these nets.

Cotton nets can be machine-washed without any problem. Shake, pre-soak, then wash. Carefully pull the net into shape to dry in full sunshine.

Holes in nets can be mended almost invisibly by covering them with a larger patch of net dipped in raw starch, that is, starch made into a thick paste with cold water. Arrange the patch over a hole, cover it with brown paper, and press with a fairly hot iron. Be very careful not to let the iron touch the surrounding net.

## NYLON

Nylon has a static electricity effect that attracts dirt and grime particles. If these work into the fiber, restoring the original clean appearance will prove more difficult.

Nylon articles should be laundered after every wear, using warm water and detergent or soap flakes. Wash thoroughly, rinse very well, and drip-dry immediately.

Stains on nylon fabrics should be treated before they set. Drycleaning fluid and spot cleaners can be used on nylon, but liquid bleach must not be used, unless advised on the label.

When nylon is blended with another fiber, for instance with cotton or wool, wash the garment according to the requirements of the weaker fabric. The labels on fabric bolts and on garments will show the percentages of each. If ironing is necessary, use only a low-set iron.

Nylon and nylon-blended fabrics will cling to the body in dry cold weather or in an atmosphere controlled by air conditioning, which reduces the amount of moisture in the air. Static cling can be reduced by adding fabric softener (*not* water softener) to the final rinse once in four or five launderings.

## ORGANDY

This is a fine, stiffened fabric usually made of cotton. Wash in plenty of hand-hot water in which mild soap flakes have been well dissolved. Push the garment up and down in the suds but do not scrub or rub. Rinse two or three times. Slip the garment onto a hanger to dry and remove it from the clothesline while still slightly damp. Press at once with a medium-hot iron to restore the garment's crispness, and continue to iron until the organdy is quite dry. An extra natural crispness can be imparted by dipping the nearly dry garment in 4 cups (1 liter) warm water containing 1 tablespoon (15 ml) borax. Then rehang until it is time to iron the garment. Light spray starch can also be applied when ironing.

Some organdy blends scorch easily. Be cautious when ironing.

## OVEN

Much has been done to improve stove finishes so that cleaning the stove is not as difficult as it once was. Lift-off oven doors and removable enameled trays fitted to line the floors of the oven and grill have simplified oven cleaning.

There is a growing demand for self-cleaning oven surfaces. These work in two ways:

1. Pyrolytic cleaning is the process by which the oven is heated to a certain high temperature, which reduces spatters and general oven soil to fine ash. There is a separate control for this cleaning cycle, which takes up to two hours. During this period, the oven door must be kept closed.
2. Continuous or catalytic cleaning is carried on with normal cooking temperatures whenever the oven is used.

For older-type ovens without these built-in cleaners, the use of a commercial cleaner is advised. These are available in spray, paste, liquid, cream, or stick form, and all work in much the same way, dissolving burnt-on grease, which can then be wiped away. The liquid cleaners should be handled carefully, and the area in front of the stove should be protected to avoid ruining the floor. Gloves should be worn when any cleaner is used.

Unless otherwise indicated by the manufacturer, the best time to clean the oven is after cooking, while the oven is still warm. Softened by heat, the grease and soil marks are more easily removed.

Oven cleaning can be minimized if a few general hints are observed:

➤ Meat and foods that have a tendency to spatter should be covered with foil or be enclosed in an oven bag.

➤ Slip a layer of foil or a tray under puddings, casseroles, or pies that might have a tendency to run over and drip.

➤ Always wipe out the oven while it is warm. This also applies to the see-through glass oven door. Dip a damp cloth in a little ammonia to aid in cleaning.

If an oven cleaner is not available, saturate a cloth with ammonia and wipe the sides, floor, and door of the oven. Put about ½ cup (125 ml) ammonia in a saucer with the cloth, and close the door. The ammonia fumes will soften the carbonized grease, and after 8 hours it can be removed by wiping with a soapy steel wool pad. Wipe clean with a damp cloth — traces of soap or detergent also bake on with heat.

Do not use caustic or gritty cleaners on the main outer surface of the stovetop. If there are stains, use an emulsion-type cleaner on a damp cloth.

If the stainless steel trays under the coils on your electric burners are irremovable, lift the coils and pour about a tablespoon (15 ml) of cloudy ammonia into each tray. Leave for an hour or longer. Wearing gloves (and working in a ventilated kitchen), scrub the trays with soapy steel wool, wiping up with paper towels as you work. Wipe the trays with a cloth wrung out in light detergent suds.

This treatment will remove burnt-on deposits. Consider the use of foil liners for these trays. They will save much work.

To clean removable trays, soak them in water with ¼ cup (60 ml) of ammonia. Scrub with steel wool.

## OXIDIZED METALS

These are found in old homes, usually as door knobs and drawer and door latches. They should *not* be treated with metal polish. Instead, rub them with a damp cloth and, after a few minutes, with a cloth sprayed with silicone cream, which will offer some protection from rust.

Rusted oxidized metals should be wiped over with a soapy cloth, and then with a clean, damp cloth. Rub in petroleum jelly, machine oil, or olive oil, and let this remain for several hours. Then wipe it off and apply silicone furniture cream.

## PAINTED SURFACES

Painted surfaces, in bathrooms and kitchens especially, are subjected to steam and condensation unless a ventilator fan is installed and utilized. An occasional washing of the walls with a commercial paint cleaner helps to restore the gloss and remove traces of grime, which are detrimental to paint.

Walls should be washed from the floor level, working upward. If you start at the top, rivulets of water run toward the floor. These drips, charged with cleaner, act as grime looseners on their way down. They are difficult to remove and stand out in contrast to the areas that have been wiped over.

Start at the bottom and working up, cover about a square yard (meter) at a time. Work with two buckets, one containing the cleaning solution, the other containing clean, warm water and a sponge. Change the rinse water frequently.

## PARQUET FLOORS

These attractive wood-block floors should never be exposed to unnecessary wetting. Water or spills can cause the wooden blocks to swell and become uneven. Sometimes sanding is necessary to restore the level of the floor.

Parquet floors can be sealed or waxed. Modern seals make the blocks less vulnerable to wetness; they enhance the beauty of the grain and provide a strong, durable finish that requires only daily dry mopping to remove dust. Damp mop occasionally to clean.

The seals wear well and can be replaced in the traffic areas as they wear, usually after some years.

If the blocks have been waxed, sanding will be necessary before a seal can be applied.

If wax polish is used, apply it in time to let it dry, then buff with a polishing machine. The surface will be harder and more brilliant, and it will last longer.

Furniture legs should be protected with plastic glides or with rubber tips to prevent scratching.

## PATENT LEATHER

Wipe patent leather with a cloth dampened with vinegar. Then wipe dry with a clean, soft cloth.

## PEWTER

Modern pewter contains a high percentage of tin, and it is more tarnish-resistant than antique pewter. It requires little maintenance except for regular dusting with a soft duster.

Pewter comes in two finishes, one with a clear high sheen resembling silver and the second with a satin finish to give an antique appearance. After use, wash both kinds in hot suds, rinse in warm water, and buff with a soft cloth.

Acids will stain pewter, so avoid using pewter bowls for salads containing lemon or any other citrus juice, vinegar, pickles, sauces, or condiments unless the bowl has a liner or unless the containers or pewter servers can be washed without delay. A liner of foil can sometimes be used to protect the finish.

Some pewter flatware cannot be cleaned in a dishwasher. Check with the retailer when making a new purchase of pewter to be sure about this.

The use of pewter or silver polish will remove light scratching to which this soft metal is susceptible, and it will restore the appearance of articles that have been exposed to sea air.

## PILLOWS

**Fiber-filled pillows** tend to flatten with use. Bounce, bulk, and softness can be restored by washing them every couple months, choosing a windy day. In an automatic machine, using the shortest cycle, these pillows can be washed in cold or lukewarm water with mild detergent suds, rinsed, and spun dry. If washing by hand, use cool suds and press out the surplus water. Rinse twice, then press and roll out as much water as possible. Hang to dry in a semi-shaded breezy position, turning frequently. If water in the casing takes a long time to drip, prick the casing with a darning needle in several places.

Placing the pillow in a dryer turned to its lowest setting will also fluff the flattened filling.

**Feather pillows** also require very cool sudsing and shade drying. Heat can release traces of oil in the feathers and cause them to smell. If the featherproofed cover is very soiled, it is advisable to undo it a few inches (centimeters) and to shake out the feathers into a clean casing or into a large paper bag until the original cover can be soaked and washed. Sometimes pillows become badly stained by medicines, beverages, and so on, and specific washing of the casing is necessary. Treat the stains according to their nature; pre-soak, then wash in hand-hot suds.

**Other fillings in pillows** should be washed according to the manufacturer's instructions.

## PLUSH

Used for upholstery and curtains, plush can be made of silk, of synthetic fibers, or of rayon. Silk and rayon plushes are best drycleaned. Synthetic plush fabrics and fake fur should be treated according to the manufacturer's label.

**Plush-covered toys.** Some soft toys can be washed in a machine; others must be hand-washed, and still others should be shampooed or drycleaned. Follow instructions on the label; these will depend on the type of filling in the toy.

For toys that can be shampooed, first shake or vacuum to remove surface dust. Dampen the plush evenly, then rub in a small amount of shampoo or mild detergent. Gently scrub the nap, then remove the suds with a series of clean damp cloths. Hang to dry in a breezy position or dry in a low-set dryer. Before and during the drying process, smooth the pile with a clean clothes brush.

## POLYESTER

This fiber is used extensively in garments. Hand wash in hand-hot water; machine wash in warm or cold water to minimize wrinkling. Try to wash in a load of similarly colored garments and those of a similar fabric. Wash before the garments are badly soiled; some soil stains are difficult to remove. Hang to dry out of direct sunlight. Except for slacks, shorts, and trousers, try to hang the garments (using plastic-coated hangers) that are not being worn.

## POLYURETHANE

Polyurethane fibers have now replaced rubber for making elasticized swimwear, brassieres, foundation garments, support stockings, stretch tights, and shorts. Polyurethane is also used for fillings and paddings.

Wash **elasticized garments** in hand-hot water with detergent, or machine wash using a short cycle and warm water. Dry in semi-shade, not in direct sunlight. Do not expose to high temperature in a dryer.

## POPLIN

Once this was made of 100 percent cotton, but now it can be made of wool, silk, or rayon. It should be washed according to the composition of the fiber.

**Cotton poplin,** often used for shirts and blouses, can be washed in hot water. Dry dyed cotton poplin garments inside out; lightly starch or spray with liquid starch when ironing.

**Silk and rayon blends** require hand washing in mild warm suds. Roll wet garments in dry towels or dry garments in wet towels and iron when a uniform dampness is obtained. Or, test an inside facing to see if steam ironing is sufficient to remove wrinkles.

**Wool poplin** can be drycleaned or carefully hand-washed in cool, mild suds. Roll in a towel to absorb surplus moisture, dry inside out on a well-padded hanger, then steam press.

**Silk poplin,** like some silks, may lose its luster after it has been laundered. This can be restored by rinsing the clean damp garment in vinegar water using 2 teaspoons (10 ml) of white vinegar to one quart (liter) of cold water before drying. If this acid rinse is used, soak the garment in clean, cold water for 30 minutes before it is laundered again. Iron while slightly damp.

## PORCELAIN

For dark marks on porcelain, mix a paste of hydrogen peroxide and a scratchless cleanser. Add to this mixture ⅛ teaspoon (1 ml) of cream of tartar. Cover the stains with this mixture and let the porcelain stand for half an hour. Rub with a sponge, then rinse.

To remove the green stains on porcelain left by copper piping, combine equal parts of scratchless cleanser and cream of tartar, then add hydrogen peroxide to make a paste. Apply to the stained area and let stand half an hour. Rinse.

## QUILTED FABRICS

Hand wash delicate quilted garments. Use plenty of water of a temperature suitable for the fabric involved and mild detergent suds. Do not wring or twist. Remove spots by rubbing in detergent and scrubbing gently with a soft-bristled brush. Rinse well, press out excess water, roll in a towel to absorb still more moisture, then hang in a breezy place to dry, or dry at low temperature in a dryer.

If washing in a machine, use the shortest cycle and cool, mild suds. Rinse and spin dry. If one or two fluffy

**Caution**

Mildew spores will develop if a damp garment is left rolled up for too long. If there is to be a delay before ironing, put the garment into a plastic bag in the refrigerator or freezer. Mildew spores will not develop in low temperatures.

towels are put in the same load (space permitting), they will act as buffers and protect the padded fabrics.

Dry jackets and robes on well-padded hangers, using old stockings to bolster the shoulder line. Distribute the weight of a bedspread over two or three clotheslines, and halfway through the drying period turn the spread. You also can put it into a dryer with a very low setting to fluff up the padding.

## RAINCOATS

Soiled nylon and plastic raincoats can be washed in warm detergent suds. Rinse thoroughly and drip-dry on a plastic hanger.

Remove mud marks on nylon coats by spreading the soiled area on a flat surface and gently scrubbing with a nailbrush.

## RAYON

These fibers can be woven to simulate such fibers as linen, wool, silk, and cotton. However, rayon is not as strong as these fibers, and it is noticeably weaker when wet. Care should be taken not to wring, twist, or scrub wet rayon. Wash rayon garments frequently to make hard washing unnecessary.

Rayon invariably requires ironing, and this should be done while the garment is slightly and evenly damp: Roll the dry garment in the folds of a damp towel. After half an hour, when the garment is evenly damp, iron it using the rayon setting on the iron — a moderately hot setting. Air the garment before putting it away.

Iron glossy rayons on the right side and dull rayons on the reverse side.

## REFRIGERATOR

Once a week, wash the refrigerator, vegetable crispers, and meat storage bins in cool detergent suds; rinse and dry well. Wipe the interior of the refrigerator with a cloth wrung out of a baking soda solution, one rounded tablespoon (15 ml) to 1 quart (liter) warm water. This is an effective cleaner that leaves no odor. Odors will develop if food is left uncovered or if it becomes bad. Wash out the interior as suggested, and place 1 tablespoon (15 ml) pure vanilla extract in a saucer on a middle shelf. Leave it there for 48 hours.

Tuck an open box of baking soda on a shelf in the back of the refrigerator where it cannot be spilled. The baking soda will absorb food odors. Change the box every four to six weeks. Pour the old box down sink or tub drains to keep them sweet-smelling. Dissolve by running warm water from the tap.

Charcoal is a cheap and effective odor absorber. Dampen a sizable lump and keep it in the egg compartment where it will not mark other foods. It helps to keep the refrigerator sweet-smelling. Hardware stores stock "odor-eaters," which are also effective.

In damp or humid weather, the outside of the refrigerator might "sweat." Wipe it frequently, using a clean, dry towel. Mold will quickly develop where there are traces of food or grime.

To clean black mold from rubber and plastic gaskets around the doors, use 3 parts cold water to 1 part household bleach. Pull a thin cloth dipped in the solution over an ice pick and run it down the pleats and grooves in the door seals. Be careful not to puncture the gaskets. Change the position of the cloth frequently. Alternatively, use an old sterilized toothbrush as a scrubbing tool.

## SATEEN

Known as "poor man's satin," sateen can be made of pure cotton, rayon, or a blend of silk and cotton.

**100 percent cotton sateen** can be treated as any cotton. Use hot water and detergent or soap suds, rinse and dry. Iron on the wrong side first with a light spray of liquid starch, then lightly on the right side to restore the sheen.

**Silk-cotton sateen and rayon sateen** should be washed by hand in lukewarm water with mild detergent or soap flakes. Rinse twice, and strip, rather than wring, out excess water. Press with a moderately hot iron while still slightly damp, or drip-dry.

## SATIN

This material is now available in several fibers, and the manufacturer's instructions should be observed.

**Silk satin** is often made into underwear. Wash silk underwear by hand in mild soap and very cold water.

**Satin made with acetate** is practically crease-resistant. It should be washed before becoming badly soiled; use warm water and liquid detergent or mild soap flakes. Do not wring or twist. Push the garment up and down in the water until soiling dissolves. Rinse twice and drip-dry until almost dry, then iron immediately or roll the wet garment in a towel until it is evenly damp and can be ironed.

**Crepe satin** has a sheen on one side and a crepe backing, and often both finishes are combined in garment making. Wash as above. While there is still a slight dampness in the garment, press with a slightly hotter iron, using long sweeps. (Slower, more deliberate strokes with the iron will leave impressions in the fabric.) If in doubt about which temperature to use, test the heat of the iron on an inside facing or seam. Drycleaning is advisable.

## SHEEPSKIN

Coats, rugs, car seats, and so on can be drycleaned to perfection by any cleaner skilled in cleaning animal skins.

If cleaning at home is desirable and the fleece is not badly soiled, try using a carpet-cleaning powder; sprinkle it into the fleece and work it in well with your fingers. Be generous with the powder, which absorbs grime and grease. Roll up the article and slip it into a plastic bag. Leave it for at least 12 hours before shaking or vacuuming to remove the powder. Brush or comb the fleece and shake again before returning the article to use.

Some articles with treated backings can be washed. Follow the manufacturer's instructions carefully. Never use hot water and try to choose a windy day so that the article will dry quickly. If using an electric dryer, set it at the lowest possible temperature.

## SHIRTS

Empty the pockets. Treat stains, if any. Rub soiled areas such as the collar band and cuffs with dampened laundry soap or treat them while they are dry with a pre-wash stain loosener. Hand wash in cool detergent suds and rinse well before drip-drying in the shade; or machine wash in the shortest cycle of an automatic machine, using cold or warm water and mild detergent suds.

When washing wash-and-wear shirts, for best results wash in a single shirts-only load, using cool suds and ample water. This gives the garments plenty of room and prevents undue creasing and wrinkling. Remove the shirts from the machine as soon as the cycle is completed and hang them at once to dry. Shirts can be tumble dried in a dryer if a low temperature setting is used, but they should be removed and hung immediately when the cycle is completed. Little or no ironing will be required.

## SHOES

Never dry wet shoes in an oven or near direct heat. Synthetic soles and uppers will become distorted and shrunken; leather shoes will shrink and crack.

Wipe mud from wet shoes and apply a coating of matching shoe polish to the damp uppers. Then stuff the shoes firmly with newspaper, pushing it compactly into the toes with the handle of a wooden spoon. This blocks the shoes into shape, and the paper will absorb some of the dampness.

For faster drying, place a low-set hair dryer or an electric fan near the damp shoes. Do not use a radiator. When the shoes are dry, buff them to a shine.

**Dyeing shoes.** The only shoes that cannot be dyed successfully are made of smooth plastic or nonporous synthetic materials. Most other shoes can be dyed to extend their life, freshen their appearance, or match a special outfit. Shoes in good condition dye best; those with creasing caused by wear will begin to crack in the creases after a short time, yet the work involved in dyeing these shoes might be justified if it saves the cost of new ones.

Apply the dye with light strokes and try not to overlap applications. Let the first coat dry, then give the shoes another application. Several coats deepen the color. Each coat should be light — heavy applications tend to crack.

If matching shoes to a specific color, test one small area first and allow it to dry. Colors lighten when dry.

Masking tape can be used to cover sole and heel edges and the inside of shoes. Wear rubber gloves and work over newspaper to avoid staining skin and countertops.

**Fabric shoes.** Canvas, denim, satin, and brocade shoes can be protected against bad soil marks by spraying them when they are new with a fabric protector. This will make them water-repellent and less likely to stain. Reapplications will be necessary if canvas and denim shoes are washed.

Brush fabric shoes after each use. An old toothbrush can be kept for this purpose. It is stiff enough to treat fabrics and it can be washed and dried easily.

Use a matching felt pen to touch up scuff marks on the heels of good shoes grated by gravel or worn while driving a car.

**Suggestion**
Turpentine will soften dried shoe polish. Pour 1 to 3 teaspoons (5 to 15 ml) over the caked polish and leave the container in strong sunlight until it softens. Stir with a twig, mixing in more turpentine if necessary.

**Patent leather.** Clean with neutral creams, silicone sprays, or a smear of petroleum jelly to restore the shine. Rub well with a soft cloth.

Do not let heels wear down to the heel coverings before having them repaired.

**Storing out-of-season shoes and boots.** Polish or clean shoes in the usual way and make sure they are quite dry before they are stored.

Vinyl footwear can be stored in plastic bags, but leather and suede footwear should be wrapped in soft cloths or tissue paper. Leather will dry out if stored in plastic.

Ideally, shoes should be blocked with paper or shoe trees. Stuff the shafts of boots with paper.

Make a point of inspecting stored footwear (and belts, bags, and travel goods) for mold in damp and humid weather.

**Fleecy, wool- and fur-lined slippers and boots.** Clean before they are stored during the summer months. Insert the hose end of a vacuum cleaner inside the footwear and vacuum well. Then dust the lining with carpet-cleaning powder, talcum powder, or powdered starch and let this remain for 24 hours before vacuuming again. This treatment will absorb grease and perspiration and will freshen the linings.

Protect these linings from moths and silverfish by slipping a few paradichlorobenzene crystals into each shoe before storing. Wrap as suggested above.

**Suede shoes and boots.** Brush the footwear thoroughly to remove dust before applying suede cleaners, which are readily available in several shades. Use according to directions. Light stains can be erased and flattened nap raised by rubbing the suede gently with fine steel wool or sandpaper. Suede footwear can be renovated by a drycleaner who specializes in the cleaning of skin garments.

Old suede shoes with flattened nap can be rejuvenated by polishing. Stuff the shoes with paper or insert shoe trees, and rub in matching paste polish. Let this dry in the sun and then apply two or three more coats, letting each dry, before finally buffing to a shine.

To treat stains on suede, use an art gum eraser. Small spots on suede can be rubbed with a nail file.

**Rubber boots.** Wipe or hose off dirt and mud each time the boots are worn. Do not apply shoe polishes of any kind. To store, stuff balls of newspaper in the toes and shaft of each boot so that they maintain their shape. Stand in a paper grocery bag and place in a cool cupboard.

Wet rubber boots will dry quickly if a low-set hair dryer is trained inside each boot. Alternatively, stuff the boots with old towels or balls of newspaper to absorb the dampness.

## SILK

Pure silk or fabrics with silken blends should be washed in warm water and mild liquid detergent or soap flakes. Care must be taken not to apply stress by rubbing, twisting, or wringing. Gently squeeze the garment in the suds. Rinse three or four times to remove all traces of soap or detergent.

If washing removes the natural sheen from a silk garment, simply rinse it in cold water containing 2 teaspoons (10 ml) white vinegar. This acid must be soaked out before the garment is washed the next time. Use cold water in a nonmetal container, and soak for 30 minutes.

Restore slight stiffness to silk by misting the surface with liquid spray-on starch while ironing. Hold the pump upright at a greater distance than is usually required and spray very lightly.

## SILVER

Silver is a metal that enhances any setting. Its appearance improves with use and its maintenance is made easy with readily available polishes.

There are several excellent silver cleaners on the market. Long-term silver cleaners and foams save much work. Silver dips should be used with caution. If silver plating is wearing thin and the base metal is exposed, the use of silver dip will cause dark stains. These can be removed by repeated applications of silver polish.

**Silver cutlery** soon becomes stained with egg, salt, vinegar, and condiments. Intensive cleaning can be avoided if silver cutlery is immersed in hot water containing a little liquid detergent as soon as it is cleared from the table.

Restauranteurs find they need to have their plated cutlery replated more frequently since the advent of commercial dishwashers. Electroplaters, the people who restore worn silverware to its pristine beauty, are unanimous in their belief that dishwashing detergents cause the erosion of the plate more quickly than does everyday use and subsequent manual washing in milder suds.

Tarnish marks on egg spoons and on the tips of fork tines can be removed quickly by placing them in an old aluminum saucepan with sufficient cold water to cover the tarnish marks. Add 1 teaspoon (5 ml) baking soda per 2 cups (500 ml) water. Bring to simmering point for a few minutes, then rub with a silver polishing cloth to restore the shine.

Larger neglected and badly tarnished articles or silver articles with ornamentation can be enclosed in crumpled foil and boiled in the same way with baking soda in an aluminum saucepan. This method of tarnish removal subjects the silver plating to less wear and tear than does sustained rubbing. The treatment will dull the silver a little, but this can be restored by rubbing lightly with a soft cloth and silver polish.

Silversmiths, usually listed in the Yellow Pages under "Electroplating," or simply "Plating," can perform miracles with dented and worn sterling or plated articles. The cost is well justified, particularly in the case of worn cutlery and teapots.

Care should be taken with **silver-plated saltshakers** during wet or humid weather. Salt will quickly erode the plating and the base metal. Make a habit of removing salt from a silver shaker that is not in regular use. Wash and dry the shaker thoroughly.

Bluish-green deposits around the shaker hole or above the glass liner of a silver or silver-plated saltshaker are a sign of corrosion. Remove the deposit as soon as possible by repeated rubbing with silver polish. A smear of olive oil over the area will protect it until the shaker is used again. Remove the oil before use.

**Silver coffee- and teapots and lidded jugs** should not be stored with the lids closed. Frequently a musty smell will develop, and this is difficult to remove.

**An End to Tarnish**

Silver cutlery will not tarnish during long storage if it is thoroughly dried and wrapped in sets in aluminum foil. Store in a cardboard box or wrap in a cloth and keep the cutlery in a dry place. Dampness and humidity cause tarnish.

You can keep a lump of sugar in an unused, stored tea- or coffeepot to prevent mustiness, but in some climates the sugar will attract pests such as ants and cockroaches. If the pot has been dried thoroughly and the lid is left open, mustiness will not develop.

A deposit of tannin in a silver teapot can be removed with a commercial tannin dissolver or with borax, using 1 rounded teaspoonful (5 ml) to 1 quart (liter) boiling water in the pot. Let the solution stand until it cools, then discard the water and scrub the inside of the pot with a nylon brush. Use pipe cleaners or a fine bottle brush to clean the spout. If the drain holes are badly corroded with tannin, work from the inside and force the pipe cleaner up the spout. Rinse several times.

**Embossed and ornamented** silver pieces benefit from an application of silver polish. To remove all traces of polish, rub with a cloth dampened with ammonia. The use of an old shaving brush helps to work polish into ornamentation. Rinse in hot suds, then in clear hot water. Dry and buff.

Not all mold spots can be removed. Once silver plating has eroded, the damage is done and replating is the only solution. Some spots will respond to rubbing with ammonia applied on a soft cloth. Another possibility is to make a paste of baking soda and warm water and to rub it into the spots with a strip of uncrumpled aluminum foil. *Note:* Crumpled foil can scratch the soft silver surfaces.

A silver-polishing cloth is useful for the quick maintenance of silver in daily use. Discount and department stores stock these, or they can be made at home.

Use an old soft dish towel or a hemmed square of old flannel dipped in a silver-cleaning solution. Dry and store the cloth in a plastic bag; use it to rub silver after it is washed. Afterwards, rewash the silver if it will be in contact with food. The cloth can be washed regularly and redipped.

## SLIPCOVERS

Most slipcovers made of linen or cotton can be washed at home. However, before washing them for the first time, multicolored materials should be tested to see if the dye is fast, particularly if the background is light.

To test for colorfastness, spread a section over the ironing board and cover it with a wet white cloth. Press with a hot iron. If the white cloth is stained with dye, have the covers drycleaned.

Having removed the covers, shake them well to remove surface dust and fluff.

Remove grease spots by spreading them over a padded towel and sponging the area with drycleaning fluid. Work outdoors and away from flame.

Wash one cover at a time. Pre-soak it in tepid detergent suds for 10 minutes. Drain that water and wash in equally cool suds, gently scrubbing the soiled arms and headrests with a soft nailbrush. If that water is very dirty, wash yet again before rinsing twice. Add half a cupful (125 ml) of vinegar to the final rinsing water to brighten fading colors.

Hang in a single thickness, as far as possible out of direct sunlight. Remove the covers from the line while they are still slightly damp.

Press with a moderately hot iron, paying particular attention to pleats. The use of spray starch will give a better appearance.

Place the covers back on the furniture while they are slightly damp. They will more readily stretch when damp; as they dry they will shrink slightly and draw out creases. When they are quite dry, an application of a fabric protector will help to make the freshly washed covers more grime resistant. Be cautious about washing loose covers in a washing machine; the pipings can abrade and come undone with the action of the machine.

## STAINLESS STEEL

Stainless steel has proved to be a most practical metal for household use. It is used extensively for cookware, flatware (cutlery), and tableware, as well as for sinks and countertops, basins, tubs, and furniture. It is durable, attractive, and easy to maintain. Stains from the few foods that do spot stainless steel — egg, citrus fruits, salt, and mayonnaise, for example — are easily removed by light rubbing with an emulsion-type cleaner.

When choosing stainless steel articles for table use, look for those with a whiter color. These contain more nickel and will retain their new look longer. Stainless steel with a blue tinge contains more chromium; it is less expensive, though still quite durable.

Sinks, tubs, and sink boards should be wiped dry after each use. An emulsion-type cleaner will remove most stains and is less abrasive than powder cleaners.

**Note:** Never let silver dip come into contact with stainless steel as the stain will be very difficult to remove.

Stainless steel saucepans might assume rainbow hues if they are exposed to great heat. It is important to watch the saucepan until the contents come to the boiling point, then reduce the heat. Stainless steel retains heat and cooks perfectly at the lower temperature.

Simply pre-soak cooked-on food in a stainless steel pot or pan; the food will lift off easily with a rubber spatula. Never use harsh pot scrubbers to clean stainless steel cookware, just soak them a little longer in hot detergent suds.

A stainless steel cleaner that will erase heat marks is available on the market.

White water spots might form inside pots and pans that have been imperfectly wiped, then stored with the lids on. For best results rinse a hand-washed pot in hot water and dry it while it is still warm.

**Caution**
Never use steel wool on stainless steel. Instead, rub hard with a sponge or cloth and liquid detergent.

To remove grease, use liquid detergent on a soft cloth. You may use an emulsion cleaner occasionally to restore the sheen. The use of powdered detergents can cause rainbow effects on stainless steel. If one must be used, rinse completely and dry the stainless steel thoroughly and immediately.

Protect stainless steel draining boards with several thicknesses of newspaper if handling undiluted chemicals and bleaches and particularly liquid silver cleaner, which will definitely cause a stain.

## STEEL

Steel articles, such as fire tongs and pokers, some barbecue tools, frames of garden furniture, and so on, rust quickly. Rub household goods with fine, dry steel wool to remove rust, then apply rust inhibitor or rust converter (available in hardware stores) according to the manufacturer's instructions.

## SUEDE. *See under Shoes*

## SWIMWEAR

Swimwear is expensive; correct washing and storage over the winter months will ensure a longer life. It is important to read the label attached to new swimwear and to follow instructions for rinsing and washing designed to suit that particular fabric.

Before storing, if the suit has been worn in chlorinated pool water, soak it for 10 minutes in cold water containing a little water softener. Rinse in cold water, then in cold liquid detergent suds. Rinse well and dry in the shade.

If the suit has been used in saltwater, soak it for a few minutes in cold water to remove traces of salt. Rinse, then launder as suggested above.

Finally, fold the suit in shape and store it in tissue paper or a perforated plastic bag.

**Keeping Swimwear Stain-Free**

Suntan oils, sunscreens, and cosmetics often cause stains. Light rubbing with liquid detergent will usually loosen them, and they can be rinsed out under a hard-running cold water tap.

## TAFFETA

The taffeta effect is now produced in so many fibers that often it is simpler to have the article drycleaned rather than experiment with laundering methods at home. The attractive stiffness of taffeta can be lost through mishandling.

**Acetate and rayon taffetas** are often made into bedspreads, curtains, and cushion covers. Hand wash them, using as much water as possible so that the folds are suspended in water and the taffeta will not crush. Push the article up and down in the water to rinse out suspended grime.

It is generally convenient to wash these articles in a tub so that after washing and rinsing the old water can be drained and fresh water run in.

Drip-dry taffetas to retain extra stiffness. Try to avoid the mark of clotheslines on large articles such as bedspreads. This can be achieved by first laying a sheet over three or four parallel lines, then placing the spread over the sheet. Alternatively, you may peg the borders of the spread between three or four lines.

**Nylon taffetas** should be hand-washed in warm water with liquid detergent suds. Rinse twice and drip-dry. Under this category of taffeta comes stiffened taffeta, which is used for half slips and linings for

**Ironing Taffeta**
Iron taffeta while still slightly damp. A light misting of liquid starch held at a distance (so that concentrated spray will not cause blotching) will help to restore lost crispness.

garments that require light, stiff bolstering.

**Stiffened taffetas** must not be overhandled. Treat dirty hemlines with prewash spot cleaner before washing while the fabric is dry. Then spread the hemline onto a flat surface, and using a soft natural-bristled nailbrush, gently scrub the grime marks.

Use equal parts of warm water and liquid detergent to do this. Then push the garment up and down in plenty of lukewarm water with mild detergent or soap suds. Rinse twice or hang it by the waist with clothespins and lightly hose away the suds. This way, the original stiffness will be retained. If ironing is necessary, press lightly just before it is completely dry using a low-set iron.

## TIES

Expensive silk ties are best drycleaned, but they can be cleaned at home using drycleaning fluid poured into a basin. This fluid is flammable, so work in a well-ventilated place away from fire or flame.

Use an old clean toothbrush to gently scrub stains. Move the ties freely in the fluid to remove grime and dirt. Wearing gloves, strip out excess fluid with your fingers, and air the tie in the shade in a breezy place.

Most ties are now lined with a washable fabric, and with care they will retain their shape. Do not twist or wring. Hand wash in lukewarm detergent suds, removing spots with an old toothbrush. Rinse well and dripdry by hanging them over a clothesline. Finger smooth while they are still wet. If ironing is necessary, first pull the tie into shape, using long tacking threads if necessary, then steam press on the wrong side.

Wool-woven ties usually need tacking along the sides and across the wider end to maintain their shape while they are being washed.

## TIN

Some kitchen tools and gadgets are made of tin, which will rust easily if the

**Treating New Tinware**
New tinware can be treated to make it more rust-resistant. Rub lard or unsalted fat evenly onto the surfaces and bake the article in a slow oven for 15 minutes.

articles are not properly dried or if they are stored under damp or humid conditions. Dry them in sunshine or in a warm oven before storing. Remove light rust marks by rubbing with dry steel wool. Wash in hot suds, then rinse in hot water and dry well.

Aluminum has replaced most tin in baking sheets, cake pans, and so on. Tin has its disadvantages — it rusts if not properly dried, and it darkens with heat and use. While this darkening detracts from its appearance, many excellent cooks and bakers believe that such utensils cook more evenly.

Wash tin articles in hot suds, rinse thoroughly, and dry well in bright sunlight or in a warm oven. To remove burnt-on stains, after soaking in deep suds containing washing soda, rub the surface with well-soaped steel wool.

## TOWELS

Dark-dyed towels are not as absorbent as light-colored towels. It is possible that there will be dye loss during the first wash or two, so avoid dye marks on lighter articles by washing new towels alone.

Very grimy towels should be pre-soaked or put through the pre-wash cycle of the machine.

Fabric softener can be used to give softness and fluffiness to towels. This should be added to the final rinse water. Do not overuse — once in three or four washes is adequate. If softener is used too frequently, towels will feel slippery and become less absorbent.

**Absorbency.** Purchasers of some shear or cropped-pile towels complain that despite a thick pile and close weave, these towels do not absorb well. The pile is too smooth, chilly to the touch, and has a slinky feel that is unpleasant. More absorbent towels have a looped pile. Although all new towels should be washed before they are used to remove the sizing and make them more absorbent, washing has no effect on close-weaved, thick-piled towels. Here are some tips on how to make these towels more absorbent:

➤ Soak them for 12 hours in plenty of cold water with 2 tablespoons (30 ml) Epsom salts, moving frequently. Wring and wash as usual in the machine, preferably using a cold water detergent.

➤ Do not spin dry. After the rinse cycle, remove the towels from the machine and drip-dry on the line. This treatment will result in a coarser, more absorbent finish.

➤ Use and wash the towels as often as possible, following these instructions. It could take up to a dozen launderings for the towels to become more absorbent.

➤ Do not use fabric softener and do not put them in a dryer.

➤ It also helps to hang these towels in heavy rain, allowing them to dry on the clothesline as the weather improves.

## TRIACETATE

This is labeled Arnel, Trilan, or Tricel. Wash in lukewarm suds made with mild soap flakes or liquid detergent. Rinse well and drip-dry.

Many triacetates can be machine-washed, but check the label inside the garment to make sure. Wash in the shortest cycle using cold or lukewarm water; rinse and either spin dry or drip-dry. Remove garments from the machine as soon as the cycle is completed to avoid unnecessary creasing. Ironing should not be necessary, but if a touch-up is required, do so with care using a low-set steam iron when the article is dry.

## TRICOT

Read the label and wash according to the fiber used—nylon or viscose rayon.

## TULLE

Tulle is now made from a variety of fibers, and washing instructions depend on whether this fine net is basically made of nylon, rayon, or cotton. Tulle soon loses its attractive stiffness. Sometimes this can be restored by ironing it while it is still damp, using a medium-hot iron. Always test a small section first. Some tulle shrivels with heat and completely disintegrates.

To avoid digging the point of the iron into this frail fabric, work over a lightly padded board, which will provide a harder base, or lead with the side or the back of the iron rather than with the point.

Tulle edges might appear bedraggled after washing. Trim these with scissors to improve their appearance.

## TWEED

Tweed made of pure wool should be drycleaned. Even blended tweeds look better if they have been drycleaned and steam-pressed. If drycleaning costs are not justified for an old garment, wash it in lukewarm suds using a wool-washing detergent or mild soap flakes. Rinse twice. Spin dry, if possible, or roll in a towel to extract surplus water, then dry quickly in a breezy place. Steam press.

## UMBRELLAS

To clean pastel-colored nylon umbrellas that have been soiled with grime and mud, work outdoors. Open the umbrella and sponge it all over with drycleaning fluid. Use a series of clean cloths and discard each as it becomes soiled.

Next, prepare a bowl of warm soapy water. Scrub the nylon gently with a soft nailbrush. Hose inside and out to remove all traces of suds.

Wipe the inside frames with an old towel and dry the umbrella in its open position without delay. Never store a closed damp umbrella as its framework will rust.

Black umbrellas look fresher if they are sponged with cold water containing a tablespoonful (15 ml) of vinegar.

Do not oil the stiff framework; oil will stain the cover. Instead, slip a sheet of paper between the frame and the cover and spray with a rust inhibitor or rub with a soft lead pencil.

## UPHOLSTERY. *See also Furniture*

Upholstered chairs and lounges never go out of style. Regular maintenance will preserve the appearance of the upholstery material and make professional cleaning unnecessary for some time.

**Fabric upholstery.** Weekly cleaning of fabric upholstery consists of vacuuming, using the special attachment that can be inserted into folds and creases and around piped areas.

An application of spray-on fabric shield will protect new and freshly cleaned fabrics against undue soiling.

**Plush velvets and velveteen upholstery** should be vacuumed regularly. This is more effective than brushing, which merely redistributes the dust. Use drycleaning fluid occasionally to remove grimy deposits, treating small overlapping areas at a time. Test the effect of the solvent on a small part of the upholstery before proceeding. Modern velvets are often a blend of synthetic fibers. Sponging with a textured cloth wrung out of

**Keeping Napped Fabrics Clean**
To remove lint, dust, and animal hairs from napped materials, use a clean pure bristle clothes brush lightly dipped in drycleaning fluid.

vinegar water — 1 tablespoonful (15 ml) in 2 cups (500 ml) cold water — is often sufficient to freshen the appearance of these napped fabrics. A steam iron held about 1 inch (3 cm) above crushed velvets will raise the nap.

Acrylic velvets have a built-in grime repellent, and cleaning consists of wiping over the fabric with a napped cloth wrung out of warm detergent suds. Go over the surfaces with a second damp cloth to remove traces of the suds.

**Blended silk and rayon upholstery** often spots if a drop of liquid falls on it. Sponge the spot with a slightly dampened cloth, working from the outside toward the center. Disturb the outline of the spot by scrubbing gently with your fingernail or an old toothbrush. If the spot is still visible, hold a steam iron just above the mark for a few seconds, then gently scrub the outline again.

**Leather upholstery** such as cowhide and pigskin needs regular polishing to keep from drying out. Matching leather polish or silicone cream will maintain pliability, gloss, and cleanliness.

To clean neglected dark leather furniture, combine ¼ cup (60 ml) raw linseed oil with ¾ cup (180 ml) vinegar in a lidded jar. Shake well. Apply with a soft cloth and keep changing the cloth as grime, perspiration, and soil marks are loosened.

**Cleaning Vinyl Upholstery**
Treat grease spots, food spills, perspiration stains, and extra grimy spots on any vinyl upholstery as soon as possible.

Saddle soap is also suitable for washing leather goods. This can be used with warm water. Remove traces of soap with a clean damp cloth.

Dried-out leathers require repeated applications of linseed oil, leather dressing, or petroleum jelly to help restore pliancy. When the dressing is quite absorbed, polish with silicone wax.

Mildew on leather furniture can be removed by working petroleum jelly into the grain and leaving it on for several hours. During damp weather, mildew or mold may form on soiled areas, perhaps where food was spilled. Treat immediately, because it can cause deterioration and bleaching of the leather.

**Vinyl upholstery.** To clean vinyl upholstery, use a small amount of baking soda or vinegar on a rough rag. Wash the vinyl, using this rag and some mild detergent. Washing vinyl in this way can prevent the hardening and cracking often caused by body oils. Regular wiping with a damp soapy cloth will help to remove traces of perspiration and hair products from the backs of vinyl seats. Perspiration tends to discolor and dry out vinyls.

If the vinyl becomes delustered as a result of any stain removal treatment, rub the area with a little glycerin or apply silicone furniture polish. Make sure that all traces of stain remover have been wiped off, first with a soapy cloth and then with a clean, damp cloth.

## VEILS

Wash veils in cool suds. Rinse three times. Dry flat on an old sheet on the lawn; or if ironing is necessary, roll in a towel and iron while slightly damp. Liquid starch will restore crispness.

## VELOUR

Usually it is advisable to have velour furnishings and articles drycleaned.

However, if velour is labeled "washable," then wash in as much water as possible. The water should be just warm. Use wool-washing detergent. Shake the articles to remove surface dust. Wash one at a time, squeezing and lifting it in the water to release loosened grime. Rinse twice. Try to choose a fine windy day when drying will be speedy. If possible, hang curtains so that the lines will not leave a mark.

Smooth with a clean clothes brush while drying and shake well when dry to raise the nap. Ironing should not be necessary.

## VELVET, VELVETEEN, AND CORDUROY

Silk velvet should be drycleaned. Cotton and synthetic fibers such as rayon and nylon are often washable. The manufacturer's tag on piece goods or the label inside a garment will indicate if drycleaning or washing is desirable.

When washing any napped goods, try to choose a breezy day. Use cool suds and liquid detergent. Move the article around in its bath until it is clean. Do not squeeze or twist; both cause creasing and crushing. Rinse three times, then drip dry. Smooth the pile with a clean clothes brush and shake the garment when it is dry.

Creases can be removed from velvet with steam. Hold a steam iron just above the creases on the wrong side of the material, or hold the underside over a pan of boiling water. You can also hang a velvet garment in a steaming bathroom.

Maroon, brown, bottle-green, navy blue, and red are colors that run. Dye loss is the result of particles suspended in and on the velvet pile.

Dark dyes can be set by pre-soaking the garment in cold water containing 1 rounded tablespoon (15 ml) Epsom salts per 2 quarts (liters) water. Soak for 20 minutes before stripping out the water and washing.

Wash velveteen and corduroy separately in cool detergent suds for the first two or three launderings to avoid tinging other garments. Rinse well and drip-dry, smoothing the pile with a clean clothes brush or your hand while it is still wet.

Ironing is often not necessary. If it is, steam press lightly or hold a steam iron just above the velveteen to raise the pile.

## WALLS

There are endless ways to clean your walls, depending on the surface. Walls can be vacuumed, or if very dirty (and washable), you can use an all-purpose cleaner. Remember to wash walls from the bottom to the top. Grimy water drips running from the top of the wall to the bottom, and fortified with a grime-loosening cleaner, will cause traces that are difficult to remove.

To remove tape from a wall, place a cloth over the area and use a warm iron. This will loosen the backing and make it easy to pull off.

Remove finger smudges before they settle in.

Clean brick walls with soap and water; or if they are really dirty, you can try bleach and water. Some stains by the fireplace can be scrubbed with an abrasive cleanser, but you will need to rinse very well to remove all the cleanser.

**Wallpaper.** Periodic dusting will help to keep all wallpapers more attractive. Use the brush attachment on your vacuum cleaner. If necessary, wash and dry the attachment thoroughly before using on wallpaper to ensure its cleanliness; or, use a freshly washed and dried nylon broom, a soft-bristled wall brush, or a mop covered with an old towel.

**Vinyl, spongeable, and washable wallpapers** should be dusted before further treatment. Then wring out an absorbent cloth in warm detergent suds and start at the baseboard, working upward in long straight strokes.

Treat one section at a time, completely finishing off that area by going over it a second time with a clean, damp cloth to remove traces of loosened grime and suds. Never overwet wallpaper; even the most washable wallpaper might bubble or lift if it is saturated.

If in doubt about the washability of your wallpaper, test it first in an inconspicuous part of the room. Dust first, then sponge it as described above, rinse, and let it dry. Judge the result carefully: Has the color run? Faded? Has the paper bubbled or lifted?

**Stain Removal Tips for Wallpaper**

☞ Mix ¼ cup (60 ml) baking soda, ½ cup (125 ml) white vinegar, and 1 cup (250 ml) ammonia. Wash the walls with this solution. Wear rubber gloves.

☞ Use rubbing alcohol, which can sometimes remove black spots from the wall. Test first in an area where it will not show in case discoloration results.

☞ Try a little lighter fluid on a cloth to remove crayon marks. Rub gently.

☞ Some spots can be removed with art gum erasers.

*Note:* Some wallpaper cannot be washed — check the manufacturer's instructions for care.

**Nonwashable papers** should be dusted only. Many grime marks can be removed by rubbing them with the inside crust of white bread. Grime and crumbs fall away together, so protect the floor covering by laying down newspapers. On small areas, art gum erasers can be used in the same way.

Detergent makes water wetter. Once the paper is saturated it will be possible to peel it off in large strips.

**Removing Wallpaper**

To remove old wallpaper easily, go over the surface two or three times with a paint roller saturated in 4 quarts (liters) of hot water containing half a cup (125 ml) of liquid detergent.

Greasy marks can be removed with the aid of absorption and heat. Cover the stain with a white paper towel and press it with a fairly hot iron. As the grease is absorbed into the paper, discard that sheet and use another to avoid redistributing it. Textured papers might require a different treatment. Make a paste of powdered starch, talcum powder, or crushed chalk using a little drycleaning fluid or carbon tetrachloride to mix it. Dab it over the stain and let it dry.

Remove the dry powder by suction with the vacuum cleaner or with a clean clothes brush. Repeat if necessary. If the wallpaper is very dark, test this treatment first on an inconspicuous part of the paper; on some surfaces, traces of the white powder might remain. If necessary, patch the stained area.

Another method to remove grease from wallpaper is to work some rye bread into a ball and put a few drops of kerosene on it. Rub the grease stain gently. To remove crayon from wallpaper, rub with a damp cloth and some toothpaste. Rinse with a clean, damp cloth.

Perspiration and grime on fingers fumbling in the dark for a light switch often leave stains on wallpaper. Rub them with a wad of fresh bread sprinkled with not more than three drops of drycleaning fluid, or protect this vulnerable area with a square of self-adhesive clear plastic.

Pollen from floral arrangements often stains wallpaper. Try to avoid this by keeping fresh flowers away from the paper. The stains can be wiped off vinyl-coated and sealed papers but are usually indelible on those that have not been treated.

Lead pencil can usually be removed with an art gum eraser. Felt pen and ink are sometimes indelible. Some inks and dyes are so fast that a solvent would certainly harm the paper. Patch the area for best results.

**Patching Wallpaper**
Torn edges are best for patches because cut edges are more clearly defined and they tend to collect dust and darken.

**Repapering.** When repapering a room, try to save roll ends as well as an entire roll for emergency repairs. It is seldom possible to match old wallpapers because dye lots vary and patterns and colors are constantly replaced.

Wallpaper darkens with exposure, and off-cuts from the roll ends look new and bright by comparison. A more "aged" effect can soon be given to new patches by exposing them to sunlight. Some papers darken quickly; others require a few days to match that on the walls.

**Patching wallpaper.** Patches are almost invisible if they are applied properly. It is not necessary to remove the stained area, although greasy marks should be sponged with grease solvent before being covered.

Obtain a strip of new paper that is larger in width and breadth than the area to be patched. Cut it roughly into shape, being careful to match the pattern.

Lay the patch face down on a clean surface and tear all around it, making it an uneven shape with tissue-thin edges. Then apply clear paste to the back of the patch, being careful to cover the fine edges. Press it in place, matching the pattern exactly. If necessary, press out air bubbles by rolling over the patch with a rolling-pin or by pressing it with the bristles of a clean clothes brush. A patch applied in this way seldom fails to blend well with the old wallpaper.

## WOOL

Woolen garments and articles must be washed carefully. Never use hot water, and do not allow the force of water to strike the garment directly. Use cold or lukewarm water only with soap flakes, mild liquid detergent, or wool-washing detergent. Do not soak woolens. Do not wring, twist, scrub, or rub woolen articles; such action mats the wool fibers and causes felting. Felting removes the elasticity from woven wool, resulting in shrinkage.

Do not dry white woolen garments — particularly fine knits such as babywear — in strong sunlight. This could cause yellowing.

Do not leave wet woolen garments in a heap. Extract surplus water as soon as possible and hang to dry, or spread flat to dry or dry at the lowest temperature in a dryer.

Some woolen garments can be machine washed; some require hand washing. If a short cycle is available on your machine, line the machine with a soft towel that will act as a buffer and will help to keep the woolen garments soft and fluffy. Use cold or lukewarm water and a wool-washing detergent. Remove the garments from the machine as soon as the cycle ends.

Stretch woolens into shape and size while wet, then hang to dry. Sweaters can be hung on old pantyhose, with the legs in the sleeves and the waist and toes pegged to the line. Special plastic-covered hangers are available at department stores.

**Before You Buy**

Read the care tag on any heavyweight sweater you are planning to buy. Some will specify drycleaning only; others will give specific washing instructions.

Hand-washed woolens can be well rinsed; then, if the timing is right, they can be dropped into a load of clean clothes in a machine approaching the final spin-dry cycle. This will extract surplus water and ensure quicker drying.

Alternatively, roll the garment in a thick towel to absorb extra moisture.

Most synthetic knits will emerge from the wash as new. Others, washed carelessly, will stretch to unwearable proportions.

**Shrunken woolens** can sometimes be stretched. Dissolve 3 ounces (75 g) Epsom salts in sufficient boiling water to cover the garment. Use a large plastic container or porcelain tub. Do not use a metal container. Allow the solution to cool to body temperature. Soak the dry shrunken garment for half an hour. During that time, keep it submerged and move it around several times. Remove the garment from the solution and roll it in a towel to extract surplus water.

Now unroll the garment and spread it flat. Stretch it methodically lengthwise and crosswise, using a well-fitting garment as a size guide. Hang to dry, using old pantyhose or a plastic-coated hanger. Stretch it several times while it is drying.

When it is almost dry, press it on a well-padded surface with a steam iron on the wool setting, and recheck the measurements.

Do not expect miracles. Some wools respond better than others, but the treatment is inexpensive and worth trying if it might salvage an otherwise valuable wool garment.

**Stretched woolens.** Some heavy woolens, particularly hand-knits, stretch after they have been laundered. Usually this is because they have been hung on the line while still heavy with water. Crimped wool or loosely knitted wools drop with the weight of the water.

Expensive cashmeres and heavy hand-knits will also stretch if you are not careful when washing them.

**Shrinking woolens.** Sometimes a woolen (but not an acrylic) garment can be shrunk. Lower the dry article into hot, not boiling, water. Let it soak for five minutes, moving it around and keeping all parts under the water. Try to do this in a tub with a plug that can be pulled out to drain the water. Do not lift the garment except in both hands, fully supporting its weight. Press out as much water as possible; then lift it onto a fluffy towel, roll it up in the folds, and press out again. Dry flat, as suggested above, on a sheet on the lawn, or on a warm path. When dry, press lightly with a steam iron using an up-and-down action, not a side-to-side movement.

## WORK CLOTHES

Heavily soiled work clothes should not be washed immediately. Dampen them evenly, then rub laundry soap deeply into the stains. Roll the garments tightly, slip them into a large plastic bag, and leave them for about 12 hours.

Wash them the next day in hot detergent suds in the longest cycle of the machine. If the machine is fitted with a pre-wash cycle, use this first, then reset the machine. Hot rinsing will also help to remove stains.

**Washing
Work Clothes**
When machine washing work clothes, allow for the maximum amount of water.

**Greasy overalls** can be dusted heavily with cheap talcum powder. Scrub it into heavy grease stains with a toothbrush or nailbrush. Roll up the overalls and leave them in a plastic bag for several hours. Shake them outside to remove the powder, which will have absorbed much of the grease, then rub them with soap and treat them as outlined above.

## WROUGHT IRON

This is used extensively for garden and patio furniture and for security doors and windows. To clean it, wipe with a cloth dampened with detergent suds. A light spraying with silicone wax will keep the surfaces more dust- and soil-resistant and will help to prevent rust. When repainting becomes necessary, use paint containing a rust inhibitor.

## ZINC

Wash with a solution of washing soda and hot water, 1 tablespoon (15 ml) per quart (liter). Rinse and rub with silicone wax.

# Part Four

# TREATING SPECIFIC STAINS

## ACID

Acids can damage fabrics permanently unless treated promptly. Rinse immediately with cold water, holding the stained area under running water so that the acid is flushed out. Spread the stained area over a folded towel and dampen it with household ammonia. Repeat several times, changing the position of the pad. Rinse again under running water. *Note:* Do not use undiluted ammonia on pure wool or silk or on blends containing wool or silk.

Acids on wool or silk should be flushed out with cold water, then sponged with equal parts of ammonia and cold water. Ammonia can restore color to fabrics bleached by acid.

Acid spills on carpets should be blotted up immediately. Fold a number of tissues and put weight on them so that still more acid is absorbed. To neutralize the acid, make a thin paste of baking soda and warm water, then work it deeply into the pile with an old toothbrush. Substitute borax if baking soda is not available. Allow the paste to dry, then sponge with a clean, damp cloth. Repeat the paste application and let it dry again. Vacuum to remove traces of the powder. Repeat the treatment as necessary.

## ADHESIVE TAPE

Sponge with eucalyptus, kerosene, or carbon tetrachloride. Finally, wash in warm detergent suds and rinse well.

## ALCOHOL, WINE, AND FRUIT BEVERAGES

Alcoholic beverages that have been spilled should be blotted up quickly, and if possible, the stain should be treated before it dries. Sponge immediately with a cloth barely dampened with warm water and containing 1 or 2 drops of liquid detergent. Rinse with a clean, damp cloth and dry as quickly as possible, using a hair dryer set on medium heat.

Spilled alcohol and fruit beverages might be invisible when dry, but stains oxidize with heat and age, and these can become indelible. Sponge or dab with soda water, or sponge with warm water containing a little detergent. Rinse well. Pre-soak dry stains in an enzyme solution and wash in the usual way.

On nonwashable garments, sponge with cold water, then take the stained garment to a drycleaner as soon as possible.

Fabric with dried-on beer stains should be sponged with a solution of equal parts vinegar and dishwashing liquid, then rinsed with warm water.

On carpets, blot up as much as possible immediately. Sponge the area with a clean towel wrung out of warm water. Then dissolve 1 teaspoon (5 ml) of laundry detergent powder in 1 cup (250 ml) warm water and use the solution to lightly wet a piece of toweling. Repeatedly sponge the stained area, blotting up with dry cloths as you work. Sponge with a series of damp cloths to remove the suds. Blot as dry as possible, then train a low-set hair dryer or an electric fan over the damp spot. Smooth the pile. New spills are sometimes barely visible, but as the stain ages it becomes brown and then it will be very difficult to remove.

To remove alcohol from carpets, blot up the spill as quickly as possible, continuing until the cloth or tissues remain dry. Mix 1 tablespoon (15 ml) of laundry detergent in 2 cups (500 ml) warm water. Sponge this into the stain, using dry tissues or cloths to blot up as you work so that the carpet does not become too wet. Sponge and blot repeatedly. Be thorough; these stains become brown and indelible with age unless they are completely removed.

On a light-colored carpet, a weak bleach solution can be used to sponge out remaining traces of the spill. Use 1 teaspoon (5 ml) bleach to ¼ cup (60 ml) cold water. Finally, sponge with clean, damp cloths and train an electric fan on the area to dry it quickly.

For red wine, blot immediately with tissues. Then make a thick paste of borax and cold water, and work it deeply into the pile with a toothbrush or nailbrush. Let the paste dry, then vacuum. Repeat as often as necessary.

Alcohol-based drinks, perfumes, and medicines attack the wood finish on furniture. Blot up the spill as quickly as possible, trying not to worsen the stain. Sponge the stain with a clean, damp cloth and blot dry; then assess the damage. If the furniture has been well maintained, the mark will be slight. Rub hard with silicone polish, working from the outside of the mark toward the center. Rub well, following the grain, with linseed oil or petroleum jelly mixed with cigarette ash. After rubbing hard for several minutes, smear the area with oil or petroleum jelly and leave this on for at least 12 hours. Then wipe it off and polish in the usual way.

## ANIMAL HAIRS

Some upholstery fabrics seem to act as magnets for animal hairs. Concentrated vacuuming is best, of course, but periodic cleaning is easier with a slightly dampened sponge or a clean, damp chamois cloth. Clothes brushes are also effective — they consist of a velvet pad with a handle and induce static electricity when they are used.

## ANTIPERSPIRANTS AND DEODORANTS

Antiperspirants that contain aluminum chloride are acidic and may interact with some fabric dyes. Color can be restored by sponging with ammonia. Rinse thoroughly. To use on wool, mohair, or silk, dilute ammonia with an equal amount of water.

Another method for removing deodorant stains is to apply rubbing alcohol to the stain and cover the area with an absorbent pad dampened with alcohol. Keep both moist and let sit.

Treat stiffened, yellowed areas with an enzyme-soaking powder. Make a stiff paste of the powder by mixing it with cold water. Rub it into the stained sections. Colored articles should be pre-tested in an inconspicuous part of the garment to see if the color is affected by the paste.

Slip the garment into a plastic bag and leave it for 8 or more hours.

These treated areas must then be washed in very hot water. Hot water might cause wrinkling or creasing in a drip-dry garment, so stretch only the stained sections over a basin in the sink and pour over each underarm about 1 quart (liter) of very hot water. Then wash the whole garment by hand or in a machine in the usual way.

Do not iron material with a deodorant stain. The heat will interact with the chemical residue from the deodorant and the fabric could be ruined.

## BABY FORMULA STAINS

Some milk and baby formula stains can be removed using unflavored meat tenderizer. Make a paste of the tenderizer and cool water, rub it into the stain, and let sit before washing as usual. This treatment is effective because meat tenderizers contain an enzyme that breaks down protein.

## BERRIES *(blueberries, cranberries, raspberries, strawberries)*

Dried berry stains on washables should be rubbed on each side with bar soap. Then cover with a thick mixture of cornstarch and cold water. Rub in well, then leave fabric in the sun until the stain disappears. Repeat the process in three days if needed.

Another way to treat berry stains is to sponge the area with lemon juice (or rub a lemon slice over the stain). Flush with water and allow to air dry. For persistent stains, soak item in a solution of 1 teaspoon (5 ml) mild detergent, 1 teaspoon (5 ml) white vinegar, and 1 quart (liter) warm water for at least 15 minutes. Launder as usual. (See also Fruit.)

## BEVERAGES

Blot up immediately until the mark is as dry as possible. Then sponge with clean, warm water containing borax — 1 teaspoon (5 ml) per cup (250 ml) of water. Avoid overwetting. Sponge and blot repeatedly. See entries for specific beverages.

## BLOOD

On washable fabrics, soak as soon as possible in salted water, or soak in an enzyme pre-soaking solution, if necessary, for 2 or 3 hours. Wash in cool suds or in cold water in a machine. Traces of the stain can be bleached in either liquid or powdered bleach depending on the fabric involved. Read labeled instructions carefully. You can also sponge with hydrogen peroxide (1 part of hydrogen peroxide to 3 parts of water) and expose the stain to fresh air, keeping moist with peroxide until the stain fades. Rinse well to remove traces of peroxide. Have good garments drycleaned.

Sponge mattresses with hydrogen peroxide and keep damp with peroxide until the stain fades.

Fresh bloodstains can sometimes be removed from washable fabrics with a solution of ½ teaspoon (2 ml) salt and 1 cup (250 ml) water. Soak the item in cold water with laundry detergent. Fresh bloodstains on white cotton fabrics should be soaked in cold water with ammonia.

If you have blood on the carpet, blot with tissues. Sponge with salted water — 1 teaspoon (5 ml) to 1 cup (250 ml) cold water. Sponge and blot until the mark fades. Sponge with a clean, damp cloth to remove traces of salt. If a stain remains, mix equal parts of peroxide and warm water, and work this into the pile with a toothbrush. Keep slightly damp for 1 or 2 hours until the stain fades, then sponge again with a clean, damp cloth. Another way to treat bloodstains on the carpet is to make a paste of borax and water or powdered bleach and water and let it dry on the pile. Vacuum to remove the dried powder.

If the blood has dried, dampen it with a little water. Sponge with laundry detergent solution — 1 teaspoon (5 ml) powdered detergent to 1 cup (250 ml) tepid water. Sponge and blot repeatedly until the mark fades. If the carpet is light, apply the peroxide treatment described above. ***Note:*** Avoid excessive wetting.

## BURN MARKS. *See also Scorch Marks*

Remove attachment from the end of the vacuum cleaner pipe and concentrate the suction over the burn. This will remove much of the charred pile. Mix 1 teaspoon (5 ml) laundry detergent powder in ½ cup (125 ml) water, and gently scrub the burn with an old toothbrush, using this solution. Blot up excess dampness and sponge again with a damp cloth. To remove remaining burn marks, lightly bleach with equal parts of peroxide and water, plus one single drop of ammonia. When this dries, sponge again with a damp cloth; if necessary, carefully snip charred pile ends with nail scissors.

Burn marks on the polished surfaces of furniture might need the expertise of a professional polisher. However, you can cover with petroleum jelly or a drop of oil until metal polish can be rubbed in with a circular movement. Wipe this off and cover again with linseed, camphorated, or olive oil or more petroleum jelly. Leave this on for 24 hours. Rub again, wipe off, and polish.

Burn marks on fabric upholstery can be camouflaged by inserting a piece of material cut from under the furniture, carefully matched, and eased under the hole with a knitting needle. Use a little fabric adhesive around the edges of the patch to keep it in position. First remove charred edges around the hole with fine nail scissors. When the patch is in position, cover the spot with waxed paper, apply a weight, and leave it there until the adhesive dries.

Small burn holes and cuts on vinyl upholstery can be treated by cutting a larger patch of matching vinyl from a fold underneath the chair or lounge. Trim the edges of the burn with a razor blade or nail scissors to remove the char mark. Smear a polyvinyl chloride (PVC) adhesive around the margins of the patch, and slip it under the hole with a knitting needle. Wipe off any excess adhesive with acetone, nail polish remover, or carbon tetrachloride before it sets; then cover the patch with a sheet of waxed paper and apply a weight for several hours.

## BUTTER AND MARGARINE

Gently scrape up any solid matter with a blunt knife.

For washable articles, dampen the stain. Rub powder detergent into the marks and scrub between two thumbs. Wash and dry. If the stain remains, spread it over a folded pad and sponge it with a cloth dampened with drycleaning fluid. Air to dry. Repeat if necessary, then wash and rinse.

Fabrics with special finishes such as drip-dry and wash-and-wear tend to retain grease stains, so patience and repeated applications of fluid over a series of clean pads might be required. Do not iron until all traces of the stain have been removed. Age and heat will cause yellowing, and the marks will be indelible.

Nonwashable articles should be taken to a drycleaner.

After scraping as much of the solid butter as you can, apply an absorbent powder. Do not press the absorbent into the fabric. Let it sit until it cakes, then lightly brush the loose material off. Repeat if necessary.

For butter on carpets, remove as much as possible with a pliable spatula or knife. Sponge lightly with drycleaning fluid, blotting with tissues as the grease dissolves. Then treat the area with carpet shampoo or sprinkle dry carpet-cleaning powder over the stain; leave it on for several hours, then vacuum.

## CANDLE WAX

Lift off solid wax. Place folded tissues under and over the remaining mark and a sheet of brown paper over the top tissue, and press with a warm iron. Repeat until no more melted wax is absorbed by the tissues. Or hold fabric taut over the sink, and pour boiling water through the fabric from a height to flush away wax. Take care not to burn yourself.

Sponge the remaining grease mark with drycleaning fluid or a similar solvent, working over a folded towel. Wash in the usual way.

Candle wax stains on linens should be rubbed with vegetable oil. Wipe off excess oil with a clean cloth, then wash as usual. To remove a lot of candle wax, scrape excess wax off the fabric. Put fabric between layers of paper towels or paper bags, and press with a warm iron.

***Note:*** Minimal heat should transfer the wax to the towel or paper. Afterward, use a cleaning solution on the remaining stain.

To remove candle wax from carpets, press an ice cube on the wax drip to harden the wax so it can be pulled up. Treat stain with drycleaning fluid. Let dry and vacuum.

Lift off as much as possible. Cover the remaining wax with half a dozen tissues and press with a cool iron. Change the tissue and repeat until no more wax is absorbed. The dye from colored candles might leave a stain; sponge this with carbon tetrachloride unless the pile is set in rubber or synthetic rubber. If it is, make a paste of powdered starch, talcum powder, or cornstarch and drycleaning fluid. Work this into the pile, vacuuming the area when the powder dries.

Wax on a polished surface can be removed without scratching the furniture if the wax is first made brittle and hard. To do this, put a tray of ice cubes in a plastic bag and let this stand on the wax for 2 or 3 minutes. Then cover the blade of a blunt knife with a piece of soft cloth and gently lift and scrape off the wax. Rub the marks with a damp cloth and a smear of soap. Sponge with a clean cloth and polish in the usual way.

## CANDY

To remove candy stains from carpets, scrape up as much material as you can. Mix 1 teaspoon (5 ml) mild detergent, 1 teaspoon (5 ml) white vinegar, and 1 quart (liter) warm water. Apply to stain, let dry, then vacuum. For removing chocolate stains, see Chocolate.

## CARBON PAPER

Sponge with carbon tetrachloride, working over a folded towel that will absorb loosened dye. Let this dampness evaporate, then dampen the mark and rub in a little detergent. Scrub lightly between two thumbs; rinse under a running cold water tap. Wash in the usual way.

Nonwashables should be taken to a cleaner. To treat them at home, try sponging them with carbon tetrachloride over an absorbent pad. Work first from the back of the stain so that it is flushed out into the pad, the position of which should be changed frequently to avoid restaining the garment.

## CHOCOLATE OR COCOA

Remove excess chocolate from the stained area without embedding the chocolate deeper into the material. Sponge with cold water or soak for 30 minutes in an enzyme pre-wash solution. Rub detergent into the remaining stain and scrub it lightly between your two thumbs. Rinse out loosened traces under cold running water and dry. If a greasy mark remains, sponge it with a solvent such as drycleaning fluid. The final stain should come out in the wash.

For nonwashables, flush the stain with club soda to prevent setting. Sponge the area with a drycleaning solvent. If stain persists, apply a few drops of dishwashing detergent and a few drops of ammonia to the stain, then scrape. Blot occasionally with an absorbent pad. Flush well with water to remove ammonia.

To remove chocolate from carpets, blot up as much as possible, then sponge with 1 teaspoon (5 ml) powdered laundry detergent dissolved in 1 cup (250 ml) warm water. Scrub the suds into the pile with a toothbrush if the stain is deep. Sponge and blot with dry tissues or cloths until the stain fades. Final traces will disappear if a paste of borax and warm water is worked into the pile and left to dry. Vacuum the area and repeat as necessary. If the beverage contains milk, sponging with drycleaning fluid might be necessary. Follow this treatment with more sponging, first with detergent suds, then with a clean, damp cloth to remove the suds.

***Note:*** Drycleaning fluid should not come in contact with rubber or synthetic backing. Instead, make a paste of powdered starch and the drycleaner, and work this into the pile.

## COFFEE AND TEA

Blot up quickly and rinse out or sponge out as much as possible with cool water. Rub detergent into the stain and scrub between your two thumbs before washing in the usual way.

If a stain remains and if the fabric will stand boiling water, spread the stain over a basin in the sink, cover it with borax, and pour on boiling water. Let the stain soak in the borax water for 30 minutes.

If the fabric will not stand boiling water, make a thick paste of borax and hot water and rub it into the stain. Leave it on for half an hour, then brush off the paste. Repeat as often as necessary.

Diluted peroxide can be used on white or light fabrics to remove final traces of the stain. Keep the mark dampened with equal parts of water and peroxide in sunlight for 2 hours or longer. Rinse to remove traces of peroxide.

To remove coffee or tea stains from china, wet the cup with white vinegar. Dip a damp rag in baking soda or salt and wipe the stain out.

Denture-cleaning tablets will remove coffee or tea stains from a cup. Drop a tablet in the cup of warm water, and let it soak for several hours. Gentle scrubbing will remove the stains. Wash and rinse cups thoroughly after treatment.

To remove coffee stains from carpet, blot the spill as soon as possible. Mix 1 teaspoon (5 ml) mild detergent, 1 teaspoon (5 ml) white vinegar, and 1 quart (liter) warm water. Apply to stain, then let dry. Follow with an application of drycleaning fluid. Allow carpet to dry, then vacuum.

## COLA AND SOFT DRINKS

A soft drink spilled on a carpet might be invisible initially, but it must be treated promptly and thoroughly, because when stains age they may become indelible.

Blot the area until no more of the stain can be absorbed. Then sponge deeply into the pile with laundry detergent powder (not liquid detergent), using a toothbrush or nailbrush if necessary. Avoid excessive wetting; blot with tissues or clean cloths as you work. Finally, sponge out the suds with a series of clean, damp cloths and when the area is dry, vacuum thoroughly.

## COSMETICS

Dampen the stain and rub in powdered detergent, or rub undiluted liquid detergent into the dry stain. Scrub between both thumbs, then rinse under cold running water. Repeat several times if necessary before washing as usual.

Send nonwashable garments to a drycleaner.

## CRAYON

To remove crayon stains from fabrics, scrape off excess material. Sponge detergent onto the stain, rinse, then dry. Persistent stains can be sponged with a cleaning fluid.

Crayon stains on acrylic, cotton, linen, polyester, nylon, and washable wool can be removed by placing the stained area between two pieces of white blotting paper and pressing with a warm iron. The blotting paper should be changed as the stain is absorbed. Take care not to spread the stain. If a stain from the crayon color remains, flush the area with drycleaning solvent.

Another method for removing crayon stains is to place the stained surface down on several paper towels. Spray with a petroleum-based solvent and let stand for several minutes. Turn the fabric and spray the other side; let stand. Apply detergent and work into stained area until the stain is gone. Hand wash the item in detergent to remove traces of the oil. Wash as usual.

Use silicone spray to remove crayon from countertops.

## DYE

Dye stains are difficult to remove, especially if the entire garment cannot be soaked in a suitable bleach.

Try spreading the stain over a large basin in an unplugged sink or tub. Turn on the cold water faucet so that a steady drip (not flow) falls on the stain. Empty the basin as it fills. Often a dye stain will vanish after 3 or 4 hours of this treatment.

Some dye stains respond to a long soak in rich, cool suds.

Articles that can be bleached should be soaked in a weak bleach solution in a nonmetal container for 6 to 8 hours. Care should be taken not to expose treated fabrics (drip-dry, wash-and-wear, noniron, and so on) to chlorine bleach.

Other stains may respond to sponging with equal parts of water and peroxide. Expose the dye stain to air or sunlight and keep it moist with peroxide solution until the stain disappears. Rinse well.

Clothing stained with hair dye should be washed in sudsy water with vinegar added. White items can later be bleached.

If the color from an item in the washing machine has run onto other items, and the items discolored were originally white or light colored, try a commercial dye remover.

## EGG

Scrape off any solid matter. Soak in a nonmetal container with an enzyme-soaking compound for as long as convenient — 6 to 8 hours if possible. If a stain remains, rub in powdered detergent and rub between both thumbs. Rinse and wash in the usual way. The stain must be totally removed before heat is applied.

Nonwashable garments should be drycleaned without delay. Be sure to advise the cleaner as to the origin of the stain.

If treating at home, dampen the stain and rub in undiluted liquid detergent. Rub between both thumbs. Spread over a pad, and sponge repeatedly with a series of damp cloths to remove the suds.

To remove egg from carpet, scrape up as much as possible and sponge the stain with salty water using ½ teaspoon (2 ml) to 1 cup (250 ml) cool water. Then sponge with a solution of enzyme laundry stain remover, followed by sponging with a series of clean, damp cloths. Blot frequently with dry cloths or tissues to absorb excess moisture.

## FOOD DYE

Fruit juices, gelatin desserts, and frozen fruit treats are just a few of the foods that leave stubborn food dye stains. If you are able to treat the stain while it is still fresh, neutralize it with a solution of 1 tablespoon (15 ml) ammonia in a cup of water. This will especially help prevent dye transfer on nylon carpeting and similar fabrics. Then rub table salt into the stain and let it sit. Remove salt, repeat if necessary, then rinse.

Stretch a small stain under cold running water and turn it on full. The force of the water will flush out much of the dye without spreading the stain. Then rub in powdered detergent and scrub between both thumbs. Rinse again under cold running water. Soak in cool detergent suds for 30 minutes, and wash in the usual way. If a stain remains and if the basic color of the garment will not be bleached by peroxide (pretest on an inside seam), keep the stain moist with equal parts of water and hydrogen peroxide in sunlight until it fades. Rinse well.

## FRUIT. *See also Berries*

These stains must be removed *before* the article is washed. Heat and age will set fruit stains and make them indelible. Sponge or spray with soda water immediately.

Rinse the stain as soon as possible while it is still wet. Rub in detergent and scrub the stain between both thumbs. Rinse under running water as hot as the fabric can stand. Hold the material taut so that the full flow of water pours onto the stain.

If the stain is still visible, make a paste of borax and warm water and work it into the stained fibers. Let this dry, then brush it off. Repeat several times if necessary.

On all washable, colored garments, sponge the fresh stain with cold water. Half-fill a basin with boiling water and add 1 tablespoon (15 ml) ammonia. Stretch the stained section taut across the top of the basin. Let the fumes permeate the stain; do not let the material touch the water. Test the effect of peroxide on an unseen part of the garment. If the dye is unaffected, pour a few drops of diluted peroxide onto the stain with the steam still rising. Lift off and keep moist with peroxide until the stain fades. *Note:* If ammonia, peroxide, and glycerin must be purchased, it will be more economical to take the garment to a drycleaner. Be sure to advise the cleaner of the cause of the stain.

Fresh fruit stains, treated promptly, usually come out in the wash. It is important to sponge them while they are fresh, especially peach, citrus, and the sap from banana palms.

**Old fruit stains.** Reconstitute the stain with glycerin. Leave this on for half an hour, then treat as above.

Glycerin rubbed into a dried stain will freshen it and make it easier to remove. Then treat as above, according to the material. Nonwashables are best treated as soon as possible by a drycleaner. Sponge the stains with cold water as soon as they occur, and take the garment promptly to a cleaner. Be sure to explain the nature of the stain.

To remove from carpets, scrape up as much of the spilled material as you can. Mix 1 teaspoon (5 ml) mild detergent, 1 teaspoon (5 ml) white vinegar, and 1 quart (liter) warm water. Apply to stain, let dry, then vacuum. Repeat if necessary.

## FRUIT JUICES AND CORDIALS

To remove from carpets, blot up as much as possible, then sponge with fresh effervescent soda water, blotting frequently. If a stain remains, sponge with 1 teaspoon (5 ml) powdered detergent dissolved in 1 cup (250 ml) water, scrubbing it in with a toothbrush or nailbrush dipped in the solution. Avoid excess wetting and blot frequently. Sponge with clean, damp cloths. These stains will become brown and often indelible with age, so all traces should be removed quickly.

Old stains need to be reconstituted with glycerin. Rub in a little glycerin and leave it on for half an hour, then sponge with the detergent solution as suggested above. A warm water and borax paste worked into the stained area will often remove final traces of the spill.

## FURNITURE POLISH

To remove from carpets, blot up immediately and continue to blot until no more is absorbed by cloths or tissues. Sponge with powdered detergent, 1 teaspoon (5 ml) dissolved in 1 cup (250 ml) tepid water. Work it into the carpet pile with a toothbrush or nailbrush, and blot up with fresh tissues as you work. Then sponge with a clean, damp cloth to remove traces of the suds.

Furniture polish usually contains dye, and this can be difficult to remove. If the stained area is large and conspicuous, call for professional help.

Smaller, lighter stains will respond to a light application of drycleaning fluid. Blot up as you sponge to remove traces of dye and oil. Avoid overuse of the fluid as it could damage the back of rubber or synthetic rubber pile or remove loose dyes. If in doubt, pre-test on an inconspicuous part of the carpet.

## GLUE, MUCILAGE, AND ADHESIVES

Modern adhesives are difficult to remove. If you need to purchase solvents, you might find that it is more economical to have the garments drycleaned. Tell the cleaner the name of the adhesive that caused the stain.

**Balsa wood (model airplane) glue.** This can be removed from most fabrics with acetone.

To remove this glue from furniture, try rubbing with cold cream or vegetable oil.

**Plastic adhesives.** Try to treat the stain before it dries. Wash in cool detergent suds. If a stain remains, bring ¼ cup (60 ml) of white vinegar to boiling point and immerse the stain. Have another ¼ cup (60 ml) of white vinegar on the stove and as the first cools, reheat it while the stain soaks in the hot vinegar. Continue this process for 15 minutes.

**Rubber cements.** Gently scrape up solid matter. Spread stain over a pad and sponge with carbon tetrachloride or drycleaning fluid. *Note:* All these substances are flammable, so observe fire precautions.

Rubber cement on furniture can sometimes be removed by rubbing with cold cream or vegetable oil.

**Other glues.** Sponge or rinse in warm water. Rub in powdered detergent and scrub the area between two thumbs. Rinse and wash in water as hot as the fabric will stand.

Soap and water will remove most synthetic glue if the stain is fresh. Acetone will dissolve most clear plastic cements, but you should pre-test on fabric. *Note:* Acetone cannot be used on acetate.

For an old or dried glue stain, soak the fabric in a boiling solution of vinegar and water — 1 part vinegar to 10 parts water — for 30 minutes. Water-rinseable paint and varnish remover will remove some model cements but should be tested on the fabric first.

If a water-soluble glue caused the stain, sponge with warm water and soap to remove as much as possible. If the stain is old or dried water-soluble glue, soak in water as hot as the fabric will allow. Remove the glue carefully as it softens in the water.

To remove from carpets, scrape up as much as possible with a knife or spatula. Sponge first with a cloth dampened with hot water, then with heated vinegar. Blot frequently to remove traces of dissolved glue.

There are many types of glues and adhesives, some of which might be damaging to synthetic carpets. Acetone may be effective on natural fibers, but always test these agents first on an inconspicuous part of the carpet. If in doubt, don't hesitate to call a professional cleaner.

## GRASS AND FLOWERS

Grass stains in washable fabrics can be removed by rubbing laundry detergent into the stained area and rinsing.

If the fabric is not washable, dampen the stained area with rubbing alcohol. Test first for colorfastness. Dilute alcohol with 2 parts water for acetate fabrics. Do not use alcohol on wool. Rinse. If stain persists, sponge with vinegar, then with water. Rinse.

Avoid alkalis such as ammonia, degreasers, or alkaline detergents on grass stains. They interact with the tannin in grass stains and can permanently set the stain.

## GRAVY

To remove from carpets, wipe up as much of the spilled material as possible. Mix 1 teaspoon (5 ml) mild detergent, 1 teaspoon (5 ml) white vinegar, and 1 quart (liter) warm water. Apply to stain, let dry, then vacuum. Apply drycleaning fluid, let carpet dry, then vacuum again.

## GREASE AND OIL

Grease, whether it is from automotive, vegetable, or animal oil, can leave a semitransparent stain that turns dark from all the soil it picks up. To remove a grease stain, first gently remove as much of the greasy substance as possible without further embedding the substance in the fabric. Apply an absorbent agent. Let the agent sit until it cakes with the greasy material. Gently brush away the absorbent, and repeat if necessary.

Spread the stained area face down over a thickly folded cloth and work from the back of the stain so that dissolved grease is absorbed into the pad rather than deeper into the fabric.

Sponge with drycleaning fluid or carbon tetrachloride. Change the position of the pad as it becomes stained. Let the dampness evaporate; repeat the treatment over a fresh pad.

Grease stains can set, and with age and heat they can develop into a yellow stain. Depending on the fabric, this can be treated with bleach or with peroxide suitably diluted. Treated fabrics (for example, those with noniron or crease-resistant finishes) retain grease marks and require longer treatment than others.

**Nonwashables.** Dryclean or, if prepared to exercise time and patience, sponge repeatedly with small amounts of drycleaning solvent. Change the absorbent pad frequently to avoid restaining the garment.

**Washables.** For washable fabrics, scrub with distilled or soft water and soap.

To remove food spills from carpets, scrape and blot up as much as possible. Sponge with powdered detergent, 1 teaspoon (5 ml) dissolved in 1 cup (250 ml) warm water, blotting up as you work; then apply drycleaning fluid, being careful not to wet the carpet backing. Finally, sponge with a damp cloth.

Light, greasy marks can often be treated with dry carpet cleaner worked well into the pile and left for several hours. Use the vacuum cleaner to remove the powder.

**Bicycle grease.** Cover with tissues and stand on them; the tissues will absorb some of the grease. Sponge with eucalyptus or with a little kerosene, blotting frequently as you work. Work from the outer rim of the stain toward the center. Try not to make the stain larger. Sponge with an old towel dipped in powdered laundry detergent dissolved in warm water, 1 teaspoon (5 ml) to 1 cup (250 ml) water. Blot frequently. If a stain remains, apply 2 or 3 applications of borax powder mixed to a paste with warm water, removing each dry application with the vacuum cleaner before reapplying.

For heavy and dark grease stains, call a professional.

Grease marks on upholstery can be absorbed with powdered chalk (not crayon), powdered starch, or talcum powder.

The white absorbents (starch and talcum powder) cause no problems on light-colored upholsteries, but on darker colors they can be difficult to remove. Crush a matching stick of chalk (from a stationery store) finely with a hammer, and rub this powder in. Another option is to fold it up in an old handkerchief, lay it over a grease stain, then press with a moderately hot iron.

An old grease stain, dried and soiled, can be treated with a paste made from one of the absorbents and a cleaning solvent such as carbon tetrachloride or drycleaning fluid. Spread this over the stain and let it dry. Vacuum or brush it away. Vacuuming is preferable; brushing will scatter the powder.

## GUM

Harden soft chewing gum before you try to remove it. One way to do this is to put the fabric in the freezer. Scrape off hard residue, and remove the stain with vinegar, dishwashing liquid, or lighter fluid.

Peanut butter will soften old or dry gum for removal, but it may leave an oily spot that will in turn need to be treated (see Grease and Oil).

For carpets, slip a tray full of ice cubes into a watertight plastic bag and stand this over the gum for a few minutes. The gum will become brittle and pieces will be easy to lift off. Snip off small stubborn pieces with nail scissors. Remove traces of the gum with carbon tetrachloride or drycleaning fluid applied *lightly* to the pile, particularly if the backing is rubber or synthetic rubber.

Remove chewing gum from upholstered surfaces by freezing it. Put a trayful of ice cubes into a watertight plastic bag and rest it on the gum. Soon it will become brittle and much of it can be peeled off. Sponge out remaining stains with carbon tetrachloride or drycleaning fluid.

## HAND CREAM

To remove from carpets, wipe up spilled material. Apply drycleaning fluid and let carpet dry. Repeat if necessary. Vacuum.

## HARD-WATER STAINS

Hard-water stains result from minerals in the water. Old stains and deposits can be thick and tough to remove. Use a cleaner with at least 9 percent phosphoric acid. Apply and allow to soak for several minutes. Repeat until the stain is gone.

To prevent further hard-water stains, consider a water softener, or apply lemon oil after cleaning to prevent buildup.

## HEAT MARKS

Heat marks on furniture are usually caused by placing hot plates, teapots, coffee pots, casserole dishes, and so forth on an unprotected table. Treat in the same way as you would water marks on furniture, repeating the treatment several times as necessary.

## ICE CREAM

Sponge with cold water or soda water as soon as possible, or place article in an enzyme-soaking solution for half an hour. Wash in the usual way. If a greasy mark remains, sponge it with grease solvent such as drycleaning fluid or carbon tetrachloride. Work over a padded cloth that will absorb loosened grease elements.

To remove from carpets, scrape up as much as possible with a spatula or knife. Sponge with tepid laundry detergent suds. Avoid excessive wetting and blot with tissues as you work. Sponge with damp cloths. If a greasy mark still persists, sponge with drycleaning fluid, being careful not to wet the backing if it is rubber or synthetic rubber. Or you can make a paste of borax and water and work that into the pile. When the paste dries, vacuum the area.

## INK

Sponge ballpoint ink stains with alcohol or a cleaning fluid. Sometimes hair spray will remove ballpoint ink from hands, leather, or plastic. Spray it directly onto the stain, rub it in, and rinse.

Hair spray sometimes removes ballpoint ink stains from clothing, but you should test it on an inconspicuous area of the item first. Hold a cloth under the stain to collect the ink, then spray directly onto the stain.

Use acetone on fabrics (but not on acetate). Some ink can be washed out. Test by staining a scrap of similar material with the same ink. Let it dry and wash in the usual way, or spray it with a pre-wash stain remover when it is dry and wash it as usual.

To remove ballpoint ink from leather, rub petroleum jelly on the spot and leave it for several days before wiping clean.

Some inks can be treated with turpentine. Work over thickly folded cloths or a folded towel. Spread the stain face down and sponge the back of it with turpentine, or use an old toothbrush with a tapping rather than a scrubbing action to drive the dissolved ink into the pad. Change the pad frequently as it becomes stained. Flush under water as hot as the fabric can stand. Rub in powdered detergent and scrub between both thumbs. Rinse and wash.

The manufacturers of some inks recommend specific solvents, so read the label on the ink bottle and follow instructions for removing stains caused by the ink involved. The recommended solvent will be more effective than others.

To remove ballpoint ink from carpets, immediately apply drycleaning fluid and let carpet dry. Repeat until stain comes out. Vacuum when dry. Use care when applying drycleaning solvents to carpets with rubber or synthetic rubber backings.

On a light carpet, make a paste of cream of tartar and lemon juice and work this into the pile. Leave it on for one minute, then sponge and responge. Blot dry.

White vinyl upholstery is a temptation to young children, who will mar these surfaces with ballpoint scribblings. The most effective first aid for this stain is ordinary saliva. Applied immediately and generously to fresh ballpoint marks, many such stains can be wiped off with a clean cloth.

First wipe over the area with glycerin. This helps reconstitute the stain, thus making it easier to remove. Leave the glycerin on for half an hour, then try one or more of the following, wiping off between treatments.

➤ Eucalyptus. Apply it with a white cloth. Persevere if the cloth becomes stained with ink, a sign that it is coming away.

➤ Acetone, usually found in nail polish remover, available in drugstores.

➤ Hydrogen peroxide. Add 1 drop of cloudy ammonia to 1 teaspoon (5 ml) peroxide.

➤ Commercial stain remover.

Pre-test on an unseen part of the upholstery. Mark an inconspicuous section with similar ink, then dampen it with acetone or nail polish remover. Immediately blot up the loosened ballpoint ink with a tissue.

This will show whether the covering would be damaged by the application of acetone; if so, substitute eucalyptus or a commercial stain remover, still experimenting on the test piece.

## LACQUER

Fold several cloths or a towel and slip it under the stain to act as an absorbent pad. Sponge the stain with acetone, working from the back of it so that dissolved lacquer is flushed into the pad. ***Note:*** Do not use acetone on acetates.

If a solvent needs to be purchased, it might prove more economical to take the garment to a drycleaner. Tell the cleaner the name of the lacquer involved.

## LINT

Sometimes an item goes through the wash with a tissue left in the pocket, leaving dark clothing covered with lint after it has been through the washing machine. To remove the lint, dampen an old handkerchief with fabric softener and put it with the articles in the dryer. Run the dryer for 5 minutes on a warm setting. Most of the lint will be caught up in the filter, and the remainder can be brushed off with a clothes brush.

Some dark fabrics seem to act as a magnet to lint, and this is particularly the case in a washing machine. Remove tissues from pockets, clean out the lint filter, and wash dark items together. Lint can be removed by hard brushing with a piece of dampened sponge or with a corrugated clothes brush, which generates static electricity when it is drawn sharply over the surface thereby attracting lint particles to its own surface.

However, much lint in the wash can be avoided if these simple rules are followed:

➤ Do not wash dark fabrics with white or light-colored clothing.

➤ Turn pockets inside out, and turn down cuffs and brush them before putting them in a machine. These are repositories for lint and, like a single paper tissue, can speckle an entire load of dark clothing.

➤ Chenille spreads and garments, towels, babies' diapers, and washable mats are typical lint creators. Wash these separately or in one load, certainly not with dark clothing in the same load.

➤ Use plenty of water when hand or machine washing. Do not overload the washer or the tub. Rinse well.

➤ Wash synthetic items (such as nylon and velveteen clothing) inside out so they will attract less lint.

## LIPSTICK

Lipstick is dye in an oily base. Water or heat or wet spotters will spread and set the stain. Rub in vegetable oil or mineral oil and let sit for 15 minutes. Sponge in a few drops of ammonia (unless the fabric is silk or wool). If the stain is old and has dried, apply petroleum jelly and wait 30 minutes.

Hair spray can be used to remove lipstick stains from clothing (test on an inconspicuous area of the item first). Spray directly onto stain, let sit for a few minutes, then wipe off gently.

To remove lipstick from carpets, carefully scrape up or lift off solid matter. If it is very soft, slip a trayful of ice cubes into a plastic bag and rest it over the mark for a few minutes. The cold will harden the lipstick and pieces will lift off.

Mix enzyme stain removing and pre-soak powder into a stiff paste with water and spread it over the mark. Leave it on for 5 minutes, then lift it off with a pliable knife. Sponge repeatedly with detergent solution — ½ teaspoon (2 ml) of powdered detergent in ½ cup (125 ml) water — continually blotting with fresh tissues as the stain is loosened. Then sponge with eucalyptus sprinkled onto a piece of old toweling. Continue this process until all the color is removed. Sponge with a clean, damp cloth.

## MAYONNAISE

To remove mayonnaise from carpets, scrape up as much as possible. Sponge with effervescing soda water, blotting up quickly. Sponge out remaining stains with powdered detergent solution — 1 teaspoon (5 ml) to 1 cup (250 ml) water — then sponge with clean, damp cloths. If an oil stain persists, sponge lightly with carbon tetrachloride or drycleaning fluid, using caution if the pile is set in a rubber or synthetic backing.

## MEAT JUICES

These are difficult to remove once they have dried. Sponge with cold water, or soak in an enzyme pre-soaking solution for half an hour after rubbing some of the pre-soak powder into the dampened stain and scrubbing between two thumbs. Wash in the usual way, but in cool water.

**Nonwashables.** Sponge with cold water. Take to a cleaner.

## MEDICINES

These differ greatly in composition. If the garment is good, take it to a cleaner, along with a piece of material deliberately stained with the same medicine (to use as a tester).

Syrupy medicines can usually be washed out with water. Dampen the stain and rub in detergent, or presoak in an enzyme solution before washing.

Spills on bedding or other articles not worth drycleaning should be sponged or soaked at once.

Oily medicines can be treated with a grease solvent.

Medicines that contain iron often cause rusty marks. Treat the stain as a rust mark (see Rust), or check your local hardware store for commercial rust-removing products.

**Medicines with an alchohol base** can stain fabrics. Treat in the same way as alcohol spills (see Alcohol).

To remove from carpets, blot up immediately with a clean hand cloth or tissues. Do not rub or scrub, as this will only work it deeper into the pile. Use carpet shampoo as directed by the manufacturer or detergent suds — 1 teaspoon (5 ml) to 1 cup (250 ml) warm water — gently scrubbed into the pile with a brush. Blot up as you work, and persist until the stain fades. Some medicine stains will require the services of a professional cleaner.

For medicine stains on furniture, blot up as quickly as possible. Treat as for *alcohol.*

## MILDEW

Mildew is a visible fungus found in warm, humid, dark conditions. The best way to avoid mildew is to be sure things are perfectly dry before they are put away.

The microscopically small spores of mildew and mold multiply astronomically when they settle on natural materials such as paper, wool, cotton, leather, and wood, and soiled areas of synthetic fabrics.

To counter mildew attack, do not crowd clothing in a hanging space. Allow air to circulate. Store only thoroughly clean clothing.

Clean leather goods such as bags, belts, travel accessories, and shoes, and leave them in strong sunlight for an hour before wrapping them in brown paper or newspaper or storing them in cardboard boxes. Do not store these items in plastic bags; plastic will absorb leather dyes, leaving the articles irremediably stained.

Check items frequently during a long spell of damp humid weather. A musty smell emanating from a closet or cupboard is always suspect.

Remove the contents of the cupboard, vacuum well, and spray for insect control. Then place a trouble-light in the wardrobe for 2 hours. The heat it generates will dry the interior. Or use a hair dryer on wood joints and corners where mildew spores could lodge.

Silica gel or camphor blocks can be placed in musty enclosures to absorb moisture.

To remove mildew, try simple measures first. Some light spots wash out when the article is laundered. If mildew covers the article, and the article will tolerate bleach, soak it in household chlorine bleach — 2 tablespoons (30 ml) to 1 gallon (4 liters) of cold water —

**Bleaching**

Rub mildew spots with lemon juice and salt, and keep moist in strong sunlight until spots fade. Diluted peroxide or vinegar can be used in the same way.

Always test the effect of bleaching agents on an inconspicuous area to see if color bleaching might occur. To avoid undue fading of the rest of the garment, expose only the part being treated.

provided the fabric has not been treated to make it drip-dry, wash-and-wear, crease-resistant, and so on. Chlorine bleach reacts on these special finishes and causes yellow-brown stains.

Mildew stains on some fabrics can be removed by moistening the stained area with lemon juice and salt, then leaving the item to dry in the sun. (It would be wise to test this cleaning solution on an inconspicuous area of the item first.)

**Winter clothes.** Sometimes winter suits and other clothing are put away in a packed wardrobe without being cleaned. In damp or humid weather, soil marks on these garments will become mildewed or moldy. Either causes rapid deterioration of the fabric. Rush these garments to a drycleaner.

**Leather.** Take mildewed leather outside and brush off powdery deposits with a clothes brush. (Stand the brush bristle down in a diluted bleach solution for 10 minutes and allow it to dry thoroughly in the sun before using on clean clothing.)

To remove surface mildew from leather, wipe the leather with a solution of equal parts rubbing alcohol and water.

**Carpets.** To remove mildew from carpets, first kill the fungus with a solution of 1 teaspoon (5 ml) disinfectant cleaner and 1 cup (250 ml) water. Apply to mildew and blot. Then, to remove the mildew stain, apply a mixture of ammonia and water — 1 part ammonia and 10 parts water. Blot, rinse, and vacuum when dry. It is important to dry carpets as quickly as possible; do not walk on wet pile.

**Painted walls and cement paths.** Use 1 part household bleach to 5 parts cold water to remove black mold from painted walls and cement paths. Leave the solution on the surface for a few minutes, then hose it off. If repainting a mold-prone area of the house, use an antifungal paint.

## MILK AND CREAM

Rinse under a cold water tap. Soak in cool detergent suds or in a pre-wash enzyme solution. Wash as usual, but in cool water; hot water will set stains. If greasy marks remain, sponge with drycleaning fluid over a thick pad; air and wash again.

For washable fabrics stained with milk, sponge with cool water. Let sit, then wash in cool water. Air dry. For drycleanables, sponge with neutral detergent solution and a few drops of ammonia (unless it is silk or wool), then cool water.

To remove from carpets, scrape up as much as possible with a spatula or knife. Sponge with tepid laundry detergent suds. Avoid excessive wetting and blot with tissues as you work. Sponge with damp cloths; if a greasy mark still exists, then sponge with drycleaning fluid, being careful not to wet the backing if it is rubber, or make a paste of borax and water and work that into the pile. When the paste dries, vacuum the area.

## MUD

For mud stains on washable fabrics, allow mud to thoroughly dry, then brush away loose dirt. Wash in warm water.

For drycleanables, sponge with neutral detergent solution, then rinse with water.

For really stubborn mud stains, sponge with equal parts of rubbing alcohol and water. For red earth mud stains, try rust remover (see Rust).

Never treat a wet mud stain beyond carefully lifting off the solid matter with a knife or spatula. Allow the stain to dry. When the mud stain is dry, remove the attachment from the vacuum cleaner hose and concentrate the suction pipe over the area. Then sponge out the remaining stain using warm detergent suds, 1 teaspoonful (5 ml) of powdered detergent in 1 cup (250 ml) of water. Sponge and blot repeatedly, then mop with clean, damp cloths.

## MUSTARD

The turmeric in mustard is a bright yellow spice that stains. Remove as much of the loose material as possible. Flex the fabric to break up embedded residue. Apply glycerin and let it sit before washing. Hydrogen peroxide can sometimes remove mustard stains. ***Note:*** Avoid ammonia or heat — they will set the stain.

Another method is to rub undiluted detergent into dry fabric, or dampen and rub in powdered detergent. Scrub lightly between both thumbs. Rinse under cold running water. If a stain remains, soak in a pre-wash solution.

Have nonwashables drycleaned.

To remove mustard stains from a countertop, rub in a little baking soda with a damp cloth.

## NAIL POLISH

To remove nail polish from carpets, blot up as much as possible with a tissue or anything handy. Then test the effect of nail polish remover on an inconspicuous part of the carpet. If there are no ill effects on the pile, apply it with an eye dropper, blotting up immediately. Sponge with warm powdered detergent suds, 1 teaspoon (5 ml) to 1 cup (250 ml) warm water. Sponge and blot many times. If a trace of color remains, make the spot as dry as possible. Slip a number of folded tissues under the stain and sponge it with nail polish remover. Change the tissue pad frequently. ***Note:*** Acetone or nail polish remover should not be used on acetates.

Any remaining dye stain can be bleached with peroxide. Keep the stain damp with diluted peroxide and expose it to sunlight.

**Nonwashables** should be drycleaned.

Another way to remove nail polish from carpets is to apply drycleaning fluid. Use caution if the carpet has rubber or synthetic backing. For persistent stains, mix 1 teaspoon (5 ml) mild detergent, 1 teaspoon (5 ml) white vinegar, and 1 quart (liter) warm water. Apply to stain, let dry, then vacuum.

## OIL. *See also Grease and Oil*

Blot up excess oil as quickly as possible. Be gentle; forceful scrubbing will just embed the oil in the fibers. For washable fabrics, wash in as hot a water as the fabric will tolerate.

For drycleanables, rub a small amount of petroleum jelly on the stain and let it sit for 10 minutes. Take to the drycleaner as soon as possible.

## PAINT

**Latex paint** on washables can be removed with soap and water. It is important to work on removing the paint before it dries.

To remove latex paint from carpets, scrape up as much as possible. Sponge with laundry detergent suds, 1 teaspoon (5 ml) to 1 cup (250 ml) water, blotting up as you work. Sponge with a series of clean, damp cloths to remove the suds, then with drycleaning fluid, being careful not to saturate the carpet backing. Professional help might be necessary.

**Oil-based paints.** Act at once. Old stains that have dried are often impossible to remove. Read the paint label, which often recommends a solvent that acts as a thinner. This is usually effective, provided a pre-testing of an inside seam shows that the fabric is not adversely affected by its use.

If expensive solvents need to be purchased, do not delay. Take the garment to a drycleaner. Supply the name of the paint or varnish involved.

Turpentine is a good paint solvent. Work from the back of the stain, which should be spread over a thick pad of tissues or folded cloth. Tamp the stain with an old nylon-bristled toothbrush dipped in turpentine. (Do not use turpentine on Arnel.)

When no more color appears on the pad under the stain, rub detergent into the area, still dampened with turpentine. Cover the stained part with hot water and let it soak for 10–12 hours. Then scrub between your thumbs and wash in the usual way.

Water-soluble paints can be rinsed out of fabrics, just as brushes can be washed in water. Rub detergent into the stain, scrub between your thumbs, rinse under running water, and wash in the usual way.

Removing oil-based paint and varnish from carpet is usually a job for a professional, but you can help by immediately scraping up as much as possible with a spatula, taking care not to spread the stain.

Sponge with thinners or turpentine, after first testing the reaction of either on an unseen section of the carpet. Try not to penetrate to the backing of the carpet; some backings will be adversely affected. Blot repeatedly to absorb as much of the loosened paint as possible.

Then sponge lightly with drycleaning fluid, blotting and sponging until the tissues remain clean. Next, gently sponge the pile with powdered detergent solution — 1 teaspoon (5 ml) dissolved in 1 cup (250 ml) tepid water; then sponge with a series of clean, damp cloths. Smooth the pile. Vacuum when quite dry.

## PENCIL

Lead pencil stains on fabrics can often be removed by rubbing with a clean, soft eraser or a sponge with carbon tetrachloride. If necessary, spray with a pre-wash stain remover.

## PERFUME

To remove perfume from carpet, first blot up. Sponge with laundry detergent solution, 1 teaspoon (5 ml) mixed into 1 cup (250 ml) tepid water, then with a series of damp cloths to remove the suds. Vacuum when dry. Perfume might yellow with age, so do not ignore spills.

## PERSPIRATION

Perspiration will weaken fabrics, so treat vulnerable areas carefully. Dampen the stains with warm water and rub in detergent, or soak in a pre-wash soaking compound. Wash in the usual way. If the color of the fabric has been changed by perspiration, try ammonia or white vinegar to restore it. Sponge fresh stains with ammonia and immediately rinse in cold water.

Perspiration stains on upholstery result in fading, bleaching, yellowing, and greasy marks. A vinegar solution can also be used quite safely. To each cupful (250 ml) of tepid water, add 2 teaspoons (10 ml) vinegar. Wring out a cloth in the solution, and sponge briskly.

Sponging with drycleaning fluid also helps. If the cover is textured, rub this in with a soft, clean nailbrush. Blot up as much as possible with absorbent cloths. After the drycleaning fluid evaporates, apply the vinegar treatment.

Vinegar water helps to revive fading colors, and it brightens upholstery after the use of drycleaning fluids.

## RUST

Rust stains on fabric can sometimes be taken out with lemon juice and salt. Apply the mixture directly to the stain and let it sit for a few minutes. Then pour boiling water through the fabric until the stain is out. Afterwards, wash as usual.

Fabrics that can be boiled can be treated in a cream of tartar solution. Use 1 tablespoon (15 ml) to 1 quart (liter) water and boil for 10 minutes or longer. Rinse well.

Clean rust from countertops with lemon juice and salt, or rub in toothpaste with your finger. Rub until the stain is gone, then rinse and wipe dry.

To remove rust stains from a slate sink, use full-strength white vinegar.

If metal furniture has accumulated rust, try scrubbing with turpentine.

## SALAD DRESSING

To remove from carpet, absorb as much of the spill as possible. Mix 1 teaspoon (5 ml) mild detergent, 1 teaspoon (5 ml) white vinegar, and 1 quart (liter) warm water. Apply to stain, let dry, then vacuum. Repeat if necessary.

## SALT

To clean salt marks off boots and shoes, wipe down with a mixture of 1 part white vinegar and 3 parts water.

Dry salt can change the color of a carpet and will attract dampness, which will suspend grime and dirt. If a spill occurs, vacuum slowly and deeply.

For salt water or salty liquids, blot up as much as possible. Make a solution using 1 tablespoon (15 ml) laundry detergent, 1 tablespoon (15 ml) white vinegar, and 1 cup (250 ml) tepid water. Sponge and blot several times, then sponge with damp cloths. Smooth the pile and vacuum when dry.

## SCORCH MARKS. *See also Burn Marks*

Pre-test the effect of peroxide on a hidden seam as it might bleach some fabrics or react on treated materials. Dampen a cloth with hydrogen peroxide (1 part hydrogen peroxide to 3 parts water). Lay it over the scorch mark and press with a moderately hot iron. Protect surrounding material with cloth or brown paper so that it will not be scorched also. Expose to full sunshine and keep moist with peroxide until the mark fades.

Scorch marks on some fabrics are less noticeable if they are rubbed lightly with very fine sandpaper. This raises the singed nap on woolens, for example, and reduces the shiny appearance. Gentle handling of scorched garments is necessary as scorching weakens the threads.

Light scorch marks can often be bleached simply by saturating them with clean cold water and exposing them to strong sunlight.

On white materials, wet the stain with diluted hydrogen peroxide, cover with a white cloth, and press with a moderately hot iron. If a stain remains, wet again with peroxide and keep moist for 2 or 3 hours in strong sunlight. Rinse thoroughly to remove traces of peroxide.

On white or colorfast materials, wet the scorch with lemon juice and expose to sunshine. Rewet with lemon juice every half hour until the mark fades. Rinse well under running water.

Actual charring might occur when woolens and heavy synthetic materials are scorched. The nap is burnt and the threads are weakened. Remember not to abrade, rub, or twist the scorch-weakened fabric.

Light scorches on trousers might respond to treatment with a paste made of borax and glycerin. Cover the scorch mark completely and let the paste dry for 12 hours before brushing it off. Wash in tepid suds and rinse well. If the glycerin leaves an oily stain, sponge this out in warm detergent suds.

When deep scorching occurs on expensive items or garments made of wool, take the garments to a good tailor. Usually these experts can patch in a matching piece of fabric cut from a turned-up cuff or from the inside facing of a coat. The repair is almost invisible, and the cost is negligible when compared with that of replacement.

Treat scorch marks on pure silk with a paste of baking soda and cold water. When the paste dries, brush it off and repeat if necessary. Rinse well. On white silk the peroxide treatment will remove a light scorch. Rinse well.

You can also cover the mark with a thick paste made of borax and warm water. Work it into the pile. When this dries, vacuum the area and sponge with a damp cloth; vacuum again.

## SCRATCHES

Scratches on furniture can often be completely camouflaged with patient treatment. Treat as you would burn marks.

## SCUFF MARKS

To clean scuff marks off shoes, wipe with toothpaste on a damp rag.

## SEWING MACHINE OIL

After oiling a sewing machine, remove the thread from the needle and run the machine over an old piece of cloth before sewing good material.

If machine oil does stain a garment in the making, immediately blot the spot with a tissue or rub it with chalk or talcum powder. Then, working over several folded tissues, which will act as an absorbent pad, sponge the mark with eucalyptus or drycleaning fluid.

## SHOE POLISH

Work laundry detergent into the fabric immediately and rinse. For persistent stains, sponge with alcohol and rinse again, or try turpentine or cleaning fluid. Test these solutions on an inconspicuous area of the item first.

Shoe polish is dye in an oily base. Water or heat or wet spotters will spread and set the stain. Rub in vegetable oil or mineral oil and let sit for 15 minutes. Sponge in a few drops of ammonia (unless the fabric is silk or wool). If the stain is old and dry, apply petroleum jelly and wait 30 minutes.

Hair spray can be used to remove shoe polish stains from clothing (again, test on an inconspicuous area of the item first). Spray directly onto the stain, let sit for a few minutes, then wipe off gently.

To remove from carpets, lift off any solid matter with a knife or spatula. Apply drycleaning fluid drop by drop, blotting rapidly so that it does not penetrate to the backing. Exercise particular caution if the backing is made of rubber or synthetic rubber. Continue until most of the color has been removed. Then scrub the area with laundry detergent suds and an old toothbrush, working in a rotary motion from the outside of the stain toward its center. Sponge with a series of damp cloths to remove further traces.

If a blotchy mark remains after the area has dried, work carpet shampoo or a thick paste of borax and water into the pile. Allow it to remain for 4 hours before vacuuming. Repeat as necessary.

**Liquid shoe polish.** On carpets, blot up immediately with anything handy. Dissolve 1 teaspoon (5 ml) of laundry detergent in ½ cup (125 ml) of warm water and work this into the pile, blotting very frequently. Remaining dye stains on a

### Stain Removal Kit

Fill a basket with any of the items you might need in a stain emergency. Some suggestions include white absorbent cloths and a spoon or butter knife to scrape away the spill. Include small bottles of the following stain removers:

- ☛ Drycleaning fluid
- ☛ Hydrogen peroxide
- ☛ Rubbing alcohol
- ☛ White vinegar
- ☛ Ammonia
- ☛ Diluted bleach
- ☛ Acetone

Keep the basket in a handy place, so when you are faced with a spill you won't lose time collecting materials.

light carpet might respond to bleach treatment. Mix 1 teaspoon (5 ml) in bleach with ¼ cup (60 ml) cold water and scrub this gently into the stained area with an old toothbrush, blotting frequently as you work. Finally, sponge with damp cloths to remove all traces of bleach.

## SMOKE STAIN

To neutralize the odor of smoke in nonwashable items, sprinkle the item with baking soda and seal it in a plastic bag for several days. For washable items, use a baking soda and water pre-soak.

## SOFT DRINKS. *See also Cola*

Soft drinks that have been spilled should be blotted up quickly, and if possible, the stain should be treated before it dries. These stains may be invisible when they dry, but they will yellow with age and heat.

Sponge immediately with a cloth barely dampened with warm water and containing 1 or 2 drops of liquid detergent. Rinse with a clean, damp cloth and dry as quickly as possible, using a hair dryer set on medium heat.

To remove from carpets, absorb as much of the spill as possible. Some drinks contain dyes that can permanently stain carpets. Mix 1 teaspoon (5 ml) mild detergent, 1 teaspoon (5 ml) white vinegar, and 1 quart (liter) warm water. Apply to stain, let dry, then vacuum. Repeat if necessary.

## SOOT

To remove from carpets, vacuum lightly by holding the vacuum extension immediately above the deposits. Do not use a pushing-pulling movement. Most traces should disappear. Carpet shampoo (used according to directions), powdered carpet cleaner, or a paste made of borax and water rubbed into the pile and left to dry before vacuuming should remove any residue.

## STICKERS

Stickers can sometimes be removed by applying vinegar directly or on a cloth dampened with vinegar. On nonabsorbent surfaces like glass and plastic, stickers are harder to remove. Nail polish remover, turpentine, and pre-wash spray are among the most effective.

Wet cotton with the solvent and apply it liberally over the sticker. Foil stickers do not absorb, so the solvent should be brushed around the edges. Leave for a minute or two, then repeat once or twice. The sticker can usually be peeled off. A smear of solvent will generally remove adhesive.

A light application of pre-wash spray will usually remove adhesive left by sticky tape, particularly from walls where posters have been hung. It will also remove masking tape marks from around glass after window frames have been painted.

Commercial jar labels can usually be soaked off except for a strip of adhesive that attaches to the ends. Many jars are purposely designed for re-use so they need to be clear of old labels. Try one of the suggested solvents or the pre-wash spray to remove final traces. Always work in a well-ventilated area when using spray.

## TAR

Lift off as much solid matter as possible immediately, using a knife to do so. Spread the stain over a thick pad of face tissues and tamp the stain with an old toothbrush dipped in eucalyptus. As the tissues become stained, discard them and substitute new ones. Finally, spread the stain over a plate or saucer, pour over a little more eucalyptus oil, and continue to tamp or gently scrape the area with a blunt knife. Blot up stained matter, and rinse the saucer. Repeat until no more tar can be extracted.

If eucalyptus is not available, use turpentine, carbon tetrachloride, or drycleaning fluid.

**Dried tar.** Soften with warmed olive oil after spreading the stain over folded tissues. Then proceed as above, preferably using eucalyptus oil as the solvent.

Rub detergent into the stain, rub between both thumbs, and rinse under running water as hot as the hands can bear. If a yellow mark remains, bleach it by keeping it moist with peroxide and exposing it to full sunlight. Rinse well.

Have nonwashable garments drycleaned as soon as possible.

To remove from carpets, lift off solid matter with a knife. If the tar has dried, it will need to be softened with warmed oil. Put a few drops on the tar and leave it until the tar feels soft to the touch. Then use tissues to blot up excess oil.

Sponge carefully with eucalyptus or with turpentine. To avoid spreading the stain, continually blot the area with tissues, which will absorb loosened tar elements.

Sponge with laundry detergent solution — 1 teaspoon (5 ml) to ½ cup (125 ml) warm water. If the tar is trodden into the pile, scrub with a toothbrush. Continue to scrub and blot for as long as tissues continue to be stained with brown sulphur traces from the tar; then sponge with a series of damp cloths. Use drycleaning fluid to remove traces of oil used to soften the tar; if these remain, they will attract grime. Blot frequently as you work.

Concentrated cleaning such as this might result in a very clean patch of carpet with grimier surroundings. Shampooing the whole carpet may prove necessary.

## TEA

If hot or boiling water can be flushed through a fresh tea stain, the stain will fade. If the fabric involved can stand boiling or very hot water, spread the stain over a large basin in the sink. Cover the mark with borax. Pour a jug or kettleful of boiling water over the stain. Let it soak in the water until it cools. You can also turn on a hot water tap. Hold the stained area taut beneath its flow; often the stain will be washed out.

Lemon juice and sunlight also will bleach tannin stains. Rub lemon juice into the marks, and hang or spread them in full sunlight. Keep moist with lemon juice, perhaps for two days, until the stains fade. Rinse well and wash.

On colored fabrics, treat tea stains with a borax paste. Mix 1 tablespoon (15 ml) of borax to a paste with hot water. Spread it over the stain. When this dries, brush it off and apply fresh paste. Continue until the mark fades; or if it persists, apply diluted peroxide and expose to sunlight, keeping it damp for several hours.

Tea spilled on woolens or on blankets should be mopped up as quickly as possible. Send lined garments to a drycleaner. Rinse a stained blanket in warm detergent suds and in a succession of warm rinsing waters. If a tea stain has dried on a blanket, soak it in a hydrogen peroxide solution. To each tablespoon (15 ml) of hydrogen peroxide, add 5 tablespoons (75 ml) warm water. Wet the tea stain thoroughly. Let the blanket soak until the stain fades; then wash the entire blanket, or rinse that section very well and roll it in a towel or blot it semi-dry before drying it completely.

Glycerin will reconstitute an old tea stain, making it easier to remove. Rub in glycerin, working it in with a scrubbing action between both thumbs. Leave it on for 10 hours. Then spread the stain over a basin in the sink, cover it with borax, and pour over it water as hot as the fabric can stand. Let it soak in the borax solution until the mark fades. (See also Coffee and Tea.)

## UNKNOWN MATERIALS

Depending on the fabric or material that is stained, you may want to try one of the following stain removal techniques.

➤ Blot with cool water.

➤ Blot with a wet sponge on which you have sprinkled a few drops of vinegar. (Do not use this on cotton or linen.)

➤ Blot with a wet sponge on which you have sprinkled a few drops of ammonia. (Do not use this on cotton or linen.)

➤ Blot with rubbing alcohol that has been diluted with an equal amount of water. Rinse well.

➤ Sponge with a solution of bleach and water.

## URINE

Fresh stains are comparatively easy to remove. First rinse well, pre-soak using an enzyme powder or powdered detergent in the water, then wash in the usual way. Or sponge immediately with salty water; later rinse well and wash in the usual way. If the color of the fabric has been changed, sponge the mark with ammonia, then rinse again. (Do not use ammonia on wool or silk.) Yellow stains on white materials such as cotton sheets can be soaked in chlorine bleach. Do not use bleach on materials with treated finishes that make them no-iron or wash-and-wear. Bleach will cause yellow-brown marks on specially treated fabrics.

Soak urine-stained fabrics in clear water for 30 minutes (hot water is best, if the care label permits). Add detergent, wash, then rinse. If necessary, use a bleach that is safe for the fabric. If fabric color changes, sponge with ammonia. If the stain remains, sponge with white vinegar. Launder again.

A mixture of white vinegar and baking soda is a good neutralizer. Sponge onto fabric or carpet.

To remove from carpets, blot up quickly so that as little as possible is absorbed. Prepare a solution of 2 teaspoons (10 ml) powdered laundry detergent, ½ cup

(125 ml) warm water, and 2 tablespoons (30 ml) white vinegar. Scrub this into the pile of the carpet, using an old toothbrush. Let it remain for 20 minutes, then sponge repeatedly with clean, damp cloths.

Urine stains darken with age, and they can bleach dark carpets. Sometimes the color can be restored by sponging with ammonia water. Use 1 teaspoon (5 ml) ammonia in a cup (250 ml) of cold water. It is advisable to first test the effect of ammonia on an inconspicuous part of the carpet before sponging a large area. After the ammonia treatment, sponge with a series of clean, damp cloths.

Pet and some baby urine will leave a recurring odor, particularly in damp or humid weather or if a room has been closed up. Drugstores stock solutions that can be used to deodorize as well as remove stains. Most can be sprayed on. For persistent odors, turn back the carpet and clean and spray the backing and underlay.

## VOMIT

To remove from carpets, attend to this stain without delay. Use a spatula to remove solid matter and an old towel to blot up as much as possible. Prepare a sponging solution using 1 tablespoon (15 ml) laundry detergent in 1 cup (250 ml) warm water, plus 1 tablespoon (15 ml) white vinegar. Scrub into the area with a nailbrush. Try to avoid overwetting. If saturation results, the wet carpet backing will absorb some of the unpleasant odor, which will be difficult to remove.

After traces of detergent have been sponged out with a series of damp cloths, use drycleaning fluid to remove greasy deposits. Blot persistently to absorb as much moisture as possible. Finally, sponge with dry towels and train an electric fan or hair dryer on the area to dry the carpet. Vacuum when dry.

## WATER

An overflowing bath or basin, a leaking pipe, a storm-damaged roof, even a knocked-over vase can cause severe carpet stains. Copious amounts of water will loosen grime and dirt deposits; the backing and underlay become saturated and the carpet is stained with dirty marks. In addition to the shrinking that can be caused by saturation, some underlays will mildew and the resulting smell is very unpleasant. Some carpet dyes might bleed; others might fade.

Absorb as much water as possible with bath towels. Walk on them to press them deeply into the pile where they will absorb still more water.

The best course of action in the event of severe flooding is to take up the carpet and dry it out or to turn back the carpet to the saturated section and train an electric fan on the backing until it is dry. Never use a radiator; synthetic carpets scorch easily, and woolen carpets will shrink.

If the carpet is a good one, have it steam-cleaned by a professional carpet cleaner. It will also need to be relaid by a professional, who might need to stretch a shrunken wall-to-wall carpet.

**Water rings on furniture.** Damp marks on furniture are often caused by leaking vases and rings of condensation from cold glasses. The polish must be removed so that the area can be buffed dry. Put a little vinegar on a damp cloth and wipe the wet mark. It will remove the old polish and darken the bleached wood. Dry well, then work in linseed oil or petroleum jelly. Rub hard from the outside of the mark toward the center. Cover with more oil or petroleum jelly, and leave for several hours before again rubbing with a heated duster. A duster can be warmed by standing a heating iron on it for a minute or two. The warmth will help the wood absorb the oil. Then polish in the usual way; or, if the mark remains, repeat the rubbing treatment.

## WINE

Treat as soon as possible. On a garment, spray or sponge with carbonated soda water. On a cloth, sprinkle heavily with salt after blotting up as much as possible. Later, follow instructions for removing tea stains. (See Tea.)

Do not hesitate to send an expensive garment to a drycleaner.

On upholstery, immediately blot up as much as possible. Sponge with warm water; blot and sponge repeatedly. Cover the stain with a dry tissue and sprinkle this with talcum powder. Cover with another tissue and apply a weight. The tissues and the powder will absorb still more of the stain. Lift off carefully. Vacuum.

To remove red wine stains from carpets, dilute the stain with white wine, then clean the spot with cold water and cover with salt. Wait 15 minutes, then vacuum up the salt.

Another method for removing wine from carpets is first to blot it up immediately, then spray with effervescing soda water. Blot persistently. Make a thick paste of borax and warm water, and scrub it deeply into the carpet pile with a nailbrush or toothbrush. Let it remain overnight before vacuuming. Repeat several times if necessary.

## YELLOW SPOTS AND STAINS

Sometimes caused by soap residue (especially in linens that are ironed). Treat the stains in the following way: Apply fresh lemon juice on stains, then sprinkle the juice with salt. Stretch the fabric tightly and pour hot water through the stains.

Tablet denture cleaners will remove yellow stains from fabrics. Fill container with warm water and add cleaning tablets according to the directions on the box. After tablets dissolve, add the stained item and soak until stain comes out.

If the exterior of a white freezer or refrigerator has yellowed with age, apply an automotive cutting compound, available from garages or hardware stores.

# APPENDIX

## Product Assistance

The U.S. Consumer Product and Safety Commission has a toll-free number, **1-800-638-2772**. To obtain information for a commercial product, you can check the product label or ask your local library for the address and telephone number of the manufacturer. Call manufacturers for information about specific products.

## Poison Information

Contact your local poison center about the health effect of products and for information about treating poisoning. The telephone number for poison control usually appears on the inside cover of your telephone directory.

# HOUSEHOLD HAZARDOUS WASTE REFERENCE

| SUBSTANCE ☞ | PROBLEM ☞ |
|---|---|
| **Bleach and liquid cleaners** | Contain strong oxidizers. Can cause burns. |
| **Cleansers and powdered cleaners** | Contain strong oxidizers. Poisonous. Can cause burns. |
| **Drain cleaners** | Poisonous. Can cause serious burns. May contain carcinogens. |
| **Dyes** | Poisonous, especially to children; don't use cooking utensils when dyeing. May be carcinogenic. |
| **Furniture polishes** | Include various poisonous solvents. One ounce (25 grams) may be lethal to an adult. |
| **Mothballs** | Contain poisonous chemical compounds. |
| **Oven cleaners** | Poisonous. Can cause serious burns. May contain carcinogens. |
| **Silver polishes** | Poisonous. May contain carcinogens. One ounce (25 grams) may be lethal to an adult. |
| **Spot removers** | Poisonous. Most are solvent-based. May be carcinogenic. |
| **Toilet cleaners** | Spray cans are the most dangerous. Poisonous. Can cause serious burns. One teaspoonful (5 ml) may be lethal to an adult. |
| **Window cleaners** | Contain harmful chemical compounds and sometimes carcinogens. May cause birth defects. |

| PROPER DISPOSAL ☞ | ALTERNATIVES |
|---|---|
| Wash down drain with lots of water. | Use powder, not liquid bleach. |
| Wrap tightly in plastic, place in a box, tape shut, and put in garbage. | Baking soda and mild detergent, elbow grease. |
| Wash down drain with lots of water or take to hazardous waste collection site. | Boiling water, plunger, metal snake. |
| Wrap tightly in plastic, place in a box, tape shut, and put in garbage. | Use vegetable dyes such as onion skins, teas, marigolds. |
| Use up according to directions or take to hazardous waste collection site. | Mineral oil with lemon oil (but this may strip finish), or Carnauba wax. |
| Use up according to directions or take to hazardous waste collection site. | Cedar chips, newspapers; wrap wool clothing in plastic bags during warm seasons. |
| Use up according to directions or take to hazardous-waste collection site. | Salt, quarter cup (60 ml) of ammonia overnight. |
| Use up according to directions or take to hazardous waste collection site. | Soak silver in water with baking soda, salt, and small piece of aluminum foil. |
| Use up according to directions or take to hazardous waste collection site. | Immediate cold water and detergent, rubbing alcohol, or a little acetone. |
| Wash down drain with lots of water. | Mild detergent or small amounts of bleach. |
| Wrap tightly in plastic, place in a box, tape shut, and put in garbage. | Vinegar and water. |

SOURCE: League of Women Voters of Marin County, California. Used with permission. For further information, contact your local solid waste authority.

# REFERENCES

Aslett, Don. *Stainbuster's Bible.* Penguin, 1990.

Barndt, Herb. *Professor Barndt's On-the-Spot Stain Removal Guide.* Doubleday, 1992.

Barrett, Patti. *Too Busy to Clean? Over 500 Tips & Techniques to Make Housecleaning Easier.* Storey Publishing, 1990.

Berthold-Bond, Annie. *Clean & Green: The Complete Guide to Non-Toxic & Environmentally Safe Housekeeping.* Ceres Press, 1990.

Chestnut Moore, Alma. *How to Clean Everything.* Simon & Schuster, 1977.

Consumer Guide, ed. *Practical Hints & Tips.* Consumer Guide, 1994.

Pinkham, Mary Ellen, and Pearl Higginbotham. *Mary Ellen's Best of Helpful Hints.* Warner, 1979.

Proux, Earl. *Yankee Home Hints.* Yankee Books, 1993.

Time Life Staff. *Cleaning & Stain Removal.* Time Life, 1990.

# INDEX